# ABNORMAL
# PSYCHOLOGY

## ESSENTIAL CASES AND READINGS

# ABNORMAL PSYCHOLOGY

## ESSENTIAL CASES AND READINGS

**Thomas Bradbury**
and
**Cindy Yee-Bradbury**

UNIVERSITY OF CALIFORNIA, LOS ANGELES

W. W. NORTON & COMPANY
NEW YORK · LONDON

The text of this book is composed in Minion
with the display set in Matrix
Composition by PennSet, Inc.
Manufacturing by Maple-Vail
Copy editor: Christine Habermaas
Manufacturing director: Roy Tedoff


Library of Congress Cataloging-in-Publication Data
Abnormal psychology : essential cases and readings / [edited by] Thomas Bradbury and
Cindy Yee-Bradbury.
        p. cm.
    Includes bibliographical references.
    ISBN 0-393-97730-7 (pbk.)
    1. Psychology, Pathological. 2. Psychology, Pathological—Case studies. I. Bradbury,
Thomas. II. Yee-Bradbury, Cindy.

RC454 .A253 2001
616.89—dc21
                                                            2001030727


W. W. Norton & Company, Inc., 500 Fifth Avenue, New York, N.Y. 10110
www.wwnorton.com

W. W. Norton & Company Ltd., Castle House, 75/76 Wells Street, London W1T 3QT

    3  4  5  6  7  8  9  0

# CONTENTS

# Chapter 3

## Anxiety Disorders 61

# Chapter 4

## Somatoform and Dissociative Disorders 87

# Chapter 5

## Mood Disorders 113

# Chapter 6

## Disorders of Childhood and Adolescence   141

# Chapter 7

## Personality Disorders   169

# Chapter 8

## Schizophrenia 205

# Chapter 9

## Aging and Psychological Disorders 233

# Chapter 10

## Eating Disorders 257

# Chapter 11

## Sexual and Gender Identity Disorders   283

# Chapter 12

## Substance-Related Disorders   323

# Chapter 13

## Treatment of Psychological Disorders   355

# Chapter 14

## Social and Legal Aspects of Abnormal Psychology  391

# Chapter 15

## Future Directions in Abnormal Psychology  415

# PREFACE

Compiling a book of readings about abnormal psychology is quite different from writing an abnormal psychology textbook. With an abnormal psychology textbook, one endeavors to be comprehensive and thorough. Although there is great variety in how the material is presented—for example, focusing more on research than practice or cultural considerations or the biological underpinnings of disorder—in the end most textbooks cover fairly similar ground: historical considerations, research methods, theoretical perspectives, legal and ethical considerations, disorders that reflect the main diagnostic categories, and treatment. Virtually all major abnormal psychology textbooks present material in an interesting and compelling manner, but completeness of coverage is the primary concern.

In our opinion, a book of readings in abnormal psychology should reverse these two priorities. The readings should, first and foremost, be interesting to students who are now encountering the field seriously for the first time. The field of abnormal psychology, or psychopathology as it is sometimes called, is endlessly fascinating. It is also a relatively new field, with a short but rich history and many discoveries and contributions waiting to be made. Our goal in collecting these readings is to capture some of what makes abnormal psychology fascinating to us, so that you might come away from the book with a greater understanding of some of the subtleties and controversies that exist in the field today. As you will see, the selections cover a wide range of topics, but we are less concerned about being comprehensive in our coverage than about presenting you with articles that show how engaging and multifaceted the study of psychopathology can be.

From our survey of the large professional and nonprofessional literature on psychopathology over the past few years, we have selected readings that captured our attention, that we believed made an important point about the field and the phenomena, and that are significant enough that we would want to share them with our colleagues and students. We have written introductions for each reading to convey why we found it interesting or important and have also provided references to additional articles that expand on the same theme or approach it from a different direction. The resulting articles—4 each for 15 chapters—come from a wide range of newspapers, magazines, and professional journals, and most of them were published within the last 3 or 4 years.

We hope that these readings will encourage you to consider a professional career in a mental health–related field, whether it be psychology, medicine, neuroscience, law, social work, or nursing. But even if you do not pursue a career in these fields, we hope that the articles will instill in you a lifelong interest in reading about human behavior and mental illness in the world around us. Doing so will make you a better-informed consumer of mental health research and treatment, and it will help you to make better decisions about your own mental health and that of your friends and family.

As you read, bear in mind that we sometimes deleted sentences or paragraphs from the original articles that did not seem essential to the main theme, and we eliminated some technical and statistical details likely to be unfamiliar to most readers. Interested readers should refer back to the original sources before citing these works and before assuming that they have read the complete text. Editing the work of others, particularly those with well-deserved reputations as journalists, professional writers, and scientists, proved to be a challenging and humbling experience. We hope that we have merely sharpened rather than distorted the authors' original messages. Except where otherwise noted, the identities of individuals depicted in these readings were disguised by the original authors, as is customary in the use of case material.

In closing we would like to express our thanks to Jon Durbin at W. W. Norton and Company for his guidance and patience, to Marissa Ordonio at UCLA for her enthusiastic assistance, and to Martin Seligman at the University of Pennsylvania and Elaine Walker at Emory University for encouraging us to undertake this project.

# ABNORMAL PSYCHOLOGY

ESSENTIAL CASES AND READINGS

# CHAPTER 1

## Scope and Focus of Abnormal Psychology

*These readings introduce key topics, distinctions, and dilemmas commonly encountered by students and scholars of abnormal psychology. They address such questions as How costly are mental disorders to our society? How can we protect research subjects while also gathering information from them that might help others in the future? To what extent can we rely upon the judgments of researchers and practitioners? How adequate is our existing approach to diagnosing mental disorders? You might be surprised to learn that seemingly simple questions like these are not fully resolved yet and, in some cases, are sources of great debate in the field. Although the ambiguity around these questions can be frustrating, it also presents exciting opportunities for future progress in the field.*

# MENTAL HEALTH: A REPORT OF THE SURGEON GENERAL—EXECUTIVE SUMMARY

## U.S. Department of Health and Human Services

*How would our world be different if serious psychopathology—schizophrenia, depression, drug and alcohol abuse, bipolar disorder, for example—simply did not exist? Had you taken a course in abnormal psychology in the 1990s, your instructor probably would have discussed the Epidemiologic Catchment Area study reported by Regier and colleagues (1988) or the National Comorbidity Study reported by Kessler and colleagues (1994). These studies are quite large and intensive for our field, as they involve 18,571 and 8,098 standardized interviews, respectively, conducted with people from the general population. They indicate that 15.4% of the population could be classified as fulfilling diagnostic criteria for some kind of mental disorder within the previous month. This figure rises to 29% when we consider the previous year and rises to 48% when we consider entire lifetimes. With almost half of the general population likely to encounter some form of mental disorder at some point in life, it becomes clear that our world would indeed be radically transformed if serious psychopathology did not exist.*

*A more recent study by Murray and Lopez (1996) makes this point by comparing the human costs associated with mental disorder with other kinds of diseases in all regions of the world. They look at an index called disability-adjusted life years (DALY) that measures ( for each disease) the sum of years lost as a result of premature death or disability. Using this index, Murray and Lopez (1997) conclude that 15.4% of all lost years are due to mental illness—more than all forms of cancer combined (15%) and second only to cardiovascular disease (18.6%). These findings are staggering, and they capture well the toll that mental illness takes on individuals, their families, and our society.*

*The first reading, which comes from the Surgeon General's first-ever report on mental health, summarizes data on the societal impact of mental illness, provides a useful analysis of mental health as contrasted with mental illness, and outlines the potent role of stigma in contending with the problem of mental illness. Thus, progress in reducing the burden associated with mental illness requires not only enhanced scientific understanding and better forms of treatment, but also a change in people's attitudes so that it becomes acceptable to seek help for psychological and psychiatric difficulties. In fact, in the National Comorbidity Study cited above, only 1 in 4 people with a lifetime history of a disorder sought any kind of professional help.*

## References

Kessler, R. C., McGonagle, K. A., Zhao, S., Nelson, C. B., Highes, M., Eshleman, S., Wittchen, M., & Kendler, K. S. (1994). Lifetime and 12-month prevalence of *DSM-III-R* psychiatric disorders in the United States Results from the National Comorbidity Study. *Archives of General Psychiatry, 51*, 8–19.

Murray, C. J. ., & Lopez, A. D. (1996). *The global burden of disease.* Cambridge, MA: Harvard University Press.

Murray , . J. L., & Lopez, A. D. (1997). Alternative projections of mortality and disability by cause 199 –2020: Global Burden of Disease Study. *The Lancet, 349*, 1498–1504.

Re er, D. A., Boyd, J. H., Burke, J. D., Rae, D. S., Myers, J. K., Kramer, M., Robins, L. N., George, L. K., Karno, M., & Locke, B. Z. (1988). One-month prevalence of mental disorders in the United States. *Archives of General Psychiatry, 45*, 977–986.

---

Rockville, MD: U.S. Department of Health and Human Services, Substance Abuse and Mental Health Administration, Center for Mental Health Services, National Institutes of Health, National Institute of Mental Health. (1999).

This first Surgeon General's Report on Mental Health is issued at the culmination of a half-century that has witnessed remarkable advances in the understanding of mental disorders and the brain and in our appreciation of the centrality of mental health to overall health and well-being. The report was prepared against a backdrop of growing awareness in the United States and throughout the world of the immense burden of disability associated with mental illnesses. In the United States, mental disorders collectively account for more than 15 percent of the overall burden of disease from *all* causes and slightly more than the burden associated with all forms of cancer (Murray & Lopez, 1996). These data underscore the importance and urgency of treating and preventing mental disorders and of promoting mental health in our society.

The report in its entirety provides an up-to-date review of scientific advances in the study of mental health and of mental illnesses that affect at least one in five Americans. Several important conclusions may be drawn from the extensive scientific literature summarized in the report. One is that a variety of treatments of well-documented efficacy exist for the array of clearly defined mental and behavioral disorders that occur across the life span. Every person should be encouraged to seek help when questions arise about mental health, just as each person is encouraged to seek help when questions arise about health. Research highlighted in the report demonstrates that mental health is a facet of health that evolves throughout the lifetime. Just as each person can do much to promote and maintain overall health regardless of age, each also can do much to promote and strengthen mental health at every stage of life.

Much remains to be learned about the causes, treatment, and prevention of mental and behavioral disorders. Obstacles that may limit the availability or accessibility of mental health services for some Americans are being dismantled, but disparities persist. Still, thanks to research and the experiences of millions of individuals who have a mental disorder, their family members, and other advocates, the Nation has the power today to tear down the most formidable obstacle to future progress in the arena of mental illness and health. That obstacle is stigma. Stigmatization of mental illness is an excuse for inaction and discrimination that is inexcusably outmoded in 1999. As evident in the chapters that follow, we have acquired an immense amount of knowledge that permits us, as a Nation, to respond to the needs of persons with mental illness in a manner that is both effective and respectful.

## Overarching Themes

\* \* \*

MENTAL DISORDERS ARE DISABLING   The burden of mental illness on health and productivity in the United States and throughout the world has long been profoundly underestimated. Data developed by the massive Global Burden of Disease study,[1] conducted by the World Health Organization, the World Bank, and Harvard University, reveal that mental illness, including suicide,[2] ranks second in the burden of disease in established market economies, such as the United States (Table 1-1).

Mental illness emerged from the Global Burden of Disease study as a surprisingly significant

### TABLE 1-2

LEADING SOURCES OF DISEASE BURDEN IN
ESTABLISHED MARKET ECONOMIES, 1990

|  | Total DALYs (millions) | Percent of Total |
|---|---|---|
| All causes | 98.7 | |
| 1 Ischemic heart disease | 8.9 | 9.0 |
| 2 Unipolar major depression | 6.7 | 6.8 |
| 3 Cardiovascular disease | 5.0 | 5.0 |
| 4 Alcohol use | 4.7 | 4.7 |
| 5 Road traffic accidents | 4.3 | 4.4 |

Source: Murray & Lopez, 1996.

contributor to the burden of disease. The measure of calculating disease burden in this study, called Disability Adjusted Life Years (DALYs), allows comparison of the burden of disease across many different disease conditions. DALYs account for lost years of healthy life regardless of whether the years were lost to premature death or disability. The disability component of this measure is weighted for severity of the disability. For example, major depression is equivalent in burden to blindness or paraplegia, whereas active psychosis seen in schizophrenia is equal in disability burden to quadriplegia.

By this measure, major depression alone ranked second only to ischemic heart disease in magnitude of disease burden (see Table 1-2). Schizophrenia, bipolar disorder, obsessive-compulsive disorder, panic disorder, and post-traumatic stress disorder also contributed . . . to the burden represented by mental illness.

### TABLE 1-1

DISEASE BURDEN BY SELECTED ILLNESS
CATEGORIES IN ESTABLISHED MARKET
ECONOMIES, 1990

|  | Percent of Total DALYs* |
|---|---|
| All cardiovascular conditions | 18.6 |
| All mental illness** | 15.4 |
| All malignant diseases (cancer) | 15.0 |
| All respiratory conditions | 4.8 |
| All alcohol use | 4.7 |
| All infectious and parasitic diseases | 2.8 |
| All drug use | 1.5 |

*Disability-adjusted life year (DALY) is a measure that expresses years of life lost to premature death and years lived with a disability of specified severity and duration (Murray & Lopez, 1996).
**Disease burden associated with "mental illness" includes suicide.

MENTAL HEALTH AND MENTAL ILLNESS: POINTS ON A CONTINUUM   As will be evident in the pages that follow, "mental health" and "mental illness" are not polar opposites but may be thought of as points on a continuum. *Mental health* is a state of successful performance of mental function, resulting in productive activities, fulfilling relationships with other people, and the ability to adapt to

[1]Murray & Lopez, 1996.
[2]The Surgeon General issued a Call to Action on Suicide in 1999, reflecting the public health magnitude of this consequence of mental illness.

change and to cope with adversity. Mental health is indispensable to personal well-being, family and interpersonal relationships, and contribution to community or society. It is easy to overlook the value of mental health until problems surface. Yet from early childhood until death, mental health is the springboard of thinking and communication skills, learning, emotional growth, resilience, and self-esteem. These are the ingredients of each individual's successful contribution to community and society. Americans are inundated with messages about *success*—in school, in a profession, in parenting, in relationships—without appreciating that successful performance rests on a foundation of mental health.

Many ingredients of mental health may be identifiable, but mental health is not easy to define. In the words of a distinguished leader in the field of mental health prevention, ". . . built into any definition of wellness . . . are overt and covert expressions of values. Because values differ across cultures as well as among subgroups (and indeed individuals) within a culture, the ideal of a uniformly acceptable definition of the constructs is illusory" (Cowen, 1994). In other words, what it means to be mentally healthy is subject to many different interpretations that are rooted in value judgments that may vary across cultures. The challenge of defining mental health has stalled the development of programs to foster mental health (Secker, 1998), although strides have been made with wellness programs for older people (Chapter 5).

*Mental illness* is the term that refers collectively to all diagnosable mental disorders. Mental disorders are health conditions that are characterized by alterations in thinking, mood, or behavior (or some combination thereof) associated with distress and/or impaired functioning. Alzheimer's disease exemplifies a mental disorder largely marked by alterations in thinking (especially forgetting). Depression exemplifies a mental disorder largely marked by alterations in mood. Attention-deficit/hyperactivity disorder exemplifies a mental disorder largely marked by alterations in behavior (overactivity) and/or thinking (inability to concen-

trate). Alterations in thinking, mood, or behavior contribute to a host of problems—patient distress, impaired functioning, or heightened risk of death, pain, disability, or loss of freedom (American Psychiatric Association, 1994).

This report uses the term "mental health problems" for signs and symptoms of insufficient intensity or duration to meet the criteria for any mental disorder. Almost everyone has experienced mental health problems in which the distress one feels matches some of the signs and symptoms of mental disorders. Mental health problems may warrant active efforts in health promotion, prevention, and treatment. Bereavement symptoms in older adults offer a case in point. Bereavement symptoms of less than 2 months' duration do not qualify as a mental disorder, according to professional manuals for diagnosis (American Psychiatric Association, 1994). Nevertheless, bereavement symptoms can be debilitating if they are left unattended. They place older people at risk for depression, which, in turn, is linked to death from suicide, heart attack, or other causes (Zisook & Shuchter, 1991, 1993; Frasure-Smith et al., 1993, 1995; Conwell, 1996). Much can be done—through formal treatment or through support group participation—to ameliorate the symptoms and to avert the consequences of bereavement. In this case, early intervention is needed to address a mental health problem before it becomes a potentially life-threatening disorder.

MIND AND BODY ARE INSEPARABLE Considering health and illness as points along a continuum helps one appreciate that neither state exists in pure isolation from the other. In another but related context, everyday language tends to encourage a misperception that "mental health" or "mental illness" is unrelated to "physical health" or "physical illness." In fact, the two are inseparable.

Seventeenth-century philosopher Rene Descartes conceptualized the distinction between the mind and the body. He viewed the "mind" as completely separable from the "body" (or "matter" in general). The mind (and spirit) was seen as the concern of organized religion, whereas the body was seen as the concern of physicians (Eisendrath & Feder, in press). This partitioning ushered in a separation between so-called "mental" and "physical" health, despite advances in the 20th century that proved the interrelationships between mental and physical health (Cohen & Herbert, 1996; Baum & Posluszny, 1999).

Although "mind" is a broad term that has had many different meanings over the centuries, today it refers to the totality of mental functions related to thinking, mood, and purposive behavior. The mind is generally seen as deriving from activities within the brain but displaying emergent properties, such as consciousness (Fischbach, 1992; Gazzaniga et al., 1998).

One reason the public continues to this day to emphasize the difference between mental and physical health is embedded in language. Common parlance continues to use the term "physical" to distinguish some forms of health and illness from "mental" health and illness. People continue to see mental and physical as separate functions when, in fact, mental functions (e.g., memory) are physical as well (American Psychiatric Association, 1994). Mental functions are carried out by the brain. Likewise, mental disorders are reflected in physical changes in the brain (Kandel, 1998). Physical changes in the brain often trigger physical changes in other parts of the body too. The racing heart, dry mouth, and sweaty palms that accompany a terrifying nightmare are orchestrated by the brain. A nightmare is a mental state associated with alterations of brain chemistry that, in turn, provoke unmistakable changes elsewhere in the body.

Instead of dividing physical from mental health, the more appropriate and neutral distinction is between "mental" and "somatic" health. Somatic is a medical term that derives from the Greek word *soma* for the body. Mental health refers to the successful performance of mental functions in terms of thought, mood, and behavior. Mental disorders are those health conditions in which alterations in mental functions are paramount. Somatic conditions are those in which alterations in nonmental functions predominate. While the brain carries out all mental functions, it also carries out some somatic functions, such as movement, touch, and balance. That is why not all brain diseases are mental disorders. For example, a stroke causes a lesion in the brain that may produce disturbances of movement, such as paralysis of limbs. When such symptoms predominate in a patient, the stroke is considered a somatic condition. But when a stroke mainly produces alterations of thought, mood, or behavior, it is considered a mental condition (e.g., dementia). The point is that a brain disease can be seen as a mental disorder or a somatic disorder depending on the functions it perturbs.

THE ROOTS OF STIGMA  Stigmatization of people with mental disorders has persisted throughout history. It is manifested by bias, distrust, stereotyping, fear, embarrassment, anger, and/or avoidance. Stigma leads others to avoid living, socializing or working with, renting to, or employing people with mental disorders, especially severe disorders such as schizophrenia (Penn & Martin, 1998; Corrigan & Penn, 1999). It reduces patients' access to resources and opportunities (e.g., housing, jobs) and leads to low self-esteem, isolation, and hopelessness. It deters the public from seeking, and wanting to pay for, care. In its most overt and egregious form, stigma results in outright discrimination and abuse. More tragically, it deprives people of their dignity and interferes with their full participation in society.

Explanations for stigma stem, in part, from the misguided split between mind and body first proposed by Descartes. Another source of stigma lies in the 19th-century separation of the mental health treatment system in the United States from the mainstream of health. These historical influences exert an often immediate influence on perceptions and behaviors in the modern world. . . .

*Public Attitudes About Mental Illness: 1950s to 1990s*  . . . In the 1950s, the public viewed mental illness as a stigmatized condition and displayed an unscientific understanding of mental illness. Survey respondents typically were not able to identify individuals as "mentally ill" when presented with vignettes of individuals who would have been said to be mentally ill according to the professional standards of the day. The public was not particularly skilled at distinguishing mental illness from ordinary unhappiness and worry and tended to see only extreme forms of behavior—namely psychosis—as mental illness. Mental illness carried great social stigma, especially linked with fear of unpredictable and violent behavior (Star, 1952, 1955; Gurin et al., 1960; Veroff et al., 1981).

By 1996, a modern survey revealed that Americans had achieved greater scientific understanding of mental illness. But the increases in knowledge did not defuse social stigma (Phelan et al., 1997). The public learned to define mental illness and to distinguish it from ordinary worry and unhappiness. It expanded its definition of mental illness to encompass anxiety, depression, and other mental disorders. The public attributed mental illness to a mix of biological abnormalities and vulnerabilities to social and psychological stress (Link et al., in press). Yet, in comparison with the 1950s, the public's perception of mental illness more frequently incorporated violent behavior (Phelan et al., 1997). This was primarily true among those who defined mental illness to include psychosis (a view held by about one-third of the entire sample). Thirty-one percent of this group mentioned violence in its descriptions of mental illness, in comparison with 13 percent in the 1950s. In other words, the perception of people with psychosis as being dangerous is stronger today than in the past (Phelan et al., 1997).

The 1996 survey also probed how perceptions of those with mental illness varied by diagnosis. The public was more likely to consider an individual with schizophrenia as having mental illness than an individual with depression. All of them were distinguished reasonably well from a worried and unhappy individual who did not meet professional criteria for a mental disorder. The desire for social distance was consistent with this hierarchy (Link et al., in press).

Why is stigma so strong despite better public understanding of mental illness? The answer appears to be fear of violence: people with mental illness, especially those with psychosis, are perceived to be more violent than in the past (Phelan et al., 1997).

This finding begs yet another question: Are people with mental disorders truly more violent? Research supports some public concerns, but the overall likelihood of violence is low. The greatest risk of violence is from those who have dual diagnoses, i.e., individuals who have a mental disorder as well as a substance abuse disorder (Swanson, 1994; Eronen et al., 1998; Steadman et al., 1998). There is a small elevation in risk of violence from individuals with severe mental disorders (e.g., psychosis), especially if they are noncompliant with their medication (Eronen et al., 1998; Swartz et al., 1998). Yet the risk of violence is much less for a stranger than for a family member or person who is known to the person with mental illness (Eronen et al., 1998). *In fact, there is very little risk of violence or harm to a stranger from casual contact with an individual who has a mental disorder.* Because the average person is ill-equipped to judge whether someone who is behaving erratically has any of these disorders, alone or in combination, the natural tendency is to be wary. Yet, to put this all in perspective, the overall contribution of mental disorders to the total level of violence in society is exceptionally small (Swanson, 1994). . . .

*Stigma and Seeking Help for Mental Disorders*
Nearly two-thirds of all people with diagnosable mental disorders do not seek treatment (Regier et al., 1993; Kessler et al., 1996). Stigma surrounding the receipt of mental health treatment is among the many barriers that discourage people from seeking treatment (Sussman et al., 1987; Cooper-Patrick et al., 1997). Concern about stigma appears to be heightened in rural areas in relation to larger towns or cities (Hoyt et al., 1997). Stigma also disproportionately affects certain age groups, as explained in the chapters on children and older people.

The surveys cited above concerning evolving public attitudes about mental illness also monitored how people would cope with, and seek treatment for, mental illness if they became symptomatic. (The term "nervous breakdown" was used in lieu of the term "mental illness" in the 1996 survey to allow for comparisons with the surveys in the 1950s and 1970s.) The 1996 survey found that people were likelier than in the past to approach mental illness by coping with, rather than by avoiding, the problem. They also were more likely now to want *informal* social supports (e.g., self-help groups). Those who now sought *formal* support increasingly preferred counselors, psychologists, and social workers (Swindle et al., 1997).

*Stigma and Paying for Mental Disorder Treatment*
Another manifestation of stigma is reflected in the public's reluctance to pay for mental health services. Public willingness to pay for mental health treatment, particularly through insurance premiums or taxes, has been assessed largely through public opinion polls. Members of the public report a greater willingness to pay for insurance coverage for individuals with severe mental disorders, such as schizophrenia and depression, rather than for less severe conditions such as worry and unhappiness (Hanson, 1998). While the public generally appears to support paying for treatment, its support diminishes upon the realization that higher taxes or premiums would be necessary (Hanson, 1998). In the lexicon of survey research, the willingness to pay for mental illness treatment services is considered to be "soft." The public generally ranks insurance coverage for mental disorders below that for somatic disorders (Hanson, 1998).

*Reducing Stigma*    There is likely no simple or single panacea to eliminate the stigma associated with mental illness. Stigma was expected to abate with increased knowledge of mental illness, but just the opposite occurred: stigma in some ways intensified over the past 40 years even though understanding improved. Knowledge of mental illness appears by itself insufficient to dispel stigma (Phelan et al., 1997). Broader knowledge may be warranted, especially to redress public fears (Penn & Martin, 1998). Research is beginning to demonstrate that negative perceptions about severe mental illness can be lowered by furnishing empirically based information on the association between violence and severe mental illness (Penn & Martin, 1998). Overall approaches to stigma reduction involve programs of advocacy, public education, and contact with persons with mental illness through schools and other societal institutions (Corrigan & Penn, 1999).

Another way to eliminate stigma is to find causes and effective treatments for mental disorders (Jones, 1998). History suggests this to be true. Neurosyphilis and pellagra are illustrative of mental disorders for which stigma has receded. In the early part of this century, about 20 percent of those admitted to mental hospitals had "general paresis," later identified as tertiary syphilis (Grob, 1994). This advanced stage of syphilis occurs when the bacterium invades the brain and causes neurological deterioration (including psychosis), paralysis, and death. The discoveries of an infectious etiology and of penicillin led to the virtual elimination of neurosyphilis. Similarly, when pellagra was traced to a nutrient deficiency, and nutritional supplementation with niacin was introduced, the condition was eventually eradicated in the developed world. Pellagra's victims with delirium had been placed in mental hospitals early in the 20th century before its etiology was clarified. Although no one has documented directly the reduction of public stigma toward these conditions over the early and later parts of this century, disease eradication through widespread acceptance of treatment (and its cost) offers indirect proof.

Ironically, these examples also illustrate a more unsettling consequence: that the mental health field was adversely affected when causes and treatments were identified. As advances were achieved, each condition was transferred from the mental health field to another medical specialty (Grob, 1991). For instance, dominion over syphilis was moved to dermatology, internal medicine, and neurology upon advances in etiology and treatment. Dominion over hormone-related mental disorders was moved to endocrinology under similar circumstances. The consequence of this transformation, according to historian Gerald Grob, is that the mental health field became over the years the repository for mental disorders whose etiology was unknown. This left the mental health field "vulnerable to accusations by their medical brethren that psychiatry was not part of medicine, and that psychiatric practice rested on superstition and myth" (Grob, 1991).

These historical examples signify that stigma dissipates for individual disorders once advances render them less disabling, infectious, or disfiguring. Yet the stigma surrounding *other* mental disorders not only persists but may be inadvertently reinforced by leaving to mental health care only those behavioral conditions without known causes or cures. To point this out is not intended to imply that advances in mental health should be halted; rather, advances should be nurtured and heralded. The purpose here is to explain some of the historical origins of the chasm between the health and mental health fields.

Stigma must be overcome. Research that will continue to yield increasingly effective treatments for mental disorders promises to be an effective antidote. When people understand that mental disorders are not the result of moral failings or limited will power, but are legitimate illnesses that are responsive to specific treatments, much of the negative stereotyping may dissipate. Still, fresh approaches to disseminate research information and, thus, to counter stigma need to be developed and evaluated. Social science research has much to contribute to the development and evaluation of anti-stigma programs (Corrigan & Penn, 1999). As stigma abates, a transformation in public attitudes should occur. People should become eager to seek care. They should become more willing to absorb its cost. And, most importantly, they should become far more receptive to the messages that are the subtext of this report: mental health and mental illness are part of the mainstream of health, and they are a concern for all people. . . .

# References

American Psychiatric Association. (1994). *Diagnostic and statistical manual of mental disorders* (4th ed.). Washington, DC: Author.

Baum, A., & Posluszny, D. M. (1999). Health psychology: Mapping biobehavioral contributions to health and illness. *Annual Review of Psychology, 50*, 137–163.

Cohen, S., & Herbert, T. B. (1996). Health psychology: Psychological factors and physical disease from the perspective of human psychoneuroimmunology. *Annual Review of Psychology, 47*, 113–142.

Conwell, Y. (1996). *Diagnosis and treatment of depression in late life.* Washington, DC: American Psychiatric Press.

Cooper-Patrick, L., Powe, N. R., Jenckes, M. W., Gonzales, J. J., Levine, D. M., & Ford, D. E. (1997). Identification of patient attitudes and preferences regarding treatment of depression. *Journal of General Internal Medicine, 12*, 431–438.

Corrigan, P. W., & Penn, D. L. (1999). Lessons from social psychology on discrediting psychiatric stigma. *American Psychologist, 54*, 765–776.

Cowen, E. L. (1994). The enhancement of psychological wellness: Challenges and opportunities. *American Journal of Community Psychology, 22*, 149–179.

DSM-IV. See American Psychiatric Association (1994).

Eisendrath, S. J., & Feder, A. (in press). The mind and somatic illness: Psychological factors affecting physical illness. In H. H. Goldman (Ed.), *Review of general psychiatry* (5th ed.). Norwalk, CT: Appleton & Lange.

Eronen, M., Angermeyer, M. C., & Schulze, B. (1998). The psychiatric epidemiology of violent behaviour. *Social Psychiatry and Psychiatric Epidemiology, 33*(Suppl. 1), S13–S23.

Fischbach, G. D. (1992). Mind and brain. *Scientific American, 267*, 48–57.

Frasure-Smith, N., Lesperance, F., & Talajic, M. (1993). Depression following myocardial infarction. Impact on 6-month survival. *Journal of the American Medical Association, 270*, 1819–1825.

Frasure-Smith, N., Lesperance, F., & Talajic, M. (1995). Depression and 18-month prognosis after myocardial infarction. *Circulation, 91*, 999–1005.

Gazzaniga, M. S., Ivry, R. B., & Mangun, G. R. (1998). *Cognitive neuroscience: The biology of the mind.* New York: W. W. Norton.

Grob, G. N. (1991). *From asylum to community. Mental health policy in modern America.* Princeton, NJ: Princeton University Press.

Grob, G. N. (1994). *The mad among us: A history of the care of America's mentally ill.* New York: Free Press.

Gurin, J., Veroff, J., & Feld, S. (1960). *Americans view their mental health: A nationwide interview survey* (A report to the staff director, Jack R. Ewalt). New York: Basic Books.

Hanson, K. W. (1998). Public opinion and the mental health parity debate: Lessons from the survey literature. *Psychiatric Services, 49*, 1059–1066.

Hoyt, D. R., Conger, R. D., Valde, J. G., & Weihs, K. (1997). Psychological distress and help seeking in rural America. *American Journal of Community Psychology, 25*, 449–470.

Jones, A. H. (1998). Mental illness made public: Ending the stigma? *Lancet, 352*, 1060.

Kandel, E. R. (1998). A new intellectual framework for psychiatry. *American Journal of Psychiatry, 155*, 457–469.

Kessler, R. C., Nelson, C. B., McKinagle, K. A., Edlund, M. J., Frank, R. G., & Leaf, P. J. (1996). The epidemiology of co-occurring addictive and mental disorders: Implications for prevention and service utilization. *American Journal of Orthopsychiatry, 66*, 17–31.

Link, B., Phelan, J., Bresnahan, M., Stueve, A., & Pescosolido, B. (in press). Public conceptions of mental illness: The labels, causes, dangerousness and social distance. *American Journal of Public Health*.

Murray, C. J. L., & Lopez, A. D. (Eds.). (1996). *The global burden of disease. A comprehensive assessment of mortality and disability from diseases, injuries, and risk factors in 1990 and projected to 2020*. Cambridge, MA: Harvard School of Public Health.

Penn, D. L., & Martin, J. (1998). The stigma of severe mental illness: Some potential solutions for a recalcitrant problem. *Psychiatric Quarterly, 69*, 235–247.

Phelan, J., Link, B., Stueve, A., & Pescosolido, B. (1997, August). *Public conceptions of mental illness in 1950 in 1996: Has sophistication increased? Has stigma declined?* Paper presented at the meeting of the American Sociological Association, Toronto, Ontario.

Regier, D. A., Narrow, W. E., Rae, D. S., Manderscheid, R. W., Locke, B. Z., & Goodwin, F. K. (1993). The de facto US mental and addictive disorders service system. Epidemiologic Catchment Area prospective 1-year prevalence rates of disorders and services. *Archives of General Psychiatry, 50*, 85–94.

Secker, J. (1998). Current conceptualizations of mental health and mental health promotion. *Health Education Research, 13*, 57–66.

Star, S. A. (1952). *What the public thinks about mental health and mental illness*. Paper presented at the annual meeting of the National Association for Mental Health.

Star, S. A. (1955). *The public's ideas about mental illness*. Paper presented at the annual meeting of the National Association for Mental Health.

Steadman, H. J., Mulvey, E. P., Monahan, J., Robbins, P. C., Appelbaum, P. S., Grisso, T., Roth, L. H., & Silver, E. (1998). Violence by people discharged from acute psychiatric inpatient facilities and by others in the same neighborhoods. *Archives of General Psychiatry, 55*, 393–401.

Sussman, L. K., Robins, L. N., & Earls, F. (1987). Treatment-seeking for depression by black and white Americans. *Social Science and Medicine, 24*, 187–196.

Swanson, J. W. (1994). Mental disorder, substance abuse, and community violence: An epidemiological approach. In J. Monahan & H. J. Steadman (Eds.), *Violence and mental disorder: Developments in risk assessment* (pp. 101–136). Chicago: University of Chicago Press.

Swartz, M. S., Swanson, J. W., & Burns, B. J. (1998). Taking the wrong drugs: The role of substance abuse and medication noncompliance in violence among severely mentally ill individuals. *Social Psychiatry and Psychiatric Epidemiology, 33*(Suppl. 1), S75–S80.

Swindle, R., Heller, K., & Pescosolido, B. (1997, August). *Responses to "nervous breakdowns" in America over a 40-year period: Mental health policy implications*. Paper presented at the meeting of American Sociological Association, Toronto, Ontario.

Veroff, J., Douvan, E., & Kulka, R. A. (1981). *Mental health in America: Patterns of help-seeking from 1957 to 1976*. New York: Basic Books.

Zisook, S., & Shuchter, S. R. (1991). Depression through the first year after the death of a spouse. *American Journal of Psychiatry, 148*, 1346–1352.

Zisook, S., & Shuchter, S. R. (1993). Major depression associated with widowhood. *American Journal of Geriatric Psychiatry, 1*, 316–326.

# THE CHALLENGE TO PSYCHIATRY AS SOCIETY'S AGENT FOR MENTAL ILLNESS TREATMENT AND RESEARCH

## William T. Carpenter Jr., M. D.

*The enormous individual and societal costs associated with mental illness is the driving motivation for many scientists and practitioners in the field of mental health. The need for systematic research to alleviate these burdens is widely recognized, but can create other problems. In order both to advance our understanding of the causes of mental disorder and develop effective treatments, it is necessary to expose people suffering from these disorders to research procedures and treatments that may be uncomfortable (such as an MRI scan) or carry some risk of harm (like a potentially valuable but untested medication). Yet researchers are personally committed and professionally required to minimize risk to research participants and protect them from adverse experiences. Where does this line get drawn? This is a dilemma for researchers in many fields, of course, but it takes on even greater significance in the field of mental health because patients might not always be able to understand fully the experimental procedures and treatments being proposed, and because treatments are sometimes in the form of potent psychoactive drugs. As a result, these people may not be able to give their* informed consent *for research participation and may not comprehend the procedures they are consenting to.*

*The next article, by William Carpenter Jr., explores these problems further and offers some useful guidelines for protecting the well-being of research participants while still permitting researchers to make progress in understanding and treating mental illness. The reference list for this article also provides recent sources in the popular media where you can read more about patients who appeared to be harmed from participation in research.*

## Suggested Readings

Appelbaum, P. S. (1998). Missing the boat: Competence and consent in psychiatric research. *American Journal of Psychiatry, 155,* 1486–1488.

Davis, K. L., Braff, D. L., & Weinberger, D. R. (1999). Protecting research subjects and psychiatric research: We can do both. *Biological Psychiatry, 46,* 727–728.

Hyman, S. E. (1999). Protecting patients, preserving progress: Ethics in mental health illness research. *Academic Medicine, 74,* 258–259.

Shalala, D. (2000). Protecting research subjects—What must be done. *New England Journal of Medicine, 343,* 808–810.

*American Journal of Psychiatry, 156,* 1307–1310. (1999).

Society has a moral responsibility for its sick and disabled citizens. Psychiatry assumes this responsibility when clinicians provide care and treatment to mentally ill patients, many of whom suffer from the worst diseases afflicting humans. But these very patients often lack insight into the nature of their afflictions, their causes, and their need for treatment. Experiencing altered perceptions, affects, and beliefs is very different from experiencing other somatic dysfunctions. Both patients and society view the latter as illness requiring medical intervention, whereas the former all too often are viewed as personal attributes rather than disease. Society is uncertain how to assert responsibility, looking simultaneously to law enforcement, religion, psychiatry, the family, and social planning. Given complex and competing themes, psychiatry's capacity to assert and validate illness models and therapeutic interventions is invaluable. A major advance over the past 40 years has been establishing society's confidence that psychiatry can identify individuals who suffer from mental disorders and intervene with effective therapeutics. At the same time, society has also advanced the cause of civil liberties for the mentally ill. Here, too, much good has been accomplished, but disquieting problems remain, problems that stir passions as the ethics and politics of personal autonomy and free will clash with the consequences of honoring these virtues.

. . . Psychiatry accepts a clinical responsibility for determining which individuals, on the basis of mental disease and law, shall be deprived of autonomy rights and dignity by involuntary commitment to receive protection and (perhaps) treatment through clinical services. This burden of judgment and responsibility weighs heavily on the physician-patient relationship and on the professional identity of the physician. Psychiatrists experience their discipline at risk when their assertion of this authority is criticized by society and by the patient whose autonomy rights are compromised. Nothing is quite as reassuring in the exercise of this responsibility as a grateful patient who has come to appreciate the physician's action. Stone's "thank you" theory (1) captured this important dynamic and has been used in support of psychiatry's wise exercise of this authority. . . .

Psychiatrists most often must accept the responsibility of denying autonomy and dignity rights without the appreciative endorsement of their patients. Clear role definition regarding clinical and social responsibility, valid concepts and assessment procedures to meet legal and clinical standards, and an acceptable degree of predictive validity regarding safety and therapeutic advantage are essential. Most important is that society sanction this role assigned to the psychiatrist in addressing the moral obligation of protection and treatment for the very ill citizen. However, the tension will remain as long as the patients we serve fail to understand their illness and the physician's purpose. Change in this regard is importantly dependent on new therapeutic advances through scientific research.

The role of the psychiatric investigator in meeting society's obligation to develop new knowledge to benefit ill citizens is also a vexing paradox: society simultaneously expresses "best hope" and "worst fear" images. No responsible commentator doubts that new knowledge through science is critical to advancing treatment and prevention of mental illness, but current attention in the popular media involves harsh criticism of psychiatric investigations (2–11). Clinical research is not a perfect endeavor, and errors in subject protection procedures and occasional fraudulent investigators have been noted. Much of the criticism, however, is based on misunderstanding of science, misrepresentation of facts, and unsubstantiated allegations. Nonetheless, there is a common ground of concern on the issue of the capacity to make decisions in providing informed consent to research participation.

Subjects in mental illness research are usually presumed to be competent. This may be viewed as respect for the autonomy and dignity rights of persons with mental illness, but the question has also been raised that the presumption of competence permits too many patients with impaired decision-making capacity to sign consent forms they do not understand. Those who believe that valid informed consent can be (and usually is) obtained believe that optimal procedures require continual evolution and that better documentation is needed to enable society to judge the adequacy of the informed consent process. Those who believe that mental illness research is substantially conducted without valid informed consent doubt that investigators and institutional review procedures can ever ensure that this lynchpin of ethical research will be routinely secured. All agree on the urgent need for data that address decision-making capacity for providing consent among prospective subjects for mental illness research. . . .

I am concerned that more harm to the future of individuals with mental illness is being caused by the rush to allegation and redress than is justified by anticipated benefit. Optimal and ever-evolving procedures for the protection of research subjects, including the mentally ill, are of fundamental importance. Stigmatizing those citizens who receive a psychiatric diagnosis, however, and creating a veil of mistrust between society and psychiatric investigator can be rationally justified only if research procedures in psychiatry are both unique and flawed. Commissions in New York (12) and Maryland (13) recently addressed issues of subject protection in medical research with populations at risk for impaired decision-making capacity. Michels (14) called attention to the substantial difference in tone and content of the New York and Maryland commissions compared with the National Bioethics Advisory Commission report, and the interested reader will see this contrast

extended when reading the companion articles by Michels (14) and by Capron (15), a member of the national commission. Michels suggested that the failure of the national commission to include any member with experience and expertise in psychiatric research may explain the difference. In this regard, the two state commissions focused on the decision-making capacity of individuals rather than diagnostic groups, on investigator and review procedures that would enhance capacity assessment and ensure adequacy of consent, on how to design protections in a more realistic relationship to risk, and on how to avoid costly new procedures that would interfere with acquisition of knowledge unless evidence for need and effectiveness was presented. Involvement of psychiatric investigators in these two commissions also reflects the field's commitment to examining problems and evolving optimal procedures.

The psychiatric investigator lives in interesting times. Although I believe much of the present public attention is ill-informed and unfair, the field has received a wake-up call. Adequate decision-making capacity for providing informed consent to research participation can be assessed and documented. But how well is this being done in all the various settings where research is conducted? What constitutes adequate capacity, and how is this to be determined and documented? Who should participate in informed consent, and how should research be conducted if the person is judged to be too impaired for competent consent? How should these procedures be reviewed, and which stakeholders should participate in the review? These and many other questions are on the table. As they are addressed in new federal procedures and regulations, there is already much to do at the local level to address subject protections. The following suggestions seem reasonable, helpful, not too demanding, and protective of both patient subjects and investigators. Not intended as comprehensive guidelines, these suggestions illustrate actions that can be initiated by clinical investigators and their institutions and have worked well at the Maryland Psychiatric Research Center.

1. Have patients or their advocates comment on proposed research and consent forms.

2. Ensure that informed consent is an educational procedure taking place in a time frame that enables the prospective subject to understand, appreciate, reason, and freely exercise choice.

3. Include clinicians other than key investigators in the informed consent process and assessment of decision-making capacity, but do not exclude the investigator from personal responsibility and participation.

4. Include significant others as the patient considers participation, but do not compromise the patient's autonomy and dignity rights if decision-making capacity is adequate.

5. Provide material to all concerned clarifying that clinical care involving research is importantly different from ordinary clinical care. Work with patient subjects to minimize the therapeutic misconception that is commonplace in biomedical research (16).

6. Ensure that patient subjects have contact with a noninvestigator who can help resolve issues relating to research participation.

7. When accepting a consent form, document understanding of basic facts relating to the protocol. . . .

8. Provide educational and sensitivity-raising sessions in ethics for investigators and staff. Include an appreciation of the fundamental role in subject protection incorporated in institutional-review-board-related procedures.

This last point merits brief comment. The media and a handful of severe critics have taken findings of procedural errors and reported them as unethical research and implied that unethical scientists are harming patients (2–11). This I condemn, but clinical investigators have also sometimes regarded such findings as merely procedural. We need to inculcate a deep appreciation of the regulations for review and approval and the monitoring of research as fundamental to the protection of human subjects. These procedures must be conducted with care, and shortcomings must be addressed as a first priority in the ethical conduct of human research.

## References

1. Stone AA: Mental Health and Law: A System in Transition. Rockville, Md, NIMH Center for Studies of Crime and Delinquency, 1975.
2. Hilts PJ: Agency faults a UCLA study for suffering of mental patients. New York Times, March 10, 1994, p. A1.
3. Hilts PJ: Medical experts testify on tests done without consent. New York Times, May 24, 1994, p. A13.
4. Hilts PJ: Consensus on ethics in research is elusive. New York Times, Jan 15, 1995, p. 24.
5. Hilts PJ: Psychiatric researchers under fire for experiments inducing relapse. New York Times, May 19, 1998, p. C1.
6. Hilts PJ: Psychiatric unit's faulted. New York Times, May 28, 1998, p. A26.
7. Wilwerth J: Tinkering with madness. Time, Aug 10, 1993, pp. 40–42.
8. Whitaker R, Kong D: Testing takes human toll. Boston Globe, Nov 15, 1998, p. AO1.
9. Kong D: Debatable forms of consent. Boston Globe, Nov 16, 1998, p. AO1.
10. Whitaker R: Lure of riches fuels testing. Boston Globe, Nov 17, 1998, p. AO1.
11. Kong D: Still no solution in the struggle on safeguards. Boston Globe, Nov 18, 1998, p. AO1.
12. New York State Department of Health Advisory Work Group on Human Subject Research Involving the Protected Classes: Recommendations on the Oversight of Human Subject Research Involving the Protected Classes. Albany, New York State Department of Health, 1998.
13. Final Report of the Attorney General's Working Group on Research Involving Decisionally Incapacitated Subjects. Baltimore, Office of the Maryland Attorney General, 1998.
14. Michels R: Are research ethics bad for our mental health? N Engl J Med 1999; 340:1427–1430.
15. Capron AM: Ethical and human-rights issues in research on mental disorders that may affect decision-making capacity. N Engl J Med 1999; 340:1430–1434.
16. Appelbaum PS, Roth LH, Lidz CW, Benson P, Winslade W: False hopes and best data: consent to research and the therapeutic misconception. Hastings Cent Rep 1987; 17:20–24.

# Comparative Efficiency of Informal (Subjective, Impressionistic) and Formal (Mechanical, Algorithmic) Prediction Procedures: The Clinical-Statistical Controversy

## William M. Grove and Paul E. Meehl

*The day-to-day activities of mental health professionals, particularly those directly treating patients, demand a wide range of decisions and judgments. What diagnosis is appropriate for this collection of symptoms? Should this patient be hospitalized? Is this person ready to be discharged from inpatient care? Is this patient likely to respond better to medication or psychotherapy, or a combination of both? How likely is it that this person will try to commit suicide? Does this test confirm the existence of a neuropsychological deficit? The accuracy of judgments such as these is very important because a series of good decisions can facilitate recovery. Consistently poor decisions, on the other hand, can compromise patients' well-being.*

*Psychologists, particularly cognitive psychologists, have questioned and debated the accuracy of clinical judgment, especially when judgments are made in ambiguous situations like those routinely encountered by mental health professionals. Many studies have been conducted in which clinical judgments are compared to judgments made with some simple equation or mechanical procedure. For example, in a classic study by Lewis Goldberg (1965), clinicians were given the results of MMPI personality tests from dozens of patients and were asked to examine them and state whether each testing profile reflected an individual who was likely to have a diagnosis of neurosis or a diagnosis of psychosis. At the same time, a clerk reviewed these same testing profiles and used a simple rule to make the same decision. The rule, which resulted from previous research studies and did not require any human judgment to apply, would be something like "add up the scores on scales A, B, and C, and then subtract the scores from scales D and E. If the score is below 45, designate this person as neurotic; if the score equals or exceeds 45, designate this person as a psychotic." Distinctions of this kind are important, as they might determine whether a person needs inpatient or outpatient care or whether they need medication (see Dawes, Faust, & Meehl, 1989). This study showed that, compared to the clinicians' judgments, the simple rule was a more accurate index of actual diagnoses that were obtained via interviews. In fact, the simple rule was accurate in 70% of the cases, and the best judge in this study was accurate only 67% of the time; on average the judges were accurate on 62% of the cases.*

*This study is important because it has been replicated time and again with many different kinds of judges and a wide range of decisions. With very few exceptions, the application of a simple rule outperforms the human judge. This is quite remarkable, and it has been a source of much research and consternation in the field of clinical psychology. This article, excerpted from a paper written by Will Grove and Paul Meehl, details the research supporting this basic phenomenon, and it outlines why it happens and why practitioners often resist employing this kind of procedure. Part of the reason that practitioners "use their heads instead of formulas" (see Kleinmuntz, 1990) is that few such rules exist. Indeed, a key task for the field is to develop and refine rules that will automate important judgments; this is already happening in other fields such as cardiology, where mechanical procedures for diagnosing a heart attack from an electrocardiogram are being devised (see Gawande, 1998).*

*As you read the Grove and Meehl article, keep in mind the distinction between human judges as collectors of information and human judges as interpreters of collected data. Grove and Meehl are primarily addressing the limitations of human judges as interpreters of information. It is difficult to imagine a machine that could replace the sensitivity, awareness, and pattern-recognizing capabilities of a human judge. Quantifying human judgment so that it can be used in a routine and automated way is, however, a more complex task.*

## References

Dawes, R. M., Faust, D., & Meehl, P. E. (1989). Clinical versus actuarial judgment. *Science, 243*, 1668–1674.

Gawande, A. (1998, March 30) No mistake. *The New Yorker, 74*, 76–81.

Goldberg, L. R. (1965). Diagnosticians versus diagnostic signs: The diagnosis of psychosis versus neurosis from the MMPI. *Psychological Monographs, 79* (9, Whole No. 602).

Klenimuntz, B. (1990). Why we still use our heads instead of formulas: Toward an integrative approach. *Psychological Bulletin, 107*, 296–310.

## Suggested Reading

Dawes, R. M. (1994). *House of cards: Psychology and psychotherapy built on myth.* New York: The Free Press.

*Psychology, Public Policy, and Law, 2*, 293–323. (1996).

Given a data set about an individual or a group (e.g., interviewer ratings, life history or demographic facts, test results, self-descriptions), there are two modes of data combination for a predictive or diagnostic purpose. The *clinical method* relies on human judgment that is based on informal contemplation and, sometimes, discussion with others (e.g., case conferences) The *mechanical method* involves a formal, algorithmic, objective procedure (e g, equation) to reach the decision. Empirical comparisons of the accuracy of the two methods (136 studies over a wide range of predictands) show that the mechanical method is almost invariably equal to or superior to the clinical method· Common antiactuarial arguments are rebutted, possible causes of widespread resistance to the comparative research are offered, and policy implications of the statistical method's superiority are discussed.

In 1928, the Illinois State Board of Parole published a study by sociologist Burgess of the parole outcome for 3,000 criminal offenders, an exhaustive sample of parolees in a period of years preceding. (In Meehl, 1954/1996, this number is erroneously reported as 1,000, a slip probably arising from the fact that 1,000 cases came from each of three Illinois prisons.) Burgess combined 21 objective factors (e.g., nature of crime, nature of sentence, chronological age, number of previous offenses) in unweighted fashion by simply counting for each case the number of factors present that expert opinion considered favorable or unfavorable to successful parole outcome. . . . Subjective, impressionistic, "clinical" judgments were also made by three prison psychiatrists about probable parole success. The psychiatrists were slightly more accurate than the actuarial tally of favorable factors in predicting parole success, but they were markedly inferior in predicting failure. Furthermore, the actuarial tally made predictions for every case, whereas the psychiatrists left a sizable fraction of cases undecided. The conclusion was clear that even a crude actuarial method such as this was superior to clinical judgment in accuracy of prediction. Of course, we do not know how many of the 21 factors the psychiatrists took into account, but all were available to them; hence, if they ignored certain powerful predictive factors, this would have represented a source of error in clinical judgment. To our knowledge, this is the earliest empir-

ical comparison of two ways of forecasting behavior. One, a formal method, uses an equation, a formula, a graph, or an actuarial table to arrive at a probability, or expected value, of some outcome; the other method relies on an informal, "in the head," impressionistic, subjective conclusion, reached (somehow) by a human clinical judge. . . .

Wittman (1941) developed a prognosis scale for predicting outcome of electroshock therapy in schizophrenia, which consisted of 30 variables rated from social history and psychiatric examination. The predictors ranged from semi-objective matters (such as duration of psychosis) to highly interpretive judgments (such as anal-erotic vs. oral-erotic character). None of the predictor variables was psychometric. Numerical weights were not based on the sample statistics but were assigned judgmentally on the basis of the frequency and relative importance ascribed to them in previous studies. We may therefore presume that the weights used here were not optimal, but with 30 variables that hardly matters (unless some of them should not have been included at all). The psychiatric staff made ratings as to prognosis at a diagnostic conference prior to the beginning of therapy, and the assessment of treatment outcome was made by a therapy staff meeting after the conclusion of shock therapy. We can probably infer that some degree of contamination of this criterion rating occurred, which inflated the hits percentage for the psychiatric staff. The superiority of the actuarial method over the clinician was marked, as can be seen in Table 1. It is of qualitative interest that the "facts" entered in the equation were themselves of a somewhat vague, impressionistic sort, the kinds of first-order inferences that the psychiatric raters were in the habit of making in their clinical work.

By 1954, when Meehl published *Clinical Versus Statistical Prediction: A Theoretical Analysis and a Review of the Evidence* (Meehl, 1954/1996), there were, depending on some borderline classifications, about 20 such comparative studies in the literature. In every case the statistical method was equal or superior to informal clinical judgment, despite the nonoptimality of many of the equa-

## TABLE 1

COMPARISON OF ACTUARIAL AND CLINICAL
PREDICTIONS OF OUTCOME OF ELECTROSHOCK
THERAPY FOR SCHIZOPHRENIC ADULTS

| Five-step criterion category | n | Percentage of hits | |
|---|---|---|---|
| | | Scale | Psychiatrists |
| Remission | 56 | 90 | 52 |
| Much improved | 66 | 86 | 41 |
| Improved | 51 | 75 | 36 |
| Slightly improved | 31 | 46 | 34 |
| Unimproved | 139 | 85 | 49 |

*Note.* Values are derived from a graph presented in Wittman (1941).

tions used. In several studies the clinician, who always had whatever data were entered into the equation, also had varying amounts of further information. . . . The publication of Meehl's book aroused considerable anxiety in the clinical community and engendered a rash of empirical comparisons over the ensuing years. As the evidence accumulated (Goldberg, 1968; Gough, 1962; Meehl, 1965, 1967; Sawyer, 1966; Sines, 1970) beyond the initial batch of 20 research comparisons, it became clear that *conducting an investigation in which informal clinical judgment would perform better than the equation was almost impossible* [emphasis added]. A general assessment for that period (supplanted by the meta-analysis summarized below) was that in around two fifths of studies the two methods were approximately equal in accuracy, and in around three fifths the actuarial method was significantly better. Because the actuarial method is generally less costly, it seemed fair to say that studies showing approximately equal accuracy should be tallied in favor of the statistical method. . . .

The purposes of this article are (a) to reinforce the empirical generalization of actuarial over clinical prediction with fresh meta-analytic evidence, (b) to reply to common objections to actuarial methods, (c) to provide an explanation for why actuarial prediction works better than clinical prediction, (d) to offer some explanations for why practitioners continue to resist actuarial prediction in the face of overwhelming evidence to the contrary, and (e) to conclude with policy recommendations, some of which include correcting for unethical behavior on the part of many clinicians.

## Results of a Meta-Analysis

Recently, one of us (W.M.G.) completed a meta-analysis of the empirical literature comparing clinical with statistical prediction. This study is described briefly here; it is reported in full, with more complete analyses, in Grove, Zald, Lebow, Snitz, and Nelson (1996). To conduct this analysis, we cast our net broadly, including any study that met the following criteria: was published in English since the 1920s; concerned the prediction of health-related phenomena (e.g., diagnosis) or human behavior; and contained a description of the empirical outcomes of at least one human judgment–based prediction and at least one mechanical prediction. *Mechanical prediction* includes the output of optimized prediction formulas, such as multiple regression or discriminant analysis; unoptimized statistical formulas, such as unit-weighted sums of predictors; actuarial tables; and computer programs and other mechanical schemes that yield precisely reproducible (but not necessarily statistically or actuarially optimal) predictions. To find the studies, we used a wide variety of search techniques, which we do not detail here; suffice it to say that although we may have missed a few studies, we think it highly unlikely that we have missed many.

We found 136 such studies, which yielded 617 distinct comparisons between the two methods of prediction. These studies concerned a wide range of predictive criteria, including medical and mental health diagnosis, prognosis, treatment recommendations, and treatment outcomes; personality description; success in training or employment; adjustment to institutional life (e.g., military, prison); socially relevant behaviors such as parole violation and violence; socially relevant behaviors in the aggregate, such as bankruptcy of firms; and many other predictive criteria. The clinicians included psychologists, psychiatrists, social workers, members of parole boards and admissions committees, and a variety of other individuals. Their educations range from an unknown lower bound that probably does not exceed a high school degree to an upper bound of highly educated and credentialed medical subspecialists. Judges' experience levels ranged from none at all to many years of task-relevant experience. The mechanical prediction techniques ranged from the simplest imaginable (e.g., cutting a single predictor variable at a fixed point, perhaps arbitrarily chosen) to sophisticated methods involving advanced quasi-statistical techniques (e.g., artificial intelligence, pattern recognition). The data on which the predictions were based ranged from sophisticated medical tests to crude tallies of life history facts. . . .

We excluded studies in which the predictive information available to one method of prediction was not either (a) the same as for the other method or (b) a subset of the information available to the other method. In other words, we included studies in which a clinician had data $x$, $y$, $z$, and $w$, but the actuary had only $x$ and $y$; however, we excluded studies in which the clinician had $x$ and $y$, whereas the actuary had $y$ and $z$ or $z$ and $w$. The typical scenario was for clinicians to have all the information the actuary had plus some other information; this occurred in a majority of studies. The opposite possibility never occurred; no study gave the actuary more data than the clinician. Thus many of our studies had a bias in favor of the clinician. Because the bias created when more information is accessible through one method than another has a known direction, it only vitiates the validity of the comparison if the clinician is found to be superior in predictive accuracy to a mechanical method. If the clinician's predictions are found inferior to, or no better than, the mechanical predictions, even when the clinician is given more information, the disparity cannot be accounted for by such a bias. . . .

What can be determined from such a heterogeneous aggregation of studies, concerning a wide array of predictands and involving such a variety of judges, mechanical combination methods, and data? Quite a lot, as it turns out. . . . Of the 136

studies, 64 favored the actuary by this criterion, 64 showed approximately equivalent accuracy, and 8 favored the clinician. The 8 studies favoring the clinician are not concentrated in any one predictive area, do not overrepresent any one type of clinician (e.g., medical doctors), and do not in fact have any obvious characteristics in common. This is disappointing, as one of the chief goals of the meta-analysis was to identify particular areas in which the clinician might outperform the mechanical prediction method. According to the logicians' "total evidence rule," the most plausible explanation of these deviant studies is that they arose by a combination of random sampling errors (8 deviant out of 136) and the clinicians' informational advantage in being provided with more data than the actuarial formula. . . .

Experience of the clinician seems to make little or no difference in predictive accuracy relative to the actuary, once the average level of success achieved by clinical and mechanical prediction in a given study is taken into account. *Professional training (i.e., years in school) makes no real difference* [emphasis added]. The type of mechanical prediction used does seem to matter; the *best results were obtained with weighted linear prediction (e.g., multiple linear regression)* [emphasis added]. Simple schemes such as unweighted sums of raw scores do not seem to work as well. All these facts are quite consistent with the previous literature on human judgment (e.g., see Garb, 1989, on experience, training, and predictive accuracy) or with obvious mathematical facts (e.g., optimized weights should outperform unoptimized weights, though not necessarily by very much). . . .

The great preponderance of studies either favor the actuary outright or indicate equivalent performance. The few exceptions are scattered and do not form a pocket of predictive excellence in which clinicians could profitably specialize. In fact, there are many fewer studies favoring the clinician than would be expected by chance, even for a sizable subset of predictands, if the two methods were statistically equivalent. We conclude that this literature is almost 100% consistent and that it reproduces and amplifies the results obtained by

Meehl in 1954 (Meehl, 1954/1996). Forty years of additional research published since his review has not altered the conclusion he reached. It has only strengthened that conclusion. . . .

## Explanation of Why Actuarial Prediction Works Better Than Clinical

What is the explanation for the statistical method being almost always equal or superior in accuracy to the informal, impressionistic, clinical method of data combination? Space does not permit more than a summary statement here; for more extensive treatment by clinical, social, and cognitive psychologists, see, for example, Arkes and Hammond (1986); Dawes (1988); Faust (1984); Hogarth (1987); Kahneman et al. (1982); Meehl (1954/1996); Nisbett and Ross (1980); and Plous (1993); for a listing of sources of error in clinical judgment, see Meehl (1992a, pp. 353–354). Assume that the clinician does not usually (except, e.g., Freud) attempt to concoct an idiographic mini theory of an individual's psyche and the environmental forces that are likely to act on that person but simply attempts to do a subjective, impressionistic, in-the-head approximating job of actuarial computation. Then the clinician's brain is functioning as merely a poor substitute for an explicit regression equation or actuarial table. Humans simply cannot assign optimal weights to variables, and they are not consistent in applying their own weights. . . .

The human brain is a relatively inefficient device for noticing, selecting, categorizing, recording, retaining, retrieving, and manipulating information for inferential purposes. Why should we be surprised at this? From a historical viewpoint, the superiority of formal, actuarially based procedures seems obvious, almost trivial. The dazzling achievements of Western post-Galilean science are attributable not to our having any better brains than Aristotle or Aquinas, but to the scientific method of accumulating objective knowledge. A very few strict rules (e.g., don't fake data, avoid parallax in reading a dial) but mostly rough "guidelines" about observing, sampling, recording, calculating, and so forth sufficed to create this amazing social machine for producing valid knowledge. Scientists record observations at the time rather than rely on unaided memory. Precise instruments are substituted for the human eye, ear, nose, and fingertips whenever these latter are unreliable. Powerful formalisms (trigonometry, calculus, probability theory, matrix algebra) are used to move from one set of numerical values to another. Even simple theories can now be derived by search algorithms (e.g., Langley, Simon, Bradshaw, & Zytkow, 1987; Shrager & Langley, 1990), although inventing rich theories postulating theoretical entities interacting in complex ways is as yet a uniquely human mind task. However theories are concocted, whether appraisal of their empirical merits is best conducted informally, as presently (except in meta-analysis, cf. Glass, McGaw, & Smith, 1981; Hunter, Schmidt, & Jackson, 1982), is not known and has been forcefully challenged (Faust, 1984; Faust & Meehl, 1992; Meehl, 1990a, 1990b, 1992a, 1992b). However, we need not look to science for the basic point to be made, as it holds—and is universally accepted, taken for granted—in most areas of daily life.

> Surely we all know that the human brain is poor at weighting and computing. When you check out at a supermarket, you don't eyeball the heap of purchases and say to the clerk, "Well it looks to me as if it's about $17.00 worth; what do you think?" The clerk adds it up. (Meehl, 1986, p. 372) . . .

## Why Do Practitioners Continue to Resist Actuarial Prediction?

Readers unfamiliar with this controversy may be puzzled that despite the theoretical arguments from epistemology and mathematics and the empirical results, the proactuarial position is apparently held by only a minority of practitioners. How is it possible that thousands of MDs, PhDs, and MSWs, licensed to practice in their jurisdictions, and even academics teaching in clinical training programs, could be so wrong, as we allege? Having answered their objections on the merits, we think it not arguing ad hominem or committing the genetic fallacy to suggest some sociopsychological factors that may help explain this remarkable resistance to argument and evidence.

*Fear of technological unemployment.* If one of 20 social workers engaged in writing presentence investigation reports is told that 18 could be dispensed with and that the other 2, supervised by a PhD-level psychologist or statistician, could do as well or better in advising the court judges, then this is cause for concern.

*Self-concept.* Income aside, most professionals have a self-image and a personal security system that are intimately tied in with the value that they and society place on their scholarly and technical functions. As an analogy, consider how unhappy senior partners in a law firm would be, even if assured of their jobs, to learn that paralegals with a few years of experience could predict the opinions of an appellate court as accurately as a partner can.

*Attachment to theory.* Most researchers and clinicians have a fondness for certain concepts and theories, and the idea that our theory-mediated predictions do not contribute anything predictively beyond what an atheoretical actuarial table could or that the theory may even make matters worse produces cognitive dissonance. Most intellectuals, whether practitioners or not, take concepts and theories seriously. . . .

*General dislike of computers' successfully competing with human minds.* Personal ego involvement and employment aside, many persons seem to have some diffuse resentment toward the very idea that a computer can duplicate human cognitive performance. Thus, for instance, that computer chess programs are now able to defeat a few grand masters sometimes bothers people who are not themselves chess masters. For some reason, people just do not like the idea that a mere machine can do better than a person at any cognitive task.

*Poor education.* Poor education is probably the biggest single factor responsible for resistance to actuarial prediction; it does not involve imputation of any special emotional bias or feeling of personal threat. In the majority of training programs in clinical psychology, and it is surely as bad or worse in psychiatry and social work, no great value is placed on the cultivation of skeptical, scientific habits of thought; the role models—even in the academy, but more so in the clinical settings—are often people who do not put a high value on scientific thinking, are not themselves engaged in scientific research, and take it for granted that clinical experience is sufficient to prove whatever they want to believe. There are probably not more than two dozen American psychology departments whose clinical training programs strongly emphasize the necessity for scientific proof, either as experiments or statistical study of file data, as the only firm foundation for knowledge. As a sheer matter of information, many psychologists, psychiatrists, and social workers are literally unaware that any controversy about the merits of prediction procedure exist or that any empirical comparisons of the two methods have been performed. The common position is, "Well, of course, a deep psychological understanding will enable a clinician to predict an individual's future behavior better than any generic mathematical equation possibly could." Even if motivational forces were absent (and they are hardly likely to be totally absent in any of us who engage in clinical work), inadequate scientific education would be more than sufficient to account for the compact majority being in error. . . .

## Conclusions and Policy Implications

We know of no social science controversy for which the empirical studies are so numerous, varied, and consistent as this one. Antistatistical clinicians persist in making what Dawes (1994, pp. 25, 30, 96) called the "vacuum argument," in which (imagined, hoped for) supportive evidence is simply hypothesized, whereas negative evidence that has actually been collected is ignored. For example, "But clinicians differ; some are better than others." Reply: "True, but even the best ones don't excel the equation." "But even the best ones were naive; they should have feedback so as to improve their performance." Reply: "The effectiveness of feedback is not a robust finding and is small." "But they were not given the right kind of feedback," and so forth. One observes a series of tactical retreats, reformulations, and ad hoc explanations, coupled with a complacent assurance that if the "right sort" of study were done, things would turn out differently. This sublime confidence in the yet-to-be-done super study persists despite the social fact that many of the published investigators (including Meehl, 1959, trying to implement Meehl, 1957) were motivated to come up with a good antiactuarial result. When we have 136 interpretable studies with only 5% deviant, ranging over a wide diversity of predictands (e.g., winning football games, business failures, response to shock therapy, parole violation, success in military training), it is time to draw a conclusion "until further notice," the more so as the facts are in accord with strong theoretical expectations. One must classify continued rejection (or disregard) of the proactuarial generalization as clear instances of resistance to scientific discovery (Barber, 1961), or, more generally, as exemplifying H. L. Mencken's dictum that most people believe what they want to believe. This seems a harsh but warranted judgment. . . .

The policy implications of the research findings are obvious. Two main theses emerge from the empirical conclusion. First, policymakers should not accept a practitioner's unsupported allegation that something works when the only warrant for this claim is purported clinical experience. Clinical experience is an invaluable source of ideas. It is also the only way that a practitioner can acquire certain behavioral skills, such as how to ask questions of the client. It is not an adequate method for settling disputes between practitioners, because they each appeal to their own clinical experience. Histories of medicine teach us that until around 1890, most of the things physicians did to patients were either useless or actively harmful. Bleeding, purging, and blistering were standard procedures, as well as prescribing various drugs which did nothing. In 1487, two Dominican monks, Kraemer and Sprenger (1487/1970), published a huge treatise, *Malleus Maleficarum*, that

gave details on how to reach a valid diagnosis of a witch. It is estimated that more than 100,000 persons were hanged, burned alive, drowned, or crushed with stones as witches; the basis for the detailed technical indications in that book was the clinical experience of inquisitors. All policymakers should know that a practitioner who claims not to need any statistical or experimental studies but relies solely on clinical experience as adequate justification, by that very claim is shown to be a nonscientifically minded person whose professional judgments are not to be trusted (cf. Meehl, in press). Further, when large amounts of taxpayer money are expended on personnel who use unvalidated procedures (e.g., the millions of dollars spent on useless presentence investigation reports), even a united front presented by the profession involved should be given no weight in the absence of adequate scientific research showing that they can do what they claim to do.

Regardless of whether one views the issue as theoretically interesting, it cannot be dismissed as pragmatically unimportant. Every day many thousands of predictions are made by parole boards, deans' admission committees, psychiatric teams, and juries hearing civil and criminal cases. Students' and soldiers' career aspirations, job applicants' hopes, freedom of convicted felons or risk to future victims, millions of taxpayer dollars expended by court services, hundreds of millions involved in individual and class action lawsuits for alleged brain impairment (Faust, Ziskin, & Hiers, 1991; Guilmette, Faust, Hart, & Arkes, 1990), and so forth—these are high stakes indeed. To use the less efficient of two prediction procedures in dealing with such matters is not only unscientific and irrational, it is unethical. To say that the clinical-statistical issue is of little importance is preposterous.

# References

Arkes, H. R., & Hammond, K. R. (1986). *Judgment and decision making: An interdisciplinary reader.* New York: Cambridge University Press.

Barber, B. (1961, September 1). Resistance by scientists to scientific discovery. *Science, 134,* 596–602.

Dawes, R. M. (1988). *Rational choice in an uncertain world.* Chicago, IL: Harcourt Brace Jovanovich.

Dawes, R. M. (1994). *House of cards.* New York: Free Press.

Faust, D. (1984). *The limits of scientific reasoning.* Minneapolis: University of Minnesota Press.

Faust, D., & Meehl, P. E. (1992). Using scientific methods to resolve enduring questions within the history and philosophy of science: Some illustrations. *Behavior Therapy, 23,* 195–211.

Faust, D., Ziskin, J., & Hiers, J. B. (1991). *Brain damage claims: Coping with neuropsychological evidence* (Vols. 1–2). Los Angeles: Law & Psychology Press.

Garb, H. N. (1989). Clinical judgment, clinical training, and professional experience. *Psychological Bulletin, 105,* 387–396.

Glass, G. V., McGaw, B., & Smith, M. L. (1981). *Meta-analysis in social research.* Beverly Hills, CA: Sage.

Goldberg, L. R. (1968). Simple models or simple processes? Some research on clinical judgments. *American Psychologist, 23,* 483–496.

Gough, H. G. (1962). Clinical versus statistical prediction in psychology. In L. Postman (Ed.), *Psychology in the making* (pp. 526–584). New York: Knopf.

Grove, W. M., Zald, D. H., Lebow, B. S., Snits, B. E., & Nelson, C. E. (1996). *Clinical vs. mechanical prediction: A meta-analysis.* Manuscript submitted for publication.

Guilmette, T. J., Faust, D., Hart, K., & Arkes, H. R. (1990). A national survey of psychologists who offer neuropsychological services. *Archives of Clinical Neuropsychology, 5,* 373–392.

Hogarth, R. M. (1987). *Judgement and choice: The psychology of decision.* New York: Wiley.

Hunter, J. E., Schmidt, F. L., & Jackson, G. B. (1982). *Meta-analysis: Cumulating research findings across studies.* Beverly Hills, CA: Sage.

Kahneman, D., Slovic, P., & Tversky, A. (Eds.). (1982). *Judgments under uncertainty: Heuristics and biases.* Cambridge, England: Cambridge University Press.

Kraemer, H., & Sprenger, J. (1970). *Malleus malaeficarum.* New York: Blom. (Original work published 1487)

Langley, P., Simon, H. A., Bradshaw, G. L., & Zytkow, J. M. (1987). *Scientific discovery: Computational explorations of the creative processes.* Cambridge, MA: MIT Press.

Meehl, P. E. (1957). When shall we use our heads instead of the formula? *Journal of Counseling Psychology, 4,* 268–273.

Meehl, P. E. (1959). A comparison of clinicians with five statistical methods of identifying MMPI profiles. *Journal of Counseling Psychology, 6,* 102–109.

Meehl, P. E. (1965). Seer over sign: The first good example. *Journal of Experimental Research in Personality, 1,* 27–32.

Meehl, P. E. (1967). What can the clinician do well? In D. N. Jackson & S. Messick (Eds.), *Problems in human assessment* (pp. 594–599). New York: McGraw-Hill.

Meehl, P. E. (1986). Causes and effects of my disturbing little book. *Journal of Personality Assessment, 50,* 370–375.

Meehl, P. E. (1990a). Appraising and amending theories: The strategy of Lakatosian defense and two principles that warrant using it. *Psychological Inquiry, 1,* 108–141, 173–180.

Meehl, P. E. (1990b). Why summaries of research on psychological theories are often uninterpretable. *Psychological Reports, 66,* 195–244, and (1991) In R. E. Snow & D. Wiley (Eds.), *Improving inquiry in social science* (pp. 13–59). Hillsdale, NJ: Erlbaum.

Meehl, P. E. (1992a). Cliometric metatheory: The actuarial approach to empirical, history-based philosophy of science. *Psychological Reports, 71,* 339–467.

Meehl, P. E. (1992b). The Miracle Argument for realism: An important lesson to be learned by generalizing from Carrier's counter-examples. *Studies in History and Philosophy of Science, 23,* 267–282.

Meehl, P. E. (1996). *Clinical versus statistical prediction: A theoretical analysis and a review of the evidence.* Northvale, NJ: Jason Aronson. (Original work published 1954)

Meehl, P. E. (in press). Credentialed persons, credentialed knowledge. *Clinical Psychology: Science and Practice.*

Nisbett, R. E., & Ross, L. (1980). *Human inference: strategies and shortcomings of human judgment.* Englewood Cliffs, NJ: Prentice-Hall.

Plous, S. (1993). *The psychology of judgment and decision making.* New York: McGraw-Hill.

Sawyer, J. (1966). Measurement *and* prediction, clinical *and* statistical. *Psychological Bulletin, 66,* 178–200.

Shrager, J., & Langley, P. (1990). *Computational models of scientific discovery and theory formation.* San Mateo, CA: Morgan Kaufman.

Sines, J. O. (1970). Actuarial versus clinical prediction in psychopathology. *British Journal of Psychiatry, 116,* 129–144.

Wittman, M. P. (1941). A scale for measuring prognosis in schizophrenic patients. *Elgin Papers, 4,* 20–33.

# How Psychiatry Lost Its Way

## Paul R. McHugh

*Bringing order and meaning to the phenomena of interest is a central task for all scientific disciplines. In the absence of mutually agreed-upon definitions and distinctions about psychopathology, researchers and practitioners cannot communicate effectively about what they see, and scientific progress will be slow. There are many barriers to establishing workable definitions and distinctions including the complexity of the phenomena themselves, the differing theoretical orientations that people adopt, and the fact that meaning can be established in many different ways.*

*Paul McHugh addresses the difficulties that have arisen with standard diagnostic practices in the domain of psychopathology. He notes that diagnostic categories were initially formalized as a way of reliably categorizing patients, who could then be compared across laboratories in treatment studies. He argues that a subtle but far-reaching shift occurred when these same categories were viewed as diseases. What was intended as a convenient shorthand for forming groups of patients who may or may not benefit from a particular treatment became a set of rules for deciding whether or not a person had a particular disorder. McHugh notes that defining disorders on the basis of collections of symptoms—what he calls "appearance-based classifications"—is relatively primitive compared to other branches of medicine, where diagnostic decisions are made on the basis of likely causes for observed symptoms. Treatments are more likely to prove effective when presumed causes are used as the basis for distinguishing between patients.*

*How exactly do we define a mental disorder? To what extent should mental disorders be viewed as discrete categories versus continuous dimensions? These and other questions about the diagnosis and classification of psychopathology are active topics of debate today. The McHugh article introduces some of these key themes, and numerous extensions of them can be found in the suggested readings.*

### Suggested Readings

Follette, W. C., & Houts, A. C. (1996). Models of scientific progress and the role of theory in taxonomy development: A case study of the *DSM. Journal of Consulting and Clinical Psychology, 64*, 1120–1132.

Hartung, C. M., & Widiger, T. A. (1998). Gender differences in the diagnosis of mental disorders: Conclusions and controversies of the *DSM-IV. Psychological Bulletin, 123*, 260–278.

Nathan, P. E., & Langenbucher, J. W. (1999). Psychopathology: Description and classification. *Annual Review of Psychology, 50*, 79–107.

Wakefield, J. C. (1992). The concept of mental disorder: On the boundary between biological facts and social values. *American Psychologist, 47,* 373–388.

*Commentary, 108,* 32. (1999).

"The desire to take medicine," noted the great Johns Hopkins physician William Osler a hundred years ago, "is one feature that distinguishes man, the animal, from his fellow creatures." In today's consumer culture, this desire is hardly restricted to people with physical conditions. Psychiatric patients who in the past would bring me their troublesome mental symptoms and their worries over the possible significance of those symptoms now arrive in my office with diagnosis, prognosis, and treatment already in hand.

"I've got adult attention deficit disorder," a young man informs me, "and it's hindering my career. I need a prescription for Ritalin." When I inquire as to the source of his analysis and its proposed solution, he tells me he has read about the disorder in a popular magazine, realized that he shares many of the features enumerated in an attached checklist of "diagnostic" symptoms—especially a certain difficulty in concentrating and an easy irritability—and now wants what he himself calls "the stimulant that heals."

In response, I gamely point out a number of possible countervailing factors: that he may be taking a one-sided view of things, emphasizing his blemishes and overlooking his assets; that what he has already accomplished in his young life is inconsistent with attention deficit disorder; that many other reasons could be adduced for irritability and inattention; that Ritalin is an addictive substance. But in saying all this, I realize that I have also entered into a delicate negotiation, one that may end with his marching angrily from my office. For not only am I not doing what he wants, I am being insensitive, or so he will claim, to what "his" diagnosis clearly reveals. Less a suffering patient, he has been transformed, before my very eyes, into a dissatisfied customer.

It is a strange experience. People normally do not like to hear that they have a disease, but with this patient, as with many others like him, the opposite is the case: the conviction that he suffers from a mental disorder has somehow served to encourage him. On the one hand, it has rendered his life more interesting. On the other hand, it plays to the widespread current belief that everything can be made right with a pill. This pill will turn my young man into someone stronger, more in charge, less vulnerable—less ignoble. He wants it; it's for sale; end of discussion.

He is, as I say, hardly alone. With help from the popular media, home-brewed psychiatric diagnoses have proliferated in recent years, preoccupying the worried imaginations of the American public: Restless, impatient people are convinced that they have attention deficit disorder (ADD); anxious, vigilant people that they suffer from post-traumatic stress disorder (PTSD); stubborn, orderly, perfectionistic people that they are afflicted with obsessive-compulsive disorder (OCD); shy, sensitive people that they manifest avoidant personality disorder (APD), or social phobia. All have been persuaded that what are really matters of their individuality are, instead, medical problems, and as such are to be solved with drugs. Those drugs will relieve the features of temperament that are burdensome, replacing them with features that please. The motto of this movement (with apologies to the DuPont corporation) might be: better living through pharmacology.

And—most worrisome of all—wherever they look, such people find psychiatrists willing, even eager, to accommodate them. Worse: in many cases, it is psychiatrists who are leading the charge. But the exact role of the psychiatric profession in our current proliferation of disorders and in the thoughtless prescription of medication for them is no simple tale to tell.

When it comes to diagnosing mental disorders, psychiatry has undergone a sea change over the last two decades. The stages of that change can be traced in successive editions of the *Diagnostic and*

*Statistical Manual of Mental Disorders (DSM)*, the official tome of American psychiatry published and promoted by the American Psychiatric Association (APA). But historically its impetus derives—inadvertently—from a salutary effort begun in the early 1970's at the medical school of Washington University in St. Louis to redress the dearth of research in American psychiatry.

The St. Louis scholars were looking into a limited number of well-established disorders. Among them was schizophrenia, an affliction that can manifest itself in diverse ways. What the investigators were striving for was to isolate clear and distinct symptoms that separated indubitable cases of schizophrenia from less certain ones. By creating a set of such "research diagnostic criteria," their hope was to permit study to proceed across and among laboratories, free of the concern that erroneous conclusions might arise from the investigation of different types of patients in different medical centers.

With these criteria, the St. Louis group did not claim to have found the specific features of schizophrenia—a matter, scientifically speaking, of "validity." Rather, they were identifying certain markers or signs that would enable comparative study of the disease at multiple research sites—a matter of "reliability." But this very useful effort had baleful consequences when, in planning *DSM-III* (1980), the third edition of its *Diagnostic and Statistical Manual*, the APA picked up on the need for reliability and out of it forged a bid for scientific validity. In both *DSM-III* and *DSM-IV* (1994), what had been developed at St. Louis as a tool of scholarly research into only a few established disorders became subtly transformed, emerging as a clinical method of diagnosis (and, presumably, treatment) of psychiatric states and conditions of all kinds, across the board. The signs and markers—the presenting symptoms—became the official guide to the identification of mental disorders, and the list of such disorders served in turn to certify their existence in categorical form.

The significance of this turn to classifying mental disorders by their appearances cannot be underestimated. In physical medicine, doctors have long been aware that appearances, either as the identifying marks of disorders or as the targets of therapy, are untrustworthy. For one thing, it is sometimes difficult to distinguish symptoms of illness from normal variations in human life. For another, identical symptoms can be the products of totally different causal mechanisms and thus call for quite different treatments. For still another, descriptions of appearances are limitless, as limitless as the number of individuals presenting them; if medical classifications were to be built upon such descriptions, the enumerating of diseases would never end.

For all these reasons, general medicine abandoned appearance-based classifications more than a century ago. Instead, the signs and symptoms manifested by a given patient are understood to be produced by one or another underlying pathological process. Standard medical and surgical conditions are now categorized according to six such processes: infectious disorders, neoplastic disorders, cardiovascular disorders, toxic/traumatic disorders, genetic/degenerative disorders, and endocrine/metabolic disorders. Internists are reluctant to accept the existence of any proposed new disease unless its signs and symptoms can be linked to one of these processes.

The medical advances made possible by this approach can be appreciated by considering gangrene. Early in the last century, doctors differentiated between two types of this condition: "wet" and "dry." If a doctor was confronted with a gangrene that appeared wet, he was enjoined to dry it; if dry, to moisten it. Today, by contrast, doctors distinguish gangrenes of infection from gangrenes of arterial obstruction/infarction, and treat each accordingly. The results, since they are based solidly in biology, are commensurately successful.

In *DSM*-led psychiatry, however, this beneficial movement has been forgone: today, psychiatric conditions are routinely differentiated by appearances alone. This means that the decision to follow a particular course of treatment for, say, depression is typically based not on the neurobiological or psychological data but on the presence or absence of certain associated symptoms like anxiety—that is, on the "wetness" or "dryness" of the depressive patient.

No less unsettling is the actual means by which mental disorders and their qualifying symptoms have come to find their way onto the lists in *DSM-III* and *-IV*. In the absence of validating conceptions like the six mechanisms of disease in internal medicine, American psychiatry has turned to "committees of experts" to define mental disorder. Membership on such committees is a matter of one's reputation in the APA—which means that those chosen can confidently be expected to manifest not only a requisite degree of psychiatric competence but, perhaps more crucially, some talent for diplomacy and self-promotion.

In identifying psychiatric disorders and their symptoms, these "experts" draw upon their clinical experience and presuppositions. True, they also turn to the professional literature, but this literature is far from dependable or even stable. Much of it partakes of what the psychiatrist-philosopher Karl Jaspers once termed "efforts of Sisyphus": what was thought to be true today is often revealed to be false tomorrow. As a result, the final decisions by the experts on what constitutes a psychiatric condition and which symptoms define it rely excessively on the prejudices of the day.

Nor are the experts disinterested parties in these decisions. Some—because of their position as experts—receive extravagant annual retainers from pharmaceutical companies that profit from the promotion of disorders treatable by the company's medications. Other venal interests may also be at work: when a condition like attention deficit disorder or multiple personality disorder appears in the official catalogue of diagnoses, its treatment can be reimbursed by insurance companies, thus bringing direct financial benefit to an expert running a so-called Trauma Center or Multiple Personality Unit. Finally, there is the inevitable political maneuvering within committees as one expert supports a second's opinion on a particular disorder with the tacit understanding of reciprocity when needed.

The new *DSM* approach of using experts and descriptive criteria in identifying psychiatric dis-

eases has encouraged a productive industry. If you can describe it, you can name it; and if you can name it, then you can claim that it exists as a distinct "entity" with, eventually, a direct treatment tied to it. Proposals for new psychiatric disorders have multiplied so feverishly that the *DSM* itself has grown from a mere 119 pages in 1968 to 886 pages in the latest edition; a new and enlarged edition, *DSM-V*, is already in the planning stages. Embedded within these hundreds of pages are some categories of disorder that are real; some that are dubious, in the sense that they are more like the normal responses of sensitive people than psychiatric "entities"; and some that are purely the inventions of their proponents.

Let us get down to cases. The first clear example of the new approach at work occurred in the late 1970's, when a coalition of psychiatrists in the Veterans Administration (VA) and advocates for Vietnam-war veterans propelled a condition called chronic post-traumatic stress disorder (PTSD) into *DSM-III*. It was, indeed, a perfect choice—itself a traumatic product, one might say, of the Vietnam war and all the conflicts and guilts that experience engendered—and it opened the door of the *DSM* to other and later disorders.

Emotional distress during and after combat (and other traumatic events) has been recognized since the mid-19th century. The symptoms of "shell shock," as it came to be known in World War I, consist of a lingering anxiety, a tendency toward nightmares, "flashback memories" of battle, and the avoidance of activities that might provoke a sensation of danger. What was added after Vietnam was the belief that—perhaps because of a physical brain change due to the stress of combat—veterans who were not properly treated could become chronically disabled. This lifelong disablement would explain, in turn, such other problems as family disruption, unemployment, or alcohol and drug abuse.

Once the concept of a chronic form of PTSD with serious complications was established in *DSM-III*, patients claiming to have it crowded into VA hospitals. A natural alliance grew up between patients and doctors to certify the existence of the disorder: patients received the privileges of the sick, while doctors received steady employment at a time when, with the end of the conflict in Southeast Asia, hospital beds were emptying. Anyone expressing skepticism about the validity of PTSD as a psychiatric condition—on the ground, say, that it had become a catchall category for people with longstanding disorders of temperament or behavior who were sometimes seeking to shelter themselves from responsibility—was dismissed as hostile to veterans or ignorant of the mental effects of fearful experiences.

Lately, however, the pro-PTSD forces have come under challenge in a major study that followed a group of Vietnam veterans through their treatment at the Yale-affiliated VA hospital in West Haven, Connecticut, and afterward. The participants in the study had received medications, group and individual therapy, behavioral therapy, family therapy, and vocational guidance—all concentrating on PTSD symptoms and the war experiences that had allegedly generated them. Upon discharge from the hospital, these patients did report some improvement in their drug and family problems, as well as a greater degree of hopefulness and self-esteem. Yet, within a mere eighteen months, their psychiatric symptoms, family problems, and personal relationships had actually become worse than on admission. They had made more suicide attempts, and their drug and alcohol abuse continued unabated. In short, prolonged and intensive hospital treatment for chronic PTSD had had no long-term beneficial effects whatsoever on the veterans' symptoms.

This report, which brings into doubt not only the treatment but the nature of the underlying "disease," has produced many agonized debates within the VA. Enthusiasts for PTSD argue that the investigators somehow missed the patients' "real" states of mind while at the same time overlooking subtle but nonetheless positive responses to treatment. They have also stepped up the search for biological evidence of brain changes produced by the emotional trauma of combat—changes that might validate chronic PTSD as a distinct condition and justify characterizing certain patients as its victims

regardless of whether a successful treatment yet exists for it. In the psychiatric journals, reports of such a "biological marker" come and go.

Yet while we await final word on chronic PTSD, the skeptics—both within and without the VA system—would appear to hold much the stronger hand. They have pointed, for example, to analogous research on war veterans in Israel. According to Israeli psychiatrists, long-term treatment in hospitals has the unfortunate tendency of making battle-trauma victims hypersensitive to their symptoms and, by encouraging them to concentrate on the psychological wounds of combat, distracts their attention from the "here-and-now" problems of adjusting to peacetime demands and responsibilities. . . .

Medical errors characteristically assume three forms: oversimplification, misplaced emphasis, and invention. When it comes to chronic PTSD, all three were committed. Explanations of symptoms were oversimplified, with combat experiences being given priority quite apart from such factors as longstanding personality disorders, independent (post-combat) psychiatric conditions including major depression, or chronic psychological invalidism produced by prolonged hospitalization. Misplaced emphasis followed oversimplification when treatment concentrated on the psychological wounds of combat to the neglect of here-and-now problems that many patients were dodging, overlooking, or minimizing. Finally, the inventive construction of a condition called chronic PTSD justified a broad network of service-related psychiatric centers devoted to maintaining the veterans in treatment whether or not they were getting better—and, as we have seen, they were not. . . .

Why are psychiatrists not more like other doctors—differentiating among patients by the causes of their illnesses and offering treatments specifically linked to the mechanisms of these illnesses? One reason is that they cannot be. In contrast to cardiologists, dermatologists, ophthalmologists, and other medical practitioners, physicians who study and treat disorders of mind and behavior are unable to demonstrate how symptoms emerge directly from activity in, or changes of, the organ that generates them—namely, the brain. Indeed, many of the profession's troubles, especially the false starts and misdirections that have plagued it from the beginning, stem from the brain-mind problem, the most critical issue in the natural sciences and a fundamental obstacle to all students of consciousness.

It was because of the brain-mind problem that Sigmund Freud, wedded as he was to an explanatory rather than a descriptive approach in psychiatry, decided to delineate causes for mental disorders that implicitly presupposed brain mechanisms (while not depending on an explicit knowledge of such mechanisms). In brief, Freud's "explanation" evoked a conflict between, on the one hand, brain-generated drives (which could be identified by their psychological manifestations) and, on the other hand, socially imposed prohibitions on the expression and satisfaction of those same drives. This conflict was believed to produce a "dynamic unconscious" whence mental and behavioral abnormalities emerged.

This explanation had its virtues, and seemed to help "ordinary" people reacting to life's troubles in an understandable way. But it was not suited to the seriously mentally ill—schizophrenics and manic-depressives, for example—who did not respond to explanation-based treatments. That is one of the factors that by the 1970's, when it became overwhelmingly clear that such people did respond satisfactorily to physical treatments and, especially, to medication, impelled the move away from hypothetical explanations (as in Freud) to empirical descriptions of manifest symptoms (as in *DSM-III* and -*IV*). Another was the longstanding failure of American psychiatry, when guided by Freudian presumptions, to advance research, a failure that led, among other things, to the countervailing efforts of the investigators in St. Louis.

At first, indeed, the new descriptive approach seemed to represent significant progress, enhancing communication among psychiatrists, stimulating research, and holding out the promise of a new era of creative growth in psychiatry itself, a field grown stultified by its decades-long immersion in psychoanalytic theory. Today, however, twenty years after its imposition, the weaknesses inherent in a system of classification based on appearances—and contaminated by self-interested advocacy—have become glaringly evident.

In my own view, and despite the obstacles presented by the brain-mind problem, psychiatry need not abandon the path of medicine. Essentially, psychiatric disorders come under four large groupings (and their subdivisions), each of them distinguished causally from the other three and bearing a different relationship to the brain.

The first grouping comprises patients who have physical diseases or damage to the brain that can provoke psychiatric symptoms: these include patients with Alzheimer's disease and schizophrenia. In the second grouping are those who are intermittently distressed by some aspect of their mental constitution—a weakness in their cognitive power, or an instability in their affective control—when facing challenges in school, employment, or marriage. Unlike those in the first category, those in the second do not have a disease or any obvious damage to the brain; rather, they are vulnerable because of who they are—that is, how they are constituted.

The third category consists of those whose behavior—alcoholism, drug addiction, sexual paraphilia, anorexia nervosa, and the like—has become a warped way of life. They are patients not because of what they have or who they are but because of what they are doing and how they have become conditioned to doing it. In the fourth category, finally, are those in need of psychiatric assistance because of emotional reactions provoked by events that injure or thwart their commitments, hopes, and aspirations. They suffer from states of mind like grief, homesickness, jealousy, demoralization—states that derive not from what they have or who they are or what they are doing but from what they have encountered in life.

Each of these distress-generating mechanisms will shape a different course of treatment, and its study should direct research in a unique direction. Thus, brain diseases are to be cured, alleviated, and prevented. Individuals with constitutional weaknesses need strengthening and guidance, and perhaps, under certain stressful situations, medication for their emotional responses. Damaging behaviors need to be interrupted, and patients troubled by them assisted in overcoming their appeal. Individuals suffering grief and demoralization need both understanding and redirection from circumstances that elicit or maintain such states of mind. Finally, for psychiatric patients who show several mechanisms in action simultaneously, a coordinated sequence of treatments is required.

But the details are not important. What is important is the general approach. Psychiatrists have for too long been satisfied with assessments of human problems that generate only a categorical diagnosis followed by a prescription for medication. Urgently required is a diagnostic and therapeutic formulation that can comprehend several interactive sources of disorder and sustain a complex program of treatment and rehabilitation. Until psychiatry begins to organize its observations, ex-

planatory hypotheses, and therapeutics in such a coherent way, it will remain as entrapped in its present classificatory system as medicine was in the last century, unable to explain itself to patients, to their families, to the public—or even to itself.

That is not all. In its recent infatuation with symptomatic, push-button remedies, psychiatry has lost its way not only intellectually but spiritually and morally. Even when it is not actually doing damage to the people it is supposed to help, as in the case of veterans with chronic PTSD, it is encouraging among doctors and patients alike the fraudulent and dangerous fantasy that life's every passing "symptom" can be clinically diagnosed and, once diagnosed, alleviated if not eliminated by pharmacological intervention. This idea is as false to reality, and ultimately to human hopes, as it is destructive of everything the subtle and beneficial art of psychiatry has meant to accomplish.

# CHAPTER 2

## Approaches to Psychopathology

*Theories are proposed explanations for some phenomenon; they are also conceptual devices that help us organize information and identify other important pieces of information. Good theories are clearly stated, testable, and, of course, explain why or how something happens. Testability is particularly important because a theory cannot be revised and improved—or perhaps rejected entirely—on the basis of research findings if it cannot first be tested.*

*Theories are like caricatures: they exaggerate certain parts of a phenomenon and ignore other features altogether. Scientists will differ in what they choose to emphasize and what they choose to ignore as they set out to explain a disorder or, more typically, some facet of a disorder. Collecting data to see which portrayal is more accurate and useful thus becomes a central task for the scientist interested in psychopathology. We often think of the scientist's job as adding small facts to some accumulating body of scientific knowledge. In a certain sense this is true, but it is equally true that the scientist's task is to conduct studies that allow him or her to eliminate explanations that are wrong. Instead of a pointillist painter, who adds small dots to a canvas to create, in the end, a complete and textured portrait, it is more accurate to think of the scientist as a sculptor, who is confronted with a large block of material—a large set of plausible explanations for some phenomenon—and then cuts off those parts that do not belong as part of the final work. The four articles in this chapter draw out and contrast a few major theoretical approaches now prominent in the study of psychopathology.*

*Theories are much more than abstract conceptual devices, however. They are important because they often guide treatment decisions. For example, if we believe that panic disorder results from the conflicting goals of the superego and the id, then we are likely to treat this disorder by talking with patients about these conflicts. On the other hand, if we believe that panic disorder results from a misconstrual of normal feelings of anxiety, then we might apply procedures to help patients reinterpret these sensations. Thus, as you will see from the articles presented here, theories are important because they organize and guide research as well as treatment.*

# DREAM WARRIORS

## Lisa Birk

*Why do we dream? Do dreams have special meaning and significance? There are no definitive answers to these questions, but the answers that are proposed—and the degree of attention given to dreams—depend on one's theoretical orientation. This article focuses specifically on theoretical approaches to dreams and dreaming, and it contrasts a psychodynamic explanation with a neurophysiological one. It does so by introducing the work of Ernest Hartmann, a psychoanalyst, and Allan Hobson, a neurophysiologist, thereby presenting two case studies about theorizing. What you will see in this article is that the same phenomenon can be viewed in dramatically different ways, and that people often adopt theories that reflect the way they prefer to make sense of the world. You may also recognize that theorizing is more than a cold, objective enterprise; scientists are very committed to their ideas and work hard to defend them.*

## Suggested Readings

Hartmann, E. (1998). *Dreams and nightmares: The new theory on the origin and meaning of dreams.* New York: Perseus Press.

Hobson, J. A. (1998). *Consciousness.* New York: Freeman.

Luhrman, T. M. (2000). *Of two minds: The growing disorder in American psychiatry.* New York: Alfred A. Knopf.

Westen, D. (1998). The scientific legacy of Sigmund Freud: Toward a psychodynamically informed psychological science. *Psychological Bulletin, 124,* 333–371.

Wood, J. M., Bootzin, R. R., Rosenhan, D., Nolen-Hoeksema, S., & Jourden, F. (1992). Effects of the 1989 San Francisco earthquake on frequency and content of nightmares. *Journal of Abnormal Psychology, 101,* 219–224.

---

*The Boston Phoenix.* (1999, January 21–28). [On-line].
Available: http://www.bostonphoenix.com/archive/features/99/01/21/dreams.html

A man dreams his mother is riding a tiny tricycle back and forth across a stage. "Love me, love me, love me," she sings operatically. To a psychoanalyst, the dream might spotlight two aspects of the mother, emotional neediness and a penchant for drama. To a neurophysiologist, the dream indicates a decrease in norepinephrine and a decrease in serotonin, leading to an increase in acetylcholine, which produced random images in the man's mind. Just like every other dream.

How we think about our dreams has always reflected how we think about our place in the universe. In ancient Greece, dreams were messages from the gods. In biblical times, dreams were prophecies. In contemporary America, experts are at odds—are dreams a meaningful system? or are they a random process, a kind of brain tic?—and have been for almost five decades.

The split is drawn vividly here in Boston, where psychiatrists Ernest Hartmann and J. Allan Hobson, former colleagues at a Harvard teaching hospital, have been rivals in the field of dream theory for nearly 40 years. Now they are battling it out again, if indirectly, on the bookshelf. Hartmann, a psychoanalyst, Tufts med-school professor, and director of the sleep-disorders center at Newton-Wellesley Hospital, describes his approach in his 1998 book, *Dreams and Nightmares: The New Theory on the Origin and Meaning of Dreams* (Plenum). Allan Hobson, a Harvard med-school professor and director of Harvard's neurophysiology lab, describes his latest approach and its implications in his book *Consciousness*, published in November by W. H. Freeman.

Both men are challenging Freud's dream theory, which is to say they are challenging not only the notion of the unconscious, but also talk therapy, free will, the muse, the nature of creativity, and the nature of madness. They are challenging, in other words, our reigning image of ourselves. But they are challenging that image in very different ways, and no one is yet sure what will be erected in its place. . . .

For nearly 50 years, psychiatry students were trained in Freud's theory of the id, ego, and superego. They were trained in Freud's theory of the unconscious, Freud's theory of free association, Freud's theory of therapy, and Freud's theory of dreaming. Dreams were central to this system; Freud himself had called dreams "the royal road to the unconscious," meaning that dreams were the best path to the otherwise hidden and unknowable recesses of the mind. During sleep, he believed, our rational mind (the ego) relaxes, allowing instincts (the id) to surface. However, if our forbidden wishes or drives became too explicit, we'd wake up. Thus, he hypothesized, dreams were coded: they occurred in symbols, and the psychoanalyst's job was to decode the dream, and so permit the dreamer insight into his true self.

Then, in 1953, came a seismic shock. Two researchers at the University of Chicago discovered that sleepers experienced bursts of rapid eye movement in their sleep. The scientists also noted that dreaming happened consistently and perhaps exclusively during these REM bursts, which suggested that the actual catalyst of dreams was not repressed memories or desires but, rather, a physiological process. Even animals, it seemed, had REM sleep.

Suddenly dreams, which according to Freud were an upwelling of powerful suppressed urges and anxieties, were being described as "automatic." Dream content might not be terribly important or even terribly individual—because dreams were triggered not by one's horrible past, but by the release of a chemical.

If the scientists who discovered REM sleep were right, if dreams were merely a chemical process, then the unconscious was—to put it bluntly—a bunch of hooey. Talk therapy was a bunch of hooey. Among psychiatrists, the more scientifically inclined retreated to one shore and studied the brain. The psychoanalytically inclined retreated to the opposite shore and studied the mind. Scholarly articles took one side or the other. The world of psychoanalysis, which had tenuously bridged two worlds—the medical and the psychological—began to pull apart.

It was at this moment that Ernest Hartmann and J. Allan Hobson entered Harvard Medical School to finish their training as psychiatrists.

The year Allan Hobson turned eight, he and his father built a lab for Allan's experiments. The family lived in West Hartford, Connecticut, near Avon Mountain, and Hobson frequently went foraging in the woods.

Sometimes he brought back snakes. Hobson was afraid of snakes, partly because he knew the woods were full of them (some of them poisonous), and partly because local wisdom had it that even if you bashed a snake's head in or chopped its head off, it wouldn't die until after sundown. Not only could snakes kill you; it seemed they also had supernatural powers.

Hobson investigated. His first set of experiments consisted of catching snakes and bashing their heads in. He'd take each snake back to the lab and wait for its body to stop wriggling. Sundown would come, and then his bedtime would come, and then sometime in the night the snake stopped twitching.

Hobson conducted a second set of experiments, which varied little from the first except that Hobson would wake himself periodically through the night to check on the snake to see exactly when it had stopped moving. He then conducted a third set of experiments, which again resembled the first except that Hobson began chopping the snake bodies into smaller and smaller bits. Still, each bit wriggled for hours.

Eventually Hobson figured out—whether through further experiments or by reading books he no longer remembers—that the snake's nervous system is segmented. The body twitches not because snakes are supernatural but because their physiology is set up that way.

By high school, Hobson was routinely dissecting brains, a hobby many of his classmates considered "weird, perverted and disgusting," he writes in the acknowledgments of his 1988 book, *The Dreaming Brain*. But adults, especially scientists, encouraged him. The first to do so was a dyslexia specialist named Page Sharp, who took an interest in the 15-year-old Hobson as a subject. Tests showed that Hobson had been born with dyslexic brain wiring but functioned normally. Sharp wanted to know why. Eventually, Sharp was so impressed with Hobson's intelligence that he hired him as a research assistant.

Some years later, Jack Ewalt, Harvard's charismatic chief of psychiatry at midcentury, must have seen something similar: an energetic, smart young scientist who was willing, even eager, to buck the trends. Ewalt partially funded Hobson's lab at Harvard's prestigious Massachusetts Mental Health Center when Hobson was still a lowly post-doc.

Hobson made good use of the funds and the lab. In 1973, 20 years after REM sleep was first linked with dreaming, he shook the psychoanalytic world with a lecture titled "The Brain as Dream Machine." No doubt the word "machine" was in-

tended to rankle those who still believed that dreaming was a most human act—that dreaming distinguished us from animals, and *definitely* distinguished us from machines.

Much of Hobson's research was based on cat brains, and many critics thought his presentation premature. Four years later, Hobson answered the critics with a flourish (some called it grandstanding): he opened "Dreamstage," a six-week "multimedia portrait of the sleeping brain" at Harvard's Carpenter Center. Crowds thronged in to see a human sleeper sleep, to see the machine that recorded the sleeper's brain waves. (The brainwave patterns, it turned out, looked a lot like a cat's brain-wave patterns). To some scholars, Hobson's exhibit bordered on the tacky. To the public, it was sexy and fun—and who'd ever thought brain science could be fun? Hobson was a force to be reckoned with.

But Hobson was not the only student singled out by Jack Ewalt in the early '60s. Ewalt also believed in another bright, promising young man, a Viennese named Ernest Hartmann.

Like Hobson, Hartmann was attracted to science. He remembers with distaste a psychiatry professor who urged students not to read books but just to "sit with the patients." Unlike Hobson, however, his approach to analysis was not shaped by chopping up snakes. It was shaped by, well, analysis.

Ernest Hartmann's father, the renowned Viennese psychoanalyst Heinz Hartmann, was an early and loyal disciple of Sigmund Freud. The junior Dr. Hartmann (at age two) even met Freud, a fact he includes on the jacket flap of his latest book.

Hartmann remembers a poll taken in the '50s or '60s, in which both psychoanalysts and the public were asked to name the best psychoanalyst in the country. The public voted for a doctor named Erik Erikson. The psychoanalysts, however, voted for Heinz Hartmann.

Hartmann senior was the psychoanalysts' psychoanalyst, and so loyal a Freudian that people nicknamed him the "son of Freud." So Ernie Hartmann is, he sometimes jokes, the grandson of Freud.

Meeting Hartmann *is* a bit like meeting Freud's grandson, or your mental image of Freud's grandson. He doesn't have the beard or the paunch, but his wispy hair sometimes stands up or out, the way really smart people's hair is supposed to. He has a Viennese accent, a courtly, almost old-fashioned kindliness, heavy red drapes, and a Newton home office lined floor-to-ceiling, wall-to-wall with books. In the middle of the office, he's placed two red leather chairs on either side of an elegant table stacked with thick books and a big rock incised with one word: DREAM.

Hartmann, however, is not such a loyal grandson when it comes to ideas. In decades of research, both as a scientist and as a psychoanalyst, he has come to reject nearly half of Freud's tenets. Hartmann does not believe, as Freud did, that dream content is irrational or even coded. He rejects the idea that all dreams are based on a repressed wish. What distinguishes Hartmann from most followers of Freud, according to J. Christian Gillin, a professor of psychiatry at the University of California at San Diego, is that Hartmann "is a more independent thinker." Hartmann has not just modernized Freud's theory, he has rebuilt it.

Hartmann goes along with neurophysiologists who say that dreaming is chemically activated; he's done some experiments along those lines himself. He just doesn't think that's very interesting. He wants to understand why we dream and what those dreams mean, and what the answers imply for a new model of the mind.

Hartmann spent years as a researcher and a psychoanalyst working with traumatized people, and over time he collected 40 dream series containing from six to a thousand dreams each. The dreams were collected in the weeks or months after a trauma or, in some cases, over five years.

The nightmares of traumatized people, he found, had certain common features: there was a strong feeling, often expressed in metaphor, and there were bits of the dreamer's past woven in.

Traumatized people often dreamed not so much about the facts of what had happened as about the way the event made them feel. This was particularly true as time went on. Sometimes people dreamed of the trauma itself—say, a rape—but the details, the setting, or the characters would be different. Later, people would dream about other traumas they hadn't experienced—tidal waves, for instance—but the dream rape and the dream tidal wave would engender a common feeling of terror.

Big losses triggered similarly metaphoric dreams. Hartmann writes of a man whose powerful mother had just died. In his dream, "This huge mountain has split apart and there are pieces lying around. I am supposed to make arrangements to take care of it." In the dream of a woman who had just lost her mother, "There was an empty house, empty and barren. All the doors and windows were open and the wind was blowing through."

These dreams, Hartmann theorized, were driven by emotion, but the content was metaphoric, and the metaphors were important. The metaphors, he writes, were a way of showing the dreamer, "It is a terrible event, yes, but is it unique? Let's look at . . . other catastrophes. . . . Awful, yes, but it's part of a whole catalog of human disasters, . . . . [and] sometimes people survive." Dreams, in other words, are a way of healing the dreamer. . . .

Hartmann collected another type of dream, too: those of scientists and artists. Among them is the story of inventor Elias Howe, who for five years had tried to invent a sewing machine. Howe could visualize most of the machine, a needle piercing fabric over and over, but he couldn't figure out how to get the machine to hold and knot the thread. Then one night he dreamed he was a missionary caught by natives carrying spears. The spears, he noticed, had holes in the tips. When he woke, he had the solution to his problem: a hole through the tip of the needle to hold and knot the thread.

Robert Louis Stevenson claimed to have dreamed the entire plot of *The Strange Case of Dr. Jekyll and Mr. Hyde.* More than 50 percent of mathematicians answering a survey said they had solved a problem in their dreams at least once. Hartmann lists famous artists, ranging from Albrecht Dürer to William Blake to Frida Kahlo, who recorded a dream as the source of their inspiration.

Hartmann began to think about the common properties of these two sorts of dreams: nightmares that made metaphors of trauma, and dreams that found solutions to problems. He began to think of dreaming as "hyperconnective," a state of mind in which we are able to make more associative leaps than we can in the waking state. And then, appropriately, he dreamed a visual representation of such a connective sort of brain. He dreamed of "a pile of Persian carpets loosely tied together."

As he developed the theory, Hartmann began to visualize the mind as composed of "neural nets" lying one on top of another. Imagine a pile of tiny electrified fishing nets. The spot where one rope knots with another is a neural connection. In the conscious mind, dreams are more likely to stay within a net; in dreams, they are more likely to leap from net to net. The mind, Hartmann believes, makes connections all the time, whether awake, asleep, or dreaming—but the dreaming mind connects "more broadly, more widely."

"The waking mind is on a hunt," says Hartmann. It is goal-directed. "The dreaming mind is on an exploration." The dreaming mind's spreading connections help people think associatively, creatively, as Howe did with the sewing machine, and Stevenson did with Jekyll and Hyde.

Allan Hobson will have none of it. "My challenge to the metaphor merchants," he says, rolling close in his office chair, "is, prove it! Show us scientifically! The whole point of science is to check belief. Rhetoric? I'm not interested. Literature? I'm not interested. Science is insurance against being fooled."

Hobson rolls around in his chair a lot, often aggressively, to emphasize a point or to ask a question. It is easy to imagine his delight nearly 30 years ago over that lecture title, "The Brain as Dream Machine," the title that tweaked establishment psychoanalysts and launched his career.

Hobson has graduated from a home lab to the neurophysiology department of Harvard Medical School, but in some sense he is still, at 60-plus, the boy who cut up snakes to challenge local wisdom. He spends his nights experimenting: he sometimes wears a "nightcap," a device made of a modified tennis headband with sensors for eye and body movement, to record his own REM sleep. . . .

"Psychoanalysts' dream theory," says Hobson, "is the most fanciful, delicious, absurb theory that anyone's taken seriously for 100 years." And they've taken it seriously, Hobson believes, because it's so seductive. So comforting. How thrilling, after all, to believe that your subconscious creates while you sleep, that your subconscious heals psychic wounds, that something wiser than your conscious self is in charge.

In place of Freud's theory and Hartmann's theory and all the other psychoanalysts' theories, Hobson offers his own: a purely physiological theory that he calls "activation-synthesis."

In its simplest form, activation-synthesis, originally formulated by Hobson and his colleague Robert McCarley, another psychiatry professor at Harvard, comes down to this: we dream because of two processes, one called activation and the other called synthesis.

In the "activation" phase, the brain stem—the lower, more primitive part of the brain—blocks most incoming sensory data (smell, touch, sound) and also blocks motor impulses (the impulse to run, for instance). This is why someone dreaming about monsters does not physically react by running away. A dreamer is effectively paralyzed.

The cycles of REM sleep are governed by the balance of three neurotransmitters: serotonin, norepinephrine, and acetylcholine. (Neurotransmitters are chemicals that communicate messages from nerve cell to nerve cell.) While the body sleeps, the brain stem's production of serotonin and norepinephrine decreases almost to the point of inactivity. This raises the level of acetylcholine, which induces REM sleep—and excites the visual, emotional, and motor centers that may be responsible for flooding the sleeping brain with images. Certainly, Hobson believes, there is a correlation between increasing acetylcholine and dreaming, but he can't yet say definitively that the one causes the other.

"Synthesis" takes place in the cortex, the seat of thinking and the higher part of the brain. The brain responds to the incoming flood of images by knitting them together as best it can, turning the random bits of data into a story, or what we know as a "dream." The reason dreams seem coherent to the dreamer—at least at the time—is because serotonin and norepinephrine, the chemicals that shut down to trigger the dreaming process, are also the chemicals that govern judgment. In other words, Hobson and McCarley believe, the very mechanism that enables dreaming prohibits us—at least while we are dreaming—from realizing how arbitrary our dreams really are.

In some sense this sounds anti-humanist. The process is automatic, the content random. Still, Hobson sees dreaming as a possible agent of creativity. We are nightly visited with spectacular visions—"literary productions," as he puts it—which, if we are good editors, we can transform into something else: a dream log, maybe even art.

Besides, Freud's theory of dreaming, says Hobson, is *boring*. Psychoanalysis is so limited. Everything is self-referential. "There are more things," he says, "than are dreamt of in your philosophy, Mr. Freud."

But the frontiers of brain science are rapidly expanding, and even as Hobson distances himself from Freud's theories, others are distancing themselves from Hobson's. Cognitive scientist David Foulkes, in a 1996 article for the journal *Sleep*, reviewed the last 40-plus years of dream research and concluded that dreaming happens not just in REM sleep, but also in other phases.

That idea may challenge some of Hobson's most fundamental principles. "What I'll conclude for you," says Gerald Vogel, a critic of Hobson and director of the sleep-research laboratory at Emory University, "is that REM sleep is not a *necessary* condition for dreaming, and it is not a *sufficient* condition for dreaming. So therefore, unique physiological events can not explain dreaming. That's it in a nutshell, kid."

And if REM's "unique physiological events" cannot explain dreaming, then certainly, says Alfred Margulies, an associate professor of psychiatry at Harvard Medical School, "it's untenable to say that [neurophysiology] proves Freud wrong. Dream physiology is a lot less clear than folks would have it."

Still, most experts believe Hobson has made a significant contribution to our understanding of REM sleep. J Christian Gillin believes that Hobson and other neurophysiologists have also strengthened traditional psychoanalysis. "In the '40s and '50s," says Gillin, "there were virtually no clinical trials ever conducted to determine the effectiveness of psychoanalytic theory. Today, nearly every theory is being tested empirically." So it seems that each side is at long last building a new methodological bridge, one that spans the conundrum of the brain-mind.

. . . [T]he two camps are still divided over content. Neurophysiologists believe that understanding the brain is our best shot at explaining the mind. Psychoanalysts believe the neurophysiologists are focused on the least interesting part of the story. . . .

"All we can say now [about dreaming from a biological perspective]," says Hartmann, "is that [the brain] lights up differently during waking and dreaming. We can say the amygdala (the center of emotion) lights up during dreaming, but. . . . " He shrugs as if to say, So what?

Margulies agrees. Studying neurophysiology to the exclusion of psychology "is like a deaf Martian studying . . . how the human auditory system works. But the Martian could never understand Mozart."

Gillin has another metaphor: If dreaming is a drama, then "[neurophysiologists] have discovered where the house manager sits, and who turns on the lights, but they don't tell you what play will go on tonight, or who the actors will be."

"Psychology is a higher level of biology," says Hartmann. "Maybe someday biology will be able to describe what's happening in the cortex. But it will take 10,000 statements to say 'defense mechanism.' Psychology is the shorthand way, and at the moment the best way, to describe what's going on in the cortex."

In the end, many researchers in both fields believe that the overriding goal of dream theorists is not to pick sides, but to find one unifying theory that explains both brain and mind. That job may very well take professionals working from both the lab and the couch.

For all their differences, Hobson and Hartmann exemplify the trend toward unification. Each expresses a kind of intellectual joy upon hearing the other's theory of creativity. When Hartmann learns that Hobson believes dreaming allows for a random recombination of data that "opens up the system for creativity," the psychoanalyst sits back, looks skyward, and says, "I like that."

When Hobson is told of Hartmann's theory of dreaming as a "hyperconnective" state, he pauses, quieted, as if rolling the concept around his mind. "It's a genial theory," he says.

The argument between them is a central question in our age. Biology or metaphor? Science or art? Which discipline better explains the "truth" of dreaming? The debate being conducted here in Boston, in our heads and often over them, is a debate not only over dreaming, but over how we should be thinking about the big questions.

"I suspect in the long run," says Gillin, "we'll have to reconcile both theories." But in the meantime, the two camps are still a long way apart.

At the very end of one long interview, Hobson told me thoughtfully, maybe even wistfully: "All complex systems are noisy. Why shouldn't the brain be noisy?" He meant that dreams might be the static in a complex system, not the music. Hobson is still going into the woods, confronting the local wisdom, chopping up the snakes to figure out what makes them wiggle and what makes them stop.

Hartmann, in one of his last calls to me, said, "You left your scarf here," and then he paused. "You know what Freud would say? Freud would say you didn't want to leave." And metaphorically speaking, he was right.

# LINKING MIND AND BRAIN IN THE STUDY OF MENTAL ILLNESS: A PROJECT FOR A SCIENTIFIC PSYCHOPATHOLOGY

## Nancy C. Andreasen

*The previous article pits a psychodynamic perspective against a neurophysiological one in explaining the nature of dreams and dreaming. Neurophysiological approaches—or more generally, biological approaches—to psychopathology are very prominent today and are dominant explanations for several major disorders. Scientists focus on the biological underpinnings of a disorder, often with the expectation that this will lead to better medications. The advent of new technologies, such as neuroimaging and electrophysiology, have given scientists unprecedented access to the structure and functioning of the human brain. This means that brain processes that were the source of speculation only a few years ago can now be measured and observed with increasing precision.*

*In the following article, Nancy Andreasen provides an overview of this approach to psychopathology. She emphasizes recent advances in understanding schizophrenia and depression and reviews how a variety of new methods are helping to clarify how the brains of individuals with these disorders differ from those of people without the disorders. Note how she strives both to describe the neurophysiology of these disorders and to link problems in specific areas of the brain with specific symptoms. This approach promises to yield new insights into the interplay between the brain and the mind.*

### Suggested Reading

Guze, S. B. (1989). Biological psychiatry: Is there any other kind? *Psychological Medicine, 19*, 315–323.

*Science, 275*, 1586–1593. (1997).

Brain research on mental illnesses has made substantial advances in recent years, supported by conceptual and technological developments in cognitive neuroscience. Brain-based cognitive models of illnesses such as schizophrenia and depression have been tested with a variety of techniques, including the lesion method, tract tracing, neuroimaging, animal modeling, single-cell recording, electrophysiology, neuropsychology, and experimental cognitive psychology. A relatively sophisticated picture is emerging that conceptualizes mental illnesses as disorders of mind arising in the brain. Convergent data using multiple neuroscience techniques indicate that the neural mechanisms of mental illnesses can be understood as dysfunctions in specific neural circuits and that their functions and dysfunctions can be influenced or altered by a variety of cognitive and pharmacological factors

In 1895, a little-known Viennese neuropsychiatrist named Sigmund Freud wrote a largely unnoticed work entitled A Project for a Scientific Psychology, in which he proposed that the cognitive mechanisms of normal and abnormal mental phenomena could be explained through orderly and rigorous study of brain systems. Freud began his career researching pharmacology (the therapeutic effects of cocaine), neurology (aphasia in children), and basic neuroscience (staining techniques for visualizing neurons), but he ultimately abandoned both the project and neuropsychiatry. During the fin de siècle 1900s, however, Freud's project is slowly being achieved. This fruition reflects the maturity of the techniques of neuroscience, as well as the convergence of efforts from multiple domains: psychiatry, cognitive psychology and neuropsychology, and clinical and basic neuroscience. Models of illness mechanisms have been developed through the use of clinical observation, experimental paradigms developed in psychology, animal and human lesion studies, anatomic studies of neural circuits, neuroimaging, and behavioral neuropharmacology. The long-term goal is to achieve a "scientific psychopathology": to identify the neural mechanisms of normal cognitive processes and to understand how they are injured in mental illnesses.

This overview provides a summary of some of the fundamental conceptual issues that are being addressed in pursuit of this long-term goal. The work of neuroscientists studying two common mental illnesses—schizophrenia and depression—illustrates the consensus that is developing among investigators who begin with different strategies originating from different disciplines in the broad field of cognitive neuroscience.

## Fundamental Conceptual Issues

*The relationship between mind and brain.* Mental illnesses have historically been distinguished from other medical illnesses because they affect the higher cognitive processes that are referred to as "mind." The relationship between mind and brain has been extensively discussed in contemporary philosophy and psychology, without any decisive resolution (1). One heuristic solution, therefore, is to adopt the position that the mind is the expression of the activity of the brain and that these two are separable for purposes of analysis and discussion but inseparable in actuality. That is, mental phenomena arise from the brain, but mental experience also affects the brain, as is demonstrated by the many examples of environmental influences on brain plasticity (2). The aberrations of mental illnesses reflect abnormalities in the brain/mind's interaction with its surrounding world; they are diseases of a psyche (or mind) that resides in that region of the soma (or body) that is the brain.

Mind and brain can be studied as if they are separate entities, however, and this is reflected in the multiple and separate disciplines that examine them. Each uses a different language and methodology to study the same quiddity. The challenge in developing a scientific psychopathology in the 1990s is to use the power of multiple disciplines. The study of mind has been the province of cognitive psychology, which has divided mind into component domains of investigation (such as memory, language, and attention), created theoretical systems to explain the workings of those domains (constructs such as memory encoding versus retrieval), and designed experimental paradigms to test the hypotheses in human beings and animals (3). The study of brain has been the province of several disciplines. Neuropsychology has used the lesion method to determine localization by observing absence of function after injury, whereas neuroanatomy and neurobiology have mapped neural development and connectivity and studied functionality in animal models (4). The boundaries between all these disciplines have become increasingly less distinct, however, creating the broad discipline of cognitive neuroscience. The term "cognitive" has definitions that range from broad to narrow; its usage here is broad and refers to all activities of mind, including emotion, perception, and regulation of behavior.

Contemporary psychiatry studies mental illnesses as diseases that manifest as mind and arise from brain. It is the discipline within cognitive neuroscience that integrates information from all these related disciplines in order to develop models that explain the cognitive dysfunctions of psychiatric patients based on knowledge of normal brain/mind function.

*Using the phenomenotype to find the biotype.* There are at present no known biological diagnostic markers for any mental illnesses except dementias such as Alzheimer's disease. The to-be-discovered lesions that define the remainder of mental illnesses are likely to be occurring at complex or small-scale levels that are difficult to visualize and measure, such as the connectivity of neural circuits, neuronal signaling and signal transduction, and abnormalities in genes or gene expression. Despite their lack of a defining objective index such as glucosuria is for diabetes, however, these illnesses are very real. Not only do they produce substantial morbidity and mortality, but advances in psychiatric nosology have produced objective, criterion-based, assessment techniques that produce reliable and precise diagnoses (5). In the absence of a pathological marker, the current definitions of mental illnesses are syndromal and are based on a convergence of signs, symptoms, outcome, and patterns of familial aggregation (6).

Finding the neural mechanisms of mental illnesses must be an iterative process; syndromal clinical definitions (or the phenomenotype) are progressively tested, refined, and redefined

through the measurement of neurobiological aspects (or the biotype) (7). This process is not fundamentally different from that used to study other diseases. The diagnosis of diabetes, for example, has evolved from the observation of glucosuria to multiple subdivisions based on age of onset, severity of symptoms and complications, degree of islet cell involvement, and genetic factors. For most mental illnesses, the task is simply made more challenging by the absence of an objective criterion that can provide an initial clue to assist in finding mechanisms, as neuritic plaques have done for Alzheimer's disease.

*Defining the boundary between normal and abnormal cognitive processes: continua versus categories.* Defining a boundary between normal and abnormal cognitive processes, which demarcates the phenomenotype of specific disorders, is often considered to be the first step in identifying the neural substrates of mental illnesses. This task has been difficult. Many of the symptoms of mental illness are on a continuum with normality. The dysphoric mood of depressive illness shares many features with the normal sadness experienced as a consequence of a personal loss such as the death of a loved one or the termination of a marriage. At what point does such normal sadness become a form of psychopathology? Most children are rambunctious and have short attention spans. At what point does this pattern become sufficiently severe to diagnose attention deficit hyperactivity disorder? Thresholds based on duration (such as dysphoria that persists for more than a month after a personal loss) or on severity (such as inattentiveness that interferes significantly with school performance) are usually applied to resolve this problem (8). These are boundaries of convenience that permit reliable definition, not boundaries with any inherent biological meaning.

This approach to defining the boundaries between mental illnesses and normality may seem imprecise. Traditional medical thinking teaches that disease processes are discontinuous from normality. One either has cancer or one does not. Categorical disease models are being challenged, however, by the recent data indicating that individuals may carry a genetic risk factor to develop a disorder that can be measured premorbidly (such as the BRCA1 and ApoE lipoprotein genes) and that may or may not ultimately be expressed as the full form of the disorder, depending on the occurrence of a variety of cofactors (9). Such observations raise questions about the discontinuity requirement for a definition of a disease process. Current models of the etiology of mental illnesses in fact share many features with cancer. In both groups of disorders, genetic factors may play a role in inducing vulnerability, but additional "hits" appear to be needed to produce a full-blown catastrophic condition that is recognized as an illness. Before the development of a full-blown catastrophic condition, however, the boundary between health and disease may be blurry.

*Focus on diseases versus symptoms.* As scientists studying mental illnesses work to give shape and focus to these apparently amorphous disease processes, they must also determine whether the problem might be made more soluble by examination of symptoms rather than disease categories. Most disease categories are constellations of symptoms. The nature of the constellation may provide a clue to mechanism (as the combination of dysphoria with diurnal dysregulation and appetitive changes suggests endocrine dysfunction in depression). An alternate strategy in the search for neural mechanisms is to reduce the field of view and examine specific components of disease processes, thereby potentially improving the focus of the investigation.

For example, hallucinations are a common symptom of severe mental illnesses. Understanding their neural mechanisms could potentially tell us something about broader aspects of brain dysfunction in these disorders. Hallucinations are defined as sensory experiences (such as seeing objects or people, or having the sensation that insects are crawling under the skin) that occur without any external stimulation. The most common form of hallucination is auditory. Auditory hallucinations are the subjective experience of hearing a voice that is clearly distinct from the person's own thoughts and has the qualities of an auditory perception

(such as volume, pitch, and intonation). The auditory hallucinations experienced during a psychotic illness such as schizophrenia are almost invariably experienced as human voices that speak in sentences or fragments of sentences. Because the brain mechanisms that control auditory perception are well understood and those governing language processing are at least partially understood, identifying the brain disturbances that produce this particular symptom could provide some leverage for understanding the nature of the brain injury in schizophrenia. Shifting the focus of investigation from disease category to specific symptoms offers the possibility of making the search for mechanisms more tractable.

This strategy also introduces other challenges, however. First, hallucinations occur in a variety of sensory modalities. Auditory hallucinations are the most common, but hallucinations may also be visual, tactile, olfactory, or (very rarely) gustatory. Does the same basic process underly all hallucinatory experiences, with some more specific process leading them to be expressed in a given sensory domain? Or is each a different discrete process? The search for the neural mechanisms of hallucinations will be driven differently, depending on which of these hypothetical alternatives is chosen. A single basic process suggests (but does not require) a subcortical locus, whereas a discrete process suggests specific cortical loci.

Second, hallucinations occur in the same modality in different disease processes. For example, auditory hallucinations are very common in mania as well as schizophrenia. Might one more powerfully seek the common basic mechanism of hallucinations by pooling patients who are traditionally studied separately? On the other hand, hallucinations also occur in different modalities in patterns that are highly characteristic of different disease processes. For example, auditory hallucinations are very common in schizophrenia and may co-occur with tactile hallucinations, whereas visual and olfactory hallucinations are much less common. Olfactory hallucinations are common in temporal lobe epilepsy, whereas visual hallucinations are common in a variety of drug-induced psychotic states (such as delirium tremens or LSD or PCP psychosis) but not in all (for example, amphetamine psychosis). The variability in patterning across disease states argues against the likelihood that hallucinations share the same mechanism in different mental illnesses, and it may argue against pooling patients for study who experience hallucinations in the same modality independently of disease process.

Finally, hallucinations have different and characteristic courses in different disease processes. The auditory hallucinations of schizophrenia tend to be relatively chronic and lifelong, whereas those of mania are brief and only occur during the euphoric mood state that defines a manic episode. This observation suggests that neuroanatomic mechanisms exert a more powerful effect in schizophrenia, whereas the mechanism driving hallucinations in mania is more rapidly reversible and plastic, and therefore neurochemical. Both types can, however, be powerfully affected by the same antipsychotic drugs and may therefore share some common neurochemical mechanism.

*Characteristics of heuristic cognitive models of mental illnesses.* Creating a scientific psychopathology requires the development of heuristic and testable models. Cognitive models of mental illnesses may develop from a variety of different vantage points, such as neurobiology, neuropsychology, cognitive psychology, or psychiatry. Whatever the point of origin, models converge on a final common pathway that leads to a shared set of characteristics. The models may begin at the level of systems, but they must also be adaptable to smaller biological scales (such as cells, membranes, and molecules), at which the primary lesions of mental illness probably occur.

Cognitive models of mental illnesses that can be heuristically applied on multiple levels share three characteristics. (i) They provide a general theory of the disease that is consistent with our current level of clinical knowledge, based on observation of signs and symptoms, response to treatment, course of illness, and familial/genetic data. (ii) They provide a theory that can be tested experimentally in human beings, preferably with several types of techniques so that comparative confirmatory or disconfirmatory data can be obtained. (iii) They provide a theory that can also be modeled and tested in animals, because animal models offer the most flexible and powerful techniques for rapidly screening new treatments and for identifying molecular mechanisms of illness.

## Linking Mind and Brain: The Examples of Schizophrenia and Depression

Advances that have been made in the study of schizophrenia and depression illustrate the power of developing cognitive models that derive from different perspectives and apply techniques from multiple domains.

*Finding the common thread in schizophrenia.* The name "schizophrenia" ("fragmented mind") was coined by Eugen Bleuler, who wished to emphasize that it was a cognitive disorder in which the "fabric of thought and emotion" was torn or fragmented, and normal connections or associations were no longer present (10). Schizophrenia poses special challenges to the development of cognitive models because of the breadth and diversity of its symptoms. The symptoms include nearly all domains of function: perception (hallucinations), inferential thinking (delusions), fluency of thought and speech (alogia), clarity and organization of thought and speech ("formal thought disorder"), motor activity (catatonia), emotional expression (affective blunting), ability to initiate and complete goal-directed behavior (avolition), and ability to seek out and experience emotional gratification (anhedonia). Not all these symptoms are present in any given patient, however, and none is pathognomonic of the illness. An initial survey of the diversity of symptoms might suggest that multiple brain regions are involved, in a spotty pattern much as once occurred in neurosyphilis. In the absence of visible lesions and known pathogens, however, investigators have turned to the exploration of models that could explain the diversity of symptoms by a single cognitive mechanism. Exemplifying this strategy are four different models that illustrate the melding of cognitive neuroscience and psychiatry, beginning at four different points of departure. The convergent conclusions of these different models are striking. . . .

The common thread in all these observations, spun from four different starting points, is that schizophrenia reflects a disruption in a fundamental cognitive process that affects specific circuitry in the brain and that may be improved through medications that affect that circuitry. The various teams use differing terminology and somewhat different concepts—metarepresentations, representationally guided behavior, information processing/attention, cognitive dysmetria—but they convey a common theme. The cognitive dysfunction in schizophrenia is an inefficient temporal and spatial referencing of information and experience as the person attempts to determine boundaries between self and not-self and to formulate effective decisions or plans that will guide him or her through the small-scale (speaking a sentence) or large-scale (finding a job) maneuvers of daily living. This capacity is sometimes referred to as consciousness.

Using diverse technologies and techniques—PET scanning, animal models, lesion methods single-cell recordings, evoked potentials—the investigators also converge on similar conclusions about the neuroanatomic substrates of the cognitive dysfunction. All concur that it must involve distributed circuits rather than a single specific "localization," and all suggest a key role for interrelationships among the prefrontal cortex, other interconnected cortical regions, and subcortical regions, particularly the thalamus and striatum. Animal and molecular models are being developed that are based on knowledge of this circuitry and the fundamental cognitive process, which can be applied to understanding the mechanism of drug actions and developing new medications.

*Dissecting the anatomy of melancholy.* Depression is the most common of the mood disorders. It is characterized by an overwhelming sense of sadness, sometimes without any obvious precipitant, accompanied by slowing of thoughts and actions (psychomotor retardation), insomnia, anorexia, alterations in normal diurnal rhythms, difficulty in concentrating, and feelings of hopelessness and guilt. Because symptoms such as insomnia or altered diurnal rhythm could be explained by a disruption in endocrine regulation, particularly involving cortisol, during the past several decades many investigators have focused on the neuroendocrinology of depression (*11*). There have been fewer cognitive models proposed for depression than for schizophrenia. However, most investigators agree on the core psychopathological feature of depression: a severe alteration in emotional tone that gives a negative coloring to many aspects of the person's thoughts and behavior. . . .

Studies of mood disorders concur on the general nature of the underlying cognitive process of depression: It is a pathological alteration in emotion. Studies using the lesion method, behavioral conditioning, and PET have begun to dissect the anatomy of emotion: Portions of the prefrontal cortex (probably anterior and inferior) and the amygdala are key nodes in the circuit, and the parietal lobes and other regions may play a role as well. Although the anatomical circuits clearly implicate frontal regions and related circuitry, the precise cognitive mechanisms are currently an area of active investigation. The data from conditioning studies and PET studies of active versus remitted patients suggest an interesting hypothesis: Memories of past pain are retained in regions such as the amygdala or parietal cortex and may lie dormant ("the trait"), predisposing an individual to developing a clinical depression ("the state") if additional factors arise. A key point in this work, however, is that the anatomy of melancholy can be modified by both psychological and chemical/molecular experiences. The depressed state can often be reversed through treatment with drugs that affect the biogenic amine systems of the brain, but it can also be treated with cognitive therapies that attempt to reverse "negative sets," and combination therapies are perhaps the most effective of all. Depression may arise as a consequence of the plastic response of mind/brain to experience, and it may also remit because of either pharmacologic or psychotherapeutic manipulations of brain plasticity.

## Summary and Conclusion

Examples of work applying diverse techniques of cognitive neuroscience to the study of depression and schizophrenia indicate that increasingly sophisticated strategies and conceptualizations are emerging as powerful new technologies are being applied. Focal regions have been replaced by circuits and static changes by plasticity and molecular mechanisms. The power of models is enhanced by efforts to design experiments that can be used in nonhuman species, in order to obtain in vivo measures that will illuminate mechanisms. The power of neuroimaging is also permitting in vivo measures of circuits and mechanisms in the human brain. These advances have created an era in which a scientific psychopathology that links mind and brain has become a reality.

## References and Notes

1. J. R. Searle, *The Rediscovery of the Mind* (MIT Press, Cambridge, MA, 1992); D. C. Dennett, *Kinds of Minds: Toward an Understanding of Consciousness* (Basic Books, New York, 1996).
2. M. M. Merzenich and K. Sameshima, *Curr. Opin. Neurobiol.* **3**, 187 (1993); W. Singer, *Science* **270**, 758 (1995).
3. M. I. Posner and S. E. Peterson, *Annu. Rev. Neurosci.* **13**, 25 (1990); E. Tulving, *Elements of Episodic Memory* (Oxford Univ. Press, New York and Oxford, 1983); J. L. McGaugh, N. M. Weinberger, G. Lynch, Eds., *Brain Organization and Memory: Cells, Systems and Circuits* (Oxford Univ. Press. New York, 1990); L. G. Ungerleider, *Science* **270**, 769 (1995).
4. L. R. Squire and S. Zola-Morgan, *The Physiological Basis of Memory* (Academic Press, New York, 1983); P. Goldman-Rakic, *Trends Neurosci.* **7**, 425 (1984); B. Milner and M. Petrides, *ibid.*, p. 403; A. L. Benton, *Contributions to Clinical Neuropsychology* (Aldine, Chicago, 1969); N. Geschwind and A. M. Galaburda, Eds., *Cerebral Dominance: The Biological Foundations* (Harvard Univ. Press, Cambridge, MA, 1984).
5. American Psychiatric Association, *Diagnostic and Statistical Manual of Mental Disorders, Fourth Edition (DSM-IV)* (American Psychiatric Press, Washington, DC, 1994); T. A. Widiger *et al.*, Eds., *DSM-IV Sourcebook, Volume 1* (American Psychiatric Press, Washington, DC, 1994).
6. E. Robins and S. B. Guze, *Am. J. Psychiatry* **126**, 983 (1970).
7. N. C. Andreasen, *Schizophr. Bull.* **13**, 9 (1987).
8. J. P. Feighner *et al.*, *Arch. Gen. Psychiatry* **26**, 57 (1972).
9. J. M. Hall *et al.*, *Science* **250**, 1684 (1990); A. D. Roses, *Annu. Rev. Med.* **47**, 387 (1996).
10. E. Bleuler, *Dementia Praecox of the Group of Schizophrenias (1911)*, J. Zinkin, Transl. (International Universities Press, New York, 1950).
11. F. Holsboer, in *Handbook of Affective Disorders*. E. S. Paykel, Ed. (Churchill Livingstone, Edinburgh, United Kingdom, 1992).

# Psychiatry's Global Challenge

## Arthur Kleinman and Alex Cohen

*The increasing prominence of biological approaches to psychopathology has encountered some resistance in the field. This is due to concerns that a biological perspective, with its strong focus on physiological processes within the body, neglects the social and physical environments in which people live. Socioculturally oriented psychologists, psychiatrists, and anthropologists claim that a westernized view of psychopathology does not recognize some of the variation in psychopathology that might be evident in developing nations, and they question the assumption that cultural and political perspectives can be ignored in the quest to understand and alleviate mental illness. As Lopez and Guarnaccia (2000, p. 590) note, "Culture is important in all aspects of psychopathology research—from the design and translation of instruments, to the conceptual models that guide the research, to the interpersonal interaction between researcher and research participants, to the definition and interpretation of symptom and syndromes, to the structure of the social world that surrounds a person's mental health problems."*

*This far more encompassing view of psychopathology provides a valuable and interesting contrast to the biological perspective. Kleinman and Cohen provide a critical analysis of existing approaches for contending with worldwide mental disorders, and they outline the challenges ahead to a culturally informed approach to psychopathology. Note in particular how they argue that, regardless of the underlying biology, mental disorders arise in social and cultural settings that can change the nature of symptoms and their outcomes.*

## Reference

Lopez, S. R., & Guarnaccia, P. J. J. (2000). Cultural psychopathology: Uncovering the social world of mental illness. *Annual Review of Psychology, 51,* 571–598.

## Suggested Reading

Lewis-Fernandez, R., & Kleinman, A. (1995). Cultural psychiatry: Theoretical, clinical, and research issues. *The Psychiatric Clinics of North America, 18,* 433–448.

*Scientific American,* 86–89. (1997, March).

Over the past 50 years, the health and living conditions of people in developing nations have improved dramatically. Average life expectancy in Egypt and India, among other countries, has risen from around 40 to 66 years. Smallpox, which once killed millions annually, has been completely eradicated, and infant mortality has fallen from about 28 to 10 percent of live births. Real average incomes more than doubled, and the percentage of rural families with access to safe water increased from less than 10 to almost 60 percent.

Unfortunately, this remarkable progress in physical well-being has been accompanied by a deterioration in mental health. In many areas outside North America and western Europe, schizophrenia, dementia and other forms of mental illness are on the rise. For example, schizophrenia—one of the most debilitating of mental illnesses, in which thoughts and emotions are sometimes disconnected or distorted by delusions—is expected to afflict 24.4 million people in low-income societies by the year 2000, a 45 percent increase over the number afflicted in 1985.

Behind this rise in the prevalence of mental illness is an array of demographic and social factors. Better physical health means, inevitably, that more people are living into the age of increased risk for some mental disorders, especially dementia. Moreover, increases in population, because of longer life spans, mean that the absolute number of people afflicted by mental disorders of all kinds is greater. In addition, the very economic and industrial development that has benefited some has also engendered massive societal changes. Rapid urbanization, chaotic modernization and economic restructuring have left many developing countries reeling. Increased rates of violence, drug and alcohol abuse, and suicide have accompanied disruptions in cultural practices, social routines, and traditional work and family roles.

Numerous studies have found that mental illness is a sharply increasing part of the health care burden for low-income societies. Depressive and anxiety disorders are the leading causes of disability around the globe, according to the World Health Organization (WHO). This United Nations agency estimates that such illnesses are responsible for approximately one quarter of all visits to health care centers worldwide. Suicide attempts and Alzheimer's disease and other dementias also cause large burdens, followed by epilepsy, psychoses, drug dependence and post-traumatic stress disorder.

The WHO study also found that, on average, general health care physicians everywhere fail to diagnose mental health disorders properly more than half the time. More dishearteningly, even when a case of mental illness is correctly diagnosed, the physician often prescribes drug treatments that are not pertinent to the condition.

## Four Persistent Myths

What is the psychiatric profession as a whole doing in response to these disturbing developments? It appears to be clinging to outmoded theories and practices, which poorly suit lower-income countries and the nonindustrial world. At present, the trend is to discount the uniqueness of symptoms that are found in a particular culture and instead to search for manifestations of mental illness that are culturally independent and are thus thought to be more closely linked to the biological basis of an illness. In turning its back on the great diversity of symptoms, however, psychiatric science is denying itself an enormous pool of data. And this failure seems to be blocking progress precisely when it is needed most.

Progress in improving mental health care in developing countries is obstructed by the persistence of several myths. Three of them have become central to psychiatry, and a fourth is current among some international health specialists. The first is that the forms of mental illness everywhere display similar degrees of prevalence. Myth number two can be described as an excessive adherence to a principle known as the pathogenetic/pathoplastic dichotomy, which holds that biology is responsible for the underlying structure of a malaise, whereas cultural beliefs shape the specific ways in which a person experiences it. The third myth maintains that various unusual, culture-specific disorders whose biological bases are uncertain occur only in exotic places outside the West. The fourth, held by many international health experts who discount mental health problems to begin with, holds that not much can be done to treat mental illness.

Myth number one has its roots in a previous, rather contradictory misconception. This earlier myth centered on the idea of the "noble savage" unencumbered by the exigencies of the "modern" world—a cornerstone of anthropology in the 19th century. As far back as the 1950s, however, the work of psychiatric anthropologists and cultural psychiatrists disproved the notion that the mental health problems of the undeveloped countries were trivial. Alexander Leighton, now professor emeritus of social psychiatry at the Harvard School of Public Health, T. A. Lambo, formerly deputy director general of WHO, and their colleagues found higher rates of depression among Nigeria's Yoruba tribe than among the people in a county in Nova Scotia. In a later study, John Orley, now at WHO, and John Wing of London's Royal College of Psychiatrists found that women living in a rural area of Uganda had higher rates of depression and suffered from more severe forms than women did in a suburb of London. Large surveys over the past 20 years of both rural and urban populations in China and Taiwan have also revealed the widespread presence of neuropsychiatric disorders. Finally, a host of studies have found that people throughout the world suffer from schizophrenia.

Eventually the mainstream of the mental health profession accepted that psychiatric illness occurs everywhere. Unfortunately, it replaced one myth with another. In the 1980s biological explanations of psychiatric phenomena were ascendant; the predominant theory maintained that the various types of mental illness were each distributed more or less uniformly on the earth. This view persists, despite the findings of many anthropological and epidemiological studies showing that the incidence and the symptoms of disorders vary markedly from one culture to another and also

with respect to class, gender and other variables. Study after study, for example, has demonstrated a correlation between socioeconomic status and health, both mental and physical.

Sex differences have been extensively documented as well. A WHO study in 14 countries (some industrial, some less so) found, overall, that women suffer from depression at almost twice the rate of men. In Santiago, Chile, however, women's risk for depression was almost five times that of men. A rather dramatic gender difference was revealed by a 1982 survey of more than 38,000 people in 12 areas in China. This research found not only that women suffered from neurotic disorders (primarily neurasthenia, dissociative neurosis and depressive neurosis) at nine times the rate of men but that the prevalence of schizophrenia was 75 percent higher among women.

This latter finding is puzzling if one regards schizophrenia as only biologically based. It may suggest that the disorder has a stronger cultural or environmental component than is generally recognized, or it may simply call into question the way in which the study was executed (although the work was regarded as rigorous, and no such criticisms have been raised). Deepening the mystery, the increased risk for schizophrenia among women has not been found in Taiwan.

Suicide rates, which have been linked to depression and substance abuse, are reported, with varying degrees of accuracy, in many countries and are sometimes used as an indicator of social health. The link between suicide rates and social upheaval was established around the turn of the century through the work of the French sociologist Emile Durkheim. Recently two Taiwanese psychiatrists, Mian-Yoon Chong of the Kaohsiung Medical College and Tai-Ann Cheng of the Academia Sinica, have revealed that Taiwan's suicide rates have varied greatly since the end of World War II. The two researchers found that the mass migration from the mainland and the rapid industrialization of what had been a rural economy were accompanied by the highest suicide rates. Those rates are now stable, although, interestingly, they are higher in rural areas than in the cities. They are also highest among the island's aboriginal peoples, who have been the most dislocated by social change.

China's suicide rate appears to be twice that of the U.S. and is most common among rural women. Elsewhere, it is men who are most at risk. Drawing on data from the World Bank, Michael Phillips, a Harvard University psychiatrist working at Hui Long Guan Psychiatric Hospital in Beijing, showed that more than 40 percent of all suicides in the world occur in China. Surprisingly, however, depression is three to five times less common in China than in the West; the country also has much less substance abuse. For troubled women in rural China, suicide appears to be almost a normative strategy for coping with distress.

Great variation has also been found, from country to country, in the most common forms of a particular mental illness. These results, too, are almost impossible to reconcile with today's emphasis on the underlying biological commonality of all mental illness. Schizophrenia, for example, has several different forms, including paranoid, which is characterized by thoughts of persecution, and catatonic, marked by immobility, such as catalepsy or stupor. Another form is known as hebephrenic; its prominent features include emotional bluntness and disorganized speech and behavior. The relative proportions of these types of the disorder vary considerably from one region to another, for reasons that are not entirely clear.

Norman Sartorius, Assen Jablensky and their colleagues at WHO recently found that paranoid schizophrenia was about 50 percent more common in the developed countries. On the other hand, the catatonic subtype was diagnosed more than six times more frequently among patients in the developing nations. (Indeed, this subtype, which was once quite common in the West, has all but disappeared there.) Hebephrenic schizophrenia was found four times as often among patients in the developed countries. Other researchers have noted that even within the industrial nations variation exists; the hebephrenic subtype, for example, is common among hospitalized Japanese patients but is unusual today in the U.S.

How do researchers account for this striking variation in the symptoms of disorders? This question brings us to our second myth. In their search for uniformity, psychiatrists and psychiatric epidemiologists have constructed a model of pathogenicity/pathoplasticity in which biology is responsible for the cause and structure of the forms of mental disease, whereas cultural factors at most shape the "content" of a disorder. For example, in paranoid schizophrenia, biology alone accounts for the fact that sufferers have delusional thoughts. Cultural beliefs, however, determine various specifics—whether the persecutor, in the afflicted's view, is the Central Intelligence Agency, evil spirits or beings from outer space.

## Too Much of a Good Model

The model is not without utility; it has allowed psychiatrists to categorize an extensive array of psychiatric symptoms into a more manageable and coherent system of diagnostic classes. Unfortunately, modern psychiatry has pushed the model to such extremes that it is counterproductive for understanding anxiety disorders and, especially, depression outside industrial regions in the West. In the developed Western world the symptoms of depression tend to be both psychological states—feelings of despair, sadness, belief that life is meaningless—and physical complaints. In general health care, patients highlight physical symptoms, whereas in psychiatric settings they emphasize psychological complaints. In non-Western societies and among traditionally oriented ethnic groups, there tends to be an emphasis primarily on bodily complaints (headaches, fatigue, dizziness, for example), and psychological symptoms are less frequent.

Modern psychiatry regards the bodily complaints as symptoms that merely mask the "real," biologically based emotional disease. But lacking a clear biological marker that could enable us to identify a specific disease conclusively, how can we be sure that the condition afflicting a Yoruba tribesman in Nigeria is the same as the disorder afflicting a lawyer in New York City or a fisherman in Nova Scotia? Furthermore, who is to say what actually constitutes the bedrock of depression: emotions or a mixture of emotional and bodily complaints with no clear organic cause?

Such questions aside, several maladies, including organic mental disorders, substance abuse, depression, manic-depression (bipolar disorder), various anxiety disorders and schizophrenia, are almost certainly global. But (turning to the third myth) as many as hundreds of other conditions appear to be culture-specific, local forms of pathology. A standard reference, the *Diagnostic and Statistical Manual of Mental Disorders* of the American Psychiatric Association, appears to acknowledge this fact in an appendix to its fourth edition. This appendix, however, with its thumbnail sketches of esoteric syndromes, is little more than a sop thrown to cultural psychiatrists and psychiatric anthropologists.

The appendix lists such exotica as amok, a condition distinguished by frenzied violent behavior directed at both people and objects, and latah, in which words and movements are repeated during sudden fright. All these conditions are presented as unique to the non-Western world. What psychiatric researchers are less willing to concede is that anorexia nervosa, multiple personality disorder, chronic fatigue syndrome and, perhaps, agoraphobia are probably culture-bound syndromes of the West, including Westernized elites in Asia. Perhaps three fourths of the manual's hundreds of diseases are, in fact, unique or most salient in North America.

The fourth and final myth comes from outside psychiatry. It contends that not much can be done to treat mental illnesses, even if they are widespread and costly. In fact, beneficial medications and therapies are becoming available at an accelerating rate, especially for the globally distributed conditions. We have effective medications for depression and anxiety. Schizophrenia can, for many patients, be managed successfully with a combination of antipsychotic medication and psychosocial interventions (family therapy or training in occupational or social skills).

Also, in the past two decades, Chinese mental health practitioners have developed a few impressive programs of psychiatric rehabilitation, notable for their ability to care effectively and humanely for people who suffer from severe mental disorders. These programs are particularly important because they appear to be applicable to other underserved populations. The incidence of several other conditions, such as mental retardation and epilepsy, could be reduced by preventing birth-related traumas, infections and nutritional deficiencies.

## An Opportunity Neglected

In an effort to base psychiatry in "hard" science and thus raise its status to that of other medical disciplines, psychiatrists have narrowly focused on the biological underpinnings of mental disorders while discounting the importance of such "soft" variables as culture and socioeconomic status. But the study of variation is a cornerstone of science, and the diversity of symptoms, outcome and prevalence of mental illness offers a tremendous opportunity to test the way human cultures and environments shape the formation, distribution and manifestation of disorders. So far this opportunity has been neglected. And in view of the hardships that mental illness imposes globally, this disinterest amounts to a tragedy of ever expanding proportions.

Of course, an enlightened view of the relation between culture and mental illness will not, by itself, suffice to improve conditions. Mental health care in the developing world is plagued by a variety of troubles, including an inability to expand small, local programs to cover more people. Additionally, low-income countries, faced with extreme poverty and limited funds, are forced to try to control such maladies as malaria and diarrhea, rather than invest in the "luxury" of mental health treatment. And although this is understandable, it is not acceptable. For depression alone, the cost of the failure to recognize and treat patients in primary care settings is enormous—depression causes more disability than arthritis, diabetes, hypertension and back pain.

Psychiatry must now confront what may be the

most damaging myth of all: that a knowledge base compiled almost exclusively from North American and European cases can be effectively applied to the 80 percent of the world's population that lives in Asia, Africa and South America as well as to the immigrant communities of North America and Europe. The need to establish cultural variation as a pillar of mental health studies comes from the empirical reality that distress, disease and treatment—however biological their roots—are experienced in contexts of cultural and social processes that make symptoms and outcomes different. Psychiatry's next challenge, then, is to formulate a perspective that better explains the interplay between the socioeconomic, cultural and biological aspects of mental illness.

# WHY BOGUS THERAPIES SEEM TO WORK

## Barry L. Beyerstein

*Well-trained young scientists learn to ask two kinds of questions. The first is "Oh yeah?" This reminds us that we need to be skeptical and critical of ideas that are put forth, of theories that are proposed, and of research findings that are published. Of course, we do not want to be so skeptical that we reject new ideas prematurely, but all claims and research findings must be scrutinized before they warrant serious scientific attention. For example, errors in logic need to be evaluated, questions about whether an idea is truly new need to be addressed, and problems with the methods that have been used need to be considered in detail. If claims pass this test, the second question—"So what?"—is asked. This question reminds us that not all legitimate claims are useful—some are tangential, irrelevant, or not testable using existing methods. It also reminds us that research is most valuable when it allows us to select between different explanations for the same phenomenon (or at least makes one of the explanations more or less plausible than the other).*

*The first three articles in this chapter refer to the content or focus of theories pertaining to mental illness. A distinct but equally important aspect of theorizing and the evaluation of theory is the degree to which we are skeptical about theoretical premises and beliefs. Theories are useful devices but only if they are open to revision—and a key ingredient motivating the revision of theories is skepticism. This article takes up the issue of skepticism (or, more accurately, the lack of skepticism) and why people believe that untested therapies work. It outlines a number of common flaws in logic that can lead to erroneous and potentially damaging conclusions. It is a reminder that few tools are as valuable as doubt and skepticism, for scientist, practitioner, and consumer alike.*

### Suggested Readings

Medawar, P. B. (1979). *Advice to a young scientist.* New York: Harper & Row.
Platt, J. R. (1964). Strong inference. *Science, 146,* 347–353.

*Skeptical Inquirer.* (1997, September/October). [On-line].
Available: http://www.csicop.org/si/9709/beyer.html

*Nothing is more dangerous than active ignorance.*

—Goethe

Those who sell therapies of any kind have an obligation to prove, first, that their treatments are safe and, second, that they are effective. The latter is often the more difficult task because there are many subtle ways that honest and intelligent people (both patients and therapists) can be led to think that a treatment has cured someone when it has not. This is true whether we are assessing new treatments in scientific medicine, old nostrums in folk medicine, fringe treatments in "alternative medicine," or the frankly magical panaceas of faith healers.

To distinguish causal from fortuitous improvements that might follow any intervention, a set of objective procedures has evolved for testing putative remedies. Unless a technique, ritual, drug, or surgical procedure can meet these requirements, it is ethically questionable to offer it to the public, especially if money is to change hands. Since most "alternative" therapies (i.e., ones not accepted by scientific biomedicine) fall into this category, one must ask why so many customers who would not purchase a toaster without consulting Consumer Reports shell out, with trusting naiveté, large sums for unproven, possibly dangerous, health remedies.

For many years, critics have been raising telling doubts about fringe medical practices, but the popularity of such nostrums seems undiminished. We must wonder why entrepreneurs' claims in this area should remain so refractory to contrary data. . . .

The answer, I believe, lies in a combination of vigorous marketing of unsubstantiated claims by "alternative" healers (Beyerstein and Sampson 1996), the poor level of scientific knowledge in the public at large (Kiernan 1995), and the "will to believe" so prevalent among seekers attracted to the New Age movement (Basil 1988; Gross and Levitt 1994). . . .

Many dubious health products remain on the market primarily because satisfied customers offer testimonials to their worth. Essentially, they are saying, "I tried it and I got better, so it must be effective." But even when symptoms do improve following a treatment, this, by itself, cannot prove that the therapy was responsible. . . .

## Ten Errors and Biases

The question is, then: Why might therapists and their clients who rely on anecdotal evidence and uncontrolled observations erroneously conclude that inert therapies work? There are at least ten good reasons.

*1. The disease may have run its natural course.* Many diseases are self-limiting—providing the condition is not chronic or fatal, the body's own recuperative processes usually restore the sufferer to health. Thus, before a therapy can be acknowledged as curative, its proponents must show that the number of patients listed as improved exceeds the proportion expected to recover without any treatment at all (or that they recover reliably faster than if left untreated). Unless an unconventional therapist releases detailed records of successes and failures over a sufficiently large number of patients with the same complaint, he or she cannot claim to have exceeded the published norms for unaided recovery.

*2. Many diseases are cyclical.* Arthritis, multiple sclerosis, allergies, and gastrointestinal complaints are examples of diseases that normally "have their ups and downs." Naturally, sufferers tend to seek therapy during the downturn of any given cycle. In this way, a bogus treatment will have repeated opportunities to coincide with upturns that would have happened anyway. Again, in the absence of appropriate control groups, consumers and vendors alike are prone to misinterpret improvement due to normal cyclical variation as a valid therapeutic effect.

*3. Spontaneous remission.* Anecdotally reported cures can be due to rare but possible "spontaneous remissions." Even with cancers that are nearly always lethal, tumors occasionally disappear without further treatment. One experienced oncologist reports that he has seen twelve such events in about six thousand cases he has treated (Silverman

1987). Alternative therapies can receive unearned acclaim for remissions of this sort because many desperate patients turn to them when they feel that they have nothing left to lose. When the "alternatives" assert that they have snatched many hopeless individuals from death's door, they rarely reveal what percentage of their apparently terminal clientele such happy exceptions represent. What is needed is statistical evidence that their "cure rates" exceed the known spontaneous remission rate and the placebo response rate (see below) for the conditions they treat. . . .

4. *The placebo effect.* A major reason why bogus remedies are credited with subjective, and occasionally objective, improvements is the ubiquitous placebo effect (Roberts, Kewman, and Hovell 1993; Ulett 1996). The history of medicine is strewn with examples of what, with hindsight, seem like crackpot procedures that were once enthusiastically endorsed by physicians and patients alike (Skrabanek and McCormick 1990; Barrett and Jarvis 1993). Misattributions of this sort arise from the false assumption that a change in symptoms following a treatment must have been a specific consequence of that procedure. Through a combination of suggestion, belief, expectancy, cognitive reinterpretation, and diversion of attention, patients given biologically useless treatments can often experience measurable relief. Some placebo responses produce actual changes in the physical condition; others are subjective that make patients feel better although there has been no objective change in the underlying pathology.

Through repeated contact with valid therapeutic procedures, we all develop, much like Pavlov's dogs, conditioned responses in various physiological systems. Later, these responses can be triggered by the setting, rituals, paraphernalia, and verbal cues that signal the act of "being treated." Among other things, placebos can cause release of the body's own morphinelike pain killers, the endorphins (Ulett 1996, ch. 3). Because these learned responses can be palliative, even when a treatment itself is physiologically unrelated to the source of the complaint, putative therapies must be tested against a placebo control group—similar patients who receive a sham treatment that resembles the "real" one except that the suspected active ingredient is withheld.

It is essential that the patients in such tests be randomly assigned to their respective groups and that they be "blind" with respect to their active versus placebo status. Because the power of what psychologists call expectancy and compliance effects (see below) is so strong, the therapists must also be blind as to individual patients' group membership. Hence the term double blind—the gold standard of outcome research. Such precautions are required because barely perceptible cues, unintentionally conveyed by treatment providers who are not blinded, can bias test results. Likewise, those who assess the treatment's effects must also be blind, for there is a large literature on "experimenter bias" showing that honest and well-trained professionals can unconsciously "read in" the outcomes they expect when they attempt to assess complex phenomena (Rosenthal 1966; Chapman and Chapman 1967). . . .

5. *Some allegedly cured symptoms are psychosomatic to begin with.* A constant difficulty in trying to measure therapeutic effectiveness is that many physical complaints can both arise from psychosocial distress and be alleviated by support and reassurance. At first glance, these symptoms (at various times called "psychosomatic," "hysterical," or "neurasthenic") resemble those of recognized medical syndromes (Shorter 1992; Merskey 1995). Although there are many "secondary gains" (psychological, social, and economic) that accrue to those who slip into "the sick role" in this way, we need not accuse them of conscious malingering to point out that their symptoms are nonetheless maintained by subtle psychosocial processes.

"Alternative" healers cater to these members of the "worried well" who are mistakenly convinced that they are ill. Their complaints are instances of somatization, the tendency to express psychological concerns in a language of symptoms like those of organic diseases (Alcock 1986; Shorter 1992). The "alternatives" offer comfort to these individuals who for psychological reasons need others to believe there are organic etiologies for their symptoms. Often with the aid of pseudoscientific diagnostic devices, fringe practitioners reinforce the somatizer's conviction that the cold-hearted, narrow-minded medical establishment, which can find nothing physically amiss, is both incompetent and unfair in refusing to acknowledge a very real organic condition. A large portion of those diagnosed with "chronic fatigue," "environmental sensitivity syndrome," and various stress disorders (not to mention many suing because of the allegedly harmful effects of silicone breast implants) look very much like classic somatizers (Stewart 1990; Huber 1991; Rosenbaum 1997). When, through the role-governed rituals of "delivering treatment," fringe therapists supply the reassurance, sense of belonging, and existential support their clients seek, this is obviously worthwhile, but all this need not be foreign to scientific practitioners who have much more to offer besides. The downside is that catering to the desire for medical diagnoses for psychological complaints promotes pseudoscientific and magical thinking while unduly inflating the success rates of medical quacks. Saddest of all, it perpetuates the anachronistic feeling that there is something shameful or illegitimate about psychological problems.

6. *Symptomatic relief versus cure.* Short of an outright cure, alleviating pain and discomfort is what sick people value most. Many allegedly curative treatments offered by alternative practitioners, while unable to affect the disease process itself, do make the illness more bearable, but for psychological reasons. Pain is one example. Much research shows that pain is partly a sensation like seeing or hearing and partly an emotion (Melzack 1973). It has been found repeatedly that successfully reducing the emotional component of pain leaves the sensory portion surprisingly tolerable. Thus, suffering can often be reduced by psychological means, even if the underlying pathology is untouched. Anything that can allay anxiety, redirect attention, reduce arousal, foster a sense of control, or lead to cognitive reinterpretation of symptoms can alleviate the agony component of pain. Modern pain clinics put these strategies to good use every day (Smith, Merskey, and Gross 1980).

Whenever patients suffer less, this is all to the good, but we must be careful that purely symptomatic relief does not divert people from proven remedies until it is too late for them to be effective.

7. *Many consumers of alternative therapies hedge their bets.* In an attempt to appeal to a wider clientele, many unorthodox healers have begun to refer to themselves as "complementary" rather than "alternative." Instead of ministering primarily to the ideologically committed or those who have been told there is nothing more that conventional medicine can do for them, the "alternatives" have begun to advertise that they can enhance conventional biomedical treatments. They accept that orthodox practitioners can alleviate specific symptoms but contend that alternative medicine treats the real causes of disease—dubious dietary imbalances or environmental sensitivities, disrupted energy fields, or even unresolved conflicts from previous incarnations. If improvement follows the combined delivery of "complementary" and scientifically based treatments, the fringe practice often gets a disproportionate share of the credit.

8. *Misdiagnosis (by self or by a physician).* In this era of media obsession with health, many people can be induced to think they have diseases they do not have. When these healthy folk receive the oddly unwelcome news from orthodox physicians that they have no organic signs of disease, they often gravitate to alternative practitioners who can almost always find some kind of "imbalance" to treat. If "recovery" follows, another convert is born.

Of course, scientifically trained physicians are not infallible, and a mistaken diagnosis, followed by a trip to a shrine or an alternative healer, can lead to a glowing testimonial for curing a grave condition that never existed. Other times, the diagnosis may be correct but the time course, which is inherently hard to predict, might prove inaccurate. If a patient with a terminal condition undergoes alternative treatments and succumbs later than the conventional doctor predicted, the alternative procedure may receive credit for prolonging life when, in fact, there was merely an unduly pessimistic prognosis—survival was longer than the expected norm, but within the range of normal statistical variation for the disease.

9. *Derivative benefits.* Alternative healers often have forceful, charismatic personalities (O'Connor 1987). To the extent that patients are swept up by the messianic aspects of alternative medicine, psychological uplift may ensue. If an enthusiastic, upbeat healer manages to elevate the patient's mood and expectations, this optimism can lead to greater compliance with, and hence effectiveness of, any orthodox treatments he or she may also be receiving. This expectant attitude can also motivate people to eat and sleep better and to exercise and socialize more. These, by themselves, could help speed natural recovery. . . .

10. *Psychological distortion of reality.* Distortion of reality in the service of strong belief is a common occurrence (Alcock 1995). Even when they derive no objective improvements, devotees who have a strong psychological investment in alternative medicine can convince themselves they have been helped. According to cognitive dissonance theory (Festinger 1957), when experiences contradict existing attitudes, feelings, or knowledge, mental distress is produced. We tend to alleviate this discord by reinterpreting (distorting) the offending information. To have received no relief after committing time, money, and "face" to an alternate course of treatment (and perhaps to the worldview of which it is a part) would create such a state of internal disharmony. Because it would be too psychologically disconcerting to admit to oneself or to others that it has all been a waste, there would be strong psychological pressure to find some redeeming value in the treatment.

Many other self-serving biases help maintain self-esteem and smooth social functioning (Beyerstein and Hadaway 1991). Because core beliefs tend to be vigorously defended by warping perception and memory, fringe practitioners and their clients are prone to misinterpret cues and remember things as they wish they had happened. Similarly, they may be selective in what they recall, overestimating their apparent successes while ignoring, downplaying, or explaining away their failures. The scientific method evolved in large part to reduce the impact of this human penchant for jumping to congenial conclusions. . . .

## Summary

For the reasons I have presented, individual testimonials count for very little in evaluating therapies. Because so many false leads can convince intelligent, honest people that cures have been achieved when they have not, it is essential that any putative treatment be tested under conditions that control for placebo responses, compliance effects, and judgmental errors.

Before anyone agrees to undergo any kind of treatment, he or she should be confident that it has been validated in properly controlled clinical trials. To reduce the probability that supporting evidence has been contaminated by the foregoing biases and errors, consumers should insist that supporting evidence be published in peer-reviewed scientific journals. Any practitioner who cannot supply this kind of backing for his or her procedures is immediately suspect. Potential clients should be wary if, instead, the "evidence" consists merely of testimonials, self-published pamphlets or books, or items from the popular media. Even if supporting articles appear to have come from legitimate scientific periodicals, consumers should check to see that the journals in question are published by reputable scientific organizations. Papers extolling pseudoscience often appear in official-looking periodicals that turn out to be owned by groups with inadequate scientific credentials but with a financial stake in the questionable products. Similarly, one should discount articles from the "vanity press"— journals that accept virtually all submissions and charge the authors for publication. And finally, because any single positive outcome—even from a carefully done experiment published in a reputable journal—could always be a fluke, replication by independent research groups is the ultimate standard of proof.

If the practitioner claims persecution, is ignorant of or openly hostile to mainstream science, cannot supply a reasonable scientific rationale for his or her methods, and promises results that go well beyond those claimed by orthodox biomedicine, there is strong reason to suspect that one is dealing with a quack. Appeals to other ways of knowing or mysterious sounding "planes," "energies," "forces," or "vibrations" are other telltale signs, as is any claim to treat the whole person rather than localized pathology.

To people who are unwell, any promise of a cure is especially beguiling. As a result, false hope easily supplants common sense. In this vulnerable state, the need for hard-nosed appraisal is all the more necessary, but so often we see instead an eagerness to abandon any remaining vestiges of skepticism. Erstwhile savvy consumers, felled by disease, often insist upon less evidence to support the claims of alternative healers than they would previously have demanded from someone hawking a used car. Caveat emptor!

# References

Alcock, J. 1986. Chronic pain and the injured worker. Canadian Psychology 27(2): 196–203.

Alcock, J. 1995. The belief engine. Skeptical Inquirer 19(3): 14–8.

Barrett, S., and W. Jarvis. 1993. The Health Robbers: A Close Look at Quackery in America. Amherst, N.Y.: Prometheus Books.

Basil, R., ed. 1988. Not Necessarily the New Age. Amherst, N.Y.: Prometheus Books.

Beyerstein, B., and P. Hadaway. 1991. On avoiding folly. Journal of Drug Issues 20(4): 689–700.

Beyerstein, B., and W. Sampson. 1996. Traditional medicine and pseudoscience in China. Skeptical Inquirer 20(4): 18–26.

Chapman, L., and J. Chapman. 1967. Genesis of popular but erroneous diagnostic observations. Journal of Abnormal Psychology 72: 193–204.

Festinger, L. 1957. A Theory of Cognitive Dissonance. Stanford: Stanford University Press.

Gross, P., and N. Levitt. 1994. Higher Superstition. Baltimore: Johns Hopkins University Press.

Huber, P. 1991. Galileo's Revenge: Junk Science in the Courtroom. New York: Basic Books.

Kiernan, V. 1995. Survey plumbs the depths of international ignorance. The New Scientist (April 29): 7.

Merskey, H. 1995. The Analysis of Hysteria: Understanding Conversion and Dissociation. 2d ed. London: Royal College of Psychiatrists.

Melzack, R. 1973. The Puzzle of Pain. New York: Basic Books.

O'Connor, G. 1987. Confidence trick. The Medical Journal of Australia 147: 456–9.

Roberts, A., D. Kewman, and L. Hovell. 1993. The power of nonspecific effects in healing: Implications for psychosocial and biological treatments. Clinical Psychology Review 13: 375–91.

Rosenbaum, J. T. 1997. Lessons from litigation over silicone breast implants: A call for activism by scientists. Science 276 (June 6, 1997): 1524–5.

Rosenthal, R. 1966. Experimenter Effects in Behavioral Research. New York: Appleton-Century-Crofts.

Shorter, E. 1992. From Paralysis to Fatigue: A History of Psychosomatic Illness in the Modern Era. New York: The Free Press.

Silverman, S. 1987. Medical "miracles": Still mysterious despite claims of believers. Psientific American (July): 5–7. Newsletter of the Sacramento Skeptics Society, Sacramento, Calif.

Skrabanek, P., and J. McCormick. 1990. Follies and Fallacies in Medicine. Amherst, N.Y.: Prometheus Books.

Smith, W., H. Merskey, and S. Gross, eds. 1980. Pain: Meaning and Management. New York: SP Medical and Scientific Books.

Stewart, D. 1990. Emotional disorders misdiagnosed as physical illness: Environmental hypersensitivity, candidiasis hypersensitivity, and chronic fatigue syndrome. Int. J. Mental Health 19(3): 56–68.

Ulett, G. A. 1996. Alternative Medicine or Magical Healing. St. Louis: Warren H. Green.

# CHAPTER 3

# Anxiety Disorders

*Anxiety disorders are characterized by excessive worry and fear and the maladaptive behaviors used to manage these feelings. This simple description masks a great deal of heterogeneity within the anxiety disorders, however, as the specific diagnoses can range from phobias, to posttraumatic stress disorder (PTSD), panic disorder, obsessive-compulsive disorder (OCD), and generalized anxiety disorder (GAD). In addition to being multifaceted, anxiety disorders are quite common. Approximately 15.7 million people in the United States between the ages of 15 and 54 suffer from anxiety disorders, and another 11.7 million people are diagnosed with an anxiety disorder and at least one other form of psychopathology. Indeed, in any given year, about 17% of the adults in the United States have one or more anxiety disorders (Kessler et al., 1994). It is no surprise that anxiety disorders are expensive to our society: Greenberg and colleagues estimated that the annual cost of anxiety disorders in the United States—including treatment costs, loss of productivity at work, and suicide—exceeded $42 billion in 1990. It is interesting to note that the largest cost, $23 billion, is associated with nonpsychiatric medical treatment costs, such as routine health costs and emergency room treatment (e.g., mistaking a panic attack as a heart attack).*

*The four readings in this chapter provide a selective introduction to anxiety disorders, including a case study of OCD, a review of research on obsessions and compulsions, an editorial on the treatment of panic disorder, and a discussion of treatment alternatives.*

## References

Greenberg, P. E., Sisitsky, T., Kessler, R., Finkelstein, S. N., Berndt, E. R., Davidson, J. R. T., Ballenger, J. C., & Fyer, A. J. (1999). The economic burden of anxiety disorders in the 1990s. *Journal of Clinical Psychiatry, 60,* 427–435.

Kessler, R. C., McGonagle, K. A., Zhao, S., Nelson, C. R., Highes, M., Eshleman, S., Wittchen, H., & Kendler, K. S. (1994). Lifetime and 12-month prevalence of *DSM-III-R* psychiatric disorders in the United States: Results from the National Comorbidity Survey. *Archives of General Psychiatry, 51,* 8–19.

## Suggested Reading

North, C. S., Nixon, S. J., Shariat, S., Mallonee, S., McMillen, J. C., Spitznagel, E. L., & Smith, E. M. (1999). Psychiatric disorders among survivors of the Oklahoma City bombing. *Journal of the American Medical Association, 282*, 755–762.

# Nightmare of the Mind

## Julie Cart

*As its name indicates, obsessive-compulsive disorder (OCD) is characterized by persistent thoughts or impulses that cause a high level of anxiety or distress and by repetitive behaviors or thoughts that the individual performs in order to control those feelings. The compulsions can be either overt behaviors, such as clapping one's hands, or thoughts, such as silently repeating a word or prayer.*

*This article describes the torment that Clint Malarchuk experienced as a result of OCD; it demonstrates that OCD is a chronic, debilitating disease that can interfere with work and social relationships. Remarkably, Malarchuk struggled with OCD while successfully playing in more than 300 games over 10 years in the National Hockey League. This article outlines the symptoms of the disease, Malarchuk's history, the stigma associated with OCD and similar disorders, and the complications that he encountered while seeking treatment. One of the psychiatrists who treated Malarchuk noted that the experience of OCD might be worse than that of schizophrenia because the person with OCD is fully aware of what is happening. It is difficult to evaluate this claim fully, but it does attest to the degree of despair and desperation in the lives of individuals afflicted with OCD.*

### Suggested Reading

Summers, M., & Hollander, E. (1999). *Everything in its place: My trials and triumphs with obsessive compulsive disorder.* New York: J. P. Tarcher.

*Los Angeles Times*, C1, C5 (1993, January 20).

SAN DIEGO—Time was when Clint Malarchuk was best known as the NHL goaltender who nearly bled to death on the ice.

On March 22, 1989, the skate of Steve Tuttle slashed Malarchuk's throat like a cutlass, severing the jugular vein. Malarchuk's blood formed a pool at his feet.

A red, ropy scar remains today, clinging like a leech to the right side of his neck, but Malarchuk came back from that incident. It used to be the one big life story for Malarchuk to retell.

Now, though, Clint Malarchuk is known as the NHL goaltender who got lost. The guy who had the problem. But no one can say exactly what it was that drove Malarchuk from the league after 10 years. That is what his problem is all about: secrecy, shame, misunderstanding and daily struggle.

A year ago, Malarchuk, 31, was found to have

obsessive-compulsive disorder, a seldom talked-about but increasingly common malfunction of brain chemistry. OCD is what drove Malarchuk from the NHL to the San Diego Gulls of the International Hockey League. OCD is also what has robbed him of his most precious possession—peace of mind.

The life of an obsessive-compulsive is one of horrifying and immobilizing thoughts and the irresistible drive to perform routines and rituals, sometimes hundreds of times a day.

There are "checkers," people who may sleep only a few hours a night because they keep getting up to make sure the doors are locked and the lights are off. There are people whose dressing routine has them putting on and taking off their clothes dozens of times. Some are convinced that they cannot walk through a doorway without twirling a certain number of times. Hand washers. Hair pullers. Counters.

The behavior of those afflicted with obsessive-compulsive disorder is difficult to understand. Many mistake the habits of OCD for interesting quirks, but they aren't. The rituals and repetitions of OCD are not the same as those of a perfectionist. Their insistence on specific patterns and methods are not superstitions.

An obsessive person cannot control his or her thoughts. A compulsive person *must* act on the thoughts.

If it all sounds strange and frightening—and Malarchuk agrees that it does—consider that OCD is more common than asthma or diabetes. It's not often talked about, but one in 40 of us have it. Doctors are calling it the disease of the '90s.

Although the disease is called OCD, it is possible to be afflicted with only the obsessions—the thoughts—and not the compulsions, the actions. According to some doctors, treating the obsessive is more difficult. It is easier to break down the rituals of a compulsive than plumb the mind of an obsessive.

"How would you like to be forced not to think about a pink elephant?" asked Dr. Stephen Stahl, a professor in UC San Diego's psychiatry department and a specialist in the treatment of OCD.

"You must not think about it. Of course, you do think about a pink elephant. You can't tell someone not to think about something. It's very difficult for these people to concentrate. They experience thoughts that are intrusive. They don't want them. It's more difficult to treat that than behavior."

Malarchuk has been living with, and hiding, the disease for most of his life. How he got through his 10 seasons with Quebec, Washington and Buffalo while struggling daily to control his thoughts is a tribute to both his love of hockey and, perhaps, his need to feel normal.

"I knew my thoughts and actions were not normal." Malarchuk said. "At times I thought I was crazy. There are [OCD] people with rituals that are beyond belief, that take them hours to perform. Yet they are able to work eight hours and put it on a shelf. That's what I was able to do. I would be terrible the day of a game, because the anxiety of the game increased the pressure. I would obsess so much easier. The night before a game it would start.

"Sometimes they give a goalie his own room. To me, that was the biggest relief in the world. I could do my preparation—which every goalie does, but in private. Pacing, acting out. Mine was a little excessive. You know what the funniest thing is? Goalies have this stigma attached to them that they are crazy and flaky. I've had more people tell me that I was the most normal goalie they'd ever met. Inside me I was saying, 'If you only knew.'"

Malarchuk saw the face of his disease in a violent and defining moment about a year ago.

By then, he obsessed all the time. It was as if he couldn't turn off his mind. He might be watching a movie on television in which a wife was being unfaithful to her husband. That would act as a powerful suggestion to Malarchuk. He would believe that his wife was being unfaithful—he would *know* it. No reassurance would satisfy him.

He could be driving down the road and hit a bump and be convinced that he had run over a pedestrian. Even doubling back and finding no body could not alleviate the real horror he felt.

That's one of the tricks of OCD. The French call it "the doubter's disease" because the obsessions are so strong that OCD sufferers don't believe their own eyes. "My hands are dirty; I must wash them. Even if they look clean I know they are still dirty."

"In a way, obsessive-compulsive people are worse off than psychotics or schizophrenics," said Bud Rickhi, a psychiatrist in Calgary who has treated Malarchuk. "Psychotics live in an unreal world. They have no point of reference. OCD patients are perfectly rational, yet they have irrational thoughts and compulsions they can't control. They are frightened because they recognize how abnormal this is. They are trapped in a kind of hell of the mind."

Malarchuk fell into that hell a year ago.

"That was a time when it was worst." Malarchuk said quietly, sitting in a coffee shop recently. "I was obsessing so bad I couldn't turn it off. It was 24 hours a day. I hadn't slept in two weeks. I would start dozing and it was like I couldn't let myself fall asleep.

"I would wake up with a start and a shock in my body. I wanted to sleep so badly, but as soon as I started to fall asleep, something would shoot into my mind and I would wake up. It was like a bolt of electricity went through my body. I can remember shaking uncontrollably and being unable to swallow.

"My eyes were burning from crying and lack of sleep. I was exhausted."

Through all this, Malarchuk remained the No. 1 goaltender for the Buffalo Sabres. Why did no one on his team recognize that Malarchuk was sick? Professional athletes are allowed—grudgingly—to be injured. But unseen diseases are the most insidious. His personality quirks were Malarchuk's business, as long as he could play. So the team was tolerant when, in Pittsburgh the night before a game, Malarchuk paced his room and cried and vomited. He couldn't stop his mind. At practice the next day, he was still throwing up. He was taken to a hospital, where it was found that Malarchuk's worrying and anxiety had produced an ulcer.

In Pittsburgh, Malarchuk was given medication that eventually put him in another hospital.

At a Super Bowl party given by a teammate, Malarchuk broke his rule of drinking during the season and had a few beers. He also took painkillers and Zantac, his ulcer medicine. More than anything, Malarchuk wanted to sleep. And having read the medicine bottles that said taking the drug with alcohol would cause drowsiness, Malarchuk, in his desperation, medicated himself—almost to death.

He left the party and went home. Confused and panicking, he begged his wife, Sandra, to help him. "What is happening?" he cried. He became incoherent, then blacked out on the bedroom floor. Sandra called paramedics and performed CPR on her husband until they arrived. Finally, at the hospital, Malarchuk's obsessive-compulsive disorder was diagnosed.

"I was in so much pain—mental pain—I was trying to put the fire out," he said. "Unfortunately, I was using gasoline. I almost died that night."

After hearing the diagnosis, OCD patients often reexamine events and patterns in their lives and are able to place eccentric behavior in the context of the disease. Malarchuk sees that he displayed classic OCD behavior as a child, although his family simply thought of him as being emotional.

"I had more [rituals] than usual, but they weren't overpowering my life yet," he said. "I can remember being very cautious. Kind of a checker. I prayed a lot. Germs were a big thing for a while. Contamination. I'm still very conscious of germs. There was a problem with bathrooms and touching doorknobs, but not to the point where it was controlling. I can remember taking stuff from home to clean the desk I was assigned to at school. I had to sterilize it.

"I was worried about everything. It wasn't normal for a 12-year-old to be so worried about everybody and everything to the point of tears. . . . Everyone just thought I had emotional problems.

"Probably, most of my problems began when I was 12. I was admitted into hospital with extreme anxiety. I was crying uncontrollably. They couldn't pinpoint anything. They just said 'What's with this kid? He's 12 years old and he's got the weight of the world on his shoulders.' I'm sure that was the beginning."

Although OCD is known as a disease that waxes and wanes, it is always present in some form. Malarchuk sees that his reputation for discipline and hard work was a byproduct of the illness. Gull Coach Rick Dudley, who also coached Malarchuk in Buffalo, recalled that his work ethic was widely known.

"Everyone always talked about how disciplined I was," Malarchuk said. "I used to work out 6–8 hours a day in the off-season. But discipline had nothing to do with it. I *had* to do it. It was part of the disease."

Recognition of OCD is only the beginning. Patients undergo lengthy trials with anti-depressant drugs, which are believed to correct the brain's chemical imbalance. The problems often compound as patients and their doctors wrestle, sometimes for years, to find the right combination of drugs. Because it can take weeks or months to determine if a drug is working, depression and anxiety are common companions to OCD sufferers.

That is Malarchuk's problem now. The drug he takes, Zoloft, leaves him groggy and sick to his stomach. Others produce side effects of blurred vision, anxiety or insomnia. Malarchuk has chafed at taking his medication because of its effect on his play. That caused a problem last month.

Malarchuk began to find his form again in November, going 5-0 with a 1.0 goals-against average. The Gulls, now 34-4-4, were rolling over opponents. And Malarchuk was playing so well that he was called up to Buffalo. That was the good news. The bad news was that he didn't play while there and didn't react well to being taken out of his environment.

When he returned to San Diego, Malarchuk began to cut back on his medication, wanting to be sharper for games. He didn't tell his doctors, or Dudley, who knew of his OCD and had been supportive. Malarchuk fell apart in a game when he gave up four goals in five shots.

The reversal was total, and Malarchuk was devastated when he thought about the effect his suddenly awful play would have on his dream to get back to the NHL.

"Everyone gave up on me real quickly," he said. "You say you have anything mental, a chemical imbalance of the brain, and you are not going to touch the guy with a 10-foot pole. It was like when I cut my throat, everyone thought, 'Is he going to be the same goalie?' I had to overcome all that, and it's the same now, only worse. We're talking about the brain."

The stigma of OCD might prove to be more difficult to overcome than the disease itself.

"The stigma is there for something people don't understand . . . don't have the information," psychiatrist Stahl said.

How realistic is Malarchuk's hope to return to the NHL? Rogie Vachon, former general manager of the Kings and now special assistant to the chairman of the club, acknowledged that Malarchuk's struggle has been discussed in the NHL. But Vachon, a former goaltender, said the bottom line was performance.

"If a player can stop the puck and win hockey games, and his problem is under control, a team will take him," Vachon said.

At the moment, Malarchuk's problem is not under control. The drug, at its new low dose, has not had any effect. But his doctor says he is optimistic, that many OCD patients do control the disease. When the drugs work, patients say, it's as if the volume in their head is turned down. Not off, but lower.

Malarchuk is facing a decision that all athletes wrestle with, the question of when to quit. Often, it is most agonizing when the decision is made for you because of injury or loss of ability. For Malarchuk, such a decision represents a burden he's not sure he wants.

"I think I'd rather not have the choice, to be honest with you," he said. "I'd rather have the doctors or the coach tell me. I wish I would break my leg. Then it would be easy.

"Ultimately, I want to keep playing. But I want to be happy, too. I would love to be able to resurrect my career and get back to the NHL. I would love that. I dream of beating the disease and beating the odds and coming back and having another year or two in the NHL. But I can't lose my life doing it. I have to be happy. It's been a struggle all my life. It's been so much pressure that I just want it to stop. Sometimes, I wish God would come down and take it all away."

# THE BIOLOGY OF OBSESSIONS AND COMPULSIONS

## Judith L. Rapoport

*This article focuses on the research conducted to understand OCD. Judith Rapoport advances the claim that OCD is the result of brain circuitry gone awry. She argues that this brain circuitry is in the basal ganglia, which appears to store a behavioral program that, as a result of our evolutionary heritage, controls how we respond to environmental stimuli that pertain to such basic functions as cleanliness, territoriality, and grooming. Normally this circuitry is essential to our everyday survival and allows us to respond efficiently and quickly to specific situations. When our hands might be contaminated with germs, for example, we wash them. For reasons that are not entirely clear, however, the manner in which these programs are turned on and off can short circuit, so that the individual is forced to enact the associated behaviors repeatedly and without discretion. This article contributes an intriguing and instructive account to the complex story of OCD.*

### Suggested Readings

Rapaport, J. L. (1989). *The boy who could not stop washing: The experience and treatment of obsessive-compulsive disorder.* New York: Dutton.

Rapoport, J. L., & Fiske, A. (1998). The new biology of obsessive-compulsive disorder: Implications for evolutionary psychology. *Perspectives in Biology and Medicine, 41,* 159–175.

Rapoport, J. L. (2000). Treatment of obsessive-compulsive disorder in children and adolescents. *Journal of Child Psychology and Psychiatry and Allied Disciplines, 41,* 419–431.

---

*Scientific American,* 83–98. (1989, March).

Sergei is a 17-year-old former high school student. Only a year or so ago Sergei seemed to be a normal adolescent with many talents and interests. Then, almost overnight, he was transformed into a lonely outsider, excluded from social life by his psychological disabilities. Specifically, he was unable to stop washing. Haunted by the notion that he was dirty—in spite of the contrary evidence of his senses—he began to spend more and more of his time cleansing himself of imaginary dirt. At first his ritual ablutions were confined to weekends and evenings and he was able to stay in school while keeping them up, but soon they began to consume all his time, forcing him to drop out of school, a victim of his inability to feel clean enough.

Sergei's condition is called obsessive-compulsive disorder, or OCD. Previously thought to be quite rare, it is now known to affect perhaps as much as 2 percent of the U.S. population. OCD is resistant to family counseling, psychotherapy and most drugs for treating anxiety and depression. Yet trials my colleagues and I have conducted at the National Institute of Mental Health show that OCD yields to certain new antidepressant medications. The capacity of these drugs to reduce obsessive-compulsive behavior is quite distinct from their effect on depression. This is one piece of evidence (among others) that OCD is not a function of mood but a specific, biologically rooted syndrome. Although the details are far from clear, a new, biological model of OCD is rapidly emerging.

A key feature of the model is the idea that certain behavioral "subroutines" related to grooming and territoriality have been programmed into the human brain over the course of evolution. Ordinarily the evidence of the senses (that one is clean or that the stove is off) are sufficient to keep such subroutines suppressed. If higher brain centers malfunction, however, the subroutines may be replayed repeatedly, and sufferers from OCD are left at their mercy, unable to stop washing or checking the stove even though consciously they understand that such behavior is "crazy." The new biology of obsessions and compulsions represents a great step forward in understanding; because of the availability of new drugs with anti-OCD activities, it has been accompanied by equally great strides in therapy.

The terms obsessive and compulsive are by now part of everyday language. People often say "He's compulsive" when what they mean is that the person is an uptight bore; they say "She's obsessed by him" when they mean that a friend is a lovesick ninny. That is not how these terms are applied here. Obsessive-compulsive disorder is a severe, chronic psychiatric problem. It manifests itself through obsessions (recurrent, persistent ideas, thoughts or impulses that are experienced, at least initially, as intrusive and senseless) or compulsions (repetitive, purposeful behaviors—perceived as unnecessary—that are performed in response to an obsession, or according to certain rules or in a stereotyped fashion).

The form these processes take in OCD typically include irresistible urges to wash, to check doors (to make sure they are locked) or appliances (to make sure they are turned off) or to count repetitively, and by the presence of intrusive thoughts (frequently of dangerous or unacceptable behaviors). The difference between OCD and the milder forms of compulsion seen in otherwise healthy people is that these behaviors have become so demanding and time-consuming that they interfere with the patient's life to a considerable degree—as in Sergei's case.

One of the surprising things about sufferers from OCD is that their disease is limited: in other areas they are quite reasonable. What is more, they understand that their obsessive-compulsive behaviors are irrational, and yet they cannot do much to control them on their own. As a result these patients suffer painfully. When the symptoms are severe, they can make the patient appear ridiculous, as Samuel Johnson, a sufferer from the disorder, must have seemed to his companions when he performed odd ritualistic hand movements before leaping through doorways. The victim of OCD may even become an unwashed hermit, as Howard Hughes did. (Although Hughes's fate seems paradoxical in light of the cleanliness compulsions of OCD patients, a plausible explanation is that his cleanliness rituals became so demanding that he could not complete them and as a result became psychologically paralyzed.)

My own medical and psychiatric training had given me little exposure to patients with OCD. The reason is not that OCD is such a rare disorder; it is that sufferers from OCD rarely seek psychiatric help. Yet as a child psychiatrist I had been intrigued even by the few cases I saw, partly because they seemed identical with the few adult cases that were familiar to me. For a psychiatric disorder to appear in identical form in children and adults is somewhat unusual; it is more common for a particular disease to appear most frequently at a specific point in the life cycle (as schizophrenia, for

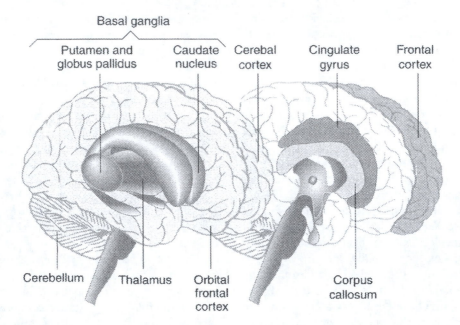

Basal ganglia

Putamen and globus pallidus | Caudate nucleus | Cerebral cortex | Cingulate gyrus | Frontal cortex

Cerebellum | Thalamus | Orbital frontal cortex | Corpus callosum

Neuroanatomy of basal ganglia is shown on a three-dimensional view of the human brain. The basal ganglia consist of several structures, including the caudate nucleus, the putamen and the globus pallidus, that lie under the cerebral cortex. The basal ganglia are connected to the frontal lobe by a variety of pathways, including one that contains tissues in the cingulate gyrus. The author proposes that aberrations in this brain circuitry may underlie the symptoms of OCD.

example, appears most frequently in late adolescence).

Yet in our study I have seen children whose odd, repetitive acts (such as walking in circles or counting or tapping a certain number over and over again—acts they felt forced to carry out against their will) began as early as the age of three. Such children have their own explanations for why they carry out these strange acts. For example, at age seven Stanley saw a television program in which friendly Martians contacted human beings by putting odd thoughts into their heads. On the basis of that program Stanley decided his compulsion to do everything in sequences of four was a sign that the Martians had picked him as their "contact man" on earth.

After two years of sterile counting rituals, no contact had been made and Stanley gave up this explanation. He did not, however, give up counting. Nor do other OCD patients generally give up their ritualistic behavior without treatment, in spite of their knowledge that the behavior is "crazy." Often, though, there will be a progression of symptoms: from counting in childhood to washing rituals in adolescence to obsessive thoughts in early adulthood. From a third to a half of all the victims of OCD first began to experience these behaviors in childhood or adolescence.

Perhaps in part because they understand that their rituals and thoughts are senseless, OCD patients may go to great lengths to hide them. These patients simulate normality as long as they can by limiting their rituals to private hours and avoiding intimate social situations in which their compulsions would be discovered. Typically the symptoms are concealed for years and help is sought only when the symptoms can no longer be managed because they have started to make the patient avoid school, work or social obligations.

Such concealment is the reason that there were initially thought to be few sufferers from OCD. Indeed, when my colleagues and I began drug trials at the NIMH, we did not know whether we would be able to find enough subjects to complete the work. Those trials began in the mid-1970's, triggered by early reports from Spain, England and Sweden that a new drug called clomipramine (CMI), formulated as an antidepressant, had specific antiobsessional activity. At the beginning we were quite skeptical that any drug could have a specific anti-OCD effect, particularly a drug that was closely related chemically to a standard antidepressant, as clomipramine is.

More than a decade later the situation is quite different. First, we now know that CMI can relieve obsessive-compulsive symptoms. Second, as a result of the publicity our trials received, we now have hundreds of patients requesting treatment. What is more, the new attention focused on the disorder has led to careful epidemiological studies that show OCD is much commoner than was once thought. The prevalence of OCD was recently measured in five U.S. communities among more than 18,000 people interviewed in their homes as part of the NIHM Epidemiological Catchment Area program. The overall prevalence of OCD ranged from 1.9 to 3.3 percent in the five communities: a rate from 25 to 60 times greater than previous estimates.

The prevalence rates in the catchment-area study were lifetime rates, that is, the rate that might be expected in a group of chronological peers at the end of their life span. That rate is supported by a study of more than 5,000 high school students carried out by my colleagues and me in collaboration with Agnes H. Whitaker of the Columbia University College of Physicians and Surgeons and her collaborators. Among this much younger group the cumulative prevalence of OCD was about 1 percent. If the two studies are correct, from four to six million people in the U.S. suffer from the disorder.

The dimensions of the problem can be appreciated when one considers how much suffering there is among those four to six million people. Even for those who can "pass" in school or on the job, OCD may mean a lifetime of worry and isolation. OCD

patients are more likely than others to divorce or not to marry in the first place—perhaps partly to avoid discovery of their private rituals. Follow-up studies of people who have been clinically treated show that the disorder is chronic and recurrent: at least 50 percent of those treated with psychotherapy or older drug therapies suffered from the disease seven to 20 years after the end of their treatment.

The experience my colleagues and I have acquired as the result of the trials beginning in 1975 have led us toward an ethological perspective on OCD. Ethology is the scientific study of animal behavior. Some of the best work in ethology has been done by Konrad Lorenz, who described nest building, grooming, courtship and defensive behavior patterns in young animals, mostly of avian species. These patterns appeared without learning models, and Lorenz hypothesized that they are "hardwired" into the brain circuitry. Many of the behaviors shown by OCD patients seem to resemble the fixed-action patterns described by Lorenz. It is obvious that cultural and physical stimuli account to some degree for a particular patient's symptoms, but the ritualized aspect of the behavior and its startling uniformity—along with the fact that children and adults show identical symptoms—suggest biological preprogramming.

In addition to the uniformity of the behaviors, certain other features of obsessions and compulsions led my colleagues and me to believe in a biological basis for OCD, which had been suggested by others but was buttressed by the new findings. For one thing, the disease is more prevalent among relatives of people with OCD than among the general population, suggesting a possible genetic cause. In addition, an association between OCD and certain neurologically rooted problems implied that the disease was closely linked to the anatomy of the nervous system. About 20 percent of patients also display motor tics: involuntary movements that are usually blinks of the eye or facial grimaces.

The connection between involuntary motor movements and obsessive-compulsive symptoms has been known for some time. In 1896 Sir William

Osler, who was then physician-in-chief at the Johns Hopkins Hospital, described a seven-year-old girl who suffered from a syndrome that included the compulsion to count as well as odd, chorealike motions. (Chorea is a general term for rapid, jerky movements that appear to be willed but are actually involuntary.) Since that time it has been shown repeatedly that OCD occurs in association with several types of neurological disorders: Sydenham's chorea, epilepsy, postencephalitic Parkinson's disease and toxic lesions of a part of the brain called the basal ganglia.

Now, this association is intriguing, in part because all the disorders affect the basal ganglia, a group of structures lying under the cerebral cortex that are known to be "way stations" between sensory inputs and the resulting motor or cognitive outputs. Is it possible that in obsessive-compulsive patients disturbances in these way stations have somehow short-circuited the loop that normally connects sensory input with behavioral output, thereby releasing stored, hard-wired behavioral packages?

In our own work we now have several independent lines of evidence implicating the circuitry of the basal ganglia in OCD. As I noted, about 20 percent of our patients show chorealike twitches resembling those of Osler's patient, and standard tests designed to identify specific neurological function indicate that our patients have functional deficits in the frontal lobes or the basal ganglia or both. We have now gone beyond such preliminary data to complete three additional types of study pointing toward the involvement of these brain regions in obsessive-compulsive disorder.

A study in which we collaborated with Jay Luxenberg of the National Institute on Aging and his colleagues compared computerized axial tomography (CAT) scans of the brains of OCD patients with those of a matched control group who did not have the disease. In particular we were interested in the volume of the caudate nucleus, one of the structures in the basal ganglia; our patients had smaller caudate volumes.

A second study took advantage of an "experi-ment of nature" that unfortunately was affecting many adolescents. There has recently been a resurgence of rheumatic fever in parts of the U.S. Rheumatic fever is a chronic inflammatory disease of the heart and joints that sometimes develops after certain streptococcal infections. About 20 percent of rheumatic-fever patients also develop Sydenham's chorea, probably as the result of an autoimmune response to the basal ganglia, leading to potential damage there.

My colleagues and I conducted a survey of 23 Sydenham's chorea patients and 14 patients who had rheumatic fever but did not have chorea (all the subjects the five collaborating pediatric departments could locate). In "blind" evaluations (in which the interviewer did not know the medical diagnosis) scores for obsessional symptoms were significantly higher among those with Sydenham's chorea. What is more, three chorea patients—but no rheumatic-fever patients—met our diagnostic criteria for full-fledged OCD. This result again suggests that OCD, at least in some patients, is due to dysfunction of the basal ganglia.

The third study was carried out by my colleague Susan Swedo in collaboration with Mark Schapiro and Cheryl L. Grady of the National Institute on Aging. The three investigators compared obsessive-compulsive patients and normal controls by means of positron-emission tomography (PET). PET scans yield brain images in which metabolic activity can be measured noninvasively in resting subjects. The study showed that OCD patients had higher levels of glucose metabolism in an area of the frontal lobe and in the cingulate pathway, which connects the frontal lobe and the basal ganglia. These results confirmed earlier ones by Lewis R. Baxter of the University of California at Los Angeles School of Medicine and his colleagues; in both studies the elevated glucose metabolism was correlated with measures of the severity of OCD.

The body of recently accumulated evidence makes it seem quite likely that obsessive-compulsive symptoms, at least in their severest form, have a distinct biological basis. Although the precise mechanism by which the symptoms are formed is yet to be elucidated, there are, as I have described, some clear hints about which brain regions are involved. At the same time as those strides were being made in elucidating the basis of the disease, corresponding advances were being made in treatment.

Two very different types of treatment may be effective in dealing with OCD. The first is behavior therapy, which entails repeated exposure of the patient to the stimulus that sets off the ritualistic acts. For example, if a patient has a compulsion that causes him to wash his hands 20 or 30 times a day, his hands may be deliberately dirtied, after which he is prevented from washing them. Although such treatment may sound cruel, it has proved to be effective in severe cases in which traditional forms of psychotherapy had failed. Behavior therapists, including Isaac M. Marks of the Maudsley Hospital Medical School in London and Edna Foa of the Medical College of Pennsylvania, have documented such improvement extensively and shown that exposure to the feared situation is crucial for recovery.

At first glance it may seem contradictory to claim simultaneously that OCD has a strong biological basis and that behavioral conditioning is effective in reversing it. Yet the contradiction is largely superficial. Ethologists have shown that many fixed action patterns in animals, which stem in part from hand-wiring, can be extinguished by repeated training. Moreover, since the brain is both a biological organ and the recipient of sensory and psychological inputs, it is only to be expected that strictly psychological causes can have biological effects.

Behavior therapy seems to be more effective in treating compulsions than in treating obsessions, which generate fewer outward signs. The new drug treatments for OCD, on the other hand, seem to be effective in lessening both obsessions and compulsions. Three drugs have been shown to have anti-OCD effects; in addition to CMI, they are fluvoxamine and fluoxetine. All three of these were formulated initially as antidepressants. Indeed, CMI differs functionally by only a single chlorine atom from a standard antidepressant called desipramine (DMI).

It might be thought that the antiobsessional effects of these new agents are simply by-products of their potency in lifting depression, but that does not seem to be the case. Most antidepressants are not particularly helpful in the treatment of obsessive and compulsive symptoms. Furthermore, the benefit seen among our patients in treatment does not depend on whether or not the patient is depressed; it seems to be an independent clinical consequence. A new psychiatric drug treatment for OCD has been established.

Of the three new drugs, CMI is the one that has been most extensively studied. In one recent study the anti-OCD effects of CMI and DMI were compared by a group of my colleagues led by Henrietta Leonard. After two weeks of receiving a placebo, two groups of patients were given either the new drug CMI or the standard antidepressant DMI for five weeks. At the end of that period the groups "crossed over" and the members of each group received the other drug for an equal period. The results of the crossover study were striking: patients improved on CMI and relapsed on DMI: those who were given DMI first improved only after receiving the newer drug.

To date 14 double-blind studies demonstrating CMI's antiobsessional efficacy have been published. As a result of such studies along with multicenter trials by the CIBA-Geigy Corporation, the drug's manufacturer, and our own multicenter clinical trials, CIBA-Geigy has received permission from the U.S. Food and Drug Administration to provide the drug to patients under a special, expedited license. (Only four drugs have had such handling by the FDA, the first of them being AZT, the anti-AIDS drug.)

CMI works. Why? The answer is not as clear as the drug's efficacy. The effectiveness of CMI (along with fluvoxamine and fluoxetine) is probably related to the physiology of the neurotransmitter serotonin. The role of serotonin in human behavior is not well understood, but there is evidence that the transmitter is important in suicide, appetite and the control of aggression, among other functions. Neurons that respond to serotonin are widely distributed in the brain; they are present in the frontal lobes and they are particularly concentrated in the basal ganglia.

Like other neurotransmitters, serotonin is released into the synapse (the gap between two nerve cells) and later must be removed from the synapse—in the process called reuptake—before the presynaptic cell can be fired again. CMI, fluvoxamine and fluoxetine all block the reuptake of serotonin in the synapse, and work by my colleague Dennis L. Murphy suggests that this may be the reason they are effective against obsessive-compulsive symptoms. Yet although serotonin or its metabolic product can be found in the blood and spinal fluid, no one has shown that OCD patients have abnormal levels of these substances there: evidence for the role of serotonin in the disease remains indirect. What is more, CMI is known to affect the action of other transmitters (particularly dopamine), and the precise mode of action of CMI remains to be elucidated.

In spite of such gaps, what is known is sufficient to formulate a hypothesis about the possible biological basis of OCD. It seems possible that latent behavioral patterns stored in the basal ganglia are somehow triggered by abnormally functioning inferior frontal lobe areas. The initiating impulse is conveyed to the basal ganglia by pathways mediated by serotonin. Successful drug treatment might alter the role of serotonin in those pathways, thereby damping the spark from the frontal regions.

The successful treatment of severe obsessive-compulsive disorder led us to try CMI as a mode of therapy in other conditions that may be biologically related. After our studies were covered on a national television program in March, 1987, we were approached by thousands of patients, among them many women with only a single compulsive symptom: they pull out their hair one strand at a time. This problem, known to physicians as trichotillomania, had not generally been linked to OCD. It may be quite severe; many women who suffer from it have never been seen by their families without a wig.

Following some initial trials, 14 women with this symptom were treated in a double-blind comparison of CMI and DMI resembling the one carried out among our OCD patients. CMI reduced the hair-pulling habit; DMI, the standard antidepressant, was not helpful. PET-scanning studies of the trichotillomaniac patients by Schapiro, Grady and Swedo are now under way, and we suspect they will reveal the same pattern of abnormalities in the frontal lobe-basal ganglia circuit that was seen in patients with the more easily recognized obsessive-compulsive disease.

The selective and successful treatment of trichotillomania raises questions about some other behaviors that are undesirable but subjectively compelling. Might nail biting, for example, respond to the same therapy? How about other "uncontrollable" impulse disorders such as kleptomania? Clinical trials in which such disorders are treated with antiobsessional drugs are waiting to be undertaken. Perhaps the new biology of OCD will one day lead to a reclassification of some other disparate behaviors under a broader category of compulsive syndromes linked by similar patterns of inheritance, by similar brain-imaging results and by the fact that they respond to specific therapeutic agents.

It is my feeling that in the even longer run this work could lead to a fundamental shift in the understanding of evolution, the mind and human rituals. In our model the basal ganglia are the repository of units of behavior that have been organized over the course of evolution. The objects of phobias have been shown to include threats to humanity that are significant from an evolutionary viewpoint (such as snakes, spiders and heights). In much the same way, I believe the formation of obsessive-compulsive rituals may be interpreted from an evolutionary and ethological viewpoint. It is clear that cleanliness, grooming and the checking of order and territorial boundaries had crucial functions during human evolution.

Perhaps under stress these fixed software packages become coupled with certain stimuli that are perceived as dangerous. Once set in motion, this loop cannot be interrupted: the patient becomes an ultimate skeptic who cannot credit his sense data or his attempts to refute the obsession by means of logic. The sufferer cannot accept reassuring information, such as the fact that the door is locked or the light is off. In effect, the patient's inability to believe sets off the ritualistic behavior that appears to be hardwired into the brain at an unexpected level of complexity. Although such thoughts are speculative, they may lead to the profoundest scientific contribution of the work on OCD: the development of a biology of doubt and ultimately a biology of belief.

# Panic Disorder—It's Real and It's Treatable

## Richard M. Glass, M.D.

*An individual having a panic attack experiences a rapid onset of very intense fear or terror, which is often accompanied by a rapid heart rate, sweating, trembling, and shortness of breath. Panic attacks can occur in a variety of different anxiety disorders, or in the absence of any disorder at all, but an individual is diagnosed with panic disorder when he or she has recurrent panic attacks that are unexpected and that lead to continuing concerns that another panic attack will occur.*

*The immediate prompt for this editorial by Richard Glass was a study conducted by David Barlow and colleagues (2000) that compared the effects of psychotherapy, pharmacotherapy, their combination, and a placebo as treatments for panic disorder. This study was particularly important because prior studies had suggested that either cognitive-behavioral therapy or tricyclic antidepressants would be effective in the treatment of panic disorder. However, little was known about their relative effectiveness within the same study or about how effective they would be when combined. Glass discusses the broader historical context of this study and provides a very useful synopsis of the key findings. One unusual finding was that those patients receiving both of the active interventions—cognitive-behavioral therapy and the antidepressant (imipramine)—fared worse than those patients receiving cognitive-behavioral therapy alone or in combination with a placebo. Glass raises the possibility that the combination of drugs and psychotherapy can actually hamper the effectiveness of the psychotherapy, though other explanations are also possible. This article also points out that what would seem to be a relatively simple task—determining which of two established interventions is preferable for treating a carefully defined disorder—is actually quite complex and requires a great deal of methodological sophistication.*

## Reference

Barlow, D. H., Gorman, J. M., Shear, M. K., & Woods, S. W. (2000). Cognitive-behavioral therapy, imipramine, or their combination for panic disorder: A randomized controlled trial. *Journal of the American Medical Association, 283,* 2529–2536.

---

*Journal of the American Medical Association, 283,* 2573–2574. (2000).

The title above, taken from a National Institute of Mental Health public service announcement, is an important message for physicians and for the public because of the common occurrence of clinical situations exemplified by the following prototypical scenario: A previously healthy young adult presents for urgent evaluation because of the most recent episode of recurrent, spontaneous attacks consisting of a rapid crescendo of intense anxiety accompanied by frightening physical sensations of "pounding heart," chest pain, sweating, shortness of breath, and dizziness, along with a fear of dying or losing control. The patient's medical history, physical examination, and electrocardiogram are otherwise unremarkable except for the presence of sinus tachycardia. The likely diagnosis is panic disorder (PD).[1]

The official recognition in 1980 of PD as a syndrome with reliable diagnostic criteria[2] replaced a number of earlier terms, such as irritable heart, soldier's heart, and hyperventilation syndrome, that had reflected the prominent cardiac and chest symptoms experienced by patients with PD. Studies demonstrating that certain substances, such as sodium lactate, carbon dioxide, caffeine, and cholecystokinin, can trigger panic attacks in patients with the disorder[3,4] and that specific drug treatments can block panic attacks from occurring[5,6] have been important in investigating the biology of PD.

The etiology of PD remains unknown, but several lines of clinical and basic research evidence suggest a dysfunctional brain alarm system, possibly involving several neurotransmitters.[3,6] Epidemiologic studies throughout the world[7] indicate a lifetime prevalence between 1.5% and 3.5%, along with high levels of social morbidity and health care service utilization.[8] As part of the usually chronic natural history of PD following the typical onset in late adolescence or early adulthood, about one third to one half of individuals in community samples who are diagnosed as having PD[7] develop agoraphobia, which commonly does include fear of the public square or marketplace but is also a much broader, irrational fear of situations in which escape might be difficult or help unavailable.

Recognition of the clinical importance and high prevalence of PD stimulated a number of controlled drug treatment trials during the past 2 decades that demonstrated the effectiveness of several classes of psychotherapeutic drugs in treating PD.[6,9] Many of the drugs initially developed and marketed as antidepressants, including the tricyclic antidepressants, the monoamine oxidase inhibitors, and the selective serotonin reuptake inhibitors (SSRIs), as well as the antianxiety benzodiazepines, can be effective medications for PD.

A growing database of randomized controlled trials also supports the efficacy of cognitive behavioral therapy (CBT) for PD.[9] This treatment usually includes patient education, monitoring of panic symptoms, breathing retraining (usually emphasizing abdominal breathing), cognitive restructuring of the catastrophic thinking associated with panic symptoms, and exposure and desensitization to somatic fear cues. This treatment program can be distinguished from the behavioral therapy of gradual exposure and desensitization to external phobic situations that has demonstrated efficacy for agoraphobia.[9] In this issue of *The Journal*, publication of the large-scale, multicenter, randomized controlled trial by Barlow and colleagues[10] provides important new information regarding treatment of PD.

Although the development and testing of effective treatments for PD have been of great benefit for patients, as Barlow et al. note, "studies of medication and psychosocial approaches have, until recently, run on parallel and sometimes hostile tracks."[10] Thus, among the values of this ambitious study are its unbiased testing of the relative efficacy of a drug treatment and a psychosocial treatment for PD and whether combined treatment with both is better than either alone. The duration of the trial (a total of 15 months for responders to acute treatment) is also unusual and is a major advance in assessing treatments for this chronic disorder.

A total of 312 evaluable patients with PD were randomized to 1 of 5 treatment arms: the tricyclic antidepressant imipramine alone, CBT alone, placebo pills alone, CBT combined with imipramine, and CBT combined with placebo. Responders to the initial acute phase (3 months) of treatment continued in a 6-month maintenance phase and were subsequently followed up for 6 months after treatment was discontinued. Ethical questions that might be raised about the inclusion of a placebo treatment arm for a disorder that has treatments of established efficacy are mitigated by an allocation procedure that assigned the smallest number of patients to the placebo arm and by provisions to remove from the study patients who experienced clinical deterioration and to offer them 3 months of active treatment at no charge. These provisions were, of course, in addition to the use of informed consent and institutional review board approval. The value of a placebo control in assessing response to the active treatments is indicated by the rather high acute phase (3 month) placebo response rates (38% based on the Clinical Global Impression Scale; 22% based on the Panic Disorder Severity Scale). As noted by the authors, placebo response was not durable, decreasing precipitously during maintenance treatment and thus providing another important comparison regarding the efficacy of the active treatments, which had much more durable maintenance treatment effects.

The main findings of the study were that drug treatment with imipramine and psychotherapy with CBT were each superior to placebo in the acute (3 month) phase—definitively so in the maintenance phase for initial responders. The 2 individual active treatments performed about equally well in the acute and maintenance phases, but follow-up analyses 6 months after treatments were discontinued tended to favor prior treatment with CBT compared with imipramine. Although this was not a robust finding, it provides some support for the intuitively appealing view that patients who receive CBT can continue to use it on their own after the treatment is stopped, whereas continued benefit from drug treatment for a chronic disorder requires continuing the drug.

The results from combined treatment (CBT plus imipramine) are not so intuitive. In the acute

phase, combined treatment was superior to the individual active treatments on several outcome measures but was not better than CBT plus placebo until the maintenance phase. Particularly surprising were the follow-up results after treatment discontinuation, which indicated that patients who had received CBT alone or CBT combined with placebo maintained their improvement significantly better than those who had received CBT plus imipramine. Does this constitute some rare empirical support for the notion that combining an effective drug treatment with a psychotherapy can inhibit the long-term benefits of the psychotherapy? Possibly it does, but the authors note that patients who continued through the maintenance phase in the most effective treatment group overall, CBT plus imipramine, might be particularly likely to relapse when both treatments were discontinued (ie, a selection-for-relapse effect).

Among the patients designated as responders in the acute phase, those who received imipramine, either alone or combined with CBT, had significantly higher levels of improvement (i.e., more complete, higher-quality responses) than responders to CBT alone. So, when it worked, imipramine worked very well. This provides at least a partial answer to those who might question the selection of the tricyclic antidepressant imipramine as the drug treatment in this study. Imipramine was the standard drug for treating PD when the study was started in 1991. However, current recommendations[9] conclude that SSRIs are the first-line medications for PD. Such recommendations are based mainly on the ease of dosage, favorable adverse effect profiles, and relative safety of overdosages offered by the SSRIs. Although usually requiring the careful dose escalation and monitoring used in this study, the efficacy of imipramine for PD is well established and appears to be comparable to that of the SSRIs.[9,10]

Moreover, while drug treatment was appropriately compared in this study with CBT—a specific set of educational, cognitive, and behavioral techniques—drug treatment works best in the context of a therapeutic patient-physician relationship. The benefits of such a relationship may explain at least part of the responses to placebo treatment observed in this and other controlled clinical trials.

The follow-up phase after treatment discontinuation in this study provides strong empirical support to recognize that, like major depression,[11] PD is usually a chronic, relapsing disorder that requires long-term treatment. Attempts to discontinue treatment should be embarked on only after careful consideration of the patient's history and then only with provisions for early detection of relapses so that treatment may be resumed quickly.

Returning to the message of the "real" and "treatable" nature of PD and the prototypical clinical scenario, it is essential that primary care physicians recognize PD, make the diagnosis after appropriate evaluation, inform patients that they have a very real disorder that can be treated effectively, and assist them in obtaining appropriate treatment. The patients and investigators involved in the study reported by Barlow et al. have contributed substantial empirical support for this important clinical message.

# References

1. American Psychiatric Association. *Diagnostic and Statistical Manual of Mental Disorders, Fourth Edition.* Washington, DC: American Psychiatric Association; 1994:394–403.
2. American Psychiatric Association. *Diagnostic and Statistical Manual of Mental Disorders, Third Edition.* Washington, DC: American Psychiatric Association; 1980:230–232.
3. Griez E, Schruers K. Experimental pathophysiology of panic. *J Psychosom Res.* 1998;45:493–503.
4. Papp LA, Klein DF, Gorman JM. Carbon dioxide hypersensitivity, hyperventilation, and panic disorder. *Am J Psychiatry.* 1993;150:1149–1157.
5. Klein DF, Zitrin CM, Werner M. Antidepressants, anxiety, panic, and phobia. In: Lipton MA, DiMascio A, Killam KF, eds. *Psychopharmacology: A Generation of Progress.* New York, NY: Raven Press; 1978:1401–1410.
6. Johnson MR, Lydiard RB, Ballenger JC. Panic disorder: pathophysiology and drug treatment. *Drugs.* 1995; 49:328–344.
7. Weissman MM, Bland RC, Canino GJ, et al. The cross-national epidemiology of panic disorder. *Arch Gen Psychiatry.* 1997;54:305–309.
8. Klerman GL, Weissman MM, Ouellette R, Johnson J, Greenwald S. Panic attacks in the community. *JAMA.* 1991;265:742–746.
9. American Psychiatric Association. Practice guideline for the treatment of patients with panic disorder. *Am J Psychiatry.* 1998;155(suppl 5):1–34.
10. Barlow DH, Gorman JM, Shear MK, Woods SW. Cognitive-behavioral therapy, imipramine, or their combination for panic disorder: a randomized controlled trial. *JAMA.* 2000;283:2529–2536.
11. Glass RM. Treating depression as a recurrent or chronic disease. *JAMA.* 1999;281:83–84.

# HIGH ANXIETY

## Consumer Reports

*The aforementioned article by Barlow and colleagues (2000) suggests that improvements in panic disorder can be accomplished with either medication or cognitive-behavioral therapy. Other studies indicate that medication and behavior therapy, when delivered separately to groups of patients with OCD, actually produce comparable changes in how glucose is used by specific structures in the brain (e.g., Baxter, et al., 1992). While it is an overstatement to say that these two forms of intervention are interchangeable, practitioners do have a real choice in whether to recommend medication versus specialized psychotherapies in the treatment of many anxiety disorders.*

*What is not immediately apparent here are important differences between medication and psychotherapy. For example, medications sometimes have side effects, they usually only work while the patient is taking them, and they are developed, produced, and patented by large corporations. All of these factors can influence how practitioners and patients select from the array of treatments available. This article is a critical analysis of the marketing and use of medications for anxiety, particularly the widely prescribed drug Xanax. It also highlights some of the tensions that arise when corporations commission and publicize scientific studies of their product, and it shows how clinical decision making is more complex than the simple identification of the best treatment for a specific patient.*

### Reference

Baxter, L. R., Schwartz, J. M., Bergman, K. S., Szuba, M. P., Guze, B. H., Mazziotta, J. C., Alazraki, A., Selin, C. E., Fering, H., Munford, P., & Phelps, M. E. (1992). Caudate glucose metabolic rate changes with both drug and behavior therapy for obsessive-compulsive disorder. *Archives of General Psychiatry, 49,* 681–689.

---

*Consumer Reports,* 19–24. (1993, January).

The woman we'll call Rachel G.—now age 31—had experienced attacks of anxiety since she was a child. But those occasional incidents did not prevent her from marrying and taking a responsible job at an East Coast bio-technology company. Then, in late 1990 and early 1991, her life took a stressful turn. There was turmoil at the lab where she worked, her mother fell seriously ill, her grandmother committed suicide, and her marriage deteriorated. In early April of

1991, after a confrontation with her boss, she had a full-blown panic attack.

"I broke into a cold sweat," she recalls. "My heart was palpitating. I swore I was having a heart attack. I was scared that I was dying. . . . I couldn't walk. I couldn't even move." The attacks went on for two days.

Rachel G. went to a psychologist for help, and simultaneously asked her regular internist for a pill to ease her suffering. Her physician prescribed *Xanax* (alprazolam). That was no surprise. In 1990, *Xanax* had become the only drug ever approved by the U.S. Food and Drug Administration for the treatment of panic disorder—repeated, intense bouts of anxiety that can make life almost unbearable.

The drug gave her some relief, but she felt it wasn't really solving her problem. After about three months on *Xanax*, she tried to cut her dose in half. Within 48 hours, she recalls, "I couldn't sleep. My heart was racing, and I was getting dizzy spells." Only going back up to an intermediate dose would suppress the withdrawal symptoms.

In February 1992, Rachel G. began having frightening thoughts of killing herself. She visited a psychiatrist, who prescribed *Tofranil* (imipramine), an antidepressant that also works against panic. Today, she is doing well, still taking imipramine—and also *Xanax*. Though she feels the *Xanax* is no longer helping her, she can't bring herself to try to quit. "I know I'm going to have to experience the withdrawal symptoms," she says, "and those are the exact symptoms that I went on it to escape from in the first place."

Rachel G.'s problem is far from unusual. *Xanax* is not only the most common treatment for panic attacks, but also the drug most often prescribed for run-of-the-mill anxiety—the kind that anyone might experience during a rough period in life. It is now the nation's largest-selling psychiatric drug; more than that, it is the fifth most frequently prescribed drug in the U.S.

Even if you've never taken *Xanax* yourself, you almost certainly know someone who has. Yet the risks are significant. Anyone who takes *Xanax* for an extended period—even as little as a few weeks—risks developing a stubborn dependency on the drug.

*Xanax* is just the latest in a long line of tranquilizers that have promised to deliver psychiatry's holy grail: relief from anxiety with no significant side effects. And like the pills that came before it, *Xanax* has fallen short. As psychiatrists and their patients are discovering, *Xanax* does have some serious drawbacks—even more than the drugs it was supposed to improve on.

Like the sleeping pill *Halcion* (triazolam), its closest chemical relative, *Xanax* demonstrates that no pill can deliver peace of mind without a price. It also raises a troubling question: How did such a flawed drug become a pharmacological superstar?

The selling of *Xanax* has been fueled by a vigorous promotional campaign. The drug's manufacturer, the Upjohn Co., has made *Xanax* highly visible in the medical community by promoting it as a uniquely effective drug for panic disorder. But *Xanax* does not represent a remarkable treatment advance so much as a marketing coup. In fact, it is little different from other, related tranquilizers—members of the drug family known as benzodiazepines, which have held an uneasy place in American culture for three decades.

## Beyond Valium

Though the word "benzodiazepine" is meaningless to most people, the trade names of the drugs in this family are almost as familiar as *Kleenex* or *NutraSweet*. The first drug in this category, *Librium* (chlordiazepoxide), came on the market in 1960; *Valium* (diazepam) came along three years later.

In 1979, a survey showed that 11 percent of Americans were taking antianxiety drugs, mostly benzodiazepines. The figure has dropped only slightly since then.

That was also the year the hazards of these drugs gained national attention through hearings held by Senator Edward Kennedy. As the hearings made clear, *Valium* and similar drugs caused two major problems: Physical dependency and sedation. People on benzodiazepines often found that they couldn't stop taking the drugs, and that they couldn't function well while they were on them. The drugs accumulated in the body; over time, they made the user more and more sluggish, drowsy, and forgetful.

Ironically, while the Kennedy hearings offered frightening testimony on *Valium*, they also set the stage for the arrival of its successor, *Xanax*. Introduced in 1981, *Xanax* was hailed as the first of a new chemical class of benzodiazepines that were completely eliminated from the body in less than half a day. Since *Xanax* didn't accumulate, the hope was that it wouldn't make people increasingly drowsy or slow them down as they continued to take it.

In addition to this chemical advantage, *Xanax* gave Upjohn a marketing edge. The patent on *Valium* expired in 1984, just as sales of *Xanax* were beginning to build. As generic competitors undercut *Valium*'s sales, the drug's manufacturer promoted it less actively, and sales of *Valium* dropped further. Upjohn took advantage of the opportunity. By 1986, *Xanax* had overtaken *Valium* as the most widely prescribed benzodiazepine. By 1987, it reached fourth place on the national sales list of all prescription drugs. And in 1991, *Xanax* accounted for almost one-fifth of Upjohn's worldwide sales.

The trouble is, *Xanax* has now turned out to be more addictive than *Valium* itself.

## Stuck on Xanax

All benzodiazepines produce physical dependency if you take them long enough. Over time, it seems, the brain "learns" to expect a certain level of the drug. If the drug is removed, the brain reacts with agitation, sleeplessness, and anxiety—the symptoms that led people to take the drug in the first place. Frequently, these symptoms are worse than the original ones, a phenomenon known as the "rebound" effect. In addition, abrupt withdrawal from the drugs can cause muscle cramps and twitches, impaired concentration, and occasionally even seizures.

Unlike people who are addicted to cocaine and heroin, users of benzodiazepines don't develop a psychological craving for the drugs, or escalate the

doses they take over time. But they do have a true physical dependency, and their withdrawal symptoms make the benzodiazepines extremely difficult to kick.

A number of clinical studies have found that *Xanax* and other benzodiazepines that are eliminated rapidly from the body produce a quicker, more severe rebound effect than drugs like *Valium* that are eliminated more slowly. Some people who take *Xanax* three times a day, a standard schedule for panic disorder, find that they even have symptoms as the drug wears off between one dose and the next.

In one major study, Dr. Karl Rickels and his colleagues at the University of Pennsylvania took 47 anxious patients who had been on benzodiazepines for a year or more and tried to take them off their medication. Fully 57 percent of the patients on *Xanax* and similar drugs simply could not stop taking them—but only 27 percent of the people on drugs like *Valium* were that physically dependent. . . .

The experience of individual doctors underscores the problem. In 1988, researchers at the Johns Hopkins School of Medicine interviewed 31 American physicians who specialized in helping people withdraw from the benzodiazepines. Asked which drugs were especially hard for patients to give up, 84 percent of the doctors specifically mentioned *Xanax*, while only 29 percent cited *Valium*. Even under the best of circumstances, clinicians have found that, to get people off *Xanax*, they must reduce the dose in tiny steps—a process that often takes months.

## An 'Eraser' for the Mind?

The fact that so many people try so hard to quit *Xanax*—as difficult as that is to do—shows that it is not an entirely pleasant drug to take. One woman we spoke with, a 41-year-old technical writer in San Francisco, started taking *Xanax* to deal with bouts of anxiety that made her feel "like I was going headlong toward some frightening and dangerous unknown." After taking *Xanax* for 14 months, she decided to stop because, as she puts it,

"It made me too stupid. I just couldn't function professionally. People would say things to me, and I'd be in a sort of fog and not be able to respond appropriately." (She ultimately succeeded in quitting, but had to go through a very difficult withdrawal process—even though she was taking a low dose, one her psychiatrist told her would not cause dependency.)

A 1990 report by the American Psychiatric Association backs up this woman's experience. It found that the benzodiazepines tend to impair memory; a person on one of these drugs may have difficulty retaining new information.

Clinicians report the same problem. "One patient of mine, a physician who took *Xanax* described it as 'a big eraser.' It sort of wipes out people's attention to things," says Dr. Robert J. Gladstone, a psychiatrist in Carlisle, Mass. "I think all benzodiazepines cause memory lapses, especially in the elderly," says Dr. Stuart Yudofsky, chairman of the Department of Psychiatry at Baylor College of Medicine in Houston.

Yudofsky also refers to evidence that the drugs impair coordination. And in his own experience, he says, patients who have used benzodiazepines for years have often suffered falls and head injuries.

*Xanax* can also have the paradoxical effect of causing rage and hostility rather than tranquility. While this is relatively rare, it's another reason for caution in using a drug that many people will be all but unable to quit.

Despite the risks, benzodiazepines have one clear use: They can be helpful for people in crisis who need short-term anxiety relief. "They're appropriate for what are called adjustment reactions," says Dr. Peter Tyrer, a professor of psychiatry at St. Mary's Hospital Medical School in London and a longtime benzodiazepine researcher. "For example, if someone has been in a car accident and is nervous afterward when he goes out into the street, he could take *Xanax* for a short time after that."

The problem, though, is that many people who start taking tranquilizers for the short term end up staying on them over the long haul. "For anxiety, in general, these medications tend to be used much too long and in too high doses," says Dr. Yudofsky. "People get put on a drug, the reason for taking it passes, but they're maintained on it week after week, year after year. That's misuse." Even Upjohn, in its own labeling for *Xanax*, cautions that the drug has never been established as effective for use over more than four months.

## Pushing the Panic Button

The people most at risk for becoming dependent on *Xanax* are those with panic disorder, because they are prescribed high doses of the drug for an extended period of time to deal with their chronic panic attacks. Since they suffer from severe or disabling anxiety, they might find dependency an acceptable price to pay for effective relief. But even though Upjohn built *Xanax*'s reputation on studies of people with panic attacks, it's not at all clear how much they were really helped.

A panic attack is intense anxiety in a concentrated dose. Victims with a severe case may suffer several full-scale attacks a day, during which their hearts race and they hyperventilate, sweat, tremble, and feel a profound sense of terror. According to the largest, most thorough survey of psychiatric problems, conducted in the 1980s by the National Institute of Mental Health (NIMH), between 4 and 7 percent of Americans have panic attacks that are frequent enough to be considered a panic disorder. The majority of people with panic disorder also have a related condition, agoraphobia—a term now used to describe a fear of ordinary activities, such as driving a car or shopping at the supermarket, that can leave the sufferer housebound.

By the early 1980s, researchers had begun to recognize that at least some types of benzodiazepines, in addition to easing ordinary anxiety, could also stop panic attacks. Upjohn proceeded to spend lavishly on studies to see whether *Xanax* could be used to treat panic disorder, and enlisted highly respected consultants in the effort. "The most senior psychiatrists in the world were . . . flooded with offers of consultancies [from Upjohn]," recalls Dr. Isaac Marks, a professor of experimental psychopharmacology at the University of London's Institute of Psychiatry.

In fact, the research could just as well have been done with another benzodiazepine—one called lorazepam (*Ativan*)—that is also cleared from the body quickly, and has also been shown to stop panic attacks. But this drug has not been under patent protection for years—and since it has not had the profit potential that *Xanax* has, it has not been aggressively tested and promoted. Today, a bottle of 100 one-milligram *Xanax* tablets costs $72.55, according to the Red Book, a standard drug price guide. The same amount of generic lorazepam in a therapeutically equivalent dose costs as little as $3.75.

Upjohn's major study on panic was a two-phase project called the Cross-National Panic Study. Phase One, conducted in the U.S., Canada, and Australia, involved more than 500 subjects with severe panic attacks; half received *Xanax* and half, a lookalike placebo. Phase Two, conducted in North and South America and Europe, enrolled 1122 subjects to compare *Xanax* not only with a placebo, but also with imipramine, an antidepressant from a different chemical class that also blocks panic attacks (even though it has never received formal FDA approval for this use). At the time, the two studies were among the largest ever done on psychiatric drugs.

Well before the results were published, Upjohn used the research to promote its drug. The company sponsored conferences and symposiums on drug treatment for panic and anxiety, and then invited its consultants to speak at them—a strategy now used by many large pharmaceutical companies. . . . Many of those meetings were then written up in Upjohn-sponsored supplements to scientific journals, sent to thousands of psychiatrists in the U.S. and abroad.

When the Phase One results were finally published, they made a huge splash: Four articles on the study consumed the better part of the May 1988 issue of the *Archives of General Psychiatry*, the most prestigious psychiatric journal in the U.S. By that time, however, the international psychiatric community had already been hearing about *Xanax*

as a treatment for panic for several years. Upjohn's publicity had made psychiatrists—and, later, general-practice physicians—more aware of *Xanax* than they were of other, similar drugs. It almost certainly was responsible for the rapid growth of *Xanax* as a drug for all sorts of anxiety problems, not just panic disorder.

"The Cross-National Study was the best advertising ever done," says Dr. Rickels of the University of Pennsylvania. "Upjohn sold millions of doses of this drug before they even got it approved for panic."

## No Panacea for Panic

Since receiving FDA approval to market *Xanax* for panic disorder, Upjohn has been using data from Phase One of the Cross-National Study in ads for the drug—including ads in journals for general-practice physicians. These doctors are likely to be unfamiliar with the actual results of the study, and to take Upjohn's word for what it showed. But despite the ads' claims, the study produced highly ambiguous results.

In the first four weeks of the eight-week study, *Xanax* looked much better than placebo treatment. By the fourth week, 50 percent of patients taking *Xanax* were completely free of panic attacks, versus 28 percent of those on an inactive placebo.

Many of Upjohn's ads for *Xanax* quote results from this midpoint of the study. But the drug's effectiveness was much less clear by the study's end. A look at the people who stayed in the study for the full eight weeks shows a remarkable picture: At the end of the study, there was no significant difference in the average number of panic attacks—or in functioning in work, home, and social life—between the people who had been taking *Xanax* and those who were taking placebos.

In addition, the Phase One study showed clearly how severe the "rebound" effect of *Xanax* withdrawal is. At the two study locations in Canada, 109 patients who had completed the eight weeks of treatment were observed as the dose of the drug (or placebo) was tapered down over a month's time. The *Xanax* group had averaged only

1.7 panic attacks a week—and the placebo group, 2.1 attacks a week—at the end of the eight-week treatment phase. But just two weeks after they stopped medication entirely, patients in the *Xanax* group were back up to 6.8 attacks a week—slightly worse off than they had been at the beginning of the study. By contrast, two weeks after the patients on placebo discontinued their "drug," they averaged only 1.8 panic attacks a week.

The findings are complicated by the Phase One study's greatest flaw: About 10 percent of the people on *Xanax* and half of those on placebo, dropped out between the fourth and the eighth week. At the time they left the study, the dropouts from the placebo group had more symptoms than people taking *Xanax*—a fact that would suggest the drug was doing some good. But many people on placebo may have been suffering from withdrawal symptoms, since many had been taking benzodiazepines just *before* they entered the study. There's also no way to tell whether they would have felt better by the end of the eight-week study if they had stuck it out, as other people in the group taking placebos did.

The findings of the Phase Two study were similar to Phase One's, except they also demonstrated that the antidepressant drug imipramine worked as well as *Xanax*. At the end of the eight weeks, 78 percent of people taking *Xanax* were panic-free, compared with 81 percent of those on imipramine and 75 percent of the people on placebo—virtually identical numbers.

Upjohn researchers and their supporters believe *Xanax* came out the clear winner in the studies. They point out that it acts much more quickly than imipramine and is easier to take. Imipramine is one of a class of antidepressants that can cause a range of unpleasant side effects, including sedation, dry mouth, severe constipation, blurred vision, weight gain, and impotence.

But other psychiatrists focus on the fact that people taking placebos did nearly as well as those on *Xanax* by the end of the study—and avoided the rebound effect that plagued people on the real drug. That suggests that, for many people, the mere act of visiting a doctor might have been reas-

suring enough to produce a measurable decrease in symptoms. It also suggests that nondrug treatment could help many other panic sufferers learn how to control their symptoms.

The same may be true for people who have more generalized anxiety—a form of chronic, excessive worrying, combined with physical and emotional symptoms, that affects about 4 percent of Americans, according to NIMH estimates. *Xanax* itself, surprisingly, has never been tested as a long-term treatment for such chronic anxiety disorders. But Dr. David Barlow, a clinical psychologist who directs the Center for Stress and Anxiety Disorders of the State University of New York at Albany, points out that the benzodiazepines in general have not proved effective for treating these problems—except to offer temporary relief of symptoms.

Barlow reviewed two decades' worth of studies that used benzodiazepines to treat chronic anxiety. He observed that patients in the "control" groups for these studies—that is, patients who received inactive placebo pills—generally improved over time. In many cases, their anxiety decreased as much as that of the people who were on the real drugs. This suggests that chronic anxiety waxes and wanes over time, and that drugs may have little effect after their initial benefit.

## Recommendations

If anxiety is an inevitable part of the human condition, then the wish for a magic potion to banish anxiety is probably a timeless human desire. In our own time, drug companies have marketed one tranquilizer after another, each one supposedly safer and more effective than the one before. But tranquilizers—in particular, the benzodiazepines—are still powerful, potentially dangerous, drugs subject to abuse and misuse.

Given the hazards and their widespread use, *we still know surprisingly little about the risks and benefits of long-term benzodiazepine use* [emphasis added]—and too little in particular about *Xanax*, now the leader of the pack.

No one knows how many people are physically

dependent on *Xanax* and how they may be affected by it. But there are some warning signs. A recent FDA analysis of reports of adverse reactions to drugs, which physicians send to the agency voluntarily, showed a number of cases in which the drug seemed to cause bouts of rage and hostility. Those side effects were rare, and were much less common with *Xanax* than with *Halcion*. But they were six times more common with *Xanax* than with *Ativan*, relative to each drug's sales. And *Ativan*'s suspected side effects have been cited in a pending British class-action lawsuit against its manufacturer.

Consumers Union believes that more information is necessary to determine the frequency of side effects from *Xanax*—not only its effects on mood, but its potential for impairing memory and causing other cognitive problems. Careful surveillance of the drug's clinical use could do much to resolve these questions.

In the meantime, if you or a loved one has a serious problem with anxiety, you need to understand your options clearly.

If you're not normally an anxious person, but are going through a particularly difficult time—a divorce or the death of a parent, for instance—you may be able to handle your anxiety with no professional help, or perhaps with a few visits to a psychotherapist to talk about the immediate stress. According to Dr. Yudofsky of Baylor, exercise, dietary changes (such as giving up caffeine), and other lifestyle changes can also help keep anxiety in check.

It can also be useful, and appropriate, to take *Xanax* or another benzodiazepine to cope with acute stress—as long as you take the drug carefully. If your doctor prescribes one of these drugs, take it at the lowest dose possible and for the shortest time possible. Remember that even a few weeks of daily *Xanax* use can lead to dependency.

*If you're suffering from panic disorder, agora-phobia, or chronic anxiety, you have a serious problem that requires professional evaluation and treatment by a psychiatrist or psychologist* [emphasis added]. It's not clear, however, that drug treatment should be your first option. CU's medical consultants recommend seeing a mental-health professional who is familiar with cognitive-behavioral therapy . . . before resorting to tranquilizers. Our consultants who have experience in both drug and nondrug therapy generally try the nondrug approaches first.

Whatever your problem is, you should avoid *Xanax* and its chemical cousins if you have any history of alcohol abuse or previous problems with other benzodiazepines. Those factors in your personal history make it more likely that you will become dependent on the drug. Alternative forms of drug therapy may be less risky. *Antidepressants like imipramine can block panic attacks as effectively as Xanax can* [emphasis added]. For people with chronic anxiety who do not have panic attacks, a drug called *BuSpar* (buspirone) can frequently reduce anxiety and does not cause the sedation or physical dependency produced by the benzodiazepines.

Finally, if your physician does prescribe *Xanax* or another benzodiazepine, question him or her closely about how long you are expected to take the medication and exactly how you are to withdraw from it. While on the medication, use extreme caution when driving, since these drugs can impair coordination. Do not exceed the prescribed dose, and do not drink alcohol while on the drug. (The interaction can be disastrous; at the least, it can worsen the slurred speech, poor coordination, drowsiness, and mental slowness that often stem from use of benzodiazepines.) Inform your doctor immediately of any unexpected side effects, such as feelings of rage or agitation. And seriously consider trying some sort of psychotherapy to gain insight into your problem.

# CHAPTER 4

# Somatoform and Dissociative Disorders

*Whereas anxiety disorders involve obvious expressions of worry and concern (specific phobias or panic attacks), there are two other classes of disorder in which anxiety is less apparent but may be just as important. The first, somatoform disorders, is characterized by the presence of physical symptoms (or the loss of physical functioning) for which there is no adequate physical explanation. Therefore, some sort of emotional or psychological conflict is inferred as the cause of the physical symptoms, as though the anxiety evoked by this conflict is expressed in bodily form. By definition, individuals with a somatoform disorder are not faking their symptoms or disorders; they usually believe they have a serious physical problem.*

*Dissociative disorders can also involve anxiety, in an indirect manner, but the prominent symptom is some disjunction or separation in mental processes that are usually connected and coordinated. For example, in dissociative fugue an individual abruptly abandons his or her daily routine (often after a highly stressful event), goes on a journey, and recalls little about his or her personal identity and history.*

*Over time, the diagnostic categories subsumed by somatoform and dissociative disorders have expanded and become more specific, but explanations for these unusual and interesting disorders remain elusive. Because somatoform and dissociative disorders tend to be rare, and because the clinical details of these disorders are so intriguing, we focus in this chapter on four case studies.*

# CASE STUDY: NEGATIVE REINFORCEMENT AND BEHAVIORAL MANAGEMENT OF CONVERSION DISORDER

## John V. Campo, M.D., and Barbara J. Negrini, M.D.

*Our first case concerns a sixth-grade boy who experiences pain and immobility in his right arm. No physical cause for these symptoms was identified after extensive testing, and the boy was subsequently diagnosed as having one type of somatoform disorder called conversion disorder. As you will see, the problem was treated successfully and quickly with a behavioral (i.e., operant or "Skinnerian") intervention.*

*This case is interesting, not only because of the nature of the problem, but also because it demonstrates that a treatment can be completely effective even when the causes of the problem are not entirely clear. Was the problem the result of the boy's receiving a shot for the hepatitis B vaccine? The mother's thyroid cancer? The father's recent unemployment? The father's tendency to worry, which the boy may have adopted? With the behavioral intervention that was used with this boy, the answers to these questions do not matter much. Instead, once a reasonably clear diagnosis of conversion disorder was made, the authors created a setting in which the boy would be rewarded for not having the symptoms. We tend to think of most rewards or reinforcements as being the presentation of positive consequences for some desired action, but in this case negative reinforcement was used: the removal of a negative experience (i.e., strict bedrest so that the boy could devote all of his energy to getting better) followed the desired action. Nevertheless, as we noted at the outset of this chapter, it is plausible to infer that somehow anxiety plays a role in the conversion of an ambiguous psychological conflict into physical symptoms. A more narrow behavioral or learning-based view would maintain that the symptoms were a way for the boy to get attention, and that the intervention tipped the scale so that he would get even more attention for the adaptive response—moving his arm freely—than the maladaptive one.*

*Notice how the therapists concentrated on ruling out plausible physical explanations for why the boy could not move his arm—the symptoms were not due to neurological damage, an arthritic condition, or problems with the bones or muscles. Even though testing for these possibilities is expensive and time consuming, it is essential because misdiagnosis and subsequent mistreatment could be even more costly to the boy's long-term well-being. It is interesting to note that the parents' behavior was also shaped by negative reinforcement, in that they were "rewarded" for agreeing with the diagnosis of conversion disorder because it meant their son no longer had to be subjected to various physical tests and procedures.*

## Suggested Reading

Razali, S. M. (1999). Conversion disorder: A case report of treatment with the Main Puteri, a Malay shamanastic healing ceremony. *European Psychiatry, 8,* 470–472.

*Journal of the American Academy of Child and Adolescent Psychiatry, 39, 787–790. (2000).*

Conversion disorder is diagnosed in the presence of one or more symptoms or deficits of voluntary motor or sensory function that suggest a neurological or other general medical condition, but which are not fully explained by the presence of physical disease, the direct effects of a substance, or another mental disorder (American Psychiatric Association, 1994). The symptoms should not appear intentionally or voluntarily produced, and they must cause distress and/or functional impairment and appear to be associated with emotional or psychological factors.

Symptoms suggestive of a neurological disorder in the absence of demonstrable disease are unusual in community samples (Garber et al., 1991; Stefansson et al., 1976), but they are not uncommon in tertiary pediatric referral centers. Nonepileptic seizures, faints, falls, and abnormalities of gait or sensation are most frequently reported (Goodyer and Mitchell, 1989; Grattan-Smith et al., 1988; Lehmkuhl et al., 1989; Leslie, 1988; Spierings et al., 1990; Volkmar et al., 1984). Conversion disorder is more common in girls (Goodyer and Mitchell, 1989) and in adolescents (Stefansson et al., 1976), but it is rare prior to 6 years of age (Grattan-Smith et al., 1988; Lehmkuhl et al., 1989; Leslie, 1988; Volkmar et al., 1984).

Although controlled treatment trials in pediatric conversion disorder are lacking (Campo and Fritsch, 1994), a behavioral approach has been described in case reports. Most have emphasized positive reinforcement for healthy behavior, as well as extinction or withdrawal of reinforcement of the symptom involving minimizing the rewards associated with the sick role (Delameter et al., 1983; Dubowitz and Hersov, 1976; Klonoff and Moore, 1986; Lehmkuhl et al., 1989; Mizes, 1985). Less well described has been the use of negative reinforcement. Negative reinforcement produces an increase in the frequency of a desired response by removing an aversive event immediately after the desired response has been performed (Kazdin, 1994). For example, restrictions theoretically imposed by illness (e.g., being confined to bed) can be lifted contingent upon functional improvement (Delameter et al., 1983; Leslie, 1988; Warzak et al., 1987). We report an illustrative case in which negative reinforcement was successfully used as a component of the outpatient behavioral treatment of a child with conversion disorder.

## Case Report

A right-handed 12-year-old boy presented with a nearly 3-month history of right arm pain and immobility. He had received a hepatitis B vaccine in his right arm approximately 1 month before the onset of pain; 3 weeks later he experienced an apparent viral syndrome with a transient, diffuse rash accompanied by pain in his knees, ankles, neck, and back in the absence of joint findings. The constant pinching or burning pain localized to the right arm and shoulder 1 week later, and he claimed he was unable to move the arm. He began using his left hand to eat and write, and he requested his mother's help with homework and dressing. He reported that constant pain interfered with his sleep, and he admitted to feeling somewhat more fatigued. His parents did not observe spontaneous arm movements during sleep. His medical history was unremarkable; he had no history of trauma, fever, or other painful symptoms. Complete blood cell count, sedimentation rate, antistreptolysin O titer, radiographs, and bone scan were unremarkable. Treatment with daily ibuprofen and physical therapy was of no benefit. Consultations with orthopaedics, rheumatology, and neurology suggested that his examination results were not consistent with physical disease, and he was referred for psychiatric evaluation by the general academic pediatrician, who agreed with the specialists when providing a second opinion.

There was no history of prior psychiatric evaluation or treatment. The boy was living with his parents and 2 siblings and was attending 6th grade, where he received special education services for reading. He missed approximately 2 weeks of school shortly after his physical symptoms began, but his attendance was regular at the time of evaluation. Occasional problems with inattention and difficulty completing assignments were reported, and he had received D's in a few subjects. He was described as an active boy who had been somewhat shy earlier in life, but who now appeared to make friends easily. Symptoms of marked hyperactivity, impulsivity, serious disruptive behavior, anxiety, depression, mania, and psychosis were denied, and there was no history of alcohol, drug, or inhalant abuse. There was no history of maltreatment of any sort. The mother had been diagnosed and treated for thyroid cancer approximately 1 year prior to presentation, and the boy admitted that he often worried about his mother's illness. The father had lost his job several months prior to the evaluation and had been treated over the previous 2 to 3 months with physical therapy for arm pain described as secondary to "tennis elbow." The family history was remarkable for "worry" in an older brother and the father, as well as a history of alcohol abuse, depression, and hypochondriasis in second-degree maternal relatives.

During a mental status examination the boy was cooperative and denied concerns about his illness. He did not appear to be troubled by his symptoms, and he expressed confidence that a serious disease was not present and that his arm would improve. He denied feelings of sadness or dysphoria, yet he rated his mood as 5 on a scale of 1 to 10. He appeared to be of average intellect, and there was no evidence of psychosis, delirium, or overt cognitive impairment. During the physical examination he held his right arm in flexion with his palm placed over his abdomen and was tender to shoulder palpation. He had no active movement except for minimal mobility of his fingers, but he did have full passive range of motion of his fingers, wrist, and elbow, with some resistance at the shoulder. He refused to grasp objects and used his left arm to reposition the right. Reflexes and muscle tone were normal, and there was no evidence of significant muscle atrophy. His strength examination was inconsistent, as he was able to overcome gravity when the examiner positioned his arm. When asked to flex the arm the boy appeared unable to do so, yet subtle movements were noted distally, and considerable muscle tension was noted in both the agonist biceps and the antagonist triceps, inconsistent with his assertion that he could not move the arm and suggesting that he was resisting flexion.

Because of the persistence of the boy's symptoms, inconsistencies in the physical examination, a possible model for illness in the father, and current stressors which included the father's loss of job, the mother's illness, and the boy's learning difficulties, conversion disorder was presumptively diagnosed and a decision was made to attempt to leverage improvement through the use of behavioral intervention. Conversion disorder was discussed with the patient and his mother as the most plausible diagnosis, and the risks and benefits of behavioral intervention were discussed. The mother was supportive of intervention given the potential to relieve symptoms and avoid additional diagnostic tests. The child did not protest, yet he seemed indifferent to the idea of treatment. Our impression that the boy's nerves and muscles were capable of functioning normally was explained, and physical therapy was continued, but it was recommended that strict bedrest be maintained when he was not performing critical functions until the symptoms resolved. Since school was not in session, he was only to leave his room to attend physical therapy sessions, use the bathroom, or join the family for meals. He was not allowed any stimulation such as reading or watching television, with the rationale being that all of his energy needed to be focused on getting well.

On the first day of treatment, the patient spent the morning quietly in his bedroom. His father worked in the yard and his mother played a video game with his sibling. After several hours, he excitedly informed his parents that he was regaining some mobility in his arm. His parents were reassuring, but they sent him back to his room to continue resting. Within 24 hours, he had regained complete mobility of his arm without any pain. He told his mother he was upset that none of his physicians had suggested this treatment earlier. He has since returned to normal activities and is symptom-free.

## Discussion

Ideally, the diagnosis of conversion disorder should be based on positive findings (Dubowitz and Hersov, 1976; Friedman, 1973; Goodyer and Taylor, 1985; Maisami and Freeman, 1987). "Clues" to the diagnosis include contiguity with psychosocial stressors or the presence of a severe stressor such as maltreatment, the presence of another psychiatric disorder, association with psychological gain for the child, existence of a symptom model within the social milieu, apparent communicative or symbolic meaning of the symptom within the patient's social milieu, the symptom's violation of known anatomic or physiological patterns, and responsiveness to placebo, suggestion, or psychological treatment (Campo and Garber, 1998; Friedman, 1973; Goodyer and Taylor, 1985).

Indifference to the symptoms ("la belle indifference") has also been considered a clue (Leslie, 1988; Maisami and Freeman, 1987; Volkmar et al., 1984), but its subjective nature limits its applicability (Dubowitz and Hersov, 1976; Spierings et al., 1990). Conversion disorder may allow a child with a learning disorder to avoid facing a skills deficit in the classroom, with the learning disorder potentially serving as both a stressor and a perpetuating factor (Silver, 1982). While virtually all the above clues to conversion disorder might be found in patients with explanatory physical disease, a constellation of clues taken together may be most persuasive (Campo and Garber, 1998; Friedman, 1973).

In this case, clues to the diagnosis included inconsistencies in the physical examination, presence of significant stressors (e.g., mother's illness and father's loss of job), a likely learning skills deficit, and a family "model" for the symptoms (e.g., the father's treatment for arm pain a few months before). The absence of a history of maltreatment was reassuring. The patient's dramatic and sustained improvement alleviated concerns regarding undiagnosed physical disease and prevented unnecessary medical tests and treatments, which can inadvertently maintain somatization by giving the impression that serious physical disease has been missed (Goodyer and Taylor, 1985; Grattan-Smith et al., 1988). While explanatory physical disease may be misdiagnosed as conversion disorder (Rivinus et al., 1975), risk of misdiagnosis is less than 10% in more recent series (Maisami and Freeman, 1987; Spierings et al., 1990; Volkmar et al., 1984). Unexplained symptoms have been reported following documented acute illnesses or accidents (Carek and Santos, 1984; Dubowitz and Hersov, 1976; Leslie, 1988). This patient may have been predisposed to conversion disorder by physical symptoms due to the vaccine or an associated viral illness, perhaps introducing him to the potential benefits associated with the sick role (Wooley et al., 1978) during a potentially stressful time in his life.

Behavioral interventions incorporating the use of negative reinforcement can be powerful in conversion disorder and complementary to a rehabilitative approach that encourages a return to usual activities and discourages sick-role behaviors (Dubowitz and Hersov, 1976; Leslie, 1988; Maisami and Freeman, 1987; Schulman, 1988). The use of negative reinforcement requires a strong therapeutic alliance with the parents, as the clinician may need to persuade family members and perhaps other professionals that such treatment is not "unfair" or "unkind" if used appropriately. In this case, the parents appeared to accept the rationale for the diagnosis of conversion disorder and were in favor of applying a behavioral intervention that had the potential to allow their son to avoid further painful tests and procedures. Negative reinforcement requires an ongoing aversive event that can be removed after the desired clinical improvement is noted to occur, though it must be remembered that an event considered aversive by one individual may not be considered so by another (Kazdin, 1994). Return to healthy functioning should also be praised and positively rewarded as an accomplishment of which the patient can be proud.

This case also highlights the importance of making a positive diagnosis of conversion disorder, discussing it directly with the patient and family, and enlisting them as partners in treatment (see Campo and Garber, 1998). Reassurance, encouragement, and optimism are useful tools and may decrease anxiety in the system (Goodyer and Mitchell, 1989; Grattan-Smith et al., 1988; Kotsopoulos and Snow, 1986; Lehmkuhl et al., 1989; Maisami and Freeman, 1987; Schulman, 1988; Thomson and Sills, 1988). Physical therapy has been advocated as a component of a rehabilitative approach (Dubowitz and Hersov, 1976; Leslie, 1988; Maisami and Freeman, 1987; Thomson and Sills, 1988). The lack of controlled trials of interventions suggests that systematic research in the treatment of conversion disorder is warranted.

## References

American Psychiatric Association (1994), *Diagnostic and statistical manual of mental disorders, 4th edition (DSM-IV)*. Washington, DC: American Psychiatric Association.

Campo JV, Fritsch SL (1994), Somatization in children and adolescents. *J Am Acad Child Adolesc Psychiatry* 33:1223–1235.

Campo JV, Garber J (1998), Somatization. In: *Handbook of Pediatric Psychology and Psychiatry: Psychological and Psychiatric Issues in the Pediatric Setting*, Ammerman RT, Campo JV, eds. Boston: Allyn & Bacon, pp. 137–161.

Carek DJ, Santos AB (1984), Atypical somatoform disorder following infection in children: a depressive equivalent? *J Clin Psychiatry* 45:108–111.

Delamater AM, Rosenbloom N, Conners CK, Hertweck L (1983), The behavioral treatment of hysterical paralysis in a ten-year-old boy: a case study. *J Am Acad Child Psychiatry* 22:73–79.

Dubowitz V, Hersov L (1976), Management of children with non-organic (hysterical) disorders of motor function. *Dev Med Child Neurol* 18:358–368.

Friedman SB (1973), Conversion symptoms in adolescents. *Pediatr Clin North Am* 20:873–882.

Garber J, Walker LS, Zeman J (1991), Somatization symptoms in a community sample of children and adolescents: further validation of the children's somatization inventory. *Psychol Assess* 3:588–595.

Goodyer JM, Mitchell C (1989), Somatic and emotional disorders in childhood and adolescence. *J Psychosom Res* 33:681–688.

Goodyer IM, Taylor DC (1985), Hysteria. *Arch Dis Child* 60:680–681.

Grattan-Smith P, Fairley M, Procopis P (1988), Clinical features of conversion disorder. *Arch Dis Child* 63:408–414.

Kazdin AE (1994), *Behavior modification in applied settings*, 5th ed. Pacific Grove, CA: Brooks/Cole.

Klonoff EA, Moore DJ (1986), "Conversion reactions" in adolescents: a biofeedback-based operant approach. *J Behav Ther Exp Psychiatry* 17:179–184.

Kotsopoulos S, Snow B (1986), Conversion disorders in children: a study of clinical outcome. *Psychiatr J Univ Ott* 11:134–139.

Lehmkuhl G, Blanz B, Lehmkuhl U, Braun-Scharm H (1989), Conversion disorder: symptomatology and course in childhood and adolescence. *Eur Arch Psychiatry Neurol Sci* 238:155–160.

Leslie SA (1988), Diagnosis and treatment of hysterical conversion reactions. *Arch Dis Child* 63:506–511.

Maisami M, Freeman JM (1987), Conversion reactions in children as body language: a combined child psychiatry/neurology team approach to the management of functional neurologic disorders in children. *Pediatrics* 80:46–52.

Mizes JS (1985), The use of contingent reinforcement in the treatment of a conversion disorder: a multiple baseline study. *J Behav Ther Exp Psychiatry* 16:341–345.

Rivinus TM, Jamison DL, Graham PJ (1975), Childhood organic neurological disease presenting as psychiatric disorder. *Arch Dis Child* 40:115–119.

Schulman JL (1988), Use of a coping approach in the management of children with conversion reactions. *J Am Acad Child Adolesc Psychiatry* 27:785–788.

Silver LB (1982), Conversion disorder with pseudoseizures in adolescence: a stress reaction to unrecognized and untreated learning disabilities. *J Am Acad Child Psychiatry* 21:508–512.

Spierings C, Poels PJE, Sijben N, Gabreels FJM, Renier WO (1990), Conversion disorders in childhood: a retrospective follow-up study of 84 patients. *Dev Med Child Neuro* 32:865–871.

Stefansson JG, Messina JS, Meyerowitz S (1976), Hysterical neurosis, conversion type: clinical and epidemiological considerations. *Acta Psychiatr Scand* 53:119–138.

Thomson APJ, Sills JA (1988), Diagnosis of functional illness presenting with gait disorder. *Arch Dis Child* 63:148–153.

Volkmar FR, Poll J, Lewis M (1984), Conversion reactions in children and adolescents. *J Am Acad Child Psychiatry* 23:424–430.

Warzak JW, Kewman DG, Stefans V, Johnson E (1987), Behavioral rehabilitation of functional alexia. *J Behav Ther Exp Psychiatry* 18:171–177.

Wooley SC, Blackwell B, Winger C (1978), A learning theory model of chronic illness behavior: theory, treatment, and research. *Psychosom Med* 40:379–401.

# "EVERYBODY LOOKS AT MY PUBIC BONE"—A CASE REPORT OF AN ADOLESCENT PATIENT WITH BODY DYSMORPHIC DISORDER

## E. Sobanski and M. H. Schmidt

*Body dysmorphic disorder (BDD) is a type of somatoform disorder in which an individual is preoccupied with an imagined defect in his or her physical appearance. The most common imagined defects involve the face or head (such as one's hair, nose, or skin), and most people with this disorder have another diagnosed disorder at the same time (usually a mood or anxiety disorder). As you might expect, people with BDD often avoid social situations, make great efforts to conceal their imagined defect, are reluctant to talk to psychologists and psychiatrists about their distress, and seek physical solutions (e.g., plastic surgery) to change their bodies. Phillips, McElroy, Keck, Pope, and Hudson (1993) provide an excellent analysis of 30 individuals diagnosed with this disorder.*

*The case we present is of a 16-year-old girl who is ashamed of her appearance and, more specifically, believes that her pubic bone attracts attention because it is dislocated and pronounced. She is also diagnosed with anorexia nervosa, an eating disorder, which we might imagine exaggerates any perceived imperfections of her pubic bone. Treatment occurred over a 10-week period in which the girl was required to gain weight, wear jeans instead of baggy clothes, and to participate in social situations that she normally avoided. As in the first article in this chapter, the intervention is successful and is based on learning theory. However, in this case, principles of classical rather than instrumental conditioning were used.*

## Reference

Phillips, K. A., McElroy, S. L., Keck, P. E., Jr., Pope, H. G., Jr., & Hudson, J. I. (1993). Body dysmorphic disorder: Thirty cases of imagined ugliness. *American Journal of Psychiatry, 150,* 302–308.

## Suggested Readings

Phillips, K. A. (1996). *The broken mirror: Understanding and treating body dysmorphic disorder.* New York: Oxford University Press.

Veale, D., Boocock, A., Gournay, K., & Dryden, W. (1996). Body dysmorphic disorder: A survey of fifty cases. *British Journal of Psychiatry, 169*, 196–201.

---

*Acta Psychiatrica Scandinavica, 101*, 80–82. (2000).

**Objective:** Body dysmorphic disorder (BDD) was described for the first time more than 100 years ago, but it is still unknown to many clinicians. Although the onset usually occurs during adolescence, BDD has received little attention in the adolescent psychiatric literature.

**Method:** The case and treatment of a 16-year-old female patient is described.

**Results:** The patient, suffering from the overvalued belief of a dislocated pubic bone, a comorbid mild depressive episode, BDD associated rituals and social avoidance, was treated successfully with a combination of exposure and response prevention and 125 mg/day of doxepine.

**Conclusion:** If BDD is diagnosed early in the course and treated appropriately, it is possible to obtain a satisfying outcome.

## Introduction

Body dysmorphic disorder is characterized by an excessive preoccupation with a real minor or imagined defect in physical appearance. The patients' degree of insight into the exaggerated nature of their dysmorphophobic concerns varies from obsessive thoughts with good insight, and overvalued ideas to delusions where insight is absent. The onset of symptoms usually occurs during adolescence and the course tends to be chronic without appropriate treatment.

## Case Report

The 16-year-old girl had been suffering for about 6 months from the belief that her pubic bone was becoming increasingly dislocated and prominent, such that everyone would stare at and talk about it. The girl could not remember a particular occurrence which had brought on the symptom and had no insight into its psychological nature. She was totally convinced that she could only be helped by a surgical correction of her pubic bone. In an attempt to achieve a smaller hip girth and also to influence the pubic bone she had reduced her body weight from 48 kg to 44 kg with a height of 1.68 m, which corresponds to a body mass index (BMI) of 15.8 kg/m². The weight reduction led to amenorrhea. One month before admission to our clinic she was admitted to a paediatric clinic where anorexia nervosa was diagnosed. She was fed with high-caloric nutrient solution and gained 2 kg. Two weeks before the referral to our clinic the girl had become totally housebound because she was extremely ashamed of her looks. She spent almost the entire day in her bedroom, wearing excessively large pyjamas. At admission her mood was depressed and her drive reduced. She cried often and reported anhedonia, hopelessness and loss of interest. She denied suicide ideation. Up to 10 times a day she lowered herself to the ground and measured, with her fingers, the distance between her pelvic girdle and the soil in order to check the position of her pubic bone. She was constantly preoccupied with thoughts about it.

The girl was the eldest daughter of a couple with university education, and had a 5-year-old sister. No particular problems in family interaction could be assessed and there was no family history for psychiatric disorders. Pregnancy and early development occurred without problems. She was described by her parents as being ambitious at school and a little reserved and shy towards her peers, with no long-term close friendships but with regular dates with her classmates. She had dated for 1 month with a boy of her age, but had discontinued the relationship because she felt too occupied by it. She had no previous sexual experience.

The patient was treated for 10 weeks at our clinic. She was obliged to gain 2 kg weight, receiving from the second week onwards 125 mg/day of doxepine and therapy with exposure and response prevention. We first set up an anxiety hierarchy of avoided situations with raising degree of difficulty: 1, wearing jeans in her own room; 2, wearing jeans in the ward and meeting others; 3, wearing jeans, going to town and visiting a pub; and 4, visiting her school and meeting classmates. She was treated with three sessions of 60–90 min per week. At first she was extremely upset by the training programme and had thoughts such as: "I am an outsider. Everybody looks at my pubic bone. If it would be normal, everything would be fine. I need a surgical correction." Gradually it became easier for her to face formerly avoided situations. At the end of treatment, the girl's BDD symptoms were distinctly improved. Despite her still being certain about the dislocation of her pubic bone, the belief was less distressing for her and no longer impaired her daily life. She had stopped camouflaging and checking her pubic bone. She dated with her peers and attended school regularly; the depressive symptoms had completely vanished. When she was seen after 6 months for follow-up the therapeutic results had remained stable.

## Discussion

Patients with BDD do not consult mental health professionals primarily because of the somatic explanation of their concerns, seeking treatment by general practitioners, dermatologists, dentists, and plastic surgeons, resulting in low prevalence in clinical psychiatric populations. To date there has been little research concerning BDD. Two cross-sectional surveys were carried out 1993 in the United States by Phillips et al. (1) and 1996 in the United Kingdom by Veale et al. (2). One epidemiological survey was carried out 1997 in Italy by Faravelli et al. (3), who reported a 1-year prevalence of BDD of 0.7%. In terms of adolescents there have been only a few case studies (4, 5), and no larger surveys at all.

Besides BDD the patient described in the case report suffered from typical comorbid features, namely a mild depressive episode (ICD-10: $F$ 32.0), associated rituals and social avoidance. According to the scientific literature depression is the most frequently related psychiatric disorder. Between 60% and 94% of patients with BDD have a lifetime diagnosis of depression (1, 2). Most individuals with BDD perform ritualistic behaviours related to

their dysmorphophobic beliefs that resemble obsessive-compulsive disorder (OCD) compulsions. Between 6% and 30% fulfil the diagnostic criteria for a concurrent OCD (1, 2, 6). Virtually always, BDD results in social impairment, in particular avoidance of social interactions. Available studies show a percentage for social phobia in BDD patients varying between 10% and 43% (1, 2, 7). In a series of 100 patients, 32 had been completely housebound for at least 1 year (6). Despite the low BMI of 15.8 kg/m$^2$ and the amenorrhea the patient described did not suffer from anorexia nervosa, because other core symptoms such as weight phobia and disturbance of the whole-body image were not present.

The dysmorphophobic symptoms were treated successfully with exposure and response prevention. At the end of treatment the girl's social and occupational functioning had improved distinctly. Several studies published in recent years report that up to 70% of patients with BDD benefit from systematic exposure to avoided situations and prevention of anxiety-reducing behaviours (8, 9). Although there is growing evidence that BDD symptoms, as well as comorbid depression, respond preferentially to SSRIs the comorbid depressive symptoms of our patient were treated with doxepine, because no data are available concerning the use of SSRIs in adolescents for this condition.

The case report shows that it is possible to obtain a satisfying outcome if BDD is diagnosed early and treated appropriately. Severe complications such as being housebound, or suicide attempts, which occur in up to 25% (10), can thereby be avoided. Therefore, it is necessary that more clinicians are informed about the disorder. More scientific data are needed concerning epidemiology, aetiology and treatment strategies.

## References

1. Phillips KA, McElroy S, Keck PE, Pope HG, Hudson JI. Body dysmorphic disorder: 30 cases of imagined ugliness. Am J Psychiatry 1993:150:302–308.
2. Veale D, Boockok A, Gournay K, et al. Body Dysmorphic Disorder, a survey of fifty cases. Br J Psychiatry 1996:169: 196–201.

3. Faravelli C, Salvatori S, Galassi F, Alazzi, L, Dree, C, Cabra S. Epidemiology of somatoform disorders: a community survey in Florence. Soc Psychiatr Psychiatr Epidemiol 1997;32:24–29.

4. Braddock LE. Dysmorphophobia in adolescence: a case report. Br J Psychiatry 1982:140:199–201.

5. Phillips KA, Atala K, Albertine RS. Case study: body dysmorphic disorder in adolescents. J Am Child Adol Psychiatry 1995:9:1216–1220.

6. Phillips KA, McElroy S, Keck P. Hudson JI, Pope G. A comparison of delusional and nondelusional body dysmorphic disorder in 100 cases. Psychopharmacol Bull 1994: 2:179–186.

7. Hollander E, Cohen LJ, Simeon D. Body dysmorphic disorder. Psychiatr Ann 1993:23:359–364.

8. Gomez-Perez JC, Marks IM, Guirrez-Fissac JL. Dysmorphophobia: clinical features and outcome with behavior therapy. Behav Psychiatr 1994:9:229–235.

9. McKay D, Todaro J, Neziroglu F, Campisi T, Moritz EK, Yaryura-Tobias JA. Body dysmorphic disorder: a preliminary evaluation of treatment and maintenance using exposure with response prevention. Behav Res Ther 1997; 35:67–70.

10. Phillips KA. The broken mirror: understanding and treating body dysmorphic disorder. New York: Oxford University Press, 1996.

# MULTIPLE PERSONALITY DISORDER FOLLOWING CHILDBIRTH

## J. M. O'Dwyer and T. Friedman

*With this article, we shift from somatoform disorders to dissociative disorders. This is the case of a 26-year-old woman, Miss B, who was diagnosed with the prototypical dissociative disorder, multiple personality disorder (which, since the arrival of the DSM-IV, is known as dissociative identity disorder). The evidence suggests that Miss B's multiple personalities began at age 10, as a way of coping with physical and sexual abuse. Miss B had never seen a psychiatrist, but shortly after the birth of her severely handicapped child she reported her behavior as being controlled by two other personalities. The authors of this report speculate that the multiple personalities became evident at this time because, as with the initial trauma, they provided Miss B with a means of managing the tremendous distress she experienced. It appears that the woman's functioning improved, though the reasons for this are difficult to discern.*

*It is a common misconception that an individual with dissociative identity disorder has schizophrenia, an error that probably results from the prefix schizo (meaning split) and from the often confusing symptoms and clinical presentations of the two disorders. Nevertheless, the two disorders are distinct in that dissociative identity disorder is marked more by amnesia and sudden shifts in identity and not by psychosis and loss of contact with day-to-day reality. This distinction should become more evident as you compare the third and fourth articles in this chapter with the case material on schizophrenia in chapter 8.*

*O'Dwyer and Friedman address the concern about the validity of multiple personalities as a real phenomenon and, in turn, whether it is being over- or underdiagnosed. There is growing evidence that alternative personalities have distinct psychological profiles (e.g., Bryant, 1995), yet the question of the scientific and clinical viability of this diagnosis remains an interesting one (e.g., see Piper, 1997).*

## References

Bryant, R. A. (1995). Autobiographical memory across personalities in dissociative identity disorder: A case report. *Journal of Abnormal Psychology, 104,* 625–631.

Piper, A., Jr. (1997). *Hoax and reality: The bizarre world of multiple personality disorder.* New York: Aronson.

## Suggested Reading

Kihlstrom, J. F., Glisky, M. L., & Angiulo, M. J. (1994). Dissociative tendencies and dissociative disorders. *Journal of Abnormal Psychology, 103*, 117–124.

*British Journal of Psychiatry, 162*, 831–833. (1993).

The first recorded case of multiple personality disorder was that of Mary Reynolds in Pennsylvania (Mitchell, 1816). There were two British cases published in 1845 (Mayo, 1845; Skae, 1845). However, the most representative cases were probably those of Janet (1907) and Prince (1900). A renewed interest in the diagnosis occurred during the 1970s, and Bliss (1986) estimated that of 300 cases in the literature, 79 were reported after 1970. During the past 20 years only two reports have appeared in the British literature (Cutler & Reid, 1975; Fahy, 1989) and, in general, psychiatrists have been rather skeptical of the validity of the diagnosis. However, it has now received recognition as a separate diagnosis in *DSM-III* (American Psychiatric Association, 1980), and in *ICD-10* (World Health Organization, 1992). We present a case of a woman who presented with features of multiple personality, in the setting of a grief reaction.

## Case Report

Miss B, a 26-year-old single woman, was admitted informally, five weeks after the birth of her son. She complained of feeling miserable, empty, low in mood, sleeping poorly, and feeling worthless, and had suicidal ideas.

She had been referred two weeks post-partum. This was her first pregnancy but labour was complicated by shoulder dystocia and the child was born with severe mental and physical handicaps. The patient became increasingly distressed leading to her admission.

Her mother was described by a general practitioner (GP) as being "rather odd, eccentric, hysterical and very manipulative," but had never seen a psychiatrist. Her father had a long history of alcohol abuse as did both the paternal grandparents, who also had histories of affective disorder, the grandmother having killed herself in her forties.

B was born in the Midlands and had an unhappy childhood, being both physically and sexually abused by her parents. She had a period of daytime enuresis when starting school, followed by truancy from school lasting seven months. She was bullied at school and described herself as a loner. At age 10 years she described her first experience of sexual abuse from her father who masturbated over her. This abuse was repeated over subsequent years, by both her father and a male babysitter. At the age of 11 years she had another period of school truancy and the following year a period of elective mutism, lasting eight months. B's school reports were poor and she had difficulty in both reading and writing, although this subsequently improved. She was frequently examined because of ill health, but no organic cause was found. At age 16 years she developed bulimia nervosa. Her weight dropped from 76 kg to 41 kg. She left school, started a training scheme, and worked as a nursing auxiliary for six years before her admission.

She had the menarche at the age of 11 years, had her first boyfriend at 18 years, and had been cohabiting with her present boyfriend for three years. She said initially she was happy with him, but he was frequently physically abusive. Her current pregnancy was initially unwanted.

Mental state examination on admission revealed a boyish-looking young woman, who was distressed throughout the interview. Her mood was depressed, with hopelessness and suicidal ideas. She wanted to die and felt she should wait in heaven for her son to join her. She had no ideas of harming the baby, but wanted him to die "to stop him suffering." She displayed marked guilt and felt totally responsible for her son's handicaps. Her speech was slow and hesitant. There were no abnormal beliefs or experiences in evidence, nor was there any disorder of her cognitive function.

The overall impression was of a young lady with symptoms suggestive of a grief reaction with pronounced depressive features since the birth of a severely handicapped child.

At times she was distressed, but other times totally dissociated from her problems, wandering about and claiming that everything was fine. This became more evident over a period of a few weeks. She then described being taken over by another person. "Susan," and then subsequently by "Helen." She claimed that she had no control over them, that at times their "coming out" embarrassed her, and that they had been there since she was ten years old. She felt they had never been so strong and they were totally independent of her will. She described three personalities:

(a) "Marie," who was good, stable, kind, loving and responsible—she coped with everything and dealt with all the problems.
(b) "Susan," who was flirtatious, mischievous and sexy—she was also naughty and irresponsible, but fun loving.
(c) "Helen," who was evil, always bad tempered, and always troublesome.

When she felt these people were "out," there were marked changes in her behaviour objectively. These changes were also noticed by her family who claimed that it had been happening for years, but was more marked while in hospital. She wrote a number of letters about the personalities.

I can't talk about Susan because she would not like it but I can write about her instead. The old Marie is just Marie but the new me is Susan. She knows she lives in Marie's body but she and Marie are very different. Marie is a sweet fun-loving girl, who cares for everybody and everything, and would never be rude or bad tempered. Susan is the opposite to Marie. Marie has been able to handle Susan over the years but sometimes Susan gets stronger and takes over.

Marie just waits until things get better and then comes back. One evening last week Susan came and pushed Marie out for a couple of days. She was stronger than she had ever been, but Marie won through in the end. I did not want to show you Susan but for 2 days I was her and I thought Marie had died. I don't want to lose Susan and I hope that by telling you the truth you will let us alone, and we will decide which way to go.

If I am not careful, when the baby dies Marie will go with him. I don't think that anybody could cope with Susan or Helen. Susan knows that he is going to die and is helping me by misbehaving like a child and jollying me along. Helen creeps in every now and then and wants to kill everything in sight, including me. Susan wants to die gracefully. Helen is now stronger than Susan, so while they battle it out, I'm stuck in the middle. Susan wants to be sexy and to look nice and does not like eating fatty or sweet foods. She likes her hair very neat and clean. She wants to do as she wants and does not care about anybody or anything. Helen wants the whole world to piss off and does not want to answer to anybody, and when she does not get what she wants she takes it out on herself. She is always hungry and upsets Susan by eating sweet things. Helen will not go to see the baby but Susan forces her to go, and I'm stuck in the middle.

At the age of 12 weeks the baby died and at this time the multiple personalities were at their most prominent. Her mood fluctuated from being exceedingly depressed with retardation, to being bright, happy, and cheerful with no evidence of a depressive illness. She received daily dynamic psychotherapy, the main aim being to reintegrate her personalities and, in spite of initial difficulties in engaging her in therapy, the aim of reintegration of the personalities was successful. She was also treated, while in hospital, with a course of antidepressants which made no difference. Because of this and her refusal to comply with further antidepressant medication, they were discontinued after six weeks.

After the death of her son, she began to improve and at the time of writing she accepted that both Susan and Helen were aspects of her own personality and were her way of coping.

She has now been discharged from hospital and appears to be coping quite well. She is pregnant again, and cautiously looking forward to the birth of another child.

## Discussion

Our patient fulfils the *DSM-III-R* (American Psychiatric Association, 1987) criteria for multiple personality disorder which are:

(a) the existence within the person of two or more distinct personalities or personality states, each with its own relatively enduring pattern or perceiving, relating to and thinking about the environment and self

(b) at least two of these personalities or personality states recurrently take full control of the person's behaviour.

According to authors such as Putnam et al. (1986), other diagnoses are quite common in patients with a diagnosis of multiple personality disorder, including depressive neurotic personality disorder, suicide attempts, etc. While our patient did have many symptoms suggestive of a depressive illness, these were inconsistent and not maintained throughout her hospital stay and were present in the setting of an acute grief reaction.

Putnam et al. (1986) also claim that many of the patients have suffered childhood trauma and this is indeed the case with our patient who suffered repeated and severe abuse. She describes the onset of the multiple personalities occurring at about the age of 10 years, which coincides with her first experience of sexual abuse, and we feel this is important in the aetiology. Her multiple personalities probably became a coping mechanism protecting her from the abuse to which she was subjected throughout her life. The fact that they became more prominent at this time probably reflects the trauma of having a severely handicapped child, and again the personalities seem to have offered her a way to cope with an exceedingly distressing situation.

Merskey (1992) disputes the existence of mul-

tiple personality disorder and suggests that other psychiatric diagnoses may apply, particularly the diagnosis of manic-depressive psychosis. He also suggests that many cases may be iatrogenic in origin. While this may have occurred in other patients, there were no previous discussions or suggestions about this diagnosis before the development of the other personalities in this patient. Subsequently, she consistently denied having heard of the disorder, prior to its onset, although one must always have some doubt in these cases. This may be the first case arising spontaneously, in the absence of other major mental illness, although she did have a severe grief reaction.

She was encouraged to acknowledge the alternative personalities as part of herself. She was also encouraged to acknowledge her relationship problems and her history of abuse openly. As time went on, the personalities of Susan and Helen seemed to recede but were still present at times. Janet (1907) claims that the multiple personalities recede with age and that the lively energetic personality becomes dominant. However, this does not appear to be the case with our patient. The rather lively and more dominant personality of Susan is receding at present. At the time of writing, she has been discharged from hospital, is pregnant again, and continuing in individual therapy where she is making considerable progress.

## References

American Psychiatric Association (1980) *Diagnostic and Statistical Manual of Mental Disorders* (3rd edn) (DSM-III). Washington, DC: APA.

———— (1987) *Diagnostic and Statistical Manual of Mental Disorders* (3rd edn, revised) (DSM-III-R). Washington, DC: APA.

Bliss, E. (1986) *Multiple Personality, Allied Disorders and Hypnosis.* Oxford: Oxford University Press.

Cutler, S. & Reid, S. (1975) Multiple personality: a single case study with a 15 year follow-up. *Psychological Medicine, 5,* 18–26.

Fahy, T. A. (1989) Multiple personality: a symptom of psychiatric disorder. *British Journal of Psychiatry,* 154, 99–101.

Janet, P. (1907) *The Major Symptoms of Hysteria* (pp. 85–92). New York: MacMillan.

Mayo, T. (1845) Case of double consciousness. *Medical Gazette New Series I,* 1202–1203.

Merskey, H. (1992) The manufacture of personalities. *British Journal of Psychiatry,* 160, 327–340.

Mitchell, S. L. (1816) A double consciousness or duality of person in the same individual. *Medical Repository*, *3*, 185–186.

Prince, M. (1900) *The Problems of Multiple Personality*. Paris: International Congress of Psychology.

Putnam, F. W., Guroff, J. J., Silberman, E. K., *et al* (1986) The clinical phenomenonology of multiple personality disor-

der—a review of 100 recent cases. *Journal of Clinical Psychiatry*, *47*, 285–293.

Skae, D. (1845) Case of intermittent mental disorder of the tertian type with double consciousness. *Journal of Medicine*, *4*, 10–13.

World Health Organization (1992) *The ICD-10 Classification of Mental and Behavioural Disorders*. Geneva: WHO.

# THERAPEUTIC MONOGAMY

## Irvin D. Yalom

*Dissociative identity disorder, or at least the strong suggestion of it, also figures into this article, which is from an engaging book of cases narrated by the well-known psychotherapist Irvin Yalom. He describes his experiences in working with a thirty-five-year-old woman he calls Marge. Marge struggles with potent feelings of inferiority and low self-worth, and, by giving us a glimpse into his stream of thought during their therapy sessions, Yalom reveals his strategy and experiences in helping her to overcome these problems. At the center of this case is the therapist's dilemma of how to respond to Me, a second personality that emerges from within Marge and that transforms the course of treatment. Perhaps the most interesting aspect of this reading is how hard Yalom works not to engage Me in any way, thus maintaining "therapeutic monogamy" with Marge. Another important feature is that, unlike the previous article, it conveys how a diagnosable disorder is not a discrete and distinct aspect of an individual but is instead part of a far more complex set of symptoms and processes. In this case it involves depression, anxiety, and personality style.*

### Suggested Reading

Kluft, R. P. (1999). An overview of the psychotherapy of dissociative identity disorder. *American Journal of Psychotherapy, 53*, 289–319.

From *Love's executioner: And other tales of psychotherapy* (pp. 213–229). New York: Harper-Collins. (1989).

I'm nothing. Garbage. A creep. A cipher. I slink around on the refuse dumps outside of human camps. Christ, to die! To be dead! Squashed flat on the Safeway parking lot and then to be washed away by a fire hose. Nothing remaining. Nothing. Not even chalked words on the sidewalk saying, 'There was the blob that was once named Marge White.' "

Another one of Marge's late-night phone calls! God, I hated those calls! It wasn't the intrusion into my life—I'd learned to expect that: it goes with the territory. A year ago when I first accepted Marge as a patient, I knew there'd be calls; as soon as I saw her, I sensed what was in store for me. It didn't take much experience to recognize the signs of deep distress. Her sagging head and shoulders said "depression"; her gigantic eye pupils and restless hands and feet said "anxiety." Everything else about her—multiple suicide attempts, eating disorder, early sexual abuse by her father, episodic psychotic thinking, twenty-three years of therapy—shouted "borderline," the word that strikes terror in the heart of the middle-aged comfort-seeking psychiatrist.

She had told me she was thirty-five, a lab technician; that she had been in therapy for ten years with a psychiatrist who had just relocated to another city; that she was desperately alone; and that sooner or later, it was just a matter of time, she would kill herself. . . .

My first impulse was to get the hell away, far away—and not see her again. Use an excuse, any excuse: my time all filled, leaving the country for a few years, embarking on a full-time research career. But soon I heard my voice offering her another appointment.

Perhaps I was intrigued by her beauty, by her ebony hair in bangs framing her astonishingly white, perfectly featured face. Or was it my sense of obligation to my career as a teacher? Recently I had been asking myself how, in all good faith, I could go on teaching students to do psychotherapy and at the same time refuse to treat difficult patients. I guess I accepted Marge as a patient for many reasons; but, more than anything, I believe it was shame, shame at choosing the easy life, shame at shunning the very patients who needed me the most.

So I had anticipated desperation calls like this. I had anticipated crisis after crisis. I had expected that I would need to hospitalize her at some point. Thank God I had avoided that—the dawn meetings with the ward staff, the writing of orders, the public acknowledgment of my failure, the trudging over to the hospital every day. Huge chunks of time devoured. . . .

But the worst thing about the calls was my ineptitude. She put me to the test, and I was always found wanting. I must have had twenty such calls from her in the past year, and not once had I found a way to give her the help she needed. . . .

I have met few people with as much self-hatred as Marge. These feelings never disappeared but during her best times merely receded to the background, awaiting a suitable cue to return. There was no cue more powerful than the publicly acclaimed success of another woman of her own age: then

Marge's self-hatred washed over her, and she began to consider, more seriously than usual, suicide.

I fumbled for words of comfort. "Marge, why are you doing this to yourself? You talk about having done nothing, having accomplished nothing, not being fit to exist, but we both know that these ideas are a state of mind. They've nothing to do with reality! Remember how great you felt about yourself two weeks ago? Well, nothing has changed in the external world. You're exactly the same person now as you were then!"

I was on the right track. I had her attention. I could hear her listening, and continued.

"This business of comparing yourself unfavorably to others is always self-destructive. Look, give yourself a break. . . . It's always possible, if you want to torment yourself, to find someone to compare yourself with unfavorably. I know the feeling, I've done the same thing.

"Look, why not just one time pick someone who may not have what you have? You've always shown compassion for others. Think about your volunteer work with the homeless. You never give yourself credit for that. Compare yourself with someone who doesn't give a damn about others. Or why not compare yourself with, say, one of the homeless people you've helped? I'll bet they all compare themselves unfavorably with you."

The click of the telephone being hung up confirmed what I instantly realized: I had made a colossal mistake. I was well enough acquainted with Marge to know exactly what she would do with my blunder: she would say that I had let my true feelings out, that I think she's so hopeless that the only persons with whom she might compare favorably would be the most hapless souls on earth.

She did not pass up the opportunity and began our next regular therapy hour—fortunately the following morning—by expressing that very sentiment. She then continued in chilling voice and staccato cadence to give me the "real facts" about herself.

"I am forty-five years old. I have been mentally ill all my life. I have seen psychiatrists since I was twelve years old and cannot function without them.

I shall have to take medicine the rest of my life. The most I can hope for is to stay out of a mental hospital. I have never been loved. I will never have children. I have never had a long-term relationship with a man nor any hope of ever having one. I lack the capacity to make friends. No one calls me on my birthday. My father, who molested me when I was a child, is dead. My mother is a crazy, embittered lady, and I grow more like her every day. My brother has spent much of his life in a mental hospital. I have no talents, no special abilities. I will always work in a menial job. I'll always be poor and will always spend most of my salary for psychiatric care. . . . You tell me to be patient. You tell me I'm not ready—not ready to stop therapy, not ready to get married, not ready to adopt a child, not ready to stop smoking. I've waited. I've waited my whole life away. Now it's too late, it's too late to live.

I sat unblinking through this litany and, for a moment, felt ashamed for being unmoved. But it was not callousness. I had heard it before and remembered how unsettled I was the first time she delivered it when, stricken with empathy and grief, I became what Hemingway has referred to as a "wet-thinking Jewish psychiatrist."

Worse yet, much worse (and this is hard to admit), *I agreed with her.* She presented her "true case history" so poignantly and convincingly that I was fully persuaded. She *was* severely handicapped. She probably *would never* marry. She *was* a misfit. She *did* lack the capacity to be close to others. She probably *would* need therapy for many, many years, perhaps always. I was drawn so deeply into her despair and pessimism that I could easily understand the allure of suicide. I could scarcely find a word of comfort for her.

It took me a week, until our next session, to realize that the litany was depression-spawned propaganda. It was her depression speaking, and I was foolish enough to be persuaded by it. . . .

So now, hearing the litany again, I pondered how to shift her from this state of mind. On similar occasions in the past, she had settled heavily into a depression and stayed there for several weeks. I knew that by acting immediately I could help her avoid a great deal of pain.

"That's your depression talking, Marge, not you. Remember that every time you've sunk into a depression, you've climbed out again. The one good—the *only* good—thing about depression is that it always ends."

I walked over to my desk, opened her file, and read aloud parts of a letter she had written only three weeks earlier when she was feeling exhilarated about life:

". . . It was a fantastic day. Jane and I walked down Telegraph Avenue. We tried on 1940s evening dresses at old clothes' stores. I found some old Kay Starr records. We jogged across the Golden Gate Bridge, brunched at Greens restaurant. So there's life after all in San Francisco. I only give you the bad news—I'd thought I'd share some of the good stuff. See you Thurs.—"

But though warm spring breezes were wafting through the open window, it was winter in my office. Marge's face was frozen. She stared at the wall and seemed hardly to hear me. Her response was icy: "You think I'm nothing. Look at your comment asking me to compare myself with the homeless. That's what you think I'm worth."

"Marge, I apologize for that. My batting average for being useful on the phone isn't great. It was a clumsy effort on my part. But, believe me, my intentions were to be helpful. As soon as I said that, I knew it was a mistake."

That seemed to help. I heard her exhale. Her tight shoulders relaxed, her face loosened, her head turned ever so slightly toward me.

I edged an inch or two closer. "Marge, you and I have been through crises before, times when you've felt just as awful as you do right now. What's helped in the past? I remember times you've walked out of the office feeling much better than when you entered. What made the difference? What did you do? What did I do? Let's figure it out together. . . . "

She said that it was important for her to be listened to, that she had no one else but me and nowhere else but my office to express her pain. She also knew that it helped when we carefully examined the incidents that precipitated a depression.

Soon we were going through, one by one, all

the unsettling events of the week. In addition to the stresses she had described to me on the phone, there had been others. For example, in an all-day meeting of the university laboratory where she worked, she had been pointedly ignored by the professional and academic staff. I empathized with her and told her that I had heard many others in her situation—including my wife—complain of similar treatment. . . .

Marge returned to the topic of her lack of success and how much more accomplished was her thirty-year-old boss.

"Why do we," I mused, "pursue these unfavorable comparisons? It's so self-punishing, so perverse—like grinding an aching tooth." I had also, I told her, compared myself unfavorably with others on many occasions (I did not give specific details. Perhaps I should have. That would have been treating her like an equal.) . . .

By the time the hour ended, she did not have to tell me how much better she felt: I could see it in her breathing, in her walk, and in her smile as she left the office.

The improvement held. She had an excellent week, and I received no midnight crisis phone calls. When I saw her a week later, she seemed almost ebullient. I've always believed that it's as important to find out what makes one better as it is to determine what makes one worse, so I asked her what had made the difference.

"Somehow," Marge said, "our last hour turned things around. It is almost miraculous how you, in such a short time, pulled me out of that funk. I'm really glad you're my psychiatrist."

Though charmed by her ingenuous compliment, I was made uncomfortable by both thoughts: the mysterious "somehow," and the vision of me as a miracle worker. As long as Marge thought in those terms, she would not get better because the source of help was either outside of herself or beyond comprehension. My task as a therapist (not unlike that of a parent) is to make myself obsolete—to help a patient become his or her own mother and father. I didn't want to make her better. I wanted to help her take the responsibility of making herself better, and I wanted the

process of improvement to be as clear to her as possible. That's why I felt uncomfortable with her "somehow," and so set about exploring it.

"What precisely," I asked, "was helpful to you in our last hour? At what moment did you begin to feel better? Let's track it down together."

"Well, one thing was the way you handled the crack about the homeless. I could have used that to keep punishing you—in fact, I know I've done that with shrinks in the past. But when you stated in such a matter-of-fact way what your intentions were and that you had been clumsy. I found I couldn't throw a tantrum about it. . . .

"The main thing that turned me around—in fact, the moment the calm set in—was when you told me that your wife and I had similar problems at work. I feel I'm so icky, so creepy and your wife so holy that we couldn't both be mentioned in the same breath. Confiding to me that she and I had some of the same problems *proved* you had some respect for me."

I was about to protest, to insist I have always had respect for her, but she intercepted me. "I know, I know—you've often *told* me you respected me, and *told* me you liked me, but it was just words. I never really believed it. This time it was different, you went beyond words."

I was very excited by what Marge said. She had a way of putting her finger on vital issues. Going "beyond words," *that* was what counted. It was what I *did*, not what I said. It was actually *doing* something for the patient. Sharing something about my wife was doing something for Marge, giving her a gift. *The therapeutic act, not the therapeutic word!* . . .

"It also helped a lot when you kept asking me what had helped me in the past. You kept putting the responsibility onto me, making me take charge of the session. That was good. Usually I sulk in a depression for weeks, but you had me, within minutes, working to figure out what happened.

"In fact, *just asking the question,* 'What helped in the past?' was helpful because it assured me that there was a way I could get better. Also, it helped that you didn't get into your role of the wizard letting me guess about questions you know the answers to. I liked the way you admitted you didn't know and then invited me to explore it together with you."

Music to my ears! Throughout my year of work with Marge, I had only a single real rule in my work—treat her as an equal. I had tried not to objectify her, to pity her, or to do anything that created a gulf of inequality between us. I followed that rule to the best of my ability, and it felt good now to hear that it had been helpful. . . .

About three weeks later, three weeks after my discovery of the importance of the therapeutic act, an extraordinary event occurred. Marge and I were in the midst of an ordinary hour. She had had a rotten week and was filling me in on some of the details. She seemed phlegmatic, her skirt was wrinkled and twisted, her hair unkempt, and her face lined with discouragement and fatigue.

In the middle of her dirge, she suddenly closed her eyes—not in itself unusual since she often went into an autohypnotic state during the session. I had long before decided not to take the bait—not to follow her into the hypnoidal state—but instead would call her out of it. I said, "Marge," and was about to utter the rest of the sentence, "Will you please come back?" when I heard a strange and powerful voice come out of her mouth: "You don't know me."

She was right. I didn't know the person who talked. The voice was so different, so forceful, so authoritative, I looked around the office for an instant to see who else might have entered.

"Who are you?" I asked.

"Me! Me!" And then the transformed Marge jumped up and proceeded to prance around the office, peering into bookcases, straightening pictures, and inspecting my furniture. It was Marge, but it was not Marge. Everything but the clothing had changed—her carriage, her face, her self-assurance, her walk.

This new Marge was vivacious and outrageously, but enjoyably, flirtatious. The strange, full contralto voice pronounced: "As long as you're going to pretend to be a Jewish intellectual, you might as well furnish your office like one. That sofa cover belongs at the Goodwill store—if they'd take

it—and that wall hanging is decaying rapidly—thank God! And those shots of the California coast. Spare me any more psychiatrists' home photos!"

She was savvy, willful, very sexy. What a relief to have a break from Marge's droning voice and relentless whining. But I was beginning to feel uneasy; I enjoyed this lady too much. I thought of the Lorelei legend, and though I knew it would be dangerous to tarry, still I visited awhile.

"Why have you come?" I asked. "Why today?"

"To celebrate my victory. I've won, you know."

"Won what?"

"Don't play dumb with me! I'm not her, you know! Not everything you say is maaaaaarvellous. You think you're going to help Marge?" Her face was wonderfully mobile, her words delivered with the broad sneer one would expect from the villain of a Victorian melodrama.

She continued in a derisive, gloating manner: "You could have her in therapy for thirty years, but I'd still win. I can tear down a year's work in a day. If necessary, I could have her step off a curb into a moving truck."

"But why? What do you get out of it? If she loses, you lose." Perhaps I was staying longer with her than I should. It was wrong to talk to her about Marge. It was not fair to Marge. Yet this woman's appeal was strong, almost irresistible. For a brief time I felt a wave of eerie nausea, as though I were peering through a rent in the fabric of reality, at something forbidden, at the raw ingredients, the clefts and seams, the embryonic cells and blastulas that are, in the natural order of things, not meant to be seen in the finished human creature. My attention was riveted to her.

"Marge is a creep. You know she's a creep. How can you stand to be with her? A creep! A creep!" And then, in the most astounding theatrical performance I have ever seen, she proceeded to imitate Marge. Every gesture I had witnessed over the months, Marge's every grimace, every action, passed in front of me in chronological order. There was Marge timidly meeting me for the first time. There she was curled up in the corner of my office. And there with large, panic-filled eyes, pleading with me not to give up on her. There she was in an autotrance, eyes closed, flickering eyelids covering frenetic REM-like activity. And there with her face in spasm, like Quasimodo's, horribly distorted, barely able to talk. There she was cowering behind her chair as Marge was wont to do when frightened. There she was complaining melodramatically and mockingly of a dreadful stabbing pain in her womb and breast. There she was ridiculing Marge's stutter and some of her most familiar comments. "I'm soooooooo g-g-g-g-glad you're my psychiatrist!" On bended knee: "D-d-d-o-o-o you like me, D-D-D-Doctor Yalom? D-d-d-don't leave m-m-m-me, I d-d-d-d-d-disappear when you're not here."

The performance was extraordinary: like watching the curtain call of an actress who has played several roles in an evening and amuses the audience by briefly, perhaps for just a few seconds, slipping back into each of them. (I forgot for a moment that in this theater the actress was not really the actress but only one of the roles. The real actress, the responsible consciousness, remained concealed backstage.)

It was a virtuoso performance. But also an unspeakably cruel performance by "Me" (I didn't know what else to call her). Her eyes blazed as she continued to defile Marge who, she said, was incurable, hopeless, and pathetic. Marge, "Me" said, should write her autobiography and entitle it (here she began to chuckle) "Born to Be Pathetic."

"Born to Be Pathetic." I smiled despite myself. This Belle Dame sans Merci was a formidable woman. I felt disloyal to Marge for finding her rival so attractive, for being so bemused by her mimicry of Marge.

Suddenly—presto!—it was over. "Me" closed her eyes for a minute or two and, when she opened them, she had vanished and Marge was back, crying and terrified. She put her head between her knees, breathed deeply, and slowly regained her composure. For several minutes she sobbed and then finally talked about what had happened. (She had good recall of the scene that had just occurred.) She had never before split off—oh yes, there had been one time, a third personality named Ruth Anne—but the woman who came today had never appeared before.

I felt bewildered by what had happened. My one basic rule—"Treat Marge as an equal"—was no longer sufficient. Which Marge? The whimpering Marge in front of me or the sexy, insouciant Marge? It seemed to me that the important consideration was my relationship with my patient—the betweenness (one of Buber's endless store of awkward phrases) of Marge and me. Unless I could protect and remain faithful to that relationship, any hope of therapy was lost. It was necessary to modify my basic rule, "Treat the patient as an equal," to "Be faithful to the patient." Above all, I must not permit myself to be seduced by that other Marge.

A patient can tolerate the therapist's being unfaithful outside of the hour that is the patient's own. Though it is understood that therapists embrace other relationships, that there is another patient waiting in the wings for the hour to end, there is often a tacit agreement not to address that in therapy. Therapist and patient conspire to pretend that theirs is a monogamous relationship. Both therapist and patient secretly hope that the exiting and the entering patients will not meet one another. Indeed, to prevent that from happening, some therapists construct their office with two doors, one for entering, one for exiting.

But the patient has a right to expect fidelity *during* the hour. My implicit contract with Marge (as with all my patients) is that when I am with her, I am wholly, wholeheartedly, and exclusively with her. Marge illuminated another dimension of that contract: that I must be with her most central self. Rather than relating to *this* integral self, her father, who abused her, had contributed to the development of a false, sexual self. I must not make that error.

It was not easy. To be truthful, I wanted to see "Me" again. Though I had known her for less than an hour, I had been charmed by her. The drab backdrop of the dozens of hours I had spent with Marge made this engaging phantom stand out with a dazzling clarity. Characters like that do not come along often in life.

I didn't know her name and she didn't have much freedom, but we each knew how to find the other. In the next hour she tried several times to come to me again. I could see Marge flicker her eyelids and then close them. Only another minute or two, and we would have been together again. I felt foolish and eager. Balmy bygone memories flooded my mind. I recalled waiting at a palm-edged Caribbean airport for a plane to land and for my lover to join me.

This woman, this "Me," she understood me. She knew that I was weary, weary of Marge's whimpering and stuttering, that I was weary of her panics, her curling up in corners and hiding under desks, and weary of her thready childlike voice. She knew I wanted a real woman. She knew that I only pretended to treat Marge as an equal. She knew we were not equals. How could we be when Marge acted so crazy and I patronized her by tolerating her craziness?

"Me's" theatrical performance, in which she regurgitated all those snippets of Marge's behavior, convinced me that both she and I (and *only* she and I) understood what I had gone through with Marge. She was the brilliant, beautiful director who had created this film. Though I could write a clinical article about Marge or tell colleagues about the course of therapy, I could never really convey the essence of my experience with her. It was ineffable. But "Me" knew. If she could play all those roles, she must be the concealed, guiding intelligence behind them all. We shared something that was beyond language.

But fidelity! Fidelity! I had promised myself to Marge. If I consorted with "Me," it would be catastrophic for Marge: she'd become a bit player, a replaceable character. And that, of course, is precisely what "Me" wanted. "Me" was . . . beautiful and intriguing, but also lethal—the incarnation of all Marge's rage and self-hatred.

So I stayed faithful and, when I sensed "Me" approaching—for example, when Marge closed her eyes and began to enter a trance—I was quick to jar her awake by shouting, "Marge, come back!"

After this happened a few times, I realized that the final test still lay ahead: "Me" was inexorably gathering strength and desperately trying to return to me. The moment demanded a decision, and I chose to stand by Marge. I would sacrifice her rival to her, pluck her feathers, pull her asunder, and, bit by bit, feed her to Marge. The feeding technique was to repeat one standard question, "Marge, what would 'she' say if she were here?"

Some of Marge's answers were unexpected, some familiar. One day when I saw her timidly scanning the objects in my office, I said, "Go ahead, speak, Marge. Speak for 'her.' "

Marge took a deep breath and revved up her voice. "If you're going to pretend to be a Jewish intellectual, why not furnish your office like one?"

Marge said this as though it were an original thought, and it was apparent that she had not remembered *everything* "Me" had said. I couldn't help smiling: I was pleased that I and "Me" shared some secrets.

"All suggestions are welcome, Marge."

And, to my surprise, she offered several good ones. "Put a partition, perhaps a hanging fuchsia plant, perhaps a standing screen, to separate your cluttered desk from the rest of the office. Get a quiet dark brown frame for that beach picture—if you must have it—and above all, get rid of that ratty tapa-cloth wall hanging. It's so busy that it gives me a headache. I've been using it to hypnotize myself."

"I like your suggestions, Marge, except that you're being tough on my wall hanging. It's an old friend. I got it thirty years ago in Samoa."

"Old friends may feel more comfortable at home than the office."

I stared at her. She was so quick. Was I really talking to Marge?

Since I hoped to establish a confederacy or fusion of the two Marges, I was careful to stay on the positive side of each. If I antagonized "Me" in any way, she would simply take her revenge on Marge. So I took pains, for example, to tell Marge (I assumed "Me" heard everything) how much I enjoyed "Me's" insouciance, vitality, brashness. . . .

Over the next several months of therapy, I continued faithful to Marge. Sometimes she would try to tell me about Ruth Anne, the third personality, or slip into a trance and regress to an earlier age, but I refused to be seduced by any of these enticements. More than anything else, I resolved to be "present" with her, and I immediately called her back whenever she started to leave my presence by slipping away into another age or another role.

When I first began to work as a therapist, I naively believed that the past was fixed and knowable; that if I were perspicacious enough, I could discover that first false turn, that fateful trail that has led to a life gone wrong; and that I could act on this discovery to set things right again. In those days I would have deepened Marge's hypnotic state, regressed her in age, asked her to explore early traumas—for example, her father's sexual abuse—and urged her to experience and discharge all the attendant feelings, the fear, the arousal, the rage, the betrayal.

But over the years I've learned that the therapist's venture is not to engage the patient in a joint archeological dig. If any patients have ever been helped in that fashion, it wasn't because of the search and the finding of that false trail (a life never goes wrong because of a false trail; it goes wrong because the main trail is false). No, a therapist helps a patient not by sifting through the past but by being lovingly present with that person; by being trustworthy, interested; and by believing that their joint activity will ultimately be redemptive and healing. . . .

So I devoted myself to being present and faithful. We continued to ingest the other Marge. I mused aloud, "What would she have said in that situation? How would she have dressed or walked? Try it. Pretend you're her for a minute or two, Marge."

As the months passed, Marge grew plump at the other Marge's expense. Her face grew rounder, her bodice fuller. She looked better, dressed better; she sat up straight; she wore patterned stockings; she commented upon my scuffed shoes. . . .

And that other Marge? I wonder what's left of her now? A pair of empty spike heels? An enticing, bold glance that Marge has not yet dared to appropriate? A ghostly, Cheshire cat smile? Where is the actress who played Marge with such brilliance? I'm sure *she's* gone: that performance required great vi-

tal energy, and by now Marge and I have sucked all that juice out of her. Even though we continued our work together for many months after the hour "Me" appeared, and though Marge and I eventually stopped talking about her, I have never forgotten her: she flits in and out of my mind at unexpected times.

Before we began therapy, I had informed Marge that we could meet for a maximum of eighteen months because of my sabbatical plans. Now the time was up, our work at an end. Marge had changed: the panics occurred only rarely; the midnight phone calls were a thing of the past; she had begun to build a social life and had made two close friends. She had always been a talented photographer and now, for the first time in years, had picked up her camera and was once again enjoying this form of creative expression.

I felt pleased with our work but was not deluded into thinking that she had finished therapy, nor was I surprised, as our final session approached, to see a recrudescence of her old symptoms. She retreated to bed for entire weekends; she had long crying jags; suicide suddenly seemed appealing again. Just after our last visit, I received a sad letter from her containing these lines:

> I always imagined that you might write something about me. I wanted to leave an imprint on your life. I don't want to be "just another patient." I wanted to be "special." I want to be something, anything. I feel like nothing, no one. If I left an imprint on your life, maybe I would be someone, someone you wouldn't forget. I'd exist then.

Marge, please understand that though I've written a story about you, I do not do it to enable you to exist. You exist without my thinking or writing about you, just as I keep existing when you aren't thinking of me.

Yet this *is* an existence story—but one written for the other Marge, the one who no longer exists. I was willing to be her executioner, to sacrifice her for you. But I have not forgotten her: she avenged herself by burning her image into my memory.

# CHAPTER 5

# Mood Disorders

*Although they affect how we think, how we feel, and how our bodies regulate such basic processes as appetite and sleep, mood disorders are so-named because their predominant features are within the affective or emotional domain. Mood disorders are quite common, and they often occur with other disorders such as alcoholism. We would expect that we all have some sense of the strong positive and negative moods that lie at the heart of mood disorders because of the range of emotional experiences in our own lives. However, as the case material in this chapter demonstrates, the highs and lows of a mood disorder are profoundly different from the happiness and disappointment that we routinely experience.*

*Mood disorders are usually equated with depression, in which an individual often experiences depressed mood, loss of pleasure, reduced appetite and weight loss, and trouble with sleep. This is not inaccurate, but it overlooks other forms of mood disorder, such as dysthymia, a chronic form of depression lasting for two or more years without an episode of major depression (for a recent study see Klein, Schwartz, Rose, & Leader, 2000), and various bipolar disorders, in which an individual may experience not only the lows of depression but also euphoria and an expansiveness of mood.*

*The readings in this chapter include a case study of major depression, a novel conceptual analysis of depression from an evolutionary point of view, a case study of bipolar disorder, and an article on the role of mood disorders and stressful life events in suicide.*

## Reference

Klein, D. N., Schwartz, J. E., Rose, S., & Leader, J. B. (2000). Five-year course and outcome of dysthymic disorder: A prospective, naturalistic follow-up study. *American Journal of Psychiatry, 157,* 931–939.

# FROM *UNDERCURRENTS: A LIFE BENEATH THE SURFACE*

## Martha Manning

*In the introduction to the first reading in chapter 1 we summarized a study by Murray and Lopez (1996) that showed that mental disorders contribute substantially to the worldwide costs of all forms of disease. One of the remarkable findings in this study is that unipolar major depression is the mental disorder that contributes most to this statistic. In fact, compared to all other forms of disease, depression is the leading cause of disability in terms of the number of people who are affected (see Holden, 2000).*

*We seek to put a human face on these statistics by presenting excerpts from a book written in diary form by Martha Manning, who struggled with depression. Manning, a clinical psychologist and former professor of psychology at George Mason University, provides poignant details about her experiences with depression and about her successful treatment with electroconvulsive therapy (ECT). The entry for July 2, 1990, in which Manning describes a racquetball match with her husband, is particularly vivid as it captures common vegetative symptoms (weight loss, psychomotor retardation); the feelings of frustration, guilt, and anger that depression can engender; and the effects of depression on a marriage. Also salient in these excerpts is how Manning makes sense of her experiences with depression, how depression and its treatment are viewed in our society, and how small gestures can have profound effects—both good and bad—on an individual's suffering.*

## Reference

Holden, C. (2000). Global survey examines impact of depression. *Science, 288,* 39–40.

## Suggested Readings

Solomon, A. (1998, January 12). Anatomy of melancholy. *The New Yorker,* 46–61.
Styron, W. (1992). *Darkness visible: A memoir of madness.* New York: Vintage Books.

San Francisco: HarperCollins. (1994).

*June 26, 1990*

In the psychological literature, depression is often seen as a defense against sadness. But I'll take sadness any day. There is no contest. Sadness carries identification. You know where it's been and you know where it's headed. Depression carries no papers. It enters your country unannounced and uninvited. Its origins are unknown, but its destination always dead-ends in you.

*June 30, 1990*

I play a perverse game with myself: What wonderful thing could snap me out of this? I have sampled all the possibilities. Millions of dollars? No. The Nobel Prize? No. Another child? No. Peace on earth? No. No good news or good times. Nothing. And all I can think of is the cruelty of it all. And the incapacitating dread that this time I won't come out. This time it will never end.

*July 1, 1990*

When you're depressed, everyone has an opinion about what you should do. People seem to think that not only are you depressed, you are also stupid. They are generous to the point of suffocation with their advice. I wonder sometimes, if I had any other illness, whether people would be so free with their admonitions. Probably not. They would concede that what they know is vastly outweighed by what they don't know and keep their mouths shut. People hear the word *depression* and figure that since they've felt down or blue at some point in their lives, they are experts, which is like assuming that because you've had a chest cold, you are now qualified to treat lung cancer.

I keep a running list of advice in my head. I sort it into categories. The first involves those behaviors that shrinks nauseatingly call "nurturance." They include such things as going away for the weekend, buying myself expensive jewelry, getting a manicure, pedicure, haircut, facial, or massage. The next category addresses my various vices: quit Diet Coke, avoid junk food, take vitamins, get more sleep, get more exercise/get less exercise. In the self-improvement domain I am told to throw myself into my work/cut down on my work, see my therapist more frequently/quit my therapist/see the advice-giver's therapist. I am advised to take more medicine/less medicine/different medicine/ no medicine. I am told to pray, to meditate, to "journal," to think of people worse off than I ("You think you've got it bad?" therapy). I have been handed the cards of spiritual advisers, chiropractors, bioenergists, herbalists, and a woman who works with crystals.

In the old days, I could shake it all off and gently refuse it. But the humiliation I feel now about being so publicly vulnerable makes me just stand there and absorb it. All their "helpful" comments imply that if I'd only do ____, my problems would be solved. Like it's all within my grasp, able to be managed and mastered, if only I would try harder, longer, better. As I nod my head in polite and pathetic appreciation for their input, I scream inside, "Shut up. Shut up. Unless you've been lost in this particular section of hell yourself, don't you dare try to give me directions."

*July 2, 1990*

Brian and I have a racquetball court reserved for 9:00. These mornings are so hard. The dread of the day, even a low-key, low-demand day, is overwhelming. I try to shake it off with activity, but my usual morning vigor has evaporated and it takes hours to dispel the clouds inside my head. I don't want to play, but I keep hoping to get a hit of endorphins from the exercise. Automatically I step on the scale in the locker room. I can't believe the reading, step off, and try again. I've lost thirteen pounds in the past four weeks. I know my usual monster appetite has been tamer lately, but I'm still surprised by such a significant loss, especially without trying. From my moldy gym bag, I pull out the unwashed shirt and shorts I wore for the last game. They are wrinkled and smelly and I don't care.

I am clumsy on the court, like I'm wearing someone else's body. My timing is off and I miss the easiest of shots. This once-simple pleasure exceeds my grasp. Brian offers continual encouragement as I attempt to make contact with the ball. I know he is trying to be helpful, but his solicitude annoys the hell out of me. As I bend down to serve, he suggests, "Maybe it would help if you varied your serves a little."

His comment blinds me with anger. "When I want your fucking advice, I'll ask for it," I retort.

His face changes quickly from surprise, to hurt, to outright anger. "Bitch," he mutters, and stomps off the court.

Now it is my turn to be surprised. I wait several minutes and determine that he has no intention of returning.

We retreat to our respective locker rooms and meet in silence at the car. The drive home is eternal. He adopts an air of righteous indignation at being undeservingly blindsided. I am broiling but can't understand why. I attempt to cut the silence with my usual conversation starter in fights, "What's your problem?"

"I am sick of having to tiptoe around you all the time. I am trying to help you and all I get is your anger. I don't deserve it," he tells me.

I know he's right, but I still feel so angry at him. I start to cry, out of a combination of frustration and guilt. I realize that I am sick of his help, of continually feeling like a patient with my own husband. I tell him, "I don't want you to help me. I want you to be with me."

He looks at me like he has no comprehension of the difference between those two things.

"I don't need a therapist-in-residence," I say. "I need a husband."

"I'm not trying to be your therapist," he replies. "What do you want from me?"

"When I tell you how lousy I feel, I don't want to run down my medications with you, I don't want to have to answer your questions, to try to put it all into words. I don't want to listen to a pep talk, or a list of suggestions."

"Then what the hell do you want?" he demands.

"Just hold me. Sit with me. Put your arm around me. Listen as I struggle to tell you what it feels like, without thinking you have to tie it all up in some cohesive clinical bundle. I don't expect you to make this better. I know you can't. But I think you feel that if you just try hard enough, that you can." We drive a few blocks in silence.

He says, "Y'know, Marth, this is hard on me too. . . . I see you slipping and I am scared. . . . I'm losing you, and nothing I try brings you back."

In our first agreement of the morning, I admit, "I know."

We say nothing the rest of the way home. Lugging our gym bags into the house, we greet a sleepy-eyed Keara who has just gotten up. "Good game?" she asks brightly. The look on our faces belies the answer Brian gives her, "Yeah, love, it was just great. . . . "

### September 3, 1990

Today is the last day of summer. What a time. What a long lonely time. I never knew the days could stretch out so endlessly. Stretch so far I think they'll break, but they only heave and sag. The weight of them bears down on me mercilessly. I wake after only two hours' sleep, into another day of dread. Dread with no name or face. Nothing to fight with my body or wits. Just a gnawing gripping fear. So hard and heavy. I can't breathe. I can't swallow.

The emptiness of the depression turns to grief, then to numbness and back again. My world is filled with underwater voices, people, lists of things to do. They gurgle and dart in and out of my vision and reach. But they are so fast and slippery that I can never keep up. Every inch of me aches. I can't believe that a person can hurt this bad and still breathe. All escapes are illusory—distractions, sleep, drugs, doctors, answers, hope. . . .

### September 6, 1990

I want to die. I can't believe I feel like this. But it's the strongest feeling I know right now, stronger than hope, or faith, or even love. The aching relentlessness of this depression is becoming unbearable. The thoughts of suicide are becoming intrusive. It's not that I want to die. It's that I'm not sure I can live like this anymore.

I was always taught that suicide is a hostile act, suggesting anger at the self or at others. I have certainly seen cases in which this was true. Suicide was a final retribution, the ultimate "last word" in an ongoing argument. But I think that explanation excludes the most important factor—suicide is an end to the pain, the agony of despair, the slow slide into disaster, so private, but as devastating as any other "act of God." I don't want to die because I hate myself. I want to die because, on some level, I love myself enough to have compassion for this suffering and to want to see it end. Like the spy with the cyanide capsule tucked in a secret pocket, I comfort myself with the thought that if this ordeal gets beyond bearing, there is a release from it all. . . .

### September 8, 1990

With our combined vacations, I haven't seen Kay in almost a month. My deterioration is obvious to her. She tells me that I need "to consider ECT."

"ECT?" my mind screams. "Electroconvulsive therapy? Shock therapy?" I flash to scenes of *One Flew Over the Cuckoo's Nest,* with McMurphy and the Chief jolted with electroshock, their bodies flailing with each jolt.

She emphasizes the severity of this melancholic depression and reminds me that ECT has by far the highest success rate in this area. I feel like she has just told me I'm a terminal case. A lost cause.

She gives me literature to read about it. She reassures me that she is not giving up on the psychotherapy, but that she believes my suffering is mostly biological and has to be addressed. "Just think about getting a consultation," she encourages.

I nod, but I have absolutely no intention of doing so. I counter her concerns with a mental list of my admittedly dubious accomplishments. I still work. I still drive. I make my daughter's lunch. I pick her up from school. I answer the phone. How bad can I be?

As if sensing my silent resistance, she says, "If it was just a matter of personal strength and determi-

nation, you'd be fine. But it's not. You have to think of this as a serious illness. One that is potentially life-threatening."

When I get to the car, my hands tremble as I skim the pages of the literature she's given me. One is a recent National Institute of Mental Health consensus report that is highly favorable toward ECT for use in depressions such as mine. The side effects are scary, particularly the confusion and memory loss. Another article cites a study in which a majority of ECT patients reported that it was no more distressing than "a dental procedure." Always the empiricist, I wonder what choices were offered to the participants. "Was ECT more like having your eyes plucked out by vultures, or undergoing a simple dental procedure?"

When I tell Brian, he looks similarly horrified. "There must be other things that can be tried," he protests.

"She said she thinks I'm past the point where any medicine is going to pull me out. The ECT is not a 'cure' for depression, but somehow it's supposed to 'reset the clock,' " I tell him, trying to remember all the things Kay told me. "She said that you can call her or make an appointment to talk about it."

"Let's wait and see what Lew says when he gets back from vacation next week," Brian offers. "Maybe there is some other medicine. . . . Some other chance. . . . "

### October 16, 1990

I am still in disbelief that I am here. The night is eternal, interrupted every fifteen minutes by a nurse doing "checks" with an annoying flashlight. But even without the interruptions, I would not be sleeping. I take a walk around the unit at 2:00 A.M. The fluorescent lights in the hall and nurses' station give an eerie cast to the place. Many people are already up, silently walking the halls in bathrobes and pajamas. We look like ghosts, lost souls inhabiting the shells of our former selves, pacing and counting out the hours till daylight.

In the middle of the night I get a roommate. She is still asleep. I know nothing about her except that she is a cheerleader, because her uniform is the only thing hanging in her closet. Being a depressed cheerleader must be as tough as being a depressed therapist. . . .

My first ECT is scheduled for tomorrow morning. I am frightened because it sets me on a course from which I cannot turn back. More than losing my memory, I am terrified that I will lose the last remnants of myself.

Immediately after breakfast, I am summoned by loudspeaker to psychodrama group. It is 8:30. Most of us are fighting off a combination of too little sleep and too much medication. Now we are supposed to express our innermost feelings and conflicts through drama. Marie, the psychodrama therapist, is loose and warm. She wears cowboy boots, and on that basis I decide that I like her. However, I have a perverse desire to say that I will participate in this stuff when she shows me hard data on its efficacy in the treatment of severe depression. But I really want the "unaccompanied" privilege, and anyway, I'm too tired to make trouble. . . .

It is rumbling and pouring down rain, echoing the mood on the unit. There is a kind of moral imperative on psychiatric units about keeping people occupied. We are divided into two groups. They call them Group 1 and Group 2, but just like in first grade, when you knew that the Red group were better readers than the Blue group, it doesn't take a Ph.D. to figure out how people are assigned. I am in the "high functioning" group, mostly depressed and manic-depressive people.

The next stop in the forced march is "support group," which is the worst so far. Two well-meaning nurses lead it and hand out the sappiest poems, which I'm sure are supposed to be inspirational. We are asked to reflect on them and then discuss them in small groups. It is like reading long greeting cards. The contrast between the mood of the group and the tone of the poems is totally wasted on the nurses, who are so perky and upbeat that I want to scream. . . .

Dr. Samuel arrives to discuss tomorrow's ECT. He leads me to a conference room and bends over the lock, fiddling with his keys. I remember all the times patients waited at locked doors while I fumbled to open them. It is strange, now, to be on the other side of the keys. . . .

Dr. Samuel explains ECT one more time before I give my written consent. Tomorrow morning I will be awakened at 5:00 A.M. for a shot of atropine, used to dry secretions before many hospital procedures. I will change into a hospital gown and be wheeled down to a recovery room, where the treatments are administered. I will be attached to monitors that will register the activity of my heart and my brain. A band will be fastened around my head. Because I am having unilateral ECT, several electrodes will be placed over the temporal region of my nondominant hemisphere. An oxygen mask will be placed over my nose and mouth. Through an IV, I will receive succinylcholine, which will immobilize me to prevent the breakage of bones, and methohexital, a short-acting anesthetic. Between 80 and 170 volts will be administered for between one-half and one second, inducing a grand mal seizure that will last for thirty to sixty-five seconds. I will awaken approximately fifteen to thirty minutes later. He warns that I may have a headache, confusion, and memory loss following the treatment.

I listen to this with the cool demeanor of a fellow professional. He asks if I have any questions and I tell him calmly that between the reading material he provided and our discussions, I feel prepared. However, on the inside I am screaming, "HOW DO I KNOW YOU'RE NOT GOING TO FRY MY BRAINS? WHAT IF THE MACHINE SHORT-CIRCUITS? WHAT IF YOUR HAND SLIPS AND YOU PUSH THE DIAL TOO FAR? WHAT IF I TOTALLY LOSE MY MEMORY? WHAT IF I DIE?" I conclude that he probably has no answers to these questions, so I spare him the hysteria. He hands me the forms to sign. My hand shakes as I take the pen. I talk to myself in my calmest, cut-the-bullshit voice. "The bottom line," I say to myself, "is that my life has already almost slipped away from me. I have two choices: I can end it or I can fight like hell to save it."

I write my name slowly and he signs as a witness. I'm scared right down to my shoes and wonder how I'll get through the night. He anticipates my concerns and offers a mild sedative to help me sleep. I tell him that over the past year we have tried every sedative, hypnotic, and tranquilizer known to medicine in doses that would knock out an Amazon for a week. None keeps me asleep for more than two hours. He gently reminds me that even two hours would be a vast improvement over what I'm getting now.

Brian and Keara come for their first visit. I cannot hold them enough. Keara surveys the unit and with her typical candor says, "Boy, Mom, I really feel sorry for you. I'd hate this place." She is fascinated with my roommate, Jennifer, whom she recognizes as several years ahead of her in school. She asks what Jennifer is "in for."

I reply sanctimoniously, "Keara, you know I can't tell you that."

She responds with dead aim. "Mom, she's not your patient. She's your roommate."

"Oh yeah," I answer, appropriately chagrined, "I guess she's depressed."

Keara is incredulous and protests, "How could she be depressed? She's beautiful!" I look at this alien being who greets each morning with a song and know that I'll never explain it to her satisfaction. . . .

*October 17, 1990*

. . . The day staff replaces the night staff. My nurse comes with a wheelchair. She must notice how frightened I am because she pats my shoulder and tells me everything will be alright. This small act of kindness makes my eyes fill up. Words stick in my throat. She wheels me through the long dark halls in silence.

The recovery room is all bright lights and shiny surfaces. There are eight beds, all empty. A group of people are assembled around a stretcher, which I assume is meant for me. Dr. Samuel introduces me to the team—two nurses and an anesthesiologist. They help me onto the stretcher and for a moment the anxiety about the ECT is replaced by the anxiety of having my bare ass visible through the open back of my hospital gown. While they un-

cross wires and plug in machines, I take a horizontal inventory of the room. In anticipation of Halloween it is decorated with orange and black crepe paper. Black rubber spiders and little skeletons are suspended from the ceiling. What were these people thinking?

I am covered with hands. They take hold of different parts of me, staking out their territory. Voices tell me this is a dance done hundreds of times before, so I need not be afraid. But their casual confidence, their ease with my body, gives me no comfort. Just as I have lost so much of myself in the past year, now I lose more. I offer myself up to these strangers in exchange for the possibility of deliverance. Someone holds my hand and slips needles under my skin. Another slides down my gown and plants red Valentine hearts on my chest. Fingers anoint my temples with cool ointment and fasten a plastic crown tightly around my head. Wires connect me to machines that hum and beep, registering the peaks and valleys of my brain and my heart. They cover my mouth and nose with plastic and instruct me to breathe. For several horrible seconds, I am paralyzed before I lose consciousness. This is the nightmare that has haunted me since I was a child. I am on a beach, caught between a tidal wave and a towering seawall. In my terror, I am frozen. I cannot run, or move, or scream. The waves slam me down and take me with them. I am drowning.

I open my eyes, squinting at the glaring white lights. A nurse smiles down and welcomes me back. She reports that I had a "good seizure," which as far as I'm concerned belongs with other psychiatric oxymorons like "uncomplicated bereavement" and "drug holiday." My head hurts and my jaw is sore. A nurse from the psychiatric unit picks me up several minutes later and delivers the best news I've had in a while. I am excused from all group activities on the days I have ECT.

My father comes for his first visit. He does his typical challenge of the nurse's authority when she tries to rifle through the things he has brought. I get vicarious pleasure from watching the retired FBI agent resist a search. He brings all kinds of goodies, which he produces one at a time, searching my face for approval. He lends me his Walkman and a tape of John Philip Sousa marches. In another bag are ten legal pads, ten pens, and a box of chocolate-covered cherries. I can tell how uncomfortable he is visiting his daughter on a psychiatric unit. If my mother were here, she'd be doing all the talking and he'd be standing around looking restless.

He surveys my miserable room and asks, "Can you go for a walk?" When I nod, he mutters, "Let's get the hell out of here."

We walk around the perimeter of the hospital. It is a gorgeous autumn day, the color of fire. The cool air against my skin is the perfect antidote for the anesthesia still lingering in my system. My father asks endless questions, "So, are you alright? Are you sure you're warm enough? Are you getting enough to eat?" He asks all the questions except the ones he'd most like to ask, "Why are you so depressed?" and "What did we do wrong?"

The day is filled with visits from brothers, sisters, and friends. Flowers and cards pile up on the windowsill. Knowing my lust for reading, everyone comes bearing books. I try to thank them enthusiastically, hoping that someday I will have enough concentration to actually read them. . . .

### March 15, 1991

Telling people I've had ECT is a real conversation killer. People seem to be more forthright these days about discussing depression. Things have loosened up, even talking about medicine. Hell, the cashier in the grocery store told me yesterday that she's on Prozac. But ECT is in a different class. For months, in my conversations with most people, I have glossed over ECT's contribution to the end of my depression. But lately I've been thinking, "Damn it. I didn't rob a bank. I didn't kill anybody. I have nothing to be ashamed of." I've started telling people about the ECT. My admission is typically met with uncomfortable silences and abrupt shifts in topics.

An acquaintance at a party is outraged. "How could you let them do that to you?"

I bristle and answer, "I didn't let them do it to me. I asked them to do it."

"But why would you ever do that?" she insists.

"Because I was trying to save my life," I answer, hoping this will end the conversation.

Emboldened by a couple of bourbons, she challenges, "Aren't you being just a bit dramatic? Depression is hardly a life-and-death condition."

"You want to bet?" I answer. "I was as close to death as I ever want to get."

"Well, it's your life, I guess."

"Yes, you bitch," I think. "It is my life and what right do you have to judge me?" In the interests of sociability, I keep my mouth shut and wander off to a cluster of people I recognize.

I fume all evening. Damn her. Damn all of them. Nobody bats an eye when electricity is delivered to a stalled heart. There is no outcry. In fact, it's considered a miracle. A person passes from life to death to life again through the application of electric current to the heart. But try talking about the same thing with the brain, and it's no miracle. Suddenly, words like *torture* and *mind control* populate the descriptions.

I'm not about to stand on street corners urging people to try electroconvulsive treatment. I will never be the ECT postergirl. I am the first to admit the downside—confusion and memory loss. But damn it, it worked. I didn't want to have it. Who would? I didn't want to have a caesarean section either. I ended up with a terrible infection, a long scar, and a difficult recovery. But I got Keara. A beautiful healthy new life. It was no picnic. But I'd do it again in a heartbeat. . . .

### July 3, 1991

Each time the darkness comes I try to remind myself that it will not last. It will hurt me, but it won't kill me. We know why this is happening. I just have to wait it out until the stronger dose of medicine kicks in.

All the romantic nonsense about depression somehow making one into a creature of unique sensibilities is easy to agree with when I feel good. Then I'm sharper, superior for having weathered something terribly difficult, or just plain pleased at having narrowly gotten away with something once again—like the snow day after the night's homework I didn't do. All of it stands up to the light, but it's bullshit in the shadows. I don't care about unique sensibilities. All I care about is surviving. My goal in life is just to get through the days.

I pull myself together and take a walk down the park road, along the winding paths of red sand packed with gravel. There is a light breeze and the plentiful Queen Anne's lace dances with it. Not all orderly, like "everyone sway this way." No, they're all mixed up in each other—dancing in a tangle of green and white that makes me smile, remembering damp gymnasiums filled with tall girls and lesser-developed boys. We always found a way to let our bodies touch—at least as much as any nun would allow—and still keep approximate time to the music.

The greater pleasures are farther ahead. I climb the slope of the dunes and see the sun over the island and the water. The sky is streaked pink and purple and yellow. There is a dark outline of children playing in the distance. I find a bench. Two boys play catch in front of me and critique each other's throws. Couples climb the dunes. Men try to capture the moment on video. The sun is huge in its departure, commanding everyone's reverent attention. I watch as it leaves the horizon and follow its descent without moving, without blinking.

Once more, I acknowledge the possibility of God. In my own narcissistic and grandiose way, I imagine that God is trying to tell me that nature is bigger than I am, that beauty will eventually win out over shit. That the sun will come up and go down despite every lousy fucked-up thing that happens on this earth. It doesn't sniff out signs of impending trouble and evacuate like I do. It departs graciously, with color and light, intermingling with shadows that contribute their own muted beauty to the scene. It always leaves and it always returns. I need to burn that into my brain.

It is hard to leave the beach. I wait for a long time after sunset, till every bit of yellow is gone and the sky is pale pink, far off in the distance. Everything around me is quiet. People speak in hushed tones. Kites come down. Children are gathered up for bed. We allow the day to come to a close.

I am tremendously reassured by what I see. Somehow it helps me to believe that I will be alright. Maybe not great. But alright.

# VIEWING DEPRESSION AS TOOL FOR SURVIVAL

## Erica Goode

*Often when psychopathologists ask why depression happens, they restrict their
answers to those factors that might be modified (for example, neurochemistry or
the pessimistic interpretations people sometimes make for adverse life events) or to
those factors that might enable identification of individuals at risk for a disorder
(via genetics or analysis of family history). This is fitting, as these strategies hold
the greatest promise for isolating a disorder within the population, for clarifying its
proximal causes, and for generating viable treatments. A rather different perspective
on this same question emerges from the application of evolutionary principles to
the phenomena associated with depression. Scientists with an evolutionary orientation are likely to ask a different set of questions, such as How is it that people
have evolved to have this kind of capacity within their repertoire? What function
does depression serve? How does it help individuals adapt to their surroundings?
Does depression enhance genetic fitness in some way?*

*Erica Goode introduces recent thinking by Randolph Nesse and others on
questions such as these. A core idea is that depression is useful because it allows
individuals to conserve their resources, to disengage from actions unlikely to help
them attain some important goal, and to "take stock" before investing in some new
enterprise. As Nesse (2000, p. 17) notes, "just as anxiety inhibits dangerous
actions, depression inhibits futile efforts." When confronted with the grim realities
of depression (as depicted in the previous article), it is difficult to conceive of this
disorder as being somehow beneficial to the affected individual. On the other
hand, the question of how we evolved to have the capacity for depression begs to be
answered, and an evolutionary perspective might shed light on how some aspects
of depression could enable us to interact more effectively with our environment.*

## Reference

Nesse, R. M. (2000). Is depression an adaptation? *Archives of General Psychiatry, 57,* 14–20.

*The New York Times,* D7. (2000, February 1).

The case, Dr. Randolph M. Nesse said, does not fit tidily with the view that depression is only a matter of disordered brain chemicals:

A woman sought help from a psychiatric clinic because she was desperately depressed. She had dedicated five years to becoming a professional musician, despite her teachers' admonitions that she lacked the talent to succeed. She persisted, the woman said, because it was her mother's dream for her.

The psychiatrists at the clinic treated her with a variety of antidepressant medications and with psychotherapy. Nothing helped. But when, one day, the woman reached a decision, giving up music in favor of a career more suited to her abilities, her depression lifted.

Dr. Nesse, director of the Evolution and Human Adaptation program at the University of Michigan's Institute for Social Research, collects many such cases (the details are altered to protect patients' identities) because he believes they offer clues to a deeper understanding of depression.

In a recent article in the journal *Archives of General Psychiatry*, Dr. Nesse argued that while some forms of depression were clearly a result of genetic vulnerability and brain abnormality, others might have their roots in evolutionary history.

Darwinian theory holds that evolution selects for fitness: organisms with traits that promote survival or reproduction pass on their genes; organisms without such traits die off.

Depression may have developed, Dr. Nesse suggested, as a useful response to situations in which a desired goal is unattainable, or, as he has put it, "when one of life's paths peters out into the woods."

Locked in pursuit of the impossible, it makes sense for an animal to hunker down, take stock and figure out what to do next, Dr. Nesse said. In some cases, depression may help a person disengage from what has proved a hopeless effort; in other cases, it may protect the person from jumping ship too rashly, perhaps landing in even less hospitable seas.

"If I had to put my position in a nutshell," he said, "I'd say that mood exists to regulate invest-

ment strategies, so that we spend more time on things that work, and less time on things that don't."

In some respects, Dr. Nesse's conception echoes that of the psychoanalyst Dr. Emmy Gut. In a 1989 book *Productive and Unproductive Depression* (Basic Books), Dr. Gut described, among other cases, the experience of a biochemist, Albert, who frequently became depressed when a research strategy he was pursuing went nowhere. When the feelings of despair passed, he said, he saw "an entirely different way to tackle the problem, or else, I have recognized that the project was unrealistic."

In an interview, Dr. Gut, who lives in Sweden, said: "I think that depression is a normal mechanism. It's an attempt toward adaptation to a problem."

Dr. Nesse and Dr. Gut are not the first to ponder what evolutionary function depression—and its close relative, sadness or low mood—might serve. Thinkers from Schopenhauer to Freud have offered their views. Over the years, scientists have speculated variously that depression represents a plea for help, a strategy for manipulating others into providing resources, a signal of submission or yielding in conflict, or a way to conserve an organism's energy and resources in hard times.

Other investigators see no point in viewing depression as anything other than a malfunction of brain chemicals.

Dr. Nesse, however, is one of a growing number of scientists who over the past decade have systematically tried to bring a Darwinian perspective to medicine, hoping to learn more about how evolution has shaped humans' vulnerability to disease.

The approach is yielding a richer understanding of illness, and in particular, is helping scientists distinguish between diseases and medical conditions that developed as defenses against other more serious threats to survival.

Coughing, for example, is not a disease in itself but is the body's attempt to rid itself of bacteria in the lungs. Diarrhea and vomiting, though unpleasant, also serve as defenses, evolving as ways to evade danger, and thus to preserve fitness. And the ability to feel pain is essential for an organism's survival. "People who are born without any capacity to feel pain are usually dead by early adulthood," Dr. Nesse said.

Similarly, emotions like anxiety, fear and depression can be viewed as defensive strategies. Such defenses make sense, Dr. Nesse noted, because they have a low cost, especially when compared with their potential for protection. Vomiting, for instance, involves only the loss of a few hundred calories, but might save an animal's life if the substance ingested is poisonous. In the same way, being frightened and anxious when no threat exists is a small price to pay for the readiness to fight or flee when true danger looms. Yet these tactics also sometimes go awry, and illness results: chronic pain syndromes or panic attacks, for example.

Dr. Nesse believes the need to gain a deeper understanding of what purpose depression might serve is especially pressing at a time when the illness is so prevalent. Surveys indicate that 10 percent of Americans suffer from clinical depression; millions more endure a darkness that is not severe enough to earn a diagnosis but still interferes with their lives.

Researchers have also found that the rates of depression have increased in people born after World War II.

"The irony," Dr. Nesse said, "is that here we have finally created a society where not many people are hungry, we stay warm, we can take baths, we can travel and have relative freedom, and yet so many people are so miserable."

One thing that has changed over the eons is the increased pressure people feel to set ever larger goals. Ancestral hominids may have striven to pick enough berries to last for a week; modern humans want to look like supermodels, make a million dollars in the stock market or produce flawless children.

In shaping his ideas, Dr. Nesse has drawn upon the work of psychologists like Dr. Eric Klinger, at the University of Minnesota, who studies how people become committed to goals, and how they reach those goals or abandon them.

Dr. Klinger's studies indicate that depression plays a crucial role in the process of disengaging from a goal. To illustrate this, he uses the analogy of a soda machine. "You put your 75 cents into the machine and nothing happens," he said. "Then you go through a series of phases: your behavior gets more invigorated, you pay more attention to the signs, you pull on levers, you put in more change. If it still doesn't work you may start to rough up the machine. But at some point," he said, "you walk away, feeling down, feeling disappointed. It's a minor depression."

The fact that depression sets in after someone is prepared to suffer a failure or a loss, Dr. Klinger said, is important. "It slows you down, and makes you take your bearings," he said, "and at the same time it's very unpleasant, so that people are not going to be attracted to giving up quickly."

Dr. Nesse believes there are many varieties of depression, not all of them captured by official diagnostic categories. An evolutionary view, he and others hope, might encourage a broader, more nuanced search for treatments.

For instance, if depression is a defense, it might not always make sense to block its defensive properties with medication. When drugs are used to treat chronic diarrhea caused by the shigella bacteria, he noted, complications often result.

"For my money," said Dr. Paul Gilbert, a psychologist at the University of Derby in England, who has written on depression and evolution, "the key thing really is recognition that the environment is key to many of these disorders. And if you really want to affect depression, it's nice to have therapies that work, and it's nice to have drugs that work. But do we really want a society where we drive everyone mad and then give them drugs to get them out of it?"

# A Homeless Person with Bipolar Disorder and a History of Serious Self-Mutilation

Cheryl A. Green, M.D., Walter Knysz III, M.D., and Ming T. Tsuang, M.D., Ph.D.

*This is a riveting case involving a man diagnosed with bipolar disorder. Formerly known as manic depressive illness, bipolar disorder is a form of mood disorder marked by episodes of major depression (of the kind illustrated in the Manning excerpt) and, at other times, euphoric and expansive moods lasting for at least a week (unless the individual is hospitalized) that are often accompanied by grandiosity, racing thoughts and ideas, and poor judgment. The man in this case, Mr. A, has a long history of hospitalizations, suicide attempts, and very serious self-mutilation, one instance of which resulted in the amputation of his right arm.*

*This man's circumstances not only underscore the havoc wrought by bipolar disorder in an individual's life—some of his hospitalizations were 10 months in duration—but also the importance of that individual's social relationships in shaping the expression of symptoms. For example, we see that one hospitalization followed the ending of a therapeutic relationship and that other hospitalizations were precipitated by Mr. A's girlfriend's suggestion that he discontinue his medication. This case also exemplifies the concept of "stress generation," or the idea that deterioration in psychological functioning can be compromised by stressors brought on by earlier episodes of the disorder (see Hammen, 1991): The disorder generates stress, which increases the likelihood of further symptoms. For instance, Mr. A's third suicide attempt (jumping into a river) appears to be the result of an inability to cope with the amputation of his arm, which itself was a consequence of self-mutilation brought on (apparently) by a strained relationship between Mr. A and his mother. Finally, we note in this case a reliable link between Mr. A's decision not to take his medication and his subsequent deteriorations. This is not at all surprising, yet it does underscore how even the most effective medications are rendered impotent when individuals do not comply with their medication regimen—the availability of effective medications and their appropriate uses are two rather separate considerations (see Montgomery & Kasper, 1995).*

## References

Hammen, C. (1991). Generation of stress in the course of unipolar depression. *Journal of Abnormal Psychology, 100,* 555–561.

Montgomery, S. A., & Kasper, S. (1995). Comparison of compliance between serotonin reuptake inhibitors and tricyclic antidepressants: A meta-analysis. *International Clinical Psychopharmacology, 9* (Suppl. 4), 33–40.

## Suggested Readings

Andreasen, N. C. (1987). Creativity and mental illness: Prevalence rates in writers and their first-degree relatives. *American Journal of Psychiatry, 144,* 1288–1292.

Helfgott, G., with Tanskaya, A. (1997). *Love you to bits and pieces: Life with David Helfgott.* New York: Penguin.

Jamison, K. R. (1995). *An unquiet mind.* New York: Knopf.

*American Journal of Psychiatry, 157,* 1392–1397. (2000).

This case report is presented to highlight the importance of recognizing the warning signs and understanding the risk factors for clinically significant self-mutilation. By recognizing the warning signs and understanding the risk factors, clinicians will be better equipped to treat patients who have a recurrent history of serious self-mutilation.

## Case History

PSYCHIATRIC HISTORY  Mr. A, a 45-year-old, single, Caucasian man who was a patient at our day hospital, is a diagnostically complex patient with a long history of brittle bipolar disorder or, possibly, schizoaffective disorder, bipolar type. Over a period of 21 years, Mr. A has been hospitalized more than 20 times and has spent a total of more than 5 years of his life in psychiatric institutions. The vast majority of his admissions have been for manic episodes, often with psychotic features. He has had only one documented admission for depression, which, along with one other self-reported episode of depressive symptoms, was early in his clinical course.

What is notable about Mr. A's history is not necessarily his three suicide attempts but his two episodes of serious self-mutilation, which occurred many years apart and under very different circumstances. The psychiatric history that follows will give a broad overview of the course of his illness, with particular focus on his suicide attempts, episodes of serious self-mutilation, and the conditions at the time that these events took place.

Mr. A had his first contact with the mental health system at the age of 24, when he was hospitalized for his first manic episode. He was in the hospital for 1 month and given lithium and haloperidol at first; eventually he was given fluphenazine decanoate on discharge. He was soon readmitted to the state facility for 9 months under the diagnosis of schizoaffective disorder (type not documented), and during this hospitalization he was given trifluoperazine and thioridazine as well as fluphenazine decanoate.

During this second hospitalization, at the age of 25, while he was taking antipsychotic medication, he made his first suicide attempt. He had obtained a pass to attend the wedding of a woman whom he had always wanted to date, and several days after the ceremony he took an overdose (without medical sequelae) of No-Doze and ingested a pint of blackberry brandy. Mr. A stated that he was neither depressed nor manic at that time and that he had been medication compliant while in the hospital. In addition, he denied any recreational drug use before that episode.

Mr. A reported that he eloped from the state hospital and after about 2 months of noncompliance with medication and outpatient treatment became so depressed that he could barely move. It was during this time, at the age of 26, that he tried to commit suicide for the second time by lighting his bed on fire while he was in it. He quickly doused the flames, but, ironically, his apartment building burned down the next day after another tenant fell asleep while smoking. This precipitated Mr. A's first period of homelessness. Mr. A denied recreational drug use or psychotic symptoms before this suicide attempt.

In his 26th year, Mr. A was hospitalized for 1 month at yet another state hospital, this time with a diagnosis of simple schizophrenia, which was treated with trifluoperazine and thiothixene. He eloped from a transitional halfway house and moved to the southeastern United States to live with his mother and stepfather.

He remained out of treatment for about 3 months and was able to find employment as a night-shift janitor. He reported that during that time he was getting very little sleep, feeling "oppressed" by the intense heat, and that there was "no privacy" in his parents' home (manifested by his recollection of his mother walking in on him one day while he was masturbating in his room). Several days after that incident, he told his mother that he wanted to quit his job and move back to New England. Mr. A reported that his mother's response was unsympathetic and that she immediately left the house to go play cards with her friends. He identified her reaction as the precipitant to his most serious act of self-injury.

Mr. A reported that he walked into the kitchen and picked up a knife that his stepfather had been using to cut tomatoes. He took the knife into the bathroom, and, in his words, "I looked into the mirror and prayed for God to forgive me." He proceeded to inflict a number of wounds on himself, beginning with his right arm. He reported that the first cut severed his hand. A second slash, to his mid-forearm, was reportedly deep enough to leave the distal end of his arm hanging. A third cut to his upper right shoulder was more superficial. He made a fourth wound by stabbing himself in the bladder, then superficially lacerated his genitals and gouged his right leg. Mr. A does not recall feel-

ing any pain while inflicting these wounds. His stepfather, who was home at the time, found him in the bathroom and called paramedics. Mr. A was hospitalized on a medical unit for 3 months, and his right arm was subsequently amputated below the elbow. When asked about this later, Mr. A was unsure whether he was trying to kill himself at the time.

Mr. A's affective state during this episode is unclear because he has given conflicting reports about it. He said that he was not using recreational drugs and that he just remembered being angry with his mother for making that comment. He denied any gross psychotic symptoms, but it is unclear from the records how disorganized he was at the time of the self-injury. It seems reasonable to suspect the presence of psychotic symptoms at the time of the serious self-injury, however, given that the medication regimen during the hospitalization before and after his auto-amputation included antipsychotics.

Mr. A described his parents as unsupportive during that difficult time, stating that his mother saw him only once or twice during those 3 months. "My mom said that if I had just made one more paycheck I could have returned to New England. I wish that she would have told me that before."

Mr. A saw his stepfather only once during this hospitalization, but during that visit Mr. A told him that all he wanted to do was go to sleep and never wake up. His stepfather reportedly replied, "But I have already spent so much money on you." That was the last time they had any contact with each other. His stepfather died of a heart attack about a month later, while Mr. A was still recuperating from the amputation.

At age 27, Mr. A was transferred from the medical unit in the Southeast to a state hospital in New England. This was his only admission for depression (bipolar type, with psychotic features), and he was given amitriptyline in addition to thiothixine and chlorpromazine. Although compliant with his treatment regimen, while hospitalized he made his third suicide attempt by jumping into a river (without medical consequences). Mr. A could not identify a particular precipitant, but it appears from the record that he was having substantial difficulty adjusting to the loss of his arm. He was discharged after 10 months, but, at age 30, he was readmitted for a manic episode with psychotic features. He later eloped during a snowstorm and became homeless again.

After his elopement, he moved to a major city in New England. During the 7 subsequent years he was never hospitalized, received no psychiatric medication or psychotherapy, and spent only 2 of the 7 years homeless. He was employed for a great deal of the time. He described himself during that period as being "happy and aggressive" and credited marijuana use (about "five joints a day") for his success.

At age 37, several weeks after his promotion to supervisor at his place of work and after an argument with his new girlfriend, Mr. A had his first hospitalization in our facility, which is funded by the Massachusetts Department of Mental Health. This manic episode terminated the 7-year period without psychiatric intervention.

Between the ages of 37 and 45, Mr. A had seven hospitalizations in our institution. The precipitants, presentation, and course of each of these episodes have been remarkably similar. Most of the admissions were precipitated by the discontinuation of his psychiatric medications at the urging of his girlfriend, or, on one occasion, in the context of losing a therapist. He usually presented as floridly manic and quite psychotic by the time he was hospitalized. He usually required an average of 4 months on an inpatient unit to recuperate, but he had several admissions that lasted longer than 10 months.

Typically, about 10 days after stopping his mood stabilizers and neuroleptics, Mr. A would become extremely manic. He was often found sweeping the streets, directing neighborhood traffic, attempting to organize a rock concert on the sidewalk, or donating his belongings to the poor by throwing them out of the window. At other times the police would find him barricaded in his apartment, walking around nude and quoting scripture.

On initial evaluation, Mr. A would endorse a history of decreased sleep, racing thoughts, feeling "on top of the world," and being able to "do anything, even become President." The records describe Mr. A as having pressured speech, as well as being expansive, irritable, and grandiose. For example, he said he was "the Prince of Peace" and that he would win the Nobel Prize for an AIDS cure.

. . . Hospital stays were typically characterized by his requiring chemical restraints and locked-door seclusion for assaulting staff. With mood stabilizers, neuroleptics, and benzodiazepines on a regular basis, he would gradually become less aggressive and intrusive.

This progress was often interrupted by elopements, multiple 3-day notices that he would sign and then retract, and visits from his girlfriend, described as an untreated mentally ill woman who did not believe in psychiatric medication. She often encouraged Mr. A to discontinue his medications, and she assisted in his elopement from several hospitalizations. During these elopements, he would stop his medications and eventually return to the hospital floridly manic.

It is notable that since the onset of his illness, Mr. A was noncompliant with outpatient treatment and medications until the last several years, when his compliance moderately improved. The seven hospitalizations over this time period were all for manic episodes (the majority with psychotic features) and precipitated by discontinuation of medications, or, once, in the context of terminating with a therapist. Mr. A admitted to becoming attached to his therapists but denied ever stopping medications in response to a change in therapists. When challenged with information from the medical record, he refused to discuss it further, saying, "They must have got it wrong." The only clear reason Mr. A gave for stopping his medications was when he was encouraged to do so by his girlfriend. His medication regimen over the last 7 years has typically consisted of one to two mood stabilizers, an antipsychotic, and a long-acting benzodiazepine.

The most striking feature of Mr. A's course is that he had no reported episodes of self-injury from ages 29 to 44. This mutilation-free period ended, however, in October 1997, when he stuck a thumbtack in his right eyelid more than 50 times. The reported precipitant was that he had seen an attractive woman in the drugstore and felt guilty about his "lustful thoughts" about her. When asked about this incident, Mr. A replied, "The Bible says that if the eye offends you, then you must pluck it out." Of note, just 3 days before this event, Mr. A's psychiatrist of 2 years had terminated Mr. A's therapy with him because he was changing jobs. Mr. A reported being "a little manic" at this time. He denied recreational drug use and, interestingly, gave variable reports about whether he was having command hallucinations at the time to enucleate himself.

Notably, Mr. A's two episodes of serious self-injury were quite different. They were separated by a span of many years. His mood was unclear in the first episode and was at least hypomanic in the second. He denied command hallucinations with the attempted auto-amputation (although it is probable that he had at least some level of psychosis at that time), and he likely had psychotic symptoms (possible command hallucinations) when he stuck the thumbtack in his eyelid. During the first episode he was not taking his psychiatric medication and had been out of treatment for several months; the second time he was taking his mood stabilizer and antipsychotic medication and was participating in outpatient treatment. Both episodes were not influenced by recreational drugs, and both were in the context of perceived abandonment: by his mother for being unsupportive and after the loss of the therapist. He reported that both episodes were impulsive and that he has never had a desire for self-injury (other than the suicide attempts and a head-shaving episode) at any other time.

After the attempted self-enucleation, Mr. A was hospitalized for several months on an inpatient unit and then moved to the day hospital program at our facility, where his care was managed in conjunction with his new out-patient providers.

FAMILY PSYCHIATRIC HISTORY  Mr. A's second-oldest sister has a history of bipolar disorder and is the only family member, other than Mr. A, who has been diagnosed with a mental illness.

SOCIAL/DEVELOPMENTAL HISTORY  What we know about Mr. A comes primarily from the records of his hospitalizations and through his self-report. Because his family has never been more than peripherally involved in his care, there has been no way to corroborate many of the details about his developmental history that he has provided.

Mr. A was born in 1953, the youngest of six children. The three oldest children were single births; his mother's fourth pregnancy resulted in nonidentical triplets, of whom Mr. A was the last born. The other two triplets were girls, one of whom died several days after birth due to complications stemming from prematurity.

According to Mr. A, his biological father was a carpet layer who had numerous extramarital affairs. Mr. A's father left the family soon after he learned of the triplets' conception, and, although he continued to interact with the older children, he never had any contact with Mr. A, who was raised by his mother and maternal grandfather.

Mr. A's mother was a nurse and devout Catholic who was described as emotionally unavailable. Mr. A stated, "She told me that she loved me, but she never spent enough time with me because she was always playing cards." He felt closer to his grandfather, with whom he engaged in activities such as playing checkers, gardening, and going to church. He described his grandfather as "very peaceful and calm" and as his primary parental figure. The records indicate that Mr. A was an active, outgoing child who did well academically in Catholic grammar school. However, he was also described as an extremely quiet child with a violent temper. With much discomfort, Mr. A himself revealed that his school years were extremely difficult because he had very few friends and was frequently picked on because he was short.

His grandfather died when Mr. A was 10 years old, of what Mr. A described as "old age." Mr. A's mother soon married a divorced alcoholic who adopted both Mr. A and his triplet sister. When asked about the impact these events had on him,

Mr. A quickly became anxious and disorganized and terminated the interview.

The relationship between Mr. A and his stepfather was tumultuous. Mr. A recalled one incident when he was 10 years old when his stepfather literally dragged him out of a Boy Scout meeting by his hair because Mr. A had not done the dishes yet.

During his high school years, the fighting between Mr. A and his stepfather increased. His stepfather would loudly and frequently belittle Mr. A about his lack of masculinity and the ever-growing length of his hair. . . .

During his last 2 years in high school, Mr. A began to use marijuana and LSD on a regular basis. Although he would continue to use drugs intermittently throughout his life, he reported that he was sober at the time of his self-injurious behavior.

After graduation from high school, Mr. A attended a state university on the East Coast where he majored in biomedical research. After a year and a half year there, he reports that he discovered that his roommate, a bowling teammate and friend, was homosexual. This, coupled with the fact that his grades were suffering because he was working long hours at a fast-food restaurant, led Mr. A to transfer to a less rigorous college.

He did well academically at the new college, despite substantial marijuana use, frequently smoking up to 10 joints daily. He eventually graduated *summa cum laude* with a Bachelor of Science degree in business administration. He described these college years as the best in his life "because marijuana gave me a lot of friends."

After graduation from college, Mr. A worked for a year in a nursing home, where he met and soon became engaged to an environmental services co-worker. They ended up moving to a large city in New England, where he began to work long hours at a fast-food restaurant. It was soon after his promotion to supervisor in the restaurant and his breakup with his fiancée that he had the first of his 20 psychiatric admissions.

TREATMENT COURSE During his day hospitalization, Mr. A continued a regimen of risperidone, divalproex, clonazepam, and benztropine mesylate. Despite his medication compliance, he was hypomanic for substantial periods of time. This was manifested by intermittent pressured speech, irritability, grandiosity (planning to launch a singing career or run for lieutenant governor), and hyperreligiosity (with frequent references to, and literal interpretations of, Biblical passages regarding sex, sinning, guilt, and punishment). When discussing religious themes, family, sexuality, and his history of self-mutilation, Mr. A frequently became anxious and disorganized.

He was an active participant in our Life Skills Track, which is composed of groups that focus on interpersonal skills and reintegration into the community. Although he complied with the program, he also frequently requested discharge. The treatment team encouraged a slower pace of transition out of the day hospital, to which he reluctantly agreed. As part of his transition, he worked part-time in the hospital gift shop and attended a community drop-in program. His insight and judgment remained poor, as evidenced by his goal to move to Oregon and grow marijuana.

During this admission he had no episodes of self-injury, but he shaved his head shortly after the case conference. When questioned by staff, he admitted that he was concerned about his "lustful thoughts" and had been thinking of poking his eye out again. He agreed to a voluntary admission to a locked psychiatric unit in the area. . . .

## Discussion

Suicide, serious suicide attempts, parasuicidal/suicidal gestures, substance abuse, eating disorders, and self-mutilation are examples of self-injurious behavior with which clinicians may be confronted (1). All types of self-injurious behavior represent serious clinical problems, but a review of Mr. A's clinical history illustrates that this type of self-mutilating behavior stands in a class by itself. Our discussion here will focus primarily on self-mutilation because this topic is most relevant to Mr. A's case. Understanding this behavior, recognizing the warning signs, and managing ongoing risk is an important challenge to mental health professionals. . . .

It is generally agreed that psychosis is a major factor in severe self-mutilation (2). Risk factors for severe self-mutilation in psychotic individuals include a history of previous self-mutilation, a dramatic change in body appearance (i.e., a sudden change in the style of clothing or a newly shaved head), delusions (often of religious or sexual content), and preoccupation with religion and sexuality (2, 3, 4). Shortly after the case presentation, the day hospital staff recognized several of these risk factors in Mr. A, most notably that he suddenly shaved his head. When staff confronted him, Mr. A stated that he wanted to poke his eye out because he was again having lustful thoughts about a woman that he had seen in a drugstore.

Command auditory hallucinations have also been suggested as increasing the risk of self-multilating behavior. A patient who is suspicious of the voices will likely appear agitated and threatened, thereby alerting the treaters (3, 5). However, a patient who trusts the voices may appear relaxed and content and possibly go unnoticed (3, 5). "Those patients showing evidence of command hallucinations from a heavenly or other trusted source (or ideas of reference from the Bible) *may* be at *greater* risk of self-mutilation" (3). The highest risk patient, therefore, may be one who experiences command auditory hallucinations but who is calm in his or her response, indicating trust in the voices and relief at the impending sacrifice of a body part (3, 5).

Finally, anticipated or perceived object loss may also increase the risk of self-mutilation (2). This can be particularly relevant in training institutions, where medical student and resident turnover can occur at regular intervals. Clinicians, therefore, should be acutely aware of losses to the patient. This includes the rotation of residents in a training institution, a therapist's vacation or graduation, anniversaries, a change in housing, and other transitions. Mr. A had just lost his psychiatrist of 2 years before his self-enucleation attempt.

## Conclusions

The case presented illustrates several risk factors for future severe self-mutilation: 1) history of previous self-mutilation, as shown by Mr. A's right arm self-amputation, 2) psychosis, as shown by his propensity to become psychotic, 3) acute intoxication, as shown by Mr. A's history of substance abuse (marijuana and LSD), 4) dramatic change in body appearance, illustrated by Mr. A's shaving his head, 5) preoccupation with religion and sexuality, as shown by Mr. A's strong religious preoccupations, literal interpretations of the Bible, and profound feelings of guilt about his own sexuality, 6) command auditory hallucinations to harm oneself, as illustrated by variable reports of Mr. A having command auditory hallucinations to hurt his eye, and 7) anticipated or perceived object loss, as shown by Mr. A's act of self-injury after rejection by his mother and one episode of medication noncompliance during provider changes.

In patients with a history of psychosis and major self-mutilation, the priority is to treat the psychosis. Critical examination of the patient's differential diagnosis will aid in optimal long-term management. Mr. A's treatment team has struggled with this issue and has attempted to clarify Mr. A's diagnosis. Cross-sectionally, it is very clear that Mr. A does meet the criteria for bipolar disorder. In order to diagnose schizoaffective disorder, there needs to be evidence of psychosis in the absence of mood symptoms. However, it is uncertain whether Mr. A can be definitively diagnosed as having schizoaffective disorder because he is still hypomanic at baseline. There is no indication in the available records that Mr. A has ever approached an euthymic baseline. Mr. A is disorganized with a chronic course, so the possibility of schizoaffective disorder still needs to be ruled out.

The differential diagnosis should also include chronic psychosis not otherwise specified, substance-induced mood disorder, and borderline personality disorder. Furthermore, given Mr. A's self-mutilation in the context of prominent religiosity, the role of organicity (i.e., temporal lobe epilepsy) should be considered. Our literature search did not reveal evidence of any role for multiple or premature birth in bipolar illness or self-mutilation. The important treatment question is, Can all the clinical features be explained on the basis of one disorder?

When considering a psychopharmacological regimen to treat Mr. A, one must take into account both mood and psychotic symptoms in the context of his history of noncompliance. The record shows that no drug so far has brought Mr. A back to a normal thought process. Clozapine would serve to treat his psychosis, stabilize his mood, and ease his anxiety. This would reduce polypharmacy, which may enhance medication compliance, which has been a problem for him in the past. Furthermore, relationships are developed in the clozapine clinic, thereby providing a source of ongoing connection. Clozapine had been offered to Mr. A in the past, but he refused because of the required blood draws. . . .

It is important to ensure that Mr. A is in treatment with a clinician who can establish a long-term relationship with him. Therapy should focus on monitoring the psychosis, managing medications, teaching alternative ways of dealing with anxiety and destructive impulses, and dealing with practical life problems (2, 6). Attention should also be paid to recognizing early warning signs of decompensation (6), and there should be a strong relapse prevention component to his treatment protocol. Finally, the treatment team should be extremely careful when scheduling reductions in his medication. Monitoring for substance abuse and substance abuse counseling should also be integrated into the treatment plan (6).

Pastoral consultation should be considered, particularly for patients with strong religious preoccupations. The focus of these consultations should be to address the harsh religious views often held by these patients (6, 7). Family and community support should be enlisted to monitor and encourage treatment compliance (6, 7). Mr. A has suffered numerous losses and experienced a lack of familial and social support in his life, other than the early relationship with his grandfather. He has no contact with his sister, who recently moved and declined to provide him with her forwarding address. This lack of family structure could very well contribute to his disorganization and lack of compliance. Although Mr. A's family is estranged, attempts to enlist their support should be pursued with cautious optimism. Family involvement, a group home, and meaningful employment should be encouraged as sources of support and empowerment for Mr. A.

Bipolar disorder is arguably one of the most difficult of mental illnesses for intimate relationships. Families must endure episodic and recurrent mood swings and may experience the patient as unreliable and/or unavailable. Furthermore, episodes of mania or depression may threaten the patient's ability to maintain employment and thereby a family's income (8). The percentage of family members estranged from patients with bipolar disorder is unclear but not small. Families can benefit from acknowledgment of their struggles (8), psychoeducation (8) (including family-focused treatment approaches [9, 10]), and support groups, including the National Alliance for the Mentally Ill and the National Depressive and Manic Depressive Association (10).

In conclusion, this case highlights the importance of recognizing the warning signs and understanding the risk factors for significant self-mutilation. Such recognition and understanding equips clinicians for the treatment of patients with a history of serious self-mutilation.

## References

1. Hingorani M, Singh A, Williams H: Oedipism and ocular self-mutilation. Irish J Psychol Med 1995; 12:144–146.
2. Sweeny S, Zamecnik K: Predictors of self-mutilation in patients with schizophrenia. Am J Psychiatry 1981; 138:1086–1089.
3. Shore D: Self-mutilation and schizophrenia. Compr Psychiatry 1979; 20:384–387.
4. Favazza AR: Why patients mutilate themselves. Hosp Community Psychiatry 1989; 40:137–145.
5. Shore D, Anderson DJ, Cutler NR: Prediction of self-mutilation in hospitalized schizophrenics. Am J Psychiatry 1978; 135:1406–1407.

6. Kennedy BL, Feldmann TB: Self-inflicted eye injuries: case presentations and literature review. Hosp Community Psychiatry 1994; 45:470–474.
7. Tobias CT, Turns DM, Lippmann S, Pary R, Oropilla TB: Evaluation and management of self-mutilation. South Med J 1988; 81:1261–1263.
8. Moltz DA: Bipolar disorder and the family: an integrative model. Fam Process 1993; 32:409–423.
9. Milkowitz DJ, Frank E, George EL: New psychosocial treatments for the outpatient management of bipolar disorder. Psychopharmacol Bull 1996; 32:613–621.
10. Lefley HP: Book review, DJ Miklowitz, MJ Goldstein: Bipolar Disorder: A Family-Focused Treatment Approach. Am J Psychiatry 2000; 157:657–658.

# FROM *NIGHT FALLS FAST: UNDERSTANDING SUICIDE*

## Kay Redfield Jamison

*Most people with mood disorders do not commit suicide, and suicide is not only committed by people who are depressed. Nevertheless, the presence of depression dramatically increases the probability that an individual will commit suicide, and thus it is appropriate to take up the issue of suicide in the context of mood disorders.*

*National statistics on suicide are staggering: For every 2 people who die by homicide each year, 3 die as a result of suicide; about 30,000 people commit suicide each year; about 500,000 people receive treatment in emergency rooms for attempted suicide each year. Suicide takes the lives of more teens and young adults than cancer, heart disease, chronic lung disease, AIDS, birth defects, stroke, pneumonia, and influenza combined. The rate of suicide among adolescents and young adults nearly tripled between 1952 and 1996 (U.S. Public Health Service, 1999).*

*Our fourth reading is by Kay Redfield Jamison, a professor of psychiatry at Johns Hopkins School of Medicine, who has written eloquently about her own experiences with bipolar disorder and attempted suicide. In this excerpt from her book, she discusses recent research on the role of stressful life events in suicide, illustrating her arguments with powerful case material from individuals who committed suicide.*

## Reference

U.S. Public Health Service (1999). *The Surgeon General's call to action to prevent suicide.* Washington, DC.

## Suggested Readings

Brent, D. A., Kerr, M. M., Goldstein, C., & Bozigar, J. (1989). An outbreak of suicide and suicidal behavior in a high school. *Journal of the American Academy of Child and Adolescent Psychiatry, 28,* 918–924.

Brown, G. K., Beck, A. T., Steer, R. A., & Grisham, J. R. (2000). Risk factors for suicide in psychiatric outpatients: A 20-year prospective study. *Journal of Consulting and Clinical Psychology, 68,* 371–377.

Poussaint, A. F., & Alexander, A. (2000). *Lay my burden down: Unraveling suicide and the mental health crisis among African-Americans.* Boston: Beacon Press.

---

New York: Knopf. (1999).

It is tempting when looking at the life of anyone who has committed suicide to read into the decision to die a vastly complex web of reasons; and, of course, such complexity is warranted. No one illness or event causes suicide; and certainly no one knows all, or perhaps even most, of the motivations behind the killing of the self. But psychopathology is almost always there, and its deadliness is fierce. Love, success, and friendship are not always enough to counter the pain and destructiveness of severe mental illness. American artist Ralph Barton tried to explain this in his suicide note:

> Everyone who has known me and who hears of this will have a different hypothesis to offer to explain why I did it. Practically all of these hypotheses will be dramatic—and completely wrong. Any sane doctor knows that the reasons for suicide are invariably psychopathological. Difficulties in life merely precipitate the event—and the true suicide type manufactures his own difficulties. I have had few real difficulties. I have had, on the contrary, an exceptionally glamorous life—as lives go. And I have had more than my share of affection and appreciation. The most charming, intelligent, and important people I have known have liked me—and the list of my enemies is very flattering to me. I have always had excellent health. But, since my early childhood, I have suffered with a melancholia which, in the past five years, has begun to show definite symptoms of manic-depressive insanity. It has prevented my getting anything like the full value out of my talents, and, for the past three years, has made work a torture to do at all. It has made it impossible for me to enjoy the simple pleasures of life that seem to get other people through. I have run from wife to wife, from house to house, and from country to country, in a ridiculous effort to escape from myself. In doing so, I am very much afraid that I have spread a good deal of unhappiness among the people who have loved me.

Barton put on his pajamas and a silk dressing gown, got into bed, opened up his copy of *Gray's Anatomy* to an illustration of the human heart, and shot himself in the head.

Difficulties in life merely precipitate a suicide, wrote Barton; they do not cause it. There is much evidence to support his belief. But which difficulties are most precipitous? And why? The reversals of fortune, the deaths or divorces that may be blamed for a suicide are the same disasters and disappointments that attend us all. Yet few of us kill ourselves in response.

A. Alvarez describes better than anyone the highly personal interpretation given to events by those who are suicidal: "A suicide's excuses are mostly casual. At best they assuage the guilt of the survivors, soothe the tidy-minded and encourage the sociologists in their endless search for convincing categories and theories. They are like a trivial border incident which triggers off a major war. The real motives which impel a man to take his own life are elsewhere; they belong to the internal world, devious, contradictory, labyrinthine, and mostly out of sight. . . ."

There are many reasons to believe that stressful events might bring on or worsen a psychiatric illness. If the underlying psychiatric illness or biological predisposition is severe enough, such events may well play a role in suicide as well. We know that stress has a profound effect not only on the body's immune system and the production of powerful stress hormones but also on the sleep-wake cycle (which, in turn, plays a critical role in the pathophysiology of mania and depression). Tom Wehr and his colleagues at the National Institute of Mental Health, for instance, have demonstrated that psychological stress, certain medications and illnesses, and significant changes in light and temperature can interfere with circadian rhythms; these disturbances can, in turn, trigger mania or depression in genetically vulnerable individuals.

The relationship between the events of life, stress, and psychiatric illness is not a straightforward one, however. People, when manic or depressed, not only are influenced by the events in their lives, they also have a strong reciprocal influence on the world and people around them: they often alienate others with their anger, withdrawal, or violence; act in such ways as to cause divorce; or get themselves fired from work. What looks like the cause of a relapse may in fact be brought about by the illness itself. (There is, for example, no consistent strong relationship between unemployment and suicide. It is clear, however, that heavy drinking, mental illness, and personality disorders all contribute to unemployment.) The causal arrows move both ways, further compounded by the fact that individuals, when depressed or psychotic, react to stress in very different ways from those who are not mentally ill. Accordingly, many researchers have narrowed their study of life events to the so-called independent life events, such as a death or serious illness in a family. Unlike "events" such as divorce or financial problems, which are more likely to be affected by mental illness, these independent events are more genuinely random.

Most research finds a significant increase in life events prior to the onset of both manic and schizophrenic episodes, although the influence of psychosocial stress appears to be less important in later stages of manic-depressive illness (by which time the illness has often established a rhythm of its own). Patients with mood disorders seem, for the most part, to be more affected by stressful life events than those who suffer from schizophrenia. Psychologist Sherry Johnson and her colleagues at Brown University found that negative life events not only increase the rate of relapse in patients with manic-depression, they also increase the length of time it takes for patients to recover from their episodes of depression or mania. Without significant causes of stress, patients take about four months to recover. If, on the other hand, significant negative life events precede the relapse, it takes, on average, almost eleven months before they are well again. This nearly three-fold increase in recovery time is not only a highly painful time for patients and their families, it is also an extended period of vulnerability for suicide.

Sudden heartbreak or catastrophe is often known to have occurred before a suicide, but the nature and extent of the crisis it causes is unclear. Almost certainly, most of the danger of the event lies in its incendiary effect on the underlying mental condition. But the ultimate impact of psychological stress is different in each individual, depending on his or her own life experiences, ease

of access to a means of death, extent of hopelessness, and type and severity of the mental illness. Difficulties and conflicts in personal relationships or imminent threats of arrest or criminal prosecution tend to occur more frequently before the suicides of alcoholics and substance abusers, for instance, than before the suicides of individuals with depression. . . .

Gender also matters. In a large Finnish study, the partners of those who had killed themselves were asked what they thought was the reason for suicide. Severe mental illness was rated as the most important cause of suicide in the women, whereas medical illness was seen as a more important reason for suicide in the men. For both men and women, intense interpersonal discord was also perceived as an important contributing factor.

Differences in gender exist at a younger age as well. Young or adolescent boys, for instance, are much more likely than girls to have experienced a crisis event in the twenty-four hours prior to suicide. Particularly common are breakups with girlfriends, disciplinary or legal crises (such as suspension from school or a pending appearance in juvenile court), and humiliating events, such as public failure or rejection. David Shaffer, a child psychiatrist at Columbia University in New York, finds that many male adolescents who kill themselves are not only depressed but aggressive, quick-tempered, and impulsive; they also tend to drink heavily, use drugs, and have difficulties in their relationships with others. Most other clinicians and researchers agree. Depressive illnesses in conjunction with substance abuse are common in these adolescents, providing a combustible fusion when triggered by an adverse or painful event. The fact that most parents are unaware of depression and suicidal thinking in their adolescent children only makes the potential for disaster worse. Recent research shows that adolescents who suffer from depression are much more likely than those with no psychiatric illness to commit suicide when they reach adulthood.

A different but not uncommon profile of an adolescent suicide is that of a high-achieving, anxious, or depressed perfectionist. Setbacks or failures, either real or imagined, can sometimes precipitate suicide. It may be difficult to determine the extent of such a child's psychopathology and mental suffering, due to the tendency to try to appear normal, to please others, not to call attention to oneself. The real reasons for suicide remain fugitive.

One fifteen-year-old boy wrote this poem two years before he killed himself:

Once . . . he wrote a poem.
And he called it "Chops,"
Because that was the name of his dog, and
    that's what it was all about.
And the teacher gave him an "A"
And a gold star.
And his mother hung it on the kitchen door,
    and read it to all his aunts . . .

Once . . . he wrote another poem.
And he called it "Question Marked Innocence,"
Because that was the name of his grief, and
    that's what it was all about.
And the professor gave him an "A"
And a strange and steady look.
And his mother never hung it on the kitchen door
    because he never let her see it . . .

Once, at 3 a.m. . . . he tried another poem . . .
And he called it absolutely nothing, because that's
    what it was all about.
And he gave himself an "A"
And a slash on each damp wrist,
And hung it on the bathroom door because he
    couldn't reach the kitchen.

Psychological pain or stress alone—however great the loss or disappointment, however profound the shame or rejection—is rarely sufficient cause for suicide. Much of the decision to die is in the construing of events, and most minds, when healthy, do not construe any events as devastating enough to warrant suicide. Stress and pain are relative, highly subjective in their experiencing and evaluation. Indeed, some people thrive on stress and are at sea without it; chaos and emotional upheaval are a comfortable part of their psychological lives. Many individuals at a relatively high risk for suicide—for example, those with depression or manic-depressive illness—function extremely well

between episodes of their illness, even when in situations of great pressure, uncertainty, or repeated emotional or financial setbacks.

Depression shatters that capacity. When the mind's flexibility and ability to adapt are undermined by mental illness, alcohol or drug abuse, or other psychiatric disorders, its defenses are put in jeopardy. Much as a compromised immune system is vulnerable to opportunistic infection, so too a diseased brain is made assailable by the eventualities of life. The quickness and flexibility of a well mind, a belief or hope that things will eventually sort themselves out—these are the resources lost to a person when the brain is ill.

We know that the brain's inability to think fluently, reason clearly, or perceive the future with hope creates a defining constellation of depression. We also know that depression is at the heart of most suicides. Neuropsychologists and clinicians have found that people when depressed think more slowly, are more easily distracted, tire more quickly in cognitive tasks, and find their memory wanting. Depressed patients are more likely to recall negative experiences and failure, as well as to recall words with a depressive rather than a positive context. They are also more likely to underestimate their success on performance tasks.

Most of the impaired cognitive functioning in depression is also apparent in highly suicidal patients, including those who have recently tried to kill themselves. Suicidal patients, for example, are less able to generate possible solutions when presented with a series of problems to solve. Their thinking is more constricted and rigid, their perceived options narrow dangerously, and death is seen as the only alternative. Occasionally death is seen not just as the only alternative but as a highly seductive and romantic one. A nineteen-year-old college student illustrates this in drawings she gave to her psychologist, which portray suicide as a tranquil surcease of pain, a lulling alternative to the problems of life.

When suicidal patients undergo psychological testing, the experiences they describe tend to be negative, vague, and diffuse, and they see the future with futility and despair. When asked to think of things they are looking forward to, suicidal patients come up with far fewer than nonsuicidal people do. Often only a sense of responsibility to other family members or concerns about the effects of suicide on their children keep some people alive who otherwise have a strong desire to commit suicide.

In short, when people are suicidal, their thinking is paralyzed, their options appear spare or nonexistent, their mood is despairing, and hopelessness permeates their entire mental domain. The future cannot be separated from the present, and the present is painful beyond solace. "This is my last experiment," wrote a young chemist in his suicide note. "If there is any eternal torment worse than mine I'll have to be shown. . . . "

On October 29, 1995, twenty-year-old Dawn Renee Befano, a talented Maryland freelance journalist who had suffered from severe depression for years, killed herself. She left behind twenty-two journals, which are now in unpublished manuscript form. Excerpts from the journal written in the weeks leading up to her death show how unbearable her world had become, how her sense of her options had constricted them to nonexistence, and how an agonizing, suffusing hopelessness pervaded all reaches of her mind:

*October 9th.*

*I will not last another month feeling as I do now. I do not question that my eyes are brown, and I do not question my fate: I will die a suicide within the next month if relief does not come relatively quick. I am growing more and more tired, more and more desperate. I am dying. I know I am dying, and I know it will be by my own hand. . . .*

*I am so bone-tired and everyone around me is tired of my illness.*

*October 10th.*

*Outside the world is crisp and blue, refreshing fall weather, beautiful weather. I feel like hell, trapped in a black free-fall. The contrast between the two makes both seem more extreme.*

*In a strange way, however, I feel at peace, resigned to my fate. If I do not feel better by the end of November, I have decided to choose death over madness. I*

*know, one way or another, that this will all be over with by the end of next month. This will all be over and done with. . . .*

*I feel everything and all is pain. I do not want to live, but I must stick it out until my deadline.*

*October 11th.*

*I'm terrified. What'll it be, death or madness? In all honesty, living like this for another two weeks is difficult to imagine. I can only take so much of this punishment. When I die, all I leave behind are these journals. . . . I don't think I'll leave a suicide note, these journals will be more than adequate.*

*October 17th.*

*I can't think. All is muddled. I want to sink into sleep, to escape. I am so tired. To care about anything takes such a tremendous effort. The fog keeps rolling in.*

*I simply want the world to leave me alone, but the world slips in through the cracks and crannies. I cannot help that. The goddamn fog keeps rolling in.*

*Insane. This waiting is truly testing my endurance. I cannot handle it for much longer. I don't want to have to handle it. Nobody around me does either. Nobody.*

*October 20th.*

*Behold, I am a dry tree.—Isaiah 56:3*

*October 23rd.*

*I want to die. Today I feel even more vulnerable than usual. The pain is all-consuming, overwhelming. Last night I wanted to drown myself in the lake after everyone in the house had gone to sleep, but I managed to sleep through that impulse. When I awoke, the urgency had vanished. This morning, the urgency is back. I live in hell, day in and day out. Every day, I break down a little bit more. I am eroding, bit by bit, cell by cell, pearl by pearl. I am not getting any better. "Better" is alien to me, I cannot get there. They can try acupuncture, they can try ECT, they can try a frontal lobotomy, none of it will work. I am a hopeless case. I have lost my angel. I have lost my mind. The days are too long, too heavy; my bones are crushing under the weight of these days.*

*October 24th.*

*I am sick, so sick. Impossibly sick. . . .*

*October 28th.*

*So this is what the* Tibetan Book of the Dead *calls "bardo," the time between lives. I don't have any taste for life because I am between lives. A more optimistic way of putting things, instead of simply, I don't want to live. . . .*

*I will not go back into a hospital. I will simply take a walk into the water.*

*The pain has become excruciating, constant and endless. It exists beyond time, beyond reality, beyond endurance. Tonight I would take an overdose, but I don't want to be sick, I just want to be dead.*

The next morning Dawn woke early. She sat at the kitchen table, ate cold cereal, and worked on the crossword puzzle from the newspaper. After a short while, she left the kitchen and was not seen alive again.

The bed in her room was made neatly, according to her mother. There was "a stack of thirteen library books on the floor, and the contents of her backpack, including keys, cash, and her driver's license, stowed in a large envelope. Her great-grandmother's crystal rosary beads were spread out on the bed."

Her body was found months later, floating in a lake.

# CHAPTER 6

# Disorders of Childhood and Adolescence

*Disorders arising in childhood and adolescence catch our attention for several reasons. First, as difficult as it is to confront the unfortunate reality of psychopathology in adults, it is doubly difficult to do so when it involves children. Second, disorders diagnosable in childhood and adolescence cover a wide spectrum and include such major categories as mental retardation, learning disorders, communication disorders, pervasive developmental disorders, attention-deficit and disruptive behavior disorders, and tic disorders. Third, study and treatment of these disorders are complicated by the fact that the individual is developing and changing while also struggling with symptoms. We should not assume that many important changes do not occur among adults, but their rate and extent pale in comparison to the dynamic and complex changes happening in children. Fourth, perhaps because of these broad and sometimes rapid developmental changes, available treatment strategies and societal reactions to them differ from those for adult disorders. Thus, for example, the topic of whether it is appropriate to medicate children diagnosed with attention-deficit/hyperactivity disorder is, predictably, controversial. Finally, disorders arising early in life can provide an important clue about their origins in adulthood. Nicolson and Rapoport (1999), for example, discuss the basic similarity or continuity of childhood-onset and adult-onset forms of schizophrenia, and they suggest that the childhood form of the disorder is a result of greater genetic vulnerability. This helps to corroborate theories of adult schizophrenia and also hints at strategies for identifying people at risk for the disorder.*

## Reference

Nicolson, R., & Rapoport, J. L. (1999). Childhood-onset schizophrenia: Rare but worth studying. *Biological Psychiatry, 46,* 1418–1428.

# THE EARLY ORIGINS OF AUTISM

## Patricia M. Rodier

*Autism is an early childhood disorder that involves impairments in social interaction, communication deficits, preoccupations and restricted interests, and repetitive behaviors. Recent publications of autobiographies by individuals with autism (e.g., Grandin, 1995; Williams, 1994) provide a fascinating glimpse into their special psychological world.*

*Scientists are now discovering that autism may be genetic in origin and that the brain structures involved in producing the symptoms of autism are affected quite early in the course of fetal development. This first article, by the embryologist Patricia Rodier, is a case study in scientific discovery; it outlines how she and her colleagues made a key observation linking disordered brainstem development to the presence of symptoms associated with autism. The speculation that a mutation in the gene HOXA1 can lead to autism has received further support since the publication of this article (Ingram, Stodgell, Hyman, Figlewicz, Weitkamp, & Rodier, 2000). A key clue in this line of research is that thalidomide, a drug prescribed to pregnant women in the 1960s for morning sickness (and later shown to cause birth defects), dramatically elevated the likelihood of autism. Therefore, a promising step forward in understanding autism emerged from the careful scientific study of the tragic thalidomide-induced birth defects of four decades ago.*

## References

Grandin, T. (1995). *Thinking in pictures: And other reports from my life with autism.* New York: Doubleday.

Ingram, J. L., Stodgell, C. J., Hyman, S. L., Figlewicz, D. A., Weitkamp, L. R., & Rodier, P. M. (2000). Discovery of allelic variants of HOXA1 and HOXB1: Genetic susceptibility to autism and spectrum disorders. *Teratology, 62,* 393–405.

Williams, D. (1994). *Nobody nowhere: The extraordinary autobiography of an autistic.* New York: Avon Books.

## Suggested Reading

Szatmari, P., Jones, M. B., Zwaigenbaum, L., & MacLean, J. E. (1998). Genetics of autism: Overview and new directions. *Journal of Autism and Developmental Disorders, 28,* 351–368.

---

*Scientific American,* 56–63. (2000, February).

Autism has been mystifying scientists for more than half a century. The complex behavioral disorder encompasses a wide variety of symptoms, most of which usually appear before a child turns three. Children with autism are unable to interpret the emotional states of others, failing to recognize anger, sorrow or manipulative intent. Their language skills are often limited, and they find it difficult to initiate or sustain conversations. They also frequently exhibit an intense preoccupation with a single subject, activity or gesture.

These behaviors can be incredibly debilitating. How can you be included in a typical classroom if you can't be dissuaded from banging your head on your desk? How can you make friends if your overriding interest is in calendars? When children with autism also suffer from mental retardation—as most of them do—the prognosis is even worse. Intensive behavioral therapy improves the outcome for many patients, but their symptoms can make it impossible for them to live independently, even if they have normal IQs.

I became involved in the search for autism's causes relatively recently—and almost by accident. As an embryologist, I previously focused on various birth defects of the brain. In 1994 I attended a remarkable presentation at a scientific conference on research into birth defects. Two pediatric ophthalmologists, Marilyn T. Miller of the University of Illinois at Chicago and Kerstin Strömland of Göteborg University in Sweden, described a surprising outcome from a study investigating eye motility problems in victims of thalidomide, the morning-sickness drug that caused an epidemic of birth defects in the 1960s. The study's subjects were adults who had been exposed to the drug while still in the womb. After examining these people, Miller and Strömland made an observation that had somehow eluded previous researchers: about 5 percent of the thalidomide victims had autism, which is about 30 times higher than the rate among the general population.

When I heard these results, I felt a shock of recognition, a feeling so powerful that I actually became dizzy and began to hyperventilate. In the effort to identify autism's causes, researchers had long sought to pinpoint exactly when the disorder begins. Previous speculation had focused on late gestation or early postnatal life as the time of origin, but there was no evidence to back up either hypothesis. The connection with thalidomide suddenly threw a brilliant new light on the subject. It suggested that autism originates in the early weeks of pregnancy, when the embryo's brain and the rest of its nervous system are just beginning to develop. Indeed, Miller and Strömland's work convinced me that the mystery of autism could soon be solved.

## Genetic Factors

At least 16 of every 10,000 babies is born with autism or one of its related disorders. Since autism was first identified in 1943, scientists have made great strides in describing its symptoms. The biological basis for autism, however, has been elusive—an unfortunate circumstance, because such an understanding could enable researchers to identify the leading risk factors for autism and possibly to design new treatments for the condition.

By examining the inheritance of the disorder, researchers have shown that autism runs in families, though not in a clear-cut way. Siblings of people with autism have a 3 to 8 percent chance of being diagnosed with the same disorder. This is much greater than the 0.16 percent risk in the general population but much less than the 50 percent chance that would characterize a genetic disease caused by a single dominant mutation (in which one faulty gene inherited from one parent is sufficient to cause the disorder) or the 25 percent chance that would characterize a single recessive mutation (in which a copy of the faulty gene must be inherited from each parent). The results fit best with models in which variants of several genes contribute to the outcome. To complicate matters further, relatives of people with autism may fail to meet all the criteria for the disorder but still have some of its symptoms. Although these relatives may have some of the gene variants linked to autism—whatever they may be—for some reason the genetic factors are not fully expressed in these individuals.

Studies of twins in the U.K. confirm that autism has a heritable component but suggest that environmental influences play a role as well. For example, if genetic factors alone were involved, monozygotic (identical) twins, who share the same genes, should have a 100 percent chance of sharing the same diagnosis. Instead, when one twin has autism, the second twin has only a 60 percent chance of being diagnosed with the same disorder. That twin also has an 86 percent chance of having some of autism's symptoms. These figures indicate that other factors must modify the genetic predisposition to the disorder.

## The Embryology of Autism

Several environmental risk factors are already known. In utero exposure to rubella (German measles) or to birth defect–causing substances such as ethanol and valproic acid increases the chances that autism will develop. People with certain genetic diseases, such as phenylketonuria and tuberous sclerosis, also have a greater chance of developing autism. None of these factors, however, is present frequently enough to be responsible for many cases. Furthermore, most exposures to diseases or hazardous substances would be likely to affect both members of a pair of twins rather than just one. Some of the environmental influences must be more subtle than those identified so far. Researchers do not know how the multiple factors combine to make some people display symptoms while allowing others to escape them. This variation makes the search for autism's causes especially difficult.

In their 1994 study Miller and Strömland added another environmental contributor to autism: thalidomide exposure in utero. All their subjects—Swedish adults born in the late 1950s and early 1960s—exhibited some of the malformations for which thalidomide is infamous: stunted arms and legs, misshapen or missing ears and thumbs, and neurological dysfunctions of the eye and facial muscles. Because scientists know which organs of the embryo are developing at each stage of pregnancy, they can pinpoint the exact days when a malformation can be induced: the thumb is affected as early as day 22 after conception, the ears from days 20 to 33, and the arms and legs from days 25 to 35. What made the new study so exciting for me was Miller and Strömland's discovery that most of the thalidomide victims with autism had anomalies in the external part of their ears but no malformations of the arms or legs. This pattern indicated that the subjects had been injured very early in gestation—20 to 24 days after conception—before many women even know they are pregnant.

For embryologists, nothing tells us so much about *what* happened to an embryo as knowing *when* it happened. In the case of thalidomide-induced autism, the critical period is much earlier than many investigators would have guessed. Very few neurons form as early as the fourth week of gestation, and most are motor neurons of the cranial nerves, the ones that operate the muscles of the eyes, ears, face, jaw, throat and tongue. The cell bodies of these neurons are located in the brain stem, the region between the spinal cord and the rest of the brain. Because these motor neurons develop at the same time as the external ears, one might predict that the thalidomide victims with autism would also suffer from dysfunctions of the cranial nerves. Miller and Strömland confirmed this prediction—they found that all the subjects with autism had abnormalities of eye movement or facial expression, or both.

The next logical question was, "Are the cases of autism after thalidomide exposure similar to cases of unknown cause, or are they different?" Aside from their behavioral symptoms, people with autism have often been described not only as normal in appearance but as unusually attractive. They are certainly normal in stature, with normal-to-large heads. The few studies that have tested nonbehavioral features of people with autism, however, have concluded that there are indeed minor physical and neurological anomalies in many cases, and they are the same ones noted in thalidomide-induced autism. For example, minor malformations of the external ears—notably posterior rotation, in which the top of the ear is tilted backward more than 15 degrees—are more common in children with autism than in typically developing children, children with mental retardation or siblings of children with autism. Dysfunctions of eye movement had been associated with autism before the thalidomide study, and lack of facial expression is one of the behaviors used to diagnose the condition.

## The Neurobiology of Autism

Is it possible that all the symptoms of autism arise from changes in the function of the cranial nerves? Probably not. It is more likely that the nerve dysfunctions in people with autism reflect an early brain injury that not only affects the cranial nerves but also has secondary effects on later brain development. That is, the injury to the brain stem might somehow interfere with the proper development or wiring of other brain regions, including those involved in higher-level functions such as speech, resulting in the behavioral symptoms of autism. Or perhaps the ear malformations and cranial nerve dysfunctions are only side effects of an injury that we don't understand. Whatever the true situation may be, the anomalies in patients with autism of unknown cause were much the same as the anomalies in the thalidomide victims with autism. The conclusion was clear: many cases of autism, if not all, are initiated very early in gestation.

The region of the brain implicated by the thalidomide study—the brain stem—is one that has rarely been considered in studies of autism or in studies of other kinds of congenital brain damage, for that matter. On a simplistic level, neurobiologists associate the brain stem with the most basic functions: breathing, eating, balance, motor coordination and so forth. Many of the behaviors disturbed in autism, such as language, planning and interpretation of social cues, are believed to be controlled by higher-level regions of the brain, such as the cerebral cortex and the hippocampus in the forebrain.

Yet some symptoms common in autism—lack of facial expression, hypersensitivity to touch and sound, and sleep disturbances—do sound like ones more likely to originate in the brain regions associated with basic functions. Furthermore, the most consistently observed abnormality in the brains of people with autism is not a change in the forebrain but a reduction in the number of neurons in the cerebellum, a large processing center of the hindbrain that has long been known to have critical functions in the control of muscle movement.

One reason for scientists' confusion about the brain regions involved in autism may be that our assumptions about where functions are controlled are shaky. For example, the laboratory group led by Eric Courchesne of the University of California at San Diego has shown that parts of the cerebellum are activated during certain tasks requiring high-level cognitive processing. Another difficulty is that the symptoms of autism are so complex. If simpler behavioral abnormalities could be shown to be diagnostic of the disorder, researchers might have a better chance of identifying their source in the nervous system.

In 1995 our research team had the opportunity to follow up on the thalidomide study by examining the brain stem of a person with autism. The tissue samples came from the autopsy of a young woman who had suffered from autism of unknown cause; she had died in the 1970s, but fortunately the samples of her brain tissue had been preserved. When we examined the woman's brain stem, we were struck by the near absence of two structures: the facial nucleus, which controls the muscles of facial expression, and the superior olive, which is a relay station for auditory information. Both structures arise from the same segment of the embryo's neural tube, the organ that develops into the central nervous system. Counts of the facial neurons in the woman's brain showed only about 400 cells, whereas counts of facial neurons in a control brain showed 9,000.

Overall, the woman's brain was normal in size; in fact, it was slightly heavier than the average brain. I hypothesized that the brain stem was lacking only the specific neurons already identified— those in the facial nucleus and the superior olive—and to test that idea I decided to measure the distances between a number of neuroanatomical landmarks. I was surprised to discover that my hypothesis was absolutely wrong. Although the side-to-side measures were indeed normal, the front-to-back measures were astonishingly reduced in the brain stem of the woman with autism. It was as though a band of tissue had been cut out of the brain stem, and the two remaining pieces had been knit back together with no seam where the tissue was missing.

For the second time in my life, I felt a powerful shock of recognition. I heard a roaring in my ears, my vision dimmed, and I felt as though my head might explode. The shock was not generated by the unexpected result but by the realization that I had seen this pattern of shortening before, in a paper that showed pictures of abnormal mouse brains. When I retrieved the article from the stacks of papers on my office floor, I found that the correspondence between the brain I had been studying and the mouse brains described in the article was even more striking than I had remembered. Both cases exhibited shortening of the brain stem, a smaller-than-normal facial nucleus and the absence of a superior olive. Additional features of the mice were clearly related to other anomalies associated with autism: they had ear malformations and lacked one of the brain structures controlling eye movement.

What had altered the brains of these mice? It was not exposure to thalidomide or any of the other environmental factors associated with autism but the elimination of the function of a gene. These were transgenic "knockout" mice, engineered to lack the expression of the gene known as *Hoxa1* so that researchers could study the gene's role in early development. The obvious question was, "Could this be one of the genes involved in autism?"

The literature supported the idea that *Hoxa1* was an excellent candidate for autism research. The studies of knockout mice showed that *Hoxa1* plays a central role in development of the brain stem. Groups in Salt Lake City and London had studied different knockout strains with similar results.

They found that the gene is active in the brain stem when the first neurons are forming—the same period that Miller and Strömland had identified as the time when thalidomide caused autism. *Hoxa1* produces a type of protein called a transcription factor, which modulates the activity of other genes. What is more, *Hoxa1* is not active in any tissue after early embryogenesis. If a gene is active throughout life, as many are, altered function of that gene usually leads to problems that increase with age. A gene active only during development is a better candidate to explain a congenital disability like autism, which seems to be stable after childhood.

*Hoxa1* is what geneticists call a "highly conserved" gene, meaning that the sequence of nucleotides that make up its DNA has changed little over the course of evolution. We assume that this is a characteristic of genes that are critical to survival: they suffer mutations as other genes do, but most changes are likely to be fatal, so they are rarely passed on to subsequent generations. Although many other genes appear in several forms—for example, the genes that encode eye color or blood type—highly conserved genes are not commonly found in multiple versions (also known as polymorphic alleles, or allelic variants). The fact that no one had ever discovered a variant of *Hoxa1* in any mammalian species suggested that my colleagues and I might have trouble finding one in cases of autism. On the other hand, it seemed likely that if a variant allele could be found, it might well be one of the triggers for the development of the disorder.

## Zeroing in on *HOXA1*

The human version of the gene, labeled as *HOXA1*, resides on chromosome 7 and is relatively small. It contains just two protein-coding regions, or exons, along with regions that regulate the level of protein production or do nothing at all. Deviations from the normal sequence in any part of a gene can affect its performance, but the vast majority of disease-causing variations are in the protein-coding regions. Thus, we began the search for variant alleles by focusing on the exons of *HOXA1*. Using blood samples from people with autism and from subjects in a control group, we extracted the DNA and looked for deviations from the normal sequence of nucleotides.

The good news is that we have identified two variant alleles of *HOXA1*. One has a minor deviation in the sequence of one of the gene's exons, meaning that the protein encoded by the variant gene is slightly different from the protein encoded by the normal gene. We have studied this newly discovered allele in detail, measuring its prevalence among various groups of people to determine if it plays a role in causing autism. (The other variant allele is more difficult to investigate because it involves a change in the physical structure of the gene's DNA.) We found that the rate of the variant allele among people with autism was significantly higher than the rate among their family members who do not have the disorder and the rate among unrelated individuals without the disorder. The differences were much greater than would be expected by chance.

The bad news is that, just as the family studies had predicted, *HOXA1* is only one of many genes involved in the spectrum of autism disorders. Furthermore, the allele that we have studied in detail is variably expressed—its presence does not guarantee that autism will arise. Preliminary data indicate that the variant allele occurs in about 20 percent of the people who do not have autism and in about 40 percent of those who do. The allele approximately doubles the risk of developing the condition. But in about 60 percent of people with autism, the allele is not present, meaning that other genetic factors must be contributing to the disorder.

To pin down those factors, we must continue searching for other variants in *HOXA1*, because most genetic disorders result from many different deviant alleles of the same gene. Variations in other genes involved in early development may also predispose their carriers to autism. We have already discovered a variant allele of *HOXB1*, a gene on chromosome 17 that is derived from the same ancestral source as *HOXA1* and has similar functions in the development of the brain stem,

but its effect in autism appears to be minor. Other investigators are scrutinizing candidate regions on chromosome 15 and on another part of chromosome 7. Although researchers are focusing on alleles that increase the risk of autism, other alleles may decrease the risk. These could help explain the variable expression of the spectrum of autism-related disorders.

Even a minimal understanding of the genetic basis of autism would be of great value. For example, researchers could transfer the alleles associated with autism from humans to mice, engineering them to be genetically susceptible to the disorder. By exposing these mice to substances suspected of increasing the risk of autism, we would be able to study the interaction of environmental factors with genetic background and perhaps compile an expanded list of substances that women need to avoid during early pregnancy. What is more, by examining the development of these genetically engineered mice, we could learn more about the brain damage that underlies autism. If researchers can determine exactly what is wrong with the brains of people with autism, they may be able to suggest drug therapies or other treatments that could ameliorate the effects of the damage.

Devising a genetic test for autism—similar to the current tests for cystic fibrosis, sickle cell anemia and other diseases—would be a much more difficult task. Because so many genes appear to be involved in the disorder, one cannot accurately predict the odds of having a child with autism by simply testing for one or two variant alleles in the parents. Tests might be developed, however, for the siblings of people with autism, who often fear that their own children will inherit the disorder. Clinicians could look for a set of well-established genetic risk factors in both the family member with autism and the unaffected sibling. If the person with autism has several high-risk alleles, whereas the sibling does not, the sibling would at least be reassured that his or her offspring would not be subject to the known risks within his or her family.

Nothing will make the search for autism's causes simple. But every risk factor that we are able to identify takes away some of the mystery. More important, new data spawn new hypotheses. Just as the thalidomide results drew attention to the brain stem and to the *HOXA1* gene, new data from developmental genetics, behavioral studies, brain imaging and many other sources can be expected to produce more welcome shocks of recognition for investigators of autism. In time, their work may help alleviate the terrible suffering caused by the disorder.

# Clinical Case Conference: Asperger's Disorder

Fred R. Volkmar, M.D., Ami Klin, Ph.D., Robert T. Schultz, Ph.D., Emily Rubin, M.S., C.C.C.-S.L.P., and Richard Bronen, M.D.

*We now turn to a case involving an 11-year-old boy, Robert, who is diagnosed with Asperger's disorder. This disorder, like autism, is known as a pervasive developmental disorder, in that there is severe impairment in functioning that affects several aspects of a young child's development. A child with Asperger's disorder is similar to one with autism because both display difficulties in social interaction and restricted, repetitive patterns of interests and activities. However, in contrast to the child with autism, the child with Asperger's disorder does not demonstrate significant delays with language acquisition or cognitive development. This distinction can be quite dramatic; you will see that Robert, at age 11, has the verbal skills of a 17-year-old but the social skills of a 3-year-old. In addition to showing that deficits can be highly specific to a particular domain of functioning—in this case the social domain—this article is valuable because it presents actual psychological testing data of the kind used to assess children. It also shows how apparent misdiagnosis can occur (in this case an earlier diagnosis of an anxiety disorder with play therapy used for treatment) and how some symptoms (such as dysphoria) appear to follow from other conditions.*

*We present this particular case because of its similarity to autism. A common dilemma for clinicians and researchers is how to make a distinction between two similar sets of symptoms that can be differentiated reliably on some other characteristic. Or, in the vernacular, should we lump (say two disorders are really the same) or should we split (say that they are different)? This article argues for maintaining the distinction between Asperger's disorder and autism (and between these two diagnoses and pervasive developmental disorder not otherwise specified) in part because children in these categories may respond to different forms of psychotherapy. Nevertheless, the two disorders could share a common biological cause. Indeed, children receiving either diagnosis are not distinguished in Rodier's work on the genetics of this class of disorder (see the first article in this chapter).*

## Suggested Reading

Szatmari, P. (2000). The classification of autism, Asperger's syndrome, and pervasive developmental disorder. *Canadian Journal of Psychiatry*, 45, 731–738.

*American Journal of Psychiatry, 157*, 262–267. (2000).

Although only recently officially recognized in *DSM-IV*. Asperger's disorder has a history nearly as long as that of autism. During World War II, Hans Asperger, a Viennese physician, described a group of boys who had marked social problems but rather good language and cognitive skills (1). These "little professors" were rather pedantic and highly verbal and had unusual, all-encompassing, circumscribed interests that were so all-consuming as to interfere with the children's development in other areas. These boys had awkward motor skills; similar problems were noted in their fathers. Asperger's original explanation for the condition *autistichen Psychopathen*, or "autistic personality disorder" (sometimes less correctly translated as "autistic psychopathy"), suggested some points of similarity with the work of Kanner on infantile autism that had appeared 1 year earlier (2), although neither man was aware of the other's work. . . .

In this report, we present a description of a patient with a relatively classic presentation of Asperger's disorder. After the case presentation, we briefly summarize current controversies in diagnosis, the validity of the diagnostic concept, implications for treatment, and current research.

## Case Presentation

Robert, age 11 years, 8 months, was seen for evaluation at the request of his parents, who were concerned that despite his apparent academic skills, Robert was increasingly isolated in school. He was the younger of two children born to his parents, both physicians. They provided historical information, including copies of previous evaluations and school records. . . .

BACKGROUND INFORMATION   Robert was born after an essentially uncomplicated pregnancy, labor, and delivery. His parents had no concerns about Robert in his first years of life. He said his first words at 1 year and spoke in sentences by 16 months. Bladder and bowel control were achieved between the ages of 3 and 4, although nighttime bladder control was not achieved until almost age 6. Although his motor skills were somewhat awkward and clumsy, his parents reported that he was an early and avid reader who seemed to learn to read through his interest in videotapes; for example, he had read the Chronicles of Narnia in kindergarten.

Social problems were a major source of concern when Robert entered preschool at age 3; in his rather unstructured program, he had major difficulties with peer interaction. His parents sought a more structured setting, where he did somewhat better but was quickly seen as a rather eccentric child, in part because of his special interests. Robert was interested in, and quite knowledgeable about, astronomy by this time. His early interest in astronomy was quite intense, and he would pursue this interest at any opportunity; the interest intruded on essentially all aspects of his life. For example, in any conversation with peers, he inevitably brought the conversation or play around to stars and planets or time and its measurement. Interests since then have included computer games—their rules, programmers, and the companies that produce them.

Robert was enrolled in regular kindergarten and was evaluated for occupational therapy at age 5, when he was noted to have low motor tone. He was seen by a psychiatrist at age 8, when a diagnosis of anxiety disorder was given. Play therapy was undertaken for approximately 1 year and then discontinued when it appeared ineffective. Robert was not identified as having any special educational needs until age 10. Psychological testing was undertaken at age 10 years, 3 months because of various concerns (poor visual-motor skills, difficulties with handwriting, and social isolation). On the WISC-III (3), his verbal IQ was 145, his performance IQ was 119, and his full-scale IQ was 135; the difference between his verbal and nonverbal abilities was statistically significant and relatively unusual. Achievement testing revealed a range of abilities—e.g., his standard score on reading composites was 134, his writing score was 125, his math reasoning score was 159, and his score for written expression was 101. He had significant difficulties with tasks that required visual-motor coordination, including writing. His gross and fine motor problems were of sufficient concern to prompt occupational and physical therapy sessions; his classroom teacher started to make accommodations for him. In some areas he did very well, e.g., he was enrolled in a math program for gifted children.

MEDICAL AND FAMILY HISTORY   Apart from a history of recurrent croup and erythema multiforme or urticaria, Robert was in good general health. He had never had an EEG or an MRI; there was no question of a seizure disorder. His hearing was within normal limits. Robert's older brother had a history of some mild motor delays. There was a family history of depression and a history of social difficulties in members of the extended family. There was no family history of autism.

CURRENT ASSESSMENT   Robert, who had traveled some distance for the assessment, was seen over a period of several days. He was accompanied by his mother, who provided historical information as well as information on Robert's current functioning.

*Mental status examination.* Robert's social difficulties were readily apparent during the course of our contact. He responded to adults' greetings with appropriate, although very short, phrases and then turned to the side with a rather unmodulated smile, which he did not vary much for quite some time. Typically, he did not always respond to other people's facial expressions or gestures and often did not attend to social stimuli. Robert actively

avoided eye contact and seemed to look through people. Most of the time his emotional expressions—vocal as well as gestural—lacked variability and modulation. One notable exception involved some conversation about sadness and hurtful feelings, during which he briefly commented on his difficulty talking about sadness with others and whether it was worth the effort.

Although initially somewhat quiet and reserved, Robert became much more animated as he felt more comfortable with the examiners (A.K., E.R., and F.R.V.) and situation. He then began to describe his interest in astronomy and, more recently, in time . . . and engaged in a long monologue describing the history of the universe and the various epochs. . . . Having begun this topic, Robert pursued it with great intensity and vigor, despite repeated attempts by the examiner to redirect the discussion. This interest also appeared repeatedly in his schoolwork, e.g., in an autobiographical statement he had recently prepared (appendix 1).

Robert was able to describe two children he considered his friends, although these relationships appeared to be based almost exclusively on their common interest in computers. His language was quite sophisticated. There were no indications of disorganized thinking. Robert did not exhibit the vegetative signs of depression, although his mood was clearly and predominantly depressed. This seemed to be most evident when he discussed his feelings about school. He described himself as quite isolated and withdrawn in a novel group situation, although he mentioned that he was an excellent public speaker as long as the presentation was a formal one that he could rehearse and memorize in advance.

Robert was not overly preoccupied with extraneous stimuli, could focus on tasks with prompting, and did not exhibit unusual motor behaviors (e.g., self-stimulatory behaviors or tics).

*Psychological and speech-language assessments.* Robert's intellectual abilities were reassessed by means of the WISC-III (3). Scores on this test, and other measures, were consistent with those from previous testing. There was a significant and very unusual discrepancy between his verbal (150) and performance (116) IQs, indicating verbal intelligence skills in the "very superior" range and nonverbal performance skills in the "high average" range. Robert's verbal skills were all within the "very superior" range, with some ceiling (i.e., perfect) scores. In contrast, there was a great variability in his skills on the performance subtests, with IQs ranging from "average" to "superior." Performance IQs on a task involving the processing of social situations presented visually and by means of visual-spatial reconstruction were only within the "average" range, and thus represented relative deficits. . . .

From the assessment of his speech and communication skills, he was found to be functioning more than 3 standard deviations above the mean in relation to his same-aged peers in terms of his receptive and expressive vocabulary (standard scores of 146 and 141, respectively). Of greater interest, in some respects, was his rather formal and pedantic communication style, e.g., when asked to provide another word for "call," Robert's response was "beckon," and for the word "thin" he provided "dimensionally challenged." As indicated previously, the overall grammatical structure and linguistic form of Robert's spontaneous language was noted to be quite sophisticated. On a formal test of his metalinguistic competence, which assessed his overall flexibility of language use, he was also noted to perform above the average range when determining multiple meanings for ambiguous sentences and interpreting a variety of idiomatic expressions. Notable difficulties were observed when a task required the integration of nonverbal information (e.g., facial expressions, gestures, and body proximity) to interpret another's perspective, to determine appropriate communicative intents, and to identify the choice of relevant topics.

Tests of social cognition and attribution were administered to obtain standard observations of Robert's ability to interpret social situations. Given the strength of his verbal skills, his performance on an experimental task of social attribution was extremely limited. He failed to appreciate nonverbal cues and to make comments about intentions, social actions, feelings, or any other social elements of a story.

Robert's mother was the informant for the Vineland Adaptive Behavior Scales, expanded edition (4). These scales assess the patient's capacity to engage in the day-to-day activities necessary to take care of oneself and get along with others. It is important to note that for this instrument, the behaviors studied represented typical, rather than optimal, performance of the individual, i.e., scores were based on the degree to which the individual actually engaged in the behavior. In contrast to his strikingly good cognitive and linguistic abilities, Robert exhibited major deficits in adaptive skills. His overall score of 58 (mean = 100, SD = 15) on this instrument was over 5 standard deviations below that of his full-scale IQ. However, his profile was quite variable, so that, for example, in the communication domain his written language skills were at the level of 14 years, 6 months, whereas the level of his interpersonal abilities was 2 years, 7 months. . . .

## Discussion

This case exhibits many of the clinical features typically seen in Asperger's disorder. Consistent with the original description of Asperger's disorder (1), the patient exhibited a very severe social disability in the context of excellent overall cognitive and verbal abilities. Although he had the verbal abilities of a 17-year-old, his social skills were at a 3-year-old's level; this was reflected in his everyday interactions with peers, in which his one-sided and socially naive overtures were rapidly rejected. His verbal ability was the patient's area of strength in the face of considerable deficits in nonverbal areas; his all-encompassing interest in the stars, planets, and time appeared to actually interfere with the acquisition of skills in other areas and with his ability to interact with others in a more reciprocal fashion. In contrast to what usually occurs with autism, recognition of his difficulties emerged only when he entered preschool, and despite his precocity in some areas, his motor awkwardness was a disability for him.

Although the patient's diagnostic assignment could be considered relatively straightforward and illustrative of Asperger's disorder, the use of this diagnostic concept in clinical practice and research has been immersed in a number of controversies; the recent advent of consensual definitions in *DSM-IV* and *ICD-10* has so far failed to resolve a number of issues.

DIAGNOSTIC CONTROVERSY Diagnostic controversy stems from several sources. First, "Asperger's disorder" has been used in very different ways to denote different types of pervasive developmental disorder, e.g., some use the term to refer, essentially, to higher-functioning autism, others to adults with autism, still others to a subthreshold pervasive developmental disorder not otherwise specified, and yet others to a condition that differs in important ways from autism or pervasive developmental disorder not otherwise specified (5, 6–8). Yet another difficulty has arisen because individuals from diverse disciplines have also struggled with the problem of categorizing individuals with severe social disability who do not display classic autism; as a result, various terms have arisen to describe similar conditions, e.g., semantic-pragmatic processing disorder (9), right-hemisphere learning problems (10), nonverbal learning disability (11), and the like (reviewed by two of us elsewhere [5]). From the viewpoint of psychiatric taxonomy, the inclusion of Asperger's disorder is only important if the use of the concept can be supported on the basis of some external validating factor or factors, e.g., differential response to treatment or differences in family history, associated features, patterns of comorbidity, outcome, and the like. While one hopes that the body of work on Asperger's disorder since Wing's classic 1981 article (12) might offer final resolution of these issues, it is, unfortunately, not to be.

As we (5) and others (13) have pointed out, various problems have complicated interpretation of the available research on the validity of this diagnosis. These problems include circularity in definition (e.g., when the external validating variable is essentially included in the definition), marked differences in diagnostic practice, and various problems in study design and group description. *DSM-IV* has been criticized as being overly restrictive (14); with *DSM-IV*, autism takes precedence over Asperger's disorder and the criteria for the onset of autism are not well elaborated. In contrast, attempts by others to simply apply the diagnosis of Asperger's disorder to a socially disabled child with communicative speech at age 2 years seems to err in the opposite direction, i.e., by failing to be more specific about the precise differences between the two conditions, thus leading to overdiagnosis of Asperger's disorder (5). In our experience, Asperger's disorder can be differentiated from pervasive developmental disorder not otherwise specified, in part, because of the greater severity of the social dysfunction, and it can be distinguished from autism by differences in history and current presentation (e.g., the much greater verbosity of individuals with Asperger's disorder). It is certain that current approaches to diagnosis will be significantly improved by the time *DSM-V* appears.

VALIDITY OF THE DIAGNOSTIC CONCEPT Although current data are somewhat contradictory, several lines of evidence suggest important differences among Asperger's disorder, autism, and pervasive developmental disorder not otherwise specified. In a *DSM-IV* field trial, for example, patients with a clinical diagnosis of Asperger's disorder were found to differ in several ways from those with autism and those with pervasive developmental disorder not otherwise specified. The patients with Asperger's disorder had higher verbal performance IQs than those with autism and significantly greater social impairment than those with pervasive developmental disorder not otherwise specified (7, 15–17). A major problem in interpreting the available work has been the recurrent problem of circularity—that is, when the external validating factors may not necessarily be independent of the definition in the first place. However, several studies have now suggested differences in Asperger's disorder in several areas. First, verbal skills are often significantly greater than nonverbal ones—a pattern different from that seen in autism, where the reverse is often true (7, 15). Also, although there are apparently strong genetic associations in both conditions, in Asperger's disorder there appears to be a significantly greater incidence of the disorder in first-degree relatives (18). Finally, there are suggestions of different patterns of comorbidity (5, 19). These differences may have important implications for treatment and research, which lend interest to the condition.

Several studies have shown that patients with Asperger's disorder have significantly higher verbal IQs than performance IQs, which are often associated with a nonverbal learning disability (6). This is in contrast to autism that is not associated with mental retardation, in which, typically, nonverbal skills are more likely to be higher than or on par with verbal skills (20). Some preliminary results suggest high rates of social disability in family members (18), although the co-occurrence of Asperger's disorder and autism in the same family has been reported. Considerable interest in various case reports has centered on the issue of comorbidity in Asperger's disorder, suggesting higher levels of psychosis or violent behavior and many other conditions. Controlled studies are lacking, and in our experience, as in our patient's case, depression is the most common comorbid condition. Depression is particularly frequent in adolescents and young adults, and, although sometimes overlooked, it can be treated pharmacologically and with structured psychotherapy (5). . . .

IMPLICATIONS FOR TREATMENT Although social disabilities in Asperger's disorder and autistic disorder are defined in the same way, there may be important differences in treatment. In Asperger's disorder, the cognitive style of treatment is heavily biased toward verbal functioning. Although language skills are relatively preserved and serve as a lifeline for social interaction, there is often a significant discrepancy between the sophistication of linguistic form and structure and the social use of language. Unfortunately, educators (and others) may be misled by the individual's verbal abilities and may attribute poor social skills and poor performance on nonverbal tasks to negativism or

other volitional behaviors; as a result, these individuals may be viewed as behaviorally disordered or "socially emotionally maladjusted" and placed in classes for children with conduct disorders. As we have noted elsewhere (5), this approach might lead to the placement of a child with Asperger's disorder, a perfect victim, with perfect victimizers. As a result of the child's growing social isolation, often in the face of some desire for social contact, it is not surprising that the child may become depressed.

In terms of intervention, the better verbal abilities associated with Asperger's disorder suggest the utility of verbally mediated treatment programs not usually indicated in autism, e.g., very structured and problem-oriented psychotherapy and counseling may be indicated. Verbal skills can be used to teach problem-solving techniques that can be generalized from one situation to another. For example, a child can be taught a set of rules to use to identify contextual cues such as location, facial expressions, body proximity, and gestures to facilitate more appropriate comments, topic initiations, and social inferences. Similar verbal problem-solving techniques can be implemented to help the child cope with more novel or emotionally charged situations. The very explicit verbal approach can be used to help an individual identify and respond appropriately to difficult situations; although such an approach can initially have a rather rehearsed and canned quality, the ability to implement such routines can facilitate an individual's adaptation. Verbal cues can also be used to help children with Asperger's disorder complete activities with more challenging motor demands by breaking down each task into specific steps and by promoting verbal self-regulation. Finally, vocational planning should encompass the individual's strengths and deficits, e.g., presenting problems in visual-motor and visual-spatial integration may be important (21). Although Asperger himself was relatively optimistic about the outcome of Asperger's disorder, follow-up studies are limited. Nevertheless, the available information suggests that although social difficulties persist, many individuals are capable of adult self-sufficiency and many marry (5). Unfortunately, studies of the differential responses to treatment are still scarce, and the interpretation of outcome studies has been difficult as a result of nosological imprecision. Substantive empirical data would help clarify these issues. . . .

### Appendix I.

AUTOBIOGRAPHICAL STATEMENT OF A BOY WITH ASPERGER'S DISORDER[A]    My name is Robert Edwards. I am an intelligent, unsociable, but adaptable person. I would like to dispel any untrue rumors about me. I am not edible. I cannot fly. I cannot use telekinesis. My brain is not large enough to destroy the entire world when unfolded. I did not teach my long-haired guinea pig Chronos to eat everything in sight (that is the nature of the long-haired guinea pig)

[a]Patient's name has been changed.

# References

1. Asperger H: Die "autistichen Psychopathen" im Kindersalter. Archive fur Psychiatrie und Nervenkrankheiten 1944; 177:76–136.
2. Kanner L: Autistic disturbances of affective contact. Nerv Child 1943; 2:217–250.
3. Wechsler D: Wechsler Intelligence Scale for Children, 3rd ed. San Antonio, Tex, Psychological Corp (Harcourt), 1987.
4. Sparrow S, Balla D, Cicchetti D: Vineland Adaptive Behavior Scales. Circle Pines, Minn, American Guidance Service, 1984.
5. Klin A, Volkmar FR: Asperger syndrome, in Handbook of Autism and Pervasive Developmental Disorders, 2nd ed. Edited by Cohen DJ, Volkmar FR. New York, John Wiley & Sons, 1997, pp. 94–122.
6. Kerbeshian J, Burd L, Fisher W: Asperger's syndrome: to be or not to be? Br J Psychiatry 1990; 156:721–725.
7. Klin A, Volkmar FR, Sparrow SS, Cicchetti DV, Rourke BP: Validity and neuropsychological characterization of Asperger syndrome: convergence with nonverbal learning disabilities syndrome. J Child Psychol Psychiatry 1995; 36:1127–1140.
8. Szatmari P, Bartolucci G, Bremner R: Asperger's syndrome and autism: comparison of early history and outcome. Dev Med Child Neurol 1989; 31:709–720.
9. Bishop DV: Autism, Asperger's syndrome and semantic-pragmatic disorder: where are the boundaries? Br J Disord Commun 1989; 24:107–121.
10. Ellis HD, Ellis DM, Fraser W, Deb S: A preliminary study of right hemisphere cognitive deficits and impaired social judgments among young people with Asperger syndrome. Eur Child Adolesc Psychiatry 1994; 3:255–266.
11. Rourke BP: Nonverbal Learning Disabilities: The Syndrome and the Model. New York, Guilford, 1989.
12. Wing L: Asperger's syndrome: a clinical account. Psychol Med 1981; 11:115–129.
13. Ghaziuddin M, Tsai LY, Ghaziuddin N: Brief report: a comparison of the diagnostic criteria for Asperger syndrome. J Autism Dev Disord 1992; 22:643–649.
14. Miller JN, Ozonoff S: Did Asperger's cases have Asperger disorder? a research note. J Child Psychol Psychiatry 1997; 38:247–251.
15. Volkmar FR, Klin A, Siegel B, Szatmari P, Lord C, Campbell M, Freeman BJ, Cicchetti DV, Rutter M, Kline W, Buitelaar J, Hattab Y, Fombonne E, Fuentes J, Werry J, Stone W, Kerbeshian J, Hoshino Y, Bregman J, Loveland K, Szymanski L, Towbin K: Field trial for autistic disorder in DSM-IV. Am J Psychiatry 1994; 151:1361–1367.
16. Lincoln A, Courchesne E, Allen M, Hanson E, Ene M: Neurobiology of Asperger syndrome: seven case studies and quantitative magnetic resonance imaging findings, in Asperger Syndrome or High Functioning Autism? Edited by Schopler E, Mesibov GB, Kunc LJ. New York, Plenum, 1998, pp. 145–166.
17. Ozonoff S, Rogers SJ, Pennington BF: Asperger's syndrome: evidence of an empirical distinction from high-functioning autism. J Child Psychol Psychiatry 1991; 32:1107–1122.
18. Volkmar FR, Klin A, Pauls D: Nosological and genetic aspects of Asperger syndrome. J Autism Dev Disord 1998; 28:457–463.
19. Ghaziuddin M, Weidmer-Mikhail E, Ghaziuddin N: Comorbidity of Asperger syndrome: a preliminary report. J Intellect Disabil Res 1998; 42(part 4):279–283.
20. Sparrow S: Developmentally based assessments, in Handbook of Autism and Pervasive Developmental Disorder, 2nd ed. Edited by Cohen DJ, Volkmar FR. New York, John Wiley & Sons, 1997, pp. 411–447.
21. Klin A, Volkmar FR: Treatment and intervention guidelines for individuals with Asperger syndrome, in Asperger Syndrome. Edited by Klin A, Sparrow SS, Volkmar FR. New York, Guilford, 2000.

# ATTENTION-DEFICIT HYPERACTIVITY DISORDER

## Russell A. Barkley

*Over the past decade, attention-deficit/hyperactivity disorder (ADHD) has received a great deal of attention. This is due in part to the large number of children that appear to be diagnosed with this condition, but also to the controversy over its defining features, whether children should be medicated for this condition, and whether it extends into adulthood. Our third reading is an excellent synopsis of what is known about ADHD. Russell Barkley, a leading scholar in the field, provides a clear clinical picture of the core symptoms of ADHD—particularly the relative inability of children to have delayed reactions to events around them— and a discussion of likely causal factors. This article gives a particularly good sense of how scientists sift through many clues as they work toward refining a causal understanding of a disorder and how this understanding can sometimes inform clinical interventions. Thus, for example, if children with ADHD are discovered to have difficulties in inhibiting their behavior in particular situations, then strategic structuring of their environments can help them become less distractible and more able to focus their attention.*

### Suggested Readings

Faraone, S. V. (2000). Attention deficit hyperactivity disorder in adults: Implications for theories of diagnosis. *Current Directions in Psychological Science, 9,* 33–36.

Hallowell, E. M., & Ratey, J. J. (1995). *Driven to distraction: Recognizing and coping with attention deficit disorder from childhood through adulthood.* New York: Simon & Schuster.

Weiss, G., & Hechtman, L. T. (1993). *Hyperactive children grown up.* New York: Guilford.

*Scientific American,* 66–71. (1998, September).

As I watched five-year-old Keith in the waiting room of my office, I could see why his parents said he was having such a tough time in kindergarten. He hopped from chair to chair, swinging his arms and legs restlessly, and then began to fiddle with the light switches, turning the lights on and off again to everyone's annoyance—all the while talking nonstop. When his mother encouraged him to join a group of other children busy in the playroom, Keith butted into a game that was already in progress and took over, causing the other children to complain of his bossiness and drift away to other activities. Even when Keith had the toys to himself, he fidgeted aimlessly with them and seemed unable to entertain himself quietly. Once I examined him more fully, my initial suspicions were confirmed: Keith had attention-deficit hyperactivity disorder (ADHD).

Since the 1940s, psychiatrists have applied various labels to children who are hyperactive and inordinately inattentive and impulsive. Such youngsters have been considered to have "minimal brain dysfunction," "brain-injured child syndrome," "hyperkinetic reaction of childhood," "hyperactive child syndrome" and, most recently, "attention-deficit disorder." The frequent name changes reflect how uncertain researchers have been about the underlying causes of, and even the precise diagnostic criteria for, the disorder.

Within the past several years, however, those of us who study ADHD have begun to clarify its symptoms and causes and have found that it may have a genetic underpinning. Today's view of the basis of the condition is strikingly different from that of just a few years ago. We are finding that ADHD is not a disorder of attention per se, as had long been assumed. Rather it arises as a developmental failure in the brain circuitry that underlies inhibition and self-control. This loss of self-control in turn impairs other important brain functions crucial for maintaining attention, including the ability to defer immediate rewards for later, greater gain.

ADHD involves two sets of symptoms: inattention and a combination of hyperactive and impulsive behaviors. Most children are more active, distractible and impulsive than adults. And they are more inconsistent, affected by momentary events and dominated by objects in their immediate environment. The younger the children, the less able they are to be aware of time or to give priority to future events over more immediate wants. Such behaviors are signs of a problem, however, when children display them significantly more than their peers do.

Boys are at least three times as likely as girls to develop the disorder; indeed, some studies have found that boys with ADHD outnumber girls with the condition by nine to one, possibly because boys are genetically more prone to disorders of the nervous system. The behavior patterns that typify ADHD usually arise between the ages of three and five. Even so, the age of onset can *vary* widely: some children do not develop symptoms until late childhood or even early adolescence. Why their symptoms are delayed remains unclear.

Huge numbers of people are affected. Many studies estimate that between 2 and 9.5 percent of all school-age children worldwide have ADHD; researchers have identified it in every nation and culture they have studied. What is more, the condition, which was once thought to ease with age, can persist into adulthood. For example, roughly two thirds of 158 children with ADHD my colleagues and I evaluated in the 1970s still had the disorder in their twenties. And many of those who no longer fit the clinical description of ADHD were still having significant adjustment problems at work, in school or in other social settings.

To help children (and adults) with ADHD, psychiatrists and psychologists must better understand the causes of the disorder. Because researchers have traditionally viewed ADHD as a problem in the realm of attention, some have suggested that it stems from an inability of the brain to filter competing sensory inputs, such as sights and sounds. But recently scientists led by Joseph A. Sergeant of the University of Amsterdam have shown that children with ADHD do not have difficulty in that area; instead they cannot inhibit their impulsive motor responses to such input. Other researchers have found that children with ADHD are less capable of preparing motor responses in anticipation of events and are insensitive to feedback about errors made in those responses. For example, in a commonly used test of reaction time, children with ADHD are less able than other children to ready themselves to press one of several keys when they see a warning light. They also do not slow down after making mistakes in such tests in order to improve their accuracy.

## The Search for a Cause

No one knows the direct and immediate causes of the difficulties experienced by children with ADHD, although advances in neurological imaging techniques and genetics promise to clarify this issue over the next five years. Already they have yielded clues, albeit ones that do not yet fit together into a coherent picture.

Imaging studies over the past decade have indicated which brain regions might malfunction in patients with ADHD and thus account for the symptoms of the condition. That work suggests the involvement of the *prefrontal cortex,* part of the cerebellum, and at least two of the clusters of nerve cells deep in the brain that are collectively known as the *basal ganglia.* In a 1996 study F. Xavier Castellanos, Judith L. Rapoport and their colleagues at the National Institute of Mental Health found that the right prefrontal cortex and two basal ganglia called the caudate nucleus and the globus pallidus are significantly smaller than normal in children with ADHD. Earlier this year Castellanos's group found that the *vermis region* of the cerebellum is also smaller in ADHD children.

The imaging findings make sense because the brain areas that are reduced in size in children with ADHD are the very ones that regulate attention. The right prefrontal cortex, for example, is involved in "editing" one's behavior, resisting distractions and developing an awareness of self and time. The caudate nucleus and the globus pallidus help to switch off automatic responses to allow more careful deliberation by the cortex and to coordinate neurological input among various regions of the cortex. The exact role of the vermis region is unclear, but early studies suggest it may play a role in regulating motivation.

What causes these structures to shrink in the brains of those with ADHD? No one knows, but many studies have suggested that mutations in several genes that are normally very active in the prefrontal cortex and basal ganglia might play a role. Most researchers now believe that ADHD is a polygenic disorder—that is, that more than one gene contributes to it.

Early tips that faulty genetics underlie ADHD came from studies of the relatives of children with the disorder. For instance, the siblings of children with ADHD are between five and seven times more likely to develop the syndrome than children from unaffected families. And the children of a parent who has ADHD have up to a 50 percent chance of experiencing the same difficulties.

The most conclusive evidence that genetics can contribute to ADHD, however, comes from studies of twins. Jacquelyn J. Gillis, then at the University of Colorado, and her colleagues reported in 1992 that the ADHD risk of a child whose identical twin has the disorder is between 11 and 18 times greater than that of a nontwin sibling of a child with ADHD; between 55 and 92 percent of the identical twins of children with ADHD eventually develop the condition.

One of the largest twin studies of ADHD was conducted by Helene Gjone and Jon M. Sundet of the University of Oslo with Jim Stevenson of the University of Southampton in England. It involved 526 identical twins, who inherit exactly the same genes, and 389 fraternal twins, who are no more alike genetically than siblings born years apart. The team found that ADHD has a *heritability* approaching 80 percent, meaning that up to 80 percent of the differences in attention, hyperactivity and impulsivity between people with ADHD and those without the disorder can be explained by genetic factors.

Nongenetic factors that have been linked to ADHD include premature birth, maternal alcohol and tobacco use exposure to high levels of lead in early childhood and brain injuries—especially those that involve the prefrontal cortex. But even together, these factors can account for only between 20 and 30 percent of ADHD cases among boys; among girls, they account for an even smaller percentage. (Contrary to popular belief, neither dietary factors, such as the amount of sugar a child consumes, nor poor child-rearing methods have been consistently shown to contribute to ADHD.)

Which genes are defective? Perhaps those that dictate the way in which the brain [regulates] *dopamine,* one of the chemicals known as neurotransmitters that convey messages from one nerve cell, or neuron, to another. Dopamine is secreted by neurons in specific parts of the brain to inhibit or modulate the activity of other neurons, particularly those involved in emotion and movement. The movement disorders of Parkinson's disease, for example, are caused by the death of dopamine-secreting neurons in a region of the brain underneath the basal ganglia called the substantia nigra.

Some impressive studies specifically implicate genes that encode, or serve as the blueprint for, dopamine receptors and transporters; these genes are very active in the prefrontal cortex and basal ganglia. Dopamine receptors sit on the surface of certain neurons. Dopamine delivers its message to those neurons by binding to the receptors. Dopamine transporters protrude from neurons that secrete the neurotransmitter; they take up unused dopamine so that it can be used again. Mutations in the dopamine receptor gene can render receptors less sensitive to dopamine. Conversely, mutations in the dopamine transporter gene can yield overly effective transporters that scavenge secreted dopamine before it has a chance to bind to dopamine receptors on a neighboring neuron.

In 1995 Edwin H. Cook and his colleagues at the University of Chicago reported that children with ADHD were more likely than others to have a particular variation in the dopamine transporter gene DAT1. Similarly, in 1996 Gerald J. LaHoste of the University of California at Irvine and his co-workers found that a variant of the dopamine receptor gene D4 is more common among children with ADHD. But each of these studies involved 40 or 50 children—a relatively small number—so their findings are now being confirmed in larger studies.

## From Genes to Behavior

How do the brain-structure and genetic defects observed in children with ADHD lead to the characteristic behaviors of the disorder? Ultimately, they might be found to underlie impaired behavioral inhibition and self-control, which I have concluded are the central deficits in ADHD.

Self-control—or the capacity to inhibit or delay one's initial motor (and perhaps emotional) responses to an event—is a critical foundation for the performance of any task. As most children grow up, they gain the ability to engage in mental activities, known as *executive functions*, that help them deflect distractions, recall goals and take the steps needed to reach them. To achieve a goal in work or play, for instance, people need to be able to remember their aim (use hindsight), prompt themselves about what they need to do to reach that goal (use forethought), keep their emotions reined in and motivate themselves. Unless a person can inhibit interfering thoughts and impulses, none of these functions can be carried out successfully.

In the early years, the executive functions are performed externally: children might talk out loud to themselves while remembering a task or puzzling out a problem. As children mature, they internalize, or make private, such executive functions, which prevents others from knowing their thoughts. Children with ADHD, in contrast, seem to lack the restraint needed to inhibit the public performance of these executive functions.

The executive functions can be grouped into four mental activities. One is the operation of *working memory*—holding information in the mind while working on a task, even if the original stimulus that provided the information is gone. Such remembering is crucial to timeliness and goal-directed behavior: it provides the means for hindsight, forethought, preparation and the ability to imitate the complex, novel behavior of others—all of which are impaired in people with ADHD.

The internalization of self-directed speech is another executive function. Before the age of six, most children speak out loud to themselves frequently, reminding themselves how to perform a particular task or trying to cope with a problem, for example. ("Where did I put that book? Oh, I left it under the desk.") In elementary school, such *private speech* evolves into inaudible muttering; it usually disappears by age 10. Internalized, self-directed speech allows one to reflect to oneself, to follow rules and instructions, to use self-questioning as a form of problem solving and to construct "meta-rules," the basis for understanding the rules for using rules—all quickly and without tipping one's hand to others. Laura E. Berk and her colleagues at Illinois State University reported in 1991 that the internalization of self-directed speech is delayed in boys with ADHD.

A third executive mental function consists of controlling emotions, motivation and state of arousal. Such control helps individuals achieve goals by enabling them to delay or alter potentially distracting emotional reactions to a particular event and to generate private emotions and motivation. Those who rein in their immediate passions can also behave in more socially acceptable ways.

The final executive function, reconstitution, actually encompasses two separate processes: breaking down observed behaviors and combining the parts into new actions not previously learned from experience. The capacity for reconstitution gives humans a great degree of fluency, flexibility and creativity; it allows individuals to propel themselves toward a goal without having to learn all the needed steps by rote. It permits children as they mature to direct their behavior across increasingly longer intervals by combining behaviors into ever longer chains to attain a goal. Initial studies imply that children with ADHD are less capable of reconstitution than are other children.

I suggest that like self-directed speech, the other three executive functions become internalized during typical neural development in early childhood. Such privatization is essential for creating visual imagery and verbal thought. As children grow up, they develop the capacity to behave covertly, to mask some of their behaviors or feelings from others. Perhaps because of faulty genetics or embryonic development, children with ADHD have not attained this ability and therefore display too much public behavior and speech. It is my assertion that the inattention, hyperactivity and impulsivity of children with ADHD are caused by their failure to be guided by internal instructions and by their inability to curb their own inappropriate behaviors.

## Prescribing Self-Control

If, as I have outlined, ADHD is a failure of behavioral inhibition that delays the ability to privatize and execute the four executive mental functions I have described, the finding supports the theory that children with ADHD might be helped by a *more structured environment*. Greater structure can be an important complement to any drug therapy the children might receive. Currently children (and adults) with ADHD often receive drugs such as Ritalin that boost their capacity to inhibit and regulate impulsive behaviors. These drugs act by inhibiting the dopamine transporter, increasing the time that dopamine has to bind to its receptors on other neurons.

Such compounds (which, despite their inhibitory effects, are known as psychostimulants) have been found to improve the behavior of between 70 and 90 percent of children with ADHD older than five years. Children with ADHD who take such medication not only are less impulsive, restless and distractible but are also better able to hold important information in mind, to be more productive academically, and to have more internalized speech and better self-control. As a result, they tend to be liked better by other children and to experience less punishment for their actions, which improves their self-image.

My model suggests that in addition to psychostimulants—and perhaps antidepressants for some children—treatment for ADHD should include training parents and teachers in specific and more effective methods for managing the behavioral problems of children with the disorder. Such methods involve making the consequences of a child's actions more frequent and immediate and increasing the external use of prompts and cues about rules and time intervals. Parents and teachers must aid children with ADHD by anticipating events for them, breaking future tasks down into smaller and more immediate steps, and using artificial immediate rewards. All these steps serve to externalize time, rules and consequences as a replacement for the weak internal forms of information, rules and motivation of children with ADHD.

In some instances, the problems of ADHD children may be severe enough to warrant their placement in special education programs. Although such programs are not intended as a cure for the child's difficulties, they typically do provide a smaller, less competitive and more supportive environment in which the child can receive individual instruction. The hope is that once children learn techniques to overcome their deficits in self-control, they will be able to function outside such programs.

There is no cure for ADHD, but much more is now known about effectively coping with and managing this persistent and troubling developmental disorder. The day is not far off when genetic testing for ADHD may become available and more specialized medications may be designed to counter the specific genetic deficits of the children who suffer from it.

# CASE STUDY: BEHAVIORAL TREATMENT OF OBSESSIVE-COMPULSIVE DISORDER IN A BOY WITH COMORBID DISRUPTIVE BEHAVIOR PROBLEMS

## Elizabeth B. Owens, M.S., and John Piacentini, Ph.D.

*This article is the case study of an 8-year-old boy, Neil, who was diagnosed with ADHD at the age of 3. Complicating Neil's clinical picture was a cooccurring diagnosis of OCD (discussed in chapter 3). Neil had a compulsive need to touch his body in a symmetrical way and also to have others touch their bodies in a symmetrical way. Thus, if he touched his right leg, he would have to "even out" this sensation by touching his left leg. These compulsions were debilitating—in one half-hour period of observation at home, Neil's mother noted 44 instances of this "evening out" behavior—and it is no surprise that Neil's touching affected his behavior and performance at school.*

*Whereas the previous article on ADHD suggested that a large proportion of children with this disorder respond successfully to medication, this case demonstrates how medication can sometimes be contraindicated—it actually made Neil's compulsions worse. The psychologist treating Neil therefore turned to a behavioral intervention, in which Neil was encouraged to resist the temptation to touch himself symmetrically, with gradually longer delays. In this way Neil learned that he could tolerate the discomfort of not responding in his usual way. One interesting aspect of the discussion following the case discussion is that, by virtue of the successful elimination of the OCD symptoms, the authors were able to conclude that this could not have been a tic disorder because the behavioral program is not usually effective for tic disorder.*

*The authors introduce a number of assessment tools that may not be familiar to you, but, because they are clearly described, this should not interfere with your understanding of this case. Note in particular that the authors describe the Child Behavior Check List (CBCL), which yields an internalizing score and an externalizing score. These are not formal diagnostic terms, but they help to describe two large categories of childhood disorders. Externalizing disorders, which we have emphasized in the readings for this chapter, involve often disruptive "acting out."*

*Whereas internalizing disorders, such as anxiety disorders and depression, involve symptoms that are less visible and more typically contained within the individual. Zahn-Waxler, Klimes-Dougan, and Slattery (2000) provide an excellent summary of the current knowledge on internalizing disorders.*

## Reference

Zahn-Waxler, C., Klimes-Dougan, B., & Slattery, M. J. (2000). Internalizing problems of childhood and adolescence: Prospects, pitfalls, and progress in understanding the development of anxiety and depression. *Development and Psychopathology, 12*, 443–466.

---

*Journal of the American Academy of Child and Adolescent Psychiatry, 37*, 443–446. (1998).

Obsessive-compulsive disorder (OCD) in children is a chronic and often debilitating disorder (Piacentini and Graae, 1997) which affects up to 1% of youngsters but remains poorly recognized and potentially undertreated. This is unfortunate because pharmacological (March and Leonard, 1996) and cognitive-behavioral (March et al., 1994; Piacentini et al., 1994) interventions have been shown to be effective. Although therapies are successful in up to 75% of cases, treatment of childhood OCD can be complicated by the presence of comorbid psychiatric disorders which occur in 62% to 84% of youths with OCD (Piacentini and Graae, 1997; Swedo et al., 1989).

Of particular significance for treatment is the comorbidity of childhood OCD and the disruptive behavior disorders, most notably attention-deficit/hyperactivity disorder (ADHD) and oppositional defiant disorder (ODD). Stimulant medications used to treat ADHD can increase the intensity and frequency of obsessions and compulsions (Dulcan and Popper, 1991), and behavior therapy for OCD is often not considered because of difficulties securing treatment compliance from hyperactive, inattentive, and/or noncomplaint children. This report describes the nonpharmacological treatment of OCD in a boy with ADHD, ODD, and a history of two unsuccessful medication trials using a behavioral program designed to address interference from his comorbid symptomatology.

## Case Study

Neil, an 8-year-old Caucasian boy, presented with a history of OCD, overactivity, inattentiveness, and oppositionality. A structured diagnostic evaluation, including clinical interview with mother and child and standardized measures such as the Child Yale-Brown Obsessive Compulsive Scale (CY-BOCS) (Goodman et al., 1989), the Child Behavior Checklist (CBCL) (Achenbach, 1991), and the Inattention/Overactivity With Aggression (IOWA) Conners Scale (Loney and Milich, 1982), revealed that Neil met *DSM-IV* criteria for OCD, ADHD combined type, and ODD.

Neil's compulsions, which he called "sensors," were behaviors aimed at establishing tactile body symmetry. Neil "evened out" tactile sensations by touching the analogous part on his body's opposite side. Neil reported that he often got an overwhelming "annoying" feeling when he touched something or was touched and that performing his compulsion got rid of this feeling. Consequently, he appeared quite fidgety and frequently touched objects. Diagnostic evaluation revealed no history of tics or tic disorder. Although Neil's symptoms resembled premonitory urges and complex motor tics, his behaviors were performed according to rigidly applied rules in an attempt to reduce significant anxiety. Consequently, his behaviors met criteria for OCD and not for a tic disorder.

Neil felt he had no control over his sensors, which occurred continuously throughout the day but seemed especially troublesome at home in the evening. At the beginning of treatment, Neil and his mother recorded 44 sensors during a half-hour period at home. His compulsions also interfered with school because he was distracted by them and found it almost impossible at times to sit still. Neil reported that his sensors had been around "forever," and his mother believed they had been bothering him for at least 5 years. According to both reporters, Neil had been bothered by one obsessional image which was not currently problematic and therefore not targeted for treatment.

Neil received the diagnosis of ADHD at age 3 years, and he was first treated pharmacologically with methylphenidate, 10 mg b.i.d. for less than a week at age 6. According to his mother, methylphenidate significantly exacerbated Neil's OCD and had no effect on his disruptive behavior. Neil was then treated with fluoxetine, 30 mg/day for 2 years, which his mother said resulted in an only very slight improvement in his OCD symptoms and notable side effects including increased irritability. . . .

Treatment was based on in vivo exposure plus response prevention (ERP) (Meyer, 1966). In ERP, patients are systematically exposed to their feared stimuli while being encouraged to resist ritualistic behavior. The most commonly proposed mechanism for the effectiveness of this approach is that over prolonged exposure to feared stimuli, physiological components of anxiety are corrected by autonomic habituation. Treatment was adapted for use with children according to Piacentini et al. (1994). These modifications included emphasis on therapist modeling, structured parental involvement, and a reward system for compliance with in-session and homework tasks.

Assessment and treatment were administered during twelve 45-minute sessions over a period of 4 months. Neil and his mother participated in each session. First, Neil was introduced to the Feeling Thermometer (FT), a 10-point (0=no distress, 10=extreme distress) subjective units of distress scale. Neil went beyond the scale's limits when he rated the annoying feeling associated with his sensors as at least "10" and sometimes as high as

"100." Although it was initially difficult for Neil to distinguish which sensors were associated with more or less anxiety, he was able to create a symptom hierarchy with the therapist during the first few sessions.

After development of his hierarchy, ERP training began with the stimulus that produced the least anxiety for him. In these initial exposures, Neil watched his mother tap her forearm on the table without "evening out." This stimulus produced a FT level of 5. At first Neil yelled at his mother to touch her other forearm and tried to touch it to the table himself. He complained, "My sensor doctor is giving me sensors!" However, with strong encouragement he was able to resist for a few minutes, within which time his FT dropped to 1 or 0. After the initial session, Neil was given an assignment to watch his mother resisting a sensor three times per day and to monitor and record his distress until it dissipated.

Securing Neil's attention and compliance during the initial sessions was highly challenging given his behavior problems. These problems were addressed with contingency management and intensive maternal involvement in treatment. Neil needed clear expectations and reinforcement for behaviors conducive to benefiting from behavior therapy. Three session rules were established and reviewed each session: use a quiet voice, answer all questions without refusing, and stay in seat. After every 15 minutes in which Neil complied with these rules and attempted the exposures, he chose two small candies. At the end of each session he chose two stickers as a reward for attending the session and practicing exposures. After the introduction of this system, Neil's behavior during sessions improved substantially. He remained difficult to manage but was able to participate in therapy to the extent that he could benefit from it.

Throughout treatment, Neil was given homework assignments to be completed approximately 5 days per week; these consisted of ERP to the situations addressed in session. Records of homework and distress ratings during ERP were kept by Neil and his mother and reviewed each session. Contingency management at home was introduced as well. Neil's mother purchased an enjoyable toy for Neil to play with only during his homework sessions. The parental intervention consisted of psychoeducation and support for the mother to ensure that she clearly understood the rationale for ERP and could assist him with homework in a positive and supportive manner.

During the remaining sessions, Neil practiced ERP with situations progressively further up his anxiety hierarchy. After watching his mother or therapist resist a sensor, Neil was asked to touch a body part to an object, resist performing sensors, and monitor his annoying feeling. At first he resisted for only a few seconds and screamed while waiting. However, by the fifth attempt his initial anxiety level was 5 and dropped to 1 within a few minutes. After this, Neil's mother or the therapist touched his arm or helped him take his shoes off and on while he resisted his compulsion and monitored his distress. Although Neil's initial anxiety level was reportedly 10, by approximately the fifth trial his initial anxiety level dropped to 2, which dissipated to 1 or less during exposures lasting several minutes.

Within a few sessions, the frequency and intensity of Neil's compulsions dropped dramatically. The annoying feeling that triggered his compulsions dropped from "100" on the FT to 2 or less. He appeared significantly less fidgety and reported being only infrequently bothered by sensors. In addition to continued ERP, homework during the later stages of treatment consisted of his mother and Neil monitoring his sensors during discrete intervals throughout the day, with Neil earning a reward for ritual-free intervals of increasing length. Neil also stopped using his special toy while practicing ERP at home so that he could learn to resist his compulsion without the use of a distracter.

Posttreatment measures of OCD symptomatology indicated minimal symptoms and almost no interference in daily activities. . . . At 6-month follow-up, Neil's mother reported a slight return of his OCD. A booster ERP session was held, and Neil practiced his exposures at home for 2 weeks. Contact with the mother 2 weeks later revealed that Neil's sensors had subsided to initial posttreatment

levels. . . . Neil's mother and his therapist concurred that further treatment was not warranted at that time.

## Discussion

This report describes the successful behavioral treatment of OCD in a boy whose clinical picture was complicated by comorbid ADHD, ODD, and two failed medication trials. At posttreatment the child no longer met criteria for OCD, and he was not experiencing any impairment from the one mild residual compulsion he called his sensors. Several treatment features, including frequent and systematic rewards for on-task behavior and participation in session, and intensive maternal involvement in treatment, were likely important in this child's treatment. Neil's mother actively participated in each session. She understood the treatment rationale well and supervised Neil's homework assignments in a supportive manner.

Despite this report's promising features, certain limitations must be noted. First, data regarding symptoms and impairment were gathered almost exclusively from the mother. While maternal report has the advantage of being based on countless hours with the child, and the clinician also provided data based on her own observations and interview with the child, additional systematic data from other sources (e.g., teachers) would have been helpful in assessing treatment outcome. Second, although this report suggests that gains were largely maintained for as long as 6 months, additional follow-up is necessary to inform long-term durability of treatment gains. Although data regarding long-term outcome in these children are limited, our clinical experience suggests that with occasional booster treatment, the majority of youngsters with OCD who are treated behaviorally continue to do well.

Two diagnostic issues also warrant comment. The decision that Neil's behaviors represented compulsions rather than tics was supported by the fact that his symptoms responded to exposure-based treatment, which has not been shown to be effective for tics. In addition, given the improvement in some of Neil's untargeted externalizing behavior problems, it could be argued that his ADHD and ODD symptoms were actually manifestations of his OCD. The CBCL and IOWA Conners Inattention/Overactivity scores changed significantly with treatment, suggesting that as Neil's OCD symptoms improved, so did some of his problems with inattention and overactivity. It seems possible that some of Neil's externalizing problems may have been related to his sensors, which were highly distracting and caused him to appear fidgety. However, there is also evidence that Neil's disruptive symptoms were at least partially independent of his OCD. His posttreatment CBCL Externalizing score remained almost two standard deviations above the mean and represents clinically significant problems despite the virtual elimination of his OCD symptoms. Also, Neil's IOWA Conners Aggression/Defiance score showed no improvement. Regardless of whether Neil's disruptive symptoms were secondary to OCD, their presence still posed treatment challenges.

In summary, this case suggests that children with OCD and comorbid disruptive behavior disorders are able to tolerate and benefit from behavior therapy with some adaptations in the absence of psychotropic medications. Although promising, the efficacy of the treatment described in this report needs to be replicated using larger samples of children with OCD and comorbid disruptive behavior disorders.

## References

Achenbach TM (1991), *Manual for the Child Behavior Checklist/14–18 and 1991 Profiles*. Burlington: University of Vermont Department of Psychiatry.

Dulcan MK, Popper CW (1991), *Concise Guide to Child and Adolescent Psychiatry*. Washington, DC: APA Press.

Goodman WK, Price LH, Rasmussen SA (1989), The Yale-Brown Obsessive Compulsive Scale, I: development, use, and reliability. *Arch Gen Psychiatry* 46:1006–1011.

Loney J, Milich R (1982), Hyperactivity, inattention, and aggression in clinical practice. In: *Advances in Developmental and Behavioral Pediatrics*, Vol 3, Wolraich M, Routh D, eds. Greenwich, CT: JAI Press, pp. 113–147.

March J, Leonard H (1996), Obsessive-compulsive disorder in children and adolescents: a review of the past 10 years. *J Am Acad Child Adolesc Psychiatry* 35:1265–1273.

March J, Mulle K, Herbel B (1994), Behavioral psychotherapy for children and adolescents with obsessive-compulsive disorder: an open trial of a new protocol-driven treatment package. *J Am Acad Child Adolesc Psychiatry* 33:333–341.

Meyer V (1966), Modification of expectations in cases with obsessive rituals. *Behav Res Ther* 4:270–280.

Piacentini J, Gitow A, Jaffer M, Graae F, Whitaker A (1994), Outpatient behavioral treatment of child and adolescent obsessive compulsive disorder. *J Anxiety Disord* 8:227–289.

Piacentini J, Graae F (1997), Childhood obsessive-compulsive disorder. In: *Obsessive-Compulsive Disorders: Etiology, Diagnosis, and Treatment*, Hollander E, Stein D, eds. New York: Marcel Dekker, pp. 23–47.

Swedo S, Rapoport J, Leonard H, Lenane M, Cheslow D (1989), Obsessive compulsive disorder in children and adolescents: clinical phenomenology of 70 consecutive cases. *Arch Gen Psychiatry* 46:335–341.

# CHAPTER 7

# Personality Disorders

There is a major distinction in the Diagnostic and Statistical Manual of Mental Disorders (DSM) *between Axis I and Axis II pathologies. Axis I disorders are known as "clinical disorders" and include such diagnoses as schizophrenia and depression. They are major forms of psychopathology that are often evident to others, are often disabling, commonly result in the individual seeing a mental health professional, and are typically diagnosed as being present or absent. Axis II disorders are known as "personality disorders" and include such diagnoses as schizotypal personal disorder, narcissistic personality disorder, and antisocial personality disorder. Axis II tend to cause less distress than Axis I disorders, are less likely to lead people to seek professional help, and are not always that obvious. There are ten specific personality disorders listed in the DSM-IV, and, compared to Axis I disorders, it is difficult to think of them as present or absent for a given individual. Instead, it is easier to think of them as dimensions rather than categories, or as being present in degrees. Personality disorders are rigid sorts of traits—the chronic suspiciousness of a paranoid personality disorder, the instability of self-image in borderline personality disorder, and the social inhibition of an avoidant personality disorder—that become so disadvantageous for an individual that they cause distress or interfere with everyday functioning.*

*In this chapter we present four articles that capture different aspects of personality and personality disorders. This includes a conceptual article on an interpersonal mechanism that might operate in some personality disorders; a case study of psychotherapy involving a woman diagnosed with borderline personality disorder; an 18-year longitudinal study on the antecedents of violent crime, which is often evident in antisocial personality disorder; and the report of a rare experiment that was designed to modify personality and clarify its underlying biology.*

## Reference

American Psychiatric Association (1994). *Diagnostic and statistical manual of mental disorders* (4th ed.). Washington, DC: Author.

## Suggested Readings

Cloninger, C. R. (1999). *Personality and psychopathology.* Washington, DC: American Psychiatric Association.
Shapiro, D. (1965). *Neurotic styles.* New York: Basic Books.

# Cyclical Processes in Personality and Psychopathology

## Paul L. Wachtel

*Most of us are familiar with the idea of self-fulfilling prophesies—we think that someone may not like us, so we act coldly toward him, which leads him to not like us—and the idea of vicious cycles—we diet or exercise to lose weight, and after we do so we decide we can eat a bit more than usual, which leads to more dieting and exercise, and so on. These are known as dynamic, reciprocal phenomena, and in the first article Paul Wachtel applies them to personality disorders in general, with specific reference to narcissistic personality disorders. This leads to such interesting, paradoxical notions as: "to a considerable extent, what makes [individuals with personality disorders] feel bad is how they go about trying to feel better" and "the solution is the problem." This article is also valuable because it picks up themes introduced in chapter 2, such as the integration of behavioral perspectives with principles of psychodynamic and family system theories.*

### Suggested Reading

Watzlawick, P., Weakland, J., & Fisch, R. (1974). *Change: Principles of problem formation and problem resolution.* New York: Norton.

*Journal of Abnormal Psychology, 103,* 51–54. (1994).

The study of psychopathology, like the theory and practice of psychotherapy, has long been characterized by competing schools and viewpoints, whose proponents are sometimes more interested in countering their rivals' arguments than in seriously considering their data. Recently, a strong integrative trend has developed seeking to overcome these divisions. The result has been not only powerful new formulations based on a broader set of observations (see Arkowitz, 1992; Gold & Stricker, 1993; Norcross & Goldfried, 1992) but also a rapidly growing international organization, The Society for the Exploration of Psychotherapy Integration. One of the conceptual tools that has been particularly useful in these evolving efforts to reconcile the disparate perspectives on personality and psychopathology has been the analysis of the cyclical processes by which internal states and external events continually recreate the conditions for the reoccurrence of each other.

The utility of such a cyclical perspective can be illustrated by its role in forging an integration of the discoveries and methods deriving from psychodynamic and cognitive-behavioral points of view. A seeming obstacle to such an integration is the apparent contradiction between, on the one hand, an approach that centers on the persistence of unmodified fragments of early psychological development that play themselves out largely independently of environmental input and, on the other, an approach that emphasizes the crucial role of that very input. Further impeding integration—but also pointing toward the need for it—is the tendency for proponents of psychodynamic theories and proponents of behavioral and social learning theories to base their formulations on rather different databases, with neither addressing the full range of observations that are encompassed by the other. This is a severe limitation on the adequacy of either theory alone—one not usually confronted by advocates of either approach because they are either scarcely aware of the observations made by the other or dismissive of those observations.

Psychodynamic theorists tend to regard the experiments that form the basis for social learning formulations as mostly trivial. They are viewed as sidestepping significant phenomena in the quest for a specious certainty. Moreover, the generalizability and applicability of the experimental findings to real-life circumstances outside the laboratory are seen as questionable; the assiduous application of experimental controls in one setting disguises the leaps of faith required in applying those findings to contexts that are sometimes radically different. Behaviorally oriented clinicians and investigators, on the other hand, tend to hew to an epistemology that is dismissive of uncontrolled clinical observation and to attempt to found their theories on experimentally verified propositions.

There is a measure of truth in each side's attacks on the other's database, but the sum of their assaults reveals the inadequacy of either alone and the need for the tempering of one with the strengths of the other, both epistemologically and in the focus of their observations (see P. L. Wachtel, 1973, 1977). The key to integrating observations accruing from both orientations within a comprehensive conceptual framework lies in paying attention to the relation between the seemingly

infantile ideas and desires observed by psychoanalytic clinicians and the actual life circumstances of the people who harbor these odd but powerful psychological anomalies. From the more typical psychoanalytic vantage point, primitive wishes or thoughts—or in more recent formulations, internalized objects or early, arrested structures of self—have a kind of priority. Although these seeming residues of early psychological organization are increasingly understood as having an origin in actual life events (especially in the contemporary formulations of self-psychology and object relations theories), past some point in early childhood they are treated essentially as independent variables. Largely fixed and inaccessible to influence, they are seen as shaping the individual's behavior and experience but as being themselves largely uninfluenced by the events of the person's life (or influenced only in the limited sense that such events serve as a trigger to release propensities whose shape is essentially independent of the events and circumstances of daily living—see P. L. Wachtel, 1981, 1993).

To illustrate, in contrast, how a cyclical formulation addresses the same set of observations, but in a way that highlights as well how the intrapsychic state is itself understandable as a function of the events of daily living, let us consider the sort of individual who might be given the increasingly common diagnosis of narcissistic personality disorder. Such individuals are characterized by sharply fluctuating self-esteem, with marked grandiosity at certain times and feelings of worthlessness at others. Their aggressive presentation of self may well be rooted in real talents and accomplishments, but in their pressured efforts to continually impress, they tend to present themselves as considerably more important, accomplished, or praiseworthy than they really are.

If such individuals are successful in impressing people with their grandiose self-presentation, they may experience some immediate feelings of gratification and enhanced self-esteem, but the victory is likely to be a Pyrrhic one. For at some level of awareness, such individuals know they are not quite what they seem. Because they have worked so hard to overplay their hand, as it were, they are likely to be plagued by a sense of fraudulence or hollowness that may well become more severe the more they manage to be admired. Moreover, that sense of fraudulence is not simply the persistence of a feeling induced in childhood but is a product of the ongoing events of their lives, including the very efforts they make in the present to quell such feelings. Thus, there is a powerful element of irony in such individuals' difficulties: To a considerable extent, what makes them continue to feel bad is how they go about trying to feel better.

Of course, not all attempts at impressing others are likely to be successful. Sometimes the other will experience such an individual as a phony or braggart or blowhard, and if this reaction is perceived by the narcissistic individual, it too will contribute to his or her sense of worthlessness or fraudulence.

In either event, the habitual (indeed, virtually compelled) response of such individuals to the painful state of uncertainty and inner vulnerability just noted is to attempt to overcome the sense of fraudulence and lack of solidity by still further efforts to bolster self-esteem via inflated self-presentations that, ironically, initiate the vicious cycle once again. For these compensatory self-inflations once more deprive the individual of the experience of being accepted and admired for who he or she *really* is, serving instead to foster again the feeling (whether fully and consciously experienced or only dimly sensed) that the foundations for his or her place in the world and sense of self are shaky and fraudulent, and thus requiring still further doses of grandiosity, which create still further feelings of fraudulence, ad infinitum.

The origins of a life pattern such as this may well lie, at least partially, in the experiences of early childhood emphasized by such theorists as Kohut (1971, 1977) and Kernberg (1975). But whatever their origins, careful attention to both the subjective state of the individual and the events of his or her life—as well as to the relation between the two—reveals a psychological structure in which the fragile internal state and the tendency to compensate via aggressive and grandiose self-presentations are each both the source and the result of an endlessly repeated pattern in which

neither has intrinsic priority but in which each is crucial to the perpetuation of the other.

## Reciprocal Relationship Between Intrapsychic and Environmental Influences

It is important to be clear that viewing intrapsychic processes as a function of the events of daily life does not render them mere epiphenomena or consign them exclusively to the role of dependent variables. It is equally the case that the events one encounters in daily living are a function of one's intrapsychic state. To begin with, our way of viewing the world and our regnant aims and wishes lead us to act in certain ways that are likely to draw predictable responses from others or, put differently, are likely to shape our interpersonal environment (Bell & Harper, 1977; Buss, 1987; Coyne, 1976; Kelly & Stahelski, 1970; Snyder, 1984; P. L. Wachtel, 1977). Moreover, our internal state influences in an even more direct way who we choose to associate with and what kinds of organizations, tasks, and challenges we choose to encounter; thus, here too the environment we respond to is in large measure our own creation (Emmons & Diener, 1986; Emmons, Diener, & Larsen, 1986; Gormly, 1983; Swann, Wenzlaff, Krull, & Pelham, 1992; P. L. Wachtel, 1973).

Finally, our internal state influences how we perceive the events of daily life, especially the highly ambiguous occurrences of interpersonal encounters, and hence shapes the subjective or perceived environment (which can differ substantially from what a putative "objective" observer might describe). It is ultimately this perceived environment that determines our choice of response and our experience of ourselves and of the world. Because our private expectations and schemas impart a skew to the perceived environment we create for ourselves out of the welter of stimuli impinging on our sensory organs, which in turn skews both the responses we make and the responses to those responses that we receive from others, the expectations with which we view the world tend quite regularly to be self-perpetuating, bringing about the very kind of environment we have learned to expect (see, e.g., Gotlib & Whiffen, 1991; Jones, 1986, 1990; McNulty & Swann, 1991; Snyder, 1981; Snyder, Tanke, & Berscheid, 1977).

Thus, for example, individuals who are inclined, in ambiguous interpersonal interactions, to experience the behavior of others as hostile are likely themselves to respond with some degree of hostility or suspicion to people who are actually, at that moment, either positively or at worst neutrally inclined toward them. This behavior, however, has an impact on the other, and increases the likelihood that before long the other person *will* act in a hostile manner. This in turn "confirms" the first person's suspicion and sets the stage for the next replay of the cycle. . . .

## Cyclical Formulations and Family Systems Theories

Cyclical formulations have also been central in the formulations of family systems theorists. Watzlawick, Weakland, and Fisch (1974), for example, argued that what perpetuates psychological symptoms is the very effort people undertake to make the symptoms go away. As Watzlawick et al. put it, "The solution becomes the problem." More generally, family therapists frequently view their work as reflecting a "new epistemology." In this view, psychological difficulties are understood in terms of recursive patterns between people in which beginning and end or cause and effect are in large measure simply a matter of how each party "punctuates" what is actually a seamless flow. Hoffman (1981), summarizing much of the basic work on which this new epistemology is based, depicted its central concept as the idea of circularity and offered the following observation:

> If one saw a person with a psychiatric affliction in a clinician's office, it would be easy to assume that he or she suffered from an intrapsychic disorder arising from the past. But if one saw the same person with his or her family, in the context of current relationships, one began to see something quite different. One would see communications and behaviors from everybody present, composing many circular causal

loops that played back and forth, with the behavior of the afflicted person only part of a larger, recursive dance. (Hoffman, 1981, pp. 6–7)

Because of the emphasis of family therapists on circular processes, they have frequently contrasted their approach sharply with that of psychodynamic thinkers, who they portray as committed to a linear perspective that sharply (and misleadingly) distinguishes cause and effect and that locates the relevant causes of present difficulties in the distant past (e.g., Hoffman, 1981). This contention has some validity when applied to most versions of psychodynamic thought, which, as described previously, portray the internalized residues of early interactions and psychological states as exerting their influence more or less independently of the events and transactions in which the individual presently participates. But the particular psychodynamic perspective that has guided much of the discussion in this article, the *cyclical psychodynamic* perspective (P. L. Wachtel, 1977, 1987, 1993), has a quite different structure. Devised as a framework for integration of the major viewpoints and clinical approaches to personality and psychopathology, cyclical psychodynamics highlights the vicious circle structure within which unconscious inclinations are embedded, and there are strong convergences between its concepts and those of family systems theories (E. F. Wachtel & Wachtel, 1986).

## Study of Personality and Research on Self-Perpetuating Processes

The conception of personality that underlies the account presented here is a dynamic interactional one. Its fundamental assumptions and the questions it asks contrast quite significantly with more trait-oriented approaches to the study of personality. Like the latter, cyclical or interactional accounts concern themselves with persistent individual differences, but the emphasis in the cyclical version is on the processes that maintain those differences.

Trait-oriented approaches to personality,

though they may provide valuable understanding of structural regularities, often present a rather static picture. Process-oriented accounts, such as that presented here, lend themselves equally well to understanding persistence and to understanding change. For this reason they are particularly useful for uniting the study of personality and psychopathology with the study of psychotherapy.

Conducting empirical research on the conceptions of personality and psychological disorder described here is difficult. Investigation of complex feedback loops and recursive bidirectional patterns does not easily lend itself to simple designs in which independent and dependent variables are clearly demarcated (P. L. Wachtel, 1973, 1980). In large measure the conceptions described here derive from clinical and naturalistic observations, and attention to such observations by personality researchers is likely to continue to be a potent stimulus for furthering our understanding. But important contributions have also been made by empirical researchers using statistical methods such as path analysis and time series analysis that are more suited to the study of reciprocal interactions and by investigators whose theoretical frameworks have especially emphasized the role of expectancies, self-fulfilling prophecies, and self-verification (e.g., Jones, 1986, 1990; McNulty & Swann, 1991; Swann et al., 1992).

As noted earlier, generalizing from the circumstances and parameters of laboratory experiments to those that bring people to therapy or produce the passions explored by a Shakespeare or Tolstoy is a riskier business than is sometimes acknowledged. But much of the empirical work cited in this article reflects efforts to incorporate more complex models into research in social and personality psychology, and sophisticated researchers in this realm are increasingly examining how the findings of the laboratory and the findings of the clinic can interact with and enrich each other (e.g., McNulty & Swann, 1991). Further experimental work along these lines, complemented by careful clinical and naturalistic observation, may point us toward a sounder understanding of the continuous shaping of who we are by experience and the continuous shaping of experience by who we are.

# References

Arkowitz, H. (1992). Integrative theories of therapy. In D. Freedheim (Ed.), *History of psychotherapy: A century of change* (pp. 261–303). Washington. DC: American Psychological Association.

Bell, R. Q., & Harper, L. V. (1977). *Child effects on adults.* Hillsdale. NJ: Erlbaum.

Buss, D. M. (1987). Selection, evocation and manipulation. *Journal of Personality and Social Psychology, 53,* 1214–1221.

Coyne, J. C. (1976). Depression and the response of others. *Journal of Abnormal Psychology, 85,* 186–193.

Emmons, R. A., & Diener, E. (1986). Situation selection as a moderator of response consistency and stability. *Journal of Personality and Social Psychology, 51,* 1013–1019.

Emmons, R. A., Diener, E., & Larsen, R. (1986). Choice and avoidance of everyday situations and affect congruence: Two models of reciprocal interactionism. *Journal of Personality and Social Psychology. 51,* 815–826.

Gold, J., & Stricker, G. (Eds.). (1993). *Comprehensive handbook of psychotherapy integration.* New York: Praeger.

Gormly, J. (1983). Predicting behavior from personality trait scores. *Personality and Social Psychology Bulletin. 9,* 267–270.

Gotlib, I. H., & Whiffen, V. E. (1991). The interpersonal context of depression: Implications for theory and research. In W. H. Jones & D. Perlman (Eds.), *Advances in personal relationships* (Vol. 3, pp. 177–206). London: Jessica Kingsley Publishers.

Hoffman, L. (1981). *Foundations of family therapy.* New York: Basic Books.

Jones, E. E. (1986). Interpreting interpersonal behavior. *Science, 234,* 41–46.

Jones, E. E. (1990). *Interpersonal perception.* New York: W. H. Freeman.

Kelly, H. H., & Stahelski, A. J. (1970). Social interaction basis of cooperators' and competitors' beliefs about others. *Journal of Personality and Social Psychology, 16,* 66–91.

Kernberg. O. (1975). *Borderline condition and pathological narcissism.* Northvale, NJ: Jason Aronson.

Kohut, H. (1971). *The analysis of the self.* New York: International Universities Press.

Kohut, H. (1977). *The restoration of the self.* New York: International Universities Press.

McNulty, S. E., & Swann, W. B., Jr. (1991). Psychotherapy, self-concept change, and self-verification. In R. C. Curtis (Ed.), *The relational self: Theoretical convergences in psychoanalysis and social psychology* (pp. 213–237). New York: Guilford Press.

Norcross. J. C., & Goldfried, M. R. (Eds.). (1992). *Handbook of psychotherapy integration.* New York: Basic Books.

Snyder, M. (1981). Seek and ye shall find: Testing hypotheses about other people. In E. T. Higgins, C. P. Herman, & M. P. Zanna (Eds.), *Social cognition: The Ontario symposium* (pp. 277–304). Hillsdale, NJ: Erlbaum.

Snyder, M. (1984). When belief creates reality. In L. Berkowitz (Ed.), *Advances in experimental social psychology* (Vol. 18, pp. 248–305). San Diego. CA: Academic Press.

Snyder, M., Tanke, E. D., & Berscheid, E. S. (1977). Social perception and interpersonal behavior: On the self-fulfilling nature of social stereotypes. *Journal of Personality and Social Psychology, 35*, 656–666.

Swann, W. B., Wenzlaff, R. M., Krull, D. S., & Pelham, B. W. (1992). Allure of negative feedback: Self-verification strivings among depressed persons. *Journal of Abnormal Psychology, 101*, 293–306.

Wachtel, E. F., & Wachtel, P. L. (1986). *Family dynamics in individual psychotherapy.* New York: Guilford Press.

Wachtel, P. L. (1973). Psychodynamics, behavior therapy, and the implacable experimenter: An inquiry into the consistency of personality. *Journal of Abnormal Psychology, 82*, 324–334.

Wachtel, P. L. (1977). *Psychoanalysis and behavior therapy: Toward an integration.* New York: Basic Books.

Wachtel, P. L. (1980). Investigation and its discontents: On some constraints on progress in psychological research. *American Psychologist, 35*, 399–408.

Wachtel, P. L. (1981). Transference, schema, and assimilation: The relevance of Piaget to the psychoanalytic theory of transference. *The Annual of Psychoanalysis 8*, 59–76.

Wachtel, P. L. (1987). *Action and insight.* New York: Guilford Press.

Wachtel, P. L. (1993). *Therapeutic communication: Principles and effective practice.* New York: Guilford Press.

Watzlawick, P., Weakland, J., & Fisch, R. (1974). *Change: Problem formation and problem resolution.* New York: Norton.

# A LITTLE CREAM AND SUGAR: PSYCHOTHERAPY WITH A BORDERLINE PATIENT

## Joan Wheelis, M.D., and John G. Gunderson, M.D.

*You may recall from the fourth article in chapter 4 how a therapist, Irvin Yalom, responded with alarm to a patient named Marge, when he suspected that she may have borderline personality disorder. If you saw the movie* Fatal Attraction, *you are familiar with the main diagnostic criteria that characterize individuals with this disorder: fear of abandonment, emotional instability, impulsivity, manipulative suicidal gestures, and strong anger. The following article is an excerpt from a case study involving a 35-year-old woman, Lotta, who is diagnosed with borderline personality disorder. This case provides an excellent depiction of this dramatic, oftentimes chaotic, disorder, along with interesting analyses of transcriptions taken from several psychotherapy sessions. Particularly evident are the high interpersonal stakes involved in this therapy, the poignant vulnerability and pain of the patient, and the constant pressure on the therapist to avoid saying things that will elicit Lotta's rage.*

## Suggested Readings

Linehan, M. (1993). *Cognitive-behavioral treatment of borderline personality disorder.* New York: Guilford.
Melges, F. T., & Swartz, M. S. (1989). Oscillations of attachment in borderline personality disorder. *American Journal of Psychiatry, 146,* 1115–1120.

*American Journal of Psychiatry, 155,* 114–122. (1998).

This case report describes selected parts of a psychotherapy with a patient diagnosed with borderline personality disorder. Although this report features aspects of psychodynamic psychotherapy, readers should recognize that this modality usually needs to be used selectively as part of a treatment program involving family, cognitive/behavioral, and psychopharmacological modalities (1). Process material has been chosen from the first year of a twice-weekly psychotherapy to highlight issues that are commonplace during the course of such therapies: establishing an alliance, managing boundaries, setting limits, and responding to rage and suicide threats. The clinical material examines how countertransference feelings arise and become enacted. Insofar as this case report documents the common, recurrent, and oft-feared problems in psychotherapy with borderline patients, the discussion is intended to offer a primer for how these problems can be effectively managed. Indeed, the testing, the combativeness, and the dangers characteristic of the borderline patient presented here provide a backdrop against which we hope to convey a larger thesis. While the depth and intensity of dependent and rageful feelings, technical challenges, and commitment inherent in such work are often seen as a reason to avoid such patients, the work can be, and with experience will be, an enriching and satisfying professional activity.

## Case Presentation

I, Dr. Wheelis, was a second-year resident on call when I first met Ms. A. At the time she was a psychiatric inpatient who had been admitted a week before for suicidality and increased alcohol abuse. I had been asked to meet with Ms. A and potentially take over her treatment, since she had recently terminated with her therapist. The inpatient psychiatrist in charge of the care of Ms. A, as well as an outpatient consultant, had recommended a confrontational dynamic psychotherapy. I had arranged a first appointment for the following morning, but as the doctor on call the evening before, I was asked to see her for medical attention. In a rage at having been put in a quiet room, Ms. A had hit her elbow on the wall and was complaining of great pain. I felt uneasy that my first contact should be under such circumstances and wondered if she knew I was the doctor on call that night. When I arrived to see her, I was met by a short, medium-built woman wearing jeans, sitting cross-legged on the floor, looking angrily at me. Before I'd had a chance to introduce myself, she snapped:

Ms. A: You could be dying before you got any help around here! My arm is killing me! This place is crazy!
THERAPIST: Ms. A, I would like to introduce myself. I am Dr. Wheelis.
Ms. A: Oh, no kidding! I didn't expect you. You're a resident? Interesting. You must be either very good or very crazy to have taken me on.
THERAPIST: I can't tell if that's an invitation, a warning, or both [she smiled at my comment], but we have an

appointment tomorrow. Why don't we discuss it then. For now, perhaps I should take a look at your arm.
Ms. A: No, it's okay, just a little bang.
THERAPIST: Are you sure? You suggested that it was giving you considerable pain.
Ms. A: No, it's fine, really. I'll see you tomorrow. By the way, I hate being called Ms. A.
THERAPIST: How would you like to be called?
Ms. A: Lotta. That's what everyone calls me.
THERAPIST: Very well, as you wish.

Already in this initial interaction with her therapist-to-be, harbingers of the therapeutic challenges are evident. Ms. A demonstrates a manipulative style that predates the first interaction by seeking help through the exaggeration of a minor physical complaint. There is also the hint that Ms. A may be taking pleasure in suggesting to the therapist-to-be that working with her will be more than a small challenge. Her final request, to be called Lotta, betrays her desire to bypass professional formality by requesting an immediate familiarity.

Ms. A was a 35-year-old, single, white librarian when I met her as an inpatient. The hospitalization was her 10th psychiatric admission. Her past history was replete with self-destructive behavior including wrist slashing as a teenager, alcohol and benzodiazepine abuse, chronic dysthymia, and suicidality. She was diagnosed with borderline personality disorder following her first hospitalization at age 18, having met seven of the nine diagnostic criteria of *DSM-IV*. At other times she had been given additional axis I diagnoses including bipolar disorder. She had had several medication trials without benefit. Her dominant symptoms were emptiness and aloneness; although she was impulsive and labile as well, these symptoms were connected to interpersonal stressors and did not fit criteria for bipolar disorder. Her current admission was precipitated by increasing depression and suicidality, but without a suicide attempt, following the loss of her boyfriend of 8 years. Her psychiatrist of 10 years had terminated treatment because of a geographic relocation. She felt increasingly withdrawn from her family, especially her mother, with whom she had been particularly close. Ms. A was quite specific as to the goals of her current hospitalization. She wanted to find a new therapist and to become involved in Alcoholics Anonymous in order to stop drinking.

After the initial meeting in the quiet room, I met with Ms. A for her first scheduled appointment the following day. She was waiting for me when I arrived on the inpatient unit.

Ms. A: Could we go where I could smoke? You'll have to get the matches from the nurse. I'm on supervised flames.

I proceeded to get the matches and found a room where smoking was permitted. I handed her the matches.

Ms. A: You're going to trust me with these?

THERAPIST: I'm going to see if I can.

Ms. A: What if I try to set something on fire? [She said this sarcastically.]

THERAPIST: Then I won't be able to trust you, and I'll ask for them back.

Ms. A: Hm! You ask a simple question, you get a simple answer. Doesn't happen so commonly around here. Do you smoke?

THERAPIST: On occasion.

Ms. A: Two for two! Most shrinks don't answer my questions.

THERAPIST: Let's not try to set a record.

Ms. A: I feel much better now that I have a therapist.

THERAPIST: I want to interrupt you; I've only a half an hour today and I wanted to speak with you about a few things. What I had in mind was to meet with you several times between now and when you're discharged and give ourselves the opportunity to see if you want to work with me and for me to see if I think I can be of help to you. If we decide we can work together, then we'll continue on an outpatient basis two or three times a week, which we can decide together. [Ms. A starts to shake her head.]

Ms. A: Let me interrupt you a minute! I'm not a nine-to-fiver. Now, I know I have trouble with limit setting and you can tell me this is out of the question, but I have in mind five times a week, and I need to know I can call you, you know?

THERAPIST: No, I don't know.

Ms. A: Well, like if I get into trouble, I want to know that I can contact you.

THERAPIST: If you feel in trouble and unable to wait until our next appointment, I would be available, but if this were to occur frequently it would not be all right. I would question the utility of the therapy and would want to reassess it.

Ms. A: Well, I never called my last therapist, but it mattered that I knew I could. You know, I always imagined I'd be in treatment forever.

THERAPIST: Is that a wish?

Ms. A: I'd just assumed since I'd been in therapy this long already, I will continue to be in therapy forever.

THERAPIST: Do you want to change?

Ms. A: Well, of course.

THERAPIST: Then I think it's a mistake to make that assumption without question.

Ms. A: Well, are you saying I won't need therapy forever?

THERAPIST: I cannot say that.

Ms. A: Well, then, are you saying I'll need therapy for the rest of my life?

THERAPIST: I can't say that, either. I don't know, but I am suggesting that if you leave the question open, your therapy might be more effective.

Ms. A: You're also telling me that you're not sure you're going to be my therapist.

THERAPIST: That's true.

Ms. A: What does it depend on?

THERAPIST: If I feel I can be of help to you.

Ms. A: What? Do I have to prove myself a good patient?

THERAPIST: I would think it more worthwhile for you to be thinking if you want to work with me.

Ms. A: I never really thought about that kind of thing.

THERAPIST: Well, time to start.

Ms. A: You're something else.

THERAPIST: How so?

Ms. A: Well, nobody really talks to me the way you do.

THERAPIST: How's that?

Ms. A: I don't know. Like you treat me like an adult, no kid gloves.

THERAPIST: Should I?

Ms. A: No. I don't know.

THERAPIST: You're not quite sure?

Ms. A: Well, most people treat me with kid gloves, you know, Lotta the sick one, the one who can't deal with anything. It makes me mad, makes me feel like a cripple. But then I think, they're probably right, and I can't handle anything anyway.

I was aware of the way in which Ms. A's style of engaging me was static and rigid. She wanted me to conform with what she deemed the appropriate treatment plan—my being actively available to nurture her without question. My efforts to encourage her capacity for critical thinking were met with resistance but not rejection. I felt that this session significantly shaped my initial treatment plan. The primary task was to encourage her as an active participant in her treatment rather than as a passive recipient of her treatment. We clarified other goals of her treatment to include improving her relationship with her mother, friends, and lovers through the examination of her conflicted feelings of neediness and anger. I told her that much of the work that we could do together would depend upon her ability to examine such problems in the context of our relationship as we had in this first session. Although reluctant, Ms. A was intrigued.

This initial session is illustrative of a couple of important issues regarding alliance building. The interactions are characterized by the therapist's repeated attempts to question Ms. A's unrelenting efforts to force an unquestioned relationship based on her needs alone. The therapist wisely sets a preliminary agenda of considering the viability of a treatment relationship. She sets the stage by underscoring that therapy is to be tied to forward progression and not to continuation of old ways. The implicit differentiation between therapist and patient suggested in this process material covertly indicates that ultimately, separation is the goal of treatment. Later in the session, specific goals of therapy were discussed. Together they agreed that their work would focus on managing her anger and impulsivity and improving her relationship with her mother.

I met with Ms. A as we had planned for a total of six sessions while she was hospitalized. I obtained the following history from her and her old records.

Ms. A was born in the Midwest and was the older of two children; she had one sister 3 years younger. Her parents both worked in the auto parts industry. She had little to say about either parent: she described her father as difficult, her mother as rigid, like herself, but her "best friend." She had always hated her sister. Her mother reported that Ms. A was the product of an unremarkable pregnancy and that her early development was normal. She also commented during one of Ms. A's hospitalizations that she had found the task of mothering to be difficult, finding it frustrating to be tied to the house and to be caring for a child.

Ms. A's earliest memory, at age 3, was of offering her mother a picture she had carefully and painstakingly drawn for her upon her arrival home from the hospital with her new little sister. She remembers shredding the picture into little pieces as her mother reached to accept it. When Ms. A was 13, her father suffered a fall at work and was paralyzed from the waist down. Whereas before she had been an active, helpful, and good-humored child who was open and talkative, she became withdrawn, solemn, and uncommunicative. Around the same time she began a friendship with a friend, Susan. She described the relationship as intense and said that its breakup after 4 years was instigated by Susan, who found the closeness suffocating. Susan apparently felt so controlled by Ms. A that Susan's mother became concerned that this was interfering in her daughter's development and so urged her to end the relationship. After the break-up of the friendship, Ms. A, then age 16, became depressed and cut her wrists for the first time, telling no one. Subsequently her schoolwork in a local public high school deteriorated, and she went from being an A student to a D student.

This history frames important issues for the subsequent treatment. Her earliest memory introduces the issue of exclusivity, rivalry, and spitefulness. Until this point, Ms. A had been the sole proprietor of the parental attention; the disillusionment occurred when she saw her mother giving attention to her sister. Ms. A's intense relationship with her friend Susan was so exclusive and controlling that Susan's mother became concerned and intervened. The immediate effect of this was that Ms. A cut her wrists for the first time. It is notable that like many people who subsequently become identified as borderline, Ms. A made the initial self-destructive gestures in private. Only later did the secondary gain (the attention drawn from family and therapists by such actions as wrist cutting) become conscious and manipulatively—even spitefully—exploited. Perhaps more telling than the cut wrists is the fact that Ms. A's schoolwork deteriorated. This might have been a signal to caretakers that she was in trouble and calling for help, but, in any event, it reflects the serious and sustained injury that the breakup of this friendship involved for Ms. A.

The loss of an exclusive relationship, as these

vignettes suggest, reveals a core vulnerability in borderline patients (2). The therapist can anticipate that the patient is likely to want to recreate an exclusive relationship and can expect that the inevitable disillusionment of such claims will be greeted with similarly spiteful actions.

Ms. A skipped many classes and began taking street drugs including marijuana and barbiturates. During her junior year of high school she began shoplifting and missing school altogether. There was increased friction at home with her parents. Despite their attempt to set limits through insisting on a curfew and other rules of conduct, they were ineffectual at controlling their daughter's behavior. The same year, at age 17, Ms. A was hospitalized for the first time after cutting her wrists and, this time, showing them to her parents. She continued to cut her wrists superficially while in a general hospital; unable to abide by the limits set on this, she was transferred to a state hospital briefly. After returning to the general hospital, she continued to violate the rules and regulations, even once setting her hair on fire in anger at a staff member. This and other breaches of agreements that she not harm herself necessitated her return to a state hospital, where she stayed for 6 months. . . .

Following her discharge Ms. A completed high school studies. As a graduation present she was given a trip to Cuba to work with other college-bound students on a sugar cane plantation. Although she had been looking forward to this trip, shortly after her arrival she found herself feeling increasingly isolated and suspicious that other people around her did not like her. After only 2 weeks there, she decided to come home and called her parents. Following her mother's reluctant agreement with her adamant wish to come home, she wrote her parents a letter in which she stated that she felt like a failure and proceeded to overdose on her antidepressant medication. Her family flew to Cuba to bring her home, and she was then hospitalized psychiatrically for 6 months. Subsequently, Ms. A, then 19, took a job and began at a local college. She saw a therapist intermittently, and her next psychiatric admission occurred 3 years later. The context of that hospitalization was related to her inability to make a contract for safety with her therapist before the latter's vacation. Found not to be actively suicidal, however, Ms. A was discharged after only 5 days.

The phenomenology of borderline psychopathology needs to be evaluated in terms of the patient's relationships to primary caregivers. When a borderline patient feels in the presence of one who is supportive or holding, the depressive features become paramount. Borderline patients can work collaboratively within a therapy, and their complaints are usually of boredom, loneliness, or emptiness. When a borderline patient feels endangered regarding the potential loss of the supportive, holding relationship involving a person or institution, then manipulative, self-destructive acts are common. These acts, then, have angry motivations as well as conscious manipulative intentions of preventing the separation from occurring by enjoining the therapist (or any other needed person who might be leaving) to respond in ways that will provide ongoing holding and support to the borderline patient. In contrast to such secondary gain associated with self-destructive acts, primary gain is evident under circumstances in which borderline patients find themselves without a holding or caring object relationship. In such cases the intention of self-mutilation is not manipulative; rather, it serves to diminish the anxieties associated with deficient self-object differentiation, boundary delineation, and dissociative experiences. On an unconscious level it may serve the purpose of exculpating themselves from the sense of profound badness. Under these circumstances, paranoid ideas of reference such as Ms. A experienced in Cuba can occur. They serve to diminish the sense of aloneness. Potentially dangerous impulsive actions can also occur that are neither intentionally manipulative nor self-destructive, e.g., promiscuity or getting into fights, often in the context of substance abuse.

At the age of 22 Ms. A began her one long-term psychotherapeutic treatment. She described this 10-year therapy as "friendly," commenting that the "boundaries were loose." She was often not billed if she was having financial difficulties, and she and her therapist occasionally met over a meal. She felt fondly toward him. She had several hospitalizations shortly into this treatment because of suicidal ideation, but for the 4 years before the index hospitalization, Ms.

A was relatively stable. She was in a long-term romantic relationship and had a stable job in a small library.

Ms. A's diminished self-destructiveness and ability to sustain employment during this earlier period are probably attributable to the stabilizing effect of this therapist's supportive availability, as well as that of her romantic relationship. As noted earlier, when borderline patients find themselves within supportive or holding relationships, their ability to work collaboratively emerges, and there is an absence of the self-destructive and impulsive behaviors that otherwise would characterize them. If these supportive relationships are sufficiently stabilizing, they allow borderline patients to find alternative stabilizing sources of support in their lives outside of their therapy. Such supportive therapy can consolidate some developmental gains, which later permits more exploratory, expressive, focused treatment around character structure and organization. The reemergence of Ms. A's full repertoire of borderline behaviors and feelings at the time of the index hospitalization for this report is a testimonial to the persistence of her basic character problems. Although it is likely that her prior therapy had an overall positive effect, the lax professional structures within the relationship may have had the unfortunate effect of making her less willing to conform and accept the boundaries of a usual therapy. They may also have robbed her of the potential benefits that more ambitious exploratory or expressive psychotherapies can sometimes offer in terms of bringing about character change (3, 4). . . .

In a session shortly before the decision would be finalized regarding our working together, Ms. A spoke of her anxiety regarding that issue.

Ms. A: I like you. If you tell me on Thursday that you will not be my therapist, I am going to be very, very upset!
THERAPIST: That sounds like a threat.
Ms. A: No, I am just telling you.
THERAPIST: Have you been thinking about your needs?
Ms. A: I really like what you said about maybe not being in therapy for the rest of my life. I've been afraid to ask you how much you charge. I won't be able to afford it when I leave.
THERAPIST: If we continue, you would be transferred to the outpatient clinic. The fee there is $28.
Ms. A: What? [She sounds disappointed.] I thought it was going to be about $100.

Ms. A's positive attitudes toward the desired therapist-to-be should be noted. In saying that she really likes the notion that she does not have to be in therapy for the rest of her life, does she really mean this? If she does, is it because it is a relief from the fear of being trapped and controlled by her therapist? One would hope that it means that she is truly interested in changing and making that therapy obsolete in time, but that would involve a loss which we can predict already that she is likely to dread. It is thus prudent to listen to such complimentary remarks with some skepticism. As Ms. A goes on to suggest that she thought the fee would be $100 and that she would not have been able to afford this, she may be hinting at her ambivalence even as she flatters the therapist-to-be. She would like her therapist to begin feeling very much needed and special.

The final meeting while Ms. A was an inpatient occurred a couple of days later.

Ms. A: So today's the day. You know, I never thought that you would need to make a decision, too. I thought that if I wanted to see you and could agree to the terms, it would be all right.

Are we hearing echoes from Ms. A's childhood? Is this a small child speaking to her mother before her sibling arrived? Did she believe that if she wanted to be with her mother, that would be sufficient to ensure its actualization? Ms. A did not and probably still does not accept the idea that her relationships can be worthwhile if they are not exclusive.

THERAPIST: Did you think I might not have some impression, too?
Ms. A: [nervous] I never thought about those things before.
THERAPIST: You seem nervous.
Ms. A: I am because I want to know what your decision is.

THERAPIST: You're worried that I might say no.

Ms. A: I'd be very upset.

THERAPIST: What are your thoughts?

Ms. A: I don't want to talk about it. But I'd be very upset! I feel like the only thing I might get out of this hospitalization is finding a therapist, and since I am leaving in a couple of days, if you don't see me, I'll be very unhappy!

THERAPIST: You sound like you're hoping I'll feel guilty.

Ms. A: No, I'm not. I've nothing more to say.

THERAPIST: You say you don't want to talk about your thoughts and feelings that upset you. That is one of the many things I was talking about the other day, when we spoke of making a contract for therapy. You're going to have to try to explore those different feelings and thoughts if I'm going to be of any help to you.

Ms. A: Listen, I'll *do* the work. You haven't even told me yet if you're going to work with me. Christ almighty, this is like torture!

THERAPIST: I am curious to know why you find yourself so confident that you can work with me when it sounds like your previous therapist had such a different style.

Ms. A: Well, just because I stay with something doesn't mean it's a good thing.

THERAPIST: So what kept you in that treatment for so long if you felt it wasn't a good thing?

Ms. A: I liked him. He was a friend and he cared about me, but I also knew I didn't do any work, certainly later on. I like you; I want to work. I'll tell you now, I'll get angry and fuss when you ask me to work, but I'll do it. I really was intrigued with the idea you put in my head that maybe I don't have to be in therapy for the rest of my life.

THERAPIST: Well, I have decided to work with you. These are my conditions: that we begin with meeting twice a week, that I am available in between appointments only in emergencies, and that you work, meaning paying attention to your feelings and that you pay your bill in a timely fashion.

Ms. A: I won't miss work to come to my appointments. I need a 7:00 a.m. or 7:00 p.m. appointment.

THERAPIST: I could see you at 7:30 a.m. or 6:30 p.m.

Ms. A: [She shakes her head.] I can't do it.

Notice the dramatic shift that takes place in Ms. A. She has started the session in a kind of plaintive, pleading way reflecting an idealized transference toward the therapist-to-be and a hungry wish to please. She then shifts into a demanding and controlling attitude reflecting a view of a therapist as someone who should be willing to sacrifice in order to see her. This is an example of what is referred to as pathological splitting. Ms. A begins the hour aware of what she wants; being needy and solicitous, she hopes to gain the therapist's commitment and to assure caretaker proximity. Once she feels that she has that, Ms. A treats the therapist with devalued contempt—insistently attempts to control her. Another way to put this is that she longs for an idealized relationship, i.e., exclusive, nurturant, always accessible. When the therapist, however, sets forth conditions, Ms. A is easily disillusioned. Those conditions are inconsistent with her idealized hope and set in motion angry efforts to impose controls on the therapist.

THERAPIST: Well, if it matters to you to come to therapy, I'm sure you will find a way.

Ms. A: All right. Can't I wait a while to pay the bill?

THERAPIST: Why do you ask?

Ms. A: Too many things to pay for now.

THERAPIST: You have a job. Seems like a matter of priorities again.

Ms. A: All right, all right, I'll pay for it.

THERAPIST: You seem troubled by this.

Ms. A: I hate talking about money.

THERAPIST: How come?

Ms. A: Because I do.

THERAPIST: That's not really an answer.

Ms. A: You'll get paid on time. It won't be an issue, all right?

THERAPIST: I'm much more interested in understanding what troubles you so much about discussing money.

Ms. A: Because it makes it seem so businesslike.

THERAPIST: What does that mean to you?

Ms. A: That you don't care about me if I have to pay.

THERAPIST: Not charging is no guarantee of caring. For me, not to charge would not be doing my job. I'm not a friend or a parent. I am your therapist. I charge you for the service I give you. That doesn't mean I don't care. You will need to find that out for yourself. You can't exact it from someone. You'd only feel like you twisted my arm.

And so I began a twice-weekly therapy with Ms. A. I liked her and felt challenged by the work. I also felt anxious that I had agreed to see her at 7:30 a.m. and 6:30 p.m. Although I had offered these hours to her,

I would have preferred more traditional hours but felt that I might lose her if I had insisted otherwise.

A subtle transformation has taken place here in which the therapist's growing concern about losing this patient has eroded and displaced the patient's abandonment concerns, i.e., that she, the patient, would become attached to someone, the therapist, whom she would then lose. By bending over backward to accommodate the patient, the therapist is enacting a reassurance about the patient's specialness and about the patient's ability to control the therapy. Such countertransference developments, a result of projective identification, are not uncommon in the treatment of borderline patients. In the material presented earlier, projective identification is evident as Ms. A attempts to distance herself from feelings of inadequacy and unlovability by accusing her therapist of "not caring." Here projective identification entails the disavowal of core identifications (low self-esteem) through the splitting off of the feared and unacceptable ("I'm not good enough to be truly cherished and valued by another") and projecting it into another ("You don't care about me") (5). There is a clear and close relationship between splitting and projective identification. The therapist's ability to recognize, acknowledge, and separate from the patient's projections allows for the possibility of their modification. . . .

> As the months of treatment proceeded, Ms. A began to speak of overwhelming physical sensations that were difficult to describe. She demanded medication and made it clear that if I did not give her anything, she would go ahead and find something to take. She began to talk more and more about suicide in a threatening way.
>
> With her increasing reluctance to speak of her feelings alongside the increasing threats to hurt herself, I suggested that she think about the hospital. Although able to acknowledge that the feeling would likely go away if she came into the hospital, she also knew it would likewise return upon discharge. Ms. A insisted that I take responsibility for making the decision. I told her that without understanding how she felt, my making such a decision for her would be unwise. I found her behavior to be manipulative and

was not sure how far she would go to force me to take action.

Demands that a therapist do something to take care of subjective states that feel intolerably bad often cause therapists to take ill-advised actions. If something is done, whether it be a medication or a hospitalization, it is important that the enactment be accompanied by a statement that while both you and the patient might do many things to diminish the patient's bad feelings, there is reason to fear that this will be harmful. Unwanted feelings are important experiences where the occasion to think about one's feelings (e.g., defining the type and the relationship to life events), to talk about them, and to improve tolerance is often more meaningful in helping such patients than are efforts to get rid of them. The therapist can say, "Insofar as you feel you need to get rid of these feelings, you'll just get angry if I don't do something to help. Rather than risk your acting out on that anger, I'm willing to do what you want. But as I also think doing what you ask may actually be bad for you, do you still want me to proceed?" The message here is that while you are willing to submit to such demands, it is associated with possible harm to the patient and with acknowledgment of the therapist's personal limitations. This robs the submission of its unconscious significance, i.e., that you agree that a painless life is possible, or that unwanted feelings can be exorcised, or that your efforts demonstrate what a good person/therapist you are. It is useful to interpret how such feelings usually relate to whether the patient feels there is adequate care and attention.

> It made me uneasy and I reminded her that if she felt unsafe, she should page me. She, in fact, did page me and told me over the phone that she felt overwhelmed inside and unable to describe what she was experiencing. She tried to engage me in deciding whether she should stay with a friend or not. With my noncommittal response that she must make such a decision herself on the basis of how she understood her current state of distress, she hung up on me. I was anxious about her safety. . . .
>
> Following her paging me over the weekend, Ms.

A returned in seemingly better spirits with a paper bag in her hand. She proceeded to unpack two cups of coffee.

Ms. A: I don't know how you like your coffee, so I brought sugar and cream in separate containers. [pause] Well, how do you like it? Well, since you are not going to answer, you do it yourself. But if I ever do this again, it would be nice to know how you like it so I don't have to ask for separate containers of cream and sugar. [She extended the coffee. I did not reach for it and noted that my hands were sweaty.]

THERAPIST: What made you decide to bring me coffee?

Ms. A: Jesus, are you going to question this, too?! I just thought I'd be nice. Can't anything be simple? I was just being courteous. It is early in the morning. I wanted coffee. It seemed rude to drink by myself. I imagine you would probably like a cup yourself. And I haven't noticed a coffee machine around here. I suggest you get one, especially if you are working so early in the morning. As a matter of fact, if you buy the coffee machine, I'll supply the coffee.

> Her pleasant demeanor was fading fast. I felt an odd twisting of emotions within. I thought perhaps Ms. A was grateful for how I had handled the past weekend and really meant the coffee to be an appreciative gift. If that were the case, it would be rude not to accept. But acceptance might make me feel in her debt, and she might refer to this gift repeatedly in an attempt to extract something from me. I felt the truth lay somewhere in between, and I decided to err on the side of gracious acceptance and take a chance on the consequences.

THERAPIST: [I reached for the coffee.] Thank you.

Ms. A: Jesus Christ, what a big deal you make everything into. So how *do* you like your coffee?

> I felt uncomfortable; to reveal how I liked my coffee at that very moment seemed like sharing the most intimate details of my personal life.

THERAPIST: A little cream and sugar.

Ms. A: There . . . was that so bad?

THERAPIST: We are here to talk about things, feelings, relationships. I think it important to take a look at how you decided to bring me coffee today.

Ms. A: I already answered.

THERAPIST: It seems a lot has been going on lately.

Ms. A: What do you mean?

THERAPIST: Do you really not know what I'm referring to?

Ms. A: Not really.

THERAPIST: You seemed to be feeling pretty badly over the weekend, so much so that you called me.

Ms. A: I'm feeling better. I just don't want to talk about it. It might jinx my mood. Just drink your coffee.

THERAPIST: I think it's important to talk about these issues. Especially since one issue for you has been about people taking you seriously.

Ms. A: Yeah, who is paying who around here? I'm paying you so that I can choose to talk about what I want.

THERAPIST: Well, that's true, but that doesn't mean I don't have opinions about this therapy.

I noted after Ms. A left that I hadn't taken a sip.

The therapist, feeling somewhat battered and not particularly self-confident, goes ahead and concedes something that really isn't true—she concurs with the patient that because she is paying, she can choose what to talk about. The therapist always retains the prerogative to judge whether the patient is spending their time in therapy usefully. The patient pays for the opportunity of coming and talking in ways that can help her learn about herself. If the patient wants to talk about the price of coffee, that's her prerogative, but it's the therapist's responsibility to insist that the patient's reasons for wanting to discuss this become the topic. It is not an issue of whether the therapist should or should not drink Ms. A's coffee. But that the patient would follow a desperate "emergency" phone call, concluded with a hang-up, by bringing it gives the meaning of this "gift" overriding importance. If one drinks the cup of coffee without exploring its meaning, it encourages the patient to believe the therapy task is not primary or that she has intimidated the therapist. During the early phase of therapy such testing of boundaries is inevitable. The therapist's responses shape the relationship and determine whether a task orientation will prevail.

> Ms. A began to talk more and more about her increasing fondness for me and attempted repeatedly and unsuccessfully to elicit some acknowledgment of my caring for her. Four months into her treatment with me, she came in complaining that she felt desperate inside and felt a need for something and requested a pill. I suggested that an upcoming 4-day

weekend might be difficult for her. With her voice raised she demanded new medication to make her feel better. When I reiterated that I needed to understand how she felt in order to be helpful, she began swearing at me. I tried unsuccessfully to halt her tirade with the suggestion that she explore her feelings and that I would have to terminate the hour if she did not stop speaking to me in that fashion. Finally, I stood up from my chair.

THERAPIST: I need to terminate the hour now. I cannot work when I'm being treated in this manner.
Ms. A: You better only bill me for a half an hour.

With that she stormed out of my office. An hour later, she called and again demanded medication. I told her that since I did not understand what was troubling her, I felt it inappropriate to treat it with medication. To this she replied:

Ms. A: Well, you're full of shit and you don't understand and you're not helping, I'm not coming Wednesday or ever again.

I urged her to keep her next appointment, so we could try together to understand her experience. She told me there was nothing further to discuss and hung up. . . .

She did return and, in a characteristic way, behaved as if nothing out of the ordinary had occurred. I persisted in pointing out the need to explore her feelings and behavior. She persisted in complaining of her inability to sleep and the unbearable feelings in her stomach. Several weeks later, Ms. A paged me several times over a weekend, complaining of suicidality. With unfortunate coincidence, that same weekend I was attending the funeral of a friend's mother who had committed suicide. I was vulnerable and found myself less certain that Ms. A would not try to hurt herself. Again she complained of an ill-defined feeling that made her want to end her life. I was sympathetic, perhaps more so than I had been, spoke with her 15 minutes at a time, and tried to help clarify her feelings, although unsuccessfully. At the end of each conversation with her, I found myself saying, "I'll see you Monday," to which she would reply, "maybe."

She was late to her next appointment but arrived in good spirits. Mine, on the other hand, were frayed, and her being late filled me with fantasies that she had, in fact, killed herself. Seeing her walk in the door heralded relief and fury on my part.

Ms. A: I did something today which I have never done before. I turned off my alarm. Usually my cat, remember her name?
THERAPIST: Samantha.
Ms. A: Good; I'm impressed. Anyway, usually Samantha wakes me, but today she didn't.
THERAPIST: Maybe you didn't want to come.
Ms. A: I knew you were going to say that.
THERAPIST: Since you knew I was going to say that, perhaps you could address the issue.
Ms. A: Because you're a shrink. All questions, no answers, reasons behind everything.
THERAPIST: That's too general.
Ms. A: Hey, how did you remember my cat's name?

I knew I was angry with her, I was angry because of her sarcastic indifference to my welfare over a weekend in which my fears had made me distinctly uncomfortable. I felt devalued and ridiculed. . . .

Over the next few months, the treatment with Ms. A settled down into a regular routine. There were still acting out behaviors, although fewer. Over one weekend, she paged me several times regarding neck pain and wanted medication or the name of a good doctor. I told her that this kind of conversation could wait until our next appointment. She threatened to quit therapy but returned, reporting that she had gone to an emergency room and had her neck attended to appropriately. She apologized for having called. With further questioning as to why she *had* called, she said:

Ms. A: I was treating you like my mother, and I wanted you to take care of it right away. I was behaving like a baby. I did call my mother, but she said she didn't know any good doctors since daddy had died, and she was too busy. She told me to just take care of it.

The stabilization of the treatment was supported by a change in Ms. A's relationship with her mother. Her mother, who had for many years felt blown around by the wishes, fears, and threats of her daughter, was now setting some limits. In this way the process of treatment involving myself was paralleled by Ms. A's evolving relationship with her mother. With this development, Ms. A's treatment became much more focused on the relationship with her mother. She became overwhelmed by feelings of pending annihilation should her mother continue insisting on claiming her own freedom and independence. Ms. A became paranoid and resistant to exploring her concerns about this. I recommended that we include her mother in our sessions for a while. There were four such meetings. In the presence of her mother, Ms. A was more able to examine her rage and dependent longings in their relationship. These meetings served to help consolidate the important changes that were occurring in that relationship.

Such conjoint meetings signal the patient's accepting the therapist as an ally. This may be particularly useful with borderline patients who experience the growing attachment to a therapist as betraying their parents. The guilt about this, combined with abandonment fears, will aggravate suicidal thinking and testing behaviors. While peripheral to this case, it is relevant to note that psychotherapists often avoid such meetings "to preserve the transference" or "protect the relationship" under circumstances in which urging such meetings can be constructive for transference control, as well as establishing a truly therapeutic relationship.

The work became more effectively focused on impaired interpersonal dynamics, both with her mother and in the transference. The work became much less taxing for me and more rewarding for us both.

My treatment of Ms. A lasted almost a year. It ended when her mother became ill with leukemia. This occurred in the context of Ms. A having only recently acquired the ability to separate from her mother. Tolerating both the associated anxiety and anger was intolerable to Ms. A in the face of a potential real loss of her mother. Ms. A experienced this possible loss as in direct conflict with her therapeutic task of exploring and tolerating her disappointments with her mother. She opted to end the treatment rather than risk damaging her ties with her now more needy mother. Ms. A felt the need to devote all of her available free time before and after work to be with her mother.

## Discussion

The problems of suicidality, substance abuse, missed appointments, silences, intersession contact, rage, and self-destructive behavior that Ms. A presented are characteristic of the early phase of a psychotherapeutic treatment with a borderline patient. These problems transform psychotherapy into what Dawson and MacMillan aptly describe as skilled relationship management (18). The therapist helps the patient recognize how his or her moods and actions are reactive to whether he or she perceives relationships as holding or withholding. Helping a borderline patient move from actions outside the therapist's office to words inside the office enables exploration and analysis of the patient's internal life to begin. While this sounds straightforward, it is invariably a complicated process, as seen with Ms. A, requiring support, interpretation, limits, and directives in the right admixture. This report illustrates how, by recognizing and accepting countertransference feelings of hate, anxiety, and vulnerability, a therapist offers invaluable help for borderline patients to better control these feelings. While the transition from acting to speaking takes place, other psychotherapeutic processes related to attachment are occurring. By the end of the first year of treatment, borderline patients should have become aware of their dependence on the therapist and have the sense that this is acceptable (7). A joint recognition of how maladaptively the patient can respond to separations should result in diminished severity and frequency of acting out, particularly in the self-destructive behaviors. By the second year of treatment, one may expect sufficient stabilization such that a patient can resume some kind of role performance in terms of work- or school-related activity. Ms. A's occupation was the best "cotherapy" available, better even than the self-help groups. A vocation structures time and encourages the development of a sense of self independent of the role of patient.

This case report describes a brief and interrupted treatment. This is not an uncommon story for a borderline patient. Affective instability and countertransference dilemmas, as presented here in the treatment of Ms. A, often result in premature terminations. While the potential progression of longer treatments with borderline patients is important, the beneficial impact of a single episode of treatment needs to be underscored. In an era of managed care and the catch phrase "episodes of illness," there is something to be said for the value of episodes of treatment to lessen the regressive pull of borderline states. . . .

## References

1. Gunderson J, Links P: Borderline personality disorder, in Treatment of Psychiatric Disorders, 2nd ed. vol 2. Edited by Gabbard G. Washington, DC, American Psychiatric Press, 1995, pp. 2291–2310.
2. Gunderson JG: The borderline patient's intolerance of aloneness: insecure attachments and therapist availability. Am J Psychiatry 1996; 153:752–758.
3. Waldinger RJ, Gunderson JG: Effective Psychotherapy With Borderline Patients. New York, Macmillan, 1987.
4. Stevenson J, Meares R: An outcome study of psychotherapy for patients with borderline personality disorder. Am J Psychiatry 1992; 149:358–362.
5. Goldstein WN: Clarification of projective identification. Am J Psychiatry 1991; 148:153–161.
6. Dawson D, MacMillan HL: Relationship Management and the Borderline Patient. New York, Brunner/Mazel, 1993.
7. Gunderson JG, Waldinger RJ, Sabo AN, Nalavits LM: Stages of change in dynamic psychotherapy with borderline patients. J Psychotherapy Practice and Res 1993; 2:64–72.

# Birth Complications Combined with Early Maternal Rejection at Age 1 Year Predispose to Violent Crime at Age 18 Years

Adrian Raine, DPhil, Patricia Brennan, Ph.D., and Sarnoff A. Mednick, Ph.D.

*Individuals with antisocial personality disorder have a chronic disregard for the rights and well-being of others. They often break the law, lie, are irresponsible, impulsive, irritable, and aggressive. How might this type of behavior come about? It is common to speculate that antisocial behavior results from some combination of biological factors and the environment in which a child is raised. In the next article, Adrien Raine, Patricia Brennan, and Sarnoff Mednick sharpen this argument by demonstrating that one component of antisocial personality disorder—violent criminal activity—appears to result from a combination of birth complications and early rejection of the child by his caretakers.*

*What is most interesting is that neither factor, when acting alone, leads to an elevated level of violent crime; both factors have to be present for a significant increase in the likelihood of violent crime. This is known as a statistical interaction, or a moderating effect—meaning that the association between one independent variable (birth complications) and the dependent variable (violent crime) changes as a function of the score an individual receives on some other independent variable (in this case, early rejection as a child). Thus, when birth complications have occurred and the child has been rejected early in life, then the probability of violent criminal activity increases dramatically. The idea of statistical interaction can be difficult to understand at first, but it is an essential tool for theoreticians and it can clarify where and when something is likely to occur.*

*This article is also marked by a sophisticated approach toward specificity in the independent variable (as the authors demonstrate that it is early rejection of the child and not poor social circumstances that confers the risk) and in the dependent variable (early rejection of the child in combination with birth complications, which can interact to predict violent crime but not nonviolent crime).*

*Finally, the conclusion demonstrates the limitations of the study (e.g., that causation cannot be inferred because this is not an experiment) and includes the startling possibility that the rates of violent crime could be lowered by the reduction of birth-related complications and the improvement of caregiver skills.*

## Suggested Readings

Black, D. W., & Larson, C. L. (1999). *Bad boys, bad men: Confronting antisocial personality disorder.* New York: Oxford University Press.
Wolman, B. B. (1999). *Antisocial behavior: Personality disorders from hostility to homicide.* New York: Prometheus Books.

*Archives of General Psychiatry, 51,* 984–988. (1994).

**Background:** This study tests the biosocial interaction hypothesis that birth complications when combined with early maternal rejection of the infant predispose to adult violent crime

**Methods:** This hypothesis was tested using a cohort of 4269 consecutive live male births on whom measures of birth complications (age 0), early maternal rejection (age 1 year), and violent crime (age 18 years) were collected.

**Results:** A significant interaction ($P<.0001$) between birth complications and early maternal rejection indicated that those who suffered both birth complications and early child rejection were most likely to become violent offenders in adulthood. While only 4.5% of the subjects had both risk factors, this small group accounted for 18% of all violent crimes. The effect was specific to violence and was not observed for nonviolent criminal offending.

**Conclusions:** To our knowledge, this is the first study to show that birth complications in combination with early child rejection predispose to violent crime. The findings illustrate the critical importance of integrating biological with social measures to fully understand how violence develops and also suggest that prenatal, perinatal, and early postnatal health care interventions could significantly reduce violence.

The recent report on understanding and preventing violence from the National Research Council suggests that birth complications may predispose to violence, [1(pp364–365)] but empirical support for this link is currently very limited. While several studies have indicated that perinatal factors are linked to later antisocial and criminal behavior,[2–7] not all studies have confirmed this relationship.[8]

There are four limitations to these important but initial studies that may help explain conflicting findings. First, samples tend not to have been representative of the general population. Second, it is unclear whether the effect is specific to violence or can be observed for nonviolent crime or repeated criminal offending; most previous research has found it difficult to isolate specific correlates of violent crime as opposed to correlates of criminal behavior in general.[1(p359)] Third, and most important, previous studies have not considered the possibility that birth complications may additionally require a negative early psychosocial environment to result in the specific outcome of violent behavior in adulthood. Research on school performance, for example, has indicated that the combination of birth complications and a negative family environment is associated with poor school performance.[9] While the interaction between biological and environmental variables is commonly believed to be important in explaining violent behavior,[1,3,10,11] there is surprisingly little hard empirical evidence to support such a view.[1(p102)] Fourth, previous studies have not assessed the potential importance of early child rejection in predisposing to violence. Maternal rejection of the infant and disruption to the mother-infant bond, in conjunction with a biological predisposition to violence, could prove critical in disrupting interpersonal development and predisposing to more callous, violent interpersonal behavior in later life.

The study reported herein attempts to overcome some problems associated with previous studies to better test the biosocial interaction hypothesis that birth complications interact with negative early psychosocial environment in predisposing to adult violent offending. In particular, the possibility that early child rejection may be a specific and important aspect of a negative psychosocial environment in predisposing to violence was tested. Specificity to violent as opposed to nonviolent crime was also assessed.

## Methods

SUBJECTS  Male subjects (N=4269) were drawn from a total cohort of 9125 consecutive births of males and females that took place in the maternity department of the State University Hospital (Rigshospitalet) in Copenhagen, Denmark, between September 1959 and December 1961. All live deliveries of over 20 weeks' gestation were included. Informed consent for human investigation was obtained from the parents. . . . Only data from males were analyzed because the very low rates of criminal violence in females (0.3%) precluded meaningful statistical analyses.

BIRTH COMPLICATIONS  Birth complications and conditions were recorded at the time of delivery by an obstetrician assisted by a midwife. This study uses a frequency birth complications score developed through the collaboration of American and Danish obstetricians and pediatric neurologists.[12,13] Examples of delivery complications on this scale include forceps extraction, breech delivery, umbilical cord prolapse, preeclampsia, and long birth duration. For analysis purposes, the subjects were divided into two groups: those with no delivery complications and those with one or more complications.

EARLY CHILD REJECTION AND SOCIAL CIRCUMSTANCE MEASURES  Demographic, family, and psychosocial variables were collected during pregnancy and when the child was 1 year old. Variables collected during pregnancy relevant to our analyses include whether the pregnancy was wanted or unwanted, the mother's attempts to abort the fetus, and the mother's age. Year 1 follow-up interview variables included home conditions, marital status, and placement of infant for care into a full-time public institution for more than 4 months of the first year. The socioeconomic status of the family (based on educational and occupational levels) was obtained at 1 year from the Danish Central Persons' Register.

A factor analysis using principal component analysis followed by a varimax rotation produced two factors with eigenvalues greater than 1. The two factors were defined as follows (factor loadings in parentheses): factor 1, "poor social circumstances": unmarried mother (.71); low socioeconomic status (.67); poor home conditions (.65); young maternal age (.64); unwanted pregnancy (.59); and factor 2, "early child rejection": public institutional care of infant (.68); attempt to abort fetus (.65); unwanted pregnancy (.44). . . .

VIOLENT CRIMINAL OFFENDING  Criminal status was assessed when the offspring were aged 17 to 19 years by a search of the Danish National Criminal Register in which all police contacts and court decisions involving Danish citizens are recorded. This is viewed as one of the most comprehensive and accurate registers in the Western world.[14] The definition of violence used by the National Academy of Sciences Panel on the Understanding and Control of Violence ("behaviors by individuals that intentionally threaten, attempt, or inflict physical harm on others") was used.[1] Consequently, violent crime was defined by the following offenses: murder, attempted murder, assault (including domestic assault), rape, armed robbery, illegal possession of a weapon, and threats of violence. Nonviolent crime was defined as theft, breaking and entering, fraud, forgery, blackmail, embezzlement, vandalism, prostitution, pimping, and narcotic offenses. One hundred forty-five subjects were classified as violent criminals (3.4%), 540 as nonviolent criminals (12.6%), and 3584 as noncriminals (84.0%). The total criminality rate of

16% in this Danish sample is similar to the rate of 17% found by Raine et al[15] for a community sample of English males.

## Results

VIOLENT OFFENDERS VS NONCRIMINALS A logistic regression analysis indicated a highly significant interaction between delivery complications and early child rejection in predicting violence ($\chi^2$ [$df$=1, N=3175]=10.4, P<.002) and indicated that those who experienced both birth complications and early child rejection were most likely to become violent. To exemplify this relationship diagrammatically, rates of violence were calculated for those subjects who had both risk factors, i.e., birth complications and severe maternal rejection (defined by mothers' negative attitude to pregnancy and either attempted abortion or institutionalization). Rates of violence for this group were compared with three other comparison groups: (1) those with neither risk factor, (2) those with severe maternal rejection only, and (3) those with birth complications only. Results of these analyses are shown in Figure [7.1]. Using this more severe criterion of maternal rejection, the interaction was again significant ($\chi^2$ [$df$=1, N=3175]=14.4, P <.0001).

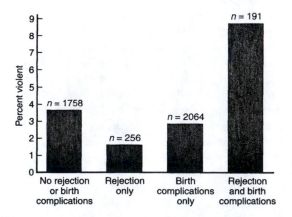

Figure 7.1. Illustration of the significant interaction (P<.001) observed between birth complications and early maternal rejection at age 1 year in predicting outcome for criminal violence at age 18 years.

The interaction was specific to early maternal rejection in that no such interaction was observed between poor social circumstances and birth complications (P>.66). As has been observed in previous research,[1] a main effect was observed for poor social circumstances ($\chi^2$ [$df$=1, N=3175]=40.6, P<.00001). No main effects were observed for birth complications (P>.90) or early child rejection (P>.62).

VIOLENT OFFENDERS VS NONVIOLENT CRIMINALS The above interaction is specific to violent offending and is not found for nonviolent crime. A significant interaction between birth complications and early child rejection was observed when violent criminals were compared with nonviolent criminals in a logistic regression analysis ($\chi^2$ [$df$=1, N=557]=6.3, P<.02). The interaction indicated that those who experienced both high birth complications and early child rejection were most likely to become violent criminals, i.e., of offenders who had both risk factors, 47.2% became violent compared with 19.7% of offenders who had neither risk factor or only one.

In this comparison of violent with nonviolent criminals, the interaction effect is again specific to maternal rejection. No interaction effect was observed for poor social circumstances and birth complications (P>.80). In addition, main effects were not found for early child rejection (P>.39), poor social circumstances (P>.08), or birth complications (P>.23). . . .

## Comment

To our knowledge, this is the first study to provide evidence from a large birth cohort to show that birth complications in combination with a negative psychosocial environment (specifically early child rejection) are associated with violent crime in early adulthood. In contrast, the very few previous biosocial studies have neither shown specificity for violence nor highlighted the specific importance of early child rejection.[9,13] The interaction between biological and social predispositions appears to be critically important in understanding violent offending[16,17] because possession of only one risk factor (i.e., birth complications alone or early child rejection alone) was not associated with increased rates of violence. This interaction effect was found to be specific to violent crime and not crime in general, whereas most previous biological research has not obtained specificity for violent crime per se.[1(p359)]

The fact that birth complications combined with child rejection but not the more general factor of poor social circumstances in predisposing to violence helps establish a more specific biosocial pathway toward violent crime. Poor social circumstances such as low social class and poor home conditions have been found to be general, weak correlates of violent and nonviolent crime, whereas there is some evidence that variables related to child rejection such as child neglect, lack of maternal warmth, and separation from parents may be more specific predispositions toward violent crime in particular.[18–20] Disruption to the mother-infant bonding processes due to institutionalization has been associated with affectionless psychopathic criminal behavior.[21,22] Poor early bonding may therefore lead to more callous, affectionless, unempathic interpersonal relationships that in turn may increase the likelihood of violent interpersonal behavior, particularly when combined with a preexisiting biological predisposition to violence.

It is not known precisely how birth complications predispose to violence, but it is possible that such complications result in brain dysfunction and associated neurological and neuropsychological deficits that in turn directly and indirectly predispose to violence.[3,23–25] For example, birth complications could lead to cognitive deficits that in turn lead to school failure, occupational failure, and ultimately violence. Similarly, birth complications may contribute to neuropsychiatric deficits and lack of self-control, resulting in explosive, impulsive aggression.[7] The effects of any such brain dysfunction may in turn be exacerbated by a negative early psychosocial environment.[3,9]

While prospective longitudinal studies can help tease out causality by establishing temporal ordering of variables, they cannot establish causal-

ity per se, and several causal pathways are feasible other than the one described above. Specifically, it is possible that a third factor underlies the link between birth complications/parental rejection and violence. For example, it is conceivable that there are genetic predispositions to birth complications, negative parenting, and violence and that genetic factors underlie the observed relationships.

It could be argued that birth complications and maternal rejection are not independent events. Specifically, children with birth complications might be more likely to be rejected by their mothers. This scenario seems unlikely, however, for two reasons. First, two of the three variables making up the construct of early child rejection precede birth in time (unwanted pregnancy, attempts to abort fetus) rather than postdating birth complications. Second, birth complications and early child rejection were not positively correlated in this sample ($\tau=-.029$), indicating that these constructs reflect processes that are largely independent.

We would caution against the overgeneralization of our findings to other populations at this stage and emphasize the need for replication of our findings in the United States. Denmark is a relatively homogeneous society and future studies are needed to confirm this biosocial interaction in countries such as the United States with its higher rates of violent crime. . . . We also would caution that these findings do not demonstrate causal links between birth complications/early child rejection and later violence, although the prospective, longitudinal nature of the study helps to provide some support for such an interpretation. Furthermore, it is recognized that birth complications and early child rejection are only two of many risk factors for violence, which also include learning deficits,[26] parental criminality,[27] low serotonin levels,[28] parental absence,[21,29] neuropsychological deficits,[23,30,31] poor parental supervision,[32,33] child abuse,[19,31] low arousal,[15] poor affective relationships,[34,35] and parental criminality.[36]

Results of this study raise two important questions with respect to efforts to reduce rates of violence that focus on biological and psychosocial risk factors. The first question concerns whether interventions aimed at providing better antenatal health care to underserved populations could have an effect in reducing rates of violence. The recent National Research Council report on understanding and preventing violence recommended that serious consideration be given to conducting such interventions to reduce perinatal complications,[1(pp 383–384)] although this recommendation was based on limited empirical data. In the present study, we found that although only 4.5% of [the] population had both birth complications and early child rejection, this small group accounted for 18% of all violent crimes perpetrated by the entire sample of 4269. Assuming early interventions could successfully reduce birth complications and the link between birth complications and violence is causal, these findings suggest that such interventions could conceivably reduce violence in the next generation by as much as 18%. The current findings lend some support for the consideration of initial perinatal intervention research studies to test whether the link between birth complications/early child rejection and violence is causal.

The second question concerns whether changing the psychosocial environment can help reduce violence in society. Very little is known regarding what factors protect a biologically predisposed individual from becoming violent. The finding that birth complications do not predispose to violence when combined with a nonrejecting early home environment is of potential importance because it suggests that a good psychosocial home environment can protect against the otherwise negative effects of birth complications. This is consistent with previous findings that good parental care and the opportunity to bond with a caregiver in the first year of life can reduce the deleterious cognitive and behavioral effects of birth complications.[2,16] Psychosocial interventions aimed at increasing caregiving skills to parents may conceivably help suppress this biological predisposition to later adult violence.

# References

1. Reiss AJ, Roth JA, eds. *Understanding and Preventing Violence*. Washington. DC: National Academy Press; 1993.

2. Werner EE, Smith RS. *Overcoming the Odds: High Risk Children From Birth to Adulthood*. Ithaca, NY: Cornell University Press; 1992.

3. Raine A. *The Psychopathology of Crime: Criminal Behavior as a Clinical Disorder*. San Diego, Calif: Academic Press; 1993.

4. Brennan P, Mednick SA, Kandel E. Congenital determinants of violent and property offending. In: Pepler DJ, Rubin KH, eds. *The Development and Treatment of Childhood Aggression*. Hillsdale, NJ: Lawrence Erlbaum Associates; 1993:81–92.

5. Kandel E, Mednick SA. Perinatal complications predict violent offending. *Criminology*. 1991;29:519–529.

6. Litt SM. *Perinatal Complications and Criminality*. Ann Arbor: University of Michigan; 1971, Doctoral dissertation.

7. Mungas D. An empirical analysis of specific syndromes of violent behavior. *J Nerv Ment Dis*. 1983;171:354–361.

8. Denno DJ. *Biology, Crime and Violence: New Evidence*. Cambridge, England: Cambridge University Press; 1989.

9. Drillien CM. *The Growth and Development of the Prematurely Born Infant*. Baltimore, Md: Williams & Williams; 1964.

10. Mednick SA, Christiansen KO. *Biosocial Bases of Criminal Behavior*. New York, NY: Gardner; 1977.

11. Raine A, Mednick SA. Biosocial longitudinal research into antisocial behavior. *Rev Epidemiol State Publique*. 1989;37:515–524.

12. Mednick SA, Mura E, Schulsinger F, Mednick B. Perinatal conditions and infant development in the children of schizophrenic parents. *Soc Biol*. 1971;18:S103–S113.

13. Baker RL, Mednick BR. *Influences on Human Development: A Longitudinal Analysis*. Boston, Mass: Kluwer; 1984.

14. Wolfgang ME. Foreword. In: Mednick SA, Christiansen KO. eds. *Biosocial Bases of Criminal Behavior*. New York, NY: Gardner; 1977:v–vi.

15. Raine A, Venables PH, Williams M. Relationships between CNS and ANS measures of arousal at age 15 and criminality at age 24. *Arch Gen Psychiatry*. 1990;47:1003–1007.

16. Eichelman B. Neurochemical and psychopharmacological aspects of aggressive behavior. *Ann Rev Med*. 1970;41:149–158.

17. Widom CS. Does violence beget violence? a critical examination of the literature. *Psychol Bull*. 1991;109:130.

18. Farrington DP. Childhood aggression and adult violence: early precursors and later life outcomes. In: Pepler DJ, Rubin KH, eds. *The Development and Treatment of Childhood Aggression*. Hillsdale, NJ: Lawrence Erlbaum Associates; 1991:5–29.

19. Widom CS. The cycle of violence. *Science*. 1989;244:160–166.

20. McCord JM. A longitudinal view of the relationship between paternal absence and crime. In: Gunn J, Farrington DP, eds. *Abnormal Offenders, Delinquency, and the Criminal Justice System*. Chichester, England: Wiley & Sons; 1982:113–127.

21. Bowlby J. *Forty-four Juvenile Thieves: Their Characters and Home Life*. London, England: Baillere Tindall & Cox; 1946.

22. Rutter M. *Maternal Deprivation Reassessed*. 2nd ed. Harmondsworth, England: Penguin; 1982.

23. Moffitt TE. The neuropsychology of juvenile delinquency: a critical review. In: Tonry M. Morris N, eds. *Crime and Jus-*

tice: A Review of the Literature. Chicago, Ill: University of Chicago Press; 1990.

24. Moffitt TE, Henry B. Neuropsychological studies of juvenile delinquency and juvenile violence. In: Milner JS, ed. Neuropsychology of Aggression. Boston, Mass: Kluwer; 1991:131–146.

25. Lewis DO, Pincus JH, Bard B, Richardson E, Prichep LS, Feldman M, Yeager C. Neuropsychiatric, psychoeducational, and family characteristics of 14 juveniles condemned to death in the United States. Am J Psychiatry. 1988;145:584–589.

26. Wilson JO, Hernstein RJ. Crime and Human Nature. New York, NY: Simon & Schuster; 1985.

27. Loeber R, Dishion T. Early predictors of male delinquency: a review. Psychol Bull. 1983;94:68–99.

28. Linnoila VMI, Virkkunen M. Aggression, suicidality, and serotonin. J Clin Psychiatry. 1992;53:46–51.

29. Ellis L. The victimful-victimless crime distinction, and seven universal demographic correlates of victimful criminal behavior. Pers Individual Differ. 1988;9:525–548.

30. Ellis L. Left and mixed handedness and criminality: explorations for a probable relationship. In: Coran S. ed.

Left Handedness: Behavioral Implications and Anomalies. Amsterdam, the Netherlands: Elsevier Science Publishers; 1990.

31. Lewis DO. From abuse to violence: psychophysiological consequences of maltreatment. J Am Acad Child Adolesc Psychiatry. 1992;31:383–391.

32. Loeber R. Development and risk factors of juvenile antisocial behavior and delinquency. Clin Psychol Rev 1990;10:1–41.

33. Loeber R, Stouthamer-Loeber M. Family factors as correlates and predictors of juvenile conduct problems and delinquency. In: Tonry M. Morris N. eds. Crime and Justice. Chicago, Ill: Chicago University Press; 1986;7:29–149.

34. McCord J. Long-term perspectives on parental absence. In: Robins LN. Rutter M, eds. Straight and Devious Pathways From Childhood to Adulthood. Cambridge, England: Cambridge University Press; 1990:116–134.

35. Farrington DP, Hawkins JD. Predicting participation, early onset, and later persistence in officially recorded offending. Criminal Behav Ment Health. 1991;1:1–33.

36. Farrington DP. Early predictors of adolescent aggression and adult violence. Violence Victims. 1989;4:79–100.

# Selective Alteration of Personality and Social Behavior by Serotonergic Intervention

Brian Knutson, Ph.D., Owen M. Wolkowitz, M.D., Steve W. Cole, Ph.D., Theresa Chan, B.A., Elizabeth A. Moore, Ph.D., Ronald C. Johnson, Ph.D., Jan Terpstra, M.D., Rebecca A. Turner, Ph.D., and Victor I. Reus, M.D.

*Most research on personality and personality disorders is correlational rather than experimental. In a correlational study, variables are observed as they exist naturally and their covariation is examined. In an experimental study, the independent variable is manipulated by the researcher, and its effects on some other variable (the dependent variable) are then examined. For ethical reasons, researchers are not usually able to manipulate variables such as quality of parenting that we suspect might have an effect on personality development, so this limits what we can know.*

*In the next article, Brian Knutson and colleagues conduct an experimental study to test the hypothesis that increases in the amount of one specific neurotransmitter, serotonin, when given to a group of research participants, will result in behavioral changes relative to a group of participants who receive a placebo. The independent variable in this case is whether or not an individual received paroxetine, which is known as a selective serotonergic reuptake inhibitor (SSRI). As this name suggests, paroxetine inhibits the reuptake of serotonin in the synaptic cleft, thus increasing the amount of circulating (or "bioavailable") serotonin in the brain. Prior studies indicate that low levels of serotonin are associated with hostility and aggression. Accordingly, the dependent variables in this study are self-reported feelings of aggression, irritability, negative and positive emotion, and observed level of cooperation in a problem-solving task.*

*By demonstrating changes in some of these variables as a consequence of the paroxetine, Knutson and colleagues are able to argue that feelings typically associated with personality might be linked to serotonergic functioning. One of the interesting aspects of this study is that the authors examine the effects of serotonin in two separate ways. First, they use the main between-groups independent variable (that is, whether or not an individual received paroxetine). Then they turn to a within-group variable: because peoples' serotonin levels vary, they measured these levels and correlated them with the self-reports of mood and the observed cooperativeness. Figures in the article present these results and they provide further evidence that serotonin levels may contribute to variability in the dependent variables.*

*American Journal of Psychiatry*, 155, 373–379. (1998).

*Objective·* The authors sought to test the causal hypothesis that serotonergic function modulates aspects of the normal spectrum of individual differences in affective experience and social behavior in humans. *Method:* A selective serotonin reuptake inhibitor (SSRI), paroxetine, 20 mg/day (N=26), or placebo (N=25) was administered to normal volunteers in a double-blind manner for 4 weeks, and personality variables and social behavior were assessed at baseline and at weeks I and 4 of treatment. *Results·* Relative to placebo, SSRI administration reduced focal indices of hostility through a more general decrease in negative affect, yet did not alter indices of positive affect. In addition, SSRI administration increased a behavioral index of social affiliation. Changes in both negative affect and affiliative behavior were significantly related to volunteers' plasma SSRI levels at the end of the experiment. *Conclusions:* Central serotonergic function may modulate a dimension of normal personality characterized by reduced negative affective experience and increased affiliative behavior. SSRI administration has significant and detectable effects on these measures even in the absence of baseline clinical depression or other psychopathology.

**R**esearch indicates that individual differences in human personality can be summarized by three to five independent dimensions (1). Status on each of these dimensions is stable over the adult lifespan (2) and typically shows heritabilities on the order of 50% (3). However, the physiological substrates underlying these personality dimensions have not yet been elucidated. Spurred by advances in psychopharmacology, several theorists have proposed that brain biogenic amine mechanisms may contribute to the phenotypic expression of some of these dimensions, particularly those which involve affective and motivational processes (4–6).

Consistent with these speculations, clinical studies of psychiatric patients suggest that low brain serotonin activity may be related to psychiatric disorders involving hostile affect and aggressive behavior. For instance, people with a history of impulsively violent behavior (e.g., arsonists, violent criminals, people who die by violent methods of suicide) have low CSF serotonin metabolite levels (7). In addition, patients with violent histories (e.g., with antisocial personality disorder) show signs of compromised brain serotonin function, as assessed by neuroendocrine probes (8). Finally, pharmacological interventions that augment serotonergic efficacy can reduce hostile sentiment and violent outbursts in aggressive psychiatric patients (9).

In contrast, the impact of serotonergic interventions on hostile personality characteristics in normal individuals has received less investigation. Impairment of brain serotonin function by means of precursor depletion can induce depressive affect (10, 11) and may potentiate hostile behavior (12, 13) in normal control subjects. At the time this study was conducted, no one had investigated whether augmentation of brain serotonin would affect hostility variables in normal volunteers. If enhancement of brain serotonergic function reduces hostility, might such effects remain focal only to hostility variables, or might they be attributable to broader changes in affective personality variables? For example, might administration of a selective serotonin reuptake inhibitor (SSRI) reduce negative affect (including sadness, anxiety, and other negative emotions in addition to hostility) or increase positive affect? To address these questions, we used a pharmacologically selective intervention to alter brain serotonin function in normal subjects and observed subsequent changes in standard affective personality variables over 4 weeks.

A second but related body of research suggests that brain serotonin function also plays a role in the social behavior of nonhuman primates. For instance, rhesus monkeys with low CSF serotonin metabolite levels show more spontaneous aggression toward conspecifics, receive more wounds, and die at a younger age (14, 15), while those with high CSF serotonin metabolite levels show greater proximity to and grooming of peers and have a greater number of neighbors living nearby (16). . . . To address the hypothesis that augmentation of central serotonergic function would increase affiliative behavior in humans, we observed the effects of our serotonergic intervention on the social behavior of normal humans in the context of a cooperative dyadic puzzle task.

## Method

SUBJECTS AND TREATMENT  We examined the effects of a serotonergic reuptake blockade on personality and social behavior in a double-blind protocol by randomly assigning 51 medically and psychiatrically healthy volunteers to treatment with either an SSRI, paroxetine, 20 mg/day p.o. (N=25), or placebo (N=26). Paroxetine was selected because of its relatively potent and specific inhibition of the serotonin reuptake mechanism in comparison with other SSRIs (17), although any SSRI may have secondary effects on other monoamine systems (18). Volunteers were recruited by advertisements in a local weekly newspaper. They gave written informed consent and were screened to exclude subjects with a history of or with first-degree relatives with a history of axis I disorders or dysthymia, as determined by the Structured Clinical Interview for *DSM-III-R— Non-Patient Edition* (19). Volunteers were also screened to exclude subjects with a history of psychotropic medication or substance abuse and sub-

jects taking concurrent medications (including birth control pills in the case of women). Volunteers were informed of the possibility of physical side effects but not of the hypotheses. After complete description of the study, written informed consent was obtained from volunteers. One man and one woman in the paroxetine group did not complete the experiment because of side effects, while a second woman in the control group did not complete the experiment because of scheduling conflicts, leaving a total of 23 volunteers in the SSRI group (nine women and 14 men) and 25 in the placebo group (11 women and 14 men). The mean ages of SSRI-treated (mean=26.7 years, SD=2.9) and placebo-treated (mean=27.9, SD= 4.2) volunteers did not differ.

PSYCHOMETRIC MEASURES  Standard psychometric and behavioral measures were administered at three times: at baseline, after 1 week of treatment, and after 4 weeks of treatment (i.e., at the end of the study). At each assessment, hostility was assessed with the assaultiveness and irritability subscales of the Buss-Durkee Hostility Inventory (20), as suggested by Siever and Trestman (21). To determine whether changes in hostility could be accounted for by more general changes in affective dimensions of personality, we also administered the Positive and Negative Affect Scales. Prior research has shown that different negative affects (e.g., hostility, fear) tend to be correlated in incidence, as do different positive affects (e.g., happiness, excitement). However, negative and positive affects tend to be uncorrelated with each other rather than inversely correlated, and so they are conceptualized as independent trait dimensions (22). To enhance the sensitivity of all psychometric measures to change over time, participants were asked to respond to the questionnaires in terms of their experience during the previous week.

BEHAVIORAL MEASURES  Objective behaviors were elicited at each assessment in the context of a standardized dyadic puzzle task. The task was designed to elicit face-valid social behaviors that could be reliably coded within the context of a cooperative interaction and subsequently compared across repeated measurement occasions. During the task, each subject collaborated with a partner in planning and implementing solutions for different spatial puzzles (also known as tangrams). Subject pairs were given 10 minutes to combine a set of seven puzzle pieces into configurations that matched as many target shapes as possible, with the stipulation that only one partner could touch the puzzle pieces at a time. Pairs always consisted of one SSRI- and one placebo-treated subject, and novel partners were assigned at each assessment. Neither the subjects nor the experimenter knew the experimental condition of pair members. One of the subjects in the SSRI group did not participate in the baseline puzzle task because of scheduling conflicts.

Puzzle-solving sessions were videotaped without volunteers' knowledge by a hidden camera placed behind a one-way mirror, so as to preserve the authenticity of the volunteers' nonverbal behavior. At the end of the experiment, an interviewer explained the rationale for the hidden camera and offered volunteers an opportunity to have their behavioral records removed from the analyses and deleted. None chose this option; all released their behavioral records for analysis. Coders who were blind to the volunteers' condition subsequently scored the videotapes for various objective social behaviors indicative of cooperation. Specifically, making suggestions while a partner handled the puzzle pieces was considered cooperative, but issuing commands while the partner handled the puzzle pieces was not. In addition, grasping the pieces with the intent of arriving at a unilateral solution was not considered cooperative. Coders attained significant agreement (intraclass $r=0.73$, $p<0.001$) on an aggregate measure composed of these behaviors (i.e., behavioral aggregate= (number of suggestions–number of commands–number of unilateral grasps), which served as the index of affiliative behavior in subsequent analyses.

PLASMA MEASURES  To determine whether individual differences in SSRI bioavailability might exist and potentially influence results, we assayed paroxetine levels in peripheral blood after 4 weeks of treatment. Assays were performed on samples of venous blood drawn at baseline and week 4. The baseline sample was drawn following an overnight fast, and the week 4 sample was also drawn following an overnight fast, 10 hours after the final dose of paroxetine. Plasma paroxetine was quantitated from these samples by using liquid chromatography with fluorescence detection following precolumn derivatization with dansyl chloride (23). Intra- and interassay coefficients of variation were all less than 10%. . . .

STATISTICAL ANALYSIS  Exploratory data analysis revealed that plasma paroxetine levels varied dramatically among treated individuals (range=0–44 ng/ml, with an approximate fivefold variation across the interquartile range: 5–24 ng/ml) and that changes in both psychometric and behavioral indices were strongly correlated with changes in plasma paroxetine level. Thus, psychometric and behavioral data were analyzed in two ways: 1) with a traditional group-based approach (i.e., a 2-by-3 [treatment-by-time within] repeated measures analysis of variance), and 2) with a similar statistical model that substituted continuous changes in plasma paroxetine levels for the dichotomous grouping variable as a predictor of psychometric and behavioral changes (24). . . .

## Results

* * *

PSYCHOMETRIC MEASURES  Group analyses indicated that assaultiveness scores on the Buss-Durkee Hostility Inventory declined significantly for the SSRI-treated group relative to placebo control subjects at both week 1 and week 4 (treatment-by-time interaction: $F=5.04$, df=2, 82, $p<0.01$) (table 1). While omnibus tests did not indicate a statistically significant decrement in irritability scores on the Buss-Durkee Hostility Inventory for the SSRI-treated group overall (treatment-by-time interaction: $F=2.45$, df=2, 82, $p<0.10$), pairwise contrasts suggested a significant reduction at week 4. There were no significant group differences in changes in either assaultiveness or irritability scores on the Buss-Durkee Hostility Inventory from week 1 to week 4. Plasma-based analyses indicated that decreases in assaultiveness and irritability scores on the Buss-Durkee Hostility Inventory at week 4 were both significantly related to increased plasma paroxetine at the end of the experiment (table 2).

Group analyses also indicated that negative affect scores on the Positive and Negative Affect Scales decreased for the SSRI-treated group relative to placebo subjects at both week 1 and week 4 (treatment-by-time interaction: F=3.30, df=2, 82, p<0.05). There were no significant group differences in changes in negative affect scores from week 1 to week 4. Plasma-based analyses also revealed that reductions in negative affect scores at week 1 and week 4 were significantly related to plasma paroxetine at the end of the experiment (table 2 and figure 1). Unlike negative affect scores, positive affect scores did not change significantly as a function of SSRI treatment (treatment-by-time interaction: F=1.38, df=2, 82, p=0.26), and changes in positive affect scores were not related to plasma paroxetine levels at the end of the experiment. . . .

BEHAVIORAL MEASURE  Group analyses indicated that the SSRI-treated group showed more affiliative behavior in the puzzle task than the placebo-treated group at week 1, but not at week 4 (treatment-by-time interaction: F=3.17, df=2, 80, p<0.05). . . . Plasma-based analyses indicated that affiliative behavior at both week 1 and week 4 was significantly related to plasma paroxetine levels at the end of the experiment (table 2 and figure 2). . . .

## Discussion

These data indicate that SSRI administration can modulate some aspects of personality in normal human volunteers. Furthermore, these changes show some functional selectivity. First, SSRI administration reduced psychometric assaultiveness relative to placebo; this finding extends the generalizability of clinical observations that SSRIs can reduce hostile sentiment and violent outbursts in aggressive psychiatric patients (25). Second, SSRI administration reduced negative affect relative to placebo, and this shift could statistically account for reductions in assaultiveness, which suggests that SSRIs may modulate a broader range of affective variables than those strictly related to hostility.

### TABLE 1

CHANGES IN PSYCHOMETRIC AND BEHAVIORAL SCORES FROM BASELINE TO WEEKS 1 AND 4 FOR NORMAL VOLUNTEERS RECEIVING PLACEBO OR AN SSRI

| | Score | | | | | | | |
|---|---|---|---|---|---|---|---|---|
| | Change From Baseline to Week 1 | | | | Change From Baseline to Week 4 | | | |
| | Placebo | | SSRI | | Placebo | | SSRI | |
| Variable | Mean[a] | SD | Mean[a] | SD | Mean[a] | SD | Mean[a] | SD |
| Hostility[b] | | | | | | | | |
| Assaultiveness | 0.11 | 0.80 | −0.47[c] | 0.76 | 0.39 | 0.95 | −0.39[c] | 0.93 |
| Irritability | 0.29 | 0.70 | −0.04 | 0.97 | 0.42 | 0.85 | −0.23[c] | 1.10 |
| Affect[d] | | | | | | | | |
| Negative | 0.24 | 0.95 | −0.51[c] | 1.02 | 0.32 | 1.35 | −0.50[c] | 1.02 |
| Positive | 0.05 | 0.85 | −0.50 | 1.14 | 0.08 | 1.05 | −0.11 | 1.06 |
| Affiliative behavior | −0.34 | 1.15 | 0.47[c] | 1.02 | −0.53 | 1.40 | 0.03 | 1.10 |

[a]Standardized.
[b]Buss-Durkee Hostility Inventory.
[c]Significant difference from placebo group (p<0.05).
[d]Positive and Negative Affect Scales.

Third, SSRI administration did not significantly alter positive affect, which indicates that global effects on arousal (as in the case of sedation) could not account for the observed reductions in negative affect. While changes in positive affect did show a nonsignificant trend toward diminution at week 1, the change was not significant and was unrelated to plasma paroxetine levels at the study's conclusion. Overall, these findings support theories which posit that separable neurochemical substrates modulate the expression of negative and positive affect (26, 27).

Besides modulating psychometric indices of negative affect, SSRI administration also enhanced behavioral indices of social affiliation in a cooperative task. While collaboratively solving a puzzle, SSRI-treated partners scored higher on an affiliative behavioral composite consisting of increased suggestions, decreased commands, and decreased unilateral solution attempts at week 1 of testing. It is unclear why this group difference did not persist until week 4, but affiliative behavior at week 4 nevertheless remained correlated with plasma paroxetine levels. Drops in affiliative behavior for both groups across time may have diminished potential group differences at week 4. These findings in human volunteers complement primate studies in which chronic SSRI treatment of male vervet monkeys enhanced a constellation of affiliative behaviors, which in turn led to increased status (28). However, affiliative behavior may raise one's status only in certain social contexts (e.g., in the absence of a preexisting dominance hierarchy, in the presence of peers who reciprocate affiliative behavior [29, 30]). Thus, while this work suggests that chronic SSRI administration can enhance affiliative behavior of normal volunteers in a cooperative task with novel partners, more research is needed on interpersonal effects of SSRI treatment in other types of social scenarios (e.g., competitive). . . .

Besides differences between groups, the magnitude of changes in psychometric assaultiveness, irritability, negative affect, and behavioral affiliation was correlated with plasma levels of SSRI among SSRI-treated volunteers. Indeed, plasma SSRI predicted functional changes more robustly than did group assignment. This association is somewhat surprising, given that plasma SSRI levels do not consistently predict antidepressant response in clinically depressed patients (31). On the other hand, depressed patients who eventually respond to tricyclic antidepressants do show early changes

| | TABLE 2 | |
|---|---|---|

RELATIONSHIP OF PLASMA PAROXETINE LEVELS TO CHANGES IN PSYCHOMETRIC ND BEHAVIORAL SCORES FROM BASELINE TO WEEKS 1 AND 4 FOR NORMAL VOLUNTEERS RECEIVING PLACEBO OR AN SSRI

| | Analysis[a] | | | | | | | | |
|---|---|---|---|---|---|---|---|---|---|
| | Omnibus Test | | | Change From Baseline to Week 1 | | | Change From Baseline to Week 4 | | |
| Variable | F | df | p | F | df | p | F | df | p |
| Hostility[b] | | | | | | | | | |
| Assaultiveness | 3.12 | 2, 92 | 0.05 | 2.07 | 1, 46 | 0.16 | 4.71 | 1, 46 | 0.03 |
| Irritability | 3.81 | 2, 92 | 0.03 | 2.85 | 1, 46 | 0.10 | 7.56 | 1, 46 | 0.01 |
| Affect[c] | | | | | | | | | |
| Negative | 5.12 | 2, 92 | 0.01 | 6.06 | 1, 46 | 0.02 | 9.12 | 1, 46 | <0.01 |
| Positive | 1.56 | 2, 92 | 0.22 | 2.44 | 1, 46 | 0.13 | <1.00 | 1, 46 | 0.79 |
| Affiliative behavior | 5.88 | 2, 90 | <0.01 | 10.69 | 1, 45 | <0.01 | 5.49 | 5, 45 | 0.02 |

[a] F ratio tests for time-by-plasma paroxetine level interaction.
[b] Buss-Durkee Hostility Inventory.
[c] Positive and Negative Affect Scales.

FIGURE 1. Correlation of Changes in Negative Affect With Plasma Paroxetine Levels at the End of the Experiment for Normal Volunteers Receiving an SSRI[a]

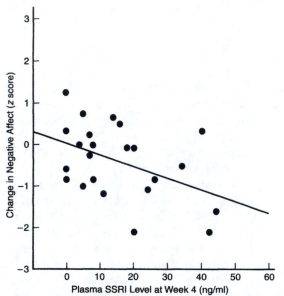

[a]r=−0.44, N=23, p<0.05. Change scores were calculated as the mean of week 1 and week 4 scores minus baseline.

FIGURE 2. Correlation of Changes in Affiliative Behavior with Plasma Paroxetine Levels at the End of the Experiment for Normal Volunteers Receiving an SSRI[a,b]

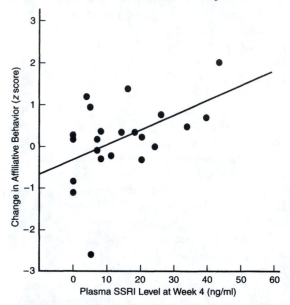

[a]r=0.65, N=22, p<0.01. Change scores were calculated as the mean of week 1 and week 4 scores minus baseline.
[b]One subject's behavioral data were not available because of scheduling conflicts.

in negative affect (e.g., at 10 days) that are more strongly associated with subsequent shifts in cerebrospinal serotonin metabolites than with depressive status per se (32). Thus, our measures may be tapping a continuum of early subsyndromal changes that either presage or bear no relation to later therapeutic responses in psychiatric patients. Others have recently reported that 6 weeks of SSRI (fluoxetine) administration did not alter the affect of normal volunteers (33), but these investigators sampled a smaller number of subjects (N=6) and did not include individual difference measures of SSRI metabolism. Verification of the utility of these measures in predicting affective change awaits further replication.

Clearly, volunteers were not all equally affected by SSRI administration. An open-ended interview at the study's conclusion revealed that SSRI effects were often manifested in subtle and seemingly idiosyncratic ways. For example, SSRI-treated vol-

unteers' responses to the question "What did you experience during the experiment?" ranged from "I used to think about good and bad, but now I don't; I'm in a good mood" (highest plasma SSRI level) to "The side effects were intense at first but then tapered off" (lowest plasma SSRI level). Individual differences in responsiveness to the manipulation may have arisen from several sources including (but not limited to) peripheral metabolic differences (e.g., enzymatic breakdown in the liver), central neurochemical differences (e.g., efficacy of the reuptake mechanism, postsynaptic receptor sensitivity), preexisting personality differences (e.g., baseline levels of chronic negative affect), or a combination of these factors. Unfortunately, the current design did not allow us to test for predisposing predictors of change, since correlation of change scores with the baseline scores used in their calculation invokes collinearity. Future studies might address these questions through repeated measures of relevant constructs at baseline.

In sum, this is the first empirical demonstration that chronic administration of a selective serotonin reuptake blockade can have significant personality and behavioral effects in normal humans in the absence of baseline depression or other psychopathology. . . . While the primary application of SSRIs lies within the realm of treating psychiatric disorders, the present work indicates that these agents may provide psychological researchers with powerful tools for the "pharmacological dissection" of distinct phenomenological aspects of normal personality (34). Studies of normal volunteers with other pharmacologically selective agents may help to further delineate the specificity of serotonergic mechanisms in modulating affect and thereby may enable researchers to elucidate other psychobiological substrates of personality.

# References

1. Digman JM: Personality structure: emergence of the five-factor model. Annu Rev Psychol 1990; 41:417–440.
2. Costa PT Jr, McCrae RR: Set like plaster: evidence for the stability of adult personality, in Can Personality Change? Edited by Heatherton TF, Weinberger JL. Washington, DC, American Psychological Association, 1994, pp. 21–40.
3. Bouchard TJ Jr: Genes, environment, and personality. Science 1994; 264:1700–1701.
4. Cloninger CR: A systematic method for clinical description and classification of personality variants: a proposal. Arch Gen Psychiatry 1987; 44:573–588.
5. Depue RA, Luciana M, Arbisi P, Collins P, Leon A: Dopamine and the structure of personality: relation of agonist-induced dopamine activity to positive emotionality. J Pers Soc Psychol 1994; 67:485–498.
6. Zuckerman M: Good and bad humors: biochemical bases of personality and its disorders. Psychol Science 1995; 6:325–332.
7. Virkkunen M, Rawlings R, Tokola R, Poland RE, Guidotti A, Nemeroff C, Bissette G, Kalogeras K, Karonen SL, Linnoila M: CSF biochemistries, glucose metabolism, and diurnal activity rhythms in alcoholic, violent offenders, fire setters, and healthy volunteers. Arch Gen Psychiatry 1994; 51:20–27.
8. Coccaro EF, Kavoussi RJ: Neurotransmitter correlates of impulsive aggression, in Aggression and Violence: Genetic, Neurobiological, and Biosocial Perspectives. Edited by Stoff DM, Cairns RB. Hillsdale, NJ, Lawrence Erlbaum Associates, 1996, pp. 67–85.
9. Fuller RW: The influence of fluoxetine on aggressive behavior. Neuropsychopharmacology 1996; 14:77–81.
10. Ellenbogen MA, Young SN, Dean P, Palmour RM, Benkelfat C: Mood response to acute tryptophan depletion in healthy volunteers: sex differences and temporal stability. Neuropsychopharmacology 1996; 15:465–474.
11. Smith SE, Pihl RO, Young SN, Ervin FR: A test of possible cognitive and environmental influences on the mood lowering effect of tryptophan depletion in normal males. Psychopharmacology (Berl) 1987; 91:451–457.
12. Moeller FG, Dougherty DM, Swann AC, Collins D, Davis CM, Cherek DR: Tryptophan depletion and aggressive responding in healthy males. Psychopharmacology (Berl) 1996; 126:97–103.
13. Cleare AJ, Bond AJ: The effect of tryptophan depletion and enhancement on subjective and behavioral aggression in normal male subjects. Psychopharmacology (Berl) 1995; 118:72–81.
14. Higley JD, Mehlman PT, Higley SB, Fernald B, Vickers J, Lindell SG, Taub DM, Suomi SJ, Linnoila M: Excessive mortality in young free-ranging male nonhuman primates with low cerebrospinal fluid 5-hydroxyindoleacetic acid concentration. Arch Gen Psychiatry 1996; 53:537–543.
15. Higley JD, King ST Jr, Hasert MF, Champoux M, Suomi SJ, Linnoila M: Stability of interindividual differences in serotonin function and its relationship to severe aggression and competent social behavior in rhesus macaque females. Neuropsychopharmacology 1996; 14:67–76.
16. Mehlman PT, Higley JD, Faucher I, Lilly AA, Taub DM, Vickers J, Suomi SJ, Linnoila M: Correlation of CSF 5-HIAA concentration with socialty and the timing of emigration in free-ranging primates. Am J Psychiatry 1995; 152:907–913.
17. Hyttel J: Pharmacological characterization of selective serotonin reuptake inhibitors (SSRIs). Int Clin Psychopharmacol 1994; 9(suppl 1):19–26.
18. Carlson JN, Visker KE, Nielsen DM, Keller RW Jr, Glick SD: Chronic antidepressant drug treatment reduces turning behavior and increases dopamine levels in the medial prefrontal cortex. Brain Res 1996; 707:122–126.
19. Spitzer RL, Williams JBW, Gibbon M, First MB: Structured Clinical Interview for DSM-III-R—Non-Patient Edition (SCID-NP, Version 1.0). Washington, DC, American Psychiatric Press, 1990.
20. Buss AH, Durkee A: An inventory for assessing different kinds of hostility. J Consult Psychol 1957; 21:343–349.
21. Siever L, Trestman RL: The serotonin system and aggressive personality disorder. Int Clin Psychopharmacol 1993; 8(suppl 2):33–39.
22. Watson D, Clark LA, Tellegen A: Development and validation of brief measures of positive and negative affect: the PANAS scales. J Pers Soc Psychol 1988; 54:1063–1070.
23. Brett MA, Dierdorf HD, Zussman BD, Coates PE: Determination of paroxetine in human plasma, using high-performance liquid chromatography with fluorescence detection. J Chromatogr 1987; 419:438–444.
24. Rogosa DR, Willett JB: Understanding correlates of change by modeling individual differences in growth. Psychometrika 1985; 50:203–208.
25. Coccaro EF: Impulsive aggression and central serotonergic system function in humans: an example of a dimensional brain-behavior relationship. Int J Psychopharmacol 1992; 7:3–12.

26. Tellegen A: Structures of mood and personality and their relevance to assessing anxiety, with an emphasis on self-report, in Anxiety and the Anxiety Disorders. Edited by Tuma AH, Maser J. Hillsdale, NJ, Lawrence Erlbaum Associates, 1985, pp. 681–706.

27. Depue RA, Luciana M, Arbisi P, Collins P, Leon A: Dopamine and the structure of personality: relation of agonist-induced dopamine activity to positive emotionality. J Pers Soc Psychol 1994; 67:485–498.

28. Raleigh MJ, McGuire MT, Brammer GL, Pollack DB, Yuwiler A: Serotonergic mechanisms promote dominance acquisition in adult male vervet monkeys. Brain Res 1991; 559:181–190.

29. Raleigh MJ, Brammer GL, McGuire MT, Yuwiler A: Dominant social status facilitates the behavioral effects of serotonergic agonists. Brain Res 1985; 348:274–282.

30. Knutson B, Panksepp J: Effects of fluoxetine treatment on play dominance in juvenile rats. Aggressive Behavior 1996; 22:297–307.

31. van Harten J: Clinical pharmacokinetics of selective serotonin reuptake inhibitors. Clin Pharmacokinet 1993; 24:203–220.

32. Katz MM, Maas JW, Frazer A, Koslow SH, Bowden CL, Berman N, Swann AC, Stokes PE: Drug-induced actions on brain neurotransmitter systems and changes in the behaviors and emotions of depressed patients. Neuropsychopharmacology 1994; 11:89–100.

33. Barr LC, Heninger GR, Goodman W, Charney DS, Price LH: Effects of fluoxetine administration on mood response to tryptophan depletion in healthy subjects. Biol Psychiatry 1997; 41:949–954.

34. Klein DF: Anxiety reconceptualized: gleaning from pharmacological dissection: early experience with imipramine and anxiety. Mod Probl Pharmacopsychiatry 1987; 22:1–35.

# CHAPTER 8

# Schizophrenia

*An article in the February 2000 issue of the* APA Monitor *listed some grim statistics: About 2.5 million Americans are diagnosed with schizophrenia. The annual costs of this illness in the United States are estimated to be between $30 billion and $65 billion. Almost 25% of all costs associated with mental illness are associated with schizophrenia. One in 10 males with schizophrenia commits suicide (McGuire, 2000).*

*What is schizophrenia? What is life like for individuals beset by schizophrenia? Does anyone recover from this condition? What kinds of research are being conducted to advance our understanding of the causes of schizophrenia? The four readings in this chapter address these questions.*

## Reference

McGuire, P. A. (2000, February). New hope for people with schizophrenia. *APA Monitor*, 24–28.

# FIRST PERSON ACCOUNT: PARANOID SCHIZOPHRENIA—A DAUGHTER'S STORY

## Jackie Powell

Schizophrenia Bulletin, *published by the National Institute of Mental Health, is a scientific journal devoted to schizophrenia and related disorders. Most of its articles present new research and theory on schizophrenia, but in several issues each year a "first-person account" is published, usually written by a person diagnosed with schizophrenia or a family member. These accounts are vivid depictions of the disorder and of the havoc it can wreak in people's lives; unlike research articles, they humanize schizophrenia.*

*The following article was written by Jackie Powell about her mother, who was diagnosed with paranoid schizophrenia. This is a short but compelling story about how, when the author was 6 years old, the symptoms of schizophrenia descended upon her mother, then in her mid-twenties. The author recounts how difficult it was to relate to her mother following her mother's first hospitalization, the schism between her life with her mother and her life outside the home, the role that her mother's condition had in her selection of a profession, and the continuing impact of the disorder on the author's life.*

## Suggested Readings

Finnegan, W. (1998, March 16). Defending the Unabomber. *The New Yorker, 52*, 54–63.
Siegel, R. K. (1996). *Whispers: The voices of paranoia.* New York: Touchstone Books.

*Schizophrenia Bulletin, 24*, 175–176. (1998).

I can clearly remember my formative years as a time of confusion, anxiety, and desperation. My mother was 25 years old when she was first hospitalized after becoming aggressive toward my father because of his adulterous ways. Their 4-year marriage had been onerous for my mother. As I remember, there was a gradual change in her behavior over a few months. She was no longer able to provide the personal fortitude needed to keep the family together. My father spent most of his time working or drinking. I remember the arguments when he would come home the next day intoxicated and smelling of smoke and alcohol. Arguments became an integral part of our family dynamics. Occasionally the arguments progressed to a pushing and shoving match, but on this particular day, it escalated into something more lethal. My mother approached my father with a shotgun after he attempted to walk away from the argument.

I do not remember the details after he ran out of the house and she continued after him. I ran to my grandmother's next door, and my uncles tried to intervene. The sheriff's entourage arrived shortly after my uncles' intervention. I vividly remember her screaming when the sheriff and deputies struggled with her on the ground as they tried to place handcuffs on her. Not really understanding the magnitude of my mother's pain and misery, I stood with my paternal relatives as people from the community gathered around whispering derogatory comments and making speculative statements.

During those few months before the hospitalization, it was difficult for my mother to remain in her work environment in a hosiery mill. Although supervisors described her as an excellent employee, she suddenly starting accusing co-workers of plotting against her. The delusions were vague but tenacious. She had exceeded the limit on all her credit cards, and long-distance phone calls exaggerated the usual expense of the phone bill. She called relatives, high school acquaintances, and any other soul who came to her mind. Some discussions were cordial and reminiscent of times shared, but other calls accused people of harassing her or of being "jealous" of her. The calls were usually made late at night or during the early hours of the morning. She was unaware of the inappropriateness of her behavior.

She slept 2 to 3 hours a night and spent most of her time pacing in the house or walking up and down the road in clothing inappropriate for the weather or for societal expectations. She altered some of her clothing into a new form of fashion. She gave other items away to people in the community or threw the items in the trash, noting that she no longer needed them. She had developed a hostile, almost sarcastic character. There was no reasoning with her at this time. To confront her meant igniting her anger and belligerence. By age 6, I realized that it was better to observe her behavior from afar and to remain confused about why she seemed to be having a conversation with

"someone" I could not hear or see even when she was not on the phone.

The small African-American community where we lived provided little support or empathy for my mother or my family; my mother merely assumed the persona of someone crazy or having "bad nerves." There was an awareness in the community of the need for medication to treat her bizarre behavior, therefore, when my mother returned and her symptoms had abated, people inquired about her compliance with her medication and her "state of mind." They would say, "Sally Mae, are you still taking your medication?"

It was 6 weeks before my mother returned home. I visited her once at the State hospital. My mother and I cried through most of the visit. To my mother, being in a State hospital was like being in an abattoir. Before the visit ended, she gave me a monkey she had made out of socks during one of her therapies. I kept this monkey for many years. Later, it reminded me of the pain I experienced seeing my mother in the hospital.

She appeared very different when she returned. She moved slowly and she had gained weight. Her eyes appeared dazed, her speech was slurred, and at times her hands trembled. I tried extremely hard not to be afraid of her, but I did not know this person who used to be my mother: The mother who made me laugh when we watched television together, the mother who listened to music and danced with my friends and me, the mother who combed my hair for school each day, and the mother who made sure I was safe at night did not return home. She was no longer exuberant, and enjoyment seemed foreign to her. She appeared numb to the world that she felt had destroyed her life. From this time forward, my life was no longer the same. Somehow we became symbiotically united, and I knew that I would always need to take care of her in some way.

My mother and father divorced shortly after her release from the first hospitalization. She returned to live with her mother. Their home was about 13 miles from the house I had called home for 4 years. My father's family decided to have my father and me stay with my paternal grandmother.

Monday through Friday, I went to school pretending to have a "normal" life, but knowing that other kids knew about my mother's hospitalization through their parents. On Friday nights my father drove me to my maternal grandmother's home where I stayed until Sunday night. This pattern continued until I went away to college.

My mother was no longer my mother. She no longer felt comfortable making the parental decisions that I needed her to make, nor was she able to set limits on my acting-out behavior. She passively allowed my father's family to be responsible for child-rearing and I merely visited her. Gradually, I found myself treating her like a child and thinking that I knew what was best for her and me. I loved her dearly, but I resented her even more for taking away my childhood. Somehow this disease stripped her of her charisma and excitement about life and left a shell that ruminated about the past, no longer connected or interested in day-to-day events. She was able to verbalize her love for me, but her affect did not demonstrate affection: Something was missing. She was no longer available to help me face the normal vicissitudes of life. There were no longer any boundaries on language or information. If my mother remembered something, she spoke it. She impulsively verbalized historical family garbage and ill deeds and dumped this information into the lap of a child.

I learned to live two lives, the life with my mother and a more superficial life in the community. I learned to call my paternal grandmother "Mother," and the community soon learned the same. During acute psychotic episodes my mother would rage about how I was taken away from her and how cruel my father's family had been to her. She would reveal frightening stories that I could not remember, such as being made to sleep on the floor, or being dragged by the sheriff. Unfortunately, there was no way to validate my mother's accusations. No family member would talk about her condition. It appeared that they wanted her medicated and paralyzed. So the task for me was to differentiate between what was delusional and what was real for my mother during these

episodes. I believed that the truth was somewhere in the middle and that for my mother her perception was 100 percent reality. I soon followed my family's strategy. My mother became a secret that I learned to avoid exposing in order to protect the two of us from being scrutinized.

After the first hospitalization, it was almost predictable that every 4 years my mother's behavior appeared to change in the fall. I would find myself becoming prepared for her to decompensate and looking for subtle changes in her behavior. In my mother's community, no effort was made to explain mental illness to family members. The effort focused instead on medicating the patient without treating the entire family, a strategy that perpetuated the lack of support and understanding in this particular community. Although my mother tried desperately to recuperate from each psychotic episode and each arrest, she became increasingly reclusive and paranoid. Each episode was precipitated by an erotomanic delusion or delusions of persecution in the workplace that followed shortly after the psychiatrist decided to taper her antipsychotic medications.

As the taper began, my mother would believe that she no longer needed to take medication and that nothing was wrong with her: Everyone else was crazy. For the first 10 years or so after her first hospitalization she worked in factories and restaurants. However, after a few years, the taper would occur and she would create elaborate stories about her co-workers plotting against her.

She would also obsess about married men, fantasizing that they were going to leave their wives to be with her. Occasionally this would progress to her calling the wife or waiting for the man at the diner. The result was usually trespassing issues and threatening behavior. Men would come and go, but my mother continued to yearn for the family she never had and the marriage she dreamed of incessantly. Eventually, she gave up the idea of maintaining a full-time job.

Now my mother's income is derived from disability Social Security income and any financial support I might give. Over the years her ability to maintain a logical conversation has diminished.

One has to search to find a connection between the theme of a dialog and my mother's response. Her language in jest is more nonsensical and tangential. She has become increasingly perseverative about minuscule things. She lives alone in an apartment, making lists (mostly the food menu for the day) and posting them on the walls. She spends most of her time cooking, thinking of new ways to "create" dishes that usually taste very strange to me. She is very cynical and critical of others. There is an obvious air of grandiosity and entitlement. She goes to the grocery store and will occasionally walk around the neighborhood to "clear her mind." She avoids going to the laundromat and now washes clothes by hand at home. She also avoids answering the phone and uses the answering machine to screen all her calls. She still feels that most people are not benevolent. After 25 years of neuroleptic treatment, she has discontinued all medications and periodically will call her case manager. She is convinced that she no longer needs medication. People in the community continue to ask her about her medication and now she lies to them.

As for my relationship as an adult with my mother, I would be lying to say that I do not think about her condition daily. I also grieve over the loss of my mother as I knew her before the first episode. For brief moments, my mother gets better and she is more aware of who I am as my own being. Sadly, I have to acknowledge the brevity of this connectedness and merely treasure the moment. I visit her once or twice a month and this seems to be enough for her. The visits are short and usually involve her cooking and updating me on what has been going on in the neighborhood. I often invite her to visit me, but familiarity is important to her and she typically declines the offer. When she does visit, I get very little rest because she is awake throughout the night eating, watching TV, reading cook books, or just sitting in a chair. When my friends happen to be around the two of us, I typically say that my mother is very odd to forewarn them in case her conversation becomes tangential or she injects a neologism. Most of my friends accept this without question, but others feel it necessary to inquire more. I usually ignore their questions or minimize the significance of her thought disorder. . . .

My mother's condition has greatly marked my career as well as my personal life. Ironically, I am a mental health professional and I work primarily with patients who have schizophrenia. I have deliberately adjusted the language of this article to reflect more of my emotional anguish and less of the psychological and psychiatric terminology that I think would take away from my personal account. I am no longer the 6-year-old who saw her mother taken away, but I struggle daily with what is real and what is delusional where my mother is concerned and how I can protect both her rights and her safety in an era of limited psychiatric involvement caused by elevated health care costs. Heavy caseloads and minimal patient contact do not allow the continuity needed to provide adequate care to the chronically mentally ill of our nation. I hope that my personal account will touch readers in a way that will encourage the reevaluation of health care systems and policies.

# THE LOST YEARS OF A NOBEL LAUREATE

## Sylvia Nasar

*This second article also describes an individual with schizophrenia, in this case John Forbes Nash Jr. Nash was a brilliant young mathematician. He received his Ph.D. on his 22nd birthday and, many years later, he received the Nobel Prize in Economics for his dissertation thesis. He was diagnosed at 30 with paranoid schizophrenia and was hospitalized. Nash struggled with the disorder into his 50s and then, for reasons that are not entirely clear, improved dramatically. This is a tragic and fascinating case study, in large part because of Nash's extraordinary mental abilities and how they were compromised by the devastating effects of schizophrenia.*

*This article, by Sylvia Nasar, is a synopsis of a detailed and compelling biography she wrote, entitled* A Beautiful Mind. *In the prologue to this book, Nasar tells the story of Nash's meeting with a fellow mathematician named George Mackay when Nash was a patient. Mackay asked, "How could you, a mathematician, a man devoted to reason and logical proof . . . how could you believe that extraterrestrials are sending you messages? How could you believe that you are being recruited by aliens from outer space to save the world? How could you . . . ?" Nash said, "Because the ideas I had about supernatural beings came to me the same way that my mathematical ideas did. So I took them seriously."*

## Reference

Nasar, S. (1998). *A beautiful mind: A biography of John Forbes Nash, Jr., Winner of the Nobel Prize in Economics, 1994.* New York: Simon and Schuster.

## Suggested Reading

Winchester, S. (1998). *The professor and the madman: A tale of murder, insanity, and the making of the Oxford English Dictionary.* New York: HarperCollins.

---

*New York Times*, F1. (1994, November 13).

PRINCETON, N.J.—Several weeks before the 1994 Nobel prize in economics was announced on Oct. 11, two mathematicians—Harold W. Kuhn and John Forbes Nash Jr.—visited their old teacher, Albert W. Tucker, now almost 90 and bedridden, at Meadow Lakes, a nursing home near here.

Mr. Nash hadn't spoken with his mentor in several years. Their hour-long conversation, from which Mr. Kuhn excused himself, concerned number theory. When Mr. Nash stepped out of the room, Mr. Kuhn returned to tell Mr. Tucker a stunning secret: Unbeknownst to Mr. Nash, the Royal Swedish Academy intended to grant Mr. Nash a Nobel for work he had done as the old man's student in 1949, work that turned out to have revolutionary implications for economics.

The award was a miracle. It wasn't just that Mr. Nash, one of the mathematical geniuses of the postwar era, was finally getting the recognition he deserved. Nor that he was being honored for a slender 27-page Ph.D. thesis written almost half a century ago at the tender age of 21.

The real miracle was that the 66-year-old Mr. Nash—tall, gray, with sad eyes and the soft, raspy voice of someone who doesn't talk much—was alive and well enough to receive the prize. For John Nash was stricken with paranoid schizophrenia more than three decades earlier.

Mr. Nash's terrible illness was an open secret among mathematicians and economists. No sooner had *Fortune* magazine singled him out in July 1958 as America's brilliant young star of the "new mathematics" than the disease had devastated Mr. Nash's personal and professional life. He hadn't published a scientific paper since 1958. He hadn't held an academic post since 1959. Many people had heard, incorrectly, that he had had a lobotomy. Others, mainly those outside Princeton, simply assumed that he was dead.

He didn't die, but his life, once so full of brightness and promise, became hellish. There were repeated commitments to psychiatric hospitals. Failed treatments. Fearful delusions. A period of wandering around Europe. Stretches in Roanoke, Va., where Mr. Nash's mother and sister

lived. Finally, a return to Princeton, where he had once been the rising star. There he became the Phantom of Fine Hall, a mute figure who scribbled strange equations on blackboards in the mathematics building and searched anxiously for secret messages in numbers.

Then, roughly 10 years ago, the awful fires that fed the delusions and distorted his thinking began to die down. It happened very gradually. But, by his mid-50's, Mr. Nash began to come out of his isolation. He started to talk to other mathematicians again. He began to work on mathematical problems that made sense. He made friends with several graduate students. He didn't get a job, but he started to learn new things, like using computers for his research.

And here he was at Meadow Lakes. Within a few weeks, Mr. Nash got the early morning telephone call from Stockholm—45 minutes late, as it turned out—telling him that he was being honored along with two other pioneers of game theory, John C. Harsanyi of the University of California at Berkeley and Reinhard Selten of the University of Bonn.

Alicia Nash, with whom Mr. Nash shares a home near Princeton even though the couple were divorced years ago and who was let in on the secret along with Mr. Tucker, breathed a sigh of relief. They called their son, also a mathematician, and Mr. Nash's sister to tell them the great news. Later, there were champagne corks and a news conference, dry Nashian jokes about the prize money not being all that good (his share is about $310,000) and consultations with other Princeton laureates about the proper way to address Sweden's King and Queen when the award is presented Dec. 10. There was even an invitation to visit the White House, on Nov. 28.

On one level, John Nash's story is the tragedy of any person with schizophrenia. Incurable, incapacitating and extremely difficult to treat, schizophrenia plays terrifying tricks on its victims. Many people with the disease can no longer sort and interpret sensations or reason or feel the full range of emotions. Instead, they suffer from delusions and hear voices.

But in Mr. Nash's case, the tragedy has the added dimensions of his early genius—and of the network of family and friends who valued that genius, wrapping themselves protectively around Mr. Nash and providing him with a safe haven while he was ill. There were the former colleagues who tried to get him work. The sister who made heartbreaking choices about his treatment. The loyal wife who stood by him when she no longer was his wife. The economist who argued to the Nobel committee that mental illness shouldn't be a bar to the prize. Princeton itself.

Together they made sure that Mr. Nash did not wind up, as so many victims of schizophrenia do, a patient in a state hospital, a homeless nomad or a suicide.

Schizophrenia usually strikes people in their teens or early 20's, often without warning, just as they are about to spread their wings. Mr. Nash was struck when he had already begun to soar.

Schizophrenia is often confused with manic depressive illness, the disease that afflicted Vincent Van Gogh, Virginia Woolf and a host of other geniuses. But that illness, primarily a disorder of mood rather than of thinking, typically arrives later in life. Sufferers can often hold high-level jobs and do extremely creative work between bouts. Schizophrenia, on the other hand, is too debilitating to co-exist with great accomplishment. Nijinsky, the Russian dancer, is one of the few known victims of schizophrenia other than Mr. Nash to have made his mark as a genius before the disease struck.

"It is always sad, but particularly when it involves someone as bright as he is," said John C. Moore, a retired mathematician who was close to the Nashes for 30 years. "These would have probably been his most productive years."

Mr. Nash has never talked about his illness publicly except to refer obliquely, at the news conference announcing his Nobel, to the fact that he had made some irrational choices in the past. He declined to be interviewed for this story, saying, "People know what they know."

But many of the people who have been close to him over the years or got to know him in the last few years have been willing, now that he has the extra protection of the mantle of a Nobel prize, to talk about his life and his achievements.

## Starting Out—The First Signs Of Genius

John Nash's West Virginia roots are often invoked by people who knew him at Princeton or at the Massachusetts Institute of Technology, where he taught for a while in the 50's, to explain his lack of worldliness. But Bluefield, the town where he grew up, was hardly a backwater. It had the highest per capita income in the state during the 30's and 40's and was home to a handful of millionaires, the Virginia Southern railroad and a four-year Baptist college.

Mr. Nash's mother, Margaret, was a Latin teacher. His father, John Sr., was a gentlemanly electrical engineer. By the time John Jr. and his younger sister were in elementary school, in the middle of the Depression, the Nashes lived in a white frame house, down the street from the country club.

Nothing was more important to the senior Nashes than supervising their children's education, recalls the sister, Martha Nash Legg. John Jr. was a prodigy but not a straight-A student. He read constantly. He played chess. He whistled entire Bach melodies.

"John was always looking for a different way to do things," said Mrs. Legg, a tall, handsome woman who is a potter in Roanoke. In elementary school, one of his teachers told John's mother that her son was having trouble in math. "He could see ways to solve problems that were different from his teacher's," Mrs. Legg said, laughing.

In the fall of 1945, Mr. Nash enrolled at Carnegie-Mellon, then Carnegie Tech, in Pittsburgh. It was there that the label "genius" was first applied to Mr. Nash. His mathematics professor called him "a young Gauss" in class one day, referring to the great German mathematician. Mr. Nash switched from chemistry to math in his freshman year. Two years later he had a B.S. and was studying for an M.S.

His graduate professor, R. J. Duffin, recalls Mr. Nash as a tall, slightly awkward student who came to him one day and described a problem he thought he had solved. Professor Duffin realized with some astonishment that Mr. Nash, without knowing it, had independently proved Brouwer's famed theorem. The professor's letter of recommendation for Mr. Nash had just one line: "This man is a genius."

## Making Waves—Game Theory And More

In 1948, the year Mr. Nash entered the doctoral program at Princeton with a fellowship, the town was arguably the center of the mathematical and scientific universe. It not only had the Institute for Advanced Study and Albert Einstein, but also there was John von Neumann, the charismatic mathematician who helped develop the modern computer as well as the mathematical theory behind the H-bomb.

At once eager to prove himself and somewhat gauche, especially compared with older students who had served in the war, Mr. Nash quickly became one of the brilliant young men who performed mental pyrotechnics in the common room of Fine Hall. Soon after he arrived he invented an extremely clever game that was played with markers on hexagonal bathroom tiles. An instant fad in the common room, it was called "Nash" or "John." Parker Brothers brought out a version a few years later called Hex.

Other students found him a loner, odd as well as brilliant. When he wasn't in the common room talking a blue streak, he paced. Around and around he would go, following Fine Hall's quadrangular hallways, occasionally dashing into empty classrooms to scribble, with lightning speed, on blackboards.

"He was always an unusual person," said Jack Milnor, an undergraduate at the time and now a mathematician at the State University of New York at Stony Brook. "He tended to say whatever came into his mind."

Lloyd S. Shapley, then a graduate student and now a mathematician at the University of California at Los Angeles, added, "He was obnoxious. What redeemed him was a keen, beautiful, logical mind."

Mr. Nash's Nobel-winning thesis on game theory was the product of his second year at Princeton. Game theory was the invention of von Neumann and a Princeton economist named Oskar Morgenstern. Their 1944 book, *The Theory of Games and Economic Behavior*, was the first attempt to derive logical and mathematical rules about rivalries. The Cold War and the nuclear arms race meant that game theory was an idea whose time had arrived.

Characteristically, Mr. Nash picked a problem for his thesis that had eluded von Neumann. Briefly, von Neumann only had a good theory for pure rivalries in which one side's gain was the other's loss. Mr. Nash focused on rivalries in which mutual gain was also possible. He showed that there were stable solutions—no player could do better given what the others were doing—for such rivalries under a wide variety of circumstances. In doing so, he turned game theory, a beguiling idea, into a powerful tool that economists could use to analyze everything from business competition to trade negotiations. "It wasn't until Nash that game theory came alive for economists," said Robert Solow, a Nobel laureate in economics at M.I.T.

Mr. Nash got his doctorate on his 22d birthday, June 13, 1950. After brief interludes as an instructor at Princeton and as a consultant at the Rand Corporation, the Cold War think tank, Mr. Nash moved on to teach at M.I.T. in 1951.

He arrived itching to show that he could solve really big problems. According to one story circulating at the time, Mr. Nash was in the common room knocking, as he often did, other mathematicians' work. An older professor is said to have challenged him to solve one of the field's most notorious problems.

The problem grew out of work done by G. F. B. Riemann, a 19th-century mathematician, and was considered virtually insoluble. But Mr. Nash wound up solving it. To do so, he invented a completely new method for approaching the problem that turned out to unlock a difficulty encountered in a far larger class of problems. Mathematicians still describe the solution as "astonishing" and "dazzling."

Most mathematicians consider this and other work Mr. Nash did in pure mathematics to be his greatest achievements, worthy of Nobels if such were given in the mathematical field. Many joke that he got his Nobel for his most trivial work. . . .

## The Disease—"It's All Over For Him"

By the mid-1950's, Mr. Nash was phenomenally productive. When he got tired of mathematicians, he would wander over to the economics department to talk to Mr. Solow and another Nobel laureate, Paul Samuelson.

And it was during this period that Mr. Nash met his future wife, Alicia Larde, an El Salvadoran physics student at M.I.T. who took advanced calculus from him. Small, graceful, with extraordinary dark eyes, Alicia looked like an Odile in "Swan Lake." "Very, very beautiful," recalls Ziporrah Levinson, the widow of Mr. Nash's mentor at M.I.T., Norman Levinson.

"He was very, very good looking, very intelligent," Mrs. Nash recalls. "It was a little bit of a hero worship thing." They were married in 1957, a year Mr. Nash spent on leave at the Institute for Advanced Study.

By the time the Nashes returned to M.I.T., John Nash had been awarded tenure. Mrs. Nash went back to graduate school and worked part time in the computer center. In the fall of 1958, she became pregnant with their son, John Charles Martin Nash. "It was a very nice time of my life," she recalled.

It is just then, when life seemed so very sweet, that John Nash got sick. Within months, at age 30 in the spring of 1959, Mr. Nash was committed to McLean Hospital, a psychiatric institution in Belmont, Mass., connected with Harvard University. . . .

Psychiatrists who treat victims of schizophrenia ask people who haven't had the disease to imagine how they would feel if unseen voices shouted, if they lost capacity to feel or to think logically. And what if on top of that, asks E. Fuller Torrey, a psychiatrist in Washington and authority on schizophrenia, those closest to them began to avoid or ignore them, to pretend that they didn't notice what they did, to be embarrassed by their behavior? And what if the treatment was ineffectual? That is what happened to Mr. Nash.

In the months leading up to his hospitalization, Mr. Nash became another person. He skipped from subject to subject. Some of his lectures no longer made sense. He fled to Roanoke at one point, abandoning his classes. He wrote strange letters to various public figures.

"It was very sad," said Professor Shapley at U.C.L.A., who ran into Mr. Nash from time to time. "There was no way to talk to him or even follow what he was saying."

The months at McLean did little to arrest the disease. "Schizophrenia is a brain disease," said Dr. Torrey, adding that it is "a real scientific and biological entity as clearly as diabetes, multiple sclerosis and cancer are." But neuroleptics, the drugs that were used to treat some, but far from all, of the symptoms for the next several decades, were just coming on the scene. And psychoanalysis, which has since been discredited as a means of treating schizophrenia, was in vogue. The causes of the disease are still not known.

As absurd as it now seems, Mr. Nash's psychiatrists thought that Mrs. Nash's pregnancy was part of the problem and hoped that he would improve after the baby's birth. "It was the height of the Freudian period—all these things were explained by fetus envy," said Mrs. Levinson. Martha Legg added, sadly, "In those days, it was all supposed to be the mother's fault."

In any event, Mr. Nash's paranoia intensified and he could no longer work. After resigning his M.I.T. post, he went to Europe, wandering from city to city. He feared he was being spied on and hunted down and he tried to give up his United States citizenship. His wife and colleagues began to receive postcards with odd messages, many concerning numbers. "I rode on bus No. 77 today and it reminded me of you," one read. Eventually, the

Nashes separated and he moved to Roanoke to live with his mother.

## The Abyss—Two Decades Of Darkness

For most of the next 20 years, Mr. Nash divided his time between hospitals, Roanoke and, increasingly, Princeton.

In 1963, Mrs. Nash divorced him but eventually let him live at her house. Mr. Nash was hospitalized at least three more times. Mrs. Nash, who never remarried, supported her former husband and her son by working as a computer programmer, with some financial help from family, friends and colleagues. "It was a pretty lean life," said Martha Legg. . . .

"Everyone at Princeton knew him by sight," recalls Daniel R. Feenberg, a Princeton graduate student in the 1970's and now an economist at the National Bureau of Economic Research. "His clothes didn't quite match. He looked vacant. He was mostly silent. He was around a lot in the library reading books or walking between buildings."

Alicia Nash believed very firmly, according to several people close to her, that Mr. Nash should live at home and stay within Princeton's mathematics community even when he was not functioning well. Martha Legg applauds her decision. "Being in Princeton was good for him," said Mrs. Legg. "In a place like Princeton, if you act strange, you're special. In Roanoke, if you act strange, you're just different. They didn't know who he was here."

Roger Lewin, a psychiatrist in Baltimore, agrees. "Some people are so disturbed that there is no way to get in touch with them, but for a significant group, compassion and receptivity of the surrounding community make all the difference."

Some former colleagues at Princeton and M.I.T. tried to help with jobs on research projects, though very often Mr. Nash couldn't accept the help. Professor Shapley at U.C.L.A. succeeded in getting a cash mathematics prize for Mr. Nash in the 70's. There were other forms of kindness, like getting Mr. Nash access to university computers or

remembering to invite him to seminars when old friends turned up on campus.

## Coming Back Finally, A Remission

Still, the people who stayed in regular contact with him eventually came to believe that his illness would never end.

Then came what Professor Kuhn calls "a miraculous remission." And as happens, for reasons unknown, in the case of some people with schizophrenia, it was not, according to Mrs. Nash or Mrs. Legg, due to any drug or treatment.

"It's just a question of living a quiet life," said Mrs. Nash.

The most dramatic sign of that remission, perhaps, is that Mr. Nash was able to do mathematics again.

And now Mr. Nash is a Nobel laureate. The story of his prize is itself testament not only to his survival but to the fierce loyalty and admiration he inspired in others. During the 20-plus years of Mr. Nash's illness, game theory flourished and it is hard to find an important article in the field that doesn't refer to his work. But mathematicians and economists who were close to the secret deliberations say that the Nobel was hardly a sure thing.

By mid-1985, the prize committee was evidently actively considering an award for game theory. (The Nobel Memorial Prize in Economic Science is not one of the prizes established in the will of Alfred Nobel, but was created as a memorial to him in 1968.)

Five years later, the committee was making discreet inquiries not just about Mr. Nash's contribution but about his state of mind. There is no formal rule that a recipient must travel to Stockholm to accept the prize in person, give a Nobel lecture there or deliver a few profundities and words of gratitude to the King at the banquet. And there is certainly no rule that the recipient must hold a university post or have maintained an active career beyond the prize-winning contribution.

But no one wins prizes without an active constituency in his field. To most young game theorists who urged that he get a prize, Mr. Nash was a demigod. But Professor Kuhn played a particular role. A noted game theorist himself, he made it clear to the committee that it would be a grave injustice if Mr. Nash's illness cost him the prize.

Early in September, Professor Kuhn got a clear signal that the prize would go to Mr. Nash when he was asked to prepare a curriculum vitae for him and to provide some photographs. At the professor's suggestion, Princeton created the title Visiting Research Collaborator to provide a ready answer for Mr. Nash to the inevitable question of his current affiliation.

The reaction to the announcement was jubilation. "The main message to the world is that the academy says mental illness is just like cancer, nothing special," said Ariel Rubinstein, a game theorist at Tel Aviv University. "It's great."

What will Mr. Nash do now? At 66, he is past the age when most mathematicians do their best work. But the researchers he now talks to say that he is interested in the major unsolved problems and that he has learned to use the computer in ingenious ways.

"The truths Nash discovered were all very surprising," said Simon Kochen, another Princeton mathematician. "Nash is a man who surprises people."

# EMPIRICAL CORRECTION OF SEVEN MYTHS ABOUT SCHIZOPHRENIA WITH IMPLICATIONS FOR TREATMENT

## Courtenay M. Harding and James H. Zahniser

*In the earlier chapter on approaches to psychopathology, we learned that how we think about a disorder has important consequences for how we treat people with a disorder. If we think that schizophrenia is a chronic condition from which recovery is rare, then this very expectation might lead us to be less aggressive in our therapeutic interventions or more accepting of lower levels of therapeutic progress. In the previous article we saw that John Nash Jr., though having lost many productive years of his life, did in fact recover from schizophrenia. How common is this? Harding and Zahniser argue that recovery is more common than most people think, and thus it is important to correct and clarify this misperception. They also address six other myths about schizophrenia, and for each rejected myth they outline the implications that a new perspective would have for treatment. As with the previous articles in this chapter, this article draws attention to the diverse forms that schizophrenia takes in people's lives, and it also provides a more hopeful and optimistic perspective.*

## Suggested Readings

Coursey, R. D., Alford, J., & Safarjan, B. (1997). Significant advances in understanding and treating serious mental illness. *Professional Psychology: Research and Practice, 28,* 205–216.

Harding, C. M., Brooks, G. W., Ashikaga, T., Strauss, J. S., & Breier, A. (1987). The Vermont longitudinal study of persons with severe mental illness: II. Long-term outcome of subjects who retrospectively met *DSM-III* criteria for schizophrenia. *American Journal of Psychiatry, 144,* 727–735.

*Acta Psychiatrica Scandinavica, 90* (Suppl. 384), 140–146.

This paper presents empirical evidence accumulated across the last two decades to challenge seven long-held myths in psychiatry about schizophrenia which impinge upon the perception and thus the treatment of patients. Such myths have been perpetuated across generations of trainees in each of the mental health disciplines These myths limit the scope and effective-ness of treatments offered. These myths maintain the pessimism about outcome for these patients thus sig-nificantly reducing their opportunities for improve-ment and/or recovery. Counter evidence is provided with implications for new treatment strategies.

There are at least seven prevalent myths about schizophrenia which often discourage clini-cians, significantly impact the view of the patient, and thus his or her treatment. All of these myths have been challenged by research data, yet they persist in training and practice across mental health disciplines. This paper endeavors to con-tribute a more balanced and contemporary view of the person with schizophrenia in order to re-energize clinicians and revitalize treatment ap-proaches.

I. MYTH: ONCE A SCHIZOPHRENIC ALWAYS A SCHIZ-OPHRENIC. REALITY: EVER WIDENING HETEROGENE-ITY OF OUTCOME ACROSS TIME. Kraepelin (1) initiated the myth by categorically splitting mental illness into either good outcome (manic depres-sion) or poor outcome (dementia praecox). Diag-nosis was verified or invalidated by the outcome. Even Eugen Bleuler (2), who was originally more optimistic about the outcome of schizophrenia, later decided that there was never "full *restitutio ad integrum.*" Harding et al. (3, 4) have explained that these two pivotal investigators suffered from "the clinician's illusion." (5) The "illusion" occurs when clinicians repeatedly see the few most severely ill in their caseloads as "typical" when, in fact, such pa-tients represent a small proportion of the actual possible spectrum. The Scandinavians have gener-ally held a broader view as evidenced by their use of the category "reactive psychosis." (6) However, even in Scandinavia, pessimism has remained about patients who were unable to fit these criteria or patients who fit these criteria, but failed to im-prove quickly.

*Evidence*: Recent worldwide studies have investi-gated the assumption of downward course and all have found wide heterogeneity in the very long-term outcome (over 2 decades) for schizophrenia, despite differences in diagnostic criteria used (e.g., 7–14). The European studies have often been dis-missed in the U.S. because of the perception that their criteria were not equivalent and because of sheer ethnocentricity. However, notwithstanding the criticisms of diagnostic differences (valid or not), all of these studies have come to the same conclusions. The longer investigators followed an identified intact cohort (whether probands were in or out of treatment), the more pronounced the picture of increasing heterogeneity and improve-ment in function. These studies have consistently found that half to two thirds of patients signifi-cantly improved or recovered, including some co-horts of very chronic cases. The universal criteria for recovery have been defined as no current signs and symptoms of any mental illness, no current medications, working, relating well to family and friends, integrated into the community, and be-having in such a way as to not being able to detect having ever been hospitalized for any kind of psy-chiatric problems. All of these investigators of long-term studies were trained in the older, more pessimistic conceptual models and were surprised by their own findings. Because the myths have been repeated so often, they had become reified. The strong belief systems and resistance, encoun-tered by these investigators, were caused by many factors and were not easily altered by one study (3, 4). However, there is now a confluence of re-sults.

*Suggested treatment strategies*: Slowly, these investi-gators have all persisted. The beliefs about course and outcome are changing. Clinical practices and programs are being restructured (e.g., 15–19). The mental health disciplines are getting the message. Given the evidence, it is suggested that treatment programs be constructed "as if" everyone will turn the corner toward significant improvement and/or recovery. This suggestion is made because the state of the art does *not* permit clinicians to triage patients on the basis of prognostic factors. In schizophrenia, particularly the multiple episodic types, the display of early symptom severity and dysfunction in illness trajectories may persist for many years. Then, as the illness lifts, the patient's energy returns, thinking clears, coping strategies for stressors improves, and he or she inches the way toward improvement in both function and symptom reduction. This is the opposite picture of a relentless downhill course for most patients as described by Kraepelin. This long process of recovery implies a revision of what the clinician tells patients and their families about prognosis ("You have a very serious illness which takes some time to work itself through. However, worldwide data shows over more than 50 percent of patients significantly improve or even recover. We will be there to walk with you on this journey toward recovery"). This new message keeps a small spark of hope alive. Hope promotes the self-healing capacity inherent in any recovery process for any illness (e.g., 20–22). Treatment also means a cohesive, comprehensive biopsychosocial approach to the whole person (23–24), and a collaborative effort between the patient, the family, the clinical team, other community agencies, and natural networks. Treatment means celebrating the small moves forward and learning from the steps backward in a manner which does not blame the patient, the team, or the family. Treatment means environmental engineering to reduce the stressors. Important to remember is the need to re-evaluate repeatedly because the same structured environment which enables a patient to organize a disorganized brain can become psychotogenic later when a now organized brain faces a much too organized environment (25).

2. MYTH: A SCHIZOPHRENIC IS A SCHIZOPHRENIC IS A SCHIZOPHRENIC. REALITY: WIDE INDIVIDUAL HETEROGENEITY WITHIN THE DIAGNOSTIC CATEGORY. Paraphrasing "Rose is a rose is a rose" (26), there is a tendency in the field to lump everyone with the same diagnosis together for treatment and research.

*Evidence*: In reality, every group of patients has substantial heterogeneity. In addition to the major

impact of gender, (27) there are considerable differences in age, developmental tasks, education levels, job histories, symptom presentation, coping skills and other personality strengths and weaknesses, meaning systems, response to stress in general and to stress of particular situations. (28) Further, it should be noted that the field has forgotten the heterogeneity of schizophrenia, itself. When E. Bleuler renamed dementia praecox, he called it "the group of schizophrenias." (29) Recently, Kendler (30) has developed several models of genetic-environmental interaction and weighting in the etiology of schizophrenia. His models make a great deal of sense given the wide heterogeneity of our patients.

*Suggested treatment strategies*: The heterogeneity, described above, requires a comprehensive, biopsychosocial assessment of each patient's unique status, the place in his or her own course trajectory, and ecological niche. Individual differences require individualized treatment planning, an appreciation of developmental achievements or strivings, and a recognition of the "person behind the disorder." (10) In order for clinicians to achieve this level of understanding, they must consider the task as a genuinely collaborative enterprise with both the patient and others who know him or her well. Continued assessment of changing, ongoing status is especially important after years of severe psychopathology and dysfunction, given the longitudinal nature of these disorders. The use of "timelines" or "life charts" is recommended in this endeavor by collecting data in a chronological life history as well as for setting a collaborative tone for treatment (31–32). Attention to individual differences, life histories, and developmental steps, will encourage patients to perceive themselves, *not* as "schizophrenics," but rather as people, who happen to have schizophrenia. Consumers repeatedly note that this recognition of their "personhood" plays a critical role in their recovery and reacquisition of their sense of well being. (33–34)

3. MYTH: REHABILITATION CAN BE PROVIDED ONLY AFTER STABILIZATION. REALITY: REHABILITATION SHOULD BEGIN ON DAY 1. This myth has been

deeply embedded within a narrow but popular version of the medical model. "Real treatment" in today's managed care climate consists of assessment, diagnosis and medication. Anything else, such as rehabilitation, must wait until stabilization and is often considered to be an ancillary service. But stabilization usually leads just to "maintenance" and not to rehabilitation.

*Evidence*: "Real treatment" has been only modestly successful in reducing symptoms, and in helping the patient by increasing the levels of functioning in self care, work, interpersonal relationships, and integration back to the community. However, there is a burgeoning field of psychiatric rehabilitation which combines with medical treatments to significantly improve the patient's level of functioning. (35, 36) The problem has been a paucity of integrated models proposed to incorporate all of these facets of care. The notable exceptions have been Engel's "biopsychosocial model" (24) and Adler et al's paper (35) which set forth an expanded medical model as a task for psychiatry. Adler's model delineates the tasks for psychiatry to be legal, societal-rahabilitative, educative-developmental, as well as medical. Anthony (36) has proposed a rehabilitation model but left out most of the illness factors.

*Suggested treatment strategies*: Rehabilitation is accruing an honored place in the treatment of patients as a key modality in partnership with psychopharmacology. Skill building (e.g., how to manage one's symptoms, managing one's medication, learning how to manage a budget, acquiring a job skill, conducting social conversation). All raise a patient's self-esteem and lower symptoms. Anything which lowers symptoms and improves function deserves to be called and reimbursed as "treatment." (17, 36–38)

4. MYTH: WHY BOTHER WITH PSYCHOTHERAPY FOR SCHIZOPHRENIA? REALITY: SUPPORTIVE PSYCHOTHERAPY IS CRUCIAL FOR INTEGRATING THE EXPERIENCE AND ENHANCING CONTINUED ADULT DEVELOPMENT. Research findings, regarding the ineffectiveness of psychotherapy in curing schizophrenia, have led to widespread discouragement in this area and to a relative lack of innovation and research. Heinrichs (39) concluded from his review that "The kindest interpretation of controlled studies to date is that the benefit of psychotherapy with schizophrenia has not yet been demonstrated." However, instead of abandoning psychotherapy altogether, the challenge is for clinicians to use psychotherapy appropriately for maximum benefit.

*Evidence*: Two main lines of evidence support the judicious use of psychotherapy. First, surveys and personal accounts of consumers have indicated that they value psychotherapy and find it to be beneficial in various ways. (40–43) Second, several different types of psychosocial interventions have demonstrated positive impact on the lives of persons with schizophrenia including family interventions (see below), group therapies tailored to the needs of persons with schizophrenia (35–36), and very specific, targeted cognitive remediation. (46–47)

*Suggested treatment strategies*: To accept that psychotherapy cannot help persons with schizophrenia reinforces the dangerous and erroneous message that such persons are separate, distinct, and deficient relative to others. On the other hand, a realistic and appropriate approach to the use of psychotherapy in the overall treatment plan can facilitate patients' recovery by integrating their experiences of a life interrupted by severe illness and by helping them learn coping strategies. Coursey (48) clarified the basis of a sound psychotherapy for persons suffering from schizophrenia: 1) psychotherapy should not be seen as competing with medication but, rather, as complementary to it; 2) psychotherapy can and should address the personal, human issues raised by having a serious mental illness; 3) psychotherapy must be practical, thus making use of educational as well as experiential approaches to help individuals learn to manage the disorder; and 4) psychotherapy should address the "normal problems of living that people with schizophrenia have to deal with just as anyone else does" (p. 351).

Neligh and Kinzie (49) have identified ten

practical approaches to accomplish the goals mentioned above. These authors suggest the following: 1) accepting the current level of functioning without pressure to change, 2) determining the appropriate frequency of contact for each patient, 3) selecting a comfortable style of relating, 4) modeling desirable social attitudes, 5) facilitating problem-solving skills, 6) providing a safe place for patients to express emotions, 7) managing dependence, 8) effecting changes in the patient's environment, 9) setting limits and discussing consequences of actions, as well as 10) establishing rules for confidentiality and the need to share information across systems of care. These authors propose a respectful, humane approach which emphasizes positive social behaviors, upbeat emotional tone, the provision of advice, information sharing, compliments, jokes, companionship, as well as sharing in the triumphs and tragedies of life. Such supportive psychotherapy may increase self-esteem, facilitate awareness of limitations, avoid deterioration and/or hospitalization, prevent undue dependence, and improve levels of function.

5. MYTH: PATIENTS MUST BE ON MEDICATION ALL THEIR LIVES. REALITY: IT MAY BE A SMALL PERCENTAGE WHO NEED MEDICATION INDEFINITELY. This myth has been generated by physicians for a wide variety of reasons. First, it is an attempt to underscore the importance of taking medication in a power struggle with the patient. Secondly, if a physician believes in Myth #1 "once a schizophrenic always a schizophrenic" or its corollary "once a broken brain always a broken brain," then the physician believes that medication is the key to maintenance of lifelong stabilization.

*Evidence*: There are no data existing which support this Myth. When analyzing the results from the long-term studies, it was clear that a surprising number (at least 25%–50%), were completely off their medications, suffered no further signs and symptoms of schizophrenia, and were functioning well. Over time, most patients altered their dosages and schedules. These behaviors often resulted in relapses early on in their illness trajectories when the illness was raging. The physicians in charge often felt justified and the patients felt defeated. Part of the trouble lay in human nature since there is usually only a 40–50% compliance rate for any kind of prescription taking in the U.S. by any kind of patient. (38) Other problems involved: 1) the patient's lack of understanding about having an illness, 2) in becoming disoriented enough not to manage taking medication, 3) in the lack of clear knowledge about the reasons for and the skills needed in taking medication, 4) in the frequent increase of covert and overt side effects which are unpleasant or undesirable (e.g., dyskinesia, dystonia, akinesia, akathisia, obesity, impotence, dry mouth, weight gain), and 5) in the lack of engineering to reduce environmental stressors. Such high stressors have been shown to increase relapse rates in some patients even if medicated intramuscularly. However, even though patients experimented with their medications and learned to use them more regularly, the long-term studies found that more subjects than not, eventually discovered through trial, error, and time, that they were able to function without medication later on in their illness trajectories.

*Suggested treatment strategies*: Most successful approaches involve the following: a strong patient-physician collaboration (49), targeted psychoeducational and skill building strategies aimed at prodromal and chronic symptom recognition and medication management (17) as well as built-in reassessment strategies and standardized side effects monitoring techniques. (49)

6. MYTH: PEOPLE WITH SCHIZOPHRENIA CANNOT DO ANYTHING EXCEPT LOW-LEVEL JOBS. REALITY: PEOPLE WITH SCHIZOPHRENIA CAN AND DO PERFORM AT EVERY LEVEL OF WORK. The idea that persons with schizophrenia are unable to work or can only achieve a low level of function because of their illness has had long standing credence especially in the U.S. Anthony et al. (50) reported in their review of the literature that only 10–30 percent of patients worked full time throughout a year or at follow-up. This finding has reinforced this perception.

*Evidence:* The early vocational approach consisted primarily of sheltered workshops designed originally for the developmentally disabled. (51) Until recently, little thought was given about whether or not these workshops were appropriate settings for these patients or for those with serious mental illnesses. In addition, there has been minimal appreciation about the power of stigma, the low priority in the vocational rehabilitation ladder, distinct systems problems at the interface (such as rigidity, isolation, compensatory ad hoc operations, and narrow frames of reference. [28, 50]). However, in their 1974 follow-up study, Strauss and Carpenter (52) found that symptoms and levels of functioning, such as work, were only loosely related to one another in an "open-linked" fashion. The Vermont Longitudinal Research Project (12) also found that, in their "improved but not recovered group," wide heterogeneity existed within the same person with some cohort members working well despite ongoing and persistent hallucinations and/or delusions. These patients had learned not to tell anyone because it "upset" others. For other patients, work became the primary treatment strategy to reduce symptomatology (25, 37, 53).

Across time, clinicians have appreciated the interactive therapeutic effects of work on illness (e.g., Galen [172 AD] "Employment is nature's best physician and is essential to human happiness" [see 54, p. 663]). Harding (28) discovered that "Despite this basic understanding of human functioning, the integration of work into systems that treat severe mental illness is limited, sporadic, and inadequately addressed." When a rehabilitation program has a strong emphasis and a cohesive approach for clients, the long-term trajectory is significantly enhanced and the work histories greatly altered. (12, 14)

*Suggested treatment strategies:* At the current time, vocational and other forms of rehabilitation are accomplished by "persistent, energetic personnel inventing ingenious solutions to the roadblocks set up at the system interfaces." (28) To treat the patient first means to "treat" the system of care in order to encourage flexibility, collaboration, data-based training, and a unified theoretical framework. Other approaches have been laid out such as the vocational strategies of "choose, get, keep" job model from the Boston group headed by Anthony et al. (50). They formulate a rehabilitation diagnosis, develop a rehabilitation plan, (which incorporates resources available and needed), and devise individually constructed interventions. This collaboration involves career counseling, skills training, placement, and work training to keep the job once the person has one (such as getting to work on time and dressing neatly and maintaining appropriate social interaction [50]).

7. MYTH: FAMILIES ARE THE ETIOLOGICAL AGENTS. REALITY: FAMILIES AS COLLABORATORS CAN PROVIDE CRITICAL INFORMATION AND PROVIDE ENVIRONMENTS TO LOWER A RELATIVE'S VULNERABILITY TO EPISODES. The myth, that families cause schizophrenia, flourished prior to the most recent biological revolution in psychiatry. Proponents of this myth targeted the family's severe dysfunctions, especially in the area of communication, as the cause of schizophrenia. For example, after observing communication difficulties in persons with schizophrenia, many theorists (55–57) reasoned that the dysfunctions were learned through interaction with disturbed family members. Although many investigators have since discarded this myth, it has survived even in the current biological era, such that numbers of clinicians and academics, who train students in the different mental health disciplines, still believe it. (58)

*Evidence:* Although family researchers have demonstrated that the emotional and interactional climate of families can help precipitate relapses in their relatives (e.g., 59) as well as the efficacy of enhanced family communication in lowering vulnerability to relapse (60), they have failed to show that family factors are necessary and sufficient causes of schizophrenia (61–62). No evidence exists that a family's psychosocial climate, communication patterns, or parenting practices are primary causes of schizophrenia. In fact, despite the finding that vulnerable individuals from families high in expressed emotion are more likely to relapse, the majority of families are not rated high on this factor. (58) Many families, who are low in EE, may very well represent a biologic protective factor. (61) Family researchers now recognize that it is the co-occurrence of an ill individual's behaviors and the various emotional/interactional characteristics of a family's response which often precipitates symptoms. The available evidence suggests that schizophrenia is an episodic disorder which, not unlike many other episodic disorders (e.g., asthma, Crohn's Disease, arthritis), is often vulnerable to environmental stresses and triggers. Stressors, such as family environment, are now not considered to be sufficient in and of themselves to be considered etiological agents of the underlying disorder.

*Suggested treatment strategies*: The optimal roles of families in treatment, and the appropriate relationships between clinicians and families are now well established, if not widely realized. Families need, and want, education, information, coping and communication skills, emotional support, and to be treated as collaborators (63). As many authors have noted (e.g., 64), scientific theories of family causation contributed to the alienation between professionals and families, as well as to the guilt and burden that families feel. For this reason, clinicians need to make a special effort to solicit the collaboration and involvement of family members. In some cases it may even be necessary to entice families into collaboration by acknowledging the difficulties they have experienced and apologizing for the way they have been treated by the mental health system. Once a relationship is established, clinician, patient, and family can work together to identify needs and appropriate interventions. Many families benefit from communication training, psychoeducation about the illness and coping strategies. Fortunately, several effective models exist (e.g., 66–67; see also 68). In addition to assisting families in the acquisition of skills and knowledge, it is important for the clinician to encourage families to develop realistic, yet optimistic expectations about their relatives' chance for improvement (see above discussion of Myth #1), and about their own

ability to contribute to the recovery process, thus helping to relieve family burden.

## Conclusion

This paper has reviewed 7 prevailing myths about the group of schizophrenias. The authors have proposed counter-evidence to each myth. Some treatment strategies were suggested to enhance the possibility of improvement and recovery through reduction of symptoms and the increase of levels of functioning for patients. It is hoped that this paper will encourage clinicians, program designers, policy makers, patients and their families to deal more effectively with these difficult and often prolonged disorders. A longitudinal perspective about schizophrenia should imbue everyone with a renewed sense of hope and optimism. After studying 508 patients across 22 years, Huber and colleagues (68) stated that ". . . schizophrenia does not seem to be a disease of slow, progressive deterioration. Even in the second and third decades of illness, there is still potential for full or partial recovery." All of the recent long-term follow-up investigators have recorded the same findings (7–14).

## References

1. Kraepelin E. Dementia praecox, in Clinical Psychiatry: A Textbook for Students and Physicians, 6th ed. Translated by Diefendorf AR. New York, Macmillan, 1902.
2. Bleuler E. Die Prognose der Dementia praecox (Schizophrenien Gruppe) Allg. Z. Psychiat. 1908: 65: 436.
3. Harding CM, Zubin J, Strauss JS. Chronicity in schizophrenia: Fact, partial fact, or artifact? Hosp Community Psychiatry 1987: 38(5): 477–486.
4. Harding CM, Zubin J, Strauss JS. Chronicity in schizophrenia revisited. Br J Psychiatry. 1992: 161 (Suppl. 18) 27–37.
5. Cohen P, Cohen J. The clinician's illusion. Arch Gen Psychiatry 1984: 41: 1178–1182.
6. Angst J. European long-term followup studies of schizophrenia. Schiz Bull. 1986: 14 (4): 501–513.
7. Ciompi L, Müller C. Lebensweg und Alter der Sizophrenen: Eine katamnestische Lonzeitstudies bis ins senium. Berlin, Springer Verlag, 1976.
8. Huber G, Gross G, Schüttler R. Schizophrenie: Verlaufs und sozialpsychiatrische Langzeituntersuchungen an den 1945 bis 1959 in Bonn hospitalisierten schizophrenen Kranken: Monographien aus dem Gesametgebiete der Psychiatrie. BD 21. Berlin Springer Verlag, 1979.
9. Tsuang MT, Woolson RF, Fleming JA. Long-term outcome of major psychoses. 1: Schizophrenia and affective disor-

ders compared with psychiatrically symptom-free surgical conditions. Arch Gen Psychiatry 1979: 36: 1295–1301.

10. Bleuler M. Die Schizophrenen Geistesstörungen im Lichte langjähriger Kranken- und Familiengeschicten. Stuttgart: George Thieme Verlag 1972: (New York: Intercontinental Medical Book Corp. The Schizophrenic Disorders: Long-Term Patient and Family Studies. Translated by Clemens SM. New Haven. Yale University Press, 1978.

11. Harding CM, Brooks GW, Ashikaga T, Strauss JS, Breier A. The Vermont longitudinal study of persons with severe mental illness: I. Methodology, study sample, and overall status 32 years later. Am J Psychiatry 1987: 144 (6): 718–726.

12. Harding CM, Brooks GW, Ashikaga T, Strauss JS, Breier A. The Vermont longitudinal study II. Long-term outcome of subjects who retrospectively met DSM III criteria for schizophrenia. Am J Psychiatry 1987: 144 (6): 727–725.

13. DeSisto MJ, Harding CM, McCormick RV, Ashikaga T, Brooks GW. Serious mental illness after 36 years: I. The Maine longitudinal study—methodology and outcome. manuscript submitted.

14. Desisto MJ, Harding CM, McCormick RV, Ashikaga T, Brooks GW. The Maine-Vermont comparison of the long-term outcome of serious mental illness. manuscript submitted.

15. Test MA, Stein LL. Community treatment of the chronic patient: research overview. Schiz Bull 1978: 4 (3): 350–364.

16. Rotelli F, Dell'aqua G. La storia della psichiatria Triestina. Il Lanternino 1991: XVI (4) Prog. 92: 1–36.

17. Liberman RP, Mueser KT, Wallace CJ. Social skills training for schizophrenic individuals at risk for relapse. Am J Psychiatry 1986: 143: 523–526.

18. Ciompi L. Catamnestic Long-term study on the course of life and aging of schizophrenics. Schiz Bull 1980: 6: 606–618.

19. Mosher LR, Burti L. Community mental health: Principles and practice. New York, W. W. Norton & Co., 1989.

20. Cousins N. Anatomy of an illness as perceived by the patient: Reflections on healing and regeneration. New York, Norton, 1979.

21. Siegel B. Love, Medicine, and Miracles. New York; Harper & Row, 1986.

22. Herth K. Fostering hope in terminally ill people. J Adv Nursing 1990: 15: 1250–1259.

23. Moyers B. Healing and the mind. New York, Doubleday, 1993.

24. Enfel G. The clinical application of the biopsychosocial model. Am J Psychiatry, 1980: 137: 535–544.

25. Strauss JS, Hafez H, Lieberman P, Harding CM. The course of psychiatric disorder: III. Longitudinal principles. (special article). Am J Psychiatry 1985: 142(3): 289–296.

26. Stein G. Sacred Emily in Portraits in Prayer. New York, Random House, 1934.

27. Seeman MV, Lang M. The role of estrogens in schizophrenia: gender differences. Schiz Bull 1990: 16 (2): 185–194.

28. Harding CM, Strauss JS, Hafez H, Lieberman P. Work and mental illness: I. Toward an integration of the rehabilitation process. J Nerv Ment Dis 1987: 175(6): 317–327.

29. Bleuler E, Dementia Praecox oder Die Gruppe der Schizophrenien. In: Hanbuch der Psychiatrie, hrsg. von G. Aschaffenburg. Leipzig, Deuticke, 1911.

30. Kendler KS, Eaves LJ. Models for the joint effect of genotype and environment on liability to psychiatric illness. Am J Psychiatry 1986: 143(3): 279–89.

31. Vaillant G. Adolf Meyer was right: Dynamic psychiatry needs the life chart. J Natl Assoc Private Psychiatr Hosp 1980: 11: 4–14.

32. Meyer A. The life chart and the obligation of specifying positive data in the psychopathological diagnosis. In: Contributions to medical and biological research, Vol. 2, Hoeber. 1919. Reprinted in The Collected Papers of Adolf Meyer (ed. E.E. Winters). Baltimore, Johns Hopkins Press, 1951.

33. Campbell, J, Schraiber R. The well-being project: Mental health consumers speak for themselves. Sacramento, CA, California Dept. of Mental Health, 1989.

34. Lovejoy M. Expectations and the recovery process. Schiz Bull 1982: 8 (4) 605–609.

35. Adler D. The medical model and psychiatry's tasks. Hosp Community Psychiatry, 1981, 32: 387–392.

36. Anthony WA, Cohen MR, Cohen BF. The philosophy, treatment process, and principles of the psychiatric rehabilitation approach. New Dir Ment Health, 1983: 67–69.

37. Breier A, Strauss JS. Self-control of psychotic disorders. Arch Gen Psychiatry 1983: 40: 1141–1145.

38. Diamond RJ. Increasing medication compliance in young adult chronic psychiatric patients. New Dir Ment Health Serv 1984: 21: 59–69.

39. Heinrichs DW. The psychotherapy of schizophrenia. IN: Handbook of studies in schizophrenia–Part 2. (eds) GD Burrows, TR Norman, G. Rubinstein. New York, Elsevier, 1986.

40. Legatt M. Schizophrenia: The consumer's viewpoint. IN: Handbook of studies in schizophrenia–Part 2. (eds) GD Burrows, TR Norman, G. Rubinstein. New York, Elsevier, 1986.

41. Ruocchio, PJ. How psychotherapy can help the schizophrenic patient. Hosp Community Psychiatry, 1989, 40: 180–190.

42. Coursey RD, Farrell EW, Zahniser JH. Consumers' attitudes toward psychotherapy, hospitalization, and aftercare. Health Soc Work, 1991: 16(3): 155–161.

43. Coursey RD, Keller AB, Farrell, EW. Individual psychotherapy and Persons with serious mental illness: The consumer perspective. University of Maryland, manuscript submitted.

44. Kanas, N. 1986: Group therapy with schizophrenics. Int J Group Psychother 1986: 36: 339–351.

45. Kanas N. Group therapy with schizophrenic patients: A short-term, homogenous approach. Int J Group Psychother 1991: 41: 33–48.

46. Chadwick PDJ, Lowe CF: Measurement and modification of delusional beliefs. J Consult Clin Psychol 1990: 58 (2): 225–232.

47. Green MF. Cognitive remediation in schizophrenia: Is it time yet? Am J Psychiatry 1993: 150: 2 178–187.

48. Coursey RD. Psychotherapy with persons suffering from schizophrenia. Schiz Bull. 1989: 15: 349–353.

49. Neligh GL, Kinzie JD. Therapeutic relationships with the chronic patient. In Effective Aftercare for the 1980's. DL Cutler (ed) New Directions for Mental Health Services San Francisco Jossey-Bass, 1883.

50. Anthony WA, Howell J, Danley KS. Chap. 13. Vocational

Rehabilitation of the psychiatrically disabled. In: The Chronically mentally ill: Research and Services. (ed.) M. Mirabi. 1984: 215–237.

51. Ciardello JA. Job placement success of schizophrenic clients in sheltered workshop programs. Vocational Evaluation and Work Adjustment Bulletin. 1981: Fall: 125–128.

52. Strauss JS, Carpenter WT. Characteristic symptoms and outcome in schizophrenia. Arch Gen Psychiatry, 1974: 30(30): 429–434.

53. McCrory DJ. The human dimension of the vocational rehabilitation process In: JA Ciardello, MD Bell (Eds) Vocational rehabilitation of persons with prolonged psychiatric disorders. Baltimore, Johns Hopkins University Press, 1988: 208–218.

54. Strauss MB. (ed) Familiar medical quotations. Boston, Little Brown, 1968: 663.

55. Bateson G, Jackson DD, Haley J, Weakland JH. Toward a theory of schizophrenia. Behav Sci 1956: 1: 251–264.

56. Wynne LC, Singer M. Thought disorder and family relations. Arch Gen Psychiatry, 1977: 9: 199–206.

57. Lidz T. The origin and treatment of Schizophrenic disorders. New York, Basic Books, 1973.

58. Lefley HP. Expressed emotion: Conceptual, clinical, and social policy issues. Hospital Community Psychiatry 1992: Vol 43 No. 6 591–598.

59. Brown GW, Birley JLT, Wing JK. Influence of family life on the course of schizophrenic disorder: A replication. Br J Psychiatry, 1972: 121: 241–258.

60. Goldstein M, Doane JA. Family factors in the onset, course, and treatment of schizophrenic spectrum disorders: an update on current research. J Nerv Ment Dis 1982: 170: 692–700.

61. Falloon IRH. Prevention of morbidity in schizophrenia. In: Falloon IRH (Ed.), Handbook of behavioral family therapy. New York: Guilford, 1988.

62. Zubin J, Spring B. Vulnerability—a new view of schizophrenia. J Abnorm Psychol 1977: 86: 103–126.

63. Bernheim KF. Supportive family counseling. Schiz Bull, 1982: 8: 634–640.

64. Beels CC, McFarlane WR. Family treatment of schizophrenia: Background and state of the art. Hosp Community Psychiatry, 1982: 33(7): 541–550.

65. Falloon IRH, Boyd JL, McGill CW. Family management of schizophrenia. Baltimore: Johns Hopkins University Press, 1985.

66. Leff J, Kuipers L, Berkowitz R et al. A controlled trial of social intervention in the families of schizophrenic patients. Br J Psychiatry, 1982: 141: 121–134.

67. Kanter J, Lamb HR, Loeper C. Expressed emotion in families: A critical review. Hosp Community Psychiatry 1987: 38: 374–380.

68. Huber G, Gross G, Schüttler R, Linz M. Longitudinal studies of schizophrenic patients. Schiz Bull, 1980: 6: 592–605.

# ON THE NATURE AND MECHANISMS OF OBSTETRIC INFLUENCES IN SCHIZOPHRENIA: A REVIEW AND SYNTHESIS OF EPIDEMIOLOGIC STUDIES

## Tyrone D. Cannon

*The causes of schizophrenia are unknown but important clues have been identified. It is known, of course, that genetic factors play a significant role in who develops the disorder. But not all individuals who are at genetic risk for the condition actually develop it, and thus consideration of other factors is necessary to explain who develops it and why. Researchers and theoreticians often work within a broad vulnerability-stress framework in their search for explanations, a framework which holds that schizophrenia occurs when an individual genetic predisposition is exposed to an environmental stressor. At one level this is a valuable perspective because it can organize many research findings, but at another level such a framework is too vague to allow the proposal and testing of specific hypotheses. Researchers aim to specify genes that comprise the heritable vulnerability to schizophrenia and the environmental factors that act upon this vulnerability (see, for example, Walker & Diforio, 1997).*

*Tyrone Cannon examines one environmental stressor that might contribute to schizophrenia: obstetric complications at birth. Cannon notes that labor and delivery complications, particularly those that result in reduced oxygen flow to the baby, are a reliable predictor of the eventual onset of schizophrenia, especially when they happen to individuals at genetic risk for the disorder. From this perspective, schizophrenia emerges from the combination of these two factors, whereas each one individually does not necessarily lead to the disorder. He speculates that the genetic risk for schizophrenia might involve specifically a heightened sensitivity to oxygen deprivation, which hinders normal growth of the brain and in turn increases the likelihood of schizophrenia later in life. This leads to the surprising but potentially important observation that schizophrenia might be prevented by exercising great care during the delivery of high-risk infants.*

## Reference

Walker, E., & Diforio, D. (1997). Schizophrenia: A neural diathesis-stress model. *Psychological Review, 104,* 667–685.

## Suggested Readings

Grimes, K., & Walker, E. F. (1994). Childhood emotional expressions, educational attainment, and age at onset of illness in schizophrenia. *Journal of Abnormal Psychology, 103,* 784–790.
McGlashan, T. H., & Hoffman, R. E. (2000). Schizophrenia as a disorder of developmentally reduced synaptic connectivity. *Archives of General Psychiatry, 57,* 637–648.

---

*International Review of Psychiatry, 9,* 387–397. (1997).

*Obstetric complications are robust correlates of schizophrenia, but it remains controversial whether more than one neurally-disruptive mechanism is involved and whether such influences covary with, depend on, or are independent of the disorder's genetic basis. Labor and delivery complications (LDCs), particularly perinatal hypoxia, are the most consistently-replicated obstetric correlates of schizophrenia and appear as risk factors in a larger proportion of cases than pregnancy complications (including viral exposure) and signs of fetal maldevelopment. However, the vast majority of individuals exposed to such LDCs, even in the extreme, do not develop schizophrenia, indicating that they are unlikely to cause the disorder on their own. In addition, unaffected siblings and offspring of schizophrenics are no more likely to have a history of LDCs than are unaffected individuals from the general population, indicating that such factors are not likely to be caused by genetic predisposition to the disorder. Findings from prospective studies of high-risk samples and representative birth cohorts are consistent in showing that the association of LDCs with schizophrenia (and with severity of its neuropathological features) is greater among those with an elevated genetic risk, suggesting that predisposing genes for schizophrenia may confer a heightened susceptibility of the fetal brain to the neurotoxic consequences of oxygen deprivation (and, possibly, other obstetric mechanisms). These findings encourage the search for candidate genes that mediate the brain's vulnerability to hypoxic-ischemic neuronal injury and suggest the use of preventive obstetric practices in high-risk pregnancies.*

## Introduction

Obstetric complications (OCs) are among the most robust environmental correlates of schizophrenia (McNeil, 1988). Ambiguity remains, however, as to whether such influences depend on (Cannon *et al.*, 1990), covary with (Fish *et al.*, 1992), or are independent of (Lewis *et al.*, 1987) genetic influences and whether more than one neurally-disruptive mechanism is involved. The answers to these questions are critical for efforts to locate predisposing genes for this disorder. If obstetric risk factors are capable of producing schizophrenia by themselves, without the participation of genetic predisposition (phenocopy model), then such cases create an unknown degree of error in analyses of covariation between DNA polymorphisms and schizophrenia within pedigrees. If obstetric risk factors are correlated with the disorder's genetic basis (gene-environment covariation model), then their influences are confounded, and precision of linkage statistics may be lost if OCs have other than an inconsequential association with schizophrenia. If an obstetric influence depends on the presence of genetic predisposition (gene-environment interaction model), then elucidating the nature of this influence should provide important clues as to the genes involved, since such genes would then be expected to confer a heightened susceptibility to the mechanism by which the particular complication increases risk for schizophrenia.

This review evaluates recent obstetric epidemiologic studies of schizophrenia to determine which of these models is appropriate in application to the various types of OCs found to be associated with schizophrenia. . . .

## Environment in Schizophrenia

... The criteria for evaluating competing models of the manner in which OCs are related to schizophrenia can be conceptualized in terms of a three-branch decision-tree. First, does the exposure reliably lead to schizophrenia? The phenocopy model does not predict that all schizophrenic patients should have the exposure, just that all individuals with the exposure should have schizophrenia. Thus, a negative result rules this model out because there would be no explanation for why some individuals with the exposure develop schizophrenia and others do not. Second, does the exposure occur more frequently in groups at elevated genetic risk for schizophrenia than those without a known genetic risk? A negative result rules out the gene-environment covariation model because gene carriers would then be no more likely to have the exposure than non-gene carriers. Third, is the exposure related to schizophrenia outcome (and to severity of its neuropathological features) only in groups at elevated genetic risk compared with those without a known genetic risk? A negative result rules out the gene-environment interaction model because the pathogenic effect of the exposure would then not depend on the presence of predisposing genes. In the latter case, a simple "additive influences" model would obtain, whereby genetic and non-genetic influences sum together in determining an individual's underlying susceptibility to schizophrenia.

## Labor and Delivery Complications

McNeil's (1988) review of the OC literature appearing prior to 1988 concluded that of the different types of OCs found to be associated with schizophrenia, labor and delivery complications (LDCs), particularly perinatal hypoxia, have the most robust association. Table 1 [not reproduced here] summarizes the results of all the studies conducted since that review which used objective birth records in comparing rates of LDCs among schizophrenics and a variety of different comparison groups (e.g., unaffected siblings, psychiatric controls, normal controls).

Three major conclusions can be drawn from the information presented in Table 1. First, despite the fact that these studies come from several different countries and utilized a variety of different LDC measures, sampling strategies and control groups, all of the odds ratios are above one and show a strong tendency to converge toward a value of three. This pattern indicates that the recent studies are replicating earlier ones in demonstrating a robust association between LDCs and increased risk for schizophrenia. ...

In strong contradiction to the phenocopy model, it is quite clear that the vast majority of individuals exposed to such complications do not become schizophrenic. In population-based cohort studies, 97% or more of individuals exposed to LDCs do not develop schizophrenia (Buka et al., 1993; Done et al., 1991). ...

The second question to address is whether LDCs occur more frequently among individuals at elevated genetic risk than among those without a known genetic risk. The most appropriate basis for examining this question is to select unaffected siblings or offspring of schizophrenics and then to compare rates of LDCs in this group to those in a sample of unaffected individuals without affected relatives. ... all such studies using objective records of birth history have found no increase in the frequency of LDCs in the high-risk compared with low-risk groups. Further, in the only study that examined individuals at three degrees of genetic risk (neither, one, both parents affected with schizophrenia spectrum disorders), rates of LDCs were equivalent across risk groups (Cannon et al., 1993). ...

We are left with the gene-environment interaction and simple additive models. Here, the critical question is whether LDCs lead to schizophrenia outcome only among individuals at elevated genetic risk compared with those without a known genetic risk. Again, the high-risk design provides the most appropriate basis for examining this question, since subjects are selected based on their genetic risk status regardless of their own diagnostic outcomes. One must discount any study that uses family-history negative schizophrenic patients as a low-risk control group in this context, since it is not valid to infer that such cases do not carry predisposing genes for the disorder. Regardless of whether risk is based on having an affected parent (Cannon *et al.*, 1990; Fish *et al.* 1992), sibling (Eagles *et al.* 1990; Gunther-Genta *et al.*, 1994; Kinney *et al.*, 1994; Pollack *et al.* 1966; Woerner *et al.*, 1973), or co-twin (Pollin & Stabenau, 1968), *all* studies using objective birth records have found that those high-risk subjects with a history of LDCs are significantly more likely to become schizophrenic than those without such a history. These findings provide evidence for one of the two logical requirements of the gene-environment interaction model; that is, given a genetic background for schizophrenia, the experience of LDCs is associated with schizophrenia outcomes. The second requirement is that this relationship should not exist in the absence of a genetic background for schizophrenia. In the only prospective study using a control group selected based on absence of schizophrenia in the parents, offspring of schizophrenic mothers who experienced LDCs were significantly more likely to develop schizophrenia than high-risk offspring without such a history, and there was no increase in risk for schizophrenia among a subgroup of the low-risk controls who had the same number and severity of LDCs as the high-risk schizophrenics (Cannon *et al.*, 1990). This model is also supported by the results of our prospective high-risk study in Denmark, in which the extent of ventricular enlargement in the subjects as adults was predicted by the interaction of degree of genetic risk for schizophrenia with LDCs (Cannon *et al.*, 1993). Among individuals without a history of LDCs, ventricular volume tended to increase linearly with the number of parents affected, but this pattern was significantly more pronounced in those with a history of LDCs. Notably, there was no difference in ventricular volume among the low-risk controls as a function of LDCs, indicating that some degree of genetic risk was required to observe the effect. In addition, high-risk subjects with SPD did not differ from those with no mental illness in the rate of LDCs (Cannon *et*

*al.*, 1990) and along with the latter had significantly smaller ventricular volumes than the schizophrenics (Cannon *et al.*, 1994).

These findings have three broad-ranging implications. First, it may be possible to prevent schizophrenia in some genetically at-risk individuals with careful prenatal and perinatal monitoring and early intervention. Claims that the incidence of schizophrenia has declined from the pre– to post–Second World War period in developed nations, with the accompanying improvement in obstetric care, are consistent with this notion (Warner, 1995); but such claims are based on analyses of hospital admissions, practices relating to which have also changed during this period. Second, some component of the genetic diathesis to schizophrenia would appear to render the fetal brain particularly susceptible to the neurotoxic consequences of oxygen deprivation (and, possibly, to other obstetric mechanisms), and, thus, the search for candidate genes that mediate the brain's vulnerability to hypoxic-ischemic neuronal injury appears warranted. The list of such candidates is likely to be relatively long, but prominent suspects might be located within the glutamatergic NMDA receptor system, as overstimulation of such receptors represents an early event in the sequence leading from hypoxia to neuronal death (Choi & Rothman, 1990). Third, because the proportion of the schizophrenic population with a history of perinatal hypoxia is quite high (i.e., 20–30%) (Buka *et al.*, 1993; McNeil, 1988), it is possible that hypoxia-ischemia represents the single most important environmental mechanism associated with increased risk for schizophrenia. . . .

## Pregnancy Complications

Taken together, pregnancy complications (PCs) are less reliably associated with schizophrenia than LDCs (Kinney *et al.*, 1994; McNeil, 1988). Most studies utilized summary scales encompassing a variety of maternal illness and disruptive events, making it difficult to isolate potential mechanisms. Among the studies that examined specific complications, fetal exposure to influenza and rhesus incompatibility are the most prominent. Numerous well-designed population and cohort studies have observed an elevated rate of schizophrenia among individuals exposed to influenza epidemics during gestation (Barr et al., 1990; Kendell & Kemp, 1989; Mednick et al., 1988; 1990; O'Callaghan et al., 1991; Sham et al., 1992; but see Crow et al., 1991; Torrey, 1992). Whether such an association reflects a neurotoxic effect of influenza on fetal brain development, an effect related to maternal immunological responses to infection, or a third factor, is not clear (Hollister & Cannon, in press). . . . Further, the proportion of the schizophrenic population showing a history of such complications is not greater than 2–3% (Hollister et al., 1996; Sham et al., 1992), indicating that if such factors do operate via mechanism(s) other than fetal hypoxia, they are likely to play a much more minor role in the etiology of schizophrenia than LDCs. . . .

## Conclusion

Epidemiologic studies rule out the possibility that fetal hypoxia and other complications of labor and delivery, which are the most robust environmental correlates of schizophrenia and are present in the histories of 20–30% of such cases, can cause schizophrenia on their own, even when experienced in the extreme. There is also no evidence that such factors covary with genetic predisposition to the disorder. In fact, all studies using objective birth records have found that rates of these complications in unaffected relatives of schizophrenics are either the same as or lower than in the general population. On the other hand, findings from prospective studies of high-risk samples are consistent in showing that high-risk individuals with a history of these complications have a greater risk for schizophrenia (and show greater severity of its neuropathological features) than those without such a history. Further, when examined, these complications have not been found to be associated with an increased risk for schizophrenia (or with its neuropathological features) among individuals without a known genetic background for the disorder. In principle, definitive rejection of

the simple additive model in favor of genotype-environment interaction must await isolation of the genes involved and demonstration that LDCs are associated with schizophrenia only in individuals who carry one or more of such genes in a predisposing configuration. However, based on the epidemiological and neuropathological evidence reviewed above, it would appear likely that some component of the genetic diathesis to schizophrenia renders the fetal brain particularly vulnerable to the effects of oxygen deprivation. These findings encourage search for molecular mechanisms underlying this association and suggest the use of preventive obstetric practices in high-risk pregnancies.

## References

Barr, C. E., Mednick, S. A. & Munk-Jorgensen, P. (1990). Exposure to influenza epidemics during gestation and adult schizophrenia. Archives of General Psychiatry, 47, 869–874.

Buka, S. L., Tsuang, M. T. & Lipsitt, L. P. (1993). Pregnancy/delivery complications and psychiatric diagnosis: a prospective study. Archives of General Psychiatry, 50, 151–156.

Cannon, T. D., Mednick, S. A. & Parnas, J. (1990). Antecedents of predominantly negative- and predominantly positive-symptom schizophrenia in a high-risk population. Archives of General Psychiatry, 47, 622–632.

Cannon, T. D., Mednick, S. A., Schulsinger, F., Parnas, J., Praestholm, J. & Vestergaard, A. (1993). Developmental brain abnormalities in the offspring of schizophrenic mothers: I. Contributions of genetic and perinatal factors. Archives of General Psychiatry, 50, 551–564.

Cannon, T. D., Mednick, S. A., Schulsinger, F., Parnas, J., Praestholm, J. & Vestergaard, A. (1994). Developmental brain abnormalities in the offspring of schizophrenic mothers: II. Structural brain characteristics of schizophrenia and schizotypal personality disorder. Archives of General Psychiatry, 51, 955–962.

Choi, D. W. & Rothman, S. M. (1990). The role of glutamate neurotoxicity in hypoxic-ischemic neuronal death. Annual Review of Neuroscience, 13, 171–182.

Crow, T. J., Done, D. J. & Johnstone, E. C. (1991). Schizophrenia and influenza. Lancet, 338, 116–117.

Done, D. J., Johnstone, E. C., Frith, C. D., Golding, J., Shepherd, P. M. & Crow, T. J. (1991) Complications of pregnancy and delivery in relation to psychosis in adult life: data from the British perinatal mortality survey sample. British Medical Journal, 302, 1576–1580.

Eagles, J. M., Gibson, I., Bremner, M. H., Clunie, F., Ebmeier, K. P. & Smith, N. C. (1990). Obstetric compilations in DSM-II schizophrenics and their siblings. Lancet, 335, 1139–1141.

Fish, B., Marcus, J., Hans, S. L., Auerbach, J. G. & Perdue, S. (1992). Infants at risk for schizophrenia: Sequelae of a genetic neurointegrative defect. Archives of General Psychiatry, 49, 221–235.

Gunther-Genta, F., Bovet, P. & Hohlfeld, P. (1994). Obstetric complications and schizophrenia: a case control study. *British Journal of Psychiatry, 164,* 165–170.

Hollister, J. M. & Cannon, T. D. (in press). Neurodevelopmental disturbances in the etiology of schizophrenia. In: M. Ron & A. S. David (Eds), *Disorders of brain and mind.* New York: Cambridge University Press.

Hollister, J. M., Laing, P. & Mednick, S. A. (1996). Rhesus incompatibility as a risk factor for schizophrenia in male adults. *Archives of General Psychiatry, 53,* 19–24.

Kendell, R. E. & Kemp, I. W. (1989). Maternal influenza in the etiology of schizophrenia. *Archives of General Psychiatry, 46,* 878–882.

Kinney, D. K., Levy, D. L., Yurgeleun-Todd, D. A., Medoff, D., LaJonchere, C. M. & Radford-Paregol, M. (1994). Season of birth and obstetrical complications in schizophrenics. *Journal of Psychiatric Research, 28,* 499–500.

Lewis, S. W., Reveley, A. M., Reveley, M. A., Chitkara, B. & Murray, R. M. (1987). The familial/sporadic distinction as a strategy in schizophrenia research. *British Journal of Psychiatry, 151,* 306–313.

McNeil, T. F. (1988). Obstetric factors and perinatal injuries. In: M. T. Tsuang & J. C. Simpson (Eds), *Handbook of schizophrenia,* vol. 3: *Nosology, epidemiology and genetics,* pp. 319–343. Amsterdam: Elsevier Science Publishers B. V.

Mednick, S. A., Machgon, R. A., Huttunen, M. O. & Bonett, D. (1988). Adult schizophrenia following prenatal exposure to an influenza epidemic. *Archives of General Psychiatry, 45,* 189–192.

Mednick, S. A., Machgon, R. A., Huttunen, M. O. & Barr, C. E. (1990). Influenza and schizophrenia: Helsinki vs. Edinburgh. *Archives of General Psychiatry, 47,* 875–876.

O'Callaghan, E., Sham, P., Takei, N., Glover, G. & Murray, R. M. (1991). Schizophrenia after prenatal exposure to 1957 A2 influenza epidemic. *Lancet, 337,* 1248–1250.

Pollack, M., Woerner, M. G., Goodman & Greenberg, I. M. (1966). Childhood development patterns of hospitalized adult schizophrenic and non-schizophrenic patients and their siblings. *American Journal of Orthopsychiatry, 36,* 510.

Pollin, W. & Stabenau, J. R. (1968). Biological, psychological and historical differences in a series of monozygotic twins discordant for schizophrenia. In: D. Rosenthal & S. S. Ketty (Eds), *The transmission of schizophrenia* (pp. 317–332). London: Pergamon Press.

Sham, P., O'Callaghan, E., Takei, N., Murray, G., Hare, E. & Murray, R. (1992). Schizophrenic births following influenza epidemics. *British Journal of Psychiatry, 160,* 461–466.

Torrey, E. F. (1992). Are we overestimating the genetic contribution to schizophrenia? *Schizophrenia Bulletin, 18,* 159–170.

Warner, R. (1995). Time trends in schizophrenia: changes in obstetric risk factors with industrialization. *Schizophrenia Bulletin, 21,* 483–500.

Woerner, M. G., Pollack, M. & Klein, D. F. (1973). Pregnancy and birth complications in psychiatric patients: a comparison of schizophrenic and personality disorder patients with their siblings. *Acta Psychiatrica Scandinavica, 49,* 712–721.

# CHAPTER 9

# Aging and Psychological Disorders

*Like any other adults, the elderly can be affected by the many disorders discussed in this book, such as depression, anxiety, schizophrenia, and alcohol abuse. However, with advancing age there is a sharp increase in the likelihood of cognitive disorders, which are disorders characterized by deficiencies in how information is stored, retrieved, and manipulated. This class of disorders takes on special significance not only because of its clear association with age, but also because large numbers of people are now living longer lives than did previous generations. Indeed this trend will continue—over the next few decades, the study and treatment of age-related changes in mental well-being will become increasingly important.*

*Cognitive disorders are usually classified as delirium, marked by inattention and a reduced awareness of the environment; the dementias, characterized by a decline in memory and other losses in cognition; and amnestic disorders, in which short-term memory is impaired severely. In this chapter we focus on the dementias in general and Alzheimer's disease in particular. We adopt this focus because of the sheer prevalence of the dementias, the corresponding breadth of literature that has been written on them, and the rapid progress that has been made recently in understanding and treating them.*

## Suggested Readings

Butler, R. N., Lewis, M. I., & Sunderland, T. (1998). *Aging and mental health: Positive psychosocial and biomedical approaches* (5th ed). New York: Allyn & Bacon.
Ricklefs, R. E., & Finch, C. E. (1995). *Aging: A natural history.* New York: W. H. Freeman.

# From *Hard to Forget:*
# An Alzheimer's Story

## Charles P. Pierce

*The first reading is a set of excerpts from a book by Charles Pierce, whose father had Alzheimer's disease. The centerpiece in this book is an incident in which the father, intending to buy flowers at a nearby store, got lost for three days. The author discusses how this forces his family to come to terms with the father's disease and how the father's deterioration forces him to re-evaluate his own future and that of his children. This article reminds us how central our memory is to who we are, and it draws attention to the anguish that results when a loved one suffers from severe memory loss.*

### Suggested Reading

Grant, L. (2000). *Remind me who I am, again.* New York: Granta Books.

---

(2000). New York: Random House.

There is no way to definitively diagnose Alzheimer's disease while the patient is still alive.

The disease usually begins in the hippocampus, the area of the brain that controls recent memory. The plaques and tangles build there first. Yesterday vanishes. A life disappears in an order reverse to that in which it was lived. Patients walk away from their houses in search of their childhood homes. Patients leave their jobs in search of their schools. Patients abandon their living wives in search of their dead mothers. But no definitive diagnosis is possible until the disease has destroyed so much of the brain that the patient has literally forgotten how to stay alive.

Then the doctors and the scientists cut out the brain and bring it to a laboratory down the hall. They section it. They stain it, so that the plaques and tangles of the disease can more easily be seen under the microscope. And then, finally, they make the diagnosis—on the death certificate. . . .

We were a solid family, but fragmented within ourselves, a fault deep in our bedrock. We weren't given either to shared introspection or to long discussions. We were private people, even to each other. Then, one day in May 1985, the fault moved. My mother sent my father out to buy flowers for our family graves. He got in his car and drove to the store, which was not two miles from his house. He was gone for three days. Practically everything I know about my family I have learned since that day. It was teased out, detail by detail, until I finally began to know what I hadn't known before, a hidden history that my father lost, one memory at a time. . . .

It was nearly Memorial Day. Every Memorial Day for almost sixteen years, my father and I had gone to plant geraniums on the family graves in St. John's Cemetery in Worcester, where the Irish in Worcester had been planting their relatives for as long as there had been Irish in Worcester to plant. Every Memorial Day, my father and I would plant them, first on the old sergeant's grave, and then on the graves of my father's aunts, and, finally, around the plot where lay Charlie Gibbons and the Duchess. And we always saved one flower for a mysterious cement cross, tiny and anonymous and mottled thick with lichens, near to where Charlie and the Duchess were buried. My father insisted on it. My mother rarely came with us. My mother was never much for graveyards.

Shrewsbury looks very much like a hundred other small New England towns. It has a pleasant, wooded common, with an old bandstand at its heart. At the head of the common is the First Congregational Church, which has dominated the common for over 200 years. They were tearing up the center of town that day. A construction crew had dug a trench across Main Street just short of the common. Traffic was being routed in an inverted U around the common and across in front of the First Congregational Church, down past the firehouse and the bandstand, and back onto Main Street along the common's westerly edge.

That morning, after stopping at the flower store, my father waved at the cop on duty—I know he did. He always waved at policemen, he was a policeman's son—and he drove northward up the east side of the common. He did not make the left turn in front of the First Congregational Church. He kept going north.

Eight hours later, Margaret and Abraham and I got home just as evening softened into night. As we walked in the door, the telephone was ringing, and that is the image that stayed with Margaret: the end of an idyllic day in the country, a new family with a baby on the way, and a little boy thrilled to have

ditched school in order to feed the ducks in a lake near the mountains, and there is a telephone ringing out of the dark at the top of the stairs.

He's gone, my mother told me on the telephone. He went to the store to buy flowers for the cemetery, and he's not home yet, and he hasn't called, and why hasn't he called? He always called before.

That brought me up short. I'd never been told about the other failed errands, or how he'd been putting on two pairs of pants. I had no idea what she was talking about—although I should have. I'd seen something there. It had come out that drunken night on the telephone. Margaret had seen it when she first met him. Everyone had seen it at the wedding. Yet this catastrophic "manifestation"—an Alzheimer's term of art that I learned later—was a complete shock to me.

I drove out to Shrewsbury. Margaret stayed behind to arrange for her sister to pick up Abraham. Meanwhile, she recalled seeing a local doctor on television, talking about the Alzheimer's Association.

She called directory assistance. The operator could find no listing for the Alzheimer's Association.

She called the television station. Nobody knew where the doctor was.

She called the Massachusetts State Police, and she asked them to put out an all-points bulletin on my father.

Well, a state policeman told her, you know that sometimes men at his age like to run off with their young secretaries.

Finally, she told them that my father had a serious brain disease, which was an exaggeration, but also the truth. She told them he had to have his medication or else he would start having seizures right there on the side of the highway. This made sense to the police. Brain disease, they could understand. Seizures, they could understand.

The newspapers told her that they could run his picture once he'd been missing for twenty-four hours.

I pulled into the driveway in Shrewsbury. I saw my mother's cigarette first, a single orange dot visible through the screens, waving through the air in the darkness of the porch. My mother was sitting in a corner. I could not see her face.

"Why hasn't he called?" she kept asking me.

I remembered Thanksgiving the previous fall, when the two of them came to dinner. I remembered my father holding on to the leash of his new and unruly puppy, refusing to take his coat off, and insisting from the time he came up the stairs that he had to go home.

"This was very nice," he said, "but I have to go home now."

But you haven't had dinner yet, I told him.

Oh, he replied. Then, he would make for the door again.

You can't walk home, I'd say. It's too far.

Oh, he replied. Then he would stand again, and look out the window, the puppy ripping at his shoes.

I remembered this as we sat on the porch the night that my father disappeared. I'd seen it and not seen it. Instead, I asked my mother if he'd ever done anything like this before, and she said, no, never, and I believed her even though, today, it seems as credible as having been told that he'd gone to the moon on a scooter.

Margaret arrived a few hours later. My mother and I were still on the porch, talking about nothing, my mother insisting that she could not understand why my father hadn't called. "If he's lost," she kept saying, "why doesn't he just call?"

My wife did not grow up with the same reflexes that I did.

"Because," she snapped, "maybe he doesn't remember his phone number."

My mother fell into a furious silence, the dancing orange dot of another cigarette the only sign that she was there. We waited on the screened porch in the dark, rain beginning to fall harder outside from the west, from the Berkshires, where the day had begun. There was an old clock ticking somewhere in the house, and the phone did not ring.

On Saturday, there was still no word. My mother had grown quite agitated, so we called the doctor in my family. Jim prescribed some Valium for my mother. Jim had retired from active practice four years earlier but, of course, this being our family, I didn't know this. He had had a bout with diabetes and a slight stroke, and I didn't know this, either. He was starting to repeat himself, and I didn't know any of this. The ground was moving in all directions beneath my feet, and I didn't feel it move.

I couldn't stay still. Margaret and I drove out, trying to retrace my father's journey, and trying to discern where he might've gone. We stopped at the flower store, where they at least remembered seeing him, and that he'd had trouble counting his change. We drove back toward the center of Shrewsbury, past the library and up toward the common. We saw the trench across Main Street, and we realized that his life had come to run on very precise rails. A detour as small as this one, no more than 200 yards in an easy loop that he'd driven for nearly thirty-five years, had been enough to send him spinning off course as surely as would have a minor navigational error early in a trip across the dark Pacific. At that point, we tried to think of anywhere he might've gone, and we drove to those places. . . .

About 200 miles away, rain pummeled Montpelier, the capital of Vermont. At two o'clock on Sunday morning, the rain awoke a woman who lived across the street from the state capitol building. She got up and idly looked out her front window. At a row of parking meters across the street, there was a man sitting in a light blue Ford Granada. He appeared to be in his mid-sixties. He had gray eyes and he had gray hair. He'd been there that afternoon, she remembered, occasionally getting out of the car to look around, being pelted by the rain. He was soaked to the bone now, and he was still there, sitting in his car, and it was two o'clock in the morning. The woman called the police.

Two cops pulled up alongside of the Granada. The man was pleasant enough, but he couldn't tell them his name. He couldn't tell them his address, his phone number. He was soaking wet and he was almost incoherent, wondering aloud about his dog. The two cops came to the obvious sidewalk conclusion. It was a good thing this guy never got his car started. They took him to the police station and they put him in the drunk tank to sleep it off.

I began to wonder if my father was dead, shot at a roadside rest stop or rolled off the highway by some cowboy trucker. Margaret was concerned about exposure—that he simply had run out of gas in the woods somewhere, and that he would either die overnight, or succumb to pneumonia soon after. I thought my mother could handle his death. It would be hard, but she could find things to do. Maybe she'd even start playing the piano again. She'd stopped mysteriously about five years earlier. Nobody in the neighborhood knew why, and she would become furious if you asked her about it.

Maybe she'd go back to the regular Tuesday-night rosary-cum-coffee klatch that had meant so much to her when I was a boy. She'd stopped going to that, too, and when the ladies in the neighborhood asked her why, she would become furious and stop talking.

Yes, I thought, my mother would be able to cope with my father's dying. She might even do fine with it.

Sitting there on the porch, as Sunday was coming up in my old neighborhood, I realized that I knew exactly where every shadow would fall. Then, the phone rang in the kitchen, and my mother said it was someone from Vermont.

In the morning, the officer on duty at the drunk tank in Montpelier checked on the man who'd been brought in the night before from in front of the capitol building. He was still pleasant, wondering about his dog. He still did not know his name, or his address. He still did not know his phone number. But he was plainly sober.

It took a while, but they finally checked the police advisories and discovered who he was. He had been reported missing in Massachusetts. Someone at the police station called the number provided and a woman answered. She said that his son would be coming up to get him and that, no, there was nothing wrong with him. He'd just gotten lost going to the store. The police handed him over to the county mental health officials. They dried him off and changed his clothes for him. They took him to Burger King, which he'd seemed to enjoy. Then they took him to a halfway house, where he sat himself in a big leather armchair and listened to a basketball game on the radio. . . .

My mother stayed home. Margaret and I drove on a great diagonal north, through New Hampshire and into Vermont. We stopped at a country store to buy sandwiches, and the counterwoman smiled at us. A young couple come into the country, the wife quite obviously pregnant. It was a bright spring afternoon, and the countryside seemed poised to bloom. Young hawks wheeled in the clear air. It was a long and lovely ride, and it was evening before we ever got to Montpelier.

We went first to the police station, where they explained that my father had been transferred. At the halfway house, there was a large sitting room with a fireplace and some overstuffed chairs. My father was sitting in one of the chairs, listening to a basketball game on the radio. One of the men who worked at the place told him that we had come to take him home. He rose to greet us.

He was smiling, but the smile never made it all the way to his eyes. The smile died before it got there, flattening out, dissipating. His eyes were blank as slate. I remember the warmth of the fire. I remember the hiss and the crackle of the wood. I remember that something happened in the basketball game that caused the announcer to get excited. At that moment, my wife took me across the room, and she introduced me to my father.

Nice to meet you, my father said.

He was very concerned about his dog. He would not leave without his dog. He wanted to show us his dog. It was such a nice dog. There he is now, my father said.

Where is your dog? we asked him.

Over there, my father said, pointing to a corner of the room.

Your dog isn't here, I told him. Your dog is at home, in Shrewsbury, at your house. My father looked around the room. He called for his dog. He's right over there, my father said, pointing toward a table. It was dark outside now, the neon in the bars along the tight little street glowed coldly. Margaret finally coaxed him into his coat, and we left.

It was too late to drive all the way home, so we took a room in a motel along the main highway. We all went to dinner in the motel's lounge. The place turned out to be a local hot spot, with a piano player telling off-color jokes to people who laughed and sang with him, even though they all seemed familiar with his act. My father took a great shine to the piano player, laughing merrily along with the crowd.

My father ordered his food and I watched him talk. His conversation ran in small circles, like a tiny loop in a country railroad. He had a series of catchphrases that would keep him on course, like station stops. He still had his manners—not society manners, like those of his Jesuit brother Michael, but a demeanor that once might have been called courtly. The waitress was charmed. He didn't exactly order his food. He waited for Margaret to order, and then he said, "I'll have that, too."

We finished dinner, and we went back to the room to go to bed. Margaret was exhausted; nearly four months pregnant, she wasn't prepared to go haring off through the north woods. My father got into bed. I lay on the other bed and watched him. Suddenly, he rose and bolted for the door.

My mother, he said. My mother is out there and she wants me.

He saw her. I have no doubt of that. She was calling to him and he was coming to her. He was out the door and running into the hallway after her in his underwear.

Margaret and I managed to catch him. He pushed back, pointing down the hallway and talking about his mother, who needed him at home. We steered him back up the hallway. He needed to go home. His mother needed him, and he had to go back. We told him he could call her on the telephone. We told him that his mother wanted him to go to bed. We told him we could settle everything in the morning. We got him back into the room. We put him back to bed, and he fell asleep, finally. We moved a dresser in front of the door.

I lay awake a long time that night. I listened to the rumble of the trucks that passed along the highway outside, shaking the walls of the motel. I watched their lights dance through the window and then move through the room, one after another, up the walls and across the ceiling, and then gone again out the window. I watched my father sleep. He slept as he'd always slept. He was not seeing dogs that were not there. He was not running to his dead mother. I knew him now. He was my father again. The next morning, before he woke, I moved the dresser away from the door.

Margaret had decided to drive my father back in our car. It was smaller, and it would not be as comfortable, but she at least was used to driving it, and she thought that I'd appreciate the chance to drive back alone in the Granada.

I drove ahead of them, concentrating fiercely on the road. I noticed every stone and tree, every bird and every barn, every degree of even the slightest bend in the road. I locked into the tiniest physical details of the trip, making pictures in my mind out of the cumulus clouds that came musc-ling in over the mountaintops, something I hadn't done since I was eight. All of this precise, nearly lunatic observation kept me where I was, where I always had been, and away from the new and frightening alternate reality that suddenly had come to exist that weekend, and that was now riding in the car behind me. I saw a blue jay go pouring across the road through the angled sunlight. I swear I counted its feathers.

Every so often, I would look in the rearview mirror. Margaret would wave at me. In the passenger seat, my father would smile. They chatted amiably, as if they'd known each other for years. My father spoke in the roundabout way that had become normal for him, and Margaret was along for the ride, following the conversation into the new reality of my father's illness. It was on this ride, I think, that she began to take care of him, leaving me behind, angry and confused. My father pointed out the windshield at me, hunched over the wheel of his car, counting blue jays and mile markers.

He's a nice little fellow, said my father to my wife.

Yes, he is, said my wife.

He's a great little fellow for helping us out, my father said.

Yes, he is, said my wife.

My wife is going to kill me, my father said.

What is your wife's name? said my wife.

I don't know, my father said, but my wife is going to kill me. She is going to kill me.

We'll explain it to her and it will be OK, said my wife.

My wife is going to kill me, my father said.

I drove on ahead of them, concentrating fiercely. Every so often, I would look in the rearview mirror.

You know, I think I'm going to give him that car, my father said.

Really, said my wife.

He's a great little fellow for helping us out, my father said.

We stopped in a McDonald's for lunch. My father liked the idea of McDonald's. He seemed to enjoy all the children darting in and out between the tables. We asked him what he wanted, and he said he would have what we were having and that would be fine. We had not ordered yet.

Margaret brought the food back to the table. I leaned across it. I thought I'd tell my father that he was going to be a grandfather. I spoke to him without thinking. I spoke to him as though he knew that I was his son and that he was my father. It would not be the only time that I did this. It would not be the last time that I did this. It was the first time that I did this.

"You know, Dad," I said, pointing at Margaret, "she's going to have a baby."

My father blanched. Plainly, he believed that we were telling him that he was the father of my wife's baby. All he had done was taken a ride with this woman. What was this nice little fellow accusing him of? He tried to speak and he couldn't, and we stopped him before he could run out of the restaurant.

He grew more anxious as we got closer to home. He kept insisting that his wife was going to kill him, and Margaret kept assuring him that everything would be fine, that his wife would understand. Even she has to notice this now, Margaret thought. He's been missing for three days. She has to see that something is not right with him.

We drove back into Shrewsbury from the north. The street was still torn up in the center of town. It was Monday afternoon, and my father was coming home from the flower store.

My wife is going to kill me, said my father.

We pulled into the driveway. My mother was sitting on the porch, smoking. My father walked up his driveway with tiny steps, as though he were barefoot on hot sand. My mother swung open the door.

"Well, Johnny," she boomed. "The next time you're leaving, why don't you send me a postcard?"

My father went back up the stairs and into his house and the screen door whanged shut behind him.

Margaret and I stood in the driveway, Margaret looking as though she'd seen something distant and dreadful behind the screen door. I knew what was going to happen. We were going to pretend now. We were going to pretend that nothing was wrong, that my father didn't go to the flower store and end up in Vermont. We were going to pretend that he could still order his own food. We were going to pretend that he didn't chase his dead mother down a motel corridor. I felt the truth bending inside me, turning the last three mad days into some familiar shape, and I realized what I was feeling was the comfort of denial.

I leaned back against the Granada. I'd driven nearly 200 miles in that car, and I'd never noticed that the backseat was full of geraniums and that, on the dashboard, my father's little compass had been moved away from the Blessed Virgin and into a spot right in front of the steering wheel. At some point, either during his drive north or even before then, my father had pulled the compass over in front of him, so that he could see it, so that it could lead him home. The compass was broken. Floating inside its little plastic bubble, the dial bobbed aimlessly, never fastening on one specific direction, floating free. . . .

Mary Ellen Pierce had had five children, and all five of them would develop Alzheimer's disease. All four of her sons would disappear and then die. One of them was my father. He died without remembering her. He died without remembering me.

I am forty-four now, the oldest of the next generation. I am married. I have three children. One of them, Abraham, does not carry my family's genes. Sometimes, at night, I'll walk down the hallway and look at the other two. Brendan has the sharp jawline that my father had, and his father before him. Molly has the round face of a Kerry farm girl. You can see what has been carried forward from the farms and hilltops to a suburb outside of Boston, carried forward as surely as was the story of the brawl in Listowel.

What else comes forward? I wonder, there in the night. What if, one day, I can't remember my son any more than my father could remember me? And what if, one day, my daughter can't remember her father any more than she can remember her own children? And what if, one day, Abraham looks into the eyes of his brother and sister, and what if he looks into mine, and we all look back at him, unknowing, eyes as blank as slate? The delicate chain of memory crumbles, link by link, until there is nothing left.

# Focus on Senior Health: The Burdens of Love

## Jane E. Allen

*With the progression of dementia comes a decline in an individual's ability to take care of him- or herself. Activities we take for granted—buying groceries, balancing our checkbook, keeping track of birthdays and holidays—can become difficult or impossible, and others—cooking, driving—become dangerous. Caregivers must make up for this loss in self-sufficiency; in many cases, responsibility falls to a spouse who is contending with his or her own age-related changes or an adult child who may be sandwiched between helping an aging parent and raising children.*

*The next article discusses the stresses and strains that accompany the caregiving role, and it outlines how caregivers can themselves be at risk for becoming overwhelmed and depressed. The article focuses specifically on caregivers among ethnic minorities and the special challenges this can present. On one hand, cultures in which caring for the elderly is expected and assumed will have the advantage of strong family involvement and a sense of obligation, but on the other hand these same people may have less access to medical services and consultation. This article also draws attention to how communities, defined either as groups of caregivers or groups of individuals sharing cultural views and beliefs or both, can ease the burden of caregivers.*

## Suggested Reading

Bernlef, J. (1989). *Out of mind.* Boston: D. R. Godine.

---

*Los Angeles Times,* S1, S5. (1999, August 2).

In the neat back bedroom of a one-story home in Bell, Josefina Pérez's face contorts as she coughs—once, twice, three times. Her eyes are clenched with the distress of pneumonia ushered in by the late-stage Alzheimer's disease that has made it nearly impossible to swallow, speak, care for herself. Her youngest daughter, Laura Padilla, rushes to the metal hospital bed, reaches for a rubber bulb to suction away phlegm in her mother's mouth, then lovingly rearranges the curly ends of her gray hair. Pérez's face relaxes once more into stony silence.

It's a ritual repeated several times an hour throughout the day. Every night, Padilla sleeps beneath a blue-flowered coverlet, just a few feet away from her widowed mother. These unrelenting routines are broken only by four hours of monthly respite care, two monthly sessions at a Spanish-language Alzheimer's support group and the hours she can get away to pray in church.

In better days, Pérez, now 72, nursed her own mother through Alzheimer's disease in Zacoalco, Mexico. A family album Padilla pulls from a high cabinet shows Pérez as a raven-haired beauty, years before the Alzheimer's. Flipping through the album, Padilla points to photos of a grandmother and an aunt who also suffered the silent ravages of the disease.

Padilla, a pretty and practical woman who has told suitors that marrying her would mean her ailing mother must come along, too, has put her own life on hold for the 15 years her mother has been sick.

"I used to assume because I was the youngest [of seven children] and not married it was my obligation," says Padilla, now 31. After struggling with being the primary caregiver in the home she shares with her 36-year-old brother, Efren, and his family, she's made peace with her role: "Now I see that it's because I want to do it."

According to social workers, Latinas like Padilla report the highest levels of stress and depression among the Alzheimer's caregivers they see. The disease, which affects an estimated 4 million older Americans, also takes a toll on the millions of loved ones who care for them. But among African American, Latino, Chinese, Japanese and Korean families, who tend to frown on nursing home care, the burdens can be even greater. Language barriers, limited access to medical services, lack of information about the disorder and poverty compound the isolation and pressure.

As the U.S. population grows older, more families will have to cope with mothers, fathers, husbands and wives who have Alzheimer's.

"This is the disease of the 21st century," says Bryan Kemp, director of gerontology programs at the Rancho Los Amigos National Rehabilitation Center in Downey and co-director of a state-funded Alzheimer's disease center. He predicts that California may see more than 1 million people with the disease by the year 2020.

Doctors, nurses, social workers and others are recognizing that a one-size-fits-all approach won't work across different cultures, races and ethnic communities, with distinct views of illness and obligation.

## Cultural Differences in Caregiving

Accommodating cultural differences has become a focus of the National Alzheimer's Assn., which devoted a recent educational conference in Long Beach to diversity in caregiving.

At that July meeting, Kemp discussed the emotional turmoil and stress that spouses of Alzheimer's patients confront in Japanese American, Mexican American, African American and white families. Researchers estimate that as many as 50% of family members who care for loved ones with Alzheimer's have to be treated for depression and anxiety.

Using Alzheimer's research funds culled from people checking a box on their California tax return to donate to such causes, Kemp and his colleagues studied stress among 202 people of various ethnic backgrounds who took care of a husband or wife with Alzheimer's. The study asked the caregivers about their ability to provide care, where they derive their support as well as their levels of religious belief, depression and stress.

Most dramatic among the findings, Kemp says, is that up to 75% of Mexican American women caregivers had a substantial mental health problem. Despite feeling they could ask for help from others, they felt the most isolated and stressed.

Among African American caregivers who responded, "spirituality was a very big buffer against their stress. They believe they're doing this for a higher purpose, that God will help them cope."

Mexican American families' reluctance to use nursing homes "may add to their stress," Kemp said. "It's more a sense of duty and feeling guilty that if they put someone in a long-term facility, they've somehow failed."

Kemp tries to intervene by helping caregivers

get treatment, find educational and support groups and use community adult day-care centers. Although Medi-Cal will pay for such respite care, Kemp said it's been tough getting the word out.

Finding the right way to approach underserved communities can be tricky, meeting participants said.

"You need to get the trust of the community," says Dr. Steven DeKosky, a neurologist and director of an Alzheimer's center at the University of Pittsburgh. "It helps if you have members of the minority community working with you."

It's highly important to debunk the myth that "it's OK and expected for old people to lose their minds" and let them know that major memory loss merits evaluation, he says.

Here in California, a state filled with immigrants who have preserved native cultures and where nearly a quarter of the elderly population belongs to ethnic minorities, many institutions and social workers are forging community links.

The Los Angeles Alzheimer's Assn. offers education and support through El Portal in the Latino communities of East and Southeast Los Angeles, and the Dementia Care Network in the African American communities around South Los Angeles and Inglewood. It also has teamed up with Korean Health Education and Information Resources to offer dementia day-care and start a support group for Korean caregivers, said Rosa Ramirez, the association's director of education and outreach.

Educational materials must be tailored not only by language, but by world view. For example, Asian families often accept memory loss as normal because acknowledging dementia can bring shame. So without using medical or biological terms, social workers have devised softer approaches that help the caregiver look for changes in behavior or daily habits that might indicate a problem, explains Dolores Gallagher-Thompson, a psychologist at a Veterans Affairs facility in Palo Alto and an associate professor at Stanford University's medical school. A program to identify early dementia within Japanese and Chinese families will ask if Grandma has forgotten how to prepare holiday foods or become confused during games of mah-jongg.

Many cultures leave caregiving to women.

In Korean families, caregiving often falls to the household of the oldest son, who usually works, leaving his wife with the ailing mother-in-law or father-in-law. J. Kim Miller, associate education director at the Roybal Institute for Applied Gerontology at Cal State-Los Angeles, interviewed 25 Korean caregivers and found most acted out of social duty: only three mentioned love.

Kim found Korean caregivers' coping skills bolstered by religious faith and sharing their difficulties with relatives. Fewer than 40% sought professional caregiving advice.

One of the hardest communities to reach with information is the Chinese community, says Dr. Tiffany Chow, a neurologist at the UCLA Alzheimer's Disease Center.

Although there are thousands of Chinese elders in Los Angeles County and the disease strikes them in numbers equivalent to other groups, she says it is rare someone Chinese walks into her clinic.

Families often keep the illness under wraps. Chinese culture values a multigenerational home, where it's an honor to take in the parents who raised you. It's easy to overlook their mental deterioration because they typically hand over most responsibilities.

"It's harder to pick up on them not being able to balance a checkbook or not being able to organize a 20-course meal because they're not being asked to do it. As long as they're quietly dementing nobody's noticing," Chow says.

Once the problem becomes apparent, social pressure kicks in. Families don't want to reveal the problem because they worry an outsider might "think we're not managing well."

However, when she brought together five Chinese American caregivers a few weeks ago, they felt comfortable enough to share their problems with each other and left her heartened that given a setting away from public scrutiny, they're open to support sessions.

Support groups often offer lifelines.

## Support Groups for Families

Latino families value "marianismo," being like the Holy Mother, uncomplaining and quietly capable, says Gallagher-Thompson, who is studying support groups and other ways to intervene with Latino and Anglo caregivers.

Latinas report "significantly higher levels" of depression and stress than Anglos. The rural women she sees, from San Francisco to Salinas, have limited education and language skills, even in their native Spanish.

That's what makes Padilla so unusual. She has tracked down help despite great odds and wants to educate other Latinos. She's become a den mother within her Latina support group—the first of its kind in the nation. It was begun by Maria Aranda, an assistant professor at the schools of social work and gerontology at the University of Southern California.

"She has several things going for her. She has a strong spiritual connection, she's able to ask for help when it is needed and she is able to find resources when the typical person would say there are none," Aranda says.

Support groups are new to Phillip DeCoud, a 70-year-old African American man who cares full time for his wife Shirley at their South-Central Los Angeles home filled with photos and other reminders of their native New Orleans and their 50 years of marriage. Shirley was diagnosed with Alzheimer's five years ago, at age 65.

DeCoud recalls that at about the time he retired from his job making braces at a Los Angeles orthopedic hospital, he started noticing that his wife "couldn't keep up with the checkbook and was forgetting things like the household chores she normally would do."

Today, he can't take his eyes off her, lest she wander away.

Their seven children, who care for 20 children of their own, help as much as they can, "but they have their responsibilities also."

He says he derives strength from faith. "Just worshipping is enough. Saying prayers and talking gets these things off my chest," says DeCoud, who walks 22 blocks to church each morning with his wife. She says the daily walks do her good, too, and help her sleep better.

Dolores Storey, a social worker with the Delta Sigma Theta Senior Center, part of the Dementia Care Network, found the DeCouds meals-on-wheels and rides to doctor's appointments and pharmacies. Storey also got DeCoud to attend his first support meetings.

"I saw my dad interacting with some other caregivers," said daughter Laurie Sands, 49, of Westchester. "It was so good for him. He was sharing things."

# Piecing Together Alzheimer's

## Peter H. St. George-Hyslop

*Alzheimer's disease is progressive and, at present, incurable. It is also fundamentally a disease of the brain. Autopsies show that the brains of those who had the disorder differ from those who were spared. Even gross examination of affected brains reveals the smoothing out of the normally convoluted surface, and microscopic analysis shows the accumulation of harmful proteins—neurofibrillary tangles and neuritic plaques—that appear to provide important clues about the origins of the disease. The following article, by Peter H. St. George-Hyslop, summarizes the nature of such clues and outlines their implications for treatment.*

### Suggested Readings

Pollen, D. A. (1993). *Hannah's heirs: The quest for the genetic origins of Alzheimer's Disease.* New York: Oxford University Press.
Selkoe, D. J. (1992, September). Aging brain, aging mind. *Scientific American*, 135–142.

*Scientific American*, 76–84. (2000, December).

Many families suffer the anguish of caring for an intellectually incapacitated parent or grandparent who, just a few years earlier, was an active, vibrant member of the family—one involved with grandchildren, hobbies and life in general. The problem typically starts with seemingly innocent absentmindedness, with questions repeated two or three times. The person then begins to have trouble following complex discussions or loses the ability to pursue challenging pastimes. Initially the family attributes these minor problems to age or fatigue. But the grandparent becomes increasingly forgetful—less able to find the way home from the corner store or even to recognize the faces of loved ones. Ultimately this once independent individual needs help with every aspect of daily living, from bathing and dressing to eating and walking outside.

This general description portrays several illnesses, called *dementias*, in which parts of the brain stop working, causing disruptions in memory, judgment, reasoning and emotional stability. Dementias are nothing new: eloquent accounts of them can be found in ancient Greek and medieval literature. Most dementias occur more frequently as people age. As a result, in societies where life expectancy has been considerably extended, these diseases are becoming a major public health concern. Approximately 15 percent of people who live to the age of 65 will develop some form of dementia; by age 85, that proportion increases to at least 35 percent.

Of all the dementias, Alzheimer's disease is the most common. Four million Americans currently suffer from the condition, and experts estimate that 22 million people around the world will be so afflicted by 2025. Until recently, researchers had almost no understanding of the disorder's causes, and it still lacks preventive or curative therapies. But findings from epidemiology, genetics, molecular and cell biology, and other disciplines are now fitting together, permitting researchers to identify some of the mechanisms that underlie it.

It appears that Alzheimer's arises because the normal processing of certain proteins goes terribly wrong, littering brain cells and the space between them with pieces of toxic protein. Intriguingly, it is becoming apparent that many other neurodegenerative disorders—among them frontotemporal dementia, Parkinson's disease and Creutztfeldt-Jakob disease—are also characterized by protein processing gone haywire. These insights are suggesting tantalizing new ways of treating Alzheimer's and other dementias, possibly including vaccines that could direct the body to rid itself of some of these toxic protein fragments.

## Reading the Brain

The foundation of today's understanding of Alzheimer's was built by researchers who directly examined patients' brains. Microscopic views have revealed a loss of nerve cells in certain regions of the brain, such as the hippocampus, a center for memory, and the cerebral cortex, which is involved in reasoning, memory, language and other important thought processes. Since the 1970s researchers have known that some of these dying neurons are *cholinergic*—that is, they communicate using the neurotransmitter acetylcholine, which is ultimately broken down by an enzyme called acetylcholinesterase. Drugs that became available in the past decade, such as tacrine and donepezil, prevent acetylcholinesterase from doing its job. By conserving acetylcholine, these compounds slow the development of impairments in people experiencing the early stages of Alzheimer's. Sadly, once cholinergic neurons degenerate fully and can no longer produce the neurotransmitter, the drugs become useless.

The other directly observable hallmarks of Alzheimer's disease are clusters of proteins in the brain. These accumulations occur in two forms: those found inside nerve cells and those found between cells. The clusters in the interior are called *neurofibrillary tangles*, and they resemble pairs of threads wound around each other in a helix. Analyses performed in the 1980s at several laboratories made it clear that these tangles consist of a protein called tau. Tau is significant because it binds to a protein named tubulin, which in turn forms structures known as *microtubules*. Microtubules are crucially important. Like the girders and pillars of buildings, they run through cells, imparting support and shape. Microtubules also provide routes along which nutrients, other molecules and cellular components such as vesicles and mitochondria move through cells.

Tangles of tau, however, are not unique to Alzheimer's disease. For that reason, even though the high density of neurofibrillary tangles in Alzheimer's patients is distinctive and strongly correlates with the severity of dementia, many investigators have not considered disruptions of tau to be as important as the second kind of protein deposits observed in Alzheimer's: *amyloid plaques*. (Tau has recently gained prominence, but I will come to that story later.)

Unlike neurofibrillary tangles, deposits of amyloid protein gather in the spaces between nerve cells. The nearby neurons often look swollen and deformed, and the clusters of protein—sometimes called senile or amyloid plaques—are usually accompanied by reactive inflammatory cells called *microglia*, which are part of the brain's immune system and might be trying to degrade and remove damaged neurons or perhaps the plaques themselves. It is unclear whether the neurons in or near these plaques function normally, because the density of plaques is only weakly correlated with the severity of dementia. Further, such plaques are present in most elderly people. Nevertheless, their extensive presence in the hippocampus and the cerebral cortex is specific to Alzheimer's patients, and they appear long before neurofibrillary tangles do.

Because of the high density of plaques and their early presence in the disease, researchers have long thought that understanding their biochemistry could yield clues about the cause of Alzheimer's. Intensive efforts to isolate the ingredients of these plaques culminated in 1984 with the discovery by George G. Glenner of the University of California at San Diego that a principal component was a peptide—that is, a very short protein fragment—made up of either 40 or 42 amino acids (the building blocks of proteins). This identification of what is now termed the beta-amyloid peptide was quickly followed by the sequencing of the gene for the longer protein from which this peptide originates: the β-amyloid precursor protein, or bAPP. These biochemical discoveries dovetailed nicely with information simultaneously coming out of another area of research: genetics.

Ever since German neurologist Alois Alzheimer identified Alzheimer's disease in 1907, epidemiologists have sought to understand its patterns. They have tried to determine, for instance, whether it runs in families, and is therefore influenced strongly by the genes, or is set in motion by something in the environment. In the 1980s research began to show that certain families are at increased risk for developing this dementia. Investigators found families in which the disease is transmitted from one generation to the next—to half the children (both male and female) of the affected patients. This pattern indicated that in some families vulnerability arises from the inheritance of a defective gene on an autosomal—or nonsex—chromosome, and it suggested that the mutant gene inherited from the affected parent is dominant over the normal gene inherited from the unaffected parent.

Epidemiologists also tracked the occurrence of Alzheimer's in people who were not from such families, establishing that genetics is not the sole cause of the affliction in the general population. The disease clearly has diverse and complex triggers—inheritance most likely plays some role in a significant proportion of cases (estimates vary from 1 to 40 percent). Yet attempts to identify environmental catalysts, which might act alone or in conjunction with heredity, have not been conclusive. The few risk factors identified so far are intriguing but not entirely illuminating. It appears that poor early-childhood education, serious head injury and—albeit much less definitively—exposure to aluminum in drinking water correlate with higher risk. Correlation, however, does not mean causality, and it may turn out that these factors are actually indicators of other agents or events. For instance, head injury might simply reduce the number of neurons, thereby causing the symptoms of Alzheimer's to appear earlier than they otherwise would have.

Nevertheless, the recognition of genetic components opened an exciting avenue of research, because any findings in that realm would have relevance for all cases of Alzheimer's. The clinical, neuropathological and biochemical abnormalities are identical in every kind of Alzheimer's—whether genetically determined or sporadic, as the other forms are called. Sure enough, when combined with the discovery of the composition of the plaques and the tangles, the genetic insights led to some seminal experiments. The isolation of the β-amyloid peptide and the isolation of the gene for bAPP were quickly followed by the discovery that the bAPP gene was located on chromosome 21. At about the same time, studies indicated that chromosome 21 might carry a defect in some families with Alzheimer's. It was known from other work that people with Down syndrome (who have three rather than two copies of chromosome 21) almost invariably display at least some features of Alzheimer's by the age of 40.

These observations suggested that the β-amyloid precursor protein gene might be the site of mutations causing some cases of Alzheimer's. This prediction was rapidly borne out in the early 1990s, when researchers—including Blas Frangione and Efrat Levy of New York Medical Center, Alison M. Goate of Washington University School of Medicine, Michael Mullan of the University of Southern Florida, Lydia Hendriks and Christine Van Broeckhoven at the University of Antwerp, and Harry Karlinsky and my colleagues of the University of Toronto—identified such mutations in individuals with familial Alzheimer's. (Because genes contain the instructions for the synthesis of proteins, a mutation in a gene can mean that the protein it specifies will turn out different than it should. This difference can lead to problems—just as substituting the wrong cog in an engine can.) It suddenly became clear that abnormal processing or activity of bAPP caused the disease. This novel idea spurred efforts to determine how the long protein was transformed into the β-amyloid peptide in the first place.

Although the precise biological role of normal bAPP molecules remains obscure, scientists now know that many kinds of cells and tissues produce bAPP and that it can be between 695 and 770 amino acids long. The protein runs through the outer cell membrane, with a short piece jutting into the cell and a longer piece sticking into the extracellular space. The β-amyloid peptide, for its part, is snipped out of the section of bAPP that spans the cell membrane. Work in a number of laboratories revealed that in the course of its life bAPP is cut in one of two ways. In one process, the protein is first cleaved by an enzyme called alpha-secretase. (Alzheimer's researchers commonly refer to this enzyme as a "putative" one, because we assume it exists—and have good evidence that it does—but we have not yet isolated it.) It is then cut by another putative enzyme, gamma-secretase. Together these cuts produce a harmless peptide fragment called p3.

## The Unkindest Cut

The second way in which bAPP is cleaved is another two-step process, one that is not always so harmless. First, an enzyme called beta-secretase—which has been isolated by Martin Citron and his colleagues at Amgen—clips the protein. One of the resulting pieces, called C99-bAPP fragment (because it is 99 amino acids long), is then snipped by gamma-secretase, and the β-amyloid peptide is born.

Under normal conditions, most of these β-amyloid strings contain 40 amino acids. But a small number of them, fewer than 10 percent, have two extra amino acids. Peter T. Lansbury and Bruce Yankner of Harvard, as well as Paul E. Fraser

and Joanne McLaurin of the University of Toronto, among others, have shown that this slightly longer form is the one that gives rise to plaques and that it has a direct toxic effect on neurons.

Studies are under way to identify exactly how the 42-amino-acid version damages nerve cells, but preliminary work suggests it acts in several ways. First, the peptide seems to disrupt calcium regulation, which can lead to cell death. Second, it may damage mitochondria, causing the release of free oxygen radicals, which then damage proteins, lipids and DNA. Finally—as noted earlier—there is evidence that the 42-amino-acid peptide and the injury it causes may bring about the release of cellular compounds. Those, in turn, may attract immune cells, engendering an inflammatory response, which could exacerbate any other injuries initiated by the peptide, creating a vicious cycle of escalating damage. Although these possible mechanisms are intriguing, their relative importance in the development of dementia remains, for now at least, a matter of disagreement.

As molecular biologists were unraveling the activities of bAPP and the β-amyloid peptide fragment, geneticists continued to home in on the mutations in the bAPP gene. They identified several that caused substitutions of amino acids at the very places along the bAPP strand where the alpha-, beta- and gamma-secretase enzymes do their cutting. Not unexpectedly, these mutations either augment the amount of both forms of β-amyloid produced or increase the production of the toxic, lengthier version.

The concept of changes in bAPP processing being central to Alzheimer's disease gained further support when investigators discovered mutations in a set of genes that interfere with the cutting of bAPP. In 1995 my colleagues and I cloned two genes, *presenilin 1* and *presenilin 2*; disruptions in these genes—which are located, respectively, on chromosome 14 and chromosome 1—cause a very aggressive form of early-onset Alzheimer's. (Early-onset forms are generally seen in about 10 to 60 percent of patients with familial Alzheimer's.) Both genes encode proteins that weave across the cell membrane several times, like a series of stitches in a piece of fabric. These proteins undergo a complicated maturation process during which they are cut into two pieces, both of which are incorporated into a complex of proteins that in turn has the job of cutting other membrane-bound proteins like bAPP and notch, which is involved in embryonic development.

## In the Wrong Place

Several studies—by Bart De Strooper of the Flanders Interuniversity Institute for Biotechnology in Leuven, Belgium, by Christian Haass of Maximillians University in Munich, by Gopal Thinakaran of the University of Chicago, and by my group at Toronto—indicate that certain induced mutations in the individual presenilin proteins disrupt the activity of these complexes and, accordingly, alter the processing of the proteins they act on. We know that bAPP is one target of the complexes, because man-made mutations in mice cause them not to produce presenilin 1. As a consequence, gamma-secretase does not make its final cut of bAPP, and the mice produce no β-amyloid. In these mice, several other membrane proteins are not cut properly either—including the notch protein.

Presenilin 1 and 2 mutations found in people with familial Alzheimer's, however, do the reverse: they bring about an increase in cutting by gamma-secretase and, consequently, an overproduction of β-amyloid peptide, especially of the destructive longer version. It is too early to know for sure, but it is possible that the presenilins are gamma-secretase itself. Or perhaps the presenilins are involved with gamma-secretase in some indirect way—maybe they activate it or mediate its activity by bringing the enzyme into contact with bAPP.

Although mutations in bAPP and presenilin genes have a dramatic effect, they are responsible for only 50 percent of the cases of early-onset familial Alzheimer's patients—that is, they account for, at most, 5 percent of all instances of the disease in the general population. It turns out that another gene is involved in a greater proportion of cases.

In 1993 studies by Allen D. Roses, now at Glaxo Wellcome, and his colleagues Margaret Pericak-Vance of Duke University and Jonathan Haines of Vanderbilt University implied the existence of a gene on chromosome 19 that is associated with the more typical form of Alzheimer's that appears late in life. Roses, then at Duke, and Warren J. Stritmatter, also at Duke, isolated *apolipoprotein E*, or APOE, which transports cholesterol in the bloodstream and is involved in cellular repair and regeneration. The gene for APOE comes in three forms, or alleles, the frequencies of which vary slightly in different populations: the e3 variant is considered normal and occurs in 40 to 90 percent of the population; e2 and e4 are less common, occurring in 2 percent and 6 to 37 percent of the population, respectively. In Alzheimer's patients, however, Roses and his colleagues found that the incidence of e4 was quite high: roughly 40 percent.

Having the e4 allele may increase risk for Alzheimer's in various ways. One explanation holds that the e4 form of the protein competes with the β-amyloid peptide for removal from the space between cells. It has been found that one molecule responsible for hauling materials away from the intercellular spaces carts off the e4 protein more efficiently than it transports β-amyloid. Consequently, β-amyloid accumulates and becomes available for biochemical troublemaking. Support for this scenario comes from the fact that patients with the e4 variant of APOE have more β-amyloid buildup than do Alzheimer's patients with the e2 or e3 versions. In addition, patients who have both a bAPP mutation and the e4 allele develop Alzheimer's disease much earlier than do people who have the same bAPP mutation but the e2 or e3 form of the APOE gene.

The accumulated evidence of the past decades definitely indicates that one of the initiating events for Alzheimer's is an abnormality in the processing of bAPP and β-amyloid peptide. Nevertheless, several important pieces of information are missing. The problems with bAPP cleavage and β-amyloid accumulation begin early in the disease. But what happens later? And why does the density of β-amyloid plaques not reflect the severity of dementia? The issue, at heart, is whether clumps of β-amyloid peptide actually give rise to dementia, and this fundamental and lingering question has for years driven both debate and research. My own view is that abnormalities of bAPP and β-amyloid peptide initiate Alzheimer's by activating a series of events that ultimately damage and kill neurons, giving rise to dementia itself. One of those later deleterious events may be the appearance of neurofibrillary tangles.

## Returning to Tau

Until recently, the abnormally entwined pairs of tau protein filaments were thought to be innocuous secondary events. But analysis of a disease called frontotemporal dementia has raised questions about this conclusion. Frontotemporal dementia is a rare form of dementia in which, in some patients, tau deposits are present. As with Alzheimer's disease, some cases of frontotemporal dementia are familial. Genetic studies done by Kirk C. Wilhelmsen of the University of California at San Francisco and others indicate that genes contribute to the familial form of the disease.

One of these genes lies on chromosome 17, home of the tau gene. By looking at patients who had the form of frontotemporal dementia characterized by the buildup of tau, Gerard D. Schellenberg of the University of Washington identified a mutation in the tau gene. Schellenberg's 1998 discovery was important because it suggested that dementia can arise directly from the abnormal processing and accumulation of tau.

Neurofibrillary tangles are therefore probably integral parts of Alzheimer's disease as well—a possibility that provides a better explanation for the fact, pointed out a decade ago by Robert D. Terry and Robert Katzman of U.C.S.D., that the density of neurofibrillary tangles in Alzheimer's disease is related to the severity of the dementia. We do not know yet exactly how mutation in the tau gene causes frontotemporal dementia, but experiments point to the idea hinted at above: mayhem in the microtubules. Errors in the tau gene may interfere with the way tau binds to tubulin— the backbone of microtubules—or they may cause an imbalance in the types of tau protein that are produced. The net effect of both events would cause a buildup of excess free tau, which accumulates in paired helical filaments. The microtubule structures would then not work properly, and the accumulated bundles of tau would throttle the cellular transport mechanism. As a result, neurons could neither transmit electrical signals nor transport nutrients and other important items to the far reaches of the cell. It seems quite likely that abnormalities in bAPP and β-amyloid peptide set in motion a series of events, a subset of which alter tau, which in turn further damages the neurons, leading to dementia.

## New Treatments

The biochemical, molecular, genetic, epidemiological and clinical discoveries of the past 10 years or so have significantly advanced our understanding of the mechanisms underlying Alzheimer's disease and make it increasingly likely that, in the years to come, useful treatments will be generated. Some of these will probably come from the recent insights into the misprocessing of tau. Indeed, the insights into bAPP and β-amyloid peptide are already fueling treatment research. For instance, some investigators are designing compounds that will block the ability of either the beta- or the gamma-secretase enzyme to cut bAPP—thus preventing the creation of the damaging β-amyloid peptide. Others are seeking to alleviate the peptide's effects once it has been created. Clinical trials are under way to see whether antioxidants such as vitamin E or nonsteroidal anti-inflammatory drugs such as ibuprofen could alleviate some of the toxic effects of β-amyloid.

A number of investigators are also working to reduce the accumulation of β-amyloid peptide by using compounds that mimic dyes such as *Congo red*, which can insert themselves into amyloid plaques, or molecules called glycoaminoglycans, which appear to be involved in the clustering of β-amyloid peptide. Such compounds could break down the aggregations of β-amyloid peptide from within.

Following this line of reasoning, Dale Schenk and his colleagues at Elan Pharmaceuticals in South San Francisco recently reported designing a vaccine based on β-amyloid. They found that in mice with a version of Alzheimer's (characterized by amyloid plaques but not tau tangles) a vaccine made of β-amyloid peptide reduced the number of plaques. In other words, they could train the body to attack and dispose of β-amyloid clusters. Whether this vaccine therapy will be effective in people with Alzheimer's disease will be the subject of interesting clinical research.

Whatever the future of treatment holds, it is gratifying that there are now so many angles to pursue at the same time. The exciting information gleaned about the different stages of the disease and the many biochemical actors that play roles has finally given researchers a better vantage point from which to examine Alzheimer's—one that seems to offer an almost panoramic view.

# ALZHEIMER'S TREATMENTS THAT WORK NOW

## Marcia Barinaga

*Until the deteriorating course of Alzheimer's disease can be eliminated, or perhaps even anticipated and prevented (see Small et al., 2000; Snowdon et al., 1996), the reality is that many patients and their families struggle with the day-to-day challenges that this disease presents. The final article in this chapter outlines some of the practical interventions that can help patients maintain as many of their skills and capabilities as possible. The sequence in which essential functions are lost—working, driving, dressing, using the toilet, feeding oneself, and so on—can be viewed as the reverse order in which these functions were acquired in childhood. Since the person with Alzheimer's disease is dependent on others in the way that a young child is, it comes as little surprise that the relationship between the patient and the caretaker has a strong effect on the patient's well-being.*

## References

Small, G. W., Ercoli, L. M., Silverman, D. H. S., Huang, S.-C., Komo, S., Bookheimer, S. Y., Lavretsky, H., Miller, K., Siddarth, P., Rasgon, N. L., Mazziota, J. C., Saxena, S., Wu, H. M., Mega, M. S., Cummings, J. L., Saunders, A. M., Pericak-Vance, M. A., Roses, A. D., Barrio, J. R., & Phelps, M. E. (2000). Cerebral metabolic and cognitive decline in persons at genetic risk for Alzheimer's disease. *Proceedings of the National Academy of Sciences, 97,* 6037–6042.

Snowdon, D. A., Kemper, S. J., Mortimer, J. A., Greiner, L. H., Wekstein, D. R., & Markesbery, W. R. (1996). Linguistic ability in early life and cognitive function and Alzheimer's disease in late life. *Journal of the American Medical Association, 275,* 528–532.

## Suggested Reading

Kasl-Godley, J., & Gatz, M. (2000). Psychosocial interventions for individuals with dementia: An integration of theory, therapy, and a clinical understanding of dementia. *Clinical Psychology Review, 20,* 755–782.

---

*Science, 282,* 1030–1032. (1998).

Alzheimer's disease is a ruthless decaying of the mind, devastating to those afflicted and to family members who witness their decline. Within the past few years, researchers have made some progress on treatments that might delay the relentless neurodegeneration, but prevention or cure is still out of reach. Millions of people suffer from the disease, and half a million of those in the final stages languish in U.S. nursing homes, incontinent, their bodies frozen by a severe stiffening called contractures, unable to speak or even recognize family members.

While neuroscientists and geneticists search for a way to turn back the clock on the ravages of Alzheimer's, another avenue of research—behavioral research conducted by psychologists, social workers, and nurses—is already providing therapies to relieve some of the suffering of the patients and their caregivers. Such behavioral therapies are far from a cure, and they may not even arrest the underlying disease process. Nevertheless, they represent "an area that cannot be ignored, because we can have such a quick, practical impact on so many people," says Zaven Khachaturian, a former associate director of the Neuroscience and Neuropsychology of Aging Program at the National Institute on Aging who is currently with Khachaturian, Radebaugh, and Associates, an international consulting group on Alzheimer's disease in Potomac, Maryland. Caregivers as well as patients stand to benefit, he notes.

Over the years, Alzheimer's experts have learned that every patient goes through a predictable decline, from forgetfulness at the early stages to an inability to speak and walk as the disease runs its course. Research suggests that patients may lose some abilities faster than necessary because their caregivers underestimate what they can still do for themselves. This is leading to a "use it or lose it" approach to Alzheimer's, in which researchers gauge what patients can still be expected to do and then help them retain those skills. Studies have shown, for example, that behavioral therapy can slow or temporarily halt patients' loss of urinary continence and of their abilities to dress themselves and communicate their needs.

Research done in the past decade also shows that behavioral strategies can reduce many disruptive behaviors common in Alzheimer's patients, such as screaming, wandering, or hitting. In the past, institutions have tried to control such problems by giving the patients antipsychotic drugs or physically restraining them—measures that can cloud the patients' minds even further or increase their agitation. The behavioral approaches instead seek to find the causes of the troubling behaviors and avoid triggering them. "What all this comes to is a new science of Alzheimer's management," says one of the pioneers of the research, New York University (NYU) psychiatrist Barry Reisberg. The next major challenge is to disseminate what researchers are learning to families and community nursing homes outside the orbit of major research centers.

## Return to Childhood

Many of the recent advances in behavioral therapy arise from viewing Alzheimer's disease as a regression toward infancy. That idea is not new: Aristophanes and Shakespeare both compared old age to a second childhood. But Reisberg and his colleagues recently have established that the stages of Alzheimer's disease accurately mimic such a regression: Patients lose the ability to hold a job, handle finances, pick out clothes, dress and bathe, control their bladder and bowels, and speak, all in faithful reversal of the order those skills were acquired as a child.

As they make this backward march through development, Alzheimer's patients can be assigned "developmental ages." Researchers have found that by providing training appropriate to those ages, they can help the patients retain longer some of the skills they would otherwise lose.

For example, a simple method originally developed to toilet-train retarded children helps Alzheimer's patients maintain continence longer. In the late 1980s, Jack Schnelle of the University of California, Los Angeles, showed that the method called "prompted voiding," in which aides visit patients every 2 to 3 hours to offer to take them to the restroom, helped some incontinent patients retain bladder control. The technique is different from merely taking the patient to the restroom on a schedule, says psychologist Louis Burgio of the University of Alabama, Tuscaloosa, who has studied prompted voiding. By asking whether the patient needs to go, he explains, "it tries to use what is left of the patient's self-knowledge, so you don't make them overly dependent on staff."

Cornelia Beck, a nursing researcher at the University of Arkansas for Medical Sciences in Little Rock, has shown that a similar approach works for another basic activity—dressing. She suspected that patients were losing skills such as dressing and feeding themselves because they were not encouraged to use them. So she set out to see if they could be retrained. Rather than dressing the patients, aides in her study would suggest that an arm goes into a sleeve, or touch the patient's arm or mimic putting their own arm into the sleeve, to encourage the patients to do it on their own.

After 6 weeks, 50% of the patients improved their ability to dress themselves by 1 to 3 points on an 8-point scale ranging from helplessness to independence; 25% improved by 4 to 6 levels. Patients who had been dependent on aides to dress them could now dress themselves, with guidance.

Even communication can be improved with behavioral strategies. For example, some typical behaviors of Alzheimer's patients, such as repeated questions or nonsensical speech, appear to be failed efforts to communicate. Michelle Bourgeois, a speech pathologist at Florida State University in Tallahassee, developed a strategy to improve communication with Alzheimer's patients, using a "memory book." This contained pictures of family members and nursing home aides and a schedule of daily activities, illustrated with a clock face showing the time and pictures of the activities.

The aides spent time with the patients looking at the book and, when the patients asked repeated questions, gently referred them to the right page of the book for the answers. Use of the memory aid "results in less nonsensical vocalization and more appropriate types of conversations" between patients and nursing home staff, says Burgio, who collaborates with Bourgeois.

## An Understanding Approach

In addition to looking at how to help patients retain skills, researchers are developing new ways to control problem behaviors. For example, NYU neurologist Emile Franssen and his wife and co-worker, nursing researcher Liduïn Souren, have found that some problem behaviors are the physical consequences of the disease itself.

By studying 2400 Alzheimer's patients at various stages of the disease, Franssen identified infantile reflexes that appear in Alzheimer's patients as they decline and a muscle stiffness that he calls paratonia, which can eventually develop into crippling contractures. Both changes can cause problem behaviors. "If you move the limbs of a patient [briskly], paratonia increases," says Franssen. "The caregiver may interpret that reaction as a willful resistance."

At least one of the reflexes—a strong grasping reflex—can also cause problems, for example when a caregiver tries to guide a patient out of a chair by the elbow and finds that the patient grabs the arms of the chair in an apparent refusal to get up. Patients may also reflexively grab a caregiver's hair or clothing. Franssen says that caregivers at nursing homes "often misinterpret [this behavior] as aggressive." But it's not. "It is an inability to cooperate rather than an unwillingness," says Franssen. Rather than struggling and upsetting the patient, the caregiver can release the grip by merely stroking the back of the patient's hand.

Other troubling behaviors arise because Alzheimer's patients are agitated. They may scream, plead, pace, disrobe, rummage through people's possessions, hit, kick, or bite. "When I started [14 years ago], people treated agitation as either a psychotic sort of behavior or a nuisance that comes with dementia," says psychologist Jiska Cohen-Mansfield of the Research Institute of the Hebrew Home of Greater Washington in Rockville, Maryland. "Their response was either psychotropic drugs, restraining, or ignoring. It made life pretty miserable for everybody."

Cohen-Mansfield suspected that the behaviors were driven by unmet needs. She had assistants watch patients around the clock, noting what triggered the behaviors. Patients tended to scream or moan, for example, when it was dark and they were alone. Thinking that this might reflect fear or loneliness, Cohen-Mansfield tried three interventions: Assistants would either stop by and visit with the patients at the problem time, play the patient a videotape of a family member talking to them, or play music they had once enjoyed. "It really made a difference," she says. The patients responded to all three approaches; as a group, their screaming or moaning dropped by roughly half in response to one-on-one interactions or the videotape, and by one-third in response to music.

In Cohen-Mansfield's study, the one-on-one interaction produced the biggest results, and in general researchers are finding that social interaction helps slow behavioral decline. Reisberg cites two striking cases: women with late-stage disease whose wealthy husbands have lavished professional attention and care on them. Normally people at their stage are bed-bound and withdrawn, but these women attend social events and appear to enjoy life. "They are doubly incontinent and say not a word, but they are happy," he says.

## Back to School

For families who can't afford costly private care, many parts of the country have day care centers for Alzheimer's patients, where they engage in developmental-age-appropriate activities, such as games or relearning daily living skills such as brushing their teeth. "The patients respond to the activities and the socialization," says Reisberg. Medication can be lowered, the patients become less agitated, "and when they come back at the end of the day, they have a lot to say to their family. It's a lot like school."

With all the new behavioral interventions, there is one caveat researchers have learned: The success of a program depends absolutely on caregivers' diligence in carrying it out. Studies by Alabama's Burgio and UCLA's Schnelle have shown that nursing home staff members tend to drop new techniques unless they are continually urged to use them. For example, a follow-up of Bourgeois's memory book study found that once the researchers left, says Burgio, "the memory book use went down."

Burgio developed a program to combat this problem, adapted from motivational programs used in industry, which combines monitoring of the nursing home staff with incentives for good performance. In a carefully controlled trial, staff members who received his program consistently used the interventions they had learned for months, while those not in the program tended to drop the interventions when the training period ended. Burgio says he tells nursing homes that are interested in behavioral therapies, "if you aren't going to use a staff motivational program, don't even bother with the behavioral intervention, [because] it won't be used."

Indeed, the new behavioral methods face many hurdles. "It is a really long road," says Teresa Radebaugh of Khachaturian, Radebaugh, and Associates, "to take something that is well tested, well described, carefully peer reviewed, and published, but done in a sophisticated setting . . . and get it out to a nursing home in a small town." Burgio agrees: "A lot of people still believe [nursing homes] should be following a custodial model, not a treatment model. It will take another 10 years before people are really accepting of the treatment model." But these researchers are committed to spreading their word and making life a bit easier for Alzheimer's sufferers and their caregivers.

# CHAPTER 10

# Eating Disorders

As a result of increased public awareness over the past decade or so, many people now know that there are two main forms of eating disorders and that an eating disorder can be lethal. In anorexia nervosa, an individual has an intense fear of gaining weight or becoming fat, refuses to maintain a minimally adequate body weight, and perceives his or her body or weight in a distorted manner. In bulimia nervosa, the individual engages in binge eating and then compensates for this increased caloric intake by self-induced vomiting, abusing laxatives (or other medications), fasting, and high levels of exercise. Physical appearance figures prominently in how individuals with bulimia nervosa evaluate themselves, but they do not misperceive their bodies in the way that those with anorexia nervosa do. Women are much more likely than men to have an eating disorder, and the age of onset is typically in late adolescence or early adulthood.

Some of us may have no difficulty remembering a time when we felt somewhat out of control when overeating or tried to restrict what we ate. Also, most of us recognize that the ideal physical image we hold of ourselves is, for better or worse, influenced by what we see on television and what we read in popular magazines. When you read case material about individuals with eating disorders, you see that these experiences and influences are magnified dramatically and that what began as a reasonable idea has spiraled out of control. An individual might start a diet (because popular people are thin, because of an off-hand comment about weight by a boyfriend, because of the need to fit into a prom dress) and experience positive reactions to initial weight loss—this could gradually lead to an obsession with the fear of weight gain and the strategies that are used to eliminate calories. The good news is that more than half of the people with an eating disorder recover; the bad news is that 30% show no substantial improvement after a decade (e.g., Keel et al., 1999). Moreover, even preteens are now engaging in potentially unhealthy practices to lose weight (e.g., Serdula et al., 1993).

The four readings on eating disorders include an authoritative review of the field, two case studies, and an article on the debate over what does and does not constitute disordered eating.

## References

Keel, P. K., Mitchell, J. E., Miller, K. B., Davis, T. L., & Crow, S. J. (1999). Long-term outcome of bulimia nervosa. *Archives of General Psychiatry, 56*, 63–69.

Serdula, M. K., Collins, M. E., Williamson, D. F., Anda, R. F., Pamuk, E., & Byers, T. E. (1993). Weight control practices of U.S. adolescents and adults. *Annals of Internal Medicine, 119*, 667–671.

# Anorexia and Bulimia Nervosa

## W. H. Kaye, K. L. Klump, G. K. W. Frank, and M. Strober

*Our first article reviews what is known about the experience, course, treatment, and biology of eating disorders and covers many recent findings in the area. One argument is that cultural factors are unlikely to be a primary cause of eating disorders. The authors base this argument on the view that the vast majority of individuals exposed to the various cultural forces implicated as causing eating disorders—depictions of beauty in the media, for example—never qualify for the diagnosis of anorexia nervosa or bulimia nervosa. Thus, while changing societal norms for thinness might account for changes in the overall incidence in eating disorders in the population, one or more additional factors must play a role in determining whether a particular individual will develop the disorder. The specific form that these factors will take is not yet clear, but the authors consider such possibilities as poor self-image, perfectionism, and genetic vulnerabilities.*

## Suggested Readings

Agras, W. S., Walsh, T., Fairburn, C. G., Wilson, G. T., & Kraemer, H. (2000). A multicenter comparison of cognitive-behavioral therapy and interpersonal psychotherapy for bulimia nervosa. *Archives of General Psychiatry, 57,* 459–466.

Becker, A. E., Grinspoon, S. K., Klibanski, A., & Herzog, D. B. (1999). Current concepts: Eating disorders. *New England Journal of Medicine, 340,* 1092–1098.

---

*Annual Review of Medicine, 51,* 299–313. (2000).

## Introduction

Anorexia nervosa (AN) and bulimia nervosa (BN) are disorders characterized by aberrant patterns of eating behavior and weight regulation and by disturbances in attitudes toward weight and shape and in the perception of body shape (1). In AN, there is an inexplicable fear of weight gain and unrelenting obsession with fatness even in the face of increasing cachexia. BN usually emerges after a period of dieting, which may or may not have been associated with weight loss.

Binge eating is followed by either self-induced vomiting or some other means of compensation for the excess of food ingested. The majority of people with BN have irregular eating patterns and satiety may be impaired. Although abnormally low body weight excludes the diagnosis of BN, some 25% to 30% of individuals with BN presenting to treatment centers have a prior history of AN. However, all BN subjects have a pathological concern with weight and shape. Common to individuals with AN or BN are low self-esteem, depression, and anxiety. Ninety to 95% of individuals with AN or BN are female.

In certain respects, both diagnostic labels are misleading. Individuals with AN rarely have complete suppression of appetite, but rather exhibit a volitional and usually ego-syntonic resistance to eating drives while eventually becoming preoccupied with food and eating rituals to the point of obsession (2). Similarly, BN may not be associated with a primary, pathological drive to overeat; rather, like individuals with AN, individuals with BN have a seemingly relentless drive to restrain their food intake, an extreme fear of weight gain, and often a distorted view of their actual body shape. Loss of control with overeating usually occurs intermittently and typically only some time after the onset of dieting behavior. Episodes of binge eating ultimately develop in a significant proportion of people with AN, whereas some 5% of those with BN will eventually develop AN. Considering that restrained eating behavior and dysfunctional cognitions relating weight and shape to self-concept are shared by both sets of patients, and that transitions between these syndromes occur in many, it has been argued that AN and BN have at least some risk and liability factors in common.

The etiology of AN and BN is presumed to be complex and multiply influenced by developmental, social, and biological processes (3, 4). However, the exact nature of these interactive processes remains incompletely understood. Certainly, cultural attitudes toward standards of physical attractiveness are relevant to the psychopathology of eating disorders (EDs), but it is unlikely that cultural influences are prominent in pathogenesis. First, dieting and the drive toward thinness are quite commonplace in industrialized countries throughout the world, yet AN affects only 0.3–0.7% of females in the general population, and BN only 1.7–2.5%. Moreover, the fact that numerous clear descriptions of AN date from the middle of the nineteenth century suggests that factors other than our current culture play an etiologic role. Second, both syndromes, particularly AN, have a relatively stereotypic clinical presentation, sex

distribution, and age of onset. This supports the possibility that there may be some biologic vulnerability to developing an ED.

## Illness Phenomenology and Course

PHENOMENOLOGY Variations in eating behavior have been used to subdivide individuals with AN into two meaningful diagnostic subgroups. In the restricting subtype of AN, subnormal body weight and an ongoing malnourished state is maintained by unremitting food avoidance; in the binge eating/purging subtype of AN, comparable weight loss and malnutrition occur, but the course of illness is marked by supervening episodes of binge eating, usually followed by some type of compensatory action such as self-induced vomiting or laxative abuse. Individuals with the binge eating/purging subtype of AN are also more likely to have histories of behavioral dyscontrol, substance abuse, and overt family conflict than are individuals with the restricting subtype of AN. Particularly common in individuals with AN are personality traits of marked perfectionism, conformity, obsessionality, constriction of affect and emotional expressiveness, and reduced social spontaneity. These traits typically appear before the onset of illness and persist even after long-term weight recovery, indicating that they are not merely epiphenomena of acute malnutrition and disordered eating behavior (5, 6).

Individuals with BN remain at normal body weight, although many aspire to ideal weights far below the normal range for their age and height. The core features of BN include repeated episodes of binge eating followed by compensatory self-induced vomiting, laxative abuse, or pathologically extreme exercise, as well as abnormal concern with weight and shape. The *DSM-IV* (1) has specified a distinction between individuals who engage in self-induced vomiting or abuse of laxatives, diuretics, or enemas (purging type), and those who exhibit other forms of compensatory action such as fasting or exercise (non-purging type). Beyond these differences, it has been speculated (7) that there are two clinically divergent subgroups of individuals with BN, which differ significantly in psychopathological characteristics: a so-called multi-impulsive type, in whom BN occurs in conjunction with more pervasive difficulties in behavioral self-regulation and affective instability, and a second type whose distinguishing features include self-effacing behaviors, dependence on external rewards, and extreme compliance. Individuals with BN of the multi-impulsive type are far more likely to have histories of substance abuse and to display other impulse-control problems such as shoplifting and self-injurious behaviors. Because of these differences, it has been postulated that individuals with multi-impulsive type BN rely on binge eating and purging as a means of regulating intolerable states of tension, anger, and fragmentation; in contrast, individuals with BN of the second type may have binge episodes precipitated by dietary restraint with compensatory behaviors maintained by reduction of guilty feelings associated with fears of weight gain.

COURSE  Most cases of AN emerge during adolescence, although the condition can occur in children. Whether prepubertal onset confers a more or less ominous prognosis is not known. Recovery from the illness tends to be protracted, but studies of long-term outcome reveal the illness course to be highly variable. Roughly 50% of individuals will eventually have reasonably complete resolution of the illness, whereas 30% will have lingering residual features that wax and wane in severity long into adulthood. Ten percent of people with AN will pursue a chronic, unremitting course, and the remaining 10% will eventually die from the disease (8, 9).

BN is usually precipitated by dieting and weight loss, but it can occur in the absence of apparent dietary restraint. The frequency of binge episodes, their duration, and the amount of food consumed during any one episode all vary considerably among patients. Age of onset is somewhat more variable in BN than in AN; most cases develop during the period from mid to late adolescence through the mid-twenties (10). Follow-up studies of clinical samples 5 to 10 years after presentation showed 50% of patients recovered whereas ~20–30% still met full criteria for BN. Following onset, disturbed eating behavior waxes and wanes over the course of several years in a high percentage of clinic cases. After remission, approximately 30% of women experience relapse into BN symptoms.

PERSISTENT PSYCHOLOGICAL DISTURBANCES AFTER RECOVERY  People who have an ED often have symptoms aside from pathologic eating behaviors. . . . Psychological symptoms include depression, anxiety, substance abuse, and personality disorders. Determining whether such symptoms are a consequence or a potential cause of pathological eating behavior or malnutrition is a major methodological issue in the study of EDs. It is impractical to study EDs prospectively due to the young age of onset and difficulty in premorbid identification of people who will develop an ED. However, subjects can be studied after long-term recovery from an ED.

The assumed absence of confounding nutritional disturbances in recovered ED women raises a possibility that persistent psychobiological abnormalities might be trait-related and potentially contribute to pathogenesis. A few studies have investigated people who have recovered from AN and BN. . . .

Investigators (5, 6, 11, 12) have found that in women who have recovered from AN, obsessional behaviors persist, as do inflexible thinking, restraint in emotional expression, and a high degree of self- and impulse control. In addition, the women are socially introverted, overly compliant, and limited in social spontaneity, and they exhibit greater risk avoidance and harm avoidance than controls exhibit. Moreover, individuals who have recovered from AN still exhibit core ED symptoms, such as ineffectiveness, a drive for thinness, and significant psychopathology related to eating habits. Similarly, people who have recovered from BN continue to be overly concerned with body shape and weight, to engage in abnormal eating behaviors, and to experience dysphoric mood (13–17). Recovered AN and BN women have greater than normal perfectionism, and their most common obsessional target symptoms are the need for symmetry and ordering/arranging. Considered together, these residual behaviors can be characterized as excessive concerns with body image and thinness, obsessionality with symmetry, exactness, and perfectionism, and dysphoric/negative affect. In general, pathologic eating behavior and malnutrition appear to exaggerate the magnitude of these concerns. Thus, these symptoms are less intense after recovery but the content of the concerns remains unchanged. The persistence of these symptoms after recovery raises the possibility that the disturbances are premorbid traits that contribute to the pathogenesis of AN and BN.

## Treatment

BULIMIA NERVOSA   Progress to date in establishing the efficacy of specific psychological and pharmacological therapies has been more dramatic for BN than for AN (18–20). With regard to psychotherapy, although controlled clinical trials are still few in number, most indicate that cognitive behavior therapy (CBT) is effective for at least 60% to 70% of individuals with BN, achieving remission of binge eating and purging in some 30% to 50% of cases. Direct comparisons of CBT with other psychological treatments suggest that this modality is more effective than psychodynamically oriented psychotherapy in reducing core symptoms of BN and that CBT is more effective than a strictly behavioral treatment in preventing early relapse into dietary restriction, binge eating, and purging. Evidence further suggests that CBT improves certain core symptoms such as body dissatisfaction, pursuit of thinness, and perfectionism.

Evidence for the efficacy of antidepressant pharmacotherapy in BN is impressive; however, the benefits may diminish over time in a significant proportion of individuals who respond initially, and only a minority have complete suppression of their symptoms with antidepressant monotherapy (21–23). The results of most double-blind, placebo-controlled, randomized trials indicate at least some superiority of antidepressants over

placebo in reducing the frequency of binge-eating episodes. In addition, some studies show a reduction in intensity of other symptoms commonly seen in BN, such as preoccupation with food and depression. These findings have been demonstrated with a variety of antidepressive medications, including tricyclic agents (TCAs) (e.g. imipramine, desipramine, clomipramine, amitriptyline), monoamine oxidase inhibitors (MAOIs; e.g. phenelzine, isocarboxazid), and serotonin-specific reuptake inhibitors (SSRIs; e.g. fluoxetine, fluvoxamine). Patients participating in these trials typically reported from 8 to 10 episodes of binge eating per week at baseline. The average decrease in binge frequency for patients receiving antidepressant medication was about 55%, with wide variation across studies. Placebo responses were similarly variable, but generally, the decrease of binge frequency was less than half the magnitude of the response for the active treatment. However, only a minority of the treated patients achieved full abstinence from binge eating and purging behaviors.

Most trials have shown no correlation between improvement in mood and reduction in BN symptoms. Additionally, antidepressants suppress BN symptoms in non-depressed BN patients, suggesting a mode of action other than through antidepressant effects. In some studies, the patients receiving the antidepressive medication demonstrated a reduction in the tendency for stressors to trigger binge eating.

A few studies (24–29) have assessed the relative efficacy of a combination of psychotherapy (CBT in most trials) and antidepressants for the management of BN, compared with each treatment by itself. Although differing in many respects, these studies suggest that the improvement in BN symptoms with CBT alone was greater than that with medication alone. Adding medication to psychotherapy generally did not improve significantly the outcome over psychotherapy alone in terms of eating behaviors, nor did it increase the speed of the therapeutic response. However, one prolonged follow-up evaluation found that combined treatment was more effective than CBT alone on a number of eating variables. Another study showed the superiority of combined therapy in reducing rates of anxiety and depression.

ANOREXIA NERVOSA   Treatment of AN has been less effective (20). The early treatment of AN derived largely from psychoanalytic, family-systems, or behavioral paradigms until the pioneering work of Bruch (30) broadened our understanding of its psychological underpinnings in impaired self-concept, body image, and interoceptive processes. Still, the first generation of controlled treatment studies focused narrowly on testing the value of behavior modification in increasing the rate of weight gain in hospitalized, emaciated patients, or the efficacy of adjunctive pharmacological treatment with either neuroleptic or antidepressant drugs. This work showed that weight gain could be achieved in many patients through a combination of supportive nursing care and behavioral techniques, whereas pharmacotherapy proved to have little incremental advantage in the treatment of severely ill patients.

A more recent series of randomized, controlled studies examined the efficacy of various types of psychological therapies in promoting weight gain in acutely ill AN patients (31, 32). Overall, the results indicate that substantial improvement in body mass and general psychosocial adjustment can be achieved in some subjects through cognitive behavioral, psychoeducational, and family therapy techniques (in some studies, coupled with dietary counseling), although treatment gains are not as robust in patients with more chronic, longstanding disability.

The evaluation of the efficacy of medications in augmenting weight gain in AN is limited because most trials have been conducted on outpatients or inpatients already participating in behavioral and nutritional ED programs, which are themselves efficient in the short run. Nevertheless, in these settings, controlled trials have not provided consistent evidence for the efficacy of antidepressant medications in the treatment of AN (21–23).

Some recent studies that have focused on preventing relapse in AN show more promise (31, 33, 34). For example, some psychotherapies specifically developed to treat AN appear to show reduced relapse at 1 to 2 years follow-up. Our group (35; WH Kaye, T Nagata, LKG Hsu, MS Sokol, C McConaha, et al., submitted for publication) found, in separate open and double-blind placebo-controlled studies, that fluoxetine improved outcome and reduced relapse after weight restoration. That is, fluoxetine was associated with a significant reduction in core ED symptoms, namely depression, anxiety, and obsessions and compulsions. In a recent double-blind, placebo-controlled study, our group found that fluoxetine, when given after weight restoration, significantly reduces the extremely high rate of relapse normally seen in AN. Ten of 16 (63%) subjects on fluoxetine remained well during 1 year of outpatient follow-up, whereas only 3 of 19 (16%) remained well on placebo ($p = 0.006$). Fluoxetine administration was associated with a significant weight gain and a significant reduction in obsessions and compulsions. Thus, fluoxetine improved outcome in AN subjects by reducing symptoms and helping to maintain a healthy body weight in outpatient treatment. . . .

## Biological Influences

EVIDENCE OF GENETIC INFLUENCES   As noted above, there is no convincing evidence that cultural factors are the primary determinants of EDs. However, emerging evidence suggests that both AN and BN are familial and that clustering of the disorder in families may arise partly from genetic transmission of risk (36). In one large family study of AN, risk of the disorder in mothers and sisters of probands was estimated at 4%, or roughly 8 times the lifetime expectancy of females in the general population (37). Moreover, we have reported recently (38) that rates of a more broadly defined ED phenotype that differs from AN or BN in severity occurs far more often in relatives of both AN and BN probands than in relatives of normal controls. Analysis of data from a large, epidemiological sample of twins obtained via the Virginia Twin Registry (39, 40) adds to evidence of a strong association between AN and BN. Specifically, it was found that the co-twin of a twin with AN was 2.6 times more likely to have a lifetime diagnosis of BN than were co-twins of unaffected twins. In short, evidence suggests at least some sharing of familial risk and liability factors between AN and BN. This finding will be important to future family-genetic research if it is confirmed that the broader, subclinical phenotype is more common among relatives than the narrow, more severe phenotype.

Paralleling these accounts are several reports of greater concordance rates of EDs in monozygotic twins than in dizygotic twins, with heritability estimates in the range of 50% to 90% for AN and 35% to 83% for BN (36, 39, 40, 41; KL Klump, KB Miller, PK Keel, M McGue, WG Iacono, et al., submitted for publication). However, with the exception of reports from the population-based Virginia Twin Registry and Minnesota Twin Family Study, existing accounts of differential concordance of EDs in twin pairs are hampered by unsystematic, and potentially biased, sampling.

A range of general psychiatric symptoms are common in patients with AN or BN. In many cases, they develop secondary to malnutrition and other disabling physiologic effects of aberrant eating psychological disability; yet, in some cases, psychiatric symptoms clearly antedate disordered eating or arise following recovery from low body weight or binge eating. Whether particular psychiatric disorders increase liability to EDs or are expressions of a shared underlying diathesis is a question of heuristic and clinical importance. . . .

## Summary

Phenomenological and etiologic research on AN and BN indicate that these disorders are characterized by a protracted course of illness, a persistence of psychological disturbances after recovery, and significant biological contributions to their development and maintenance. Treatment research suggests that both psychological and pharmacological treatment may help to ameliorate these disorders. Future research should continue to explore their biological and genetic underpinnings and should develop additional treatment approaches that may improve the efficacy of currently available treatment techniques.

## Literature Cited

1. American Psychiatric Association. 1994. In *Diagnostic and Statistical Manual of Mental Disorders*, Washington, DC: Am. Psychiatr. Press. 4th ed.
2. Schweiger U, Fichter M. 1997. Eating disorders: clinical presentation, classification and etiologic models. See Ref. 2a, pp. 199–216.
2a. Jimerson DC, Kaye WH, eds. 1997. *Balliere's Clinical Psychiatry*. London: Balliere Tindall Press.
3. Garner DM. 1993. Pathogenesis of anorexia nervosa. *Lancet* 341:1631–35.
4. Treasure J, Campbell I. 1994. The case for biology in the aetiology of anorexia nervosa. *Psychol. Med.* 24:3–8.
5. Srinivasagam NM, Kaye WH, Plotnikov KH, et al. 1995. Persistent perfectionism, symmetry and exactness after recovery from anorexia nervosa. *Am. J. Psychiatry* 152:1630–34.
6. Strober M. 1980. Personality and symptomatological features in young, nonchronic anorexia nervosa patients. *J. Psychosom. Res.* 24:353–59.
7. Vitousek K, Manke F. 1994. Personality variables and disorders in anorexia nervosa and bulimia nervosa. *J. Abnorm. Psychol.* 103:137–47.
8. Strober M, Freeman R, Morrell W. 1997. The long term course of severe anorexia nervosa in adolescents: survival analysis of recovery, relapse and outcome predictors over 10–15 years in a prospective study. *Int. J. Eating Disord.* 22:339–60.
9. Sullivan PF. 1995. Mortality in anorexia nervosa. *Arch. Gen. Psychiatry* 152:1073–74.
10. Keel PK, Mitchell JE. 1997. Outcome in bulimia nervosa. *Am. J. Psychiatry* 154:313–21.
11. Casper RC. 1990. Personality features of women with good outcome from restricting anorexia nervosa. *Psychosom. Med.* 52:156–70.
12. O'Dwyer AM, Lucey JV, Russell GFM. 1996. Serotonin activity in anorexia nervosa after long term weight restoration: response to d-fenfluramine challenge. *Psychol. Med.* 26:353–59.
13. Collings S, King M. 1994. Ten-year follow-up of 50 patients with bulimia nervosa. *Br. J. Psychiatry* 164:80–87.
14. Fallon BA, Walsh BT, Sadik C, et al. 1991. Outcome and clinical course in inpatient bulimic women: a 2- to 9-year follow-up study. *J. Clin. Psychiatry* 52:272–78.
15. Johnson-Sabine E, Reiss D, Dayson D. 1992. Bulimia nervosa: a 5-year follow-up study. *Psychol. Med.* 22:951–59.
16. Kaye WH, Greeno CG, Moss H, et al. 1998. Alterations in serotonin activity and psychiatric symptomatology after recovery from bulimia nervosa. *Arch. Gen. Psychiatry* 55:927–35.
17. Norring CEA, Sohlberg SS. 1993. Outcome, recovery, relapse and mortality across six years in patients with clinical eating disorders. *Acta Psychiatr. Scand.* 87:437–44.
18. Arnow B. 1997. Psychotherapy of anorexia and bulimia. See Ref. 2a, pp. 235–57.

19. Fairburn CG, Marcus MD, Wilson GT. 1993. Cognitive-behavioral therapy for binge eating and bulimia nervosa: a comprehensive treatment manual. In *Binge Eating: Nature, Assessment and Treatment*, ed. CG Fairburn, GO Wilson, pp. 361–404. New York: Guildford.

20. Herzog DB, Keller MB, Strober M, et al. 1992. The current status of treatment for anorexia nervosa and bulimia nervosa. *Int. J. Eating Disord.* 12:215–20.

21. Jimerson DC, Wolfe BE, Metzger ED, et al. 1996. Medications in the treatment of eating disorders. *Psychiatr. Clin. N. Am.* 19:739–54.

22. Mitchell JE, Raymond N, Specker S. 1993. A review of controlled trials of pharmacotherapy and psychotherapy in the treatment of bulimia nervosa. *Int. J. Eating Disord.* 14:229–47.

23. Walsh BT. 1991. Psychopharmacological treatment of bulimia nervosa. *J. Clin. Psychiatry* 52:34–38.

24. Agras WS, Rossiter EM, Arnow B, et al. 1992. Pharmacologic and cognitive-behavioral treatment for bulimia nervosa: a controlled comparison. *Am. J. Psychiatry* 149:82–87.

25. Fichter MM, Leibl K, Rief W, et al. 1991. Fluoxetine versus placebo: a double-blind study with bulimic inpatients undergoing intensive psychotherapy. *Pharmacopsychiatry* 24:1–7.

26. Goldbloom DS, Olmsted M, Davis R, et al. 1997. A randomized controlled trial of fluoxetine and cognitive behavioral therapy for bulimia nervosa: short-term outcome. *Behav. Res. Ther.* 35:803–11.

27. Leitenberg J, Rosen JC, Wolf J, et al. 1994. Comparison of cognitive-behavior therapy and desipramine in the treatment of bulimia nervosa. *Behav. Res. Ther.* 32:37–45.

28. Mitchell JE, Pyle RL, Eckert ED, et al. 1990. A comparison study of antidepressants and structured intensive group psychotherapy in the treatment of bulimia nervosa. *Arch. Gen. Psychiatry* 47:149–57.

29. Walsh BT, Wilson GO, Leob KL, et al. 1997. Medication and psychotherapy in the treatment of bulimia nervosa. *Am. J. Psychiatry* 154:523–31.

30. Bruch H. 1973. *Eating Disorders. Obesity, Anorexia Nervosa and the Person Within.* New York: Basic Books.

31. Russell GF, Szmukler GI, Dare C, Eisler I. 1987. An evaluation of family therapy in anorexia nervosa and bulimia nervosa. *Arch. Gen. Psychiatry* 44:1047–56.

32. Treasure J, Schmidt U, Troop N, Todd G. 1996. Sequential treatment for bulimia nervosa incorporating a self-care manual. *Br. J. Psychiatry* 168:94–98.

33. Strober M, Freeman R, DeAntonio M, et al. 1997. Does adjunctive fluoxetine influence the post-hospital course of restricting-type anorexia nervosa? A 24-month prospective, longitudinal follow up and comparison with historical controls. *Psychopharmacol Bull.* 33:425–31.

34. Treasure J, Todd G, Brolly M, et al. 1995. A pilot study of a randomized trial of cognitive analytical therapy vs educational behavioral therapy for adult anorexia nervosa. *Behav. Res. Ther.* 33:363–67.

35. Kaye WH, Weltzin TE, Hsu LKG, Bulik CM. 1991. An open trial of fluoxetine in patients with anorexia nervosa. *J. Clin. Psychiatry* 52:464–71.

36. Lilenfeld LR, Strober M, Kaye WH. 1997. Genetics and family studies of anorexia nervosa and bulimia nervosa. See Ref. 2a, pp. 177–97.

37. Strober M, Freeman R, Lampert C, et al. 1999. A controlled family study of anorexia nervosa and bulimia nervosa: evidence of shared liability and transmission of partial syndromes. *Am. J. Psychiatry.* In press.

38. Lilenfeld LR, Kaye WH, Greeno CG, et al. 1998. A controlled family study of restricting anorexia and bulimia nervosa: psychiatric disorders in first-degree relatives and effects of proband comorbidity. *Arch. Gen. Psychiatry* 55:603–10.

39. Kendler KS, MacLean C, Neale M, et al. 1991. The genetic epidemiology of bulimia nervosa. *Am. J. Psychiatry* 148:1627–37.

40. Walters EE, Kendler KS. 1995. Anorexia nervosa and anorexic-like syndromes in a population-based twin sample. *Am. J. Psychiatry* 152:64–71.

41. Bulik CM, Sullivan PF, Kendler KS. 1998. Heritability and reliability of binge-eating and bulimia nervosa. *Biol. Psychiatry* 44:1210–18.

# OUT OF CONTROL

## Kim Hubbard, Anne-Marie O'Neill, and Christina Cheakalos

*In 1999* People *magazine ran a cover story called "Wasting Away: Eating Disorders on Campus." This article reported the results of a survey that documented the extent of eating disorders among college women, and it presented the experiences of four young women and how they struggled with their weight, their eating, and their self-image. We present the introduction to this story and the experience of one of the women. As you will read, Lisa Arndt was anorexic in high school, fell into a cycle of bingeing and purging in college, and then struggled with anorexia once again. This is a vivid example of the symptoms associated with anorexia and bulimia, and it also shows how these disorders can be overcome.*

### Suggested Readings

Gottlieb, L. (2000). *Stick figure: A diary of my former self.* New York: Simon & Schuster.
Hornbacher, M. (1999). *Wasted: A memoir of anorexia and bulimia.* New York: HarperCollins.

People, 52–72. (1999, April 12).

*A*t first it seemed like a minor, if mystifying, problem: In the spring of 1996, plastic sandwich bags began disappearing by the hundreds from the kitchen of a sorority house at a large northeastern university. When the sorority's president investigated, she found a disturbing explanation: The bags, filled with vomit, were hidden in a basement bathroom. "I was shocked," says the president (who later learned that the building's pipes, eroded by gallons of stomach acid, would have to be replaced). "Yet in a way it made sense." Most of her 45 housemates, she recalls, worried about weight. "It was like a competition to see who could eat the least. At dinner they would say, 'All I had today was an apple,' or 'I haven't had anything.' It was surreal."

And, sadly, all too typical of scenes at colleges across the country. Since singer Karen Carpenter's death from complications of anorexia nervosa first jolted the nation into an awareness of the disease in 1983, the numbers of women seeking treatment for eating disorders has skyrocketed. Sufferers—5 to 10 million females and 1 million males—tend to be young (from 14 to 25), white, affluent, "perfectionistic, type-A personalities," says Marcia Herrin, codirector of Dartmouth College's Eating Disorders Education, Prevention and Treatment Program.

It's a problem that is raging on college campuses. In a People poll done last fall of 500 coeds, the figures were alarming: More than half of the young women respondents said they knew at least two schoolmates with an eating disorder. In a second poll, of 490 college health officials, commissioned by People, 70 percent said the problem was "common" on their campuses. According to Seattle's Eating Disorders Awareness and Prevention group (EDAP), an estimated 5 to 7 percent of America's 12 million undergraduates are afflicted with anorexia (a pathological fear of weight gain leading to extreme weight loss), bulimia (bingeing followed by purging) or binge eating (compulsive overeating). "College women are away from their families, and there's tremendous pressure to find their way in the world," says Jennifer Biely, EDAP's director. "Food is one thing they can control."

The idolization of wispy models and actresses adds to the problem. "I can tell a girl that what matters is what's going on in her head and heart," says sociologist Traci Mann, author of a 1997 study on campus prevention programs. "But when she turns on the TV, she sees that what matters is how you look."

Many schools are working to counter the media message. Freshman orientation programs routinely include information, once nonexistent, on eating problems, and "virtually every college has some kind of program, either a student-run group or treatment options through health services," says Charles Murkofsky, president of the New York City–based American Anorexia Bulimia Association. In February 1998 more than 600 college campuses participated in a National Eating Disorders Screening Program; of the 26,000 students who filled out questionnaires, 4,700 were referred for treatment.

Yet girls at risk often deny the problem or avoid getting help because of the stigma attached. And many college administrators "are not aware or don't want to become aware of the extent of the problem," says William Davis, a vice president of Philadelphia's Renfrew Center, a private eating disorder treatment facility. "They have to make choices about how they use funds: for education on drug and alcohol abuse or date rape or eating disorders." What's more, treating eating disorders is usually lengthy and expensive. A recent UCLA study found that the median recovery time from anorexia is seven years; many insurance companies cover only a fraction of the estimated $150,000 cost.

As colleges are discovering, however, not intervening can be far costlier. Bulimics may develop heartbeat irregularities from vomiting and laxative use, and anorexics have a mortality rate of nearly 20 percent, the highest of any mental disorder. Then there's the psychological toll. "I finally realized I didn't want to keep living like that," says Laura Mislevy, a recent Michigan State University graduate and a recovered anorexic. "There's more to worry about in life than what's for dinner. . . . "

As a sophomore at the University of California, Santa Cruz, Lisa Arndt followed a menu of her own making: For breakfast she ate cereal or fruit, with 10 diet pills and 50 chocolate-flavored laxatives. Lunch was a salad or sandwich; dinner: chicken and rice. But it was the feast that followed that Arndt relished most. Almost every night at about 9 P.M., she would retreat to her room and eat an entire small pizza and a whole batch of cookies. Then she'd wait for the day's laxatives to take effect. "It was extremely painful," says Arndt of those days in 1992. "But I was that desperate to make up for my bingeing. I was terrified of fat the way other people are afraid of lions or guns."

For Arndt, 26, in her fifth year of recovery and working as a counselor at the Rader Institute, an L.A. eating disorders clinic, bulimia began with the college cafeteria line. As a freshman, "there was plenty of food all the time and it seemed like it was free," she says. Her initial weight gain—from 100 pounds to 115 pounds, which suited her 5'6" frame—won compliments from friends. But Arndt, who had been an anorexic in high school, didn't buy it. "I felt ugly and ashamed," she says. Yet she gorged on junk food, thinking, "Oh, well, screw it, because I'm a big fat failure."

Back in high school, a friend who was the homecoming queen had confided that she was hooked on 75 laxatives a day and weighed 92 pounds. "She was trying to reach out for help," Arndt says now. But at the time the girl's despair only inspired Arndt. "I was supportive," she says. "But in the back of my mind I thought it was a great idea." Within a year of starting college, Arndt was trapped in an obsessive cycle of bingeing and laxative purging that did nothing to reduce her weight, which climbed to 140 pounds. "I would sit in class fantasizing about the cookies I'd make for myself or whether to have pepperoni on my pizza," she recalls. Grocery shopping—with four boxes of cookies and 10 boxes of laxatives in her cart—raised eyebrows. "I was so embarrassed, I went to different stores," she says. And excruciating abdominal pains weren't the sole side effect. "You start to smell," Arndt says matter-of-factly. "There's nothing you can do about it."

Later that year, Arndt got a loud wake-up call. At the age of 20, her friend, the laxative-gulping homecoming queen, suffered a heart attack. She survived, but "I remember seeing her all ghostly and pale and shaky," Arndt says, "and I thought, 'That could happen to me.'" After seeing a flyer for an on-campus support group for students with eating disorders, Arndt, a psychology major, opted to join. With the help of the group, she eventually weaned herself off the laxatives one at a time.

The weekly meetings also forced her to confront the anorexia she had suffered as a teen. Like many anorexics, her disorder had its seeds in a troubled childhood. After years of squabbling, her mother, a licensed therapist, and her father, a physician, divorced acrimoniously when Arndt was 15. "My home wasn't just broken," she says. "It cracked in 17 different places, then shattered."

Life at Santa Monica High was also fraught. "To be famous, to be Hollywood is what was cool," says Arndt. And that meant being thin. Already insecure about her features, she began dieting after a boyfriend suggested she lose five pounds and then dumped her. Arndt bought a powdered diet drink and lost five pounds in one week—only to regain the weight the next. "All of a sudden it was war," she says. She then tried combining fasting and up to 15 over-the-counter diet pills a day, followed by what Arndt calls "the half theory: I could eat half of what everybody else ate, because I wanted to be half the size of everybody else."

Before long, she stopped eating with others altogether. "I couldn't carry on a conversation," she says. "I'd get too distracted." Family meals were rare, and neither Arndt's mother nor father confronted her about her problem. Isolated and depressed at 16, she attempted suicide by slashing her wrists. "I thought I was too fat to live," she says. "I hated myself." Hospitalized for three months, she was treated for depression. It wasn't enough. "The voices in my head," she recalls, "said, 'You are fat. Failure. Pig. Bitch. Greedy.'"

By the end of her senior year in high school, Arndt weighed 92 pounds and was living on a daily diet of one fat-free blueberry muffin, which she would cut into eight parts and eat ritualistically with a knife and fork, taking up to an hour to finish. "I had lost touch with my physical sensation of hunger," she says. Her body, however, hadn't. One night, Arndt passed out as she left a movie theater with her then boyfriend, Andy Gersick, who had been badgering her about her eating habits for some time. She came to on a stretcher being lifted into an ambulance. "I was looking around at all these people and thinking, 'Oh, my God, they can all see how fat I am.' I couldn't stand up, so I couldn't hold myself in a position where I looked thinner." Though tests at St. John's health center showed that she was anemic and dehydrated (she had stopped drinking water for a week because it made her feel bloated), Arndt's denials of having an eating disorder were accepted, and she was released. Over the summer, with Andy's help, she gained eight pounds and, by the time college began, considered herself cured.

In truth, she had a long way to go. Though the college support group helped Arndt face her eating disorder in part, she says, "there was competition to be the sickest. I always wanted to be the thinnest." By graduation she had succeeded. A diet prior to graduation sent Arndt spinning back into full-blown anorexia. Before long, her hair began falling out and osteoporosis, brought on by malnutrition, had left her half an inch shorter. She joined a new support group and began working with a medical team at UCLA, where she had taken a job as a researcher in the psychology department. A nutritionist put her on a plan of foods less likely to alarm her, such as salads, lean meats and nonfat milk; a doctor tended to her illnesses, which included anemia and low blood pressure; a therapist helped her overcome her fears about food. "I took them on," she says, "one meal at a time."

Within a year, Arndt says, she was in recovery. And not a day passes that her patients at Rader don't remind her of just what that means. "They're great people," she says, "but all of them are killing themselves. Now that I'm finally free of anorexia and bulimia, life is so much better, brighter and worthwhile. I want to share that with everyone who is caught in the thinness trap so that they too can live life for real and experience true laughter and love."

# DYING TO WIN

## Merrell Noden

*If it is true that various cultural pressures increase the risk for anorexia nervosa and bulimia nervosa, then it seems plausible that athletes would be particularly susceptible to these disorders. Some sports, such as long-distance running or wrestling, place a high value on low body weight, and other sports, such as figure skating and gymnastics, emphasize a slender physique. It is easy to see how other activities, such as cheerleading, bodybuilding, and swimming, might also promote eating disorders in some situations.*

*The next article presents the disturbing story of Christy Henrich, a world-class gymnast who died at the age of 22, weighing only 61 pounds. It describes the circumstances surrounding her relentless push toward better performance and lower weight, her symptoms of anorexia, and the more general problem of eating disorders among athletes.*

### Suggested Readings

Johnson, C., Powers, P. S., & Dick, R. (1999). Athletes and eating disorders: The National Collegiate Athletic Association Study. *International Journal of Eating Disorders, 26,* 179–188.

Picard, C. L. (1999). The level of competition as a factor for the development of eating disorders in female college athletes. *Journal of Youth and Adolescence, 28,* 583–594.

*Sports Illustrated,* 52–56, 58–60. (1994, August 8).

Christy Henrich's fiancé, Bo Moreno, loved her for her sweet side, but he also knew her demons. That's why, when Henrich's parents were preparing to check her into the Menninger Clinic in Topeka, Kans., two years ago for treatment of her eating disorders, Moreno warned them to inspect her suitcase carefully. "It had a false bottom," he says. "She had lined the entire bottom of the suitcase with laxatives. That was part of her addiction." Henrich weighed 63 pounds at the time.

At another treatment center about a year later, the staff had to confine her to a wheelchair to prevent her from running everywhere in an attempt to lose weight. "Another part of the addiction," says Moreno. "Constant movement. Anything to burn calories."

At the peak of her career as a world-class gymnast, the 4' 10" Henrich weighed 95 pounds. But when she died on July 26, eight days past her 22nd birthday, of multiple organ failure at Research Medical Center in Kansas City, she was down to 61 pounds. And that actually represented improvement. On July 4, the day she was discharged from

St. Joseph's (Mo.) Medical Center, she had weighed 47 pounds.

"She was getting intensive supportive care," says Dr. David McKinsey, who treated Henrich during the last week of her life, the final three days of which were spent in a coma. "But a person passes the point of no return, and then, no matter how aggressive the care is, it doesn't work. The major problem is a severe lack of fuel. The person becomes so malnourished that the liver doesn't work, the kidneys don't work, and neither do the muscles. The cells no longer function."

Henrich had been in and out of so many hospitals over the past two years that Moreno lost count of them. Her medical bills ran to more than $100,000. There were occasional periods of hope, when she would gain weight and seem to be making progress. But for the most part, as Henrich herself told Dale Brendel of *The Independence* [Mo.] *Examiner* last year, "my life is a horrifying nightmare. It feels like there's a beast inside me, like a monster. It feels evil."

Henrich's funeral was held last Friday morning at St. Mary's Catholic Church in Independence. Her pink casket sat at the front of the church as several hundred mourners filed in. Some were fellow gymnasts; some were friends and relatives; some were former classmates at Fort Osage High, where Henrich had been a straight-A student. In his eulogy Moreno asked those present to do what most people had always had trouble doing when Henrich was alive: to think of her as more than just a gymnast. "She was a talented artist and an unbelievable cook," he said. "But I must admit, her favorite hobby was shopping, for herself and others."

Moreno closed by reading the lyrics to *I Believe in You*, a song he wrote and recorded for Henrich last summer:

> America's sweetheart brought to her knees
> Willing to do anything to please
> A product of our country
> Pushed too far
> You've got to be Extra-Tough, little lady
> Now look this way and grin
> Remember to hold your head up high
> And hold the pain within

Eating disorders are easily the gravest health problem facing female athletes, and they affect not just gymnasts but also swimmers, distance runners, tennis and volleyball players, divers and figure skaters. According to the American College of Sports Medicine, as many as 62% of females competing in "appearance" sports (like figure skating and gymnastics) and endurance sports suffer from an eating disorder. Julie Anthony, a touring tennis pro in the 1970s who now runs a sports-fitness clinic in Aspen Colo., has estimated that 30% of the women on the tennis tour suffer from some type of eating affliction. Peter Farrell, who has been coaching women's track and cross-country at Princeton for 17 years, puts the number of women runners with eating disorders even higher. "My experience is that 70% of my runners have dabbled in it in its many hideous forms."

Eating disorders, however, are by no means limited to athletes. The Association of Anorexia Nervosa and Associated Disorders reported before a U.S. Senate subcommittee hearing earlier this year that 18% of females in the U.S. suffer from eating disorders. The illnesses tend to strike women who, like Henrich, are perfectionists and they often seize those who seem to be the most successful. In 1983 singer Karen Carpenter died following a long battle with eating disorders, and for years Princess Diana waged a well-publicized fight against bulimia.

Girls or women who suffer from depression or low self-esteem are particularly susceptible to eating disorders, as are victims of sexual abuse. The expectations of society, particularly those regarding beauty, also play a role. Not coincidentally, the ideal of the perfect female body has changed dramatically in the past several decades. Marilyn Monroe, as she sashayed away from Jack Lemmon and Tony Curtis in *Some Like It Hot*, looked like "Jell-O on springs." Lemmon's description was a compliment in 1959. A decade later it would make most women cringe.

Given the importance that sport attaches to weight—and, the subjectively judged sports, to appearance—it isn't surprising that eating disorders are common among athletes. Nor is it surprising that they exact a far greater toll among women than men. In a 1992 NCAA survey of collegiate athletics, 93% of the programs reporting eating disorders were in women's sports. It is true that some male athletes—wrestlers, for example—use extreme methods of weight loss, but there is an important difference between these and the self-starvation practiced by anorexics. A wrestler's perception of his body is not distorted. When he is not competing, he can return to a healthy weight. That is not the case with anorexics, trapped as they are behind bars they can't see.

A study conducted a few years ago at Penn found that while both men and women tend to be unrealistic about how others perceive their bodies, men's perceptions tend to be distorted positively, while women's are more likely to be negative. "Someone feeling really good about herself isn't going to find her self-worth in her looks alone," says Farrell. "But how many girls between the ages of 16 and 22 [when eating disorders tend to strike] feel really good about themselves?"

"Men grow into what they're supposed to be," says Mary T. Meagher, the world-record holder in the 100- and 200-meter butterfly events. "They're supposed to be big and muscular. A woman's body naturally produces more fat. We grow away from what we're supposed to be as athletes."

Though laymen tend to lump anorexia and bulimia together—perhaps because experimentation with bulimia often leads to anorexia—the two are markedly different. "In a way bulimia is more dangerous," says Pan Fanaritis, who has coached women's track at Georgetown, Missouri and Villanova and is now the men's and women's coach at Denison. "Anorexia you can see."

What you see is frightening. Anorexia is self-starvation driven by a distorted perception of one's appearance. It is not unusual for an anorexic who is 5' 8" to weigh 100 pounds or less—and still think she's too fat. In the women's distance races at the Penn Relays this April, it was not hard to pick out the anorexics: Their arms were shrunken like the vestigial forelimbs of some dinosaurs. And on some a thin layer of downy fur had begun to form as their bodies struggled to compensate for the layers of fat they had lost.

The long-term consequences of anorexia are catastrophic. Deprived of calcium, the body steals it from the bones, leading to osteoporosis. "I've seen X-rays where the bones look like honeycomb," says Fanaritis. "X-rays of an anorexic of four or five years and those of a 70-year-old are very similar." Anorexics have suffered stress fractures just walking down the street.

Bulimia is a binge-purge syndrome in which huge quantities of food—sometimes totaling as much as 20,000 calories in a day—are consumed in a short period of time and then expelled through self-induced vomiting, excessive exercise, the use of diuretics or laxatives, or some combination of those methods. Stomach acids rot the teeth of bulimics and, if they are sticking their fingers down their throats to induce vomiting, their fingernails. Their throats get swollen and lacerated. Electrolyte imbalances disrupt their heart rates. But since bulimics are usually of normal weight, years may pass before a parent, roommate or spouse learns the terrible secret.

"You can always find an empty bathroom," says one recovering bulimic who was an All-America distance runner at Texas. During her worst period of self-abuse she was visiting bathrooms five or six times a day, vomiting simply by flexing her stomach muscles. "It's like a drug," she says of the syndrome. "It controls you. An overwhelming feeling comes over you, like a fog."

In the 1992 NCAA survey 51% of the women's gymnastics programs that responded reported eating disorders among team members, a far greater percentage than in any other sport. The true number is almost certainly higher. Moreno says he knows of five gymnasts on the national team who have eating disorders. Bob Ito, the former women's gymnastics coach at Washington, has estimated that on some of his teams 40% of the athletes had "outright eating disorders." One world-class gymnast has admitted that while she was at UCLA the entire team would binge and vomit together following meets. It was, she said, a "social thing."

Why might gymnasts be more vulnerable to eating disorders than other athletes? The subjectivity of the judging system can't help; nor can the fact that to reach the top, gymnasts must sacrifice having normal childhoods. Moreno also points to authoritarian coaches.

"A large percentage of coaches tell the girls how to count calories, how to act, what to wear, what to say in public," he says. "It becomes a control issue for the girl. They feel the only thing they control is the food they put in their bodies."

Anorexia offers a convenient antidote to what young gymnasts dread most—the onset of womanhood. Not only do anorexics keep their boyish figures, but many go months or even years without their menstrual periods, a side effect that contributes to osteoporosis. "This is a matter of locked-on adolescence," says Scott Pengelly, a psychologist from Eugene, Ore., who has treated athletes with eating disorders. "Chronologically, they may be adults. But they have a 13-year-old's way of looking at life."

In the Lilliputian world of gymnastics, arrested development seems to be an occupational necessity. Women gymnasts "are the most immature people on a college campus," says Rick Aberman, a psychologist and a consultant to the University of Minnesota's athletic department. "They're treated like little kids. When you have 18- or 19-year-old women trying to deny they've matured, you get problems. If [gymnasts] have hips or breasts, it creates inner turmoil that's so destructive. They're trying to deny something that's natural."

No one knows that better than Cathy Rigby, who 20 years ago was the darling of U.S. gymnastics and paid for it with 12 years of bulimia. "As much as [the news of Henrich's death] makes me sad, it makes me angry," Rigby says. "This sort of thing has been going on for so long in our sport, and there's so much denial."

When Rigby competed, every story celebrated her girlishness, which she worked so hard to maintain that she pinned her pigtails back from her face, fastening them so tightly that she got headaches. And the image of the world-class gymnast as waif has only become more exaggerated in the two decades since. The average size of the women on the U.S. Olympic gymnastics team has shrunk from 5' 3", 105 pounds in 1976 to 4' 9", 88

pounds in 1992. At last year's world championships the all-around gold medalist, 16-year-old Shannon Miller, was 4' 10", 79 pounds.

What chance would Vera Caslavska have had in such company? Caslavska, who won the all-around titles at the 1964 and '68 Olympics, was a geriatric giant by today's standards. In Mexico City the 26-year-old Czech was 5' 3", 121 pounds. What's more, she and Ludmila Turischeva of the Soviet Union, who succeeded Caslavska as all-around champion, looked like women. Gold medal or not, Turischeva was upstaged in '68 by 13-year-old Olga Korbut, who was 4' 11" and 85 pounds. Gymnastics has not been the same since.

At its highest levels gymnastics has evolved in a direction that is incompatible with a woman's mature body. That was plain when Nadia Comaneci, the darling of the 1976 Olympics, showed up at the world championships two years later having grown four inches and put on 21 pounds. She had become a woman, and as John Goodbody wrote in *The Illustrated History of Gymnastics*, "We learnt that week how perfection in women's gymnastics can be blemished by maturity."

By the 1979 world championships, where she won the combined title, Comaneci was her old svelte self, having lost nearly 40 pounds in two months. Eating disorders originate in the mind, and like any disease of self-deception, they are difficult prisons to escape. That was suggested in 1990, in Barbara Grizzuti Harrison's story on Comaneci in *Life* magazine. "I am fat and ugly," Comaneci, then 28, told the writer, although she was a size 6. When they went to dinner, Grizzuti Harrison wrote, "Her appetite for food is voracious. She eats her own food and [her companion] Constantin's too. After each course, she goes to the bathroom. She is gone for a long time. She comes back, her eyes watery, picks her teeth and eats some more. She eats mountains of raspberries and my crème brûlée. She makes her way to the bathroom again. When she returns, she is wreathed in that rank sweet smell."

Henrich's career followed a pattern not unlike that of thousands of little girls who fall in love with gymnastics the first time they see it on television. Henrich started at the age of four. When she was eight she enrolled at the Great American Gymnastics Express in the neighboring suburb of Blue Springs. Al Fong, a 41-year-old former LSU gymnast, founded Great American in 1979, one year before Henrich joined. Even in a sport dominated by monomaniacal men, Fong's determination to produce champion gymnasts is extraordinary. "I work at this seven days a week," he told reporter last year, "and I look forward to doing it for the next 25 years. It's an obsession with me."

Fong's elite gymnasts are renowned for the hours they train—one three-hour session at six in the morning and then four more hours at five in the afternoon. On meet days they are in the gym to work out two hours before the meet begins. "He pushed them really hard," says Sandy Henrich, Christy's mother. "He wanted them to train no matter what. He didn't want them to get casts [for fractures] because it took away their muscle tone."

For intensity Fong met his match in Henrich. Her nickname at the club was E.T.—hence the Extra-Tough allusion in Moreno's song—and she more than lived up to it, competing with stress fractures and placing second all around in the U.S. nationals just three months after she broke her neck in 1989. "No one can force someone to train 32 hours a week unless they really want to," Fong said last week. "The sacrifices are too great. Christy worked five times harder than anybody else. She became so good because she worked so hard and had this kind of focus."

Henrich made sensational progress. In 1986, at age 14, she finished fifth at the national junior championships and competed in her first international meet, in Italy. In early 1988, when she finished 10th in the all-around competition at the senior nationals, her dream of making the U.S. team at that year's Olympics seemed attainable.

"What's a [high school] dance compared to the Olympics?" she said when she was 15. "It's what I want to do. I want it so bad. I know I have a chance for the Olympics, and that gets me fired up." But Henrich didn't make the Olympic team in 1988.

She missed a berth by 0.118 of a point in a vault in the compulsories.

About the same time, her best friend, Julissa Gomez, saw her Olympic dream vanish forever, in devastating circumstances. Gomez broke her neck while performing a practice vault at a meet in Tokyo in May 1988, then went into a coma when an oxygen hose hooked to her respirator became disconnected after she had been given a tracheotomy. She died three years later without ever regaining consciousness.

"Julissa's death devastated Christy," says Moreno. "Christy's condition went downhill after this. She went to the gym and got a photo of Julissa and hung it in her room. It's still there."

Despite the tragedy that had befallen Gomez, in 1989 Henrich had her best year as a gymnast. She finished second in the all-around at the U.S. championships and fourth in the world championships in the uneven parallel bars. By that time she also had a serious eating disorder.

Its inception can be traced in part to an incident in March 1988, at a meet in Budapest, when a U.S. judge remarked that Henrich would have to lose weight if she wanted to make the Olympic team. Sandy Henrich recalls meeting her daughter at the airport upon her return: "The minute she got off the plane, the first words out of her mouth were that she had to lose weight. A judge had told her she was fat. Christy was absolutely devastated. She had a look of panic on her face. And I had a look of panic on my face. She weighed 90 pounds and was beautiful."

Henrich began eating less and less, an apple a day at first, and then just a slice of apple—this while continuing to work out six, seven hours each day.

In one important respect Henrich was different from many anorexics, who tend to live solitary existences. During her junior year at Fort Osage High she began to date Moreno, a friend of her older brother, Paul, and a wrestler on the Fort Osage team. "She was always very tough on herself," says Moreno, "and I could relate to that." Indeed, he recalls that Henrich got jealous when she learned that his body fat was 8%, while hers was 9%. "I had to tell her men just have lower body fat," he says. They got engaged in 1990 and were to be married later that year, but the wedding had to be postponed when Henrich fell ill. "She wanted to live in Florida and become a nurse," says Moreno. "We'd even named our children. Jesse Joseph and Maya Maria."

Soon after they began dating, Henrich asked Moreno how wrestlers lost weight. "I told her we'd wear plastic. Run in the shower with the steam on. Take Ex-Lax. And," he recalls with a wince, "every one of the things I told her, she tried. That laid real guilt on me, but I had no idea she'd do it. I had always told her how stupid it was."

Moreno says Fong might have spotted the danger signals of anorexia and bulimia earlier. "I find it hard to believe Al would not notice that every day Christy would work out, run five miles and come back. She truly loved Al and would have done anything for him. He'd say, 'Tuck your stomach in. You look like the Pillsbury Doughboy.' "

Kelly Macy, the 1991 NCAA champion on the uneven bars who trained regularly with Henrich at Fong's gym when both were in their early teens, recalls, "Everything was weight, weight, weight. He'd say, 'You could do this if you weighed less.' "

Fong denies ever harping on Henrich's weight or making the Doughboy comment. "It's just not true," he says. "I've heard those comments. Where in the world does that come from?"

Moreno and Sandy and Paul Henrich agree that the blame for Christy's obsession with weight should not fall only on her coach. "It's the whole system," says Sandy. "No matter what you do, it's never, never enough. The whole system has got to change—parents, coaches, the federation."

Christy lived at home, and a former USA Gymnastics official suggests that her parents might have pushed harder for intervention. As Christy's weight dropped precipitously, "they had to be aware of it," the official says, adding that the federation received no complaints from the family. Some of Henrich's friends question if they, too, should have seen the signs earlier.

"I think Christy had a problem a long time before [the obvious symptoms appeared]," says Macy, who herself suffered from anorexia while competing for Georgia and now travels the country speaking about the dangers of eating disorders. "I just didn't realize it. She was always working out, always doing extra stuff after practice. We'd finish, and she'd jump right on the exercise bike. Even my mother commented on it. She said, 'That Christy Henrich looks like she puts 150,000 percent into everything.' "

Moreno has come to understand Henrich's compulsion. "Christy's also to blame for her perfectionist attitude," he says. "The disease strikes people like that. I can remember Christy telling me, 'There's only one first place. Second place sucks.' "

Gail Vaughn, the director of Reforming Feelings, a counseling service in Liberty, Mo., worked with Henrich for six months last year. "Probably one of the things that worked against her most was that label, E.T.," says Vaughn. "She learned to deny pain. She competed in one of her biggest meets with a stress fracture. So when her body broke down and screamed in pain, she ignored it. Because she had learned to push past the pain."

For women, eating disorders are "like steroids are for men," says Liz Natale, a recovering anorexic who was a member of the Texas team that won the 1986 NCAA cross-country title. "You'll get results, but you'll pay for it."

For a time you do get results. That's part of the seduction. As an athlete's weight falls, his or her aerobic power increases. And psychologically there is no lash like anorexia. "To be a great competitor, you need that tunnel vision that anorexia feeds on," says Farrell. "Anybody who can starve herself can run a 10,000 really well."

But ultimately eating disorders exact a severe psychological toll. Distance runner Mary Wazeter was so tormented by constant thoughts of food that in February 1982, after withdrawing from Georgetown in her freshman year, she jumped from a bridge into the ice-covered Susquehanna River in her hometown of Wilkes-Barre, Pa. Her suicide attempt failed, but she broke her back and will spend the rest of her life in a wheelchair.

It does not take much to trigger an eating disorder. Natale recalls watching the mile run at the 1983 NCAA championships while sitting in the stands with her coach. "I remember her telling me to notice how thin all the women in the final were," says Natale. "I hadn't qualified, and I felt bad because I hadn't. I remember thinking if I wanted to run well, I needed to lose weight."

Many coaches aren't that subtle. Some divide their athletes into Lean Machines and Porkers. Tonya Chaplin, an assistant gymnastics coach at Washington, recalls that her club coach would punish female team members if they went much over their assigned weight by abusing them verbally, withholding meals and confining them to a "fat room." Before she quit the team, Chaplin was vomiting 12 times a day.

Regrettably, too many coaches see only what they want to see. Says Fanaritis: "How about the football coach who has the kid come back from summer vacation and he's gained 60 pounds and his neck has grown two inches, and the kid says, 'I lifted my ass off'? It's the same issue. You're not the one who said, 'Go home and use steroids.'

You're not the one who said, 'Get skinny so you can run fast.' But you're in that middle ground."

Spurred by Henrich's case, USA Gymnastics has begun to take measures seeking to help prevent eating disorders. Last year the federation measured the bone density of all 32 national team members and found that three of them had deficiencies. It says it is trying to teach young gymnasts that they can say no if they feel too much is being asked by a coach. But how realistic is it to expect children to stop themselves from doing something they love? Especially when, as famed women's gymnastics coach Bela Karolyi once put it, "The young ones are the greatest little suckers in the world. They will follow you no matter what."

Christy Henrich was buried at St. Mary's Cemetery in Independence last Friday afternoon. A line of cars half a mile long moved slowly through the tombstones, which marked the graves of those who had lived 70, 80, even 90 years. For Henrich the time was tragically short. The inscription on her stone will read: 1972–1994.

# Watching Volunteers Eat, Psychiatrists Seek Clues to Obesity

## Erica Goode

*While most of us would agree that the compulsive fear of weight gain evident in anorexia nervosa and the regular binge-purge cycle in bulimia are cause for significant concern and intervention, what position should we take on obesity? Is it a form of psychopathology? When binge eating is not followed by compensatory purging or extreme dieting, is it a source of real distress for the individual?*

*Of course, these questions raise the broader issue of how we decide whether any set of symptoms qualifies as a formal disorder. At least for obesity, if it does not cause significant distress for the individual, then it is not considered a psychological disorder. In the words of the DSM-IV (p. 539), "simple obesity is included in the International Classification of Diseases (ICD) as a general medical condition, but it does not appear in DSM-IV because it has not been established that it is consistently associated with a psychological or behavioral syndrome." Binge eating has not achieved the status of a formal diagnosis, but the DSM-IV now recognizes and defines it in an appendix as a "criteria set" provided for further study.*

*This article tackles these questions and the issue of where the lines should be drawn in determining whether or not an eating pattern constitutes an eating disorder.*

## Suggested Readings

Fairburn, C. G., Cooper, Z., Doll, H. A., Norman, P., & O'Connor, M. (2000). The natural course of bulimia nervosa and binge eating disorder in young women. *Archives of General Psychiatry, 57,* 659–665.

Wilfley, D. E., Friedman, M. A., Dounchis, J. Z., Stein, R. I., Welch, R. R., & Ball, S. A. (2000). Comorbid psychopathology in binge eating disorder: Relation to eating disorder severity at baseline and following treatment. *Journal of Consulting and Clinical Psychology, 68,* 641–649.

*New York Times*, D1. (2000, October 24).

In a small room on the ninth floor of St. Luke's-Roosevelt Hospital in Manhattan, volunteers come to eat in the name of science.

They sip milkshakes through polyethylene straws. They munch on baked chicken, sliced apples, potato chips and chocolate cake. They finish off meals composed entirely of Breyer's ice cream.

Sometimes, following instructions, they eat as much as they would in a normal meal. Other times they "binge," consuming as much as they can, or they eat continuously until an experimenter tells them to stop.

All the while, machines measure their food intake. Questionnaires, filled out at regular intervals, gather information on how hungry or full they feel, how much they feel in control of their eating, how much they like or dislike what they eat.

This orchestrated frenzy of deglutition has a purpose: through such studies, researchers at centers like the hospital's Human Ingestive Laboratory, which is affiliated with Columbia University's College of Physicians and Surgeons, hope to answer critical questions about one of life's most basic activities.

Why are some people able to control how much they eat while others seem helpless to stop? How do the eating patterns of people with anorexia or bulimia differ from those of other people? How does dieting to lose or maintain weight, an activity that more than two-thirds of Americans report engaging in, relate to more extreme eating behavior? And in a culture where fattening food is everywhere, thinness is a national ideal and 55 percent of the population is officially overweight, what is normal and what is abnormal?

Over the last two decades, scientists have progressed both in their understanding of eating disorders and their ability to treat them.

Researchers have found, for example, that cognitive therapy and antidepressants are effective therapies for bulimia nervosa. They have uncovered abnormalities in the biological systems controlling hunger and satiety that may play a role in many eating disturbances. And they have learned that eating disorders tend to run in families, sug-

gesting that the vulnerability to such problems may be at least in part genetic.

Yet despite these advances, researchers still know surprisingly little about how normal eating should be defined, or where its exact boundaries lie. And in many areas, debates continue over how severe symptoms must be to be called "disordered," how eating disorders intersect with other psychiatric diagnoses like anxiety, depression or obsessive compulsive disorder, and how different types of eating problems relate to one another.

"There's no question that there's an arbitrariness in the way the lines are drawn in these disorders," said Dr. B. Timothy Walsh, director of the eating disorders research program at New York State Psychiatric Institute in Manhattan. "And while we have made progress, we have also recognized how much we don't know, even about who should be considered as having an eating disorder."

Part of the difficulty is that for most people, eating is not just a matter of stoking up on fuel. Instead, from early childhood food becomes tied up with other things, with love and hate, power and control, with culture, religion, social circumstance and personal belief. A piece of chocolate cake can be an oasis of comfort, a reliever of stress, a cure for boredom, a balm to loneliness. French fries can be Prozac on a plate.

"Food is obviously the staple of our lives and we need it in order to keep our glucose levels up," said Dr. C. Peter Herman, a professor of psychology at the University of Toronto, who studies dieting and eating disorders. "But it quickly goes beyond its biological aspect and basically runs riot through our lives."

Adult humans display an impressive array of eating styles and preferences. In any random sample of people, some will eat fast, some slowly. Some will pick at their food, others will behave more like human vacuum cleaners. In stressful situations, some people will stop eating, others break out the banana cream pie.

Moreover, in the panoply of human diners there are broccoli haters and meat avoiders, health food addicts and carbohydrate phobics. There are those who will eat only foods that have not touched on the plate, who eat the same thing for lunch every day of the year, who always eat their carrots first and their meatloaf second.

One Philadelphia woman, interviewed as part of a study of picky eaters by Dr. Paul Rozin and Dr. Marcia Pelchat at the University of Pennsylvania, refused to eat anything with lumps, effectively ruling out beef stew, most forms of spaghetti sauce and chocolate chip cookies.

Such gastronomic eccentricities are widespread, Dr. Rozin and Dr. Pelchat have found, and largely benign. But for other people, food becomes a torment.

Anorexics starve themselves to emaciation. Bulimics binge eat uncontrollably, then induce vomiting, abuse laxatives or exercise frantically to compensate for their overindulgence.

Others who seek help at eating disorder clinics chew their food and then spit it out, or count calories compulsively, or are unable to eat in public. Or perhaps they suffer from "night eating syndrome," a disorder described by Dr. Albert Stunkard, a professor of psychiatry at the University of Pennsylvania, and other researchers, which involves nearly constant nibbling, beginning in the late afternoon, coupled with depression and insomnia.

Mark Roth, a 50-year-old pharmacist in Philadelphia, is one of those who sought treatment for the condition at the university. His eating problem, he said, "felt like a compulsion." He would skip breakfast, eat a "haphazard" lunch at work, then go home and begin munching, extending his repeated trips to the refrigerator into the wee morning hours. He edged up from 180 pounds to a chunky 230.

Sometimes he would fantasize about the pork chop left over from dinner, eventually retrieving it and devouring it hungrily. Other times he would make do with nuts, potato chips, popcorn, or other tempting snacks. "Basically, I'd eat just about anything," Mr. Roth said.

## What Is Normal?

For mental health professionals, parsing a landscape of such vastness and diversity is not always an easy task. Traditionally, psychiatrists have limited the definition of "disordered" eating to behaviors that threaten health or are distressing enough to drive people into treatment.

Anorexia and bulimia, the two eating disorders included in the *Diagnostic and Statistical Manual of Mental Disorders*, the American Psychiatric Association's official roster of psychiatric illness, clearly fit these criteria. The two involve extreme behaviors—self-starvation in the case of anorexia, frequent bingeing and purging in bulimia—that most people would agree are aberrant. And each has a significant effect on health.

Anorexia, which surveys find affects half of 1 percent to 1 percent of adolescent and young adult females, is perhaps the deadliest of mental disorders: in one long-term study, 7 percent of the anorexic subjects who participated had died within 10 years. Bulimia, two to six times as common as anorexia, has less severe health consequences, but takes over patients' lives and destroys their psychological well-being. Obesity, on the other hand, also impairs health, but it is not considered an eating disorder.

To be sure, psychoanalysts once treated obesity as a symptom of neurosis, the legacy of unresolved childhood conflict. But in the last two decades, the consensus of medical experts has been that the obese are as normal as anyone else—they just weigh more.

Obese people, experts agree, are no more likely to binge eat than their less adipose counterparts, though, in proportion to their size and energy demands, they eat more. And though studies have found that the incidence of anxiety and depression is slightly higher among the obese, they are, as a group, no more prone to psychiatric illness than other people.

Perhaps reflecting this, obesity has never been included in the psychiatric association's diagnostic manual, which insurance companies use to guide their coverage.

"It was always understood that there were many reasons that people were obese," said Dr. Michael First, a professor of psychiatry at Columbia and one of two editors of the association's manual, known as *DSM-IV*.

Still, some obese people seek help from mental health professionals because they feel that their overeating is out of control. Others come for treatment because the stigma associated with their heft has itself caused psychological distress. And while research increasingly suggests that obesity has genetic roots, like anorexia and bulimia it is also influenced by environmental factors. As a result, at least a few experts argue that it makes no sense to omit obesity in discussions of eating disorders.

In a recent editorial in the journal *TEN: The Economics of Neuroscience*, for example, Dr. Myrna M. Weissman, a professor of epidemiology at Columbia, suggested that obesity be added to the psychiatric diagnostic manual.

"Obesity," Dr. Weissman argued, while not a psychiatric disorder in itself, "is associated with psychopathology, social morbidity and stigmatization."

Treatment for obesity, she pointed out, often involves behavioral therapies, antidepressant drugs and other tools of the psychiatric profession. And basic research on why people become obese is intertwined with the investigation of the biological underpinnings of other eating disorders.

## The Binge Eater

Dr. Weissman's proposal is bound to be controversial. But so is "binge eating disorder," a diagnosis increasingly given to obese people who identify their eating patterns as a problem.

The disorder, now listed in the appendix of *DSM-IV* as a provisional diagnosis in need of further study, is defined by recurrent episodes of binge eating that occur at least two days a week for at least six months.

In addition, to qualify for a label of binge eating disorder, patients must feel distressed about their overeating, and meet three of six other criteria, including experiencing guilt or depression over eating too much, eating more rapidly than usual, eating until uncomfortably full, eating when not feeling physically hungry or eating alone because of embarrassment over the quantity being consumed.

Surveys indicate that about 2 percent of the population qualify for a diagnosis of binge eating disorder using these criteria. More than half of those are obese. And about 30 percent of obese people unhappy enough to seek treatment for their obesity engage in binge eating, according to studies. In patients who undergo a drastic weight reduction procedure called gastric bypass surgery, that figure rises to more than 50 percent.

Binge eating disorder appears to be distinct from bulimia: binge eaters do not engage in extreme measures like vomiting or abusing laxatives to compensate for their overeating, nor do they restrict their food intake when not bingeing, as many bulimics do.

Yet labeling binge eating as pathological is problematic in a culture of Big Macs, super sundaes and all-you-can-eat buffets, where overeating is a staple of every college dorm, and a routine way for adults to celebrate, recreate and respond to stresses of all kinds.

Supporters of the binge eating disorder diagnosis contend that it describes an identifiable group of people, who are troubled and in need of treatment.

"If you actually talk with people who have binge eating disorder, it takes over a large part of their lives," said Dr. Susan Yanovsky, director of the obesity and eating disorders program at the National Institute of Diabetes and Digestive and Kidney Diseases. "They don't want to go out because of it. They feel distressed about it. I think this is distinguishable from the normal, everyday binge eating that so many women go through." But the diagnosis also has more than a few critics.

"Outside North America, it's basically a laugh," said Dr. Christopher Fairburn, a professor of psychiatry at Oxford University in England, who has studied binge eating disorder in the general population. "No one thinks it's a serious condition. There is no literature on it. There are no meetings."

Arguing against the usefulness of binge eating disorder as a diagnostic category are some studies that suggest that the condition, as defined in the diagnostic manual, responds to virtually any type of treatment, including no treatment or treatment with sugar pills.

"These are overeaters," Dr. Fairburn said, "and the times when their life gets difficult, they overeat more, and they get very low about it. Then things improve and they stop. And whatever you do, including nothing, the bingeing goes away."

Still, many scientists believe more research will clarify how binge eating disorder fits into the eating disorder spectrum, and whether it should be included as a formal diagnosis in future editions of the manual.

"I think everybody is agreed that there is something out there," said Michael Devlin, a Columbia University psychiatrist who studies the disorder.

## Mapping the Unknown

The difficulties associated with drawing a clean line between normal and abnormal are not limited to overeating.

A parade of help seekers arrive at eating disorder clinics distressed by symptoms not quite severe enough to meet the diagnostic criteria for anorexia or bulimia.

Some come because they are endangering their health through dieting, for example, but do not stop menstruating or drop enough weight to qualify for an official diagnosis. Others eat large amounts of food and then try to get rid of it by vomiting, extreme exercise or abusing laxatives, but do not do so twice a week for three months—the frequency required in the manual's diagnosis of bulimia.

Countless more never seek treatment at all, but, buffeted by the cultural pressures to eat too much on the one hand and to be unrealistically slim on the other, play out in their daily lives some variation of an anorexic or bulimic theme.

"Picture a tug of war with a massive, muscular giant at each end of the rope," said Dr. Kelly Brownell, director of the Yale University Center for Eating and Weight Disorders. "People are caught in the intersection of these forces. There are the healthy few who manage not to yield, but

nearly everybody has at least a little of one problem or another."

At present, symptoms that do not fit neatly into the currently available diagnostic pigeonholes are lumped under a catch-all diagnosis, "Eating Disorder Not Otherwise Specified," a category regarded by many health insurance companies as not severe enough to warrant reimbursement.

Yet eventually, scientists may know enough to map with some certainty those behaviors that are simply the far end of normal eating and those that represent a step into illness. One way they hope to gain such knowledge is to bring patients with different diagnoses into the laboratory and study their eating patterns. And scientists at St. Luke's-Roosevelt Hospital, which recruits volunteers to eat under scientific scrutiny, are trying to do just that.

Dr. Harry Kissileff, an associate professor of clinical psychology in psychiatry and medicine at Columbia, who is director of the lab, said his research team was one of the first to ask subjects to binge eat in a laboratory setting.

"People didn't think it could be done because it was such a private behavior," he said. "But we just brought people in and asked them to do it."

With Dr. Walsh and other collaborators, Dr. Kissileff has studied bingeing in patients with diagnoses of bulimia and binge eating disorder, in the obese and in control subjects, whose eating patterns are supposedly "normal."

Through such studies, they have been able to tease out some differences between diagnostic groups, discovering variation in how much food they consume, what foods they select and how quickly they eat.

In studies where subjects were asked to binge, eating as much as they possibly could, subjects with binge eating disorder ate slightly less than bulimic subjects, and were more fussy about the foods they chose to binge on, Dr. Kissileff said.

Bulimic subjects, though they ate substantially more when told to binge than both control subjects and those with binge eating disorder, actually ate less than the other groups when asked to eat normally.

And, presented with a smorgasbord of foods to choose from, bulimic subjects structured their meals differently from normal subjects and those with binge eating disorder.

"Normal folk tend to eat meat early in the meal and toward the end of the meal eat dessert foods," said Dr. Walsh. "In contrast, people with bulimia got to dessert much earlier."

The results of such studies have led researchers at Columbia and elsewhere to form a number of hypotheses about the mechanisms that underlie bulimia. Studies have found, for example, that bulimic subjects produce abnormally low amounts [of] a hormone called cholecystokinine, or CCK, released by cells in the wall of the small intestine when food is present, indicating that the disorder may involve a disruption in the physiological signals that normally tell people when they have eaten enough.

But scientists still have a long way to go in understanding the ways that one of life's most pleasurable activities can derail. In the meantime, Dr. Yanovsky said, what is an eating disorder can be defined very simply: "If it's something that's having an impact on your life or your health or your ability to function," she said, "you ought to go out and get help."

# CHAPTER 11

# Sexual and Gender Identity Disorders

In one form or another, sexuality cuts a wide swath through our culture, our lives, and the field of abnormal psychology. For such a fundamental behavior that perpetuates our species and affects the way we relate to others and how we view ourselves, no less an impact would be expected. Of course, sex and gender in human functioning can also be a source of great concern and distress, and problems in this arena can take many different forms.

Disorders relating to sexuality and gender fall into three main categories: paraphilias, which are disorders that arise when sexual arousal derives from unusual objects or situations (these include pedophilia, exhibitionism, masochism, voyeurism, and bestiality); gender identity disorder, which is marked by a discrepancy between an individual's physical anatomy and his or her self-perceptions as being a male or female; and sexual dysfunctions, in which problems are encountered with one's desire for sex, with sexual arousal, with achieving orgasm, or with experiencing pain during sexual intercourse. These descriptions demonstrate the considerable breadth and variety of the diagnoses in this domain, almost to the point that these three diverse subcategories can be viewed as having little in common. Good prevalence estimates of paraphilias and gender identity disorder are not yet available, but it is clear that they are rare relative to sexual dysfunctions, which are estimated to affect about 31% of men and 43% of women between the ages of 18 and 59 (Laumann, Paik, & Rosen, 1999). The first three articles provide case material and analysis pertaining to sexual dysfunction, gender identity disorder, and a paraphilia, respectively; the final article is on compulsive sexual behavior which, surprisingly, is not well represented in the current diagnostic system.

## Reference

Laumann, E. O., Paik, A., & Rosen, R. C. (1999). Sexual dysfunction in the United States: Prevalence and predictors. *Journal of the American Medical Association, 281,* 537–544.

# Unusual Case Report: Nonpharmacologic Effects of Sildenafil

## David Mintz, M. D.

*A man with erectile disorder (ED) is unable to get or keep an erection that is suffi-
cient for sexual activity. ED is common, particularly as men enter middle age, and
it is made more likely by a host of conditions—stress, high blood pressure, prostate
surgery, diabetes, depression—that can restrict blood flow to the penis. Effective
behavioral approaches to ED have long been available and accepted, such as
Masters and Johnson's (1970) sensate focus and graded sexual exercises, in which
partners work together to help the man feel more relaxed and comfortable during
intimate interactions. However, with the introduction of Viagra, a medication that
restores blood flow to the penis, a great deal of attention has been brought to this
disorder and its treatment. Viagra should help a wider range of people than
behavioral approaches, though a medication-based intervention does not require
any communication between the person with ED and his partner.*

*This reading presents two brief case studies involving men who, as an indirect
effect of taking Viagra, threatened to harm their partner. Although these are likely
to be highly unusual and rare responses to Viagra, these case studies demonstrate
that although medications do operate on the biological mechanisms involved in an
individual's sexual performance, their prescription must take into account the
connections between these mechanisms and the interpersonal domains in which
they operate.*

## Reference

Masters, W., & Johnson, V. (1970). *Human sexual inadequacy*. Boston: Little, Brown.

## Suggested Reading

Heiman, J. R., & Verhulst, J. (1990). Sexual dysfunction and marriage. In F. D. Fincham and T. N. Bradbury (Eds.), *The psychology of marriage: Basic issues and applications* (pp. 299–322). New York: Guilford.

*Psychiatric Services, 51, 674–675. (2000).*

Sildenafil (Viagra), by virtue of its conflict-laden symbolic meanings, may be particularly likely to have psychosocial consequences, either therapeutic or disruptive The author presents two cases of men in their mid-seventies who took sildenafil and who were admitted to a locked geropsychiatry unit because of homicidal ideation toward their wives that occurred while they were not under the direct effect of the drug. In one case, a wife's rejection of her husband's advances seemed to uncover many hidden resentments that they bore toward each other. In the other, sildenafil failed to restore potency to a patient with diabetes, and he developed a jealous delusion that his wife was having an affair.

With a media circus accompanying the approval of sildenafil (Viagra) in 1998 by the U.S. Food and Drug Administration, 2.3 million prescriptions written in the first three months, and first-year sales of about $1 million, sildenafil seemed well on the way to being one of the most enthusiastically received drugs since penicillin. The immediate popularity of this medication and the ardor of the political struggles waged around it in the months after its release have been a testament to the powerful symbolic meanings that sexuality and male sexual potency bear individually and in our society.

One might expect a drug that holds the promise of restoring potency to exert profound psychosocial as well as physiological effects on men and on their relationships with their partners. Prescribers are likely to assume that, barring significant medical side effects, these psychosocial effects will be positive. However, the idiosyncratic meanings that specific drugs hold for patients may result in negative consequences, even in the presence of a positive drug response (1).

In the first three months after the release of sildenafil, two men were admitted to a locked geropsychiatry unit for treatment of problems apparently related to the drug. Neither had a history of psychiatric hospitalization or illness. Both were in their mid-seventies. Both had signs of early dementia on mental status testing. Both were admitted with homicidal ideation toward their spouses. In both cases, the most significant change, or psychosocial stressor, of the past several months was

the prescription of sildenafil. Neither was under the direct effect of the drug at the time that the homicidal threats were made.

## Case 1

Mr. A was an engaging and healthy-appearing black man who showed no signs of mental illness on mental status testing except for homicidal ideation toward his wife and minor deficits in executive cognitive function. He had a history of having made a homicidal threat toward his wife some 30 to 40 years earlier. The relationship had been stormy, but the hostilities in the relationship had settled into a truce.

As in a recent cartoon of a couple driving home from the gerontologist with the husband thinking "Viagra!" and the wife thinking "Viaggravation," Mr. A's wife was not enthusiastic about the patient's reawakened interest in sex. Her rejection of his advances seemed to uncover many of the hidden resentments that they bore toward each other, and open hostilities again broke out in the relationship, culminating in the patient's homicidal threats and subsequent hospitalization.

## Case 2

Mr. B was an immigrant to the United States who had a limited social system and spoke no English. His wife had made tremendous strides in mastering English, and he had become increasingly dependent on her. He worried that he had little to offer her in the relationship, and his concerns were worsened by his diabetes-induced erectile dysfunction. The prospect of restored potency had brought him some hope, but when sildenafil failed, he became frantic about his inability to please her and feared she would leave him.

What emerged and consolidated over the next several months was Mr. B's jealous delusion that his wife was having an affair, and he threatened to kill her. On mental status testing, he was initially quite guarded, but he wept spontaneously when the subject of his impotence came up. No evidence of major depression or other psychotic signs or symptoms was found. Mr. B was poorly oriented; however, not speaking the language left him without many orienting cues. At the same time, his recent memory for events in the relationship seemed relatively intact and coherent. As he described it, his homicidal threats were a desperate attempt to control his wife and reestablish a sense of security.

## Discussion

In both of these cases, the emergence of impotence in the male partner over the preceding decades had exerted a significant influence on the dynamics of the marital relationship. Long-term adaptation occurred, which allowed these couples to function but which obscured many of the deeper and unresolved conflicts in the relationship. In both cases, the prescription of sildenafil appears to have disrupted a fragile solution, made perhaps even more fragile by the declining cognitive functioning of the patients and their subsequent rigidity.

The conflicts symbolized in sexuality for these couples—desire and desirability in one case, dependency and usefulness in the other—were un-leashed by the meaning of the drug, and the result was homicidality. However, it is not difficult to imagine that because sildenafil can symbolize many different meanings, it may evoke and exacerbate similar conflicts for other patients, although without such drastic consequences. The psychosocial effects of sildenafil or other medications may be more pronounced and potentially destructive for patients who lack flexibility in their ability to adapt to novel stressors. Such patients would include those with declining cognitive functioning, like the patients in these cases, but they might also include those whose relationship reflects a long-term adaptation to personality disorder in one or both partners or to impaired communication. Mental health professionals and other physicians should be aware that the effects of sildenafil, or any drug, may go far beyond its direct pharmacologic actions.

## Reference

1. Nevins DB: Adverse response to neuroleptics in schizophrenia. International Journal of Psychoanalytic Psychotherapy 142:227–241, 1977.

# Through the Gender Labyrinth: How a Bright Boy with a Penchant for Tinkering Grew Up to Be One of the Top Women in Her High-Tech Field

## Michael A. Hiltzik

*Our gender is an important part of who we are and how we are perceived by others, and for most people the way they experience their gender is consistent with their physical sex characteristics. Indeed, for most people, the idea is probably quite foreign that there could be a divergence between these two aspects of who they are. For others, however, there is a mismatch between their gender identity and their physical sex, and they struggle to hide this fact or to resolve this disparity. It is difficult for most of us to imagine what it is like to be a woman in a man's body or, as is relatively more common, a man in a woman's body. It is also difficult to imagine the adjustments and accomodations that one might make—perhaps even changing one's physical sex—in order to bring one's physical sex and psychological gender in line with one another.*

*As more is learned about the physiology of sex and the mechanisms that contribute to the physical and psychological aspects of our sexuality during embryonic development, societal acceptance of individuals who may not conform to traditional heterosexual expectations grows. With this acceptance comes a greater willingness of people with diverse gender- and sex-related backgrounds to share their experiences and push for increasingly informed professional assistance to lessen their distress. The next article is about Lynn Conway, a professor emerita of electrical engineering and computer science at the University of Michigan, who was once a boy named Robert. This reading describes the complex social and physical transformation that she underwent as she changed from man to woman. As it turns out, Lynn was highly influential in the field of computer science. This adds to the interest of her story, but, as we learn more about transsexualism, it becomes apparent that the struggles Lynn faced are common and affect people from all walks of life.*

## Suggested Readings

Colapinto, J. (2000). *As nature made him: The boy who was raised as a girl.* New York: HarperCollins.
Brown, M. L., & Rounsley, C. A. (1996). *True selves: Understanding transsexualism.* New York: Jossey-Bass.
Middlebrook, D. W. (1998). *Suits me: The double life of Billy Tipton.* New York: Houghton Mifflin.

---

*Los Angeles Times Magazine,* 12–17, 38, 40, 42, 44. (2000, November 19).

Late in 1998, a young researcher delving into the secret history of a 30-year-old supercomputer project at IBM published an appeal for help. As Mark Smotherman explained in an Internet posting, he knew that the project had pioneered several supercomputing technologies. But beyond that, the trail was cold. IBM itself appeared to have lost all record of the work, as if having experienced a corporate lobotomy. Published details were sketchy and its chronology full of holes. He had been unable to find anyone with full knowledge of what had once been called "Project Y."

Within a few days, a cryptic e-mail arrived at Smotherman's Clemson University office in South Carolina. The sender was Lynn Conway, one of the most distinguished American women in computer science. She seemed not only to know the entire history of Project Y, but to possess reams of material about it.

Over the next few weeks, Conway helped Smotherman fill in many of the gaps, but her knowledge presented him with another mystery: How did she know? There was no mention of her name in any of the team rosters. Nor was any association with IBM mentioned in her published résumé or in the numerous articles about her in technical journals. When he probed, she would reply only that she had worked at the company under a different name—and her tone made it clear there was no point in asking further.

What Smotherman could not know was that his appeal for strictly technical information had presented Lynn Conway with a deeply personal dilemma. She was eager for the story of IBM's project to emerge and for her own role in the work to be celebrated, not suppressed. But she knew that could not happen without opening a door on her past she had kept locked for more than 30 years.

Only after agonizing for weeks did Conway telephone Smotherman and unburden herself of an extraordinary story.

"You see," she began, "when I was at IBM, I was a boy."

## Part I: Robert

Nature directs living things into a vast maze of sexual diversity from which our culture provides only two acceptable exits: male and female. Gender is the most fundamental component of our self-image, the foundation of the personality we present to everyone around us. Think of the very first question one asks about a newborn: "Is it a boy or a girl?"

Today the intricacies of gender have worked their way into cultural, scientific, even political debate. Why shouldn't girls compete against boys in math, or on the playground? Would little boys be less beastly if society discouraged rough play? Where, in fact, does our gender identity reside: In our physique? Our brain? Or somewhere deeper, in our soul?

That society has begun to grapple openly with these issues suggests how profoundly absorbing the subject is. "There's a little bit of each gender in each person, so there's something intriguing about what exists on the other side," says George Brown, a psychiatrist at the Veterans Administration Medical Center in Johnson City, Tenn. "But there's also a threat that in exploring the subject I might find out something I feel is very dangerous." This implicit threat may explain why, over the past 30 years, science has learned less about the mysteries of gender than about the origins of the universe.

Transsexualism, the most extreme expression of gender discordance, may be our last taboo. At least 40,000 Americans have undertaken the surgery and therapy to make the transition from male to female and as many as 20,000 more may have gone from female to male. But so strong is the stigma, so blatant the discrimination, that most keep the change a secret by shedding their old lives, jobs and friends along with their old gender. Lynn Conway, among the first Americans to undergo a sex change, came to give the secret life into which it forced her a name: "stealth."

Today Conway lives in a home outside Ann Arbor, where she is professor of computer science emerita at the University of Michigan. Slim and tall, with light brown hair, long, slender fingers and an engineer's unsentimental directness, she says she knew that the operation that changed her gender would consign her to a life of hardship. And she knew it would be worth it. Peering out over the 24 acres of meadow, marsh and woodland she shares with her boyfriend of 13 years in a rural district of lower Michigan, she recalls the risks she confronted three decades ago. "The prediction by everyone then was that what was happening to me would be a disaster," she says. "But sometimes in your gut, you know something is right."

A child, whom for reasons of family privacy we shall call Robert Sanders, was born in Mt. Vernon, N.Y., to a schoolteacher and a chemical engineer who divorced when he was 7. A round-faced little boy with direct blue eyes, Robert by the age of 4 was giving off signals—faint to outsiders but alarming to his parents—that he was not a normal male child. He shunned the other boys and preferred the sedate play of girls in groups. One day, walking through a clothing store in Scarsdale with his mother, he stopped, transfixed by a girl's cotton print dress, one with puffy sleeves like his little friend Janet wore.

"Can I have one like that?"

He had just gotten out the words when he felt as though every eye in the store was fixed on him. "No, you may not have that dress," his mother snapped. "You are *not* a girl!" It was obvious even to his 4-year-old ears that he had committed some terrible blunder, but he did not know what.

From that point on his parents watched carefully for any signs of effeminacy, which they mercilessly exterminated. They cut his hair back almost to the scalp, leaving just enough in the front to be combed back. His mother stopped cuddling him, barely touched him anymore, as though fearing that her previous expressions of maternal love had somehow softened him. He ended up feeling that he was being watched all the time.

The vigilance ebbed slightly after his parents' divorce. Robert's mother was so busy teaching that he and his younger brother, Blair, were left to their own devices after school. The brothers shared an unquenchable interest in nature and science. The house was full of the flotsam and jetsam of their mother's schoolroom assignments—scrap lumber, galvanized tin, all kinds of junk that became the raw material for countless backyard projects. Whatever was not on hand they scrounged during weekend forays to the public dump.

When school ended for the summer, the projects started, fueled by Robert's precocious talent for design and construction. He hand-built a hi-fi system, and then a wood-framed enlarger for the brothers' hobby of photography. In high school he resolved to build a radio-telescope. It was 1952, and searching the skies for radio waves emitted by cosmic bodies—now an indispensable tool of modern astronomy—barely ranked as an authentic scientific application. Nevertheless, Robert studied nonstop, drafted a design, acquired the necessary lumber and aluminum sheeting and, with Blair's help, erected in the backyard a working contraption, 12 feet in diameter. "Robert had this very strong personality trait of studying things well, coming up with a plan and carrying the plan through to completion," Blair says. "There's no stopping a person who continually does that."

What Blair did not comprehend was that his older brother's determination shrouded—or perhaps counterbalanced—deep inner turmoil. With puberty Robert's unremitting feelings of girlishness boiled over, setting up a violent conflict with the inexorable masculinization of his body. He did everything he could to forestall what was happening—surreptitiously shaving his legs, shaping his eyebrows, pilfering women's clothes from relatives' homes. But these pitiable cosmetic measures only sharpened his internal conflict.

In 1950s Westchester County, sex remained firmly outside the bounds of polite discussion, even within families. There was no one he could talk to for support, encouragement or explanation. His mother glared at any signs of incipient effeminacy but never raised the issue in conversation. The denial within Robert's family was fully reflected in society at large.

The prevailing view of transsexualism as a psychological disturbance is both the cause and the result of the poverty of scientific research into the foundation of gender identification. What is known is that there are four broad and somewhat related elements. These can be categorized as genetic, hormonal, physical and neurological. In most cases all four are in sync. A female child inherits one X chromosome from each parent and develops, under the influence of the "female" hormone estrogen, secondary sex characteristics such as breasts and the ability to ovulate. This child has a vagina, uterus and ovaries, and considers herself psychologically a girl. A male child inherits one X and one Y chromosome and develops facial hair and greater muscle mass under the influence of testosterone. This child has a penis and testes and psychologically considers himself a boy. But it sometimes happens that nature, usually so efficient at managing the cascade of biological events that produces a newborn, leaves one or more of these elements out of sync. The Y chromosome might lack a gene allowing the body to respond to the male hormone, in which case the result is an XY female—outwardly indistinguishable from a normal female. The reproductive system is susceptible to a wide range of defects that come under the category of "intersex"—the presence of biological elements of both genders. In a surprisingly high number of births—as many as one in 500, according to pediatric surgeons—a child is born with anomalous genitalia that in the most severe cases leave its gender hard to determine.

In the rarest cases the sole element out of sync is the neurological. The cause and, therefore, the remedy for the mental conviction that one is a whole being trapped in a perfect, but profoundly inappropriate, body is a mystery buried deep in the labyrinth of the mind.

Robert could do little to explore this maze until he left home at 17 to study physics at MIT. University life was liberating. He thrived in the rarefied competition of 900 of the country's brightest high school graduates, finishing his freshman year in the top 2% of his class. For the first couple of years he kept one foot planted uneasily in the "normal" life of a young heterosexual, going out occasionally with groups of male and female friends. On these dates, "he was as normal as any innocent kid," recalls Dorothy Hahn, who married Robert's closest MIT friend, Karl. "He was awkward with girls, but not excessively so."

But release from his mother's repressive scrutiny also gave him the space to air what he sensed was his truer self. He gave his increasingly assertive female persona the name Lynn—a derivative of his middle name—and clandestinely purchased women's clothing from the Sears catalog. When he learned that a group of acquaintances was burgling pharmacies for narcotics, he did a characteristically thorough survey of the endocrinological literature and presented them with an order, crafted with a physician's precision, for injectable estrogen. The hormones did their job. Robert's skin and features softened, his body hair thinned, he began to develop breasts. Gingerly, he began coming out to a few close friends, then wearing women's clothing in public, where his androgynous femininity attracted male attention. A photographic self-portrait from this period shows a waif-like "Lynn" in a modest black dress, hair tucked behind one ear, bare legs shod in simple pumps. Some of his new male friends became lovers, yet Robert never saw these as homosexual relationships, for although his partners knew he was male, they regarded him not as a boy but as a girl, as "Lynn."

This lonely experimentation anticipated what has since become the professional standard in the treatment of transsexuals—the "real life experience," in which the medical and legal systems require patients to live for a year in their "psychological gender" before being judged ready for sex-change surgery. Without professional support, however, Robert's double life—he still attended class as a man—only intensified his profound psychic confusion. By his senior year the strain was starting to tell. His female identity and his black-market hormones were increasingly at war with his body's determination to create the brow ridge and other features that telegraph masculinity to others on a subconscious level.

He started drinking heavily, self-medicating his psyche with buck-a-bottle fortified wine the way he self-medicated his body with estrogen. He expressed abhorrence of his physique and talked about castrating himself to arrest his body's relentless output of testosterone, going so far as to investigate how to create a germ-free environment to undertake the surgery. Karl Hahn, who had transferred to a premedical program at Boston University, was sufficiently alarmed that he found Robert a psychologist.

The man Karl had in mind was a professor at the medical school who reputedly knew something about transsexuality and the available options. (News of Christine Jorgensen's Danish sex-change operation had broken not long before.) At the very least, Karl reasoned, this would provide Robert with a professional shoulder to lean on, someone to assure him that he wasn't going insane, that he need not grapple with his bewildering condition in hopeless isolation.

The consultation began auspiciously. Robert described his feelings of sexual disjunction as the doctor listened tolerantly. Then, abruptly, with a serene detachment that gave his words a horrible finality, he punctured Robert's hopes.

"Unfortunately, there isn't anything you can do to become a woman," he said. Crisply he outlined the stark choices. Robert could cease the hormone-taking and resolve to end this phase of sexual experimentation on his own, or the state of Massachusetts would do it for him, by institutionalizing him as a sexual deviant.

"But I've heard about these operations,"

Robert protested. "I thought you would tell me where to go to get them."

"Those operations don't make you into a woman," came the reply. "They just make you into a freak."

Robert hit bottom. He flunked out of MIT. On what was to have been his graduation day he was in San Francisco, living on the fringes of the gay community, still desperately searching for where he fit. But he found no answers there, because he did not see himself as a gay man attracted to other men, but rather as a woman attracted to men—if only he could rectify nature's dirty trick.

After his hormone supply ran out the following winter, he ended up back home, working days as a repair technician at a hearing-aid company. With Blair away at college, Robert and his mother occupied the house alone, coexisting uneasily in mutual avoidance, rarely speaking, rarely even passing through the same room, lest the slightest physical encounter remind them of the unaddressed issues between them. Having failed to find a community that would have him, Robert felt degraded and humiliated. The silence of the house settled on him like a reproach.

Again, it was intellectual restlessness that stirred him from his torpor. The deadening busywork of hearing-aid repair could not keep him for long, so in 1961 he enrolled at Columbia University. There he once again excelled, earning bachelor's and master's degrees in electrical engineering after only two years. More important, his sterling work landed him a job offer from Herb Schorr, a Columbia instructor who was also a research executive at IBM.

Schorr's secret "Project Y" team was engaged in designing the world's fastest supercomputer. Soon to be renamed ACS, for "Advanced Computing System," the project had the special status of being a pet of IBM's chairman, the imperious Thomas J. Watson Jr., who was irked that his company had fallen behind its rivals in its efforts to reach and hold this prestigious beachhead.

As elite and insular as the Manhattan Project, ACS was shortly relocated to Menlo Park, Calif., where the team of 200 engineers occupied its own building on Sand Hill Road—a stretch of highway famous today as the center of Silicon Valley's venture capital community. For Robert the sheer cerebral bravado of the group was a revelation. Energized by the pioneering work taking place around him, one day he experienced a flash of insight that at a stroke solved one of the team's hardest problems.

The issue, vastly simplified, was how to allow the machine to execute more than one instruction—say, adding, multiplying, or comparing two numbers—at a time. A computer can handle several instructions at once if they are independent—say, if two instructions involve adding two unrelated pairs of numbers. But often one instruction cannot be executed until another is completed—for example the addition of two numbers, one of which is the sum of two others summed by a prior instruction. The trick is to figure out which instructions can be jumped ahead in line.

Robert's insight, which became known as "dynamic instruction scheduling," or DIS, was a way of constantly analyzing a string of instructions and ordering them efficiently while keeping the number of transistors performing these logical tests—still, in the mid-1960s, extremely expensive—to a minimum. Within days the team had incorporated DIS into the ACS architecture. Over the years it would filter into generations of high-performance, so-called superscalar, computers.

Yet as he reached this pinnacle of professional achievement Robert's personal life was coming apart. For he had not moved to California alone.

During the summer between Columbia terms Robert had befriended a co-worker at the hearing-aid company named Sue. (Her name has been changed.) She was a pretty brunet, from a Catholic family working to raise tuition for nursing school. When school resumed that fall they continued meeting socially in the city. They took walks in the park and enjoyed casual lunches, forging a relationship that the inexperienced Robert, oblivious to Sue's real feelings, considered platonic. One night after one of their non-date "dates," Sue

got affectionate and Robert, despite himself, got aroused. The next thing they knew, Sue was pregnant. For months Robert fended off Sue's insistence that they marry, but finally gave in. "I felt like it was a trap," Lynn says. "But the fact there was going to be a baby seemed like a miracle. I really looked forward to it. It was, like, 'Robert's getting trapped, but Lynn gets to have a baby.' I didn't realize the implications."

To friends aware of Robert's psychological struggle, his marriage suggested that he had decided to surrender to living with a permanent dichotomy in his sexual being. For a while that might have been true, as Robert immersed himself in the mundane demands of married life. Their daughter Kelly was born in February 1964. (The daughters' names have been changed.) Amid the excitement of his new work and the daily routine of raising a family on his $15,000 salary, the conflicts of gender seemed to recede. . . .

Meanwhile, the medical establishment was finally starting to acknowledge gender identity issues. In his 1966 book, *The Transsexual Phenomenon*, Harry Benjamin, a prominent New York endocrinologist, not only gave the syndrome a name but also chided his peers for their ignorance: "Even at present, any attempt to treat these patients . . . in the direction of their wishes—that is to say 'change of sex'—is often met . . . with arrogant rejection and/or condemnation." Benjamin wrote of patients he had treated with hormones and steered toward surgery. Robert, however, reacted to this glimmer of professional understanding not with relief but despondency.

As physical masculinization was catching up to him, his marriage to Sue was faltering under the pressure of mutual frustration. Their sexual relations had been rare and unsatisfying, although not nonexistent: A second girl, Tracy, was born in 1966.

He was 28, already raising a family, manacled so firmly into the role of father, husband and man that he felt it would take a Houdini's skills to extricate himself. . . .

On a drive home from a dinner party one evening, he pulled to the side of the road, overcome by feelings of alienation. Breaking down in tears he blurted: "I need to be a woman." It was the first time Sue had heard her husband put his feelings of disaffection into words. But that did not make them easier to talk about. The isolation only seemed to increase. Brooding alone one night in 1967 as Sue and the children slept, he broke down again. Weeping uncontrollably, he dug out a Colt .45 automatic pistol he had used for target practice and placed it to his head. He was holding it when Sue, awakened by the wailing and sobbing coming from the next room, appeared at the door, frozen in shock. The next thing Robert knew, the gun was on the table and Sue was assuring him that they would do anything they could to relieve his torment.

With Sue's consent, Robert contacted Benjamin, then in his 80s and on the eve of retirement. Benjamin agreed to accept him as one of his last patients. Under Benjamin's care, Robert resumed estrogen therapy and prepared for an operation that would remove the physical signs of his maleness and give him female genitalia, the "change of sex" he so ardently desired. The operation would prove to be the easy part.

Robert had visualized a nearly seamless transition from male to female. At IBM he would have his supervisors change his records so that he was no longer Robert, but Lynn, and he would transfer to another lab to start afresh. At home, following the separation and divorce he knew were unavoidable, he would simply visit as "Aunt Lynn"; at 2 and 4 the children should be young enough to barely register the change. But problems surfaced immediately. At work, his supervisor, an engineer named Don Rozenberg, recognized instinctively that IBM possessed exactly the wrong culture to indulge Robert's unprecedented proposal. "It was still white shirts, blue serge suits and wingtip shoes," Rozenberg says. "This simply wasn't the IBM image."

Indeed, IBM corporate management, unable to see how Robert could keep his past secret from his co-workers, feared disruption. "The decision was made," Rozenberg recalls, "to quietly move him

out of the company." For Robert the loss of his job could not have come at a worse time. His sex reassignment surgery, as it was formally known, was scheduled to take place in a few months. It would cost about $4,000—an enormous sum in 1968—not including several thousand dollars in ancillary costs: electrolysis, counseling, hormone therapy. Beyond the financial implications, the stigma of banishment from one of the world's most respected corporations fell upon him like an excommunication.

The few friends and colleagues Robert told of his medical situation identified with Sue, berating him for misleading her and exposing his young family to shame and disgrace. Nevertheless, Robert felt he had to go through with the surgery; it was change or die. In November 1968 he boarded a PSA plane for San Diego, then a bus to the Mexican border and a taxi through Tijuana to the medical clinic of Dr. Jose Jesus Barbosa, a plastic surgeon with an elite practice among affluent Americans. Barbosa also had experience performing the so-called penile inversion procedure, in which the sensitive skin of the penis is used to construct a vaginal canal. In a 4½-hour operation Barbosa transformed Robert's genitalia into those of a woman, fully sensitive and even capable of orgasm.

But the surgery failed to address another issue. Under pressure from family and friends who saw Robert's choice as something depraved, Sue wavered about letting "Aunt Lynn" stay in the girls' lives. Her doubts grew when, after Robert left IBM, the family spent three months on welfare. The troupe of county social workers thus introduced into their lives were openly appalled at Robert's decision. Sue, worried that the children might be taken from her, finally barred the girls' father from their lives on threat of obtaining a court order.

Lynn, now living as a woman, did not underestimate the threat. An encounter with the law would mean public exposure and the undoing of all her efforts to start life over. So she capitulated. Sue granted her a final visit with the children in late January 1969. Dressed as a man for the last time in her life, Lynn spent a few hours watching her towheaded toddlers chase their shadows across the playground of a Palo Alto park and tried to stifle the flood of family memories that washed over her, such as the camping trips on which Robert would hike Yosemite's trails with little Kelly strapped into a carrier on his back.

When the setting sun signaled that the afternoon was drawing to an end, Lynn called to them, enveloped each girl in hugs, and tried casually to deflect their questions about why Daddy had to leave so soon and where he was going. Finally, her heart breaking, she walked away. She would not see either of them again for 14 years.

## Part II: Lynn

... After the operation, Lynn had moved "Robert" out forever. She had her surname legally changed to Conway, after the dynamic heroine of a favorite Helen MacInnes adventure novel, and began life anew.

It was not easy. For one thing her medical history proved a formidable obstacle to employment. Firm after firm made tentative job offers, only to change their minds as soon as she disclosed her condition on medical questionnaires. A local RCA research lab, intrigued by her skills but nervous about her history, offered her a position on condition she pass a psychiatric examination. Years later Lynn produced a copy of the psychiatrist's report from her meticulous files: two stapled pages, with the faded, grainy quality that bespeaks repeated photocopying: "Lynn Conway is a 31-year-old transsexual . . . articulate, composed, attractive, and neatly attired . . . comfortable and optimistic about her life . . . no indication of any abnormal mental trends . . . very superior intellectual capacity . . . [nothing] that would preclude her appropriateness for employment."

RCA withdrew the offer.

Eventually she hooked up with a small company desperate for experienced programmers. That job led to one at Memorex, the recording equipment company, which had decided to plunge into the computer manufacturing business and needed an experienced designer. Her reputation grew, and

in 1972 she found herself weighing the most intriguing offer of her career.

The offer had come from a new electronics lab established by Xerox Corp. in an industrial park adjacent to Stanford University. Xerox, anxious that the emerging technology of digital computing might render obsolete its monopoly in office copying, had hired a few score of the smartest young engineers and scientists it could find, placed them in a California glade as far from its Connecticut headquarters as geography allowed and instructed them to follow their imaginations. The Palo Alto Research Center, or PARC, would eventually oblige by inventing the personal computer, the laser printer, Windows-style computer displays and much more in a legendary burst of innovation.

When Lynn joined PARC in 1973, much of this work was underway. The lab's revolutionary personal computer, the Alto, was already established as an indispensable office tool, each one linked to scores of others via the lab's ingenious data network known as Ethernet. But her own work would follow a slightly different path.

One of PARC's outside consultants, Caltech engineering professor Carver Mead, had proclaimed a revolutionary technical advance in computing. By imprinting ever more miniature circuits on silicon wafers, scientists had turned the traditional axioms of computer design on their heads. Computers were made of devices (transistors) and wires (their connections). Historically the transistors were expensive and the wires cheap, which dictated not only the architecture of the computer but the uses to which it was put—largely sequential, arithmetical computation. But silicon reversed the costs. Transistors, printed on layers of silicon, became cheap, while the infinitesimal connections became the cost bottlenecks. Mead foresaw that the difference would require a new kind of design but would open the possibility of nonarithmetic computation. Computers, Mead wrote, would no longer be big machines, useful only for crunching numbers, but tiny ones "deep down inside our telephone, or our washing machine, or our car."

Lynn was among the few engineers at PARC

to buy into Mead's dramatic rethinking of computing's potential. To his crystalline intuition she contributed the hands-on engineering experience and deep understanding of computer architecture she had gained at IBM and Memorex. ("I had never designed a computer," Mead says. "She had.")

She also contributed the concept of design rules for the new technology of "very large-scale integrated circuits" (or, in computer shorthand, VLSI). These were principles that could be applied to almost any particular VLSI design, the way one can use the same-sized bricks to build an infinite variety of walls. Lynn and Carver Mead codified their work in a textbook that was issued in 1979 as *Introduction to VLSI Systems* or, as it became known to a generation of engineering students, "Mead-Conway."

Mead was already a national figure in engineering, but the book cemented Lynn's reputation. Even before its formal publication she had begun proselytizing about VLSI at universities across the country, including a semester spent teaching at none other than MIT (where she kept her previous matriculation a secret). "It really did change the view the technical world had of the potential of silicon," Mead says. This set the stage for a genuine computer revolution and the ultimate realization of VLSI principles: the Pentium chip, which today powers millions of desktop computers.

In the broadest sense, the intellectual energy of Silicon Valley mirrored Lynn's own flowering, which had begun with her operation. Her mind and body finally synchronized, she felt as though she had been reborn as a new emotional being. "I was experiencing a complete and profound new internal and external reality," she says, "going through what amounted to a second puberty."

Her social life blossomed. She frequented singles bars, sampled the novel technology of computer dating, stayed out dancing and socializing into the small hours. A photograph from the period shows her nestled in the driver's seat of her new red Datsun Z-car in a miniskirt and purple blouse, the prototypical single professional. She

carried on an active sex life and, like any woman in her 30s, contemplated love and marriage.

But she was not like any other woman, and her expectations gradually faded. She got close enough to a number of boyfriends to share her past with them. At that point the relationships typically stalled out. "I backed off, thinking I would never find anybody," she says. "I felt good about myself, but I was also thinking that someone might not want to marry someone like me."

Such episodes reminded her of the ever-present danger of exposure. For the most part she kept the truth behind a shroud. At PARC, a place where your academic credentials were as much a part of your identity as the music you listened to or the books you read, she managed never to let on that she had attended MIT and worked on a pioneering supercomputer at IBM. No one ever probed too deeply: It was as if she emitted some imperceptible signal telling colleagues that there were places in her past where one did not go.

Paul Losleben, a computer engineer who worked with her in a 1980s government program, recalls hiking with her one afternoon in the Palo Alto foothills. "I came away just brimming with new ideas without being really sure where they came from," he says. "I was just overwhelmed by her intelligence, her creativity, her grasp of topic." Only later did he reflect on how little she had given up of herself. "It was as though she was a totally professional person," Losleben recalls, "without any personal side."

For all that, through the '70s and '80s Lynn detected hints that social attitudes toward transsexuality were changing. In 1983, when Lynn was recruited to head a supercomputer program at the Defense Department's Advanced Research Projects Agency, or DARPA, she sailed through her FBI background check so easily that she became convinced that the Pentagon must have already encountered a transsexual or two in its work force.

Transsexualism may not have achieved mainstream acceptance, but at least it was no longer universally viewed as a transgression against nature. For one thing, there was more public awareness of the condition. Eugene Biber, an American plastic surgeon, had performed his first sex-change operation at his clinic in Trinidad, Colo, in 1969. ("Then the grapevine started," says Biber, who has since performed more than 4,500 operations.) Meanwhile, Harry Benjamin's teachings on transsexualism had spread. Stanford University established a program studying the condition, lending transsexuals valuable credibility. From time to time a prominent transsexual was "outed"—in 1976 it was the tennis player Renee Richards—and to the extent she managed to come through the attendant derision with her dignity intact, transsexualism shed a bit more of its eccentricity. By the late 1970s an estimated 1,000 Americans were undergoing the surgery every year.

Lynn had to forge this path herself. Her mother and father died in the 1970s, still refusing to accept Robert's transition. But by then she had already reconnected with her brother Blair, visiting him while he was in San Francisco for an academic conference.

Blair had been aware of her transition, but they had never had a conversation about it. Now they sat in his hotel room, facing the mutual challenge of brother and brother recalibrating their lifelong relationship—this time as brother and sister. For years Blair, now an astronomer at the University of Wisconsin, would struggle to reconcile the male role model of his formative years with this accomplished woman who was part stranger. Over time he found the answer that allowed them to come together again as family. "I think of them now as two different people," he says.

And then, in 1983, Lynn arrived at the most disquieting stretch of uncharted familial territory.

For Kelly and Tracy, their father's absence was a mystery that reasserted itself at regular intervals. At Christmastime, Lynn paid for presents that would appear under the tree marked "Love, Dad"—apparently so designated by Sue without Lynn's knowledge. Kelly recalled blurting to a teacher in kindergarten or nursery school that she had once glimpsed her father wearing women's clothes (the teacher summoned Sue to warn her against such loose talk). And there were the monthly checks of child support, signed by a "Lynn Conway," whom the girls imagined to be a lawyer or agent of some sort.

"I had no memory of my father," Tracy recalls, "although I had the image in my mind of someone really fabulous." Of the two children, it was she who showed the greater interest in their father. When she turned 15 she began peppering her mother with questions. "I was a teenager watching all my friends be Daddy's little girls, and I wanted to know who my dad was."

But her mother, who had spent more than a decade carefully dodging the painful issue of the phantom Robert, was not about to confront it head-on. Instead she chose to deal with the questions at a safe remove. One day while traveling on business, Sue set down the broad details of Robert's transformation in a letter and mailed it home, addressed to Tracy.

Tracy opened the envelope and moments later burst into her older sister's room. "You're not going to believe this!" They read the letter together. There was something about how their father was "no longer a he, but a she," and how their mother knew something was not right with Robert but not exactly what. The letter could not help but raise more questions than it answered, but Sue remained loath to fill in the gaps. The girls struggled with wrenching questions, including the bedrock riddle of why their father, whatever his condition, had stayed out of their lives.

Finally, when Kelly turned 18 in 1983, Lynn made contact. She reintroduced herself via a series of short notes, then called to invite her daughter to their first face-to-face meeting since that desolate day at the playground. The bafflement and denial that had swept over Kelly upon reading her mother's letter two years earlier had given way to a wary curiosity. They met at a French restaurant in Palo Alto, where Kelly, who had never been to such a place, marveled at how every dish seemed slathered in rich sauce. As they ate, neither knew quite what to say. "It was almost like two strangers meeting, because we really *were* strangers," Kelly recalls.

Guardedly she brought Lynn up to date on her

own life—she was already married and had a baby boy at home. But the strained formality of the setting prevented her from raising the most painful issues between them, including the girl's profound feelings of abandonment. Throughout the dinner she stole glances at the unfamiliar woman across the table, as though searching for signs of herself. "I was trying to come to terms with what our relationship was supposed to be," Kelly recalls. "Was she a friend? My dad? An aunt?" The encounter left Kelly impressed by Lynn's humor and intelligence, but also left too many ancient hurts unhealed. "I didn't know after that night if I'd ever see her again," Kelly says. "She'd been away forever, and I didn't know if she'd really be around."

They met a few more times in California. Then in 1985, after Lynn moved to the University of Michigan as a professor and associate dean, she invited Kelly and Tracy to her new home in Ann Arbor, treating them to a shopping trip, lunch at the university, a day of canoeing, a hint of what she had become during all those years offstage.

## Epilogue

The rewards and professional accolades of a distinguished career kept coming in. Lynn received appointments to the board of trustees of MIT's Draper Laboratory and the board of visitors of the U.S. Air Force Academy (commemorated on her kitchen wall by a group photograph of the trustees, all in flight suits, lined up against the red-mountained landscape of Colorado Springs). A figure of undisputed authority in some of the most abstruse corners of computing, Lynn won election to the National Academy of Engineering in 1989.

There was, however, a lingering resentment. DIS, the logic system she had invented at IBM, had become a standard of computer design. Yet others were now claiming credit for the process, years after her brainstorm. Reflecting on her life's tortuous path and wondering if her achievements and those of her IBM colleagues had ever surfaced, she typed the word "superscalar" into an Internet search engine and came up with Mark Smotherman's Web

page. It was headed: "ACS—The first superscalar computer?"

Lynn was not surprised that Smotherman had problems unearthing ACS' history. Shortly after Robert Sanders' firing, the project had landed on the wrong side of an internal power struggle at IBM and been shut down. The team members dispersed and IBM's own institutional memory faded. The one place where that memory resided, as it happened, was in Lynn's files. The corporation had been so intent on ushering Robert Sanders out the door that it had neglected to ask him to return any of the project documents in his possession. Lynn still had them: reams of minutes, memos, diagrams—the complete history of a forgotten breakthrough in computer science.

Lynn wrestled with the infinite complications that would be raised should she make the cache public, thereby "outing" herself. Was she entirely comfortable in her role as a woman? Was there perhaps some hint still of shame? Was she a transsexual who happened to be a woman? A woman who happened to be transsexual? Or simply, at last, a woman?

There were many reasons to remain quiet, but threaded through her own life experience, Lynn also glimpsed a reason to step forward. Tens of thousands of transsexuals—whether they had had their operation, were contemplating one, or had chosen to live as the opposite sex without undergoing surgery—still were forced to make their way alone, as she had. Who could know how many suffered in solitude, unaware of their options and opportunities, of what their predecessors had learned about living with their condition? Only when homosexuality had come out of the closet did enlightenment start to ease the burden of gays and lesbians. Maybe it was time for transsexuals to benefit from the same process. Almost before knowing it, she had decided. Lynn copied the most important papers. After carefully eradicating her old name and inserting the new on every title page, she sent them to Smotherman and a few old colleagues. She was emerging from stealth.

With the same determination she once devoted to designing and building backyard radiotelescopes and room-sized computers, she made contact with old friends, revealed her past and challenged them to see her whole. She directed some to her Web site *www.lynnconway.com*, where she posted a candid "retrospective" of her life. Many were surprised at the information, but no one shunned her. "I reassured her that I had known about it and it was OK then and it was OK now," Carver Mead says.

For Lynn herself, the process meant reexamining a lifetime of decisions and choices. Recently, on a drive home from her office in Ann Arbor, Lynn reflected on the path onto which nature had steered her. "I sometimes think that all this stuff"—the achievements of a hard-fought career—"is overcompensation. If I'd been born 20 years later and transitioned at the age of 20, I probably would have found a husband and adopted kids. But I was just too early, and the transition came just too late." She stopped for a few moments. The tears passed. "But I've got to the point where that's just a fact of life."

Besides, she will tell you, she has too much to cherish now to dwell on regrets.

One day in 1987, at a canoe shop in Ann Arbor, she fell into conversation with a fellow nature enthusiast. She ran into him again a few weeks later at a canoeing outing on the Huron River. He was a professional engineer named Charlie, a hunter and outdoorsman who would introduce her to a passion that resonated with her past: amateur motocross racing.

A new possibility, long renounced, reappeared. Within a few months, they were living together, and by 1994 they were looking for a house to buy. In a rural township about a half hour from Ann Arbor, there was a trim little cottage set on marsh, meadow and wild woodland. Tentatively, as though testing a stove top that had burned before, Lynn sat Charlie down one night and broached a subject she knew she had left too long unaired.

"I think there's something you need to know about me," she said.

"She began filling me in on things I'd never begun to suspect," Charlie recalls. "I've got to say it was a little bit stunning. I was in a fog for a while, absorbing it. But I knew it was probably as hard for her to get into as it was for me to hear it."

He was a single man, never married, distant from his family. Like her, he was a soul looking for companionship, and more. Despite his confusion, he offered reassurance. "On the Huron when we met," he said later, "we were both at a point in our lives where we needed someone like the person we saw the other to be."

That's all Lynn had ever wanted. To be seen by others as she had always seen herself. And that's the person her friends and family members have now accepted. Tracy and Kelly have welcomed her into their lives. To their children she is, at last, their beloved "Aunt Lynn." Says Kelly, "I love her and love for her to be in our lives. We're very close and very similar. To us what happened in the past doesn't matter anymore."

# CHARLES: THE SOUL OF LOVE

## Robert U. Akeret

*Although it would be highly advantageous for psychotherapists to learn whether their interventions are effective over time, in practice this kind of information is rarely available in any systematic form. In an interesting departure from this tradition, Robert Akeret revisited several patients whom he had worked with decades earlier. Dr. Akeret, in the prologue to his book, states that "My world is lopsided with prologues, bereft of endings. It is as if someone had ripped the last pages from all the novels in my library. . . . After devoting my entire adult life to helping people examine and change their lives, I don't really know if I have been effective. . . . Do the changes hold? Or when my back is turned, does it all unravel?"*

*The next reading is an excerpt from one of the chapters in his book, which describes a man named Charles who has a paraphilia. Charles's paraphilia is bestiality, or the sexual attraction to an animal—in this case, a polar bear. Bestiality is very rare, and no doubt sexual attraction to a polar bear is far rarer still. But this reading is remarkable because we learn how this paraphilia came about, the intervention that Dr. Akeret used to eliminate the paraphilia, and Charles's psychological status many years later.*

### Suggested Reading

Laws, D. R., & O'Donohue, W. T. (Eds.). (1997). *Sexual deviance: Theory, assessment, and treatment*. New York: Guilford.

From *Tales from a Traveling Couch: A Psychotherapist Revisits His Most Memorable Patients* (pp. 59–100). New York: Norton. (1995).

\*   \*   \*

"Robi, I've got a thorny case I'd like you to take a look at. Rollo thought you might be the right man for the job. Thinks it needs an unorthodox approach."

It was Dr. Goldman, head of New York University Counseling Services, on the phone. The year was 1965. I was now in private practice.

"What can you tell me about it?" I asked.

"I'd rather not say much. Let you make your own assessment. The young man's name is Charles Embree. Former college student." Goldman paused a second before adding, "He currently works in a circus. . . ."

Embree first came to see me early on a Friday morning. He was a large young man with a round, shaggy-bearded face, long hair, and a rotund torso. There was a broad white bandage above his left eyebrow reaching to his hairline. He ambled up to me lugubriously, turning his head from side to side as he took in the furnishings of my office. . . . I gestured to the seat across from me, and we both sat down.

"So, what brings you here?" I asked mildly.

"I guess I'm having a little trouble making up my mind if I want to stick with my job," Charles replied. He looked me straight in the eye without any visible anxiety as he spoke. His voice was low, a touch gravelly but pleasant. "You know, sometimes I think I should move on to something else. . . . " I nodded to Charles, encouraging him to go on.

"But I love the circus," he said with obvious enthusiasm. "I love just about everything about it—the smells, the cotton candy, the animals." He shrugged and smiled shyly. "I don't know, maybe I just never grew up. I wanted to run away to the circus ever since I was a boy, and now that I'm there, I don't really want to leave."

So far his situation sounded eminently reasonable to me. Heaven knows, I had no trouble identifying with it. In my mind I was jumping ahead, wondering what the problem could be. Did young Charles have parents with more conventional career plans in mind for him? Could this possibly be the "thorny" problem that required the intervention of an "unorthodox" therapist?

"And what's the argument against staying with the circus?" I asked.

Charles shrugged again.

"It's—it's kind of a chancy business," he said, lowering his eyes from mine.

"Chancy?"

"Well, hazardous, actually," Charles said, still not looking back into my eyes.

Aha, that was it. Charles worked in a dangerous act—the high wire, perhaps, or the trapeze. But he did not appear to have the right body type for either of those. Maybe he was the human cannonball. That line of work could make a man seriously consider a career change.

I waited. Charles sighed, dropping his woolly head lower; then he shrugged again.

"I've fallen in love with someone at work," he finally said miserably.

So, it was a hazard of a different sort—a hazard of the heart. Again I waited, but when Charles did not speak for several minutes, I prodded him with "And how is it going?"

"Up and down. Well, not very good, actually." Charles wagged his large head back and forth. Then, with a sudden burst of passion, he said, "I have never been so in love in my life, Doctor. *Never!*"

I looked at Charles sympathetically. For all the hundreds of times the broken heart of unrequited love has revealed itself to me in my office, it is always painful to behold.

"Tell me about—" I stopped myself before I had to commit to pronoun gender.

"She's an incredible beauty." Charles jumped in ardently. "Voluptuous. Intense. Provocative. I've wanted her desperately since the first time I saw her."

"And she?"

"I have to win her over. It's all I really want in life," Charles said breathlessly. "And I think I can. It's just a matter of time."

Charles was now fumbling with something in his shirt pocket. It was a photograph. He regarded it a moment with obvious fondness, then passed it to me.

The photograph showed Charles, thinner and beardless, in a circus ring standing next to a polar bear that was upright on its hind legs. For several seconds the significance of what I was looking at did not register on me. But then, when it finally did, I summoned up every ounce of self-control I had within me to smile calmly and say in a natural-sounding voice, "She's lovely."

Charles's face radiated relief. I had accepted his romance on his own terms.

"Her name is Zero," he offered in a confidential tone, as if this bit of information were a gift of gratitude.

It was then, in delayed response, that my panic set in. By every diagnostic criterion I knew, Charles was a very seriously ill young man. Furthermore, on the basis of my professional experience to date,

I was not well prepared to treat such an unusual disorder. . . .

And then a second wave of panic swept over me. I was starting at the bandage on Charles's forehead, and I suddenly knew why his job had become so hazardous.

"Why did she scratch you?" I asked softly.

Charles looked down at the floor shame-faced.

"She wasn't ready for me," he replied in a hurt voice. "I rushed her, and she wasn't ready."

Without further prodding, Charles went on to tell me exactly how it had happened. . . .

On the night in question—just two weeks before Charles was referred to me—he had remained late in the animal area of the grounds where the circus was playing nearby in New Jersey. Sitting outside Zero's cage, he had guzzled down a six-pack of beer, all the while speaking softly to the bear, telling her how much he cared for her, occasionally tossing her a "bear cookie" through the bars. And then, his courage finally plucked up, he unlocked the cage door and entered, speaking words of love to Zero. She responded by immediately clubbing him on the shoulder with her right paw. Fortunately he had been wearing his leather jacket, and his only injury came from a glancing claw scratch on his forehead. It required fourteen stitches.

I listened to Charles's long narrative with the same outward calm that I had mustered when he initially revealed the identity of his beloved to me. Interestingly, it had already become somewhat easier for me to do this. Had the shock already begun to wear off? I leaned toward Charles.

"What had you hoped would happen between the two of you?" I asked.

Charles shrugged shyly. "I just wanted to show her some affection," he said. "To nuzzle with her a little bit."

"That's all?"

Charles shrugged again, but said nothing.

"Were you sexually excited?" I asked.

Charles looked back at me with an even gaze.

"Genuine affection always leads to sex, doesn't it?" he said, raising his voice in what sounded like a challenge. "That's only natural."

*Natural?* My head was spinning. It was only by transcending the very question of what is "natural" that I had been able to carry on this conversation with such equanimity.

"Natural, maybe, but it certainly does sound hazardous," I replied, offering a benign smile.

Charles hesitated; he was, I think, carefully studying my face for signs of disapproval or derision. He finally smiled back at me.

"The hazards of love." He sighed softly.

I now knew with perfect clarity that above all else, my job with Charles was to save his life, to prevent him from being crushed to death in his paramour's embrace. Whatever work we might do together would be either in service of that goal or secondary to it. In a sense that focus should have made my initial therapeutic decisions easier. It didn't. . . .

Our fifty minutes were nearly over.

"If we are going to work together, you are going to have to make me a promise," I said.

Charles raised his eyebrows.

"You have to promise not to attempt to make love to Zero in any way until our work is over. After that you can do whatever you wish."

Charles scratched at his beard.

"Okay, I promise," he said.

"Good." At that moment I believed him.

Charles rose heavily from his chair.

"By the way, I can only see you for five weeks," he said in an offhand manner.

"Why is that?"

"Because that's when the circus leaves town."

After Charles left, I sat still for several minutes, my mind churning as I tried to make sense of Charles's predicament. What in the name of God did it mean to be in love with a polar bear? What was its emotional content? And what were Charles's emotional expectations for it? Did he really believe that his love for the animal could be reciprocated? Did reciprocation even matter?

I certainly understood what it was to have a personal relationship with a domesticated animal; I had had one with my horse when I was a boy. I knew what it was to go alone into a stable and tell my deepest secrets to a four-footed animal and to believe that the look in his eye showed that he comprehended every word I said that he empathized with me totally. . . . But what Charles had described to me was love of an entirely different order. It was deep and romantic. It was an alternative to loving another human being. And yet, like the most mature interhuman love, it was a love that led "naturally" to sex.

Zoophilia, the drive to have sexual relations with animals, is a subcategory of paraphilia, so named because the deviation (*para*) lies in that to which the individual is attracted (*philia*). Also included in this category are the more common disorders of exhibitionism, fetishism, frotteurism (compulsive "mashing" of strangers), pedophilia, sexual masochism, sexual sadism, transvestism, and voyeurism. What all these disorders have in common, the *Diagnostic and Statistical Manual of Mental Disorders* declares, is sexual arousal in response to objects or situations "that are not part of normative arousal activity patterns."

But on that day in 1965 none of the books on my shelf had an entry for "paraphilia," only for "sexual deviations and perversions." And there, listed along with pedophilia and fetishism, was an "abnormal arousal activity pattern" called homosexuality.

Incredible. . . .

There was one intriguing clue in the general definition of perversion offered in the *Diagnostic Manual*. It said that these disorders "in varying degrees may interfere with the capacity for *reciprocal, affectionate activity*." Indeed, that was certainly a serious problem for Charles with Zero.

But that was also a problem for the great majority of my patients with their husbands, wives, and lovers.

There really was only one diagnostic question I needed to answer about Charles, and that was whether he was sexually attracted to his bear *in spite* of the danger she represented or because of it. Was he the very soul of love that he claimed to be? Or was he self-destructive—a sexual masochist? This was not an academic question that I could puzzle over at my leisure. My five-week clock was already ticking.

When Charles came in the following Monday, I immediately sensed something different about his appearance, but several minutes passed before I could identify what it was: His beard was several shades lighter than it had been on Friday. He had bleached it, and I instantly knew why: Charles wanted to look more like a polar bear. I now realized that this was what his beard was about in the first place. *And* his shaggy hair. *And* his increased girth. It was all part of Charles's campaign to win Zero over. I complimented him on the job he had done on his beard.

"Looks good," I said. "Maybe it will help."

Charles smiled, obviously pleased.

I was sticking with my first instinct, to take Charles's courtship of Zero seriously. I was going to proceed as if I had two equal choices to consider: either to help Charles make his relationship with Zero more fulfilling or to help him release himself from an impossibly dangerous liaison with her. If I pressed for only the latter goal, I was certain I would lose Charles's trust. Truth to tell, deep in my "unorthodox" heart, I believe that if I had discovered there really was a way that Charles could have lived with Zero happily and safely ever after, I would have helped him seek it.

I decided to move ahead with Charles as I would have with any other case, by drawing out his personal history. I would listen, alert to clues to how he got into his "hazardous" situation in hopes of finding a clue to resolving it. I certainly did not expect to come up with some comprehensive theory that accounted for why this particular man had become eroticized by a bear. I doubted there was any such theory that I would find acceptable, just as, for example, I am skeptical of theories that purport to explain why this particular person became gay and this one did not. Such theories usually strike me as circular, ultimately citing the effect as proof of the cause.

But again I was in for a surprise.

This is the story Charles told me.

He was the sole and unexpected child of an older couple. His father, Padraic, a wealthy industrialist, was already retired by the time Charles was born, and his mother, Katherine, sickly and depressive, spent most of her time in bed. They all lived on a remote country estate where day after day would pass with barely a word exchanged, even at meals. Charles could recall only one occasion when he saw his parents touching each other. He could not remember his father ever touching him.

His father had a singular obsession: his college, Bowdoin. He felt he owed his enormous success to that institution and so was deeply involved in alumni affairs—fund raising, organizing reunions, recruiting talented applicants. His home, his clothing, even his car were replete with the Bowdoin emblem, a legacy of its most illustrious alumnus, the Arctic explorer Robert Peary, '77. That emblem was a polar bear.

"There were polar bears everywhere," Charles told me. "On the lamps, on the ashtrays, the glassware, the hooked rugs. We had Bowdoin chairs with polar bears painted on the backs in all twenty-two rooms of the house. Father had a carved polar bear pipe stand. He had polar bears painted on the sides of the station wagon that the chauffeur drove me to school in. And for my birthdays and Christmas, I always got a stuffed polar bear. I can't remember ever getting anything else. I had a good thirty of them by the time I was thirteen."

These images of the polar bear had the status of powerful totems in the Embree household: They were loved and worshiped for the gift of success that the Great Polar Bear had bestowed on Padraic. And for young Charles, these bears were more than gods; they were his sole companions. The fact is there were far more polar bears in young Charles's life than there were people, and those bears were infinitely more accessible to him than people for both intimacy and comfort.

"When I was about five, Father gave me this stuffed polar bear who was bigger than I was." Charles went on. "Her name was Lucky, and I took her with me everywhere. I had these conversations with her that would go on for hours. We'd talk about everything, absolutely everything. Lucky made jokes and gave me advice about stuff. And sometimes, when something sad happened or when we were feeling particularly lonely, we would cry together. . . . Every night I fell asleep in Lucky's arms. I loved that bear. *We loved each other.*"

I asked Charles if he spoke for Lucky during his conversations with her, but he shrugged without answering. He went on.

"When Mother gave me a bath, she called my behind Big Bear and my penis Little Bear," he said. "You know, like, 'Make sure you wash Little Bear or he'll feel left out.' "

Later in the hour he reported, "Sometimes, when Mother was feeling well enough, she liked to play this game with me where she'd put on a big fur coat—usually, she'd just put it on over her slip—and she would hunt me. She'd hide behind a door waiting for me, and when I got close, she'd suddenly pounce on me. She'd wrap her arms around me and nip at my stomach with her mouth, growling all the time."

"Like a bear," I commented.

Charles turned up his palms, as if to say, "Of course."

"And you enjoyed this game?" I asked.

"Sure. It was scary, but I loved it."

*Incredible.* Could Charles be making all of this up? It was beginning to sound almost comic, as if a Hollywood scriptwriter had been asked to cook up a plausible etiology of Charles's sexual obsession. I was little surprised by what Charles told me next.

"I was still sleeping with Lucky when I was twelve. She was all worn down from years of handling. Anyhow, one night when I was stroking her. I started to get excited. You know, an erection. And the next thing I knew I came all over her. A wonderful surprise. It was my first orgasm."

This soon became a regular practice. . . .

Charles saw his first live polar bear at the age of fourteen, when his father took him to the zoo for the first time.

"It was overwhelming," he told me. "I felt so excited, I couldn't stop dancing around in front of the bars. She was so big. She was alive. She moved on her own. She looked right at me. I couldn't believe it. I told my father that when I grew up, I wanted to take care of bears."

"And what did he say?"

"Oh, I'll never forget what he said," Charles

told me, leaning his heavy body forward in his chair. "He said that polar bears were incredibly dangerous. But that the greatest test a man can have is to face real danger."

"And do you remember how that made you feel?"

"Yes. I was sure he was dead wrong," Charles said. "I thought you didn't need to be brave to face a bear. You just needed to be kind and loving."

It was at this point in Charles's life that both his parents began warning him about the dangers of women. They were gold diggers, his father had solemnly informed him, his mother adding that most of them had contagious, fatal diseases.

Seven years later, at the age of twenty-one, Charles had his fateful first encounter with Zero. He had gone to the circus with a college friend. There, late in the evening, Glorious Glorianna came into the center ring with three polar bears and proceeded to put them through their act of dancing, juggling, and jumping through hoops.

"I was mesmerized by Zero from the first moment I saw her," Charles told me. "I couldn't take my eyes off her. My heart started pounding. I broke into a sweat. It was like kismet or something. I fell in love with her right then and there. That night, when I got home, I couldn't get her out of my mind."

"Did you masturbate?"

"Yes."

"While thinking about her?"

"Yes."

"Did she remind you of Lucky?" I ventured.

Charles shrugged.

"I'm just wondering why Zero and not the other two bears." I pressed on.

For the first time that day Charles glared at me scornfully.

"*Why does anybody fall in love with anybody?*" he retorted, raising his voice. "There is just a connection, that's all. You know, like, 'Strangers in the Night. . . . ' "

So ended my second session with Charles. It left me feeling even dizzier than the first.

Did I now have a theory accounting for why Charles had become sexually fixated on a polar bear? The question is almost laughable. The truth is that if I had been asked to design a developmental model for creating a human being who would become sexually fixated on a polar bear, I could not have done a better job. In fact, considering the progression that Charles had just described to me, it was hard to imagine his having developed a primary sexual attraction to anything *other* than polar bears. Certainly not to human beings.

It was as if Padraic and Katherine Embree had deliberately covered all their bases. No brothers, sisters, or other playmates for Charles—just lifelike stuffed polar bears to talk to and play with. No loving parental contact—just bears to cuddle with. Even in her rare physical contact with Charles, Katherine had pretended to be a bear, a thrilling furry bear who nipped seductively at his naked belly. Charles was specifically taught to identify his genitalia with bears, making the sexual connection complete. And just in case Charles had any budding attraction to human women, he was informed that they were evil disease carriers. . . .

Things did not go well in the following weeks.

Charles struck me as so conscious and rational that I thought I could try dead-on logic with him. Yes, you love Zero, I argued, but there is no way you can ever get her to love you. Surely, you see that? But Charles argued back bitterly that I had no faith in the power of love. It would ultimately prevail over Zero's resistance.

On the surface this sounds like a pathological delusion, but in fact, Charles's response was no different from most of my other patients who were stubbornly stuck in impossible relationships. It will work out, they would insist. It just needs time. Love is never easy, but it conquers all.

Another week passed, and Charles was getting plumper with every visit. His hair and beard were now bleached completely white. I again complimented him on his bearlike appearance. I was getting absolutely nowhere.

Then I came up with what I thought was an ingenious approach. Look, I suggested in reasonable tones, Zero most certainly loves you, too, but she cannot control her dangerous beastly impulses no matter how much she would like to. So you have to help her control them, and this will necessarily entail extreme measures. Why don't you subdue her with an injection of tranquilizers whenever you want to be intimate with her?

As I expected, Charles found this idea extremely repugnant. It was disrespectful of Zero; it amounted to nothing less than premeditated rape. Charles became furious with me because my approach "dehumanized" Zero. But she wasn't human; that was my point. Couldn't Charles see that his novel situation required novel rules of conduct? How, indeed, did he intend to make Zero "safe"? If not this extreme measure, then what?

But Charles would not budge beyond his fury at my "insulting" suggestion, and he remained angry at me for the next four sessions. Three weeks had passed, and I was running out of ideas.

On Monday of the fourth week Charles did not show up for his scheduled hour. Nor did he that Friday or the following Monday. I became so concerned about him that I would sometimes find myself worrying about him while I was working with other patients—a cardinal sin in my profession. On Monday I finally called the circus in New Jersey. The woman who took my call was surprisingly circumspect. She would tell me nothing about Charles, just that she would take a message for him.

On Friday Charles came into my office at his appointed hour with a wide white bandage circling his neck and his right arm in a sling. He let himself down in his chair gingerly, flinching from pain. I did not ask him what had happened. I did not need to.

"I thought we had a deal," I said after a long silence.

Charles shrugged. "We weren't getting anywhere anyhow," he replied, not looking at me.

"We still have time."

"We're virtually finished," Charles said.

"*You* are virtually finished," I retorted sharply. "Look at you! . . ."

I now suspected that I had done absolutely everything wrong with Charles. By initially accepting his love of Zero as "normal," by demonstrating that it was a "natural" outcome of his upbringing, I had given Charles corroboration of his passionate impulse. In a sense I had given his love the one thing it was missing: "parental" approval. Then, by turning around and hammering away at Zero's dangerous "bestial" nature, I had pushed Charles into the position of defending her, of "standing up for the one he loved." He certainly did sound as though he were more attached to her now than when he had come in four weeks ago.

I looked over at Charles. With his neck swathed in white bandages and his bushy beard whiter than ever, he did indeed look wild and woolly, half man, half beast. At that moment he looked to me as if he really did belong in a cage.

It was not too late for that. I could suggest that now, and if Charles refused to commit himself to a mental hospital—and I was pretty sure he would refuse—I probably could convince his parents that it was in Charles's best interest that *they* commit him. I would tell them that he needed to be incarcerated as a form of "protective custody." There was not a doubt in my mind that one more nocturnal trip into Zero's cage would finish Charles off for good. I no longer cared if his incarceration amounted to an admission of my own failure. I would not be able to live with myself if a lapse in my professional judgment were to contribute to Charles's death.

I was literally within seconds of putting this plan into action when a remarkable idea popped into my head—remarkable yet, in retrospect, totally obvious.

"You know, Charles, neither of us has really been fair to Zero in here," I said. "I mean, you're always talking about how you feel about Zero, and I'm always talking about how I feel about your relationship to Zero. But she's always left out of it."

Charles eyed me warily. "What are you talking about now, Doctor?"

"I'm talking about respect," I said. "I'm talking about there always being two sides to every relationship, and I've been hearing only one."

Charles looked apprehensive. I took that as a good sign.

"You see, I think you are right, Charles: You and I have done just about all we can do together at this point." I went on. "So let me tell you what I usually do with couples who are having problems like yours: I see them together. So I can hear both sides. Couple therapy."

Charles's jaw had sagged. I did not want to give him a chance to argue with me, so I immediately stood up, walked over to my closet, and withdrew my jacket.

"Let's go," I said.

Charles remained seated.

"I—I don't really see—" he stammered.

"What have we got to lose?" I interjected, opening my office door. I knew *I* had nothing to lose; this was my last chance.

Charles hesitated a moment longer, then lifted himself heavily out of his chair and followed me out the door. . . .

Charles drove us to New Jersey in his car, a Volkswagen "beetle" that barely accommodated his hefty torso behind the wheel. I offered to drive, considering that Charles's injury left him with only one arm to steer, but he declined, saying that he felt uneasy when other people drove. He immediately switched on the radio to an "easy listening" station. I was happy not to have to talk. . . .

The circus was set up on fairgrounds not far from the Palisades. . . . Charles silently led me past the closed concession stands, their red and gold trim glinting in the late-morning sun, to the rear of the big top. There, on the far side of a parking lot, was the animal area. As we approached, I could see the heads of several elephants parading inside their pen. One of them looked directly at me with a single beady black eye as we walked by, then raised his trunk and gave a short toot. Horses were next, then lions. The final three cages were somewhat removed from the others; each contained a single polar bear. . . .

Zero was in the last cage in the row. She was sitting upright, her legs bowed in front with her heels together, her arms resting easily in her lap. In this position she looked remarkably benign, almost like an oversized teddy bear. She was considerably smaller than either of the males, only about six hundred pounds.

She immediately turned her head toward Charles as we came into view. Charles smiled, nodding gently, but said nothing. For a couple of seconds they silently regarded each other. I would not presume to guess what was going on in that bear's mind or heart, but what I saw went beyond mere recognition, even beyond the acknowledgment of long-standing comfortable familiarity that, say, transpires between my horse and myself when I approach her. What I saw passing between Charles and Zero looked remarkably like human intimacy.

At that moment I tried with all of my imagination to empathize with Charles, to feel what it would be like to love this bear as a man loves a woman. To lust after her. I confess that I could not do that. I could not even get a sense of what it would be like. I can pop myself into the leading role in many a strange fantasy, but this was not one of them.

Now Zero saw me and rose on all fours, emitting a soft growl. She clearly was not pleased with my presence. I quickly surveyed the area. There was no one else in sight. I turned to Charles.

"Okay, let's get started," I said.

Charles folded his arms across his chest. I could see a sneer of resentment forming on his lips.

"You came all the way out here to make a fool of me, didn't you?" he said, spitting out the words.

"No, that's not true," I replied softly.

"Well, this is ridiculous, and you know it." Charles continued bitterly. "You don't understand Zero. You can't possibly understand her."

"I know that," I said. "But *you* understand her. I can see that very clearly."

"And what's that supposed to mean?" he said challengingly.

"It means that you can help her out," I said. "Help her express what she feels. Give her a voice."

My heart was pounding. I was flying by the seat of my pants, improvising as I went along.

"What are you talking about now, Akeret?"

"I have some questions for Zero," I said. "Some

things that might be helpful to know. I wondered if you could help her answer them."

Charles stared back at me. I noticed that under his beard his cheeks were reddening. He did not protest. I jumped in.

"What I would like to know," I said quietly, "is what it feels like being locked up in there?"

"I hate it!" Charles shot back. He looked surprised at the vehemence of the words that came out of his mouth.

"Why's that?"

"Why? Because it drives me crazy, that's why. Stir crazy. I can barely turn around in here. And I don't have a shred of privacy. It's degrading!"

I did not have time to wonder how or why Charles had entered so completely into his role as Zero. It was incredible. It was wonderful. I pressed on.

"You must be angry then," I said.

"You bet I am!"

"Who are you angry at?"

Charles took a deep breath. He hunched his shoulders, then shot his right hand forward, as if pawing the air.

"Glorianna," he replied. "Most of all, Glorianna and her goddamned whip. But the others, too. Jack and Tulio."

"And Charles?" I said.

Charles hesitated. He slowly turned back to the cage and looked at Zero. She had come up to the bars and was standing on her hind legs, looking out at us.

"No, not Charles," Charles replied softly. "Charles cares for me."

"Is that so?" I said. I was operating on sheer instinct. "Then why don't you ask Charles to let you out of there? If he loves you, he should be willing to do that for you."

Charles's face flushed, and I could see beads of sweat forming on his forehead. . . .

Suddenly Charles turned back to me. He was trembling, and there were tears in his eyes.

"I don't like this game, Akeret," he said. "It stinks. You're a cruel man. Very cruel."

I stared back at him.

"I could kill you, Charles," I said.

"What?"

"I am speaking for Zero now," I said. I let this sink in and then repeated, "I could kill you, Charles."

Charles turned slowly back to the cage. He was looking directly into Zero's eyes.

"Maybe you should," he whispered. "Maybe you should kill me, Zero. God knows, I've failed you over and over again."

He loved her. He really did. And that, of course, was all I had to work with.

"Sometimes I really would like to kill you," I said. "But if I did, they would kill me. Put me down immediately. They always do that when an animal kills a human, no matter whose fault it really is. They have to."

Charles's chest was heaving. I could see that tears were slipping down his cheeks now.

"I—I'm sorry, Zero," he stammered.

"Leave me alone, Charles," I said softly, tenderly. "Leave me in peace. Please, please, just leave me."

Charles was sobbing. Several minutes passed before he spoke.

"All right, Zero," he whispered. "I'll leave you in peace."

Charles turned slowly back to me, still crying hard. I walked up and hugged him, like a father embracing a long-neglected son.

I stayed with Charles for the rest of that day while he packed up his things and made his goodbyes, then helped him move into a friend's apartment in Manhattan that afternoon. In my judgment, our work had just begun that day, and I was eager to see where we would go with it next. Perhaps I had saved his life, but only for now. In the long run I hoped to help him live not only a longer life but a more fulfilling one.

Charles said he would see me the next day at his scheduled hour, but he did not show up. Nor did he show up the next day or the next. I tried calling him, but to no avail. Two weeks later a letter arrived from him posted in London. It contained a postal order for sixty dollars, his outstanding bill. His note read: "I wish I could say that I was happy, but I can only say that I am alive.

Yet for that you have my undying gratitude. Charles."

The hallway outside Charles's Sarasota apartment was strewn with open cartons containing books, folders, newspaper clippings, and photographs. I hesitated in front of his door. Over the past thirty years I had often been visited by terrifying images of Charles's creeping back into Zero's cage for one final fatal assignation. When I located Charles in Florida and discovered that he was alive and well and holding joint appointments at the theater department of the University of Florida and at Clown College, I felt a terrific burden lift off me. That, I thought as I stood at Charles's door, was as much satisfaction as I could ask for. . . . I was seized by the urge to turn around and leave well enough alone.

I didn't, of course.

Charles opened after a single knock, grabbed my outstretched hand, and shook it hard.

"My savior!" He laughed.

He was heavier than when I saw him last and was completely bald on top with a short white fringe of hair on the sides and a neatly trimmed white beard. Obviously he no longer needed bleach for this effect. He wore metal-rimmed glasses that gave him a decidedly Kriss Kringle appearance. He looked cheerful and surprisingly old. He removed a pile of circus posters from an upholstered chair and gestured for me to sit down.

"One of these years I'm going to clean this place up," he said with a smile. "Not that anybody ever comes up here."

The hallway had only been a preview of Charles's interior decorating style. His entire duplex apartment was overflowing with books, papers, and various models and artifacts of circus life, including scores of juggler's balls and clubs. The decor may have been typical of an eccentric professor's retreat, but I could not help seeing it as an animal's lair.

Before he said another word, Charles rubbed the sleeve of his shirt over the cover of a book and handed it to me. It was a text on the history and art of juggling. The authors were Charles Embree and Yvonne Armato.

"It's in its ninth edition," he said proudly.

"Fabulous!" I replied, much impressed. "You've certainly made a life of it, haven't you? The circus, I mean."

"It's my whole life," Charles replied, clearing a spot on the sofa so he could sit down across from me.

"So, who was your coauthor, this, uh, Yvonne Armato?" I asked, consulting the cover again.

Charles's face flushed. "You always did have a nose for the nub of things," he said.

I nodded.

"It's a long story," Charles said, looking a bit uncomfortable.

"I like long stories."

"Yes, I remember that, too," Charles said. He took a couple of slow, deep breaths, like an acrobat preparing for a dangerous jump.

"I've been thinking about your visit ever since you called me up out of the blue," he said. "What I was going to tell you and what I wasn't. Rehearsing. That's something I always tell my juggling students: Performance is easy; rehearsal is hard."

I smiled.

"Anyhow, I decided that one thing I wasn't going to talk about was Yvonne," he said.

"That's certainly your privilege," I said.

Charles abruptly laughed. "But I've suddenly changed my mind," he said. "I always tell my students that the best performances are pure improvisation."

I laughed with him.

"But let's start first with day one, uh?" he said. "I suppose you know that little trip we took out to New Jersey a couple hundred years ago sort of gave me a new perspective on my life. An epiphany you'd probably call it. Although I've always wondered if you really had any idea what was going on in my mind that day."

He eyed me critically over the tops of his glasses.

"Probably not," I said. "But for the record, I thought that you got a very hard look at what could happen if you didn't change."

"You believed I was operating out of love, didn't you?" he said, an edge to his voice.

"Yes, I do," I replied.

"Well, I'm afraid you were wrong," he said triumphantly. "The only love I felt that day was for myself. Self-love. My little epiphany was nothing more than the remarkable realization that living was better than dying. That there was more of a future in it."

I smiled. I did not entirely believe that was all there was to Charles's change of heart that long-past day in front of Zero's cage, but I could very well understand his need to deny a more selfless motive. I still believed that his basic decision had been to sacrifice his love for his beloved's sake, but I also knew that would have been a terrible decision to live with for the rest of his life; a selfish change of heart is less susceptible to the pain of regret.

"So, where did you disappear to after that?" I asked.

"I trekked all over Europe for months," he said. "I took in every circus I could find, from Copenhagen to Sardinia. It was the first time I ever saw small, one-ring circuses, and they were a wonder to behold. Artistic, not glitzy. Intimate. Full of real drama, not just effects. I fell in love with the circus all over again. . . .

"When I came back to New York, I landed two jobs right off the bat. Two perfect jobs. One was cataloging masks in Low Library up at Columbia University. They have this incredible mask collection. And my other job was at this club Andy Warhol had just started downtown, The Electric Circus. I juggled and did a little mime I'd picked up in Europe. This was the sixties, and the clubs were all strobe lights. Let me tell you, just about anybody can look good doing mime under strobe lights."

Charles chuckled. . . .

"All right, now we come to Yvonne." Charles said after a moment. "She was a student of mine at Fordham. That was my first teaching job, probably the first position teaching circus arts at any major university. Yvonne was a drama major who wanted to be a juggler, and she was a natural. Great balance, great reflexes. Quick learner. I immediately put her in my act at The Electric Circus. We passed seven clubs at a time. Big hit.

"She was my student for four years, and then I married her. It seemed like the natural thing to do. We had big plans. We created our own commedia company in the Venice style—stilt walking, masks, mime, juggling. We gave performances in a loft down in the Bowery and sometimes in Central Park. Those were fabulous years, the best circusing I've ever done."

Charles sighed a deep and troubled sigh. The Yvonne story was not going to end well, that was for sure.

"We wrote the juggling book together just a couple years after we were married. Yvonne did the photographs. That was in '72. That means it's been in print for over twenty years, right? Well, a couple of years ago I told the publisher to change Yvonne's last name on the new edition. Make it her maiden name again."

"How long were you married?"

"Ten, almost eleven years." Charles gave me a hard look. "She left *me*, if that's what you're wondering. Ran off with a handsome young man, an actor. She broke my heart. Completely and utterly broke my heart. Smashed it right in two."

Charles's Kriss Kringle twinkle had completely vanished.

"The hazards of love, eh, Akeret?" he said caustically.

That line echoed across thirty years. I was once again reminded that a fourteen-stitch claw cut was nothing as compared with a broken heart. One question after another surged in my mind: Had he loved Yvonne the same way that he had loved Zero? How had the sex gone with Yvonne? What was the transition from bear to woman like? Had he ever completely gotten over Zero?

But Charles had started talking again, and now the source of that edge in his voice was becoming clear: It was bitterness. . . .

"Anyhow, it took me ten years to get over Yvonne." Charles suddenly went on, his voice vulnerable-sounding again. "God knows, I tried to win her back. I asked her what had gone wrong, and she just said that there wasn't enough feeling there for her. Not enough *passion*. I guess she found that with this other guy. The sex, the passion."

This was the opening I'd been waiting for, but I hesitated, not sure how wise it was to press on. My curiosity won out.

"And was the passion there for *you*, Charles?"

Charles lowered his eyes. For a long moment he was silent.

"You mean, like it was with Zero?" he said.

"Yes, like with Zero."

Charles took a deep breath and let it out slowly. "She's dead, too, you know," he said. "Died young. Caught the flu and died."

"I'm sorry to hear that."

Charles was again silent.

"So, you want to know about me and passion, uh?" he said at last. "Well, there's not a whole lot to say. Remember that movie *A Clockwork Orange*? Remember at the end when they conditioned that boy to cut off his feelings the moment he felt them? Well, that's me. If you flashed a picture of a polar bear, I'd respond, all right. I'd get excited, but then right away I'd get cut off. That was my cure. Instant cutoff from all passion. . . . Hey, it saved my life, right, Akeret?"

I did not answer. I just sat there, stunned. For thirty years I had worried that my therapy with Charles had failed in the worst possible way—that overcome with passion, he had searched out Zero and sneaked back into her cage for a final, fatal encounter. That was not hard to imagine. After all, how long did I expect the effects of a few minutes of therapy in front of a bear cage to last? Improvised therapy at that?

But what Charles was telling me was that our therapy had worked beyond my wildest expectations. It was as if I had subjected him to the most extreme form of aversion conditioning, complete with electric shocks. And it had worked so well that *all* of Charles's sexual passion had been cut off. To save his life, I had amputated his soul—his soul of love. I very much doubted that this was the whole story; it could not possibly be as simple as that. But I was sure that was the way Charles saw it. Little wonder he felt so bitter toward me.

Yet now I saw that Charles was looking at me with a warm smile, a smile that seemed to promise the possibility of forgiveness. . . .

"Are you as hungry as I am?" he asked.

"I sure am."

"You buying, Doctor?"

"You bet."

Charles took us to a café called The High Wire, up near Venice. The walls were covered with photographs of circus people and circus acts going back a hundred years. Prominent among them was an enlarged photograph of the famous midget Tom Thumb, standing on the flexed biceps of a strong man. It was midafternoon, but the place was packed, and Charles seemed to know everyone there. After I had spent the morning with him in his solitary, claustrophobic apartment, it was a pleasure to see him out among people with whom he seemed so comfortable. . . .

It was only a few minutes later that two tall, leather-clad young women—one blond, the other a redhead—approached our table. Charles introduced them as Rikki and Gretchen.

"Are you circus performers, too?" I asked.

"Why, of course," Rikki replied rather haughtily. "We work with Charles. Didn't he tell you?"

Charles's face flushed. Gretchen gave his beard a playful yank, and the two women moved on to friends at another table. Charles lowered his eyes. I busied myself with my salad.

"Look, I'm just wired differently from other people," Charles said quietly, not looking up. "Always have been."

"And I don't judge people," I replied. "Never did."

Without thinking why, I reached my hand across the table. Charles took it, and we shook warmly. A few minutes later he jotted a downtown Sarasota address on a napkin and handed it to me.

"It's called the Pyramid Club," he said. "Our act goes on at around midnight."

I said that I would be there. . . .

I would not be telling the truth if I claimed that I felt perfectly at ease inside the Pyramid Club. For starters, I was overdressed, if that is the right word.

Much of the clientele, men *and* women, wore tight-fitting leather pants and open leather vests over bare torsos. I was also easily the oldest person there, a good thirty years above the average age. Some of the couples were obviously gay; others I was not so sure of, in part because the cross-dressers among them were so artful.

Rather than take a table, I sat at the bar and ordered a glass of white wine. The music was loud and strident; the dancers on the narrow space in front of the stage were athletic and introspective; although they danced in couples, they all seemed to be doing solos. I looked at my watch: five to twelve.

Moments later the music stopped. A muscular young man in lederhosen rolled out a drum set, sat down, and beat a fanfare. Then another young man, wearing tails but no shirt, stepped to the microphone.

"The best things in life go around in circles," he said sardonically. "That is why we all love the circus so." And then, after another drumroll, he introduced the first act, "Gretchen, Rikki, and *the Professor*!"

Charles came out alone, dressed as Pierrot in white tights, three-cornered hat, and mask. He took a deep bow to scattered applause. The march from Prokofiev's *Love for Three Oranges* issued over the sound system. Charles produced three oranges and proceeded to juggle them, then added another and another until there were seven in all. He was very good, casually adept and quite funny; he would act as though he'd completely forgotten one of the airborne oranges until it was almost too late, then dive and catch it just before it hit the ground. The audience seemed unimpressed, restless.

Then Rikki, the tall blond woman I had met that afternoon at The High Wire, stepped out onto the stage. In opera hat, red tails, and knee-high boots over fishnet stockings, she reminded me of Marlene Dietrich in *The Blue Angel*. All she wore under her jacket was a lace half bra, bikini panties, and a garter belt. In her right hand was a black, long-handled whip. Rikki was the circus ringmaster/mistress, and she found her juggler wanting.

"Higher!" she demanded of Charles. "Can't you get it up any higher?"

Laughter rippled through the audience. They were watching the show attentively now. Charles looked beseechingly at Rikki and trembled, then tossed the oranges higher. I felt a knot twisting in the pit of my stomach.

A high-flying orange sailed out of Charles's reach and landed with a splat at the ringmistress's feet. She immediately lashed out at Charles, the long whip wrapping around his torso, the tip snapping sharply against his chest. Even from where I was standing at the bar, I could see Charles wince, his eyes smart. Suddenly all the oranges were falling to the floor. Rikki snapped the whip at Charles again and again. The audience was spellbound.

The knot in my stomach had risen to my throat. I swallowed hard, trying to hold it down. I wanted to turn away, but I forced myself to keep watching as now Gretchen paraded out onto the stage and joined them. Gretchen peeled off her black stockings and proceeded to bind Charles's hands and feet with them. Both women began whipping him hard, as the music blared on. I felt nauseated. I was utterly revolted by the spectacle of this aging, white-bearded man being beaten—this misbegotten, frail-hearted boy I had once tried so desperately to save from his own tragic impulses.

*Disgust . . . revulsion . . . nausea.* Was this the reaction of a man who did not judge? Of a therapist who had prided himself throughout his long career on always being suspect of "official" concepts of normal behavior? When it came down to cases, was I a prude in liberal's clothing? Did I find some "perversions" acceptable, while I found others disgusting? Forget about the paraphiliacs with innocent victims, the pederasts and rapists; their acts, of course, are unacceptable. But what of this willing whipping boy? Why was this behavior revolting, while, say, loving a polar bear was not? Was it simply a matter of my own personal taste? Was I soft on polar bears?

"He is so bad!" Gretchen was screeching.

"We should teach *him* how to juggle," Rikki cried, aiming her whip at Charles's groin. "Show him what *we'd* do with a pair of balls!"

The audience howled.

I dropped my money on the bar and walked out of the Pyramid Club into the warm night air. I had finally understood where my revulsion was coming from. It was not simply the brutality of the whipping that offended me. It was something deeper and more personal than that. I knew Charles; I knew his true desires. And this sado-masochistic farce I had just witnessed was a *per-version* in the basic sense of that word: It was a *misdirection of desires*. Not of statistically "normal" desires but of *Charles's original and true desires*.

With my help Charles had forsaken his most passionate desire—and its object—a long time ago. God knows, he had attempted to modify his nature, to adapt it to loving Yvonne, a woman with whom he apparently had so much in common. But without genuine sexual desire for her, that relationship had failed.

Still, Charles wanted to feel *something*, so he had turned to this perverse circus game in an attempt to get his passion back. "Where poetry fails, brutality doth succeed." And in the grand scheme of things, playing whipping boy to a pair of dominatrices was more socially acceptable—and far safer—than attempting to make love to a polar bear. After all, there were clubs like the Pyramid in cities all over the world, but I doubt that there was a single one for polar bear lovers.

And so ultimately these S-M games were a substitute for the feeling Charles could not permit himself: his "bestial" love of Zero. Ironically, that original feeling *was* romantic, *was* poetic, while this substitute with human beings was a crude and spurious love. I still did not believe that Charles's attraction to Zero was masochistic, that its potential for punishment was what excited him. Yet Charles's pure love for the bear had perforce been perverted and in the process something truly bestial had been born in him.

That, above all, was what pained me. I mourned the loss of pure love, of poetry in Charles's heart.

I slept poorly most of that night, then fell into a deep sleep near morning. When I awoke, the red light on my telephone was flashing. Charles had called, the desk clerk told me. He wanted me to meet him in the big top down in Venice at noon. I had less than an hour to dress and get there. . . .

Charles was standing just inside the center ring. He was wearing dark slacks and an open Oxford shirt. He nodded to me as I sat down, then continued with his lecture. He was comparing circus acts with other types of dramas—with Shakespearean comedies and French bedroom farces, with Pirandello and Beckett. It was a wonderfully entertaining lecture. Charles would quote a passage from a play, then do a piece of mime or a round of juggling that somehow paralleled the quoted scene. The students clearly loved it, and so did I.

I must remember this, I told myself. I knew that I would never be able to shake off completely the grotesque images of Charles from the night before, but I must remember this, too. For if ever a man transformed his beastly drives into something beautiful and intelligent and inspiring, it was Charles. He was among only a couple dozen American men and women who had brought circus arts into the universities, who had heralded the renaissance of the intimate, magical circus on this side of the Atlantic. It was a fine achievement, and it was, in a very true sense, the product of a personal passion, of love. This, too, is part of the picture of what became of Charles Embree.

When the class was over and the students had left, I went up to Charles. I told him how much I had enjoyed his lecture, how impressed I was with his work.

"You left early last night," he said, looking me straight in the eye.

"Yes, I did," I replied. I hesitated a moment and then added, "It's just a personal thing, but I liked today's performance much better than that one."

Charles smiled warmly at me. "Me, too," he said.

A few minutes later we shook hands again, and I walked back to my van.

Driving off, I found myself smiling. It had suddenly occurred to me that maybe Charles's performance at the Pyramid Club had been inspired by true love after all. Maybe as he entertained the audience under Rikki's cracking whip, Charles was totally identifying with his beloved Zero, the performing bear. Perhaps this was his ultimate tribute of love.

# How Do You Cure a Sex Addict?

## Lauren Slater

*This chapter concludes with a reading about compulsive sexual behavior and its treatment. As broad as the category of Sexual and Gender Identity Disorders is within the DSM-IV, there is little reference in it to compulsive sexual behavior or sexual addictions. This will probably change in the near future as more is learned about this class of behaviors and the pain it causes people. According to one definition (Goodman, 1992), sexual addiction is characterized by a lack of control over one's sexual behavior and by engagement in sexual behavior even with the realization that harmful consequences can result. Paraphilias can sometimes have this compulsive quality, but most people who identify themselves as having compulsive sexual behavior do not report paraphilias, but report instead constant cruising for sex partners, compulsive sex within relationships, and overly frequent masturbation (Black, Kehrberg, Flumerfelt, & Schlosser, 1997).*

*This article outlines the nature of sexual addictions and presents the approach used by Dr. Martin Kafka for treating patients with this problem. The article focuses on Bill Morill, his compulsive urges for sex, his despair and the shame he felt for his actions, and his successful treatment with medication. The rapid elimination of the compulsive sexual behaviors in Dr. Kafka's practice is quite remarkable, and it underscores how an advance in treatment can lead to testable questions about how that treatment works, which may lead in turn to even better interventions.*

## References

Black, D. W., Kehrberg, L. L. D., Flumerfelt, D. L., & Schlosser, S. S. (1997). Characteristics of 36 subjects reporting compulsive sexual behavior. *American Journal of Psychiatry, 154,* 243–249.

Goodman, A. (1992). Sexual addiction: Designation and treatment. *Journal of Sex and Marital Therapy, 18,* 303–314.

*New York Times Magazine,* 96–104. (2000, November 19).

* * *

His name, in all seriousness, is Dr. Kafka. No relation, he says. Martin Kafka treats and studies paraphiliacs at McLean Hospital in Belmont, Mass. Paraphilias are disorders characterized by persistent deviant sexual arousal—think exhibitionism, fetishism and pedophilia. Closely related to the paraphilias are what Kafka calls the paraphilia-related disorders (P.R.D.'s).

Those suffering from P.R.D.'s are, in common vernacular, sex addicts, who may not be breaking the law but are driven by libidos so excessive that they are pinned beneath their weight.

Kafka, senior attending psychiatrist at McLean Hospital and a clinical assistant professor at Harvard Medical School, where he lectures to residents on hypersexuality, is a nationally renowned expert in his field. . . .

In his practice he sees about 40 patients a week, more than three-quarters of whom have what by current cultural standards at least are perversely heightened libidos. His most serious cases are sexual predators; his "lite" cases include the old standbys of masculine misery: compulsive porn-watchers, compulsive clients of prostitutes, men incapable of monogamy. The middle range is composed of guys we call creeps, the ones who peer in your bedroom window, the guy in the red raincoat parting the slicker's flaps.

Kafka started out at McLean in 1983 as the medical director of the cognitive-behavior therapy unit, which is a fairly grand beginning, given that McLean is to mental hospitals what Harvard is to colleges. In fact, McLean is affiliated with Harvard, and its gracious grounds reflect that. Originally, Kafka worked with women who had eating disorders, women so thin that the bones rose in ridges under their skin. "One day, a sex offender was admitted," Kafka says. "There were no other beds in the hospital, maybe, so they put this guy on my unit, with all the eating disorders, and that's when I had my eureka moment. I began to see that the sex offenders were just like the bulimics. Both groups were suffering from a disregulation of appetite. I began to think that paraphilias and the P.R.D.'s are to men what eating disorders are to

women. I was so excited by this breakthrough, I didn't sleep for two nights."

In fact, there are interesting inverse relationships between eating disorders and sexual-impulse disorders. The sex distribution of paraphilias and related disorders is about 95 percent male, 5 percent female, whereas the sex distribution for eating disorders is the opposite. Both disorders involve difficulty experiencing satiation, as well as a general disregulation of appetite drives.

"T.S.O.," Kafka says. "Total sexual outlet." We are sitting in his damp basement office.

"So you have to look at total sexual outlet as one way of diagnosing a paraphiliac or a P.R.D.," he says. "How many times does he masturbate a week? What are the number of orgasms he has per week. Anything over six and my ears perk up."

"Six?" I say. By this definition, my husband may be in trouble.

"What's the average amount a man masturbates?" I ask.

"Three," he says. "It varies."

"There must be a lot of paraphiliacs out there that we don't know about," I say.

"There probably are," he says.

In one study, 33 percent of normal men admitted to having rape fantasies. In another study, penile tumescence was measured for both normal men and convicted pedophiles when both groups were shown deviant stimuli. Twenty-eight percent of those in the normal group were sexually aroused, some of them by pedophiliac images. . . .

"Sex," Kafka says, "can be a curse."

We have heard, of late, so much about sex and hormones; testosterone shot slowly into layered, striated muscle; estrogen rubbed on labial skin. One of Kafka's most significant contributions to the chemistry of perversity may be that he has been able to look beyond the obvious culprits—our grease-based sex steroids—to the more nuanced chemical messengers and the complex roles they play in mediating our desires.

In a 1969 study published in *Science*, a scientist shoots up some rats with parachlorophenylalanine, a compound that lowers serotonin levels in both blood and brain. Within minutes of its administration there's a veritable drought of serotonin. What happens to the rats? They become sexually aroused. They mount each other compulsively. Conversely, feed rats a serotonin-laced snack, thereby raising their levels, and almost all sexual appetite disappears. "In other words, this isn't just about testosterone," Kafka says. "It used to be thought sexual deviants had just testosterone abnormalities, but they may really have serotonin abnormalities. It may be that the lower the serotonin, the higher the sex drive, or it may be something much more complex, that sexual deviance is linked to an as-yet-unidentified disregulation affecting the serotonin system."

Other studies on male animals bear this hypothesis out; before copulation, there is an increase in dopamine and a decrease in serotonin. Postcopulation, the opposite occurs. If this proves to be the case in the human species as well, afterward, when the man is smoking his cigarette or snoring as if he had chowed down a turkey dinner, he may be experiencing a serotonin surge. In a culture in love with the idea of "high" serotonin, it might surprise us to know that passion, and its distant cousin lewdness, may lie not in the dosed-up but in the dosed-down version of being.

Kafka calls his theory of sexual-impulse disorders "the monoamine hypothesis" because he is looking at the central role our monoamines—dopamine, norepinephrine and, specifically, serotonin—play in mediating desire. One of the more interesting studies he cites involves castrated rats that are injected with parachlorophenylalanine, which depletes central nervous system serotonin, and are subsequently able to resume normal mounting behavior with little or no testosterone additives. In other words, at least as far as animal analogues go, serotonin deprivation and its hypothesized partner, depression, appear to be powerful aphrodisiacs. . . .

"The brain is such an incredibly complex organ, so largely beyond our understanding," says Dr. Laurence Kirmayer, professor of psychiatry at McGill University. "It's ridiculous to think that any one chemical causes, or is responsible for, this or that. It's patently reductive."

But Kafka isn't so sure. "Of course it's complex," he says. "All of these systems are interrelated. But because these men respond so well to drugs like Prozac or other S.S.R.I.'s"—selective serotonin reuptake inhibitors—which alter serotonin transmission in the brain, it's reasonable to point to that monoamine as central in sexual-impulse disorders."

That Kafka treats male sexual-impulse disorders biologically is nothing new. "Chemical castration," the administration of testosterone-suppressing compounds that eradicate desire, has been used legally in this country for some time. However, Kafka does not want to castrate his patients. What he aims to do is far nobler, complex and chemically questionable. He aims, through the use of serotonin-selective drugs, to whitewash deviance but somehow spare conventional sexuality.

Drugs like Prozac and Paxil specifically target the serotonin systems, thereby avoiding the widespread side effects of the older generations of antidepressants. But in Kafka's conceptualization, selectivity has reached new heights. Kafka claims that the drugs are capable of reducing or eradicating pathological desire while preserving or enhancing what are culturally considered "normal" sexual urges. How can this be? Does deviant lust reside in one part of the brain, affiliative, conventional lust in another? Is a man's erection when he fetishizes powered by, say, the pituitary, while some other, friendlier lobe raises the tumescent tissue when he makes love? Kafka is by no means claiming this as fact, but his statements imply that it is one of myriad possibilities.

"You give a man with sexual problems Prozac," I ask, "and his deviance disappears while his affiliative sexuality emerges?"

"I've seen it happen, over and over again," he says.

Bill Morrill is not a handsome man. This is the first thing he says to me after he shakes my hand. "I am not a handsome man," he says, lowering his bulky body into the seat across from me, fingers gripping the sides.

"I'm nervous," he says, "and when I'm

nervous, my nose twitches," which it is, twitching like a libidinous rabbit's while he snuffs and dabs with a huge hankie pulled from his pants pocket.

Morrill is 49. He has a jowly face and wears square glasses. There is something frankly appealing about him, his palpable anxiety, his willingness to talk. "People need to know," he says. "Go ahead, use my name. Use my story. This is a sickness, and people need to know, but God, I'm nervous to tell you." Twitch, twitch.

He touches his throat, as though to take measure of his pulse, which, I imagine, is bebopping at a rate too rapid for his comfort. "All right," he says, "this is what I did."

Morrill is a carnival man. He sets up and then disassembles the gear of other people's pleasure: moonwalks, painted carousels, Ferris wheels that jingle and sway.

"I felt my first wave," Morrill says, "when I was in my 30's." It came on slowly, a clenching in the stomach, "and then I was totally out of control—I had to have a woman."

The waves, the waves. Morrill talks at length about the waves, a total corporeal takeover that resulted in picking up prostitutes, cruising for hours on end, woman after woman, in a Dionysian but dystonic frenzy. Ambers and Jo Jos and Mandys and Sunshines. "Exhausting," Morrill says. "And I was married."

Morrill describes a life before treatment of crippling obsession, a life in which he was driven to repeated exhibitionistic bouts of intercourse in bus stations, in the back seats of Greyhounds, in elevators with the stop button engaged. He describes sitting at the dinner table with his wife and feeling himself jerked upward by a powerful, invisible hand, reeling out into the night, leaving behind him a thick trail of lies. "I never got anything done," he says. "I was totally unreliable. Sex was to me what sleep was to a narcoleptic. I was in horror of it. Desire would come on. I'd drop down and wake up and have lost a whole day. Who knows? I lost 20 years of my life."

In the mornings, after getting up, he had to watch at least one hour of porn. "But it was mostly the waves," he says. "I could get them anywhere. I

kept a mattress in the back of my van just so I could get a prostitute as quick as possible. My van has more mileage inside than out."

At first, Morrill thought he was simply oversexed. "But then I noticed that in my 40's the waves started coming more and more," he says. "They were especially bad after rainstorms."

"And did your wife know about this behavior?"

"Oh, no," he says.

"Did you have sex with your wife as well?"

"Sure," he says, adding: "Married sex is vanilla. I needed something dangerous. Anne, though, my wife, she's a super person. A super person. She's a Sagittarius. I'm a Gemini. We just blend."

Finally, at the age of 47, Morrill succumbed to what he says was the vilest deed, repeated sex with an 18-year-old.

"I was in a wave, which is why it happened," Morrill says. "She was so young. You've gotta understand. In a wave, anything can be sexual to me." He points to the lamp on the desk. "Like that lamp," he says. "In a wave, that lamp could turn me on."

Dr. Peter R. Martin of the Addiction Center at Vanderbilt University elucidates. Using M.R.I.'s, Martin, along with his colleague Dr. Mitchell Parks, has begun studying the parts of the brain involved in arousal. "If we can classify what parts of the brain are involved in normal arousal," he says, "then maybe we can see if these parts are different in normal volunteers versus men with sexual addictions or paraphilias." He has a hunch that "sex addicts" may show activation in a larger—or smaller—portion of the brain in response to a stimulus than a normal volunteer. On an M.R.I. color-coded image, the aroused paraphiliac brain might look like a lobe of scarlet activity, whereas the aroused normal brain might look like, well, a normal brain. If this proves to be true, then in men like Morrill sex may bleed into the brain's more general geography, and thus such brains may be more capable of turning everyday events, and even objects, into erotic tools. Morrill's brain, perhaps, can make an aluminum lamp from Staples into some fluid fantasy object.

I reach over and switch off the lamp. Morrill

laughs. "I like you," he says. "I feel you're on my side. Now, before treatment, if I had feelings of liking you, they'd go elsewhere. I'm not a handsome man, but before treatment I was so out of control, and I could get any woman. . . . "

"I tried to kill myself," Morrill says. "I lit my trailer on fire, with me in it. When that didn't work, I decided to jump off the crane in the Quincy shipyard. It's called a Goliath Crane, 384 feet tall." He stood at the top of the crane for some time before deciding maybe he could kill a part of himself instead of the whole package. "I went to a doctor and told them to take care of it." He points to his groin. "Cut it off. Kill it. No doc would touch me."

Morrill finally found his way to Kafka. "Kafka is a great man. He knew just what questions to ask. I filled out a million questionnaires. He looked at them and said: 'I think I know what's wrong with you. You are a sexual compulsive.' "

Common wisdom has it that the sexually compulsive or the sexually deviant were often themselves victims of abuse. "The fact is," Kafka says, "only one-quarter to one-third of my patient population suffered physical or sexual abuse, and many of them had unremarkable childhoods, as far as I can see." Which is why Kafka, who acknowledges the need for a multimodal approach and does refer men for psychotherapy, treats his patients with medication. In Morrill's case, the pill was Celexa, a newer version of Prozac.

Morrill went home and swallowed a pill. The next day he swallowed a second pill. Kaboom. Morrill No. 1 melted away, and Morrill No. 2 stepped forward, the only live wire his twitching nose. "On these pills, I am a different man," Morrill says. "My head is clear as a bell. But the weirdest thing is," and here his voice drops in wonder, "the weirdest thing is how huggy I am now. I hug people left and right."

For one moment I think he is going to hug me, but he collapses back, exhaling out his astonishment. "Really, it's quite amazing," he says.

"What about your wife?" I ask. "How's sex with her?" I've been waiting to get here, to see how "affiliative sex" perseveres or, in Morrill's case, is enhanced in the face of this chemical assault, as Kafka has described it to me.

"Listen, sex is dead," he says, patting his crotch as if it were a pet. "It's gone."

"So you don't have sex with your wife either?"

"Only when she insists," he says. "And then, I'm good for maybe a minute, if at all."

Prozac and its chemical cousins have been hailed as many things: antidepressants, PMS drugs, better-than-well drugs. Here's a new use for them, as far as I can tell—chemical castrators. This idea flies directly in the face of Kafka's pioneering efforts, which are meant to restore normal sex drive while wiping out deviance. But Morrill's case points to another possibility. The selective serotonin reuptake inhibitors work in the treatment of paraphiliacs and sex addicts because they dampen if not destroy all libido, along with all sorts of other excessive behaviors. It makes sense that one day Prozac may be approved for chemical castration. After all, many say that S.S.R.I.'s cause sexual dysfunction in 80 percent of users, so why not use them to, well, dysfunction an overly functioning man?

"Sexual dysfunction is not the same as chemical castration," Kafka says. "These men can function sexually—it's just sometimes difficult. Furthermore, chemical castration came out of a need to punish these guys, whereas my aim is to help and value these men."

Apparently, then, pharmacology, like crime, can be judged not only by outcome but also by intent. If you did not intend to murder the person, then it's manslaughter. If you don't intend to castrate the person, then it's . . . what? But Kafka has a point. You cannot easily tease apart the cure from the cure giver; medicine is an amalgam of hopes, intentions and observable results. The placebo effect underscores this. The drug is inextricably bound up with the patient's expectations. In Kafka's scheme, the doctor's expectations get thrown into the mix, as well they should. A drug is as much a wish as a fact.

All philosophizing aside, Morrill is happy with his outcome. "It's dead, and I love it," he says. He is not the first man to bow down in gratitude to his ruined sexuality. Many sex addicts and sex offenders hate their sexuality. They see it as "the Devil." It is horrific to the humane sides of their personality, which are everywhere in evidence. Morrill holds hands with his wife and walks on the beach. Jim, a convicted sex offender, designs dahlia gardens with his daughter. Bob, an exhibitionist, who, like Jim, requested anonymity, takes pride in his brand-new Hyundai, polishing its black armor until it shines like onyx. Kind men. Careful men. "Sick men we are," Morrill says. . . .

In 1985, a group of scientists reported on a brain-damaged subject who could recall everything but the names of fruits and vegetables. This case, among others, has raised the possibility that our brains are modular and store information in category-specific locales. And this modular notion of brain function appears to expand beyond the domain of language recall. Other scientists have written extensively about separate memory systems, short term versus long term, declarative versus implicit.

Why, then, might not forms of sexual appetite, or desire, be divided as well? There has been one reported case of a patient with a right thalmic-hypothalmic infarction that led to hypersexuality and another of a midbrain hypothalmic glioma leading to pedophilia. Women who develop seizure disorders, which are often linked to lesions in a specific part of the brain, may also display exhibitionistic behavior. There is a very rare disorder called Kluver Bucy syndrome, in which the amygdala is damaged and the patient may experience intense sexual desire for objects—pins, cups, maybe even lamps. . . .

Kafka [says] . . . "it is interesting to speculate that normal male sexual arousal resides in one area of the brain, deviant sexual arousal in another, and that the S.S.R.I.'s work by targeting one arousal system while sparing another," he says. "That's an interesting, plausible hypothesis, and one that wouldn't surprise me."

Another possibility is this: the higher the intensity of any drive, the more polymorphous its manifestations. The S.S.R.I.'s may work in paraphilias

and sexual addiction not by deleting but by pruning, so that the person's core sexuality is finally free to emerge. This hypothesis lies close to the idea some psychiatrists hold that the paraphilias are simply another form of obsessive compulsive disorder (O.C.D.) and that the S.S.R.I.'s work not because they target sexual arousal but because they reduce ruminative thoughts and repetitive behaviors in all kinds of conditions.

"I hate that idea," Kafka says. "The paraphilias and P.R.D.'s are not a form of O.C.D. People who have O.C.D. do not have an appetite-disregulation disorder. O.C.D. is not about appetite. Sexual-impulse disorders are all about appetite."

In the end, we have these men and their appetites. We have just a few facts. That these men feel better is a fact. That Prozac and its chemical cousins appear to have yet another use is a fact. That its uses are so widespread as to present us with a boggling contradiction is a fact; here we have a drug celebrated for its specificity but employed for every nook and cranny of our multiple miseries—that, surely, is a fact. That, when we think of sex, or brains, we are sometimes reductive is also a troublesome fact.

However, reductive or not, Kafka is doing something right. He appears to have "cured," or restored to better balance, hundreds of men, many of whom are dangerous, all of whom are, by their own standards at least, terribly twisted. Kafka's patients love him. "He is the guy," Jim says. "He saved my life," Bob says. But where, I wonder, is the history, the culture in this story? Is this just one more tale of the brain? . . .

On my last visit to Kafka, I notice what I have oddly not noticed in all my visits before: large and very beautiful photographs on almost every inch of wall space. "I took these pictures myself," Kafka says. He has traveled all over the world. Here, above me, a Peruvian boy holds his little naked brother—fat, dimpled buttocks, a sweet grin. Across the way, Italian women play cards beneath flags of laundry on a line, the photo shot in saturated yellow light, the fabric as human as flesh, vivid, living. I walk around the room, staring.

There is a photo of a zebra, an extreme closeup of the animal's face, the dark, dilated eye.

"I took this picture at the Kenya zoo," Kafka says. "The zebra was wounded, in a cage, so I could get real close to him, put the camera right up next to his face, and I got this shot of his eye."

The eye, of course, is a part of our brains, a little bit of the visual cortex poking through our flesh. Now Kafka seems to forget that I'm here. He pulls into himself. I recall how he told me, over lunch a few days ago, that in this line of work he has seen the Devil, and that the Devil has neural substrates, but something more, as well. "I have become theistic," he said, looking troubled. And then he said: "You know, my patients are my boys. They're all my boys."

Kafka reaches out and touches his photograph, the eye, this bit of animal brain exposed, unknowable. I think of how he says "my boys," and into my mind comes the old tale of Pinocchio, and the island of bad little boys, those spectral males becoming part donkey, hard hoof, the horror of that. He touches the zebra's eye tenderly, almost sadly, and watching him do this, I have to wonder if it's the proffered pill, or his hand held out, that, for these men, finally does the trick.

# CHAPTER 12

# Substance-Related Disorders

*The final class of disorders that we consider are those involving the use and abuse of psychoactive substances. Substance-related problems are caused by a wide range of potentially harmful substances, including marijuana, heroin, inhalants, and alcohol. These drugs are prevalent in our society and, because they interfere with work and social relationships, the problems they incur are costly in our society. Efforts to address substance-related problems, while increasingly successful, are complicated by the fact that drugs can have powerful positive effects (e.g., they make us feel good, they allow us to forget our problems) and by the fact that substance abuse is often interwoven with other psychological disorders and personal struggles. In many cases, mental illness appears to precede addiction to substances (e.g., Kessler et al., 1996), so that substance use becomes a means by which an individual attempts to regulate his or her other symptoms (e.g., Dalack, Healy, Meador-Woodruff, 1998).*

*Rather than attempt any kind of comprehensive coverage of the various forms of substance abuse, we present two articles that emphasize biological approaches to understanding these disorders and two articles that draw attention to the interpersonal and environmental factors that give rise to them. As you will see, adherents of either approach are unlikely to discount entirely the value of the other perspective, but each does tend to argue for the primacy of either biological or social factors as the starting point for understanding and treating substance abuse and dependence.*

## References

Dalack, G. W., Healy, D. J., & Meador-Woodruff, J. H. (1998). Nicotine dependence in schizophrenia: Clinical phenomena and laboratory findings. *American Journal of Psychiatry, 155,* 1490–1501.

Kessler, R. C., Nelson, C. B., McGonagle, K. A., Edlund, M. I., Frank, R. G., & Leaf, P. J. (1996), The epidemiology of co-occurring addictive and mental disorders: Implications for prevention and service utilization. *American Journal of Orthopsychiatry, 50,* 36–43.

## Suggested Reading

Brown, V. B., Ridgley, M. S., Pepper, B., Levine, I. S., & Ryglewicz, H. (1989). The dual crisis: Mental Illness and substance abuse. *American Psychologist, 44,* 565–569.

# ADDICTION IS A BRAIN DISEASE, AND IT MATTERS

## Alan I. Leshner

*Alan Leshner, director of the National Institute on Drug Abuse, makes the argument that addiction is, first and foremost, a disease of the brain. He supports this point by summarizing research that shows how addictive substances affect the mesolimbic reward system in the brain. At the same time, in this article and elsewhere (Leshner, 1997), Dr. Leshner acknowledges that the addicted brain is embedded in a complex network of social and behavioral factors that are implicated in the genesis and treatment of these disorders. Finally, he notes that the public response to people with substance use and abuse problems is closely linked to the implicit theory that is adopted: if the disorder is a "sin" and is believed to be a personal choice, then people will be blamed and scorned; if the disorder is a "sickness" for which the individual is not responsible, then people will receive sympathy and concern (see Weiner, 1993). Thus, the broad theoretical agenda that underlies the study and treatment of substance-related disorders has repercussions that go far beyond the scientist's laboratory and the practitioner's office.*

### References

Leshner, A. I. (1997). Drug abuse and addiction treatment research: The next generation. *Archives of General Psychiatry, 54*, 691–694.

Weiner, B. (1993). On sin versus sickness: A theory of perceived responsibility and social motivation. *American Psychologist, 48*, 957–965.

---

*Science, 278,* 45–47. (1997).

Scientific advances over the past 20 years have shown that drug addiction is a chronic, relapsing disease that results from the prolonged effects of drugs on the brain. As with many other brain diseases, addiction has embedded behavioral and social-context aspects that are important parts of the disorder itself. Therefore, the most effective treatment approaches will include biological, behavioral, and social-context components. Recognizing addiction as a chronic, relapsing brain disorder characterized by compulsive drug seeking and use can impact society's overall health and social policy strategies and help diminish the health and social costs associated with drug abuse and addiction.

Dramatic advances over the past two decades in both the neurosciences and the behavioral sciences have revolutionized our understanding of drug abuse and addiction. Scientists have identified neural circuits that subsume the actions of every known drug of abuse, and they have specified common pathways that are affected by almost all such drugs. Researchers have also identified and cloned the major receptors for virtually every abusable drug, as well as the natural ligands for most of those receptors. In addition, they have elaborated many of the biochemical cascades within the cell that follow receptor activation by drugs. Research has also begun to reveal major differences between the brains of addicted and nonaddicted individuals and to indicate some common elements of addiction, regardless of the substance.

That is the good news. The bad news is the dramatic lag between these advances in science and their appreciation by the general public or their application in either practice or public policy settings. There is a wide gap between the scientific facts and public perceptions about drug abuse and addiction. For example, many, perhaps most, people see drug abuse and addiction as social problems, to be handled only with social solutions, particularly through the criminal justice system. On the other hand, science has taught that drug abuse and addiction are as much health problems as they are social problems. The consequence of this gap is a significant delay in gaining control over the drug abuse problem.

Part of the lag and resultant disconnection comes from the normal delay in transferring any scientific knowledge into practice and policy. However, there are other factors unique to the drug abuse arena that compound the problem. One major barrier is the tremendous stigma attached to being a drug user or, worse, an addict. The most beneficent public view of drug addicts is as victims of their societal situation. However, the more common view is that drug addicts are weak or bad people, unwilling to lead moral lives and to control their behavior and gratifications. To the contrary, addiction is actually a chronic, relapsing illness, characterized by compulsive drug seeking and use (1). The gulf in implications between the "bad person" view and the "chronic illness sufferer" view is tremendous. As just one example, there are many people who believe that addicted

individuals do not even deserve treatment. This stigma, and the underlying moralistic tone, is a significant overlay on all decisions that relate to drug use and drug users.

Another barrier is that some of the people who work in the fields of drug abuse prevention and addiction treatment also hold ingrained ideologies that, although usually different in origin and form from the ideologies of the general public, can be just as problematic. For example, many drug abuse workers are themselves former drug users who have had successful treatment experiences with a particular treatment method. They therefore may zealously defend a single approach, even in the face of contradictory scientific evidence. In fact, there are many drug abuse treatments that have been shown to be effective through clinical trials (1, 2).

These difficulties notwithstanding, I believe that we can and must bridge this informational disconnection if we are going to make any real progress in controlling drug abuse and addiction. It is time to replace ideology with science.

## Drug Abuse and Addiction As Public Health Problems

At the most general level, research has shown that drug abuse is a dual-edged health issue, as well as a social issue. It affects both the health of the individual and the health of the public. The use of drugs has well-known and severe negative consequences for health, both mental and physical. But drug abuse and addiction also have tremendous implications for the health of the public, because drug use, directly or indirectly, is now a major vector for the transmission of many serious infectious diseases—particularly acquired immunodeficiency syndrome (AIDS), hepatitis, and tuberculosis—as well as violence. Because addiction is such a complex and pervasive health issue, we must include in our overall strategies a committed public health approach, including extensive education and prevention efforts, treatment, and research.

Science is providing the basis for such public health approaches. For example, two large sets of multisite studies (3) have demonstrated the effectiveness of well-delineated outreach strategies in modifying the behaviors of addicted individuals that put them at risk for acquiring the human immunodeficiency virus (HIV), even if they continue to use drugs and do not want to enter treatment. This approach runs counter to the broadly held view that addicts are so incapacitated by drugs that they are unable to modify any of their behaviors. It also suggests a base for improved strategies for reducing the negative health consequences of injection drug use for the individual and for society.

## What Matters in Addiction

Scientific research and clinical experience have taught us much about what really matters in addiction and where we need to concentrate our clinical and policy efforts. However, too often the focus is on the wrong aspects of addiction, and efforts to deal with this difficult issue can be badly misguided.

Any discussion about psychoactive drugs inevitably turns to the question of whether a particular drug is physically or psychologically addicting. In essence, this issue revolves around whether or not dramatic physical withdrawal symptoms occur when an individual stops taking a drug, what is typically called physical dependence by professionals in the field. The assumption that often follows is that the more dramatic the physical withdrawal symptoms, the more serious or dangerous the drug must be.

This thinking is outdated. From both clinical and policy perspectives, it does not matter much what physical withdrawal symptoms, if any, occur. First, even the florid withdrawal symptoms of heroin addiction can now be easily managed with appropriate medication. Second, and more important, many of the most addicting and dangerous drugs do not produce severe physical symptoms upon withdrawal. Crack cocaine and methamphetamine are clear examples: Both are highly addicting, but cessation of their use produces few physical withdrawal symptoms, certainly nothing like the physical symptoms accompanying alcohol or heroin withdrawal.

What does matter tremendously is whether or not a drug causes what we now know to be the essence of addiction: compulsive drug seeking and use, even in the face of negative health and social consequences (4). These are the characteristics that ultimately matter most to the patient and are where treatment efforts should be directed. These behaviors are also the elements responsible for the massive health and social problems that drug addiction brings in its wake.

## Addiction Is a Brain Disease

Although each drug that has been studied has some idiosyncratic mechanisms of action, virtually all drugs of abuse have common effects, either directly or indirectly, on a single pathway deep within the brain. This pathway, the mesolimbic reward system, extends from the ventral tegmentum to the nucleus accumbens, with projections to areas such as the limbic system and the orbitofrontal cortex. Activation of this system appears to be a common element in what keeps drug users taking drugs. This activity is not unique to any one drug; all addictive substances affect this circuit (5).

Not only does acute drug use modify brain function in critical ways, but prolonged drug use causes pervasive changes in brain function that persist long after the individual stops taking the drug. Significant effects of chronic use have been identified for many drugs at all levels: molecular, cellular, structural, and functional (6, 7). The addicted brain is distinctly different from the non-addicted brain, as manifested by changes in brain metabolic activity, receptor availability, gene expression, and responsiveness to environmental cues. Some of these long-lasting brain changes are idiosyncratic to specific drugs, whereas others are common to many different drugs (6–9). The common brain effects of addicting substances suggest common brain mechanisms underlying all addictions (5, 7, 9, 10).

That addiction is tied to changes in brain structure and function is what makes it, fundamentally, a brain disease. A metaphorical switch in the brain seems to be thrown as a result of prolonged drug use. Initially, drug use is a voluntary behavior, but when that switch is thrown, the individual moves into the state of addiction, characterized by compulsive drug seeking and use (*11*).

Understanding that addiction is, at its core, a consequence of fundamental changes in brain function means that a major goal of treatment must be either to reverse or to compensate for those brain changes. These goals can be accomplished through either medications or behavioral treatments [behavioral treatments have been successful in altering brain function in other psychobiological disorders (*12*)]. Elucidation of the biology underlying the metaphorical switch is key to the development of more effective treatments, particularly antiaddiction medications.

## But Not Just a Brain Disease

Of course, addiction is not that simple. Addiction is not just a brain disease. It is a brain disease for which the social contexts in which it has both developed and is expressed are critically important. The case of the many thousands of returning Vietnam war veterans who were addicted to heroin illustrates this point. In contrast to addicts on the streets of the United States, it was relatively easy to treat the returning veterans' addictions. This success was possible because they had become addicted while in a setting almost totally different from the one to which they had returned. At home in the United States, they were exposed to few of the conditioned environmental cues that had initially been associated with their drug use in Vietnam. Exposure to conditioned cues can be a major factor in causing persistent or recurrent drug cravings and drug use relapses even after successful treatment (*13*).

The implications are obvious. If we understand addiction as a prototypical psychobiological illness, with critical biological, behavioral, and social-context components, our treatment strategies must include biological, behavioral, and social-context elements. Not only must the underlying brain disease be treated, but the behavioral and social cue components must also be addressed, just as they

are with many other brain diseases, including stroke, schizophrenia, and Alzheimer's disease.

## A Chronic, Relapsing Disorder

Addiction is rarely an acute illness. For most people, it is a chronic, relapsing disorder. Total abstinence for the rest of one's life is a relatively rare outcome from a single treatment episode. Relapses are more the norm. Thus, addiction must be approached more like other chronic illnesses—such as diabetes and chronic hypertension—than like an acute illness, such as a bacterial infection or a broken bone (*1*). This requirement has tremendous implications for how we evaluate treatment effectiveness and treatment outcomes. Viewing addiction as a chronic, relapsing disorder means that a good treatment outcome, and the most reasonable expectation, is a significant decrease in drug use and long periods of abstinence, with only occasional relapses. That makes a reasonable standard for treatment success—as is the case for other chronic illnesses—the management of the illness, not a cure (*1*, *2*).

## Conclusion

Addiction as a chronic, relapsing disease of the brain is a totally new concept for much of the general public, for many policymakers, and, sadly, for many health care professionals. Many of the implications have been discussed above, but there are others.

At the policy level, understanding the importance of drug use and addiction for both the health of individuals and the health of the public affects many of our overall public health strategies. An accurate understanding of the nature of drug abuse and addiction should also affect our criminal justice strategies. For example, if we know that criminals are drug addicted, it is no longer reasonable to simply incarcerate them. If they have a brain disease, imprisoning them without treatment is futile. If they are left untreated, their recidivism rates to both crime and drug use are frighteningly high; however, if addicted criminals are treated while in prison, both types of recidivism can be reduced dramatically (*14*). It is therefore counterproductive to not treat addicts while they are in prison.

At an even more general level, understanding addiction as a brain disease also affects how society approaches and deals with addicted individuals. We need to face the fact that even if the condition initially comes about because of a voluntary behavior (drug use), an addict's brain is different from a nonaddict's brain, and the addicted individual must be dealt with as if he or she is in a different brain state. We have learned to deal with people in different brain states for schizophrenia and Alzheimer's disease. Recall that as recently as the beginning of this century we were still putting individuals with schizophrenia in prisonlike asylums, whereas now we know they require medical treatments. We now need to see the addict as someone whose mind (read: brain) has been altered fundamentally by drugs. Treatment is required to deal with the altered brain function and the concomitant behavioral and social functioning components of the illness.

Understanding addiction as a brain disease explains in part why historic policy strategies focusing solely on the social or criminal justice aspects of drug use and addiction have been unsuccessful. They are missing at least half of the issue. If the brain is the core of the problem, attending to the brain needs to be a core part of the solution.

## References and Notes

1. C. P. O'Brien and A. T. McLellan, *Lancet* 347, 237 (1996).
2. A. T. McLellan *et al.*, in *Treating Drug Abusers Effectively*, J. A. Egertson *et al.* Eds. (Blackwell, Maiden, MA, 1997), pp. 7–40.
3. R. Booth *et al.*, *Drug Alcohol Depend.* 42, 11 (1996); H. M. Colon *et al.*, *AIDS Educ. Prev.* 7, 195 (1995); R. C. Stephens *et al.*, in *Handbook on Risk of AIDS*, B. S. Brown and G. M. Beschner, Eds. (Greenwood, Westport, CT 1993), pp. 519–656; W. W. Wiebel *et al.*, *J. Acquired Immune Defic. Syndr.* 12, 282 (1996).
4. American Psychiatric Association, *Diagnostic and Statistical Manual of Mental Disorders*, (American Psychiatric Association Press, Washington, DC, ed. 4, 1994); Institute of Medicine, *Pathways of Addiction* (National Academy Press, Washington, DC, 1996).
5. G. F. Koob, *Trends Pharmacol.* Sci. 13, 177 (1992); G. F. Koob *et al.*, *Semin. Neurosci.* 6, 221 (1994).
6. S. E. Hyman, *Neuron* 16, 901 (1996); E. J. Nestler, *ibid.*, p. 897; W. P. Melega *et al.*, *Behav. Brain Res.* 84, 259 (1997); J. Ortiz *et al.*, *Synapse* 21, 289 (1995); N. D. Volkow *et al.*, *Am. J. Psychiatry* 147, 719 (1990).
7. E. J. Nestler *et al.*, *Mol. Psychiatry* 1, 190 (1996); D. W. Self and E. J. Nestler, *Annu. Rev. Neurosci.* 18, 463 (1995).
8. E. J. Nestler, *J. Neurosci.* 12, 2439 (1992); T. E. Robinson and K. C. Berridge, *Brain Res. Rev.* 18, 247 (1993); R. Z. Terwilliger *et al.*, *Brain Res.* 548, 100 (1991).
9. G. F. Koob, *Neuron* 16, 893 (1996).
10. A. I. Leshner, *Hospital Practice: A Special Report* (McGraw-Hill, Minneapolis, MN, 1997).
11. The state of addiction—both the clinical condition and the brain state—is qualitatively different from the effects of large amounts of drugs. The individual, once addicted, has moved from a state where drug use is voluntary and controlled to one where drug craving, seeking, and use are no longer under the same kind of voluntary control, and these changes reflect changes in brain function. The exact mechanisms involved are not known. For example, it is not clear whether that change in state reflects a relatively precipitous change in a single mechanism or multiple mechanisms acting in concert, or whether the shift to addiction represents the sum of more gradual neuroadaptations. Moreover, there are individual differences in the vulnerability to becoming addicted and the speed of becoming addicted. For some individuals, the metaphorical switch moves quickly, whereas for others the changes occur quite gradually (*6–10*).
12. L. B. Baxter *et al.*, *Semin. Clin. Neuropsychiatry* 1, 32 (1996).
13. A. R. Childress *et al.*, *Natl. Inst. Drug Abuse Res. Monogr.* 84, 25 (1988); D. C. Daley and G. A. Marilatt, in *Substance Abuse: A Comprehensive Textbook*, J. H. Lowinson *et al.*, Eds. (Williams & Wilkins, Baltimore, ed. 3, 1997), pp. 458–467; C. P. O'Brien, *Pharmacol Rev.* 27, 535 (1975); C. P. O'Brien *et al.*, *Addict Behav.* 15, 355 (1990); S. Grant *et al.*, *Proc. Natl. Acad. Sci. U.S.A.* 93, 12040 (1996).
14. J. A. Inciardi *et al.*, *J. Drug Issues* 27, 261 (1997): H. K. Wexler and D. S. Lipton, in *Drug Treatment and Criminal Justice*, J. A. Inciardi, Ed. (Sage, Newbury Park, CA, 1993), pp. 261–278.

# GENETIC STUDIES PROMISE A PATH TO BETTER TREATMENT OF ADDICTIONS

## Linda Carroll

*Our second article continues the theme of how the brain is implicated in addictions and focuses primarily on cocaine abuse and the role of the mesolimbic system. The receptors in this system are sensitive to one neurotransmitter, dopamine. Genes appear to determine the density of these receptors and, in turn, the susceptibility to addictive substances. The essential premise is that some people are born with a defective gene responsible for determining the density of dopaminergic receptors; thus, their subjective well-being improves dramatically when they take substances such as cocaine. Learned experiences with the drug and the cues associated with taking the drug elicit positive reminders—and small amounts of dopamine—which lead to further craving and heavier substance use. Within this model, treatment is undertaken by administering a drug—in this case baclofen—that reduces the craving by dampening the dopamine response. This article summarizes an elegant research program, and it is also an excellent example of scientific journalism.*

## Suggested Reading

Leutwyler, K., & Hull, A. (1997, November 24). Closing in on addiction: New findings suggest a biochemical common ground. *Scientific American*, 26–29.

---

*New York Times*, D6. (2000, November 14).

In a quiet, dark room at the University of Pennsylvania, Edward Coleman, 30, lies back and watches a videotape of addicts like him smoking crack while a PET scanner records each neurochemical nuance of his brain.

Normally, the images would spark an irresistible craving for the drug. His heart would start to race; his ears would begin to buzz; and a spot deep inside his brain would flash brightly on the scan. But today it is different. Before starting the videotape, Dr. Anna Rose Childress gave Mr. Coleman a medication that may someday help him, and others, combat the craving that lures so many back to their addictions.

After the video Mr. Coleman admits the images evoked an urge to use cocaine, but not such a strong one. And the PET scan backs him up: his amygdala—the small almond-shaped brain structure that helps humans and animals remember all the details associated with pleasurable events—flickers only weakly.

"Edward can still remember what the cocaine high is like, but while taking baclofen in the right dose range, he doesn't feel pulled to go out and find it," said Dr. Childress, a research associate professor . . . at the Treatment Research Center of the University of Pennsylvania. "For a patient wishing to stop cocaine, this could provide a desperately needed tool."

As the war on drugs has marched into the scientist's lab, researchers have devised a paradigm that may help explain why some people get hooked after a single "taste" of an illegal drug while others can use it for years and quit when they choose. Once thought of as weak-willed people who lacked the moral strength to just say no to drugs, addicts are now viewed as victims of genes that make them susceptible to the powerful pull of mind-altering substances.

Scientists in research centers around the country are studying how drugs affect the brain. They tweak various neurotransmitters, searching for ways to alter both an addict's genetic wiring and the rewiring of the brain that drugs initiate. Some researchers seek ways to rev up the "stop" circuitry of the forebrain—the part that considers consequences—while others look for ways to tune down the "go" circuitry of the limbic system—a part of the brain involved in processing emotion.

While researchers emphasize that environmental factors are also crucial, many population studies have pointed to the importance of genetics. For example, studies of twins have found that identical twins are more likely than fraternal twins to share a tendency to become addicted. But the predilection may be even more specific. Dr. Ming Tsuang, a professor of psychiatry at Harvard Medical School, has found that people inherit not only a general susceptibility to substance abuse but also a vulnerability to particular drugs.

"Our group is interested in finding the actual gene that is specific for heroin addiction," Dr. Tsuang says. "If we can find the gene and learn what the gene's products are, we may be able to prevent people from abusing heroin."

When it comes to a general genetic susceptibility, the leading suspect is a defect in the dopamine system, experts say. In the past decade or so, researchers have discovered that although drugs affect a variety of neurotransmitters, virtually all of them increase the levels of dopamine in the brain's mesolimbic region, which is involved in pleasure, reward and motivation.

Research has also shown that compared with those who do not use drugs, addicts tend to be deficient in a certain type of dopamine receptor, dubbed DR2. That receptor leads to feelings of pleasure when stimulated by dopamine. Some scientists have assumed that this deficiency was simply the result of the brain's reaction to a drug-induced overload of dopamine by cutting back on the number of receptors available to pick up the neurotransmitter.

And an experiment that followed with monkeys that were allowed to self-administer cocaine for a year showed that this was at least partly true. The five addicted monkeys ended up with a 15 percent to 20 percent decrease in dopamine receptors, says Dr. Michael Nader, an associate professor of physiology and pharmacology at the Wake Forest University's medical school in Winston-Salem, N.C. Nine months after the monkeys were deprived of cocaine, three had returned to normal, but two had not.

Still, several recent studies have suggested that some people may be born with a defect in the gene that doles out dopamine receptors. Those born with the defect end up with fewer DR2s and as a consequence experience life with less intensity and joy, said Dr. Ernest P. Noble, a professor of psychiatry and biobehavioral sciences and the director of the Alcohol Research Center at the University of California at Los Angeles.

"These people often say they don't feel the normal rewards and pleasures in life," Dr. Noble said. "For example, a man will describe the experience of going to the beach with a girlfriend to view a beautiful sunset and say, 'I hardly felt anything.' Or he will describe how he went to a concert where his buddies all feel exhilarated, but not him."

These patients often report that the first time they really felt normal was after their first drink or dose of an illegal drug, Dr. Noble said.

After determining that severe alcoholism was associated with a mutation of the gene that doles out DR2s, Dr. Noble and his colleagues tried treating alcoholics with bromocriptine, a medicine that boosts the amount of dopamine available to the brain. The medication quieted craving and ultimately helped alcoholics fight their addiction, Dr. Noble said.

In another experiment designed to discover whether the "taste" for drugs might be related to inherited brain chemistry, researchers at Brookhaven National Laboratory tested a group of people who had no experience with illegal drugs. After using a PET scanner to determine how many dopamine receptors each person had, the researchers injected each with a small amount of the stimulant Ritalin.

"And, lo and behold, the people with low levels of dopamine receptors in their brains were the ones who liked the way the Ritalin made them feel," said Dr. Nora Volkow, associate laboratory director for life science at Brookhaven National Laboratory. "Those who had high concentrations of receptors in their brains said the Ritalin made them feel very unpleasant. They felt like they were losing control. One almost had a panic attack."

In a follow-up experiment designed to test whether an increase in dopamine receptors could prevent drug abuse, Dr. Panayotis Thanos, a scientist at Brookhaven, used gene therapy to boost the number of dopamine receptors in rats that had developed a taste for alcohol. The result: the rats quit drinking, Dr. Volkow said.

In New York, researchers are looking at a different dopamine receptor—DR1. Scientists suspect that DR1, which gives a sensation of satiety when stimulated by dopamine, is a sort of check to DR2, said Dr. Marc Laruelle, an associate professor of psychiatry and radiology at the Columbia College of Physicians and Surgeons. In an attempt to discover whether DR1 levels can make a difference in

an addict's ability to postpone gratification, Dr. Laruelle and his colleagues are giving volunteer addicts small doses of cocaine and then offering them the choice of a $5 dose of the drug or a $10 bill.

"We want to see if they go for the money or the cocaine," Dr. Laruelle said. "The hope is that the ratio of DR1 to DR2 will be predictive. And then, perhaps, we will be able to identify addicts with very low levels of DR1 and give them a drug to stimulate DR1 more effectively."

Perhaps as important as the issue of genetic susceptibility is the effect drugs have on the wiring of the brain. Drugs lure people back because they tap into a very primal system in the human brain. In essence, drugs of abuse hijack the brain circuitry that has evolved to help people find their way back to food sources or sexual partners to reproduce, Dr. Childress said. Once people experience a pleasurable—or terrible—moment, the amygdala helps the brain remember how it got that feeling and how to get it or avoid it in the future.

"Monkeys with amygdalar damage stare expressionless at a banana across a Plexiglas screen," Dr. Childress said. "Normally this would drive them into a frenzy of excited anticipation. People with severe amygdalar damage quite literally have difficulty staying alive. They will cross the street in front of oncoming cars, as the normal signals for fear have been undone."

And when we see cues to positive experiences—a picture of a syringe or a mound of white powder, in the case of the addict—the brain releases a small spurt of dopamine that reminds us of the pleasurable experience, Dr. Childress explained.

"This increase in dopamine feels similar to a small dose of the drug itself," she added. Some even feel they can taste the drug in the back of their throats.

For many recovering addicts; that little "taste" of the drug is often too strong a temptation to ignore, Dr. Childress said.

A possible therapy is to find a drug to tone down the dopamine system and give the thinking part of the brain a better chance at remembering the consequences of drug use.

Baclofen is one candidate. An older medication, used for years to treat muscle spasms, baclofen latches onto the GABA receptor, which acts as a set of brakes to the dopamine system. It appears to quiet craving and to blunt the high associated with drugs of abuse.

In a pilot study, Dr. Childress found that baclofen can soothe craving. She was about to start a study of the long-term effects of the medication to determine, among other things, whether it would continue to quiet the desire for drugs when she discovered Mr. Coleman.

Mr. Coleman, a paraplegic, had been taking baclofen for spasms in his legs for years. On his own, Mr. Coleman had discovered the powers of baclofen. He had experimented with different doses and discovered that it would block his high if he took the baclofen too close to the time he took cocaine. He learned that the medication could reduce his craving when cocaine was unavailable. He also figured out that it quieted his craving for alcohol and cigarettes.

"In a way," Dr. Childress said, "he's done my experiment for me."

# Adolescent Drug Use and Psychological Health: A Longitudinal Inquiry

## Jonathan Shedler and Jack Block

*This article reports on a longitudinal study that links the parenting one experiences at age 5, with personality characteristics at ages 7, 11, and 18, and drug use at age 18. This study is noteworthy for two reasons: First, because of the methods it employs—data are collected over a relatively long span of time, involving psychologists, parents, and the children themselves, using an array of interview, observational, and self-report procedures; second, because of this study's design—the authors can demonstrate that there are important personality differences between those 18-year-olds who abstain from drugs, those who experiment with drugs, and those who are frequent users. The roots of these different patterns of adolescent drug use can then be traced back to early parenting and personality development. Perhaps the most intriguing findings in this research are that the highest level of psychological adjustment was attained by those adolescents who experimented with drugs, rather than by those who abstained, and that frequent users and abstainers tended to have cold, unresponsive mothers. In the context of the two preceding articles, these data force us to think whether prevention and treatment of substance abuse is more likely to succeed via an understanding of the neurophysiology of the brain, the family environment and its effects on the developing child, or some complex combination of these two distinct systems.*

## Suggested Readings

Bruner, A. B., & Fishman, M. (1998). Adolescents and illicit drug use. *Journal of the American Medical Association, 280,* 597–598.

Judge, M. G. (1997). *Wasted: Tales of a GenX drunk.* Center City, MN: Hazelden.

*American Psychologist, 45,* 612–630. (1990).

ABSTRACT: The relation between psychological characteristics and drug use was investigated in subjects studied longitudinally, from preschool through age 18. Adolescents who had engaged in some drug experimentation (primarily with marijuana) were the best-adjusted in the sample. Adolescents who used drugs frequently were maladjusted, showing a distinct personality syndrome marked by interpersonal alienation, poor impulse control, and manifest emotional distress. Adolescents who, by age 18, had never experimented with any drug were relatively anxious, emotionally constricted, and lacking in social skills.

Psychological differences between frequent drug users, experimenters, and abstainers could be traced to the earliest years of childhood and related to the quality of parenting received. The findings indicate that (a) problem drug use is a symptom, not a cause, of personal and social maladjustment, and (b) the meaning of drug use can be understood only in the context of an individual's personality structure and developmental history. It is suggested that current efforts at drug prevention are misguided to the extent that they focus on symptoms, rather than on the psychological syndrome underlying drug abuse.

D rug abuse among young people is one of the greatest challenges of our time. Almost daily, we are besieged by media reports of drug-related tragedy, of shootings in our schools, gang warfare, and overdose-related deaths. Many see the drug problem as epidemic (Robins, 1984). As an increasing share of society's resources is diverted toward coping with the drug problem and its consequences, the need for sound, scientific information on the factors contributing to drug use is urgent.

Considerable research has already been directed toward studying the causes and correlates of drug use, and important recognitions have developed (for reviews, see Bush & Iannotti, 1985; Cox, 1985; Hawkins, Lishner, & Catalano, 1985; Jessor, 1979; Jones & Battjes, 1985; Kandel, 1980). Nevertheless, many studies to date have been interpretively constrained by various research-design or empirical limitations.

Large-scale epidemiological studies (e.g., Jessor, Chase, & Donovan, 1980; Johnston, O'Malley, & Bachman, 1984, 1986; National Institute on Drug Abuse [NIDA], 1986) have provided much-needed information about the prevalence and patterns of drug use, about the demographics of drug users, and about certain psychosocial characteristics of drug users. In general, however, these studies have been unable to provide the kind of in-depth, psychologically rich, clinically oriented information needed to inform intervention efforts. And by their very nature, cross-sectional studies and panel studies of relatively brief duration can offer only limited or confounded understandings of the antecedents of drug use.

Recognizing the crucial importance of prospective inquiry into the psychological antecedents of drug use, a number of longitudinal studies of adolescent development have been undertaken and have deepened our understanding of the interplay of psychosocial forces during adolescence (e.g., Brook, Gordon, & Whiteman, 1985; Brook, Whiteman, Gordon, & Cohen, 1986; Jessor & Jessor, 1977, 1978; Smith & Fogg, 1978; see Kandel, 1978, for a review). In general, however, these studies have also been interpretively constrained because they have studied adolescents already well along in years (subjects have rarely been younger than age 13) and because they have tended to track these adolescents for no more than three or four years, from junior high school into high school or from high school into college. Also, these studies have tended to depend, perhaps too heavily, on self-administered, mailed, or impersonally offered questionnaires.

To date, only two *truly* long-term investigations into the childhood antecedents of drug use have appeared. The Woodlawn study of Kellam and his associates (Kellam, Branch, Agrawal, & Ensminger, 1975; Kellam, Brown, Rubin, & Ensminger, 1983) traced the development of a group of poor, Black, urban children beginning at ages 6 to 7. In the Woodlawn study, Kellam et al. found that psychological characteristics assessed at ages 6 to 7 foretold drug use at ages 16 to 17, a decade later. The longitudinal study initiated by Jeanne and Jack Block (see J. H. Block & J. Block, 1980) followed a group of San Francisco Bay area children from nursery school on and found numerous, theoretically coherent relations between psychological characteristics assessed in nursery school and subsequent drug use in early adolescence, at age 14 (Block, Block, & Keyes, 1988). These studies converge in demonstrating the existence of important psychological antecedents of drug use, antecedents dating to the earliest years of childhood. Conjointly, they suggest that early psychological factors may be central to an understanding of drug use, and they highlight the need for prospective research.

The present study further reports on the Block and Block sample, studied again in late adolescence when the subjects had reached age 18. This later age represents a different developmental era, one in which the implications of drug use and nonuse can well take on psychological significance different from the significance of drug use and nonuse in early adolescence. The findings we report span 13 years, from preschool through age 18. By virtue of their prospective nature, these data allow inferences about the antecedents of drug use that cannot be made from retrospective, cross-sectional, or short-term panel studies.

Beyond the length of time spanned by the present investigation, the study differs from previous studies in two important ways. In most empirical studies, psychological descriptions are limited to a small number of variables that are selected by researchers on a priori grounds. In the present study, psychological descriptions are, for all practical purposes, comprehensive and open-ended. They are based on extensive evaluations of participants by panels of psychologists, and they encompass the full range of constructs subsumed by the California Adult Q-sort (CAQ; Block, 1961/1978) and the California Child Q-sort (CCQ; J. Block & J. H. Block, 1980)—personality assessment instruments specifically designed to allow clinicians to provide in-depth, comprehensive psychological descriptions. The intention was to gather information psychologically rich enough to speak to clinical concerns and to inform intervention efforts.

The study also differs from previous studies in its approach to data analysis. Previous investigators have tended to assume (and test for) linear relations between level of drug use and measures of psychosocial disturbance. In effect, such an approach assumes that occasional experimentation with drugs is psychologically problematic, if not quite as problematic as regular use, and that complete avoidance of drugs is psychologically optimal.

However, the majority of young adults in the United States, nearly two thirds, have experimented with marijuana at one time or another (Johnston et al., 1986; Johnston, Bachman, & O'Malley, 1981a, 1981b; Miller et al., 1983; NIDA, 1986), and the vast majority of these young people do not subsequently become drug *abusers*. Little is known about the relative psychosocial adjustment of adolescents who have experimented with drugs on an occasional basis and of adolescents who have avoided drugs entirely. Indeed, a number of researchers have suggested that occasional drug use among adolescents may be best understood as a manifestation of *developmentally appropriate* experimentation. Newcomb and Bentler (1988), for example, have observed that

> one defining feature of adolescence is a quest for or establishment of independence and autonomous identity and functioning. This may involve experimentation with a wide range of behaviors, attitudes, and activities before choosing a direction and way of life to call one's own. This process of testing attitudes and behavior may include drug use. In fact, experimental use of various drugs, both licit and illicit, *may be considered a normative behavior among United States teenagers in terms of prevalence, and from a developmental task perspective.* (p. 214, emphasis added)

These empirical and developmental considerations suggest that the relations between psychological variables and level of drug use may not be linear at all. To the extent that drug experimentation may represent normative behavior during the prolonged adolescent period, as individuals seek a sense of self and possibility, it may be wrong to pathologize adolescents who experiment with drugs by assuming that they fall between nonusers and drug abusers on a continuum of psychosocial adjustment. To evaluate this conceptual possibility in the present study, we identify and contrast discrete groups of nonusers, experimenters, and frequent drug users. Additionally, we employ quadratic regression methods to formally test for curvilinear relations, when the data indicate that such relations may exist. These approaches permit the emergence of findings not discernible through conventional correlational methods with their assumption of linearity.

## Method

SUBJECTS   Subjects were 101 18-year-olds, 49 boys and 52 girls, from an initial sample of 130 participating in a longitudinal study of ego and cognitive development. The subjects were initially recruited into the study at age 3, while attending either a university-run nursery school or a parent-cooperative nursery school in the San Francisco Bay area. They were assessed on wide-ranging batteries of psychological measures at ages 3, 4, 5, 7, 11, 14, and 18 (see J. H. Block & J. Block, 1980, for an extended description of the study). Because so few subjects were lost over the years, there can be little influence of differential attrition.

The subjects live primarily in urban settings and are heterogeneous with respect to social class and parent education. About two thirds are White, one fourth are Black, and one twelfth are Asian. Not all subjects are used in all analyses to be reported, as will be discussed.

MEASURING DRUG USE   Information about drug use was collected at age 18 during individual interviews with the subjects. Skilled clinicians conducted these interviews, which ranged over a variety of topics including schoolwork, peer relations, family dynamics, personal interests, dating experiences, and so on. Total interview time was typically four hours per subject, and all interviews were videotaped.

The subjects were asked whether they "smoked pot or used it in another form." Their responses were coded from the interview videotapes as follows: (0) never used marijuana; (1) used once or twice; (2) used a few times; (3) used once a month; (4) used once a week; (5) used two or three times a week; and (6) used daily. The subjects were also given a list of other substances and were asked to check which (if any) they had used at least once on a "recreational" basis. The list included inhalants (e.g., glue, nitrous oxide), cocaine, hallucinogens, barbiturates, amphetamines, tranquilizers, heroin, and an open-ended category for "other" drugs not specifically listed.

Although self-report data on drug use are always subject to underreporting, the findings of a number of investigations indicate that such data have high validity (e.g., Block et al., 1988; Haberman, Josephson, Zanes, & Elinson, 1972; Jessor & Jessor, 1977; Perry, Killen, & Slinkard, 1980; Single, Kandel, & Johnston, 1975). Additionally, there is every reason to believe that the subjects in this investigation answered our questions honestly. The interviewers were skilled in gaining rapport and in eliciting information without inducing discomfort. Moreover, the subjects had been involved in the longitudinal study from earliest childhood; they not only had been assured that their individual responses would be held in confidence, but they knew from years of prior experience that this promise had been honored.

MEASURING PERSONALITY   Age 18 assessment. At age 18, the personality characteristics of each subject were described by four psychologists, using the standard vocabulary of the California Adult Q-sort (Block, 1961/1978). The CAQ is a personality assessment instrument that allows psychologists to provide comprehensive personality descriptions in a conceptually systematic, quantifiable, and readily comparable form. The CAQ consists of 100 personality-descriptive statements, each printed on a separate index card. The psychologist sorts these statements into a fixed nine-step distribution, according to their evaluated salience vis-à-vis the person being described. Thus, the CAQ yields a score of 1 through 9 for each of 100 personality-descriptive statements; higher scores indicate that a statement is relatively characteristic of a person, and lower scores indicate that it is relatively uncharacteristic. The validity and usefulness of Q-sort personality descriptions has been demonstrated frequently (see, e.g., Bem & Funder, 1978; Block, 1961/1978; Block, 1971; Gjerde, Block, & Block, 1988; Mischel, Shoda, & Peake, 1988).

The psychologists based their CAQ descriptions of each subject on observations made while administering a variety of experimental procedures designed to tap various aspects of psychological functioning. These psychologists were *not* the interviewers who gathered information about drug use; they had no knowledge of subjects' drug use or of any other information elicited during the interviews. Each of the four psychologists who provided CAQ-based personality descriptions saw the subjects in a different assessment context, so that four entirely independent Q-sort descriptions were available per subject. The scores assigned to each Q-sort item were then averaged across the four psychologists, to yield a final, composite Q-sort for each subject. These composite Q-sorts thus represent the consensual judgment of four independent assessors. The reliabilities of the composite Q-sorts differed somewhat from subject to subject and were of the order of .70 to .90.

*Childhood assessments.* At ages 7 and 11, the personality characteristics of the subjects were described in a similar manner, each time by entirely different sets of psychologists, using the standard vocabulary of the California Child Q-sort (CCQ). The CCQ is an age-appropriate modification of the California Adult Q-sort, and consists of statements describing the personality, cognitive, and social characteristics of children (see J. Block & J. H. Block, 1980; J. H. Block and J. Block, 1980). At age 7, the standard 100-item CCQ was used; at age 11, an abridged 63-item version was used. Three psychologists observed the children at age 7, and five psychologists observed the children at age 11, while administering a variety of age-appropriate experimental procedures. The scores assigned to the CCQ items were averaged across the psychologists to produce a composite Q-sort for age 7 and a composite Q-sort for age 11. Again, the reliabilities of the composite Q-sorts were of the order of .70 to .90.

MEASURING THE QUALITY OF PARENTING When the subjects were five years old they participated in a joint assessment session with their mothers and in a separate joint assessment session with their fathers. The purpose of the joint sessions was to allow observations of parent-child interactions under standard conditions.

During each joint assessment session, the children were given a variety of age-appropriate tasks to perform, such as assembling objects from wooden blocks, arranging plastic pieces according to shape and color, solving mazes, and so on. The parents were instructed to respond to their child's eventual difficulties with the tasks and to provide whatever help they felt was needed. The tasks were designed to be of interest to parent and child, to be appropriately challenging to the child, and to be readily understandable to all parents. The order of the sessions and the order of tasks within sessions were counterbalanced. The joint assessment procedure has been described in more detail elsewhere (Block & Block, 1971; Gjerde, 1988).

Parent and child were left alone to work on the tasks while a trained observer watched the interaction through a one-way mirror. Additionally, the sessions were videotaped. After the session, the observer described the parent's manner of interacting with the child using a 49-item Parent-Child Interaction Q-sort (PCIQ) specially developed for this purpose (Block & Block, 1971). A second observer provided an additional Q-sort description after watching the session on videotape. The two Q-sorts describing the mother-child interaction were composited, as were the two Q-sorts describing the father-child interaction.

## Results

RATES OF DRUG USE The primary purpose of this study was to investigate the relations between drug use and psychological characteristics. However, it is first useful to consider the rate of drug use in the sample in absolute terms.

Of the 101 subjects for whom information about drug use was available, 68% had tried marijuana (four years earlier, 51% of the subjects had used marijuana; see Keyes & Block, 1984). Thirty-nine percent of the subjects reported using marijuana once a month or more, and 21% reported using it weekly or more than weekly. These figures are comparable to figures obtained in nationwide probability samples of adolescents and young adults (Johnston et al., 1986; Johnston, Bachman & O'Malley, 1981a, 1981b; Miller et al., 1983; NIDA, 1986).

Approximately 37% of the subjects reported trying cocaine, and 25% reported trying hallucinogens. Approximately 10% of the subjects reported trying amphetamines, barbiturates, tranquilizers, or inhalants. Only one subject reported that she had used heroin.

CREATION OF COMPARISON GROUPS  Based on the drug use information collected at age 18, the subjects were divided into three nonoverlapping groups, as follows.

*Abstainers* were defined as subjects who had never tried marijuana or any other drug. This group contained 29 subjects, 14 boys and 15 girls.

*Experimenters* were defined as subjects who had used marijuana "once or twice," "a few times," or "once a month," and who had tried *no more* than one drug other than marijuana. This group contained 36 subjects, 16 boys and 20 girls. The mean number of other drugs tried by the subjects in this group was 0.31 (i.e., 11 of the 36 subjects had tried one drug other than marijuana).

*Frequent users* were defined as subjects who reported using marijuana frequently, that is, once a week or more, and who had tried *at least* one drug other than marijuana. This group contained 20 subjects, 11 boys and 9 girls. The mean number of other drugs tried by the subjects in this group was 2.70.

Sixteen subjects "fell between the cracks" of the classification scheme, and did not meet the definitional criteria for any of the groups. In general, these were subjects who were excluded from the abstainer and experimenter groups because of their use of drugs other than marijuana. . . .

The groups were first compared on the control variables of socioeconomic status, as assessed by both the Duncan (1961) and Warner, Meeker, and Eells (1949) indexes and IQ, as measured by the Wechsler Preschool and Primary Scale of Intelligence (WPPSI) at age 4, the Wechsler Intelligence Scale for Children (WISC) at age 11, and the Wechsler Adult Intelligence Scale (WAIS) at age 18. No associations approaching significance were observed; consequently, these variables cannot be readily invoked to explain subsequent findings.

## Personality Concomitants of Drug Use

. . . Findings are presented using the experimenters as a reference group, and the personality characteristics associated with the other groups are elucidated through comparison with them. The experimenters are used as a frame of reference for two reasons: (a) they constitute the largest group and reflect the pattern of drug use most typical for this sample and most typical for adolescents in the nation as a whole; (b) the group of experimenters lies between the other groups on the continuum of frequency of drug use; therefore, its use as a reference group facilitates the discernment of possible curvilinear relations between drug use and personality measures. As will be seen, this second consideration takes on considerable importance.

PERSONALITY CHARACTERISTICS OF FREQUENT USERS  The frequent users were compared with the experimenters on each of the 100 Q-sort items, by means of separate $t$-tests. The number of statistically significant differences between the groups is striking and far exceeds the number to be expected by chance. Fully 51 of the 100 Q-sort items revealed differences at the .05 significance level (hypothesis tests are two-tailed unless otherwise noted) . . .

*When the Q-sort descriptions are considered as a set, the picture of the frequent user that emerges is one of a troubled adolescent, an adolescent who is interpersonally alienated, emotionally withdrawn, and manifestly unhappy, and who expresses his or her maladjustment through undercontrolled, overtly antisocial behavior.*

## PERSONALITY CHARACTERISTICS OF ABSTAINERS

The abstainers were compared with the experimenters on each of the 100 Q-sort items, by means of separate *t*-tests. Once again, the number of statistically significant CAQ items well exceeds chance, with 19 of the 100 CAQ items showing differences between the groups at the .05 level. . . .

*When the Q-sort items are considered as a set, the picture of the abstainer that emerges is of a relatively tense, overcontrolled, emotionally constricted individual who is somewhat socially isolated and lacking in interpersonal skills.*

## Personality Antecedents of Drug Use

An unusual feature of the present study is that psychological descriptions of subjects are available from early childhood on. Moreover, the psychological descriptions obtained at different ages are wholly independent of one another. We wish to emphasize this independence: The psychologists who saw the subjects at different ages were different people, they saw the subjects under different conditions, they saw the subjects only at the age at which they served as assessors, and they had no contact with one another. Because of the safeguards taken to ensure the independence of the data, relations between psychological characteristics observed at age 18 and psychological characteristics observed in early childhood must be attributed to continuities in psychological development over time (and not to artifacts of the research design).

On the basis of the CAQ descriptions obtained at age 18, a priori directional hypotheses were generated for virtually all of the age 11 and age 7 California Child Q-Sort items. Specifically, it was hypothesized that abstainers would show signs of impulse overcontrol, and frequent users would show signs of impulse undercontrol, relative to experimenters; and that abstainers and frequent users would both show signs of interpersonal alienation and psychological distress, relative to experimenters. . . .

## THE CHILDHOOD PERSONALITY OF FREQUENT USERS

The frequent users were compared with the experimenters on each of the CCQ items by means of separate *t*-tests. At age 11, frequent users were described (in comparison to experimenters) as visibly deviant from their peers, emotionally labile, inattentive and unable to concentrate, not involved in what they do, stubborn (preceding items significant at the .05 level), unhelpful and uncooperative, pushing and stretching limits, not eager to please, immobilized under stress, not curious and open to new experience, likely to give up easily, likely to withdraw under stress, not having high performance standards, suspicious and distrustful, and overreactive to minor frustrations (preceding items significant at the .10 level).

At age 7, the frequent users were described as not getting along well with other children, not showing concern for moral issues (e.g., reciprocity, fairness), having bodily symptoms from stress, tending to be indecisive and vacillating, not planful or likely to think ahead, not trustworthy or dependable, not able to admit to negative feelings, not self-reliant or confident (preceding items significant at the .05 level), preferring nonverbal methods of communication, not developing genuine and close relationships, not proud of their accomplishments, not vital or energetic or lively, not curious and open to new experience, not able to recoup after stress, afraid of being deprived, appearing to feel unworthy and "bad," not likely to identify with admired adults, inappropriate in emotive behavior, and easily victimized and scapegoated by other children (preceding items significant at the .10 level).

*In short, the frequent users appear to be relatively maladjusted as children. As early as age 7, the picture that emerges is of a child unable to form good relationships, who is insecure, and who shows numerous signs of emotional distress. These data indicate that the relative social and psychological maladjustment of the frequent users predates adolescence, and predates initiation of drug use.*

## The Childhood Personality of Abstainers

The abstainers were compared with the experimenters on each of the CCQ items. At age 11, the abstainers were described as relatively fearful and anxious, using and responding to reason, not physically active, not vital or energetic or lively, inhibited and constricted, not liking to compete, not curious and open to new experiences, not interesting or arresting, physically cautious, neat and orderly (implies fussiness), anxious in unpredictable environments, not having a rapid personal tempo, looking to adults for help and direction, not responsive to humor, not self-assertive, not self-reliant or confident, shy and reserved (preceding items significant at the .05 level), cold and unresponsive, immobilized under stress, obedient and compliant, not calm or relaxed, planful and likely to think ahead, not cheerful, not talkative, and not aggressive (preceding items significant at the .10 level).

At age 7, the abstainers were described as relatively eager to please, inhibited and constricted, conventional in thought, neat and orderly, planful and likely to think ahead, not verbally expressive, not seeking to be independent and autonomous (preceding items significant at the .05 level), not proud of their accomplishments, not physically active, immobilized under stress, obedient and compliant, not self-assertive, not competent and skillful, and not creative (preceding items significant at the .10 level).

*These descriptions present a picture of a child who is relatively overcontrolled, timid, fearful, and morose. While the characterizations of these children as "anxious," "inhibited," and "immobilized under stress" are telling, more telling, perhaps, may be the descriptions of what these children are not; relative to the reference group of experimenters, they are not warm and responsive, not curious and open to new experience, not active, not vital, and not cheerful. . . .*

## Quality of Parenting

\* \* \*

### Quality of Parenting: Frequent Users

Compared with the mothers of the experimenters, the mothers of the frequent users are described as hostile, not spontaneous with their children, not responsive or sensitive to their children's needs, critical of their children and rejecting of their ideas and suggestions, not supportive and encouraging of their children, tending to dramatize their teaching, making the test situation grim and distasteful rather than fun, pressuring their children to work at the tasks, underprotective of their children, overly interested in and concerned with their children's performance, conducting the session in such a way that their children do not enjoy it (preceding items significant at the .05 level), appearing to lack pride in and be ashamed of their children, seeming to be confused about what is expected of them in the test situation, conducting the session in unusual or atypical ways, not giving their children praise, and not having a clear and coherent teaching style (preceding items significant at the .10 level).

*In brief, the mothers of the frequent users are perceived as relatively cold, unresponsive, and underprotective. They appear to give their children little encouragement, while, conjointly, they are pressuring and overly interested in their children's "performance." The apparent net effect of this double-bind is that they turn a potentially enjoyable interaction into a grim and unpleasant one.*

Few items discriminated between the fathers of frequent users and the fathers of experimenters.

### Quality of Parenting: Abstainers

Compared with the mothers of the experimenters, the mothers of the abstainers were described as hostile, not responsive or sensitive to their children's needs, critical of their children and rejecting of their ideas and suggestions, frustrated by an inability to find adequate strategies for teaching their children, not valuing their children's originality, not supportive and encouraging of their children, overly interested in, and concerned with, their children's performance, impatient with their children (preceding items significant at the .05 level), appearing to lack pride in and be ashamed of their children, seeming to be confused about what is expected of them in the test situation, conducting the session in unusual or atypical ways, not giving their children praise, not having a clear and coherent teaching style, pressuring their children to work at the tasks, and conducting the session in such a way that their children do not enjoy it (preceding items significant at the .10 level).

*Like the mothers of the frequent users, these mothers are perceived as relatively cold and unresponsive. They give their children little encouragement, while, conjointly, they are pressuring and overly interested in their children's performance. Again, the apparent net effect is that they make the interaction grim and unenjoyable.*

A variety of PCIQ items discriminated between fathers of abstainers and fathers of experimenters. . . . Compared with the fathers of the experimenters, the fathers of the abstainers were described as relatively attentive to the cognitive elements in the test situation, not responsive or sensitive to their children's needs, not allowing open disagreement between parent and child, maintaining tight control of the session, critical of their children and rejecting of their ideas and suggestions, appearing to lack pride in and be ashamed of their children, not encouraging their children to proceed independently, not valuing their children's originality, using physical means (e.g., body language and facial expression) to communicate with their children, overly interested in, and concerned with, their children's performance, impatient with their children, conducting the session in such a way that the children do not enjoy it, not deriving pleasure from being with their children, intruding physically into their children's activities (preceding items significant at the .05 level), setting too fast a pace for their children, seeming confused about what is expected in the situation, not easy and relaxed, and pressuring their children to work at the tasks (preceding items significant at the .10 level).

The picture that emerges is of an authoritarian and domineering father who squelches spontaneity and creativity and who demands that things be done *his* way. He does not appear to enjoy being with his child, and he ensures that his child does not enjoy being with him.

## Underlying Personality Factors: Linear and Curvilinear Relations

Up to this point, we have taken a *person-centered* approach in presenting our findings. That is, we focused on discrete groups of subjects (e.g., frequent users) and attempted to provide comprehensive and psychologically rich characterizations of these subjects. Such a person-centered approach is congruent with the orientation of clinical practitioners and facilitates the often difficult task of translating empirical findings into usable clinical insights.

The more common analytical approach is nomothetic or *variable-centered*. Such an approach emphasizes *variables* rather than persons. In the context of the present study, drug use is treated as a continuum, and the research inquiries become: "What are the major personality variables associated with drug use?" and "What is the *form* of the relations between these variables and drug use?"

Person-centered and variable-centered approaches can inform and complement one another, each illuminating different facets of the problem at hand. The variable-centered analyses that follow examine concomitant relations only (i.e., relations between drug use and personality characteristics, both assessed at age 18). . . .

### MONOTONIC AND NONMONOTONIC RELATIONS

. . . The pattern of monotonic and nonmonotonic relations appears to be orderly. Specifically, it appears that (a) items reflecting the Quality of Interpersonal Relations factor show somewhat U (or inverted U) shaped relations with level of drug use, such that experimenters are judged to have healthier interpersonal relationships than either abstainers or frequent users; (b) items reflecting the Subjective Distress factor manifest somewhat

U- (or inverted U) shaped relationship with level of drug use, such that experimenters are judged to have a greater sense of emotional well-being than either abstainers or frequent users; and (c) items reflecting the Ego-Control factor are related monotonically to level of drug use, such that abstainers are judged to be relatively overcontrolled with respect to impulse expression and frequent users are judged to be relatively undercontrolled. Finally, the U-shaped relations described here do not appear to be symmetric: Although both abstainers and frequent users are evaluated relatively unfavorably in terms of the Quality of Interpersonal Relations and Subjective Distress factors, it also appears that frequent users are evaluated less favorably by far.

To test these observations formally, three separate hierarchical multiple regressions were performed, in which level of marijuana use served as a predictor of the Quality of Interpersonal Relations, Subjective Distress, and Ego-Control scales, respectively.[1] Each regression equation included both a linear and a quadratic term. The regressions were "hierarchical" in the sense that the linear term entered the regression equation first, followed by the quadratic term, which provided a test of curvilinearity. The regression analyses are based on the full sample of 101 subjects for whom drug use and personality data were available; the previous distinctions between abstainers, experimenters, and frequent users were ignored. . . .

Figure [12.1] graphically illustrates the best-fit regression lines to predict Quality of Interpersonal Relations, Subjective Distress, and Ego-Control. It can be seen that both Quality of Interpersonal Relations and Subjective Distress show somewhat U- (or inverted U) shaped relations with level of drug use (i.e., moderate experimentation with marijuana is associated with more positive interpersonal relationships, and greater subjective well-being, than either no marijuana use or heavy use). These U-shaped relations are clearly asymmetric, with heavy marijuana use associated with much greater intrapersonal and interpersonal disturbance than abstention. It can also be seen from Figure [12.1] that the relation between drug use and Ego-Control is linear: the more impulsivity, the greater the level of drug use. . . .

## General Discussion

* * *

ON THE RELATION BETWEEN DRUG USE AND PSYCHOLOGICAL HEALTH    When the psychological findings are considered as a set, it is difficult to escape the inference that experimenters are the psychologically healthiest subjects, healthier than either abstainers or frequent users. Psychological health is meant here in a global and nonspecific sense, consistent with ordinary conversational usage, and consistent also with empirical recognitions by mental health researchers that a general psychological health/psychological distress factor underlies diverse clinical syndromes (e.g., Dohrenwend, Shrout, Egri, & Mendelsohn, 1980; Tanaka & Huba, 1984; Watson & Clark, 1984). . . .

The finding that frequent users are relatively maladjusted has been obtained by many other investigators. The finding that abstainers also show some signs of relative maladjustment (albeit of a very different kind) is, perhaps, unusual. In order to understand this latter finding, we suggest it is important to consider both the *meaning* of drug use within adolescent peer culture, as well as the psychology of adolescent development.

First, it is necessary to recognize that in contemporary American culture, there is wide prevalence and apparent acceptability of marijuana use in late adolescence. The majority of the 18-year-olds in our sample—approximately two thirds—had tried marijuana at one time or another. Such a high usage rate is consistent with the findings from

---

[1]Marijuana use is an ordinal variable (0 = never tried marijuana, 6 = daily marijuana use; see Method section). Level of marijuana use is used as the predictor variable in these regression analyses because it carries the most fine-grained information regarding drug involvement and because it is the primary variable upon which classification as abstainer, experimenter, or frequent user was based.

FIGURE 12.1. *Relations Between Level of Marijuana Use and (a) Quality of Interpersonal Relations, (b) Subjective Distress, and (c) Ego-Control*

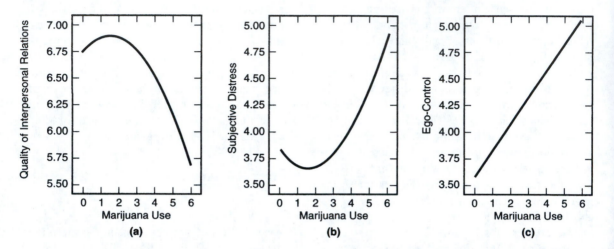

national probability samples (Johnston et al., 1986; Johnston, Bachman, & O'Malley, 1981a, 1981b; Miller et al., 1983; NIDA, 1986). Thus, some experimentation with marijuana cannot be considered *deviant* behavior for high school seniors in this culture at this time. In a statistical sense it is *not* trying marijuana that has become deviant.

Second, the extended period of adolescence is a time of transition, a time when young people face the developmental task of differentiating themselves from parents and family and forging independent identities. Experimenting with values and beliefs, exploring new roles and identities, and testing limits and personal boundaries are normative behaviors during adolescence, and they serve important developmental ends (cf. Erikson, 1968; Havinghurst, 1972).

Given these factors—the ubiquity and apparent acceptability of marijuana in the peer culture and the developmental appropriateness of experimentation and limit-testing during adolescence—it is not surprising that by age 18, psychologically healthy, sociable, and reasonably inquisitive individuals would have been tempted to try marijuana. We would not expect these essentially normal and certainly normative adolescents to *abuse* the drug (and it is crucial to distinguish between experimentation and abuse) because they would have

little need for drugs as an outlet for emotional distress or as a means of compensating for lack of meaningful human relationships—but we should not be surprised if they try it. Indeed, not to do so may reflect a degree of inhibition and social isolation in an 18-year-old.

Although no prior study has focused explicitly on the psychology of adolescent abstainers, there is some empirical precedent for the present finding that abstainers are not the most well-adjusted of adolescents. Hogan, Mankin, Conway, and Fox (1970), using a self-report personality inventory, compared marijuana users with nonusers in a college population and found that users "are more socially skilled, have a broader range of interests, are more adventuresome, and more concerned with the feelings of others" (p. 63). Nonusers were characterized as "too deferential to external authority, narrow in their interests, and overcontrolled" (p. 61). These findings, based on entirely different methodology, are strikingly similar to our own. In a similar vein, Bentler (1987) reported a small but reliable association between marijuana use and the development of a *positive* self-concept. . . .

The U-shaped relations between psychological health and drug use are reminiscent of U-shaped relations between psychological health and alcohol use noted in an earlier generation of subjects.

Thus, Jones (1968, 1971) found that moderate drinkers were psychologically healthier than either problem drinkers or abstainers. Moreover, the undercontrolled, alienated personality attributes of problem drinkers and the overcontrolled, diffident personality attributes of alcohol abstainers were quite similar to the personality attributes that characterize frequent drug users and drug abstainers in the present study. Given the prevalence and apparent acceptability of marijuana use among adolescents today, it would seem that marijuana use has taken on psychological and sociological meanings for young people that, in earlier generations, were associated with alcohol use.

TOWARD AN UNDERSTANDING OF FREQUENT DRUG USERS . . . At age 18, the frequent users appear unable to invest in, or derive pleasure from, meaningful personal relationships. Indeed, they seem fortified against the possibility of such relationships through their hostility, distrust, and emotional withdrawal. Neither do they appear to be capable of investing in school and work, or of channeling their energies toward meaningful future goals. They are, then, alienated from the "love and work" that lend a sense of satisfaction and meaning to life. Consistent with this, they appear to *feel* troubled and inadequate. It is easy to see how these characteristics could create a vicious cycle: Feeling troubled and inadequate, these adolescents withdraw from work and relationships, and alienated from work and relationships, they feel all the more troubled and inadequate.

Such a pattern of alienation can be expected to go hand in hand with an impaired ability to control and regulate impulses. When there is little investment in either work or relationships, that is, when there is little connection with those things that give life a sense of stability and purpose, then the impulses of the moment become paramount. The impulses are not adequately transformed or mediated by a broader system of values and goals because such a system is lacking. . . .

Drugs would have a special appeal to the alienated and impulsive individuals we are discussing. The temporary effects of various drugs "numb out" feelings of isolation and inadequacy; they offer transient gratification to individuals who lack deeper and more meaningful gratifications (i.e., through relationships and work); and given the poor ability of these individuals to regulate impulse, the urge toward drug use would meet with little inner resistance and would be little modified by a broader value system. . . .

This relative maladjustment perhaps may be traced, at least in part, to the maternal parenting that the frequent users received, as assessed by direct observations of mother-child interactions when the subjects were five years of age. Relative to the mothers of experimenters, the mothers of frequent users were perceived as hostile, critical and rejecting, and not sensitive or responsive to their children's needs. Moreover, they seemed to place their children in a double-bind: Although they gave their children little support and encouragement, they were simultaneously pressuring and overly concerned with their children's "performance."

TOWARD AN UNDERSTANDING OF ABSTAINERS Adolescents who have never experimented with marijuana or any other drug have not been the subject of research attention, if only because their behavior does not pose an obvious, confronting societal problem and because it has been presumed categorically that *not* using drugs goes hand in hand with psychological health. However, our data suggest that, relative to experimenters, abstainers in late adolescence are somewhat maladjusted. Unlike the patent, blatant maladjustment of frequent drug users, however, the psychological inadequacies of abstainers are largely a private matter, limiting of life as it is led, and do not attract societal attention. The constriction, uneasiness with affect, and interpersonal deficiencies of abstainers are recognizable more by way of *omission* than commission.

By omission, we refer to personal potentialities that seem to remain unfulfilled, specifically, potentialities for emotional gratifications, friendship, and human warmth and closeness. It is the relative capacity (or rather, *incapacity*) to experience these positive qualities of life that distinguishes abstainers from experimenters. Relative to experimenters, the abstainers are described at age 18 as overcontrolled and prone to delay gratification unnecessarily, not able to enjoy sensuous experiences, prone to avoid close interpersonal relationships, not gregarious, not liked and accepted by people, and so on. Thus, their avoidance of drugs seems less the result of "moral fiber" or successful drug education than the result of relative alienation from their peers and a characterological overcontrol of needs and impulses.

It seems likely that the relative overcontrol and emotional constriction of the abstainers serves the psychological purpose of containing or masking feelings of vulnerability. . . . At age 11, for example, prior to initiation of drug use, the abstainers are described (relative to experimenters) as fearful and anxious, inhibited and constricted, immobilized under stress, anxious in unpredictable environments, not curious and open to new experience, not vital or energetic or lively, not confident, not responsive to humor, and not cheerful. These traits would appear to reflect a susceptibility to anxiety and, perhaps, a consequent avoidance of circumstances or behaviors perceived as risky.

The hypothesis that emotional constriction serves the purpose of "containing" feelings of vulnerability is reinforced further by observations of mother-child interactions when the children were age five: The mothers of the abstainers were perceived (relative to the mothers of the experimenters) as unresponsive, cold, critical, and rejecting. Such parenting clearly has negative implications for psychological resiliency and well-being. It is interesting that the descriptions of the mothers of abstainers are strikingly similar to the descriptions of the mothers of the frequent users. . . .

The question of why abstainers and frequent users traveled such different developmental pathways remains an open one. Character formation is a matter of complex temperamental and developmental vicissitudes, and such questions have no straightforward answer. Our findings suggest the speculation that the fathers of the abstainers played a telling role in their character development. They acted toward their children in ways that would seem to increase anxiety, but their stern, authoritarian, and autocratic manner may have also provided a model for dealing with that anxiety. It is conceivable that the children internalized their fathers' attitudes, adopting an attitude toward their own impulses that paralleled their father's attitudes toward them.

IMPLICATIONS FOR THEORY AND SOCIAL POLICY
Taken as a whole, the present data indicate that drug use and drug abstinence have theoretically coherent antecedents and must be understood within the context of an individual's total psychology. Because experimenters and frequent users are, psychologically, very different kinds of people, the meaning of drug use in these two groups is very different. In the case of experimenters, drug use appears to reflect age-appropriate and developmentally understandable experimentation. In the case of frequent users, drug use appears to be a manifestation of a more general pattern of maladjustment, a pattern that appears to predate adolescence and predate initiation of drug use. Undoubtedly, drug use exacerbates this earlier established pattern but, of course, the logic of a longitudinal research design precludes invocation of drug use as causing this personality syndrome.

Current theories (e.g., Akers, Krohn, Lanze-Kaduce, & Radosevich, 1979; Jessor & Jessor, 1977, 1978; Kaplan, Martin, & Robbins, 1982) tend to emphasize the role of peers in influencing drug use. The importance of peers in providing an encouraging surround for *experimentation* cannot be denied, but "peer-centered" or "environmental" explanations of *problem* drug use seem inadequate, given the present longitudinal findings (cf. Margulies, Kessler, & Kandel, 1977). . . .

The recognition that *problem* drug use (and, for that matter, abstinence) has developmental antecedents, that it is a part of a broad and theoretically coherent psychological syndrome, and that it is not adequately explained in terms of peer influence has important implications for social policy.

Current social policy seems to follow from the

assumption that peer influence leads to experimentation, which in turn leads to abuse. Thus, efforts at drug education are aimed at discouraging experimentation by emphasizing the need to "just say no" to peer influence. But adolescent experimentation in and of itself does not appear to be personally or societally destructive (see also Kandel, Davies, Karus, & Yamaguchi, 1986, and Newcomb & Bentler, 1988), and peer influence does not appear to be an adequate explanation for *problem* drug use. Moreover, given the developmental tasks of the prolonged adolescent period, efforts aimed at eliminating adolescent experimentation are likely to be costly and to meet with limited success.

Current efforts at drug "education" seem flawed on two counts. First, they are alarmist, pathologizing normative adolescent experimentation and limit-testing, and perhaps frightening parents and educators unnecessarily. Second, and of far greater concern, they *trivialize* the factors underlying drug *abuse*, implicitly denying their depth and pervasiveness. For so long as problem drug use is construed primarily in terms of "lack of education," so long is attention diverted from its disturbing psychological underpinnings: the psychological triad of alienation, impulsivity, and distress. Paradoxically, then, the "just say no" approach may be concerned with a "problem" that, from a developmental viewpoint, need not be seen as alarming (adolescent experimentation), and it may be dismayingly oblivious to a serious problem that is extremely alarming (the ubiquity of the psychological syndrome that appears to underlie *problem* drug use).

The concept of drug "education" may have its current popular appeal in part because the link between the problem (drugs) and the attempted solution (drug education) is self-evident and thus reassures concerned parents, educators, and policymakers that "something is being done." But educational approaches to drug prevention have had limited success (Tobler, 1986), and society's limited resources might better be invested in interventions focusing on the personality syndrome underlying problem drug use.

Given current understandings of personality development, it would seem that the psychological triad of alienation, impulsivity, and distress would be better addressed through efforts aimed at encouraging sensitive and empathic parenting, at building childhood self-esteem, at fostering sound interpersonal relationships, and at promoting involvement and commitment to meaningful goals. Such interventions may not have the popular appeal of programs that appear to tackle the drug problem "directly," but may have greater individual and societal payoff in the end.

FORFENDING MISINTERPRETATION The finding that experimenters are the psychologically healthiest adolescents, and the observation that some drug experimentation, in and of itself, does not seem to be psychologically destructive, may sit badly with some. In particular, it may sit badly with drug counselors who "know" from clinical experience that there is no level of drug use that is safe, that it is dangerous to suggest otherwise, and that the most effective intervention is one aiming at total abstinence. To avoid any misunderstanding, we wish to make clear that there is no contradiction between this therapeutic perspective and the findings we have reported. On the contrary, we are in agreement with the therapeutic perspective.

The present data indicate that in a nonselected late-adolescent sample, occasional experimentation with marijuana is not personally or societally destructive. This view is supported by longitudinal studies of the consequences of drug use (as well as by the present study of the antecedents and concomitants of drug use; see, e.g., Kandel et al., 1986; Newcomb & Bentler, 1988), and by the fact that the majority of adolescents in the United States have experimented with marijuana but have not subsequently become drug abusers. The apparent contradiction between clinical wisdom, on the one hand, and the present findings, on the other, is resolved when it is recognized that individuals who present themselves for drug treatment are *not* representative of the general population of adolescents, but instead constitute a special, highly selected subpopulation. The psychological meaning of drug use is very different for this fractional group existing within the larger population of adolescents. For them, experimentation with drugs is highly destructive because drugs easily become part of a broader pathological syndrome. For adolescents more generally, some drug experimentation apparently does not have psychologically catastrophic implications.

In closing, one final clarification is in order. In presenting research on a topic as emotionally charged as drug use, there is always the danger that findings may be misinterpreted or misrepresented. Specifically, we are concerned that some segments of the popular media may misrepresent our findings as indicating that drug use might somehow improve an adolescent's psychological health. Although the incorrectness of such an interpretation should be obvious to anyone who has actually read this article, our concern about media misrepresentation requires us to state categorically that our findings do *not* support such a view, nor should anything we have said remotely encourage such an interpretation.

# References

Akers, R. L., Krohn, M. D., Lanze-Kaduce, L., & Radosevich, M. (1979). Social learning and deviant behavior: A specific test of a general theory. *American Sociological Review, 44,* 636–655.

Bem, D. J., Funder, D. C. (1978). Predicting more of the people more of the time: Assessing the personality of situations. *Psychological Review, 85,* 485–501.

Bentler, P. M. (1987). Drug use and personality in adolescence and young adulthood: Structural models with nonnormal variables. *Child Development, 58,* 65–79.

Block, J. (1971). *Lives through time.* Berkeley, CA: Bancroft.

Block, J. (1978). *The Q-sort method in personality assessment and psychiatric research.* Palo Alto, CA: Consulting Psychologists Press. (Original work published 1961)

Block, J., & Block, J. H. (1980). *The California Child Q-set.* Palo Alto, CA: Consulting Psychologists Press.

Block, J., Block, J. H., & Keyes, S. (1988). Longitudinally foretelling drug usage in adolescence: Early childhood personality and environmental precursors. *Child Development, 59,* 336–355.

Block, J. H., & Block, J. (1971). *Manual for the Parent-Child Interaction Procedure.* Berkeley: University of California, Department of Psychology. CA.

Block, J. H., & Block, J. (1980). The role of ego-control and ego-resiliency in the organization of behavior. In W. A. Collins (Ed.), *Minnesota symposia on child psychology* (Vol. 13, pp. 39–101). Hillsdale, NJ: Erlbaum.

Brook, J. S., Gordon, A. S., & Whiteman, M. (1985). Stability of personality during adolescence and its relationship to stage of drug use. *Genetic Social and General Psychology Monographs, 111,* 317–330.

Brook, J. S., Whiteman, M., Gordon, A. S., & Cohen, P. (1986). Dynamics of childhood and adolescent personality traits and adolescent drug use. *Developmental Psychology, 22,* 403–414.

Bush, P. J., & Iannotti, R. (1965). The development of children's health orientations and behaviors: Lessons for substance use prevention. In C. L. Jones & R. J. Battjes (Eds.), *Etiology of drug abuse: Implications for prevention* (Research Monograph No. 56, pp. 45–74). Rockville, MD: National Institute on Drug Abuse.

Cox, W. M. (1985). Personality correlates of substance abuse. In M. Galizio & S. A. Maisto (Eds.), *Determinants of substance abuse: Biological, psychological, and environmental factors* (pp. 209–246). New York: Plenum.

Dohrenwend, B. S., Shrout, P. E., Egri, G., & Mendelsohn, F. S. (1980). Nonspecific psychological distress and other dimensions of psychopathology. *Archives of General Psychiatry, 37,* 1229–1236.

Duncan, O. (1961). A socioeconomic index for all occupations. In A. J. Reiss, Jr. (Ed.), *Occupation and social status* (pp. 109–138). New York: Free Press.

Erikson, E. H. (1968). *Identity: Youth and crisis.* New York: Norton.

Gergen, K. J. (1973). Social psychology as history. *Journal of Personality and Social Psychology, 36,* 309–320.

Gjerde, P. F. (1988). Parental concordance on child-rearing and the interactive emphases of parents: Gender differentiated relationships during the preschool years. *Developmental Psychology, 24,* 700–706.

Gjerde, P. F., Block, J., & Block, J. H. (1988). Depressive symptomatology and personality during late adolescence: Gender differences in the externalization-internalization of symptom expression. *Journal of Abnormal Psychology, 97,* 475–486.

Haberman, P. W., Josephson, E., Zanes, A., & Elinson, J. (1972). High school drug behavior: A methodological report on pilot studies. In S. Einstein & S. Allen (Eds.), *Proceedings of the First International Conference on Student Drug Surveys* (pp. 103–121). Farmingdale, NY: Baywood.

Havinghurst, R. J. (1972). *Developmental tasks and education* (3rd ed.). New York: McKay.

Hawkins, J. D., Lishner, D. M., & Catalano, R. F. (1985). Childhood predictors and the prevention of adolescent substance abuse. In C. L. Jones & R. J. Battjes (Eds.), *Etiology of drug abuse: Implications for prevention* (Research Monograph No. 56, pp. 75–125). Rockville, MD: National Institute on Drug Abuse.

Hogan, R., Mankin, D., Conway, J., & Fox, S. (1970). Personality correlates of undergraduate marijuana use. *Journal of Consulting and Clinical Psychology, 35,* 58–63.

Jessor, R. (1979). Marijuana: A review of recent psychosocial research. In R. L. Dupont, A. Goldstein, & J. O'Donnell (Eds.), *Handbook on drug abuse* (pp. 337–355). Washington, DC: Government Printing Office.

Jessor, R., Chase, J. A., & Donovan, J. E. (1980). Psychosocial correlates of marijuana use and problem drinking in a national sample of adolescents. *American Journal of Public Health, 70,* 604–613.

Jessor, R., & Jessor, S. L. (1977). *Problem behavior and psycho-*

logical development: A longitudinal study of youth. New York: Academic Press.

Jessor, R., & Jessor, S. L. (1978). Theory testing in longitudinal research on marijuana use. In D. B. Kandel (Ed.), Longitudinal research on drug use: Empirical findings and methodological issues (pp. 41–71). Washington, DC: Hemisphere.

Johnston, L. D., Bachman, J. G., & O'Malley, P. M. (1981a). Highlights from student drug use in America 1975–1981. Rockville, MD: National Institute on Drug Abuse.

Johnston, L. D., Bachman, J. G., & O'Malley, P. M. (1981b). Student drug use in America 1975–1981. Rockville, MD: National Institute on Drug Abuse.

Johnston, L. D., O'Malley, P. M., & Bachman, J. G. (1984). Drugs and American high school students, 1975–1983 (National Institute of Drug Abuse, DHHS Publication No. ADM 84–1317). Washington, DC: Government Printing Office.

Johnston, L. D., O'Malley, P. M., & Bachman, J. G. (1986). Drug use among American high school students, college students, and other young adults: National trends through 1985. Rockville, MD: National Institute on Drug Abuse.

Jones, C. L., & Battjes, R. J. (Eds.). (1985). Etiology of drug abuse: Implications for prevention. (Research Monograph No. 56; DHHS Publication No. ADM 85–1335). Rockville, MD: National Institute of Drug Abuse.

Jones, M. C. (1968). Personality correlates and antecedents of drinking patterns in adult males. Journal of Consulting and Clinical Psychology, 31, 1–12.

Jones, M. C. (1971). Personality antecedents and correlates of drinking patterns in women. Journal of Consulting and Clinical Psychology, 36, 61–69.

Kandel, D. B. (1978). Convergences in prospective longitudinal surveys of drug use in normal populations. In D. Kandel (Ed.), Longitudinal research on drug use: Empirical findings and methodological issues (pp. 3–38). Washington, DC: Hemisphere.

Kandel, D. B. (1980). Drug and drinking behavior among youth. Annual Review of Sociology, 6, 235–285.

Kandel, D. B., Davies, M., Karus, D., & Yamaguchi, K. (1986). The consequences in young adulthood of adolescent drug involvement. Archives of General Psychiatry, 43, 746–754.

Kaplan, H. B., Martin, S. S., & Robbins, C. (1982). Application of a general theory of deviant behavior: Self-derogation and adolescent drug use. Journal of Health and Social Behavior, 23, 274–294.

Kellam, S. G., Branch, J. D., Agrawal, K. C., & Ensminger, M. E. (1975). Mental health and going to school: The Woodlawn program of assessment, early intervention, and evaluation. Chicago: University of Chicago Press.

Kellam, S. G., Brown, C. H., Rubin, B. R., & Ensminger, M. E. (1983). Paths leading to teenage psychiatric symptoms and substance use: Developmental epidemiological studies in Woodlawn. In S. B. Guze, F. J. Earls, & J. E. Barrett (Eds.), Childhood psychopathology and development (pp. 17–47). New York: Raven.

Keyes, S., & Block, J. (1984). Prevalence and patterns of substance abuse among early adolescents. Journal of Youth and Adolescence, 13, 1–14.

Margulies, R. Z., Kessler, R. C., & Kandel, D. B. (1977). A longitudinal study of onset of drinking among high school students. Journal of Studies of Alcohol, 38, 897–912.

Miller, J. D., Cisin, I. H., Gardner-Keaton, H., Harrel, A. V., Wirtz, P. W., Abelson, H. I., & Fishburne, P. M. (1983). National survey on drug abuse: Main findings 1982. Rockville, MD: National Institute on Drug Abuse.

Mischel, W., Shoda, Y., & Peake, P. K. (1988). The nature of adolescent competencies predicted by preschool delay of gratification. Journal of Personality and Social Psychology, 54, 687–696.

National Institute on Drug Abuse. (1986). Capsules: Overview of the 1985 household survey on drug abuse. Rockville, MD: Author.

Newcomb, M., & Bentler, P. (1988). Consequences of adolescent drug use: Impact on the lives of young adults. Newbury Park, CA: Sage.

Perry, C. L., Killen, J., & Slinkard, L. A. (1980). Peer teaching and smoking prevention among junior high students. Adolescence, 15, 277–281.

Robins, L. N. (1984). The natural history of adolescent drug use. American Journal of Public Health, 74, 656–657.

Single, E., Kandel, D., & Johnson, B. D. (1975). The reliability and validity of drug use responses in a large scale longitudinal survey. Journal of Drug Issues, 5, 426–443.

Smith, G. M., & Fogg, C. P. (1978). Psychological predictors of early use, late use, and nonuse of marijuana among teenage students. In D. B. Kandel (Ed.), Longitudinal research on drug use (pp. 101–113). New York: Wiley.

Tanaka, J. S., & Huba, G. J. (1984). Confirmatory hierarchical factor analysis of psychological distress measures. Journal of Personality and Social Psychology, 46, 621–635.

Tobler, N. S. (1986). Meta-analysis of 143 adolescent drug prevention programs: Quantitative outcome results of program participants compared to a control or comparison group. Journal of Drug Issues, 16, 537–568.

Warner, W. L., Meeker, M., & Eells, K. (1949). Social class in America. Chicago: Science Research Associates.

Watson, D. W., & Clark, L. A. (1984). Negative affectivity: The disposition to experience aversive emotional states. Psychological Bulletin, 96, 465–490.

# Tribe Sends Kids Away to Dry Out

## Maggie Farley

*If we had to guess, most of us would probably say that substance use is more prevalent in urban areas than in small towns and rural areas. However, this supposition is false. According to a report by the National Center on Addiction and Substance Abuse (2000), drug use by adults does not differ markedly across the two settings, but 8th graders in small-town and rural America are more likely than those in cities to use methamphetamine, crack cocaine, cocaine, marijuana, alcohol, cigarettes, and smokeless tobacco. Similar results are obtained for 10th graders and 12th graders.*

*One rural population that has been hit hard by substance abuse is Native Americans; Native American adolescents between the ages of 12 and 17 are more likely than comparably aged children in a national sample to use virtually every substance (Beauvais & Segal, 1992). For example, 80.5% of young Native Americans have used alcohol compared to 50% of a national sample; 61.1% have used marijuana compared to 17.4% in a national sample; and 23.8% have used inhalants compared to 8.8% in a national sample. What is going on here? This question cannot be answered yet, but the following article provides a glimpse into the lives of children and adolescents who live on a reservation in Canada and use gasoline as an inhalant. Their situation is so tragic that one young girl only took up sniffing gasoline because being brought to a treatment center off the reservation was her surest way of leaving the community. We can certainly maintain the view that addiction is a brain disease, but this article makes it clear that some environments are far more challenging than others in treating this problem.*

## References

Beauvais, F., & Segal, B. (1992). Drug use patterns among American Indian and Alaskan native youth. In R. W. Edwards (Ed.), *Drug use in rural American communities* (pp. 77–94). New York: Hawthorne.

National Center on Addiction and Substance Abuse. (2000). *No place to hide: Substance abuse in mid-size cities and rural America.* Unpublished report from Columbia University available at www.casacolumbia.org.

*Los Angeles Times*, A1. (2000, December 19).

SHESHATSHIU, Canada—Charles Rich, 11, was sniffing gasoline with his two brothers in their basement during the summer when he dropped the bag of gas near a candle. His gas-soaked clothes exploded into flames. Fumes from his breath ignited, and the fire screamed down his throat to his lungs. He burned to death in front of his brothers.

That should have been enough to scare anyone straight. But brothers Carl, 11, and Phillip, 13, still sniff gas. Phillip told CBC Television that he does it because that way he can see Charles again, a comforting angel in a gasoline mirage.

But others in this small native Canadian community on Newfoundland's Labrador barrens see nothing but danger and sickness and death spreading like a plague they can't control. More than half of the town's 636 children say they have sniffed gas, used illegal drugs or contemplated suicide, a recent study found. Nearly a quarter said they have tried to kill themselves. Three in the past year have committed suicide.

The community of Sheshatshiu decided it had no choice. The tribe could not ban gasoline. Many of the parents, struggling with alcohol problems of their own, were unable or unwilling to help their kids. And so on Nov. 15, Innu leaders—who have long lamented that the Canadian government took away their land and their culture—begged the provincial government to take away their gasoline-addicted children.

A week later, a dozen kids—the youngest only 8—boarded a blue school bus thinking they were going to a pizza party in nearby Goose Bay. Instead they were taken to an air force barracks to begin their wrenching withdrawal. Now, joined by seven others, they are continuing treatment in foster homes and wilderness camps. No one knows when they'll return.

"It's crisis intervention," says Leila Gillis, the tribe's director of Community Health Services, who led the recent study. "We're looking at it like an epidemic, a contagious disease that has to be stopped." Removing the core sniffers for treatment in effect places them in quarantine so they won't infect others. But will it work?

"If you take a dying fish out of a polluted river and put it in clean water, it will get better," says Jack Penashue, the director of the newly built Charles J. Andrew Youth Restoration Center here, who says he beat his own gas-sniffing and drinking problems. "But if you put it back in the poisoned water, what happens? It's not just a matter of healing a person, we have to treat whole families. The whole community needs healing."

It's not that they haven't tried. In this town of 1,200, whose name in the Innu language means "mouth of the river," new buildings line the few roads, each one a monument to misery: the youth drug treatment center, an alcohol rehabilitation facility, a hospital, a women's shelter, a group home. But the newest additions are simple white crosses in the cemetery—10 this year, all of them marking alcohol- or drug-related deaths.

Irene Penunsi, 19, is one of two in the group of the hardest-core gas sniffers who are of legal age and not under supervision of the provincial social services. She is living temporarily in a shelter for battered women with her mother.

There's a blizzard outside, with a sharp wind that makes you aware of your bones; it's too cold to go out and sniff gas, though Penunsi and a friend are craving its noxious fumes and sweet escape. Penunsi says the cold usually doesn't stop them.

"Sometimes at night, our parents lock us out. They say, 'You smell like gas' and close the door," she said. "So we go to the woods, build a fire and sniff all night long. We don't feel the cold." Penunsi was hospitalized three weeks ago with frost-bitten feet.

### If the Gas Tank Is Locked, They Just Bore a Hole

She describes the ritual of inhaling gas siphoned from cars, chain saws and snowmobiles; if there's a lock on the gas tank, they just bore a hole. And they take no pains to hide: They sniff right in front of the youth center, at a hot-water tank in the middle of town or in the woods between the new houses of the tribe's chief and the council president.

"You put it in a garbage bag and breathe it in," Penunsi says. "It burns your throat a little, it makes you cough. But pretty soon you hear things, like singing. You see things, as real as a movie. I see my cousin who died. He talks to me. He says he misses me."

Penunsi knows that sniffing gas is extremely damaging: that it kills brain cells with every whiff, that it weakens the heart, that it stays in the system so long that six months after you quit your sweat still smells like gasoline. With her friends all in detox, it's the perfect time to quit. But she chooses to keep sniffing.

"I'm never going to stop," she says.

Life here offers few options. Only 20% of adults have jobs, and the main business is building or working in one of the town's treatment centers. Just 5% of students graduate from high school, and five people in Sheshatshiu have college degrees. Many children can't read or write English, and their parents fret that the kids are even losing the Innu language, its vocabulary inadequate outside the bush.

One mother says her 13-year-old daughter took up sniffing after the other kids were taken away, for the chance to go away to a treatment center. She worries that addiction, not achievement, has become the ticket out of town.

If substance abuse is an epidemic in Sheshatshiu and other native communities in northeastern Canada, it is one that has been germinating for decades. The Innu were a nomadic people, traveling in small groups following herds of caribou. But a cyclical drop in the caribou population in the 1930s made it harder to keep up the traditional way of life. When an air force base was built on their land during World War II, bringing a non-Innu community with it, the hospitals and jobs attracted some Innu to settle down. In the 1950s and '60s, missionaries hungry for converts put them in religious schools and a government eager for a supply of factory laborers gave them houses.

But it turned out to be a bad bargain for the Innu.

Priests confiscated their sacred drums, scorned their gods and abused their kids. Government agents seized their shotguns, dammed their rivers and mined their land for nickel. By taking away the land, which is all the Innu knew, the government stripped away the Innu's identity.

That, the Innu say, was the beginning of their problems. After scores of lawsuits, this year Canada's four major churches compensated and apologized to Newfoundland's natives for long-term sexual and physical abuse. Negotiations with the government over the land and its riches drag on. But the Innu still have trouble reconciling their old ways with their new life.

Francis Penashue is typical of those in that first generation who tried to make the transition to a settled existence.

"In the country, my father was peaceful and strong, an educator and a good father," says Jack Penashue, 33, the youth center director. "In town, he was a mean alcoholic who beat me and my brothers. When you're in the bush, you know exactly who you are and what your duties are. But when he came here, he lost control of his life, his identity. No wonder my dad turned out the way he did."

Francis Penashue passed on his knowledge of the country—but also his drinking problem. Three of his sons—Jack, Peter and Max—told *The Times* that they also have been treated for alcoholism. Francis Penashue's wife, Elizabeth, contributed to a book on Innu women called *It's Just Like the Legend*, in which she discussed her own and her family's battle with alcohol.

In this younger generation, it seems, it's mostly the sickness that is passed along, the heritage becoming lost in a miasma of addiction, abuse and neglect. Solutions have been stifled by a culture of noninterference. In the bush, when two parties had a disagreement, one would simply move away. The community still has not come up with a good way to solve its collective problems.

"Innu people don't talk truth to each other," said Jerome Jack, a 38-year-old former tribal council member with the telltale purple-veined nose of a long-term alcoholic. He has been sober since Nov. 7, he says, when he and his 15-year-old, two-six-packs-a-night son made a pact to stop drinking.

"We're not really honest with each other, not even with ourselves," Jack says. "We just let things happen and only act when there's a crisis."

After two alcohol-related suicides in the summer of 1999, the community decided to act. Sheshatshiu banned alcohol with the help of the Mounties, setting up a 24-hour watch and roadblocks to search cars. But many town leaders were smuggling in alcohol themselves, other people challenged the prohibition as a violation of human rights, and the ban lasted only two weeks.

The community hopes that the children can do better.

"I recognize that to keep blaming the past means we won't be able to move forward. We have to take responsibility ourselves," says Peter Penashue, the president of the Innu Nation. "But to do that, we have to have resources."

## Some See an Effort to Extract Guilt Money

Penashue and tribal chief Paul Rich, a cousin of Charles Rich's father, have been effective at bringing national attention to their people's plight. But some say sending the children away was a well-timed maneuver by community leaders to wring money from a guilt-stricken government as the tribal coffers are running low; a recent provincial audit revealed financial irregularities.

The children were taken away at the height of the federal election campaign, turning the Innu's problems into a political issue. On the eve of the Nov. 27 elections, Innu leaders from Davis Inlet, about 160 miles north of here, presented Prime Minister Jean Chretien with a videotape of their kids sniffing and stumbling.

Chretien, a former Indian affairs minister, pledged to help and quickly used the issue to score political points against his leading challenger, free-market candidate Stockwell Day. "We still have some very difficult social problems in the land," he said election night, "and that type of problem will never be resolved by market forces."

Since the day the children were taken away, the provincial government has promised Sheshatshiu a new local detoxification facility, along with a family treatment center to address broader problems behind the symptoms. The federal government also pledged more funding, but even more important, it agreed to include the Innu under the Indian Act. The tribe had refused inclusion under the act in 1949 when Newfoundland became a province, fearing its members would be put on a reservation.

The act will exempt the Innu from taxes, include them in federal programs and give the tribe authority to ban the sniffing of gasoline, which is not a controlled substance in Canada.

## Innu Being Killed by Kindness, Critics Say

But critics say Canada is killing the Innu with kindness. Noting that the government last year gave the town $6.6 million (U.S.), or about $5,500 per person, the *National Post* said in an editorial: "A mountain of government money has done nothing but create a culture of dependency and a financial black hole. . . . If the government stops undermining their self-reliance with free money, they will prove tough enough to build a future for themselves."

Said Peter Penashue: "Consider the money as royalties for what the government has taken from our land."

With or without government support, many in the community still have hope. The most important factor in changing the behavior of youth, health care director Gillis found in her study, is whether parents talk to their kids about substance abuse, even if the adults have their own problems with alcohol.

"Half the kids may have alcoholic parents or sniff gasoline," Gillis notes. "But half of the kids do not."

Douglas Michelin, 13, is one who doesn't. He sits in his grandparents' house, a simple home heated by an iron-piped stove and adorned with family photos nailed into wood walls. He shows off the ginger pelt of a fox he snared a few days ago, stroking its velvety black ears. Trapping, hunting and surviving the winter in a tent are skills he learned from his grandparents, Madeleine and James Michelin, who work hard to keep the old arts alive.

"These young people don't know what to do anymore," says Madeleine Michelin. "If you put one of them in the bush, they'd starve."

So what is the difference between Douglas and the kids who gather around the hot-water tank down the road, a gas bag in one hand, a glowing cigarette in the other? Douglas thinks it's hardly a worthy question.

"I go to school. I can trap. I don't sniff gas. That's the difference."

Though the clash between modern and traditional ways may have been the root of the community's problems, Innu elders and social psychologists agree that holding on to cultural identity makes all the difference in coping with settled life.

For some of the kids who were sent away, part of the treatment will be a month in the woods with elders who will reintroduce them to the spirit of the land and teach them to recognize the natural forces within themselves. With the provincial funding, town leaders plan to buy a lodge for the new treatment center, where entire families can go back to the country and address issues without the distractions of sniffing and drinking.

"The Innu have two lives," says Jack Penashue. His memories of tents glowing like lanterns against the snow while his grandfather smoked a pipe and told the children stories around the fire have an almost mythic power.

They contrast sharply with the shadows of his other life, sniffing gas in a shed thick with fumes, dark days of hunger and alcohol. "It is up to us, and only us, to figure out how to live the right one."

# CHAPTER 13

# Treatment of Psychological Disorders

*The driving force in the mental health professions, whether accomplished indirectly via research or directly via clinical practice, is to reduce human suffering and improve others' mental well-being. Several treatment orientations are evident in the preceding chapters, but, because of its central role in the field, treatment merits its own consideration. This topic is vast, of course, but in this chapter we focus on two facets of psychological treatment that are particularly important: what happens during the course of therapy (addressed by the first two articles) and the tension that exists between scientists and practitioners as they strive toward better interventions (addressed by the last two articles). As you read, keep in mind that the treatments and orientations represented in these articles—that is, various forms of one-on-one psychotherapy—are only one small slice of the interventions that are available in our communities. Interventions to promote mental health can take many forms: a billboard that advertises a depression screening day, an Internet-based program for people with panic disorder, group therapy for elderly adults, counseling sessions between priests and parishioners, or crisis management by police officers. Each intervention can play a unique role in the prevention and treatment of mental illness.*

## Suggested Reading

Christensen, A., & Jacobson, N. S. (1994). Who (or what) can do psychotherapy: The status and challenge of nonprofessional therapies. *Psychological Science, 5,* 8–14.

# MAN GOES TO SEE A DOCTOR

## Adam Gopnik

*The genius of Sigmund Freud is, at least, two-fold: He recognized that important sources of emotion, thought, and motivation can exist outside of conscious awareness, and he maintained that we can gain greater awareness of this unconscious material (and understand how it influences us) by talking with another person. Although his classic model of psychoanalysis is no longer as prominent as it once was—in large part because it does not jibe well with prevailing short-term, results-oriented psychotherapies or biological interventions—there remains a fair degree of interest in this form of treatment and those that derive from it.*

*Nevertheless, it is rare to have a glimpse into what happens during analysis and how the patient experiences it (but also see Rabinowitz, 1998; Yalom & Elkin, 1974). The first article in this chapter is an interesting and sometimes humorous account of a course of psychoanalytic treatment, which took place in twice-weekly sessions held over six years. The author and patient, Adam Gopnik, is a well-known author and social critic, and in this article he describes the sometimes oblique tactics that his analyst, Dr. Max Grosskurth, used in treatment; it remains a mystery whether these tactics were intentionally used to achieve the changes that did result. As Gopnik notes, it did not appear to be orthodox Freudian analysis, and his experience with the treatment was also affected by Dr. Grosskurth's advanced age.*

### References

Rabinowitz, I. (Ed.) (1998). *Inside therapy: Illuminating writings about therapists, patients, and psychotherapy.* New York: St. Martin's Press.
Yalom, I. D., & Elkin, G. (1974). *Every day gets a little closer: A twice-told therapy.* New York: Basic Books.

### Suggested Readings

Dolnick, E. (1998). *Madness on the couch: Blaming the victim in the heyday of psychoanalysis.* New York: Simon & Schuster.
Westen, D. (1999). The scientific status of unconscious processes: Is Freud really dead? *Journal of the American Psychoanalytic Association, 47,* 1061–1106.
Wheelis, A. (1999). *The listener: A psychoanalyst examines his life.* New York: Norton.

*The New Yorker,* 114–121. (1998, August 24 and 31).

Lately, a lot of people in New York—why, I'm not entirely sure—have been sending me clippings about the decline and fall of psychoanalysis. Most of the reasons given for its disappearance make sense: people are happier, busier; the work done by the anti-Freudian skeptics has finally taken hold of the popular imagination, so that people have no time for analytic longueurs and no patience with its mystifications. Along with those decline-and-fall pieces, though, I've also been sent—and in this case I don't entirely want to know why—a lot of hair-raising pieces about mental illness and its new therapies: about depressions, disasters, hidden urges suddenly (or brazenly) confessed and how you can cure them all with medicine. Talking is out, taking is in. When I go back to New York, some of my friends seem to be layered with drugs, from the top down, like a pousse-café: Rogaine on top, then Prozac, then Xanax, then Viagra. . . . In this context, my own experience in being doctored for mental illness seems paltry and vaguely absurd, and yet, in its way, memorable.

I was on the receiving end of what must have been one of the last, and easily one of the most unsuccessful, psychoanalyses that have ever been attempted—one of the last times a German-born analyst, with a direct laying on of hands from Freud, spent forty-five minutes twice a week for six years discussing, in a small room on Park Avenue decorated with Motherwell posters, the problems of a "creative" New York neurotic. It may therefore be worth recalling, if only in the way that it would be interesting to hear the experiences of the last man mesmerized or the last man to be bled with leeches. Or the last man—and there must have been such a man as the sixteenth century drew to a close and the modern age began—to bring an alchemist a lump of lead in the sincere belief that he would take it home as gold.

So it happened that on a night in October, 1990, I found myself sitting in a chair and looking at the couch in the office of one of the oldest, most patriarchal, most impressive-looking psychoanalysts in New York. He had been recommended to me by another patient, a twenty-year veteran of his couch. The choice now presents itself of whether to introduce him by name or by pseudonym, a choice that is more one of decorum than of legal necessity (he's dead). To introduce him by name is, in a sense, to invade his privacy. On the other hand, not to introduce him by name is to allow him to disappear into the braid of literature in which he was caught—his patients like to write about him, in masks, theirs and his—and from which, at the end, he was struggling to break free. . . .

His name, I'll say, was Max Grosskurth, and he had been practicing psychoanalysis for almost fifty years. He was a German Jew of a now vanishing type—not at all like the small, wise-cracking, scared Mitteleuropean Jews that I had grown up among. He was tall, commanding, humorless. He liked large, blooming shirts, dark suits, heavy handmade shoes, club ties. He had a limp, which, in the years when I knew him, became a two-legged stutter and then left him immobile, so that our last year of analysis took place in his apartment, around the corner from the office. His roster of patients was drawn almost exclusively from among what he liked to call creative people, chiefly writers and painters and composers, and he talked about them so freely that I sometimes half expected him to put up autographed glossies around the office, like the ones on the wall at the Stage Deli. ("Max—Thanks for the most terrific transference in Gotham! Lenny") When we began, he was eighty, and I had crossed thirty. . . .

Why was I there? Nothing interesting: the usual mixture of hurt feelings, confusion, and incomprehension that comes to early-arriving writers when the thirties hit. John Updike once wrote that, though the newcomer imagines that literary New York will be like a choir of angels, in fact it is like the Raft of the Medusa—and he was wrong about this only in that the people on the Raft of the Medusa still have hope. In New York, the raft has been adrift now for years, centuries, and there's still no rescue boat in sight. The only thing left is to size up the others and wait for someone to become weak enough to eat.

I spilled out my troubles; told him of my sense of panic, anxiety; perhaps wept. He was silent for a minute—not a writer's minute, a real one, a long time.

"Franz Marc was a draftsman of remarkable power," he said at last: the first words of my analysis. His voice was deep and powerful, uncannily like Henry Kissinger's: not quacky, pleading Viennese but booming, arrogant German.

The remark about Franz Marc was not *quite* apropos of nothing—he knew me to be an art critic—but very near. (Franz Marc was the less famous founder of the German Expressionist movement called Der Blaue Reiter; Kandinsky was the other.) He must have caught the alarmed look in my eyes, for he added, more softly, "There are many worthwhile unexplored subjects in modern art." Then he sat up in his chair—swallowed hard and pulled himself up—and for a moment I had a sense of just how aged he was.

"You put me in mind," he said—and suddenly there was nothing the least old in the snap and expansive authority of his voice—"you put me in mind of Norman Mailer at a similar age." (This was a reach, or raw flattery; there is nothing about me that would put anyone in mind of Norman Mailer.) " 'Barbary Shore,' he thought, would be the end of him. What a terrible, terrible, terrible book it is. It was a great blow to his narcissism. I recall clearly attending dinner parties in this period with my wife, an extremely witty woman, where everyone was mocking poor Norman. My wife, an extremely witty woman . . ." He looked at me as though, despite the repetition, I had denied it; I tried to look immensely amused, as though reports of Mrs. Grosskurth's wit had reached me in my crib. "Even my wife engaged in this banter. In the midst of it, however, I held my peace." He rustled in his chair, and now I saw why he had sat up: he suddenly became a stiff, living pillar, his hands held before him, palms up—a man holding his peace in the middle of banter flying around the dinner table. A rock of imperturbable serenity! He cautiously settled back in his chair. "Now, of course, Norman has shown great resourcefulness and is receiving extremely large advances for his genre studies of various American criminals."

From the six years of my analysis, or therapy, or whatever the hell it was, there are words that are as permanently etched in my brain as the words "E pluribus unum" are on the nickel. "Banter" and "genre studies" were the first two. I have never been so grateful for a *mot juste* as I was for the news that Mrs. Grosskurth had engaged in banter, and that Norman Mailer had made a resourceful turn toward genre studies. Banter, that was all it was: criticism, the essential competitive relations of writers in New York—all of it was *banter*, engaged in by extremely witty wives of analysts at dinner parties. And all you had to do was . . . refuse to engage in it! Hold your peace. Take no part! Like him—sit there like a rock and let it wash over you. . . .

I came away from that first session in a state of blissful suspended confusion. Surely this wasn't the way psychoanalysis was supposed to proceed. On the other hand, it was much more useful—and interesting, too—to hear that Norman Mailer had rebounded by writing genre studies than it was to hear that my family was weird, for that I knew already. I felt a giddy sense of relief, especially when he added, sardonically, "Your problems remind me of"—and here he named one of the heroes of the New York School. "Fortunately, you suffer neither from impotence nor alcoholism. That is in your favor." And that set the pattern of our twice- and sometimes thrice-weekly encounters for the next five years. He was touchy, prejudiced, opinionated, impatient, often bored, usually high-handed, brutally bigoted. I could never decide whether to sue for malpractice or fall to my knees in gratitude for such an original healer.

Our exchanges hardened into a routine. I would take the subway uptown at six-thirty, I would get out at Seventy-seventh Street, walk a couple of blocks uptown, and enter his little office, at the corner of Park Avenue, where I would join three or four people sitting on a bench. Then the door opened, another neurotic—sometimes a well-known neurotic, who looked as though he wanted to hide his face with his coat, like an indicted stockbroker—came out, and I went in. There was the smell of the air-conditioner.

"So," he would say. "How are you?"

"Terrible," I would say, sometimes sincerely, sometimes to play along.

"I expected no less," he would say, and then I would begin to stumble out the previous three or four days' problems, worries, gossip. He would clear his throat and begin a monologue, a kind of roundabout discussion of major twentieth-century figures (Freud, Einstein, and, above all, Thomas Mann were his touchstones), broken confidences of the confessional, episodes from his own life, finally snaking around to an abrupt "So you see . . ." and some thunderously obvious maxim, which he would apply to my problems—or, rather, to the nonexistence of my problems, compared with real problems, of which he'd heard a few, you should have been here then. . . .

Mostly, he talked about what he thought it took to survive in the warfare of New York. He talked about the major figures of New York literary life—not necessarily his own patients but writers and artists whose careers he followed admiringly—as though they were that chain of forts upstate, around Lake George, left over from the French and Indian War: the ones you visited as a kid, where they gave you bumper stickers. There was Fort Sontag, Fort Frankenthaler, Fort Mailer. "She is very well defended." "Yes, I admire her defenses." "Admirably well defended." Once, I mentioned a famous woman intellectual who had recently got into legal trouble: hadn't she been well defended? "Yes, but the trouble is that the guns were pointing the wrong way, like the British at Singapore." You were wrung out with gratitude for a remark like that. I was, anyway.

It was his theory, in essence, that "creative" people were inherently in a rage, and that this rage came from their disappointed narcissism. The narcissism could take a negative, paranoid form or a positive, defiant, arrogant form. His job was not to cure the narcissism (which was inseparable from the creativity) but, instead, to fortify it—to get the drawbridge up and the gate down and leave the Indians circling outside, with nothing to do but shoot flaming arrows harmlessly over the stockade.

He had come of age as a professional in the forties and fifties, treating the great battlers of the golden age of New York intellectuals, an age that, seen on the couch—a seething mass of resentments, jealousies, and needs—appeared somewhat less golden than it did otherwise. "How well I recall," he would begin, "when I was treating"—and here he named two famous art critics of the period. "They went to war with each other. One came in at ten o'clock. 'I must reply,' he said. Then at four-thirty the other one would come in. 'I must reply,' he would say. 'No,' I told them both. 'Wait six months and see if anyone recalls the source of this argument.' They agreed to wait. Six months later, my wife, that witty, witty woman, held a dinner party and offered some pleasantry about their quarrel. No one understood; no one even remembered it. And this was in the days when *ARTnews* was something. I recall what Thomas Mann said. . . ." Eventually, abruptly, as the clock on the wall turned toward seven-thirty, he would say, "So you see . . . this demonstrates again what I always try to tell you about debates among intellectuals."

I leaned forward, really wanting to know. "What is that, Doctor?" I said.

"*No one cares*. People have troubles of their own. We have to stop now." And that would be it.

I would leave the room in a state of vague, disconcerted disappointment. *No one cares?* No one cares about the hard-fought and brutally damaging fight for the right sentence, the irrefutable argument? And: *People have troubles of their own?* My great-aunt Hannah could have told me that. *That* was the result of half a century of presiding over the psyches of a major moment in cultural history? And then, fifteen minutes later, as I rode in a cab downtown my heart would lift—would fly. That's right: *No one cares! People have troubles of their own!* It's O.K. That doesn't mean you shouldn't do it; it means you should do it, somehow, for its own sake, without illusions. Just write, just live, and don't care too much yourself. No one cares. It's just *banter. . . .*

Sometimes Dr. Grosskurth would talk about his own history. He was born in Berlin before the First World War, at a time when German Jews were German above all. His mother had hoped that he would become a diplomat. But he had decided to study medicine instead, and particularly psychiatry; he was of that generation of German Jews who found in Freud's doctrines what their physicist contemporaries found in Einstein's. He had spoken out against the Nazis in 1933 and had been forced to flee the country at a moment's notice. One of his professors had helped him get out. (He was notably unheroic in his description of this episode. "It was a lesson to me to keep my big mouth shut" was the way he put it.) He fled to Italy, where he completed medical school at the University of Padua.

He still loved Italy: he ate almost every night at Parma, a restaurant nearby, on Third Avenue, and spent every August in Venice, at the Cipriani. One spring, I recall, I announced that my wife and I had decided to go to Venice.

He looked at me tetchily. "And where will you stay?" he asked.

"At this *pensione*, the Accademia," I said.

"No," he said. "You wish to stay at the Monaco, it is a very pleasant hotel, and you will have breakfast on the terrace. That is the correct hostel for you."

I reached into my pockets, where I usually had a stubby pencil, and searched them for a stray bit of paper—an American Express receipt, the back of a bit of manuscript paper—to write on.

"No, no!" he said, with disgust. My disorderliness was anathema to his Teutonic soul. "Here, I will write it down. Oh, you are so chaotic. Hand me the telephone." I offered him the phone, which was on a small table near his chair, and he consulted a little black book that he took from his inside right jacket pocket. He dialed some long number. Then, in a voice even deeper and more booming than usual—he was raised in a time when long-distance meant long-distance—he began to speak in Italian.

"*Sì, sono Dottore Grosskurth.*" He waited for a moment—genuinely apprehensive, I thought, for the first time in my acquaintance with him—and then a huge smile, almost a big-lug smile, broke across his face. They knew him.

"*Sì, sì,*" he said, and then, his voice lowering, said, "No," and something I didn't understand;

obviously, he was explaining that Mrs. Grosskurth had died. "*Pronto!*" he began, and then came a long sentence beginning with my name and various dates in *giugno*. "*Sì, sì.*" He put his hand over the receiver. "You wish for a bath or a shower?" he demanded.

"Bath," I said.

"Good choice," he said. It was the nearest thing to praise he had ever given me. Finally, he hung up the phone. He looked at the paper in his hand and gave it to me.

"There," he said. "You are reserved for five nights, the room has no view of the canal, but, actually, this is better, since the gondola station can be extremely disturbing. You will eat breakfast on the terrace, and there you will enjoy the view of the Salute. Do not eat dinner there, however. I will give you a list of places." And, on an "Ask Your Doctor About Prozac" pad, he wrote out a list of restaurants in Venice for me. (They were mostly, I realized later, after I got to know Venice a bit, the big old, fifties-ish places that a New York analyst would love: Harry's Bar, Da Fiore, the Madonna.)

"You will go to these places, order the spaghetti *vongole*, and then . . ."

"And then?"

"And then at last you will be happy," he said flatly.

He was so far from being an orthodox Freudian, or an orthodox anything, that I was startled when I discovered how deep and passionate his attachment to psychoanalytic dogma was. One day, about three years in, I came into his office and saw that he had a copy of *The New York Review of Books* open. "It is very sad," he began. "It is very sad indeed, to see a journal which was once respected by many people descend into a condition where it has lost the good opinion of all reasonable people." After a few moments, I figured out that he was referring to one of several much discussed pieces that the literary critic Frederick Crews had written attacking Freud and Freudianism.

I read the pieces later myself and thought them incontrovertible. Then I sat down to read Freud, for the first time—"Civilization and Its Discontents," "Totem and Taboo," "The Interpretation of Dreams"—and was struck at once by the absurdity of the arguments as arguments and the impressive weight of humane culture marshalled in their support. One sensed that one was in the presence of a kind of showman, a brilliant essayist, leaping from fragmentary evidence to unsupported conclusion, and summoning up a whole body of psychological myth—the Id, the Libido, the Ego—with the confidence of a Disney cartoonist drawing bunnies and squirrels. I found myself, therefore, in the unusual position of being increasingly skeptical of the therapeutic approach to which I fled twice a week for comfort. I finally got up the courage to tell Grosskurth this.

"You therefore find a conflict between your strongest intellectual convictions and your deepest emotional gratification needs?" he asked.

"Yes."

He shrugged. "Apparently you are a Freudian. . . ."

On behalf of his belief, Grosskurth would have said—did say, though over time, if not in these precise words—that while Freud may have been wrong in all the details, his central insight was right. His insight was that human life is shaped by a series of selfish, ineradicable urges, particularly sexual ones, and that all the other things that happen in life are ways of toning down these urges and giving them an "acceptable" outlet. An actual, undramatic but perilous world of real things existed, whose essential character was its indifference to human feelings: this world of real things included pain, death, and disease, but also many things unthreatening to our welfare. His project—the Freudian project, properly understood—was not to tell the story of our psyche, the curious drawing-room comedy of Id and Ego and Libido, but just the opposite: to drain the drama from all our stories. He believed that the only thing to do with the knowledge of the murderous rage within your breast was not to mythologize it but to put a necktie on it and heavy shoes and a dark-blue woollen suit. Only a man who knew that, given the choice, he would rape his mother and kill his father could order his spaghetti *vongole* in anything like peace.

There was, however, a catch in this argument, or so I insisted in the third year of my analysis, over several sessions and at great length. Weren't the well-defended people he admired really the ones at the furthest imaginable remove from the real things, the reality, whose worth he praised so highly? Did Susan Sontag actually have a better grasp of things-as-they-are than anyone else? Would anybody point to Harold Brodkey as a model of calm appraisal of the scale of the world and the appropriate place of his ego in it? Wasn't the "enormous narcissistic overestimation" of which he accused me inseparable from the "well-defended, internalized self-esteem" he wanted me to cultivate? The people who seemed best defended—well, the single most striking thing about them was how breathtakingly out of touch they were with the world, with other people's feelings, with the general opinion of their work. You didn't just have to be armored by your narcissism; you could be practically entombed in it, so that people came knocking, like Carter at King Tut's tomb, and you'd still get by. Wasn't that a problem for his system, or, anyway, for his therapy?

"Yes," he said coldly.

"Oh," I said, and we changed the subject.

My friends were all in therapy, too, of course—this was New York—and late at night, over a bottle of red wine, they would offer one "insight" or another that struck me as revelatory: "My analyst helped me face the recurring pattern in my life of an overprotectiveness that derives from my mother's hidden alcoholism," or "Mine helped me see more clearly how early my father's depression shaped my fears," or "Mine helped me see that my reluctance to publish my personal work is part of my reluctance to have a child." What could I say? "Mine keeps falling asleep, except when we discuss Hannah Arendt's sex life, about which he knows quite a lot."

His falling asleep was a problem. The first few years I saw him, he still had a reasonably full schedule and our sessions were usually late in the day; the strain told on him. As I settled insistently (I had decided that if I was going to be analyzed I was going to be analyzed) into yet one more tiresome recital of grievances, injustices, anxieties, childhood memories, I could see his long, big, partly bald head nodding down toward the knot of his tie. His eyes would flutter shut, and he would begin to breathe deeply. I would drone on—"And so I think that it was my mother, really, who first gave me a sense of the grandiose. There was this birthday, I think my sixth, when I first sensed . . ."—and his chin would nestle closer and closer to his chest, his head would drop farther, so that I was looking right at his bald spot. There was only one way, I learned, after a couple of disconcerting weeks of telling my troubles to a sleeping therapist, to revive him, and that was to gossip. "And so my mother's relationship with my father reminds me—well, in certain ways it reminds me of what people have been saying about Philip Roth's divorce from Claire Bloom," I would say abruptly, raising my volume on the non sequitur.

Instantly, his head would jerk straight up, his eyes open, and he would shake himself all over like a Lab coming out of the water. "Yes, what are they saying about this divorce?" he would demand.

"Oh, nothing, really," I would say, and then I would wing it for a minute, glad to have caught his attention.

Unfortunately, my supply of hot literary gossip was very small. So there were times (and I hope that this is the worst confession I will ever have to make) when I would invent literary gossip on the way uptown, just to have something in reserve if he fell asleep, like a Victorian doctor going off to a picnic with a bottle of smelling salts, just in case. ("Let's see: what if I said that Kathy Acker had begun an affair with, oh, V. S. Pritchett—that would hold anybody's interest.") I felt at once upset and protective about his sleeping. Upset because it was, after all, my nickel, and protective because I did think that he was a great man, in his way, and I hated to see him dwindling: I wondered how long he would go on if he sensed that he was dwindling. . . .

As we went on into our fourth and fifth years, all the other problems that I had brought to him became one problem, the New York problem. Should my wife—should we—have a baby? We ag-

onized over it, in the modern manner. Grosskurth listened, silently, for months, and finally pronounced.

"Yes, you must go ahead and have a child. You will enjoy it. The child will try your patience repeatedly, yet you will find that there are many pleasures in child-rearing." He cleared his throat. "You will find, for instance, that the child will make many amusing mistakes in language."

I looked at him, a little dumb-founded—that was the best of it?

"You see," he went on, "at about the age of three, children begin to talk, and naturally their inexperience leads them to use language in surprising ways. These mistakes can really be *extremely* amusing. The child's errors in language also provide the kinds of anecdotes that can be of value to the parents in a social setting." It seemed an odd confidence on which to build a family—that the child would be your own, live-in Gracie Allen, and you could dine out on his errors—but I thought that perhaps he was only defining, so to speak, the minimal case.

So we did have the child. Overwhelmed with excitement, I brought him pictures of the baby at a week old. ("Yes," he said dryly, peering at my Polaroids, "this strongly resembles a child.") And, as my life was changing, I began to think that it was time to end, or anyway wind down, our relationship. It had been six years, and, for all that I had gained—and I thought that I had gained a lot: if not a cure, then at least enough material to go into business as a blackmailer—I knew that if I was to be "fully adult" I should break my dependence. And he was growing old. Already aged when we began, he was now, at eighty-five or -six, becoming frail. Old age seems to be a series of lurches, rather than a gradual decline. One week he was his usual booming self, the next week there was a slow deliberateness in his gait as he came to the office door. Six months later, he could no longer get up reliably from his chair, and once fell down outside the office in my presence. His face, as I helped him up, was neither angry nor amused, just doughy and preoccupied, the face of a man getting ready for something. That was when we switched our sessions to his apartment, around the corner, on Seventy-ninth Street, where I would ring the bell and wait for him to call me in—he left the door open, or had it left open by his nurse, whom I never saw. Then I would go inside and find him— having been helped into a gray suit, blue shirt, dark tie—on his own sofa, surrounded by Hofmann and Miró engravings and two or three precious Kandinsky prints.

About a month into the new arrangement, I decided to move to Europe to write, and I told him this, in high spirits and with an almost breathless sense of advancement: I was going away; breaking free of New York, starting over. I thought he would be pleased.

To my shock, he was furious—his old self and then some. "Who would have thought of this idea? What a self-destructive regression." Then I realized why he was so angry: despite all his efforts at forti-fication, I had decided to run away. Fort Gopnik was dropping its flag, dispersing its troops, surren-dering its territory—all his work for nothing. Like General Gordon come to reinforce Khartoum, he had arrived too late, and failed through the unfor-givable, disorganized passivity of the natives.

In our final sessions, we settled into a non-aggression pact. ("Have we stopped too soon, Doc-tor?" I asked. "Yes," he said dully.) We talked neutrally, about art and family. Then, the day be-fore I was to leave, I went uptown for our last ses-sion.

It was a five-thirty appointment, in the second week of October. We began to talk, amiably, like old friends, about the bits and pieces of going abroad, visas and vaccinations. Then, abruptly, he began to tell a long, meandering story about his wife's illness and death, which we had never talked about before. He kept returning to a memory he had of her swimming back and forth in the hotel pool in Venice the last summer before her death.

"She had been ill, and the Cipriani, as you are not aware, has an excellent pool. She swam back and forth in this pool, back and forth, for hours. I was well aware that her illness was very likely to be terminal." He shook his head, held his hands out, dealing with reality. "As soon as she had episodes

of dizziness and poor balance, I made a very quick diagnosis. Still, back and forth she swam. . . .

"Naturally, this was to be the last summer that we spent in Venice. However, she had insisted that we make this trip. And she continued to swim." He looked around the room, in the dark—the pic-tures, the drawings, the bound volumes, all that was left of two lives joined together, one closed, the other closing.

"She continued to swim. She had been an ex-ceptional athlete, in addition to being, as you know, an extremely witty woman." He seemed lost in memory for a moment, but then, regaining himself, he cleared his throat in the dark, profes-sionally, as he had done so many times before.

"So you see," he said, again trying to make the familiar turn toward home. And then he did some-thing that I don't think he had ever done before: he called me by my name. "So you see, Adam, in life, in life . . ." And I rose, thinking, Here at our final session—no hope of ever returning, my bag packed and my ticket bought to another country, far away—at last, the truth, the point, the thing to take away that we have been building toward all these years.

"So you see, Adam, in retrospect . . . " he went on, and stirred, rose, on the sofa, trying to force his full authority on his disobedient frame. "In retro-spect, life has many worthwhile aspects," he con-cluded quietly, and then we had to stop. He sat looking ahead, and a few minutes later, with a goodbye and a handshake, I left.

Now I was furious. I was trying to be moved, but I would have liked to be moved by something easier to be moved by. That was all he had to say to me, *Life has many worthwhile aspects*? For once, that first reaction of disappointment stuck with me for a long time, on the plane all the way to Paris. All these evenings, all that investment, all that hu-manism, all those Motherwell prints—yes, all that money, my money—for that? *Life has many worth-while aspects*? Could there have been a more fatu-ous and arrhythmic and unmemorable conclusion to what had been, after all, *my* analysis, my only analysis?

Now, of course, it is more deeply engraved

than any other of his words. In retrospect, life has many worthwhile aspects. Not all or even most aspects. And not beautiful or meaningful or even tolerable. Just *worthwhile*, with its double burden of labor and reward. Life has *worth*—value, importance—and it takes a while to get there.

I came back to New York about a year later and went to see him. A woman with a West Indian accent had answered when I called his number. I knew that I would find him declining, but still, I thought, I would find him himself. We expect our fathers to take as long a time dying as we take growing up. But he was falling away. He was lying on a hospital bed, propped up, his skin as gray as pavement, his body as thin and wasted as a tree on a New York street in winter. The television was on, low, tuned to a game show. He struggled for breath as he spoke.

He told me, very precisely, about the disease that he had. "The prognosis is most uncertain," he said. "I could linger indefinitely." He mentioned something controversial that I had written. "You showed independence of mind." He turned away, in pain. "And, as always, very poor judgment."

In New York again, five months later, I thought, I'll just surprise him, squeeze his hand. I walked by his building, and asked the doorman if Dr. Grosskurth was in. He said that Dr. Grosskurth had died three months before. For a moment I thought, Someone should have called me, one of his children. Yet they could hardly have called all his patients. ("But I was special!" the child screams.) Then I stumbled over to Third Avenue

and almost automatically into Parma, the restaurant that he had loved. I asked the owner if he knew that Dr. Grosskurth had died, and he said yes, of course: they had had a dinner, with his family and some of his friends, to remember him, and he invited me to have dinner, too, and drink to his memory.

I sat down and began an excellent, solitary dinner in honor of my dead psychoanalyst—seafood pasta, a Venetian dish, naturally—and, in his memory, chewed at the squid. (He liked squid.) The waiter brought me my bill, and I paid it. I still think that the owner should at least have bought the wine. Which shows, I suppose, that the treatment was incomplete. ("They should have paid for your wine?" "It would have been a nice gesture, yes. It would have happened in Paris." "You are hopeless. I died too soon, and you left too early. The analysis was left unfinished.")

The transference wasn't completed, I suppose, but something—a sort of implantation—did take place. He is inside me. In moments of crisis or panic, I sometimes think that I have his woollen suit draped around my shoulders, even in August. Sometimes in ordinary moments I almost think that I have become him. Though my patience is repeatedly tried by my child, I laugh at his many amusing mistakes in language—I have even been known to repeat these mistakes in social settings. I refer often to the sayings of my wife, that witty, witty woman. On the whole, I would say that my years in analysis had many worthwhile aspects.

# DOUBLE FANTASY

## John Colapinto

*Psychotherapy is a relationship unlike any other. The psychotherapy sessions are private, the interactions between patient and therapist usually take place in the therapist's office and nowhere else, the emotions discussed and experienced can be quite powerful and sustained, there is relatively wide latitude in what is permissible as therapy, and one of the parties in this relationship may be either acutely or chronically distressed. The next article describes a widely publicized case involving a young man, Paul Lozano, and his psychiatrist, Dr. Margaret Bean-Bayog. It illustrates the intensely private and emotional nature of psychotherapy, not only for the patient but also for the therapist. The case ends tragically, with the suicide of Mr. Lozano; as a consequence, strong charges were leveled against Dr. Bean-Bayog because of the nature of the regressive psychotherapy that she provided. As the article notes, Dr. Bean-Bayog maintained her innocence of any wrongdoing, asserted that she did not have a sexual relationship with Mr. Lozano, and stated that her treatment of him fell within accepted standards of care. She turned in her license to practice medicine rather than participate in a hearing in which her license might be revoked, so all of the details about what happened in this case, and why Mr. Lozano committed suicide, cannot be known. In reading this article, remember that the therapeutic relation- ship it depicts is not intended to be representative of therapy in general but rather that it helps to delineate the wide boundaries within which therapy can take place.*

### Suggested Reading

Pope, K. S. (1987). Preventing therapist-patient sexual intimacy: Therapy for a therapist at risk. *Profes- sional Psychology: Research and Practice, 18,* 624–628.

*Rolling Stone, 652,* 19–25, 48. (1993, Spring).

He emerged from the Harvard Square sub- way station into the sunshine. Hurrying along Massachusetts Avenue, he cranked the volume on his Walkman, closing himself in with the song he'd been listening to obsessively for months: "Starry, starry night, paint your palette blue and gray/Look out on a summer's day, with eyes that know the darkness in my soul. . . ."

It was July 3rd, 1986, and Paul Lozano, a twenty-three-year-old Harvard Medical School student, was in trouble. For weeks he had been too nervous and upset to sleep or eat. He'd been skipping classes. And lately, whenever he closed his eyes, he saw visions of violent death: car accidents, gunshots, bodies plummeting from buildings. Which is why he was on his way toward Mount Auburn Street, to the row of brownstones where several Harvard-affiliated psychiatrists rented offices.

At first glance, there was nothing particularly unusual about a medical student seeking psychiatric help. Every year, up to half of all med students receive some form of counseling to cope with the long hours and punishing workload. But the relationship that Paul Lozano embarked on that day would five years later spark one of the most incendiary cases of psychiatric malpractice in the profession's history. The Lozano family charged that Paul's therapist used a bizarre "regression" therapy to reduce him to a toddler state, then lured him into a "sordid" sexual relationship that unhinged his mind and led in April 1991 to his suicide by massive cocaine overdose. The case made headlines a year later not only because of the salacious allegations but because the accused, Dr. Margaret Bean-Bayog, a psychiatrist with an impeccable fifteen-year record of treating patients, was one of four or five nationally recognized experts in the field of alcoholism and addiction. Past president of the American Society of Addiction Medicine, she was a candidate for the exclusive Boston Psychoanalytic Society and Institute and one of the fast-rising stars in America's psychoanalytic scene.

But as the case unfolded, some 3000 pages of evidence, including Bean-Bayog's treatment notes, letters and sexual fantasies, were made public and provided an unprecedented glimpse into the shadowy world of psychotherapy. To the Lozano family, the paper trail documented a Svengali-analyst's destruction of a confused but otherwise stable young man. A closer look at the lives of Paul Lozano and Margaret Bean-Bayog suggests a truth considerably more complicated but no less chilling

for what it says about the emotional chaos that can be unleashed, in both patient and doctor, by the dangerous chemistry of psychoanalysis.

She greeted him in her office at 143 Mount Auburn Street and invited him to sit in one of the comfortable armchairs. At forty-two, Bean-Bayog was a tall, attractive woman with blond hair that she wore in bangs. She carried herself with confidence, but she also radiated a warmth that distinguished her from the caricature of a grim, humorless shrink. Paul remembered this warmth from two years ago, when he'd first met her. Back then, he'd been too ashamed to speak of his problems to anyone, so he'd simply picked her name off the top of an alphabetical list provided by Harvard Medical School. He'd come for two evaluative sessions, and she had urged him to start therapy. He had been too scared to probe into his seething psyche and had refused. But he hadn't forgotten Bean-Bayog.

And she hadn't forgotten him—the brilliant but deeply depressed young man who had come to her complaining of loneliness and inadequacy. She saw that he had changed: thinner, paler, with bags under his eyes that suggested he hadn't been sleeping. At the top of the eight-by-ten pad that she used for her treatment notes, she scrawled: "Not same person as seen September 24, 84." Then she settled in and listened as he described the feelings of panic and despair that had brought him back to her. Offhandedly, he mentioned an accident. Last January. He'd been hit by a car and cracked his knee and head. She asked how it happened.

He shrugged: "Car came around the corner [and] smacked me."

She jotted this down. But at the bottom of the page, she wrote, "Actually suicidal." At session's end, she again urged him to begin a course of regular therapy. This time he didn't refuse—thus setting in motion the sequence of events that would lead eventually to their mutual destruction.

For the first few months Bean-Bayog saw Paul twice a week. Her notes paint a picture of a high achiever whose accomplishments belied inner turmoil.

Paul Lozano was born and raised in the town of Upper Sandusky, Ohio, the younger in a family of six children. His father, Marcos, a Mexican immigrant bricklayer, built up a construction business, then moved the family to El Paso, Texas, when he went bankrupt in the recessionary Seventies. As a child, Paul had been something of a prodigy. He taught himself to read at the age of three. He played for hours with his chemistry set in the basement. He graduated high school with straight A's and received a congressional nomination to West Point. In his second year, he transferred to the University of Texas at El Paso, where he racked up a 4.0 GPA and earned a full scholarship to Harvard Medical School.

An unimpeachable résumé, but behind it misery hived. Paul told Bean-Bayog that his brilliance had always made him feel different, freakish, a misfit. His siblings, he said, were cruel. He was locked in closets, called a nerd. His mother, he said, was emotionally distant and given to bouts of depression. She sent him to school when he was feverish. She beat him when he was bad. West Point, he admitted, had been a disaster; he'd disobeyed orders, gotten mediocre marks, drunk a lot and quit, he said, after receiving a greater number of demerits than any other plebe in his year. El Paso wasn't much better. He'd secretly married a girl from his chemistry class—just to spite his parents, who disapproved of her. He had the marriage annulled three weeks later but remained alienated from his parents over the episode. At Harvard he felt alienated among the WASPy Ivy Leaguers and trust-fund kids. He felt like the school's token Mexican. He felt like he wasn't smart enough for Harvard: he worried about flunking out and devastating his family, which he believed was counting on him to become a rich doctor so that he could support it. He got no love from his family, just crushing pressure to succeed. He felt alone. Totally alone. He had felt this way for as long as he could remember. He said he had attempted suicide first at age six. He'd swallowed a bottle of aspirin. At thirteen he'd tried to hang himself. In college he tried to gas

himself. Eventually, Paul would locate the roots of his despair in childhood sexual abuse. He claimed to recall disturbing incidents in which his mother fondled his penis and allowed him to crawl under her skirts and touch her sexually.

When Bean-Bayog's treatment notes became public, the Lozano family was aghast at Paul's tales of childhood suicide attempts, family abuse and incest. "I don't deny Paul said those things to Bean-Bayog," says Paul's older sister Pilar. "He may very well have, within the confines of her office, when he was under her control. But the young man who went to her initially was merely very depressed. The family history presented within those sessions was a figment of Bean-Bayog's fantasies. Paul had an incredibly strong ethnic family. There was no abuse, no suicide attempts."

Charlotte Leeth, Paul's English teacher at Upper Sandusky High School, concurs. "That's not the Paul I knew and loved," she says. "He was probably the brightest kid I ever had. I never saw him without a smile." Math teacher Dick Lab taught Paul's older siblings and knew his parents. "It would be very difficult to find anyone in our community who believed his family mistreated him," Lab says.

"I knew the whole family very well," says school secretary Evie Hall. "You could walk up and down the streets of Upper Sandusky and not find one person who would agree with the terrible things that were said." Pediatrician Thomas Watkins performed regular checkups on Paul and his siblings between 1970, when Paul was eight, until 1979, when the family moved to El Paso and Paul was seventeen. Watkins says that there was never any sign of unhappiness, mental illness or sexual abuse in Paul. "This family was a joy to know," Watkins has said. "If there was anyone suicidal or depressed, it wasn't Paul."

Yet as the 987 pages of Bean-Bayog's treatment notes reveal, Paul's fraught, almost melodramatically gruesome tales seemed to multiply with each therapy session.

Two months into the therapy, Paul admitted that his suicidal urges were returning. He'd started jogging at night in isolated areas, hoping to be mugged. He was reading in veterinary journals about methods of killing big animals painlessly by injection. By the middle of September, he said that he'd contemplated jumping off a building. He told Bean-Bayog: "There's a defect in the machinery. It's important to be logical about this. Some people just aren't going to make it. When a computer shorts out, no one makes a fuss." She decided, for his own protection, to hospitalize him. On September 24th, 1986, she admitted him to McLean Hospital, in suburban Belmont.

At McLean, Paul repeated to doctors and nurses his tales of childhood abuse and suicide attempts. He also displayed odd mood shifts. He joked "inappropriately" about a recent mass slaying and laughed in a way that seemed incongruous with his suicidally depressed mood. But he responded to antidepressants. His mood lifted, his suicidal urges faded. On November 19th, after eight weeks in the hospital, he was released. He returned to therapy with Bean-Bayog and resumed his studies at Harvard. For several weeks he seemed, as the doctors at McLean had described him, "much improved."

But in January, when Paul began clinical rotations in pediatrics, working weekends and nights, he stopped taking his antidepressants. He said they made him drowsy. His mood rapidly declined. Soon he was speaking again of suicide. He told Bean-Bayog that he'd been stockpiling narcotics pilfered from the hospital. When she took these from him, he threatened to get a gun and shoot himself. He laughed at the thought of his landlady having to clean his brains off the wallpaper.

Bean-Bayog increased his sessions to three, then four, then five times a week, so that she could personally administer his antidepressants. She gave him her home and office phone numbers and encouraged him to call whenever he felt suicidal. It was soon obvious to both of them that she was crucial to his continued existence. "Even tiny decreases in [my availability to him] can trigger panic, regression, despair and increased suicide risk," she wrote.

But in mid-April, a rift developed between them. When Paul was accused of overinvolvement with one of his patients (a child in the intensive-care unit of the hospital where he was on rotations), Bean-Bayog suggested he take a leave of absence from school. He flew into a rage. His family would call him a failure. On May 3rd, when she again urged him to take a leave of absence, he stalked out of her office, vowing never to return.

Paul immediately spiraled into an acute panic. That evening, at a bar near his apartment, he gulped several beers, then headed off alone to the Harvard School of Public Health, the tallest building near the med-school campus. It was a Sunday, near midnight; the place was deserted. He buzzed himself in with his ID card, then rode to the thirteenth floor, a warren of drab offices devoted to air-pollution studies. He entered an unlocked seminar room, climbed onto the sill of a window and dangled his legs over the edge. On the brink of jumping, he suddenly climbed back into the room, hurried into the library across the hall and phoned Bean-Bayog at home. He told her where he was and that he was going to jump.

She calmed him and told him to meet her at her Mount Auburn Street office. "Mercifully, he came," she wrote in her notes, "and mercifully did not run when I told him we had to go to the hospital." But at McLean Hospital, Paul panicked. He scrambled from the car and ran. Tackled by guards, he was dragged, kicking and screaming, inside. He was shackled to a bed in four-point restraints and locked in an isolation unit.

Bean-Bayog immediately met with Dr. Frances Frankenburg, the McLean psychiatrist in charge.

"I think it would be a good idea," Frankenburg said, "if you didn't visit him for treatment for the next few days, while he's in restraints."

When the therapists met three days later, Frankenburg had sharpened her opinion. "You're over-involved," she told Bean-Bayog, "You're inappropriate and dangerous to this patient. And he's torturing you. How would you feel if he had killed himself?"

"Upset," Bean-Bayog said, "but I'd get over it." (In her notes she recorded that she was "not believed.")

Frankenburg persisted: "Who pays for his treatment?" The question carried an implicit accusation; allowing a patient free sessions is a sign of overinvolvement.

"He's running up a tab," Bean-Bayog admitted. "Currently he isn't paying."

Ignoring Frankenburg's advice to stay away, Bean-Bayog slipped in for a brief visit. Paul was still pinned to his bed. Their conversation, recorded in her notes, marked a new level of emotional intimacy between them.

"I know I can't marry you," he told her, "but someday I want to find someone like you and get married and have a family. That's why I didn't jump."

She told him that while he was in hospital they could "cool down" what was happening between them.

"But they want to take you away from me!"

"It's confusing," she agreed. "We'll talk about this. Otherwise, it's not safe, and you need a safe place."

"You're very careful," he said. Then he added: "It really helped the other night when you touched my hand when you left. I was so frightened I couldn't move."

"Even shaking hands is too confusing," she told him.

"Lozano was the most severely mentally ill and suicidal patient Bean-Bayog ever treated," her lawyers would later state. Yet she continued to treat him, even after being urged to give it up. She was known for her willingness to take on the toughest patients, the ones no one else wanted. In part this was a sign of her considerable ambition. But it also pointed to her belief that psychotherapy could work miracles. It was more than a professional conviction. It was a personal one, since she believed that she herself was a living example of how psychotherapy could rescue a life from unhappiness.

Born Margaret Bean in 1943 in Louisville, Kentucky, she grew up in Iowa City, the youngest of three children of a doctor father and a poet mother. Like Paul Lozano, she was studious, shy, scientifically inclined; and as with Paul, there are those who insist that there was never anything out of the ordinary about her, except her brilliance. "I've known Margaret all my life," says Carlyle Hedrick, who attended boarding school and college with Margaret Bean. "She had a normal childhood. She took piano lessons; we took a little ballet, read a lot and did all the things that any normal child does. I find it absolutely unbelievable what it's been suggested that she did." A medical-school classmate, Penny Krenner, echoes these sentiments: "She has become fresh meat for the people. The whole thing is just disgraceful. Margaret was, and is, an energetic, hard-working, diligent, very devoted person."

But as with Paul Lozano, Margaret Bean's diligence and accomplishments masked a considerably less successful emotional and personal life. In an essay written in 1990 for her twenty-fifth college reunion, she wrote: "I didn't expect, when I was at Radcliffe, that I would be a happy woman. I certainly wasn't then." Pam Webb, one of Margaret's few college confidantes, suggests the sources of Bean-Bayog's unhappiness: "We were young, and we were good-looking, and we just were on top of the world. Yet we were at Harvard. I didn't even realize then what kind of a place it was for women and what kind of messages were being given to us. Guys would not date Radcliffe students because they were all 'dogs.' We weren't getting the feedback we wanted in our courses, we weren't getting mentored the way we should have been. If we did well in our course work, we got totally jerked around by the men in our lives. Or we got very negative feedback from classmates. I know that bothered Margaret. . . . I know she was insecure about those issues." Webb describes Margaret Bean as a "relatively vulnerable friend." "Margaret had a lot of internal battles in her life that have taken a lot of her energy," Webb explains. "It took her a little bit longer to deal with all of them than it took some of us. And her struggles were compounded, in her early life, by problems with alcohol."

Margaret Bean graduated *cum laude* from Radcliffe in 1965 and entered Harvard Medical School that fall, later specializing in psychiatry. In 1975, as part of her psychoanalytic training, she underwent her first psychotherapy. She would remain in therapy for ten years, and she would credit the process with having "transformed my inner and outer opportunities." In June 1984, at forty, she married ("to my family's surprise and relief") fellow psychiatrist Rogelio Bayog, a widower with two children. Kathryn Kogan, a clinical psychologist who was in a supervisory group run by Bean-Bayog from 1989 to 1992, says, "As a recovering-alcoholic psychiatrist, Dr. Bean-Bayog brought a lot of new energy to the field of substance-abuse treatment." Bean-Bayog wrote and edited books on alcoholism, published papers in leading psychiatric journals and became a nationally recognized expert on addiction. To the Radcliffe classmates who saw her at their twenty-fifth reunion, in 1990, one impression prevailed: "She seemed," says Elise Bruml, "like a much happier person than she'd been in college."

Not that Margaret Bean-Bayog's life was without dissatisfactions. Indeed, for all her transformations, inner and outer, she was apparently capable of surrendering to the demons that troubled her youth. For instance, in June 1984, she was convicted in the Boston suburb of Newton for driving under the influence of alcohol. Three months later, she met Paul Lozano for the first time.

Paul's eight-week hospitalization at McLean was rocky. He raged at the staff, nurses and doctors. He threatened suicide.

In mid-May, Frankenburg arranged a family meeting attended by Paul's mother and his sister Pilar, who had flown in from El Paso. "Pilar and the mother told Paul repeatedly that he was loved for who he was and that the family had no expectations of him other than that he try to be happy," Frankenburg wrote in her notes of the meeting. But Paul "was at his most hostile, sarcastic and rageful." Frankenburg and the rest of the staff began to question the accuracy of Lozano's stories of childhood neglect and abuse. That Paul might be, in Frankenburg's words, "merely a liar" contributed to a refinement in his diagnosis. To his previous condition of major depression was added "borderline personality disorder," a diagnosis that would go far to solve the riddle of Lozano's mystifying life, his paradoxical mix of brilliance and madness; the disparities between his life as he remembered it and as others saw it.

Located on the border between neurosis and psychosis, BPD is a disorganization of the emotions originating often in a sense of childhood abandonment. Characterized by clinging dependencies, vast mood swings, explosive bouts of anger, low tolerance for frustration and suicidal fear of abandonment, BPD appears first in young adulthood, typically when sufferers first leave home for college, a separation from family and an assumption of adult pressures that trigger their first breakdown.

In light of Paul's new diagnosis, many of the mysteries of his life seemed to clear up. Paul's descents into despair when far from home (first at West Point, then Harvard); his impulsive marriage and annulment; his chronic depressions, sudden rages, panic attacks, suicidal gestures and apparent fabrications about his family—all were classic borderline behavior. Another symptom, first noted a year earlier during his first hospitalization at McLean, was "regression." An unsigned nursing note described how Paul, in conversation, "seemed to lapse into almost 'baby talk,' " evidence that he was prone to a reversion to a childlike state common to BPD. If untreated (or worse, exacerbated), regression in such patients can lead to psychosis.

Despite Frankenburg's reservations, Bean-Bayog was determined to keep Paul as a patient. She sought support for her treatment methods from Dr. Daniel Buie, an expert on BPD. "The patient shouldn't lose you, for goodness' sake," Buie told her during Paul's second hospitalization. "You have a flexibility in treating him that includes the frequent visits, seeing him for deferred payment and bringing him to the hospital yourself, which is capable of being seen as overinvolved by other people but which I think is working." Meanwhile, Frankenburg registered her concern in a discharge summary. She wrote that Paul's "complete dependence" on Bean-Bayog's therapy was troubling since it was not clear whether it was "supporting him or rather stirring up almost inconsolable yearnings and conflictual feelings."

There was legitimate reason to wonder whether Paul might be stirring similar yearnings and feelings in Bean-Bayog. Borderlines are notoriously difficult to treat. Their wild mood swings and heightened emotions often disorient therapists. The analytic relationship can, in effect, become reversed: The therapist begins subconsciously to use the patient as a way of working through his or her own unmet needs, unresolved conflicts and fantasies. Otto Kernberg, M.D., a leading authority on BPD, described this phenomenon in his groundbreaking book on the diagnosis and treatment of BPD: "The analyst may revert to former neurotic patterns in his interaction with a particular patient which had been given up in his contact with other patients and in his life outside the analytic hours. The analyst, so to speak, becomes his worst in his relationship with a certain patient. . . . It is tempting to write the whole reaction off as a character problem of the analyst and not consider sufficiently the specific way in which the patient provokes this reaction in the analyst."

Emotionally fragile therapists are at particular risk when treating borderlines. Whether Bean-Bayog was at her strongest, emotionally, is moot. Shortly before Paul's hospitalization at McLean, Bean-Bayog had discovered she was pregnant, but later she miscarried. At the age of forty-three, she was now facing the grim possibility that she would never have her own biological child.

Upon Paul's release from the hospital on July 28th, 1987, he returned to regular therapy with Bean-Bayog. They met now at her new home office in her large white colonial-style manse in suburban Lexington. Reached by a separate entrance to the left of the classically columned front porch, the office was restful, with a pastel-colored wall hanging, plants, armchairs, a couch. A sound-masking machine muffled the whoosh of traffic on the road out front. There was no receptionist.

It was at this point that she intensified what she would later describe as her "unique" therapy. It hinged on her playing the role of a nonjudgmental, loving mother to his three-year-old boy. "Her objective," Bean-Bayog's lawyers would later state, "was to support Lozano's functioning as an adult while allowing the childlike part of his personality to mature and become integrated with his adult self." The therapy was based on the psychotherapeutic technique known as "the corrective emotional experience," but it would later be difficult to distinguish *whose* emotional experience was being corrected: his or hers. To some who have reviewed her treatment, her techniques seem to have slipped into something that bears a frightening affinity to brainwashing.

"Run over these cards every day until you know them all by heart and are starting to believe them," she wrote on a stack of index cards labeled "Handy Multipurpose Emergency and Reference FLASHCARD DECK." The first card read: "I'm your mom and I love you and you love me very very much. Say that ten times." She gave him a blanket from her couch and some twenty children's books. She furnished him with audiotapes of her voice reading hypnotically vivid accounts of domestic events that cast him as a baby, her as his mother. "The sun is slanting through the bars of your crib," she wrote in a story titled "Morning." "You are lying on your back, singing and talking away to yourself, waving your feet. . . . You hear me coming down the hall. 'Mama?' You swing to your feet. 'Mama?' "

"You can too feel and act like three years old when you're twenty-five," she exhorted him in a letter. "You can curl up with the blanket, the sweater, the Pound Puppy, all the notes I've written you and all the books. You can breast-feed and be cozy. No one can take those feelings away from you." She listed things to avoid: "Do not drink. Do not call your family. If they call you, be brief. Notice what they are doing to you. Don't let them do in our boy. If you begin to believe you can't be three years old, it's because you're losing contact with me." She reminded him to keep up with his "programming."

Bean-Bayog wrote him a series of letters to be read during their first extended separation—a two-week vacation that she and her husband took to Manila over Christmas 1987. "I'm beginning to feel like it's too long and it's only five days," she wrote. "You're probably doing fine. I'm the one who's having trouble. . . . This drives me nuts. I miss you. . . . I miss all of you."

As the therapy progressed, Paul, in those moments when he wasn't "the boy," began to describe sexual fantasies he was having about her. . . .

"I want to really have sex with you," Paul told her in July of 1987. "I'm tired of talking about it."

"All the work we've done together would go all to smash," Bean-Bayog told him. "You can want to, you can make me want to, but we can stay in our chairs and keep baby safe."

Patients commonly develop strong sexual feelings toward their therapists. This is part of a phenomenon Freud dubbed transference, which also includes love, hate, jealousy, respect. If reciprocated by the therapist for the patient, the feelings are called countertransference and can be an important tool for exploring the patient's psyche. Bean-Bayog's countertransference for Paul became strong enough that she began to vent them in a series of written fantasies. "You have me always on the edge of climax, but you won't let me go over," she scribbled on one of her pads. In this fantasy she is shackled, spread-eagled on the floor, his mouth on her vagina. "I am ecstatic with the pleasure of it, helplessly pliant in your hands. . . . I lick along the crack between your leg and your body. I come to the base of your penis, which is erect by now. I begin to trace over it with my fingers and mouth." In some of her fantasies, Paul is the doctor issuing judgments on her sanity. " 'You don't handle stress well,' " she imagines him barking at her. " 'It's only to be expected. Character-disordered people have a low frustration tolerance.' "

These writings (copies of which were later discovered in Paul's apartment) blanketed fifty-five pages and grew increasingly frenetic. "I feel all the more bonded to you," she wrote in a scene in which she is hogtied, whipped and teased. "I can see your erection and the expression on your face of sheer sensuality. . . . I want you to keep on punishing and arousing and humiliating me. I would

do anything to be able to keep that expression on your face. Anything."

Griggs Road, in the tree-shaded Boston suburb of Brookline, is a secluded, winding street far from the tumult of campus life. It was to this restful enclave that Paul Lozano moved in the summer of 1988 as his therapy with Bean-Bayog entered its third year. He occupied the top floor of a house. His landlady lived on the first two floors with her husband and two sons. The woman recalls Paul as the perfect tenant: quiet, hard-working. So it was a jarring surprise when, one day, he arrived home with a woman old enough to be his mother, a woman in conservative attire, who smiled politely when Paul introduced her as his "friend."

He said she would be "around for the next couple of days." When asked, the landlady could not identify the woman as Bean-Bayog but remembers thinking she was too old for Paul. Nevertheless, he seemed happier than she'd ever seen him. In the days after this weekend visit, Paul received an unusual influx of mail. Cards and letters came every day. On two occasions, flowers arrived. The landlady, who prided herself on her discretion, never looked to see who all this mail was from, but one day she couldn't resist an attempt to draw him out.

"Are you having a birthday or something?" she asked teasingly.

Paul just smiled and moved on to his room.

Paul's suicidal ideas and gestures abated. During his leave of absence from med school, he worked on a Ph.D. in microbiology and in the fall of 1989 was well enough to resume his medical studies at Harvard. Throughout, he was seeing Bean-Bayog daily. Then, in November 1989, she began to insist that he pay, according to her notes, "at least overhead" of $100 to $120 a week or suffer a cutback in sessions. He objected, saying she had other pro bono patients. She also insisted that he join the impaired-physicians committee, a monitoring group. He angrily refused. He didn't want the stigma. Their therapy sessions became bickering matches. Her flashcards and letters took on a markedly cooler tone: "There is a safe place for the baby here, but there also needs to be a safe place for me," she wrote on a flashcard. She explained that she wished to start limiting his off-hours calls to her home.

After two years of being encouraged to think of her as an all-supporting, all-loving mother, he responded poorly to this sudden clinical chill. And when in early 1990 she announced to him her plans to adopt a child, his panic flared. "*I want to be your baby!*" he told her in a session on March 8th. He grew more distraught as Bean-Bayog spoke about taking a four-month maternity leave. He began stealing drugs from the hospital. On the evening of March 13th, he had a serious psychotic breakdown. Unable to reach Bean-Bayog on the phone, he tore off in his car. He arrived at her home around 9:00 p.m. and pounded on her doors and windows, screaming, "Dr. Bean! Dr. Bean!" Her teenage stepchildren were home alone, terrified.

Two days later, Paul missed an appointment. Bean-Bayog phoned his apartment. He sounded groggy and admitted to having injected himself with a combination of hallucinogens and anesthetics stolen from the hospital. She phoned the police, who arrived at Griggs Road and took him to Faulkner Hospital. There the admitting physician noted that the patient—"a tearful, childlike Latin American man sitting quite anxious, embracing himself, tearful and in much distress"—was hearing voices that had commanded him to "harm himself." He was diagnosed with "schizo-effective illness" and was hospitalized. He would remain hospitalized, on and off, for the next four months. During this time, Bean-Bayog visited him twice a week and discussed terminating his therapy, a topic she had first brought up the previous fall.

Paul made several efforts to keep Bean-Bayog as his therapist. He tried begging her. "Is this the last time I'll ever see you?" he asked. "I feel like it never really happened. What should I do with all the stuff you gave me? I can't bear to read those notes because they remind me. I'll give them back to you. These feelings are horrendous. I can't believe I might never see you again. How can

you inflict so much pain on a person?" He had already asked his parents for the money to pay her. In the fall of '89 Paul's father had flown to Boston with $9000. Bean-Bayog accepted the money but said it merely covered back payment. Eventually, Paul seemed to give in to the inevitable. On June 12th, 1990, he asked her: "Why did you let me in so close? It makes it ten times worse now."

"Because I thought you'd kill yourself," Bean-Bayog answered. "I can't be in a position where if you didn't get what you want, you get suicidal."

Six days later, on June 18th, 1990, Bean-Bayog terminated Paul Lozano's therapy. "Take care of yourself," she wrote to him. "Let me know from time to time what has become of you. Love, Dr. B."

For Paul Lozano, the summer and fall of 1990 passed in a blur of suicide threats and hospital psych units—Faulkner; Human Resource Institute; Massachusetts Mental Health; Malden; Massachusetts General; Carney—until finally, on October 19th, 1990, he entered Boston's Newton-Wellesley Hospital. He was referred to Dr. William-Barry Gault. The diagnosis was psychotic depression. Electroshock therapy was recommended. Paul consented. During October and November, he underwent nine treatments. Pilar flew in from El Paso to lend support. She had not seen her brother in months. The change in him was startling. He lay, dazed and weeping, on his hospital bed, begging for "Dr. Bean," for "Margaret."

Pilar had heard Paul mention Bean-Bayog's name, but she had not been apprised of the "unique" therapy. She asked her brother to explain his relationship with Bean-Bayog. He stared at her, as if to say: *Where do I begin?*

"Just go to my apartment," Paul said, finally. "That will explain everything."

In the bedroom on Griggs Road, Paul's sister found a large cardboard box containing Bean-Bayog's letters and tapes; her children's stories, stuffed animals, valentines, photographs and sexual fantasies. But perhaps the most startling item was the flashcard, in Bean-Bayog's handwriting, that read, "I'm going to miss so many things about you, the closeness and the need and the *phenomenal sex*. . . ."

Pilar brought the materials to Gault, who began gently to question Paul about them. Over several weeks, Paul disclosed details of the therapy: the mother-son role-playing, the flashcards, the books and letters. On December 12th, 1990, Gault sent a complaint to the Massachusetts Board of Registration in Medicine alleging the possibility of misconduct. A month later, he followed this with a letter to the hospital's lawyers, repeating the charges and adding that Bean-Bayog had discussed her sex fantasies, masturbated and "engaged with [Paul] in sexual activity." It would take the board more than a year to officially respond to the letter. Not until the case had exploded in the media last spring did the board call an emergency session to consider the charges against Bean-Bayog. But by then it was too late—at least, for Paul Lozano.

After the nine electroshock treatments he received in the fall of 1990, Paul did improve briefly. On January 31st, 1991, he returned to El Paso with plans to do a medical rotation at a local hospital. He took an apartment at the senior citizens' retirement home managed by his parents. But within twenty-four hours of his arrival, he was hospitalized for suicidal thoughts. He managed to get through his rotation, but by the end of March, he began to speak obsessively of Bean-Bayog. His despair over losing her was now compounded with guilt that he had betrayed her to Gault and the board of registration. From unprovoked shouts of "She lied to me! She betrayed me!" he would revert to baby talk. "Is Margaret my mommy?" he asked Pilar. "Where's Margaret?" At times he seemed to *become* a toddler. Walking bowlegged, teetering, arms out for balance, he would follow Pilar from room to room, clutching his Pound Puppy. He told Pilar that he could hear Bean-Bayog's voice in his head. "What's she saying?" Pilar asked.

"She's telling me to kill myself."

On the morning of April 1st, Paul seemed miraculously lucid. He made phone calls to family members. (His twenty-two-year-old nephew would later say that Paul had not sounded so normal in years.) That night he ate dinner with his parents, then retired to his apartment, where he showered, donned a pair of clean white jockey shorts and sprayed himself with Calvin Klein cologne. He then sat at his desk, opened his medical books and settled down as if to study.

Instead, he took from his desk drawer a hypodermic needle and a vial of liquid cocaine. He was found the next morning by his father. He had injected his hands, arms and wrists seventy-five times with the cocaine. Still at his desk, he was sitting back in his chair, head tipped over the backrest, arms hanging loosely by his sides, feet propped on his open medical books. The coroner would set the date of his death as April 2nd, 1991. Pilar believes he died in the waning hours of the day before: April Fool's Day.

On March 31st, 1992, in a preliminary hearing of the Massachusetts Board of Registration, Bean-Bayog issued a prepared statement proclaiming her innocence of any sexual contact with Paul Lozano and stating that her treatment of him fell within accepted standards of care. She insisted that Paul always knew that she was not his *real* mother, that the role-playing was simply to help him "contradict his depressive and suicidal thoughts." The flashcard referring to "phenomenal sex" was, she said, dictated by Paul and reflected what he wanted to hear from a girlfriend. The sadomasochistic fantasies were never intended for his eyes. He had, she said, stolen them from her office. She insisted that his charges were motivated solely by vengeance for her terminating his therapy. Paul Lozano, she reminded the board, was an acute borderline and by definition his utterances could not be believed.

The board, in its preliminary ruling, found Bean-Bayog's care of Paul Lozano "did not conform to accepted standards," rebuked her for calling herself his "mom" but allowed her to keep her license, pending a fuller investigation scheduled for fall 1992. To accommodate the expected crowds and perhaps to quell criticism that it had originally tried to sweep the messy case under the rug, the state of Massachusetts hired a special prosecutor and secured a 600-seat theater. Court TV planned national gavel-to-gavel live broadcast of the proceedings.

In July, Bean-Bayog had vowed to fight the charges. But on September 17th, four days before the hearings were to begin, she wrote to the state board, resigning her license. "What has changed since July," she wrote, "is not my innocence, which remains, but the way this particular case is being conducted by the state. It has changed from having some semblance of fairness into a media circus." She cited the same fears of a media feeding frenzy last December, when she settled out of court in the civil suit. Her insurance company paid $1 million damages to the Lozanos, effectively ending the investigation.

Bean-Bayog has, throughout, refused to speak to the media. Her brother, Bennett Bean, also refuses comment, except to proclaim his sister's innocence and to say that she has not yet decided what to do with her life. Dumped by Harvard, her reputation destroyed, her medical license gone, she is suffering, he says, "post-traumatic-stress syndrome." For twenty years her existence was defined by her work as a healer. She has lost her identity. In her impassioned, elegiac letter of resignation, she compares her ordeal to "my own funeral" and says: "I can't imagine life without my career as a physician. It is in my bone marrow, my ancestry and all my dreams. I loved it so."

# DAVID AND GOLIATH: WHEN EMPIRICAL AND CLINICAL STANDARDS OF PRACTICE MEET

## Larry E. Beutler

*In an ideal world, scientific research would test increasingly effective interventions for various forms of psychopathology, and practitioners would employ these interventions in their clinical work and, in turn, suggest ways that subsequent scientific studies might be conducted. The current relationship between science and practice in the field of abnormal psychology begins to approximate this ideal, but the system often breaks down because of incompatibilities between how scientists and practitioners have been trained and what they are working to accomplish. Thus, the scientific method is optimized when there is a high degree of control over many variables so that the effects of one or two variables can be discerned; as a consequence the resulting experiments tend not to resemble how therapy is conducted by practicing clinicians. For example, an experiment to test different interventions for depression is likely to be conducted with people who meet diagnostic criteria for depression and few, if any, other disorders. However, in their actual clinical work, practitioners usually will not see a "pure depressive" but patients who are depressed and have other significant problems such as anxiety, substance use, and personality disorders as well. Because of the perceived irrelevance of findings from such studies to the population they treat, the results may be ignored or dismissed by practitioners. Another reason why the interplay between research and practice is not more harmonious is that even when demonstrably effective interventions are developed through careful research, practitioners are sometimes resistant to giving up the approaches with which they are most familiar and comfortable, particularly if the new interventions constrain the practitioners' options.*

*Although this summary oversimplifies the situation as it actually exists— many scientists are also practitioners, for example—it is accurate to say that scientists and practitioners want to improve the well-being of patients, but they often disagree on the intermediate steps needed to achieve this goal. Dr. Larry Beutler, a leading scholar and commentator on the interface between science and practice, jumps into this fray by summarizing the need for treatment standards and offering a set of 18 guidelines that can inform the empirical evaluation of clinical work. A key point in his argument is that these guidelines should reflect basic principles of what is likely to bring about change in psychotherapy, regardless of the theoretical orientation of the practitioner.*

## Suggested Readings

Goldfried, M. R. (Ed.). (2001). *How therapists change: Personal and professional reflections.* Washington, DC: American Psychological Association.

Soldz, S., & McCullough, L. (Eds.). (2000). *Reconciling empirical knowledge and clinical experience: The art and science of psychotherapy.* Washington, DC: American Psychological Association.

Weisz, J. R., Donenberg, G. R., Han, S. S., & Weiss, B. (1995). Bridging the gap between laboratory and clinic in child and adolescent psychotherapy. *Journal of Consulting and Clinical Psychology, 63,* 688–701.

*American Psychologist, 55, 997–1007. (2000).*

*Traditional clinical methods of assessing the effectiveness of psychological treatments have come under attack. Experience and strong belief frequently lead to false confidence in treatments and sometimes result in damage to patients. Advocates have called for a scientific standard to replace the extant standards based on expert opinion and cost. Yet there are costs to the use of both the old standards and scientific standards based on manualized treatments and associated research. This article proposes a set of criteria for determining whether a treatment is scientifically credible based on empirically informed principles rather than on techniques or single-theory formulations This proposal offers a way to overcome the problems of rigid manuals as well as those associated with forcing clinicians to adhere to theories and practices that are outside of their interest, experience, and expertise Instead, scientifically sound, cross-cutting principles of treatment selection are proposed by which a treatment could be evaluated for scientific credibility and applied from a number of theoretical frameworks*

In 1995, the Public Broadcasting System (PBS) presented an exposé on a therapy that addressed the sequelae of satanic abuse (Bikel & Dretzin, 1995). The broadcast reported on the treatment program developed at the Multiple Personality Disorders Treatment Unit at Rush-Presbyterian Medical Center in Chicago under the direction of Bennett Braun, a psychiatrist, and Roberta Sachs, a clinical psychologist. This treatment was based on the theory that the symptoms of multiple personality disorder (MPD; now, dissociative identity disorder [DID]) were indicators that the patient so diagnosed may have been satanically abused (Braun, 1990; Young, Sachs, Braun, & Watkins, 1991).

Although Braun's deprogramming therapy was exceptional among the psychotherapies, his theory earned him many accolades, and his viewpoints were accepted as factual by a substantial minority of professional practitioners during the late 1980s and early 1990s. This theory asserted that generalized distress accompanied by ambivalence and dissociation provided reliable evidence that a patient had come under the influence, albeit subsequently repressed, of a coven of witches, one of several families of witches dating back to the Middle Ages. These families had preserved their satanic rituals and evil powers by systematically programming their children—through a process of human sacrifice, cannibalism, and sexual rituals—to pursue a lifelong mission of slaying nonbelievers. Most remarkable in this theory, because of the use of hypnosis and other powerful persuasion-based procedures, no one—neither the witches who carried out the programming nor the children who were the recipients of it—had any memory of this plot or of the rituals necessary to ensure that the plan of destruction was successful.

The witches in these satanic covens, operating on their own programmed histories, allegedly were induced to awaken from a hypnotically induced state of repression when a priest or priestess in the coven presented them with certain satanic signals or cues, usually letters of the Greek alphabet. Having awakened, they next assumed the roles of priest and priestess themselves, to initiate the human sacrifices and sexual rituals necessary to program their children or kill the uninitiated. Having done so, they then lapsed again into a state of programmed repression, assuming the mantle of normal bankers, homemakers, professors, teachers, plumbers, and the like until their hidden programs were reactivated. MPD (or DID) was a side effect of this process.

The PBS story documented the case of Mary, who was identified by Braun as being a high priestess in an ancient coven. Her identity as a witch who had killed others and who had programmed her children, by subjecting them to rituals of human sacrifice, cannibalism, and sex, to murder her enemies, was secured and confirmed by the presence of two major symptoms, dissociation and depression, along with a strong suspicion of incest. As a result of Braun's diagnosis, Mary was subjected to several years of deprogramming therapy, an intensive inpatient treatment that included withholding food, unusually high doses of medications, four-point restraints, and deprogramming groups including several therapists who attacked her denials until she confessed to being a witch. These treatments were then extended to her husband and her two sons. Ultimately, her treatment cost her insurance carrier over two million dollars and resulted in the dissolution of her marriage and her estrangement from her two sons. It also resulted in her bringing suit against Braun for malpractice.

It should be noted that most medical treatments are subject to specific empirical tests before they are or can be offered as treatments in the United States. These tests are designed by the Food and Drug Administration (FDA) to assure that the treatment is first of all safe and second, effective. Laypersons and alternative medicine practitioners frequently criticize the FDA standards of proof for being so demanding that they often exclude from the U.S. market treatments that are routinely available without prescription in European and South American countries. Yet, from a scientific perspective, the criteria used by the FDA are rather lax and sometimes have been applied in such a way that evidence of harm has been overlooked.

The FDA criteria require only that two independent, controlled studies have been published, demonstrating statistically (not necessarily clinically) significant findings when the treatment is compared with an inactive or placebo treatment. Critics point out that this standard does not weigh negative findings if positive ones are available. As a result, for example, in 1998, the FDA was forced to remove three drugs from the market because they had dangerous side effects that had been overlooked by adherence to the FDA's criteria. Redux, a popular dietetic drug, along with Posicor and Duract, was removed because the FDA criteria, in relying only on evidence of two studies in which there were positive effects, overlooked evidence that the three drugs caused serious heart and liver damage.

In the PBS exposé (Bikel & Dretzin, 1995), Braun spoke of evidence underlying his theory and practice. However, the evidentiary base to which Braun referred does not even approach the modest standard set for medical treatments by the FDA. It was based on supposedly clinical evidence, supplemented by a review of books and early writings on satanic cultures in Europe and by a plethora of letters from believers. The so-called research did not include systematic research to determine the validity of the assumptions of satanic abuse, nor did it include studies of whether memories of this type could actually be suppressed by the hypnotic techniques of the coven, tests of the potential negative effects of treatments, or an assessment of how effectively the proposed deprogramming therapy either reduced symptoms of dissociation or improved one's quality of life. In short, Braun's research did not include what psychologists would conventionally consider to be minimally necessary to certify any medical treatment as either safe or effective.

Braun's treatment was composed of psychosocial methods of deprogramming and psychotherapy. In this domain, two fundamental myths have always been accepted and applied whenever new treatments are introduced: First, psychosocial treatments are not strong enough to cause real harm, and second, all psychosocial treatments are all pretty much the same—a position that was labeled the "dodo bird verdict" by Luborsky, Singer, and Luborsky (1975)—or, in other words, all have won, and all must have prizes. Notably, these myths have been extended to and implicitly incorporated by managed care and service delivery programs when treatment decisions are made. If nothing else, the Rush-Presbyterian Medical Center experience should testify that neither of these assumptions should be accepted as universally true.

Although empirical comparisons of most structured treatments do result in similar mean effects (see, e.g., Wampold et al., 1997), there is good evidence that hidden within these mean effects are widely disparate outcomes (see, e.g., Howard, Krause, Saunders, & Kopta, 1997). Specifically, psychotherapeutic interventions, as a rule, increase the possibility of both benefit and deterioration (Lambert, 1992), and some practices (and practitioners) are consistently associated with a deterioration of patients' conditions—they are psychonoxious and sometimes dangerous (Bergin, 1963; Bergin & Lambert, 1978). If psychologists, or the health care enterprise, accept the propositions that some treatments do in fact cause harm and that all treatments are not equally damaging, then they are faced with the problem of identifying what treatments work best, for whom, and under what circumstances. That is, there would be costs.

On one hand, health care programs would be obliged to ensure that their cadre of practitioners was trained in these procedures and that they were practiced correctly. On the other hand, practitioners would have to face the possibility of giving up favored positions and theories for which scientific evidence of effectiveness is lacking and adopting others that might be less interesting to increase the scientific credibility of their work (Beutler, Kim, Davison, Karno, & Fisher, 1996).

## Clinical Standards as Criteria of Truth

Unfortunately, in determining the value and validity of clinical practice, those who practice psychosocial treatments have held themselves to exceedingly low but implicit standards based on so-called clinical evidence. Shared, strong beliefs and the personal sincerity of those who advocate these beliefs have been held as sufficient evidence to ensure the truth of a treatment recommendation. Treatment practices have been validated by reference to clinical experience, but the nature of this experience has usually been unstated, and the beliefs that are attributed to it have varied widely among similarly experienced clinicians. Extensive research evidence supports the conclusion that, among clinicians, personal beliefs, thus developed, are almost always given greater credence than scientific evidence and are considered to be the real or moral truth when the two sources of evidence are at variance (see, e.g., Garb, 1998; Singer & Lalich, 1996). To leave the future of professional practice to the dubious validity of sincere beliefs and appealing clinical theories is to risk that there will be more experiences like the one illustrated in the aforementioned PBS program. History confirms that if one believes a position very strongly and is sincere in proposing this point of view, the viewpoint is bound to be accepted as true by someone. Accepting scientifically credible approaches may well mean relinquishing any commitment to the truth of some theories that have been constructed wholly from clinical experience.

## Public Standards of Treatment Effectiveness

In a world that values beliefs over evidence, it may be no surprise that legal and quasi-political bodies, rather than professional clinicians or scientists, often make decisions about what treatments are valuable or effective. Such decisions are made daily by health insurance agencies and legal bodies as they determine what practices are covered by third-party payers and what ones are defined as malpractice

(Aaron, 1996; Beutler, Bongar, & Shurkin, 1998; Nathan, 1998). Three standards have been reified in U.S. professional practices and reinforced in U.S. courts of law, and none of the three requires scientific study or empirical evidence.

1. *Cost-effectiveness* is a criterion developed by health care systems and reflects political concerns with rising health care costs. From this perspective, the treatment considered good enough or effective enough to be covered by managed care is the one that serves a large number of people but costs less than the average services offered to those who share a given diagnosis (Aaron, 1996; Munoz, Hollon, McGrath, Rehm, & VandenBos, 1994). At this criterion's logical extreme, the most acceptable, valuable, and cost-effective treatment is one that is offered to many people but used by no one.

2. *The standard of common practice* is one that has been applied by legal bodies and by professional organizations that are concerned with minimalist criteria. The definition of malpractice arises from this so-called clinical standard. That is, court systems and peer review groups alike equate good-enough practice with what is most frequently done. This is the concept of the common or usual practice (Malcolm, 1986; Robertson, 1988). Stated another way, a treatment's effectiveness is equated with its popularity; taken to the standard's extreme, no new treatment could ever be judged to be appropriate or good enough.

3. *The principle of the respectable minority* was developed by the courts to acknowledge the vagaries in professions that foster divergent perspectives on any given problem. According to this principle, a treatment cannot be held to constitute malpractice if the treatment has an explicit theoretical foundation, a standard of delivery, and a significant number of followers. By case law, a good-enough treatment is one that is believed by as few as six professionals (Klerman, 1990; Malcolm, 1986). Under this principle, almost all treatments are good enough.

None of these criteria excludes treatments whose effects are harmful. Indeed, in the medical malpractice case by which the principle of the respectable minority was defined, scientific evidence indicated that the treatment was harmful and was not known to have any positive effects (*Hood v. Phillips*, 1976; *Leach v. Braillar*, 1967). Likewise, neither the standard of common practice nor the standard of cost-effectiveness has proposed a successful solution to the situation in which a popular or cost-efficient treatment is ineffective. Thus, when a treatment fails to meet these standards, a practitioner may be censured, but the treatment is neither corrected nor removed from the list of acceptable practices. Even in the case of the deprogramming therapy of Braun, the treatment continues to be practiced though the courts did, in 1998, act to remove Braun's medical license (Grumman, 1998), a decision that is under appeal by Braun at this writing. Interestingly enough, Braun's appeal cites the court's intrusion into matters that are best left to clinical judgment.

It is apparent that another standard of effectiveness is needed to replace the ones based on good intentions and strong belief. This standard must account for the actual benefit induced and the actual danger of deterioration imposed. This alternative is generally thought to be found in the rigors of the scientific method. . . .

## The Search for Scientific Standards

The development of a standard of evidence based on scientific findings and principles is a logical alternative to the problems encountered by reliance on the criteria of supposedly clinical evidence and experience. Yet this road, too, is uneven. Although professional practice and ethical guidelines have insisted that psychological practices be in accordance with scientific knowledge, psychologists seem unable to agree on what constitutes reasonable and adequate scientific evidence of a treatment's safety and benefit. Research studies vary in quality, often reach different conclusions, and do so with varying levels of relevance for clinical practice. How much evidence exists? What methodology was used? How strong must the evidence be relative to the presence of inconclusive and non-supportive evidence? As judged by what criteria? These are among the questions that one must address to have reasonable assurance that the scientific evidence indicates that a psychosocial treatment is safe and effective. . . .

## An Alternative Empirically Informed Criterion

Numerous scholars (e.g., Goldfried & Padawer, 1982; Prochaska, 1984) have argued that the treatment of behavioral problems would be advanced if research focused on principles of change rather than on supporting various theoretical models. Implementation of this recommendation has been hampered by the absence of commonly accepted principles. In an effort to overcome this problem and to respond to the recommendation, John Clarkin, Bruce Bongar, and I (Beutler, Clarkin, & Bongar, 2000) have recently completed a large-scale study of depression and depression-related conditions with the objective of defining the principles of change that can cut across theoretical boundaries and enhance the practices of clinicians without them having to alter their theoretical frameworks. Our intent was merely to begin the process of defining principle-based guidelines. We had no illusions that the principles we defined would be either exhaustive, exclusive, or immutable. Indeed, we sought to define principles in terms that could be subjected to additional research and added to or modified as evidence accumulates.

In this initial effort (Beutler et al., 2000), we first directed our attention to extant research. We were able to distill 15 hypothetical principles from an extensive review of literature on depression, cross-checked against research on chemical abuse and generalized anxiety. These initial principles were then subjected to an independent empirical test in a large, combined sample of over 250 outpatients representing a variety of disorders and problems. With this process, we confirmed the validity of 13 of the original principles. Five additional principles were incorporated from a survey (Peruzzi & Bongar, 1999) that defined the ethical and legal guidelines for treating individuals who are at risk for self-harm. . . .

We (Beutler et al., 2000) constructed the hypotheses so that they resembled suggestions or guidelines for constructing and planning treatment and divided them into two classes. One class addressed what we called *basic guidelines*. These are treatment-guiding principles that do not require direct observation of the clinical treatment session to monitor. They apply to the modality, format, and intensity of the treatment offered but cut across patient diagnoses.

The second class reflected what we called (Beutler et al., 2000) *optimal and enhanced guidelines*. Adherence to these guidelines could be assured only if one looked at what the clinician was actually doing in the treatment session. They applied to the use of various psychotherapy strategies exclusively, including level of directiveness, symptom- versus insight-focus, and abreactive versus supportive interventions. . . .

BASIC GUIDELINES The basic guidelines reflect treatment decisions attendant on patient prognosis, level of risk imposed, and the recommendation for using various modalities and formats of treatment. For example, the guidelines suggest that three factors are associated with a good prognosis: (a) good social support systems, (b) low functional impairment, and (c) low chronicity or complexity.

1. The likelihood of improvement (prognosis) is a positive function of social support level and a negative function of functional impairment.

2. Prognosis is attenuated by patient complexity/chronicity and by an absence of patient distress.

The level of functional impairment also has some implications for the differential assignment of psychoactive medication versus psychosocial intervention.

3. Psychoactive medication exerts its best effects on those patients with high functional impairment and high complexity/chronicity.

Functional impairment also serves as an indicator for increasing the length and intensity of treatment.

4. Benefit corresponds with treatment intensity among functionally impaired patients.

The variable of patient chronicity also carries the weight of some specific treatment recommendations as suggested by the direct finding supporting the recommendation that people with chronic problems respond better to multiperson therapy than to individual therapy.

5. Likelihood and magnitude of improvement are increased among patients with complexity/chronic problems by the application of multiperson therapy. . . .

6. Risk is reduced by a careful assessment of risk situations in the course of establishing a diagnosis and history.

7. Risk is reduced and patient compliance is increased when the treatment includes family intervention.

8. Risk and retention are optimized if the patient is realistically informed about the probable length and effectiveness of the treatment and has a clear understanding of the roles and activities that are expected of him or her during the course of treatment.

9. Risk is reduced if the clinician routinely questions the patient about suicidal feelings, intent, and plans.

A final, more general principle based on clinical safety and protection rather than directly on research findings is also included.

10. Ethical and legal principles suggest that documentation and consultation are advisable.

OPTIMAL AND ENHANCING GUIDELINES  The eight optimal and enhancing guidelines were all empirically derived first from the literature review and then from the cross-validation study. The first such principle reflects on the nature of the therapeutic relationship and on the importance of the therapeutic alliance. Although this is only one principle, it is both consistent with Basic Principle 8 above, and probably the foundation for much or even most treatment. Indeed, the other principles, at least those identified as optimal, may well be dependent on this first principle to become active.

1. Therapeutic change is greatest when the therapist is skillful and provides trust, acceptance, acknowledgment, collaboration, and respect for the patient within an environment that both supports risk and provides maximal safety.

The second principle for optimal treatment confirms the importance of exposure as a general principle of change.

2. Therapeutic change is most likely when the patient is exposed to the objects or targets of behavioral and emotional avoidance.

The third principle directs attention to the role of patient coping style in defining whether the treatment should be symptom focused or insight focused.

3. Therapeutic change is greatest when the relative balance of interventions favors the use of either skill-building and symptom-removal procedures among externalizing patients or insight- and relationship-focused procedures among internalizing patients.

The fourth principle emphasizes that all treatments should begin with a focus on symptoms, even though patients with certain coping styles must subsequently be treated with insight-oriented and conflict-focused interventions rather than strictly symptomatic ones.

4. Therapeutic change is most likely if the initial focus of change efforts is to build new skills and alter disruptive symptoms.

The next two principles address ways to respond to patient resistance. These principles emphasize the desirability of first avoiding resistant behaviors and then responding to the resistance-prone patient either with tolerance and low levels of directiveness and authoritativeness or with paradoxical interventions.

5. Therapeutic change is most likely when the therapeutic procedures do not evoke patient resistance.

6. Therapeutic change is greatest when the directiveness of the intervention either is inversely correspondent to the patient's current level of resistance or authoritatively prescribes a continuation of the symptomatic behavior.

Finally, the last two principles relate to patient motivation and specifically address the role of emotional arousal or distress in motivating change. These principles suggest the differential ways of addressing patients with high and low levels of distress and motivation.

7. The likelihood of therapeutic change is greatest when the patient's level of emotional stress is moderate, neither excessively high nor excessively low.

8. Therapeutic change is greatest when a patient is stimulated to emotional arousal in a safe environment until problematic responses diminish or extinguish.

## Conclusions

Clinical experience has proven to be an indefinite and sometimes dangerous guideline on which to base clinical work in the 21st century. The development of scientifically informed guidelines is a frequently touted alternative. As translated to contemporary practice, this means that clinicians must learn several different manual-based treatments to conduct a practice that includes individuals who fit a variety of diagnostic conditions. It is commonly accepted by some authors (e.g., Barlow, 1994; Luborsky & DeRubeis, 1984; Wilson, 1996) that treatment can be advanced by this practice and specifically, by the use of treatment manuals whose focus is on particular symptoms or diagnostic groups. Although some manual-based treatments may be sufficiently flexible to be translated for use across diagnostic groups, I do not believe that this approach works well for most practitioners and for most patients. For a variety of reasons, clinicians are unlikely to become either manual driven or diagnosis driven in their work.

I believe that procedures that enhance the quality of a healing relationship are immanently more powerful than the theory-based techniques to which contemporary manuals are addressed. Indeed, the power of any set of techniques may well be to enhance the quality of the therapeutic relationship; if this is so, then selecting techniques that fit the expectations and response dispositions of a given person is of utmost importance. It may be more important to tailor the treatment specifically to enhance the therapeutic relationship than to be consistent with a theoretical model of psychopathology. I find little evidence that either the theoretical model used, the clinical theory adopted by the clinician, or the patient's diagnosis provides much guidance in how well an intervention serves either to enhance the therapeutic bond or to facilitate outcome.

Thus, as a nonexclusive alternative to applying a different theoretically derived manual to each diagnostically distinct group of individuals, my colleagues and I (Beutler et al., 2000) have proposed the use of guidelines specifically designed to cut across theoretical models by identifying empirically informed principles of change that are relatively independent of clinical theory. Although these principles may exert much of their effect by enhancing the therapeutic alliance, this is unclear at this time. At this point, they are empirically informed and clinically sensible.

I anticipate that the initial list of principles articulated in the foregoing will be expanded and modified. I urge investigators and clinicians alike who seek to do so to ensure that the added principles are expressed in a way that both allows them to be verified and permits their disproof. This initial list is designed to avoid the problems of being bound by either techniques or theories. It allows the therapist and the clinician to use their own favored procedures to accomplish objectives that are consistent with the principles. This, I have come to believe, is what separates the skilled and artful clinician from the technician. The artful clinician follows principles and can thereby transcend situations and create novel interventions to fit new demands, all in concert with the principles. The technician and, to a lesser extent, the theoretician are bound by their techniques and may find it difficult to transcend the situation to develop new applications.

In psychotherapy, the task is to use the principles that allow the patient to explore new ideas in the safety of the office also to change this person's complex and multisymptomatic life, to make the patient feel and act better, and to overcome the problems imposed by the patient's particular, complex environment. The art of psychotherapy is taking simple principles of relationship and interpersonal influence and applying them in creative ways that fit the endless permutations and complexities that characterize the people who seek the therapist's services. If a person is just a technician, he or she will never transcend the use of techniques in a simple environment. Only an artist can apply these scientific principles to the complexity of lives and can find creative and new ways of making them relevant and workable in complex environments.

The principles that I have articulated are representative of what can be accomplished to blend science with practice and to bring diverse theoretical views together. They are also expressed in a form that I believe allows them to be subjected to further empirical test. Whatever modified form this list eventually takes, its principles must be applied in creative and novel ways to be responsive to the endless variations of behavior presented by patients. This is the true art of psychotherapy and the true challenge of using empirically supported treatments to bridge science and practice: inducing real and meaningful change.

# References

Aaron, H. (1996). End of an era. *Brookings Review, 14*, 35–37.

Barlow, D. H. (1994). Psychological interventions in the era of managed competition. *Clinical Psychology: Science and Practice, 1*, 109–122.

Bergin, A. E. (1963). The effects of psychotherapy: Negative results revisited. *Journal of Counseling Psychology, 10*, 244–250.

Bergin, A. E., & Lambert, M. J. (1978). The evaluation of therapeutic outcomes. In S. L. Garfield & A. E. Bergin (Eds.), *Handbook of psychotherapy and behavior change* (2nd ed., pp. 139–189). New York: Wiley.

Beutler, L. E., Bongar, B., & Shurkin, J. (1998). *Am I crazy or is it my shrink?* New York: Oxford University Press.

Beutler, L. E., Clarkin, J. F., & Bongar, B. (2000). *Guidelines for the systematic treatment of the depressed patient.* New York: Oxford University Press.

Beutler, L. E., Kim, E. J., Davison, E., Karno, M., & Fisher, D. (1996). Research contributions to improving managed health care outcomes. *Psychotherapy, 33*, 197–206.

Bikel, O., & Dretzin, R. (Producers). (1995). The search for Satan. In *Frontline.* Boston, MA: Public Broadcasting System.

Braun, B. G. (1990). Dissociative disorders as sequelae to incest. In R. P. Kluft (Ed.), *Incest-related syndromes of adult psy-*chopathology (pp. 227–245). Washington, DC: American Psychiatric Press.

Garb, H. N. (1998). *Studying the clinician: Judgment research and psychological assessment.* Washington, DC: American Psychological Association.

Goldfried, M. R., & Padawer, W. (1982). Current status and future directions in psychotherapy. In M. R. Goldfried (Ed.), *Converging themes in psychotherapy* (pp. 3–49). New York: Springer.

Grumman, C. (1998, August 13). Controversial psychiatrist's license in peril. *Chicago Tribune*, p. 1.

Hood v. Phillips, 537 S.W.2d 291 (Tex. Civ. App. 1976).

Howard, K. I., Krauze, M. S., Saunders, S. M., & Kopta, S. M. (1997). Trials and tribulations in the meta-analysis of treatment differences: Comment on Wampold et al. (1997). *Psychological Bulletin, 122*, 221–225.

Klerman, G. L. (1990). The psychiatric patient's right to effective treatment: Implications of Osheroff v. Chestnut Lodge. *American Journal of Psychiatry, 147*, 409–418.

Lambert, M. J. (1992). Implications of outcome research for psychotherapy integration. In J. C. Norcross & M. R. Goldfried (Eds.), *Handbook of psychotherapy integration* (pp. 94–129). New York: Basic Books.

Leach v. Braillar, 275 F. Supp. 897, 537 S.W.2d (D. Arizona 1967).

Luborsky, L., & DeRubeis, R. J. (1984). The use of psychotherapy treatment manuals: A small revolution in psychotherapy research. *Clinical Psychology Review, 4*, 5–14.

Luborsky, L., Singer, B., & Luborsky, L. (1975). Comparative studies of psychotherapies. *Archives of General Psychiatry, 32*, 995–1008.

Malcolm, J. G. (1986). Treatment choices and informed consent in psychiatry: Implications of the Osheroff case for the profession. *Journal of Psychiatry and Law, 14*, 9–107.

Munoz, R. F., Hollon, D., McGrath, E., Rehm, L. P., & Vanden-Bos, G. R. (1994). On the AHCPR Depression in Primary Care guidelines. *American Psychologist, 49*, 42–61.

Nathan, P. E. (1998). Practice guidelines: Not yet ideal. *American Psychologist, 53*, 290–299.

Peruzzi, N., & Bongar, B. (1999). Assessing risk for completed suicide in patients with major depression: Psychologists' views of critical factors. *Professional Psychology, 30*, 576–580.

Prochaska, J. O. (1984). *Systems of psychotherapy: A transtheoretical analysis* (2nd ed.). Homewood, IL: Dorsey Press.

Robertson, J. D. (1988). *Psychiatric malpractice: Liability of mental health professionals.* New York: Wiley.

Singer, M. T., & Lalich, J. (1996). *Crazy therapies.* New York: Jossey-Bass.

Wampold, B. E., Mondin, G. W., Moody, M., Stich, F., Benson, K., & Ahn, H. (1997). A meta-analysis of outcome studies comparing bona fide psychotherapies: Empirically, "all must have prizes." *Psychological Bulletin, 122*, 203–215.

Wilson, G. T. (1996). Manual-based treatments: The clinical application of research findings. *Behavior Research and Therapy, 34*, 295–314.

Young, W. C., Sachs, R. G., Braun, B. G., & Watkins, R. T. (1991). Patients reporting ritual abuse in childhood: A clinical syndrome: Report of 37 cases. *Child Abuse and Neglect, 15*, 181–189.

# How Useful for Psychotherapists Are Randomized Controlled Experiments?

## George Silberschatz and Jacqueline B. Persons

*We now delve more deeply into the merits of randomized controlled experiments. These are formal experiments, also called clinical trials, that are conducted by randomly assigning some people to receive one form of treatment and other people to receive another form of treatment, often including some kind of control group for comparison. The assumption (usually tested directly) is that these groups are equivalent prior to treatment; they are then compared at some point following treatment on a measure relating to the presenting problem—for example, depressive symptoms in the case of people who initially met diagnostic criteria for depression. It is this method that serves as the central tool in many fields for determining whether one approach or treatment is better than another, and indeed the experimental method has withstood the test of time in many applications. However, the value of this method for identifying which form of psychotherapy is better than another remains a matter of discussion and debate. George Silberschatz and Jacqueline B. Persons take different sides of this argument, and each makes a reasonably strong case for his or her point of view. Which position do you find more compelling? Does your response change depending on whether you adopt the perspective of a patient, a therapist, or a researcher?*

## Suggested Readings

DeRubeis, R. J., Gelfand, L. A., Tang, T. Z., & Simons, A. D. (1999). Medication versus cognitive-behavioral therapy for severely depressed outpatients: A mega-analysis of four randomized comparisons. *American Journal of Psychiatry, 156,* 1007–1013.

Jacobson, N. S., & Christensen, A. (1996). Studying the effectiveness of psychotherapy: How well can clinical trials do the job? *American Psychologist, 51,* 1031–1039.

Seligman, M. E. P. (1996). Science as an ally of practice. *American Psychologist, 51,* 1072–1079.

*Harvard Mental Health Letter, 16,* 5–7. (1999).

# The Results of Randomized Controlled Trials Are Useless to Clinicians by George Silberschatz

Randomized controlled trials have had little influence on the practice of psychotherapy because their methods and findings are not addressed to the needs of clinicians. These trials are a powerful tool for evaluating drug treatments, agricultural techniques, and certain medical procedures, but psychotherapy does not lend itself to this approach. As Martin Seligman, the president of the American Psychological Association, has pointed out, the very characteristics that make randomized controlled trials scientifically rigorous make them "the wrong method for empirically validating psychotherapy as it is actually done." Controlled trials do not tell therapists what they most want to know: what is troubling the patient, what the patient hopes to accomplish, what has prevented the patient from achieving that goal, and how the therapist can help. This research does not reveal how to cope with underlying personality problems or resolve a clinical impasse. It is also irrelevant to the treatment of patients with multiple disorders. Research subjects are screened to find those with a single diagnosis, but practicing clinicians usually treat complex cases with many problems and several diagnoses—precisely the kind of person most likely to be eliminated from a controlled study.

Another deficiency of randomized controlled trials is the lack of attention to individual differences. Because the treatment must be as uniform as possible, the number of sessions, the techniques, and the timing of interventions are carefully spelled out. But good clinical practice requires flexibility rather than uniformity. Psychotherapy patients choose a therapist rather than accept a random assignment. There are no artificial time constraints; therapy continues until the patient improves or quits. If one approach does not work, the therapist can take a different one. Our research clearly shows that effective therapists adapt their methods to the problems and needs of individual patients. Close adherence to treatment manuals constrains this spontaneity, creativity, and flexibility.

Although individual trials occasionally suggest that one type of psychotherapy is superior to another, these results are rarely replicated. Large-scale literature reviews and meta-analyses (combined analyses of large numbers of studies) show no consistent superiority of one school over another. The reason is that certain effective ingredients are common to different schools, and successful therapists of all schools have an intuitive understanding of what those ingredients are. To judge how psychotherapy works in practice and whether it works for a given patient, we need a type of research that is different from controlled studies. My colleagues and I have developed a strategy that concentrates on critical junctures in the relationship between patient and therapist. We analyze these incidents to identify effective ingredients and processes of therapeutic change. We have discovered that they include accurate empathy, the therapeutic relationship, and the refutation of irrational or harmful beliefs.

Randomized controlled trials and horse-race studies of psychotherapy are a waste of valuable time and resources. Instead of trying to decide which technique or school of therapy should win the biggest prize, we must discover the effective ingredients of psychotherapy and learn how therapists can be taught to use them productively.

# The Results of Randomized Controlled Trials Are Vital to Clinicians by Jacqueline B. Persons

Randomized controlled trials are needed to identify the most effective psychotherapies. Without random assignment to treatment conditions, we cannot be confident that patients in different groups do not differ systematically. In naturalistic studies, patients are usually making the choice, and patients who make different choices may differ in other ways. For example, suppose some patients at a clinic choose drug treatment and others choose psychotherapy. Those who choose drugs may want a solution that requires little effort on their part, and those who choose psychotherapy may be more highly motivated to work to overcome their symptoms. These differences may be responsible for any differences in outcome.

Clinicians must use this method if they are to offer the most effective treatments. For example, cognitive therapy and interpersonal therapy are the psychotherapies for depression that are best supported by controlled studies. Both have been shown to be as effective as medication, and cognitive therapy has been . . . shown superior to medication in preventing relapse. These therapies were developed in the mid-1970s. Clinicians who were trained before this time and do not pay attention to the controlled research will not update their skills to include these methods. Similarly, controlled studies have shown that the behavioral technique of exposure and response prevention is effective for obsessive-compulsive disorder. Again, therapists who do not read about these results may be providing ineffective treatment.

Psychotherapists sometimes say that controlled studies generally show no difference between therapies. Many older trials comparing psychotherapies in a "horse race" did result in a tie, but numerous recent studies have shown superior outcomes for one treatment or another. They show that panic control, a method developed by David Barlow, is more effective than relaxation training in the treatment of panic disorder. Cognitive-behavioral therapy is more effective than nondirective therapy, short-term psychodynamic therapy, or drugs in treating bulimia. Behavior therapy is superior to insight-oriented psychotherapy in the treatment of bedwetting. Cognitive-behavioral therapy and applied relaxation are both more effective than non-directive psychotherapy in treating generalized anxiety. These are only a few examples.

Many psychotherapists, unfortunately, use methods that have not been proven in controlled studies. They rarely use the therapies for anxiety disorders that have been shown to be effective. The alcoholism researcher William Miller has recently observed that in the treatment of drug and alcohol abuse, "the negative correlation between scientific evidence and application in standard practice remains striking, and could hardly be larger if one intentionally constructed treatment programs from those approaches with the least evidence of efficacy." The methods actually in use may be ineffective or even harmful.

Clinicians have a professional and ethical responsibility to offer therapies that have been shown to be effective before providing treatments that have either been found less effective or have not been studied. I recommend that patients ask their psychotherapists the following questions: Has the treatment you recommend been shown to be effective for my symptoms in a randomized controlled trial? Have other treatments been found equally or more effective in such studies? What are the goals of this treatment? What methods will be used to measure my progress toward those goals?

It is true that patients in controlled studies are a highly selected sample. In a study of therapies for depression, for example, people with serious medical problems, suicidal tendencies, psychotic symptoms, drug abuse problems, or panic disorder are usually screened out. Although this process would exclude many of the patients seen in routine clinical practice, that does not invalidate the results. As an analogy, suppose you have been diagnosed with bladder cancer, for which there are approved treatments that have been confirmed in randomized controlled trials. You do not meet the selection criteria for these studies because you also have diabetes. Do you still want your physician to be guided by the trials? Or would you prefer whatever methods the physician is familiar with, was taught in medical school, or has found helpful before? I would want my physician to follow the results of the latest controlled trials, and I suspect most readers would agree.

Nevertheless, Dr. Silberschatz is correct in observing that the results of these trials do not always apply to individual cases. To deal with this problem I have two recommendations for therapists. First, they should inform patients about the results of the relevant studies and state why these studies may not be fully applicable in the patient's case. Second, they should adapt the treatment to the patient's individual needs in a systematic fashion, as if the therapy were a scientific experiment with a sample size of one. In collaboration with the patient, the therapist should evaluate the situation, specify goals, and choose ways to measure progress. Both patient and therapist should moni-tor the treatment as it proceeds—the data collection phase of the experiment. If the results are poor, the plan should be revised and more data collected to evaluate the new plan. This is one way to adapt the empirical approach used in controlled research to the treatment of individual cases.

# CHAPTER 14

# Social and Legal Aspects of Abnormal Psychology

*Recognizing a few simple facts about psychopathology—it affects many people; it can diminish our capacity to manage ourselves, our relationships with others, and our work; it may involve deviant or illegal behavior—leads naturally to the observation that psychopathology must intersect significantly with many social systems that are designed to govern and promote human welfare. Understanding psychopathology completely therefore requires that we look beyond the affected individual and his or her immediate context to consider what their behavior means with reference to the law, education, the helping professions, public safety, and religion. In this chapter we attempt to scratch the surface of this complex topic by presenting articles on the legal obligations of psychotherapists, the prevalence of mentally ill people in prison, the uncertainty over whether to punish or treat sex offenders, and how religious dilemmas can interfere with the duties of medical and mental health professionals. Perhaps more than any other readings in this book, these articles emphasize that psychopathology is woven deeply into the fabric of our society and that it affects us all to different degrees.*

## Suggested Readings

Otnow-Lewis, D. (1999). *Guilty by reason of insanity: A psychiatrist explores the minds of killers.* New York: Ivy Books.

Winchester, S. (1998). *The professor and the madman: A tale of murder, insanity, and the making of the Oxford English Dictionary.* New York: HarperCollins.

Szasz, T. S. (1997). *Insanity: The idea and its consequences.* Syracuse, NY: Syracuse University Press.

# TO WARN, OR NOT TO WARN

## Barry Siegel

*The psychotherapist's job is gratifying in many respects. There are diverse settings in which to work, people of all kinds seek help with a seemingly endless variety of problems, the professional literature offers new ideas and challenges, and the opportunity to have a beneficial impact on people's lives is present in every working hour. But these positives are counterbalanced by demands on the psychotherapist's time and emotional energy. Talking with highly distressed patients can be draining, patients attempt suicide and sometimes succeed, other patients are a danger to others and must be hospitalized against their wishes, and there is not always adequate time to compare notes and commiserate with colleagues.*

*The following article addresses the psychotherapist's role as gatekeeper—in this instance determining whether or not an emotionally distraught police officer should continue to work—and the dilemmas involved in the psychotherapist's "duty to warn" another person if his or her patient threatens harm. How does the psychotherapist balance the patient's right to confidentiality against the right of a potential victim? At what point should confidentiality be broken by the psychotherapist? This case provides no easy answers to these questions, but it does provide a valuable illustration of the well-known Tarasoff vs. Regents of the University of California decision (see Blum, 1986) while also presenting an interesting portrait of psychotherapists as decision makers and the legal ramifications their decisions can have.*

### Reference

Blum, D. (1986). *Bad karma: A true story of obsession and murder*. New York: Atheneum.

---

*Los Angeles Times*, A1. (2000, September 9).

SMYRNA, Ga.—Anthony Stone's predicament began on the summer afternoon he first met Gordon "Jack" Garner III. Stone was a clinical psychologist, Garner a police officer who'd come to him for an evaluation. As they sat together in Stone's office here, the therapist began to realize that this cop suffered from more than the usual stress and burnout.

Much in life left Jack Garner disgruntled and frustrated. He had to deal with an unsympathetic supervisor and whiny citizens. He didn't fit in. He rarely slept well. It was a chore to get his uniform on some mornings. He felt himself "on a roller coaster." Some days he felt "out of control." Also—he had fantasies.

Stone, taking notes, looked up. What kind of fantasies?

This very morning, Garner reported, he had an image of shooting his precinct captain, Mike Cowart. He envisioned going to Cowart's office. He'd use his service revolver. He'd shoot Cowart lots of times. He'd hit him in his fat gut. He also might go to police headquarters. If he decided to kill himself, he'd take with him the police chief, the assistant chief and anybody else who got in his way.

Garner fixed Stone with a steady eye. He'd had other violent thoughts before, but nothing so vivid as the one about Cowart. "That's when I caught myself. . . . I scared myself thinking that way." It's fair to say that Garner was scaring Stone as well. Were Jack Garner's thoughts mere fantasies, or harbinger of a coming massacre? It was a nearly unanswerable question—but one Tony Stone had to answer.

If he concluded Garner was truly dangerous, his dilemma only deepened. A therapist in Stone's position is obliged to keep his clients' revelations confidential. Yet he also has a moral, professional and possibly legal duty to protect third parties from harm. "Duty to warn" rules are sometimes defined by state statute, sometimes by case law, sometimes by professional boards, sometimes not at all. The model is a 1976 California Supreme Court ruling, Tarasoff vs. Regents of the University of California. Yet the Tarasoff rule is tricky. It's unclear how direct the threat must be, how imminent the danger, how "reasonably" certain the mental health professional. So counselors grope about. So Stone groped.

After Garner left his office, days passed. One week stretched to two. In 23 years of practice, seeing some 30,000 people, Stone had never once issued a Tarasoff warning. Yet now he picked up the phone and called those whom Garner had imagined harming.

What followed has confounded Stone and many of his colleagues. Instead of the usual pitfall—being sued for failing to warn—he ended up

being sued for violating confidentiality. What's more, he lost: In a civil trial that was possibly the first of its kind in the country, a DeKalb County jury in December delivered a $280,000 judgment against the psychologist.

That summer in 1995, Jack Garner knew he needed help. The weather, so uncommonly hot and humid, was wearing him down. He was working in a fast-growing county northeast of Atlanta, in its busiest precinct. His job was a grind—call after call after call. At 51, he was the oldest patrol officer, working with cops half his age. His colleagues resented him because he was making more than others, because he once was a big city police officer in Atlanta. A supervisor called him a loner. A written evaluation indicated that he wasn't "sociable." Well, sure, he didn't backslap and tell jokes like when he was in his 20s. What could he say? Older cops did seem to be loners. That's just the way he was.

Garner's father died when he was 9, turning his mother to drink. He quit high school to join the Navy. Then he worked 12 years on the Atlanta force, until he got demoted from a sergeant's post over what he saw as "racial politics." Later he left a suburban police department because it was "full of cliques." He went through a difficult divorce— "like a death." After that came a suicide attempt and solitary drinking. Twenty-eight days of inpatient rehab got him sober. He remarried. He had a son. His problem now wasn't his personal life but his job. He hated work; he didn't trust his supervisors; he didn't like the public. He was going after citizens, making excessive traffic stops, running background checks. He felt tired, stressed out. He didn't know how much longer he could keep going.

That's why, on the morning of Aug. 17, 1995, he went to see James Gonzales, an ex-cop turned psychologist whose business card promised "solutions for change." On and on Garner talked, animated and expressive. This officer, Gonzales recorded in his notes that day, had a history of suicidal and violent, aggressive thoughts. He currently had feelings of violence toward the Gwinnett County Police Department. He had "passive suicidal thoughts" and "nonspecific urges to hurt someone."

Gonzales thought Garner depressed, paranoid and—most disturbing—highly agitated. While talking, Garner had stared at him—long stares and infrequent blinking. The therapist saw anger; he sensed instability. Two days later, Gonzales, wanting help, called Tony Stone, a psychologist who specialized in police evaluations. Tony Stone was an expert—the expert in their region.

I've got a troubled Gwinnett County police officer, Gonzales explained. Would you do a fitness for duty evaluation?

Stone hesitated. These fitness for duty exams often were so ambiguous, so painful. Sometimes his judgment cost a cop his job. It couldn't be avoided, of course. You had to play the gatekeeper.

OK, Stone said. I'll see him.

As he rose to greet Jack Garner that Aug. 30, Anthony Stone had good reason to feel assured about himself and his accomplishments. He'd grown up in Washington, D.C., the son of a physicist and a social worker. He'd been drawn to psychology for its insights into human behavior, for the way it resonated with his own introspective bent. Armed with a master's degree in public health and a doctorate in clinical psychology, he'd worked as staff psychologist for the Atlanta police force, then had rolled the dice and opened his own private practice.

The gamble had paid off: At 48, he now lived with his wife, a criminal justice professor, and their two children in a big comfortable home set in the woods just north of Atlanta. He wrote journal articles, he contributed chapters to textbooks, he gave speeches. Working with police officers fascinated him. He liked cops, he enjoyed the intensity of their work. That the Atlanta force had sent him through the police academy and given him a squad car with siren and emergency lights pleased him no end. So did his ability to help troubled officers.

Jack Garner's casual attire, shorts and a T-shirt, caught Stone's attention. It didn't look as if this officer had shaved that morning. Garner appeared younger than his 51 years. Although listed as 5 feet 10 and 180 pounds, he seemed smaller, lighter—

not the least imposing. Stone thought him intense and distraught, hardly able to contain himself. He was talking loudly and rapidly, his words rambling. Yet he was quite open, and clearly wanted to be helped.

Right near the start, Garner told of his latest problem: "My captain called me a liar." The day before, he'd been summoned to Capt. Mike Cowart's office to discuss a citizen abuse complaint. Cowart hadn't believed Garner's account. He drove home deeply disturbed. He changed clothes. He sat back. He felt so mad. He began to envision walking into Cowart's office. He imagined saying, "What about this? Is this a liar in uniform?" He imagined pumping bullets into the fat SOB. He imagined pumping bullets into eight to 10 others.

Stone stiffened at Garner's words. This officer had his full attention now. He began writing faster on his note pad. Garner talked on. He expressed a hatred for his job. He railed at individuals on the force. He griped about "crybaby" citizens who "complain if you look the wrong way." He described various compulsions, among them washing his hands as many as 20 times a day.

When Garner finished, Stone reflected. It was fairly common for him to hear violent fantasies. Usually, though, they were vague and general. Garner had gone further. Garner had offered names of specific potential victims. No, he hadn't said he intended to kill these people. Yet hardly anyone ever did. Most threats were conveyed as vague metaphors. Who knew? Maybe Garner had a simmering plan, or maybe he had a daydream.

Stone—as do most clinicians—freely admits he can't predict violent behavior. He only can offer opinions based on probabilities. Not until someone kills can therapists know. Then they look back and do studies. Then fingers get pointed. Then anguished cries fill the air, and lawsuits the courtroom. Stone did what he could: He searched for patterns and signposts. What he saw was a man with massive amounts of pain. One way to deal with such feelings is through compulsive rituals. Another way is to attack those you feel are causing them. Stone thought Garner might just do that. He was naming names. He was saying he felt scared of his fantasies. He was saying he wanted someone to intervene.

Stone weighed his options. He'd never violated a client's confidence. If he did it now, he'd likely end Garner's career. The prospect made Stone uncomfortable—enough so that he cast about for a compromise. He didn't believe Garner qualified for involuntary commitment, but what if Garner were willing on his own to enter structured treatment? That might be a way to protect Garner and those he imagined hurting.

As their session drew to a close, Stone recommended to Garner an increased level of care, a hospital or day program. When Garner agreed, Stone relaxed. He still had strong concerns, but given Garner's cooperation, he didn't see an imminent danger. He didn't think a Tarasoff warning was warranted. Later, in court, he said of this moment: "I did not feel that it was the time to do it."

Tony Stone had good reason to waver over his course with Jack Garner. Ever since the 1976 Tarasoff case first established the duty to warn, mental health professionals have struggled with issues of confidentiality and their questionable ability to predict behavior. Tarasoff left many therapists worrying that they were caught in a no-win situation. They could be liable for a patient's violence, or they could be liable for breaching that same patient's confidentiality.

In the Tarasoff case, two therapists treated an obsessed patient who told them of his intention to kill a former girlfriend. They informed not the girlfriend but the police, who questioned and then released the patient when he denied plans to harm anyone. Two months later, he killed his former girlfriend. When the victim's family sued, the court found that "once a therapist does in fact determine . . . that a patient poses a serious danger of violence to others, he bears a duty to exercise reasonable care to protect the foreseeable victim of that danger." Tarasoff applies only in California, but has proved a model and prod elsewhere around the country. A duty to warn has become part of the professional standards of care outlined by various boards and associations. It also has become the law in some states.

Yet responses by state courts and legislatures have varied widely: Some have restricted the application of the Tarasoff rule, some have broadened it, and some have not addressed it in any fashion. Georgia, as it happens, is among those that have done nothing. As Anthony Stone agonized over Jack Garner, he knew only that his state Board of Examiners of Psychologists did recognize situations in which therapists should reveal a confidence "to protect the patient, client or others from harm." He could choose his lawsuit. Which would he rather face, a client suing for breach of confidentiality, or widows suing after a massacre?

Early on the morning after he met Jack Garner, Stone called the referring therapist, Gonzales. He thought Garner clearly unfit for duty. He also thought they might have a Tarasoff situation. As Gonzales recalls it, Stone wanted to notify right then and there. Gonzales didn't. He wasn't in the session with Stone and Garner, he didn't know firsthand what Stone had experienced. All he knew was that Garner hadn't told him about specific violent fantasies. In fact, to him, Garner had denied any intent to harm.

Let's hold off, Gonzales proposed to Stone. Let me work with Garner. Let's get him into a structured program. Based on that, we can reevaluate.

Stone embraced this notion, it being his own first impulse. Things are going to be OK, he told himself. There are issues, but we've got a handle on them.

What transpired in the two weeks after Stone saw Garner remains, even now, murky at best. Notes are scarce, memories are blurred. It's known that Gonzales, on that first day, wrote a letter recommending that Garner be placed on 30-day paid leave. It's known that, as a result, Garner went on leave. The rest is open to some conjecture.

Stone says he thought he was "handing Garner off to Gonzales," and that "something would happen imminently, in a day or two." Yet Gonzales' records contain no references to any contact with Garner between Aug. 31 and Sept. 11, 1995. As the days passed, Stone kept calling Gonzales, only to learn that Garner had neither come for another visit nor entered a structured program. Things weren't playing out as Tony Stone thought they would. Events weren't allowing him to set aside his Tarasoff concerns.

Stone's customary assurance began waning. One evening, he spoke of the case to his wife as they sat in their lush backyard garden, a labyrinth of ponds and paths that he'd designed and built himself. Azaleas and coleus teemed; a dense stand of pine and magnolia and Japanese maple reached to the sky. Psychology had always given Stone a way of looking at things that made sense; now it didn't. "This is not OK," he said. "I don't know quite what to do."

Jack Garner, meanwhile, was sitting at home enjoying his leave. By all accounts he was feeling better. He spent time with his 2-year-old son. He did chores around his apartment building. He cooked dinner for his wife—lots of outdoor grilling. He still had a key to all the precincts and headquarters. He also still had his own guns. "I could do anything," he later pointed out. "But I'm just sitting there, thinking, 'I'm glad I'm off.'"

Days turned into a week. Late on Sept. 6, Stone learned Garner still hadn't entered a program. The next morning, as much to protect himself as to inform, he wrote Gonzales: "This officer . . . verbalized recent vivid fantasies of murdering his captain and discussed vague fantasies of gunning down his chief, assistant chief and others, in part so he could be killed. It seems appropriate to notify the captain consistent with Tarasoff guidelines and possibly the chief and assistant chief. I strongly recommend that his level of care be increased. I suggested to [Garner] that full or partial hospitalization made sense to me and that I would talk to you [which I did last week]."

Still, Gonzales didn't act. Four more days passed. Stone was rushing around—a steady stream of clients, his kids' school plays, racquetball with friends, golf and biking with his son. At the start, Garner had only occupied his mind in a few quiet moments, driving home or late at night. Now, more and more, Garner commanded his central attention. He was there when Stone awoke in the morning. He was there shooting people whose names Stone knew.

On Sept. 11, 1995, Stone sent Gonzales a formal report, with a cover letter that betrayed his sense of desperation: "I want to reemphasize my intention to notify specific persons named by Officer Garner in reference to his homicidal thoughts; however, I wish to do this in a way that is minimally disruptive to your treatment of him. Hence, I will wait your review of this report and your next session to plan the next move. I have no choice but to warn named persons under the Tarasoff guidelines, and it may be that you have no choice either, being the recipient of my report."

The next day, at their appointment, Gonzales told Garner about Stone's intent to issue Tarasoff warnings. Garner grew agitated and animated. His voice rose. He'd made no threats, he insisted. He had no intent to act violently toward himself or others. He and Stone had only discussed hypothetical situations. He'd be hung out to dry by the department if anyone issued warnings. Gonzales urged Garner to enter a structured program. Tony Stone will feel better then, he said. Tony Stone might not follow through.

Garner consented. Gonzales called a psychiatrist, Dr. Jeffrey Flatow, to arrange the necessary admitting appointment. Flatow could see Garner in two days—on Sept. 14.

After Garner left, Gonzales punched in Stone's number. "Good news," he said. "Jack has agreed to go into a program." Stone celebrated. Suddenly the world was a lot cleaner, a lot simpler.

Or so it seemed. Not until he was driving home from Gonzales' office did everything hit Jack Garner squarely in the face. He'd overheard Gonzales on the phone to the admitting people using the word "homicidal." He didn't believe that's what he was. Yet his therapists did. Stone and Gonzales obviously had been doing a lot of talking together, not including him.

That night, Garner shared his concerns with his wife. "Something's not kosher," he said. "They're setting me up for an involuntary commitment."

It's most likely that Tony Stone learned late on the morning of Sept. 14 that Garner had canceled his 3:30 p.m. appointment with Flatow. It's also possible that Stone learned then that Garner intended to terminate his relationship with Gonzales. Whatever the exact timing, on this morning Stone saw a crippling cloud of ambivalence evaporate. Now he didn't have a choice: He and Gonzales had lost the ability to control the situation, to control Jack Garner. Stone had to act, had to give the warnings.

Yet still he paused. For one last confirmation, he called the law firm that provides legal advice to members of the Georgia Psychological Assn. Yes, a lawyer there advised, you have an affirmative duty to warn. Sitting in his office, Stone reached for the phone. It felt sort of like diving into cold water, yet it wasn't hard now, it wasn't a struggle.

At 4:07 p.m.—37 minutes after Garner failed to show for his appointment—Stone made his first call, to Capt. Mike Cowart. At 4:30, he made his second, to the Gwinnett County police chief. At 3 p.m. the next day, he called the assistant chief. The Police Department responded with dispatch. Within hours, Chief Carl D. White wrote Garner, ordering him "to remain on leave." Soon after, a sergeant arrived at Garner's home to seize everything from his badge to his battery charger. Weeks later, White, rejecting recommendations from Garner's new therapists to take him back, instead offered a job at the county pound.

There, Garner lasted just four months before getting fired. He eventually moved to Savannah, where he now drives a truck, delivering pharmaceuticals each night over a 400-mile route. He makes half his police salary, with no benefits. "After a 31-year police career," he asks, "what else am I going to do?"

When Garner vs. Stone came to trial, lawyers, jurors and judges found themselves in midair, creating rules on the come, just as Tony Stone had. All the relevant case law involved doctors who failed to warn, not one who did warn. "A case of first impression," the lawyers call it. Stone won every battle along the way.

Garner's attorneys first asked for summary judgment, arguing there was no Tarasoff provision in Georgia code, so no exception to confidentiality. The judge turned them down. Then they argued

that if the judge was going to recognize a Tarasoff rule, he should tell the jury it requires a specific threat and imminent danger. Again the judge turned them down. All you need to violate confidentiality, he essentially ruled, is a reasonable chance of harm.

Stone, though, took a few hard blows inside the courtroom. The opposing attorneys and expert witnesses pointed out that Stone had seen Garner for just one session, with no follow-up, not even a call before issuing the warnings. They pointed out that Garner described fantasies, not threats; that Garner hadn't been Stone's patient; that Garner had been feeling much better since going on leave. Garner didn't represent imminent danger, two therapists suggested, and nothing indicated he would ever become violent.

"Grandstanding," one lawyer called Stone's conduct; "unbridled arrogance."

In the end, these criticisms weren't what cost Stone. Despite the therapist's possible missteps, lawyers and jurors alike agree they would have allowed him his clinical judgment if he'd reached it right away. Stone's two-week delay was his undoing. One of Garner's attorneys, William G. Quinn III, said: "If Stone had issued his warnings on the first day, we'd have no case."

Instead, Stone, recognizing ambiguity, wavered. That left him obliged—at least by the lawyers—to point to an intervening act that changed the equation, that drove him finally to act. It's when we lost control, Stone claimed. It's when Garner canceled his hospital appointment and terminated Gonzales. Courtroom testimony, however, didn't serve Stone well here. What Gonzales said on the stand obscured just when Garner terminated him—before or after Stone began making his calls. Stone's letters to Gonzales didn't help either: They made clear he felt compelled to issue Tarasoff warnings days before Garner broke relations.

That Stone had struggled with ambivalence for two weeks was obvious. So was the fact that the events of Sept. 14 provided a final impetus. Yet in the courtroom, this untidy tale got squeezed between two therapists' poor record keeping and the exacting rules of law. Gonzales, for one, was stupefied: "The way psychologists think and lawyers think is entirely different. Human behavior is just more complex than the legal system or written laws. What goes on in a courtroom is just not a rational process, though it tries to appear rational."

Quinn had his own interpretation: "I think Stone just thought on it some more and changed his mind. Over time, he stewed. He should have just said that: It would have worked."

The DeKalb County jury ended up awarding Garner and his wife $176,471 in damages and $103,779 in attorneys' fees. Rather than try to appeal, Stone settled in early May this year: Garner got paid, and in exchange, the judge vacated the formal judgment. That means there technically is no legal finding against Stone. Yet he remains on a national database of malpractice settlements. He also remains seized by a new reticence when he hears clients in his office voice possible threats. It all has become a matter of legal chess to him, rather than trying to do the right thing.

"It makes me feel sad and cynical," Stone said. "It's like I'm in this kind of crazy world that doesn't make sense. I have obligations but no protection. I did the right thing; I would do it again. Maybe not all my I's were dotted. But it's not like there's a preset method for doing this."

In the end, Garner vs. Stone highlighted rather than resolved a difficult situation. Instead of setting legal precedent, it fueled an already confused debate, and the sense among many therapists that they had better get it right whichever way they land. In fact, what therapists really must do, at least for the lawyers, is carefully document their reasoning process. Yet that won't ease the underlying problem. No matter how many sessions or phone calls, therapists cannot with certainty answer Garner vs. Stone's most haunting question: Were Jack Garner's vivid fantasies just that, or harbinger of a coming tragedy? Only if Garner had sprayed a volley of bullets would that be known. That he didn't could mean he never would have. Or it could mean that Stone's intervention had an impact.

Talking about all this one recent afternoon in Savannah, Jack Garner offered a sort of confession: "When we won the case, I actually felt sorry for Anthony Stone. It's true, I felt sorry for him. Now tell me—is that weird?"

# EXPERTS SAY STUDY CONFIRMS PRISON'S NEW ROLE AS MENTAL HOSPITAL

## Fox Butterfield

*Thousands of people beset by psychopathology are also prisoners in American jails. The next article documents the extent of this disturbing problem and points out several reasons that a recent statistic—16% of the total prison population, or more than 275,000 prisoners, have a mental illness—may underestimate its severity. The incarceration of the mentally ill appears to be an inadvertent consequence of the development of effective antipsychotic medications, such as Thorazine, in the 1950s. Availability of these drugs led to a massive deinstitutionalization of severely mentally ill patients from state-supported hospitals. This by itself was desirable, but, unfortunately, the other half of this solution—implementation of community mental health facilities—never fully materialized.*

### Suggested Reading

Torrey, E. F. (1998). *Out of the shadows: Confronting America's mental illness crisis.* New York: John Wiley.

*New York Times*, A10. (1999, July 12).

The first comprehensive study of the rapidly growing number of emotionally disturbed people in the nation's jails and prisons has found that there are 283,800 inmates with severe mental illness, about 16 percent of the total jail population. The report confirms the belief of many state, local and federal experts that jails and prisons have become the nation's new mental hospitals.

The study, released by the Justice Department on Sunday, paints a grim statistical portrait, detailing how emotionally disturbed inmates tend to follow a revolving door from homelessness to incarceration and then back to the streets with little treatment, many of them arrested for crimes that grow out of their illnesses.

According to the report, mentally ill inmates in state prisons were more than twice as likely to have been homeless before their arrest than other inmates, twice as likely to have been physically and sexually abused in childhood and far more likely to have been on drugs or alcohol.

In another reflection of their chaotic lives, the study found that emotionally disturbed inmates had many more previous incarcerations than other prisoners. More than three quarters of them had been sentenced to jail or prison before, and half had served three or more prior sentences.

Many of them were arrested for bizarre public behavior or petty crimes like loitering or public intoxication. But the report, by the Justice Department's Bureau of Justice Statistics, also found that mentally ill inmates in state prisons were more likely than other prisoners to have been convicted of a violent crime.

Moreover, once incarcerated, emotionally disturbed inmates in state prisons spend an average of 15 months longer behind bars than other prisoners, often because their delusions, hallucinations or paranoia make them more likely to get in fights or receive disciplinary reports.

"This study provides data to show that the incarceration of the mentally ill is a disastrous, horrible social issue," said Kay Redfield Jamison, a professor of psychiatry at the Johns Hopkins School of Medicine. "There is something fundamentally broken in the system that covers both hospitals and jails," said Jamison, the author of *Night Falls Fast: Understanding Suicide. . . .*

With the wholesale closings of public mental hospitals in the 1960s, and the prison boom of the past two decades, jails and prisons are often the only institutions open 24 hours a day and required to take the emotionally disturbed.

The hospitals were closed at a time when new antipsychotic drugs made medicating patients in the community seem a humane alternative to long-term hospitalization. From a high of 559,000 in 1955, the number of patients in state hospitals dropped to 69,000 in 1995.

But drugs work only when taken, and many states failed to build a promised network of clinics to monitor patients. To compound the problem, for-profit hospitals began turning away the psychotic. At the same time, the number of jail and prison beds has quadrupled in the last 25 years, with 1.8 million Americans now behind bars.

"Jails have become the poor person's mental hospitals," said Linda A. Teplin, a professor of psychiatry and director of the psycho-legal studies program at Northwestern University.

All previous estimates of the number of emotionally disturbed inmates have been based on research by Teplin in the Cook County Jail in Chicago. She found that 9.5 percent of male inmates there had experienced a severe mental disorder like schizophrenia, manic depression or major depression, four times the rate in the general population.

Teplin said that while she welcomed the Justice Department count, it was open to question because the study relied on reports by the inmates themselves, who were asked whether they had a mental condition or had ever received treatment for a mental problem. People with emotional disorders often are not aware of them, or do not want to report them, she said, so the Justice Department estimate of more than a quarter million inmates with mental illness may actually be too low, Teplin said.

In addition, Teplin said, the study was not conducted by mental health professionals using diagnostic tests, so it was impossible to tell what mental disorders the inmates suffered from, and whether they were severe illnesses, like schizophrenia, or generally less severe problems, like anxiety disorders.

One of the most striking findings in the study, and the one most likely to be disputed, is that mentally ill inmates were more likely to have been incarcerated for a violent offense than other prisoners, with 53 percent of emotionally disturbed inmates in state prisons sentenced for a violent crime, compared with 46 percent of other prisoners.

Specifically, the report found that 13.2 percent of mentally ill inmates in prisons had been convicted of murder, compared with 11.4 percent of other prisoners, and 12.4 percent of mentally ill inmates had been convicted of sexual assault, compared with 7.9 percent of other prisoners. Emotionally disturbed inmates in state prisons had also been convicted of more property crimes, but were only half as likely to have been sentenced for drug crimes.

Advocates for the mentally ill have worked hard to show that emotionally disturbed people are no more violent than others, to try to lessen the stigma surrounding mental illness. But recent research, while confirming that mentally ill people may not be more violent than others, suggests that they can become violent in a number of conditions, including when they are off their medications, are actively psychotic or are taking drugs or alcohol.

In another important finding, also subject to differing interpretations, the study found that reported rates of mental illness varied by race and gender, with white and female inmates reporting higher rates than black and male inmates. The highest rates of mental illness were among white female state prisoners, with an estimated 29 percent of them reporting emotional disorders, compared with 20 percent of black female prisoners. Overall, 22.6 percent of white state prisoners were identified as mentally ill, compared with 13.5 percent of black prisoners.

Dr. Dorothy Otnow-Lewis, a psychiatrist, said the differences were a result of white psychiatrists "being very bad at recognizing mental illness in minority individuals." Psychiatrists are more likely to dismiss aggressive behavior in men, particularly black men, as a result of their being bad, rather than being mad, said Otnow-Lewis, who is a senior criminal justice fellow at the Center on Crime, Communities and Culture of the Soros Foundation.

Michael Faenza, president of the National Mental Health Association, said the finding that mentally ill inmates tend to have more previous incarcerations than other prisoners "shows that the criminal justice system is just a revolving door for a person with mental illness, from the street to jail and back without treatment."

Jamison noted that jails and prisons are not conducive to treatment, even when it is available. "Inmates get deprived of sleep," she said, "and isolation can exacerbate their hallucinations or delusions. . . ."

# SLAMMING DOOR ON PREDATORS

## Beth Shuster

*Much of what makes the juxtaposition of legal systems, societal needs, and psychopathology challenging is the delicate balancing of priorities: confidentiality of psychotherapy versus the need to disclose potentially violent acts to an intended victim, the individual liberties of suicidal patients versus the moral obligation to hospitalize such patients against their will so that they do not kill themselves, the desire to punish an individual who has broken a law versus the desire to treat those who suffer from psychopathology.*

*In the next reading we return to the issue of mental illness and imprisonment, but with a twist. After someone has served time for a sex crime, how do we balance the need to protect the public against the individual's right to privacy? Mental health professionals are routinely involved in trials and parole hearings to determine whether someone will continue their deviant behavior once released from prison, and the stakes for either decision are high. This article introduces the main points of view in these debates—from the prison officials, state legislators, and mental health professionals to the sex offenders themselves—and, in the end, it raises more questions than it answers. One of the experts makes a distinction between mental illnesses (like schizophrenia or bipolar disorder) and mental disorders, such as a paraphilia that would lead to a sex crime. Is this a valid distinction?*

## Suggested Readings

Ressler, R. K., Burgess, A. W., Douglas, J. E., & Heafner, H. J. (1995). *Sexual homicide: Patterns and motives.* New York: Simon & Schuster.

Simon, R. I. (1999). *Bad men do what good men dream: A forensic psychiatrist illuminates the darker side of human behavior.* Washington DC: American Psychiatric Association.

---

*Los Angeles Times,* A1. (2000, May 2).

Inside an odd Los Angeles County courthouse, perhaps the most vexing problem facing the criminal justice system plays out several times a week. It's a place where constitutional liberties, society's right to protect itself and the ever-changing science of abnormal psychology collide. And there are no good solutions.

This is the courtroom, the only one of its kind in the county, devoted to cases involving violent sexual predators, the child molesters and repeated rapists who have finished their prison sentences but are liable for civil commitment. These are the ones no institution wants. These are also the ones whose risk of reoffense is so high almost nobody wants to let them go, either.

In an unprecedented use of the legal system, the state allows sex criminals to be locked away based not on crimes they have committed, but on the possibility they might offend again. And that, simply, is the root of the controversy: Is society going too far, as the judge who oversees these cases believes, or are vulnerable people being rightfully protected from dangerous sex criminals?

California approved its sexually violent predator law four years ago after a number of high-profile cases, such as that of the so-called Pillowcase Rapist, stirred politicians and activists into action. Christopher Hubbart, who was linked to about 30 rapes in which he typically covered victims' faces with a pillowcase, was the first to be held under the law. The politicians' goal was to keep sex criminals who were convicted before stricter sentencing laws were enacted from reentering society. The law allows the state to civilly commit repeated sex criminals to a state mental hospital where they must remain for at least two years, and might be held indefinitely.

As in 16 other states with similar statutes, California's law has been tested time and again in the courts. The California Supreme Court upheld the law last year. The U.S. Supreme Court found in 1997 that Kansas's law, which is similar to California's, could not be considered punishment if sex offenders are held in state treatment facilities. The justices agreed in March to review Washington state's statute based on a case brought by a man who contends that he has been unduly punished by being held for nine years without treatment.

The state's mental health department contends that the program will eventually require construction of a new state hospital devoted to the treatment of sex criminals. Until then, however, "a clash of tensions" is resulting, according to Steven Mayberg, the department's director. The inmates are angry about being detained when they are nearing the end of their prison terms; the Los An-

geles Country Sheriff's Department chafes under the difficulties of keeping them as they await commitment proceedings; some judges and lawyers question the constitutionality of the law while even some civil libertarians argue that these offenders should be kept in some kind of controlled environment. Advocates for the mentally ill, meanwhile, believe the statute is diagnosis by legislation, rather than a determination of a true medical disorder. Sex offenders, they say, are taking up valuable space in a state mental hospital. Public sentiment appears to lean toward keeping sex offenders detained, anywhere, at any cost.

"When you say to a person sitting on a jury: child molester on the streets, child molester in jail? . . . They're going to say that we should never have let them out to begin with," said John J. Vacca, head deputy of the mental health branch of the public defender's office.

## All Agree No Cure Exists

Although a range of disagreement exists over the merits of the sex offenders law and treatment, everyone agrees that no cure exists. Many experts say treatment can reduce the risks of reoffense but that a deviant sexual behavior is more of an addiction than an illness.

"It's not a mental illness like schizophrenia or bipolar disease," said Dr. Craig Nelson, the clinical administrator at Atascadero State Hospital, "but it's clearly a mental disorder. It's a fine distinction that gets lost on most people." Sex offenders are typically diagnosed as having paraphilia, a relatively generic term used to describe deviant sexual behavior.

Research shows that sex offenders whose victims are male and who have a history of violent sex crimes have high recidivism rates. One study conducted by Canadian researchers found that sex criminals probably will reoffend the first few years after being released, and that the rates keep increasing with time. The sexually violent predator program begins with the Department of Corrections, which refers repeated sex criminals at the end of their prison terms to the Department of

Mental Health for psychiatric examinations. Since the law became effective, the corrections department has screened more than 36,000 inmates.

Those evaluations must determine whether inmates have a history of violent sex acts toward strangers or casual acquaintances and whether they have a mental disorder making them "likely" to re-offend if they are released. If inmates meet those criteria, they are determined to be sexually violent predators and they typically are referred to the county where they were last sentenced to await hearings and finally jury trials to determine whether they will be civilly committed. More than 3,100 inmates statewide have been referred to the program since 1996, and about 300 offenders have been committed. Each inmate at Atascadero State Hospital costs the state about $107,000 a year, about four times more than a regular convict.

In Los Angeles County, sex offender cases are heard in an oddly located Superior Court, a decaying former pickle factory between the Golden State and Pasadena freeways, isolated miles away from the downtown courts. Superior Court Judge Harold Shabo presides. On a recent day, Eli Delray, a repeat child molester, sat quietly listening as a psychologist explained why he believed Delray would run a significant risk of committing more sexually violent crimes if he were released from custody.

"He has a pattern of arrests for similar behaviors . . . and we also know that many sex offenders commit crimes for which they are not arrested," said Hy Malinek, a Beverly Hills clinical and forensic psychologist and member of a state panel of experts on risk assessments. Malinek is frequently called as an expert witness for the prosecution in these cases. In an interview later, Malinek said the law requires "a highly complex judgment call."

"Every single day, people convicted of murder and all kinds of heinous crimes do their time and then are free," Malinek said. "In these cases, because of the underlying mental disorder, the state has this kind of protective measure. . . . No doctor can tell the future . . . but I think the law means well."

Delray's rap sheet includes numerous convictions and charges of sexually deviant behavior, including molesting children as young as 4 and even a case of indecent exposure while he was being held at the Atascadero hospital. Like most of the sex offenders in the county, Delray, 43, is represented by the public defender's office. None of those attorneys would allow their clients to be interviewed for this article.

But those lawyers say they have difficulties with the way the law treats sexual offenders. They note that tougher sentencing laws passed in 1994 mean that most violent sex offenders convicted today are sentenced to life in prison. For those already in prison before 1994, the civil commitment statute can produce virtually the same result. In addition, they point out that other laws allowing involuntary commitment require some proof that the person exhibits a present danger to society, and usually that requires evidence of a dangerous act within two weeks before confinement. To some, all of this amounts to a double standard or worse.

"Here we are saying sorry you've already served your term but we still won't let you out," said Vacca of the public defender's office. Shabo goes further, saying the law is essentially feel-good legislation intended for politicians and crusading activists. "If we're going to have preventive detention, let's call it that and deal with that," Shabo said recently during a break in court proceedings. "A healthy society doesn't lie to itself and that's what we're doing. . . . No one wants to see another victim but at the same time we don't want to have a meat-ax approach, assuming everyone is dangerous."

Shabo acknowledged that he sees a need for the law in some cases but said he doesn't believe the majority of these offenders are mentally ill. Rather, he believes they need psychological treatment immediately after they have been convicted, "before the person can rationalize the crime and/or shift the responsibility to the victim."

Perhaps what is needed, the judge said, is an alternative facility to house these offenders once they've been convicted. That way, they might more quickly receive needed treatment and the state won't rely on what the judge views as subjective criteria to detain them after their prison sentences.

Los Angeles County Sheriff Lee Baca, and those who run the jails, would also prefer to have the sex criminals kept elsewhere. Instead, they have to deal with the inmates' repeated requests and sophisticated tactics in working the system. "Undoubtedly I want them out of my jail," Baca said. But the sheriff said he doesn't want these offenders on the streets "because I'll have to deal with them again."

Currently, 47 sex criminals awaiting civil commitment, ages 29 to 70, live together as so-called K-10s—or keep-aways—in Twin Towers because sheriff's officials say they would come under attack from other inmates if they were left to live within the general jail population. Some of the sex offenders refer to themselves as "political prisoners." These inmates are a tough group for the Sheriff's Department, officials say, partly because of the sex offenders' personal knowledge of the criminal justice system and partly because of the judge's compassion for them. They frequently pass notes, write letters and file complaints to Shabo, the judge; he in turn writes orders to the Sheriff's Department. To deal with the numerous requests, the department has added two additional positions.

"We are inundated," said Cmdr. Bob Hoffman, who oversees Twin Towers, among other duties. "As we give them more privileges, that causes them to believe they're special . . . it reinforces their feeling that they don't belong in jail." So far, the department has agreed not to handcuff or shackle the sex offenders when they're in Twin Towers, even though most of the other segregated inmates in the special keep-away unit are restrained that way. The department readjusted the television sets allowing these inmates access to more major stations than others in the jail, and they now have different—and more frequent—visiting hours than the general population. They also are allowed hot water to make coffee, tea and soup. The latest dispute focuses on strip searches: The sex offenders are searched when they return from court—as are all inmates—but they object to being searched in an outdoor area when it is cold.

"Many of them are sitting in sheriff's custody in limbo," Shabo said. "To manage their frustration and bitterness has been a goal of mine. . . . It [ultimately] helps maintain order in the courtroom."

## Inmates File Class-Action Suit

One of the Twin Towers inmates filed a class-action federal lawsuit this year alleging that the sexually violent predators are being wrongfully incarcerated in a penal institution.

"I don't believe a facility exists [that is] designed for capable, competent mental health commitments," said Kenneth Ciancio, 39, who was incarcerated in state prison for 17 years for three rape and oral copulation cases. He has been held in Twin Towers for 18 months. The civil commitment law is "a sham," said Ciancio, who is representing himself in the federal case and who has filed 61 complaints since November against the Sheriff's Department.

While the offenders and Shabo are outspoken in their criticism of the law, the Los Angeles County district attorney's office finds itself caught in a tricky position. Prosecutors say they continuously battle delays and other rulings sought by the defense and agreed upon by the judge. In four years, the district attorney's office has appealed decisions and other rulings by Shabo in up to 40 cases, said Pam Booth, who oversees the district attorney's sex crimes division.

"Look, he's a very kind man and he cares passionately about these people," Booth said. "He wants to lighten their burden. . . . But they wouldn't be in this program if they weren't deemed to have a risk of reoffense." That risk is not lost on advocates of the mentally ill but they believe the sex offenders should not take up valuable space in the state's mental health system. Moreover, they contend that the program takes precious state funding; last year the state Legislature allocated nearly $42 million for the commitment program.

"It's not because I don't want society protected from dangerous people, but I think it's using the mental health treatment system as a form of social control," said Carla Jacobs, who serves on the board of the National Alliance for the Mentally Ill. "It's a legislated diagnosis and a political commitment." Regardless, Rep. James E. Rogan (R-Glendale), who sponsored the legislation while in the state Assembly, has no regrets. In fact, he said that repeated violent sex offenders should "probably get the death penalty" and that the legislation was the most important he ever carried.

"Sorry, go hold the hands of parents whose children's lives have been scarred forever," Rogan said. "I'm afraid if they're looking for sympathy from me, they'll be hard-pressed to get it."

# CLINICAL CASE CONFERENCE: WHEN RELIGION COLLIDES WITH MEDICINE

## Nada L. Stotland, M.D.

*We conclude this chapter with the gripping case study of a woman who, because of her religious beliefs, refuses medical care that would have saved her life. The physicians in this case faced a dilemma—fail to intervene and allow the patient to die, or save the woman's life but violate her religious convictions—and they called in a psychiatrist accustomed to working in medical inpatient settings to provide guidance and consultation. This case does not involve psychopathology in any way, but the mental health professional still plays a vital role by working closely with the medical personnel to evaluate the patient's mental status and capacity for making informed decisions about her care. Just as interesting are the notion that the medical staff would have been sued for malpractice had they intervened to save the woman's life and the graphic depiction of how religious beliefs can be so strong that they lead a patient and her family to choose death over life.*

### Suggested Reading

Pargament, K. I. (1997). *The psychology of religion and coping: Theory, research, and practice.* New York: Guilford.

*American Journal of Psychiatry, 156,* 304–307. (1999).

Some years ago, at the height of public concern about religious cults, a television comedy program aired a parody on a family game show. Two characters representing irate parents complained to the host about their young adult son. They wanted help in influencing him to leave a cult. They painted a picture of the crazy behaviors required by the cult. It seems their son was required to dress in a sort of long dress, more like women's clothing than men's. He had been forbidden to marry. He had had to turn his worldly possessions over to the group. Members of the cult spoke some sort of archaic language that no one in the family could understand. The leaders of the cult controlled nearly every moment of his day and decided where he would live and what he would do. All the members of the cult were expected to give their allegiance to some far-off supreme leader. After the audience had been whipped into a fine furor about the depredations of this weird cult, the "son" was brought from back stage. He was immediately recognizable as a Roman Catholic priest.

This skit captures a recurrent and unresolved

question in society. One person's religion is another person's cult or silliness. The medical setting is one in which belief systems can collide. The physician is taught that in the domain of health and disease, life itself is the highest priority. But some religions place a higher priority on specific religious tenets and proscriptions. A psychiatrist is most often called into these collisions to address questions of competence, but there are other psychological issues involved: the grief of the patient and family, the impact on dependents, and the emotional reactions and interactions of medical staff. Ethical conflicts can present as psychiatric consultations.

When it comes to competence and consent, the standards for determining the acceptability or normalcy of a patient's belief seem to be the sharing of the religion by a larger population and the longevity of the patient's religious affiliation. These criteria do not substantively address the content of the beliefs. And they provide limited solace to medical professionals caring for patients who refuse life- or limb-saving treatments or to the psychiatrists whom those medical professionals involve, like the parents on the television spoof, in hopes of either changing those patients' minds or finding a psychiatric rationale for overriding their wishes. Only the specifics of an actual case can capture the psychological, sociological, and ethical realities of these dilemmas. Following is a presentation and discussion of such a case.

## Case Presentation

The high-risk obstetrical unit of a university medical center received an urgent call. A 26-year-old woman, Ms. A, had been delivered of twins, by Cesarean section, 2 days earlier in a town some distance away. The infants were normal and thriving. The mother had seemed to tolerate the procedure well at the time, but she had now, suddenly, "crashed." Her blood pressure and pulse were approaching the level of hemodynamic shock. The presumptive diagnosis was interal hemorrhage, but the referring hospital did not have the facilities to determine the origin of the hemorrhage or to stem

it. The referring hospital urgently requested that a helicopter be dispatched to pick up Ms. A and bring her to the university hospital, which was a regional perinatal center.

Within the hour Ms. A was wheeled into the university hospital emergency room and rushed immediately to the operating room. She was weak and frightened but conscious and seemingly lucid. As the gurney sped down the corridors, she gave verbal consent for whatever diagnostic and therapeutic measures would prove necessary, but with one exception. She asked that no blood be administered, because she was a Jehovah's Witness. She was too weak to press the point, and the staff was too concerned about her immediate survival to discuss it. Without articulating it, they took the position that they would keep all options open and worry about philosophical discussions later.

In the operating room, contrast solution was introduced into Ms. A's pelvic circulation so as to identify the bleeding point radiographically. At the same time, she was typed and cross-matched for transfusion. Her hemoglobin and hematocrit were dangerously low. Type O negative blood had been hand-delivered from the blood bank and was on hand. The pelvic angiography revealed that a vessel ligated during the surgical delivery had ruptured and was actively spilling blood into the pelvic space.

Just then, the patient's husband, Mr. A, and brother-in-law, Mr. B, arrived at the hospital and appeared on the unit. They quickly thanked the staff for their prompt attention to Ms. A and echoed her objection to the use of blood and blood products. They stressed that she was a Jehovah's Witness. Her husband reported that he and she had three children, ages 4 and 3 years and 18 months, in addition to the newborn twins. All were doing well. They were being cared for by close relatives and members of the congregation. The obstetrical resident, reluctant to leave Ms. A's side, dashed out to explain that her life was probably at stake. Under these circumstances, he was certain, her husband and relatives would understand that there was no alternative to blood transfusions. No, Mr. A and Mr. B repeated, blood products were not to be used, no matter what the consequences.

Hardly able to believe what he had heard, the resident went back into the operating room to see how his patient was faring and to prepare to close off the source of the hemorrhage. By this time, the attending obstetrician had arrived. He had been informed about the clinical situation and had considered it in the few minutes it took him to reach the operating room. He was not inclined to let the life of a healthy young mother of five slip through his hands because of a completely irrational religious belief, conveyed by a woman in shock and two men who claimed to be relatives, but whom he had never seen before and whose background and motivations he had no time to explore. For all he knew, the whole family had become Jehovah's Witnesses impulsively, only weeks or even days earlier. Didn't Jehovah's Witnesses come around ringing doorbells and converting people? The attending obstetrician had his own religious beliefs; he had gone to medical school, taken the Hippocratic oath, and spent countless sleepless nights learning how to save the lives of mothers and babies. He knew what his duty was. Just to be on the safe side, he told the clerk to reach the hospital attorney and administrator-on-call.

In the operating room, the attending obstetrician and invasive radiologist prepared to perform a newly developed procedure. At the same time, the obstetrician ordered that the blood that was on hand be administered quickly, under pressure, both because of the gravity of the clinical situation and because he wanted to do what he could for Ms. A before the situation was further complicated by relatives, lawyers, and administrators. The intravenous pole with the hanging bag of blood was kept out of Ms. A's direct view, and she did not appear to notice that she was about to receive a transfusion. In any event, her consciousness and strength were waning. Soon she would not be able to consent, or object, to anything. How could anyone be sure that her refusal to accept blood was fully informed? All that could be discussed if her life could be saved. If she died, it would be a moot point.

Under radiographic control, using the catheter through which the contrast material had been injected, the obstetrician directed a bolus of a synthetic agglutinizing material to the site of the rupture in the pelvic blood vessel. Just as the procedure was being performed, Mr. A and Mr. B, who had, unbeknownst to the staff, been watching through the window in the operating room door, burst into the operating room. Before anyone inside could react, they had slipped the clamp onto the tubing conveying the blood transfusion into Mrs. A's arm and were about to pull the intravenous connection out altogether.

There was an uproar. Mr. A and Mr. B had intruded into an area off limits to nonmedical personnel and had actively interfered with medical treatment. Some members of the staff began shouting at them; others set out to remove them physically; and still others called for help from the hospital security team. Mr. A and Mr. B were equally outraged but more controlled. They left the room quietly but only after assuring themselves that no blood was flowing into Ms. A's veins. Outside the door of the operating room, they reminded any staff members who approached them that both they and Ms. A had explicitly forbidden the use of blood in her care. They questioned how they could be expected to leave her unprotected in the care of the staff in the face of incontrovertible evidence that her directive had been violated. Over the quiet but determined voices of Ms. A's family members, staff members were shouting: "Don't you understand your wife could die? Don't your babies need their mother? This is no time for philosophy; it's a life-and-death situation!"

In the operating room, meanwhile, staff had regained their wits and resumed caring for Ms. A. They resumed the radiographic studies. They were relieved, and exhilarated, to see that the procedure had worked; it appeared that the hemorrhage had been stayed. After some minutes of observation, they decided it would be safe to remove the angiographic catheter and conclude the procedure. With a few stitches and a pressure dressing, Ms. A was ready to leave the operating room for the intensive care unit. She was extremely pale, weak, and exhausted from the blood loss, the unexpected emergency, the procedure, and the hullabaloo. She made few spontaneous comments, but she did ask for word about her twin newborns and her other young children.

The staff were beside themselves. The intern, especially, was undone. She had chosen obstetrics as a specialty because of the attraction of bringing children into the world and protecting mothers and babies from harm. She was enormously impressed by the technical procedure that had saved her patient's life. She had been taught that treatments could not be administered without the informed consent of the patient, but it had never really occurred to her that a patient would refuse a straightforward, painless infusion that was necessary to save her life. How could she possibly comply with such a refusal? It flew in the face of everything she had trained for, everything she believed in, everything she cared about, everything she had sworn an oath to do. How was she to care for this patient now? She did not know whether she was relieved that she was not on call that evening or sorry that she could not follow this case through the night.

In the midst of this melee, a member of the staff thought to call for psychiatric consultation. Into the fray came the consultation psychiatrist. The attending obstetrician, patience worn thin, demanded, "You talk to these people. They must be crazy." The resident pleaded, "Isn't there some way to diagnose a mental problem in this patient?" Although several people were trying to speak at once, and despite the atmosphere of alarm, the psychiatrist managed to piece together the story. Ms. A's relatives were not, themselves, patients, and they had neither asked for nor agreed to consult with a psychiatrist. Although no formal mental status examination had been performed, there was nothing in the account to raise concern about a psychosis or even a delirium in the patient. But this was, or had been, a life-and-death matter. The psychiatrist had young children of her own. She could not begin to imagine making a treatment decision that would leave them motherless. She would see what she could do. She went to the patient's bedside.

Ms. A was deathly pale and weak, but she readily agreed to a psychiatric interview. She proved to be well-oriented, lucid, of normal intelligence, and well aware of her medical situation. She expressed love and concern for her children. She reiterated her objection to blood transfusion and suggested that the psychiatrist ask her husband and brother-in-law to explain her feelings. The interview had further exhausted her by this point, and the psychiatrist was reluctant to press her to talk further. She went into the corridor to speak to the relatives. Mr. A and Mr. B were patient and cooperative but quite anxious. They informed the psychiatrist that the patient had been born a Jehovah's Witness. Mr. B was a minister, and Mr. A a leader, in their congregation. Their lives, and those of the patient and the children, revolved around the church. The whole community at home was praying for the survival and health of Ms. A.

The psychiatrist went to check on Ms. A's condition. The artificial clot seemed to be holding fast. Ms. A's hematocrit and hemoglobin were stable. The psychiatrist and the obstetrical staff began to hope that the transfusion problem would go away. As the furor abated, however, there was one problem: a stable hematocrit is not equivalent to a hematocrit compatible with life. House staff and attending physicians searched the literature. No patient with blood indexes as low as these had ever been reported to survive. It seemed incredible that a person could be basically healthy and currently very much alive and lucid but be doomed to die. She might be terribly weak and vulnerable to infection and other complications, but surely, with proper protection, now that the crisis was over, she had a chance of gradually regenerating her own blood cells.

Accepting that approach would have simplified the psychiatrist's job. One could argue for the powerful healing power of hope. But the literature made it clear that this would be denial, not optimism. A new round of interviews and discussions began. Even as she lay exhausted from her terrifying ordeal, Ms. A and her family had to be informed of the scientific realities. The attending physician, hoping that the powerful facts would jolt the family into reconsidering their stance, conveyed the results of the literature review in no uncertain terms. They were saddened, but they did not budge.

At the same time, the staff had to deal afresh not only with their intense and highly internally and interpersonally conflicted feelings about Ms. A's decision, but also with an unusually wrenching clinical situation. Here was a young and previously perfectly healthy woman, a woman for whom the difference between life and death was the administration of a substance, blood, which staff members perceived as a commonplace medical treatment (this event took place before the HIV era) with no emotional or moral valence. The death of this woman would leave five preschool children motherless—an eventuality she dreaded. The reasons for the woman's refusal to accept the simple, available treatment were utterly incomprehensible. And the woman was going to die, over a period of many hours, while in their care.

A new round of legal approaches were proposed and considered. Although some staff members voiced the opinion that patients who refused the treatment recommended should be discharged or transferred, that option was not clinically or legally feasible. Could the psychiatrist not find some pretext for declaring Ms. A incompetent? The psychiatrist had to consider at what point repeated mental status examinations and queries about the patient's religious beliefs and understanding of the clinical situation and prognosis would become harassment. Although Ms. A's state of consciousness was likely to deteriorate, there was no reason to believe that her basic competence or convictions had changed.

What about the rights of the children to their mother's care? That was a worthy concern, with possible legal consequences for the hospital, but, in the final analysis, it did not supercede her right to refuse medical treatment. Ms. A and her relatives were repeatedly confronted with arguments about the interests of the children. They rejoined that the living relatives, and, indeed, all the members of the church were ready and willing to provide loving, comprehensive care and support to the children,

especially since their mother would have died a martyr to the religious convictions they all shared.

The lawyers and hospital administrator, in addition to these specific arguments, considered the overall algorithm: what was the hospital's liability if it should accede to Ms. A's wishes, and if it should supercede them? The relatives would actively intercede in any attempt to obtain or implement a court order for blood administration, and the relatives and patient would doubtless bring and publicize legal action against the hospital were blood to be given without such an order. On the other hand, the relatives in this particular case would be extremely unlikely to bring suit, or to prevail in a suit, if Ms. A were allowed to die. The documentation of the hospital's efforts to explain and persuade was extensive.

How would a jury react to each of the alternatives? It is generally difficult to rouse a jury's indignation over an intervention that saved a life, and a jury's respect for life-saving interventions would presumably be increased by the presence of five children who still had their mother. But juries also respect the law, and the law was clear. Ms. A had a lifelong affiliation with an established and recognized religion that mandated her behavior, and she had made an informed and competent decision.

Back at the bedside and in the nurses' station, new tensions had broken out. The nursing staff had not been invited to participate in the medical, ethical, and legal deliberations. Decisions were conveyed to them, verbally and in written orders in Ms. A's chart. It seemed to them that doctors and administrators could go off into conference rooms and make philosophical and legal decisions while they had to remain with a conscious, young, basically healthy patient and watch while her life slipped away under their care. What about their ethical responsibilities?

Over the hours of medical intervention, persuasion, and discussion, they had gotten to know their patient. She was a brave and personable young woman, a model patient, and they had grown to like her. They were tortured by the thought of her unnecessary death, her little children at home, and her sadness at the prospect of leaving them. As with the physicians and administrators, some thought she had no right to abandon her own life and those responsibilities she had taken on, and others felt strongly that her wishes should be respected.

These conflicts were also enacted in struggles about the presence of Ms. A's family. Family involvement was a fairly new, and therefore emotional, concept on the obstetrical unit. The healing power and support of family members for a patient who was laboring or ill had just been "discovered" by researchers and incorporated into hospital policy. Family members were permitted to remain at the bedsides of dying patients without regard to visiting hours. These particular family members were extremely involved and dedicated, but these particular family members seemed to be the factor that stood between life and death for their patient. When they were out of Ms. A's room pressing their case with the staff, Ms. A's resolve weakened. When they returned, her determination to avoid blood transfusions was reinforced. Should the nurses encourage the family to remain with the patient or attempt to exclude them?

One veteran, kind, and well-respected nurse, herself the mother of a large family, turned out to be a Jehovah's Witness. She had not made her religious affiliation public until this time, but now she began to advocate for respect for the patient's religious beliefs. But she did not feel entitled to explain or justify those beliefs. She was surrounded by staff members who repeatedly expressed strong negative feelings, ranging from utter bafflement to outright hostility, about the patient's stance: "She must be crazy."

Meanwhile, the nurses at the bedside watched as Ms. A had a final visit with her little children, held her husband's hand, and, alert to the end, declined. Her clinical course followed the descriptions in the literature. Approximately 24 hours after admission, she died.

## The Psychiatric Postmortem

The death of Ms. A did not resolve the feelings and conflicts of the participants in this real-life drama.

Each person who had been involved was wondering whether he or she might not have done something, somehow, to save Ms. A's life and was blaming others as well. Nurses were upset with other nurses, physicians with other physicians and with administration, and each discipline was upset with the others. The conflicts hung over the department. Instruments were slapped into the hands of gynecologists in the operating room without the usual comfortable banter. When the nurses changed shifts, reports were given through clenched teeth. Residents wrote orders in charts, flagged them, and slammed the charts on the desks in nursing stations. Discussions about patients were curt. Most exchanges consisted of comments like these:

"We're just waiting for that lawsuit."

"You aren't the one who will be accused of malpractice."

"What about the rights of those children?"

"You didn't have to sit at the bedside and get to know [Ms. A] and then watch her die."

"Why did you have to create such an uproar? [Ms. A's] wishes were clear. Why couldn't you let her die in peace with her family? You made a circus out of her last hours on earth."

"How could you let that healthy young woman die?"

"This is a hospital, not a church."

"That isn't a religion, it's insanity. This death was the fault of psychiatry."

At this point the consulting psychiatrist stepped in once more. She recognized that despite all the talk, there had been no real discussion. Nor did any of the major participants, including herself, understand the beliefs of Jehovah's Witnesses better now than they had at the outset. Should another, similar clinical situation arise, the institution would be no more prepared to handle it than it had been before Ms. A was admitted. The consulting psychiatrists proposed that a special, 2-hour grand rounds be devoted to a review of the case and of the issues it had posed. Each perspective would be presented by its adherents. She would invite representatives of the Jehovah's Witness Church to present a formal explanation of their position.

Plans for the grand rounds, which was a suggestion readily accepted, channeled the feelings of the various factions into preparations for their presentations. The scholarly context and the lapse of several weeks, which allowed tempers to cool, enabled people to listen to each other with respect. The sentiments that had been muttered in anger were articulated and now made sense to people who had taken opposing positions. The representatives from the Jehovah's Witness Church brought copies of several brochures written for the medical profession. Both the brochures and their oral presentation were impressive. It was not that Jehovah's Witnesses were suicidal, unappreciative of the value of life, or unaware of the safety of blood products or their life-saving properties. They elaborated the biblical passages from which the proscription on the use of blood is derived. They explained that the use of blood products was, for them, as great a sin as murder. They asked the medical staff to imagine how they would feel if they could live through a medical emergency only by causing the death of an innocent child. One might be desperate to live—but not desperate enough to commit such a sin.

The Jehovah's Witnesses were well aware of the problems their beliefs caused for the medical profession. They understood that it was somewhat unfair to ask the medical profession to care for sick patients, and sometimes watch them die, without access to an important and readily available part of their armamentarium. The clinicians and administrators had had no idea that the Jehovah's Witnesses were empathic with their situation. They had assumed that church members, like members of some other religions, would believe that they and they alone had the correct interpretation of the scripture and that those who did not share their interpretation were unenlightened or misled.

## Conclusions

The psychiatrist's roles in this difficult episode were several: ascertainment of mental status, evaluation of religious affiliation, assessment of competence, education, advocacy for the patient's autonomy, facilitation of communication, and conflict resolution.

The psychiatrist, although called upon to override or circumvent them, could not, and cannot, expunge the ethical and religious conflicts from the medical arena. Psychiatric intervention cannot substitute for the appreciation of cultural and religious differences—an appreciation that was insufficient in many of the medical staff members involved in this case—and that should be an integral part of medical school, residency, and continuing medical education. Psychiatrists can advocate for and participate in this integration.

## Epilogue

Several years later, a member of the nursing staff was invited to the wedding of a family member who had recently joined the Jehovah's Witnesses. At the reception, she noticed Ms. A's husband and brother-in-law, whom she remembered very well. Also present were Ms. A's five children. Beautifully dressed, well-behaved, and smiling, they were in the care of their aunt, with whom they appeared to be close and comfortable. By all accounts, they were the darlings of the entire church community. This news evoked mixed reactions at the hospital. The members of the staff were glad that the children were doing well, but they did not want this relatively happy outcome to obscure the fact that the refusal of a blood transfusion could kill a healthy young mother and orphan innocent children. Yet they understood that religious and medical value systems could genuinely collide.

# CHAPTER 15

# Future Directions in Abnormal Psychology

*We hope these readings have shown that psychopathology is real, common, distressing, and complex. They also show that there are many futures in the field of abnormal psychology, and many ways that stories might be told from this point forward. Which ones will become prominent depends on a host of factors: the development of advanced research procedures and technologies; the persistence and creativity of scientists; the availability of federal support for developing and testing new treatments; the structure of our health care system; and the recruitment of bright and compassionate students for the fields of science, medicine, and psychology. The final four readings serve as lenses that help us envision what the future of abnormal psychology may look like. They cover the misuse of psychiatric diagnoses by social institutions, long-term trends in mental illness as indicated by survey data, the possible rapprochement between biological and environmental views of psychopathology, and the intricacies of the human brain.*

# Mental Illness by Mandate

## Maggie Farley

*We begin our foray into the future of abnormal psychology by first looking back into the recent past. During the 1950s, the Roman Catholic Church in Quebec altered their records for some 3,000 orphans so that they would be officially classified as mentally ill or retarded; doing so provided the church with more money because government reimbursements were greater for the care of mentally ill and retarded people than for orphans. This change led to substandard care and even child abuse, and many orphans still suffer as a result of their experiences.*

*We include this article for several reasons. First, it is a reminder that social policies, even those with good intentions, can have devastating consequences; all possible consequences should be anticipated, particularly for those who are not able to defend themselves. Second, this article shows that, as distasteful as it is to contemplate the poor treatment of the mentally ill, it is all the more difficult to think about powerful social institutions using the designation of mental illness to further their own financial ends (also see Smith & Oleszczuk, 1996). Third, it is a harsh lesson in the fact that labels matter; when the children were designated as mentally unfit, their care—which was probably not ideal even from the start— appears to have worsened dramatically. Finally, the continued justification by some church officials of this decision—on the grounds that the children, as orphans, were already victims of parental neglect and thus not deserving of better care— emphasizes that injustices can abound even in times of growing scientific enlightenment.*

### Reference

Smith, T. C., & Oleszczuk, T. A. (1996). *No asylum: State psychiatric repression in the former USSR.* New York: New York University Press.

*Los Angeles Times,* A1. (2000, February 10).

MONTREAL—Herve Bertrand remembers the day when his life at a Quebec orphanage turned inside out. "On March 18, 1954, the nuns came in and said, 'From today, you are all crazy.' Everyone started to cry, even the nuns. Then everything changed: Our lessons stopped, and work—they called it therapy—began. I saw the bars go on the windows, the fences go up around the compound. I saw the autobuses pull up full of psychiatric patients—our new roommates.

It was like a prison. And that's where I spent a quarter of my life."

Bertrand, 57, was among more than 3,000 children living in 12 Quebec orphanages that the Roman Catholic Church transformed—some virtually overnight—into mental hospitals in the 1940s and '50s to reap more generous government subsidies. A policy ordained by Quebec's then-premier, Maurice Duplessis, granted the institutions more than three times the amount of money to care for a mental patient as they received for orphans. So, in order that the children would qualify, their medical records were altered to declare them mentally unstable or retarded.

But that was not just a change of labels, say the now-middle-aged orphans: The church sold their souls. Many were treated like mental patients, with unnecessary drugs and straightjackets. It took the orphans nearly 40 years to organize and ask the church and state for redress. They finally got an answer last year. Quebec Premier Lucien Bouchard apologized for his predecessor's mistakes and offered nominal compensation. But he also praised the "great deal of devotion" of the nuns who cared for the children.

Church officials were less contrite. "They don't deserve an apology," said Cardinal Jean-Claude Turcotte, adding that real responsibility lay not with the religious community, but with the parents for their wayward lifestyles. While the government and the church resist confronting the past, members of this damaged generation are still trying to find closure and compensation for the childhood they will never recover.

Montreal is a city of churches, a riverside capital where the skyline is crowded with steeples, a place, it is said, where you can't throw a rock without breaking a stained-glass window. Until the last few decades, the Catholic Church held sway here just as surely as the government did. It ran not only orphanages but schools and hospitals, and it handled most social services.

Duplessis, for his part, ran the province with an iron hand, forsaking civil liberties for a strong state. Today, his intermittent reign between 1936 and 1959 is referred to as "the Great Darkness."

The children affected by his decree—now in their 50s and 60s—have become known as "the orphans of Duplessis." Not all the children were orphans. Many, like Bertrand, had been born out of wedlock and were viewed by the church as children of sin. Others came from families too poor to care for them who were urged to put them in the hands of nuns for a proper religious upbringing.

But the sisters were overwhelmed—a single nun was typically in charge of 50 children, say people who were familiar with the institutions at the time. They were women with no child-rearing experience, undertrained and overworked. They transferred their culture of penitence and self-discipline to children who didn't understand. In an institutional setting, this could quickly turn into abuse, and few of the children had family visitors who could intervene.

## A Dark Memory of Cells and Straitjackets

St.-Julien Hospital was one of the earliest psychiatric institutions to take orphans, starting in the 1940s. Alice Quinton, 62, was born of an incestuous relationship and transferred to St.-Julien from an orphanage in 1945. On her admission form, the reason for her entry is written in a nun's precise cursive: "Cause of scandal." That year, when Quinton was 7, the nuns told Alice that her parents were dead, and in turn reported to her mother that Alice had died. And in a way, Quinton says, she did die that year. Her childhood, spent amid 500 other orphans and 900 mentally ill adults, is a dark memory of cells, tranquilizers and straitjackets. She says she was punished for asking questions, for wetting her bed, for not doing her work fast enough.

"I asked, 'Why am I here?' No one ever had an answer. I thought to myself: 'Am I going crazy? Am I going to grow up to be like these mental patients?' " Today, Quinton carries a binder of grievances, a catalog of injustice. She opens it to show an architectural diagram of St.-Julien, featuring the layout of her ward and the location of the bed where she says she was strapped in a straitjacket on the cold metal springs for three weeks. She presents childlike drawings of "the humiliation chair," depicting a girl in a straitjacket strapped onto a potty chair, with a gag in her mouth and tears springing from her eyes in dotted lines. The detail is precise, down to the number of fasteners on the straitjacket, as clear in Quinton's mind as her memory of a nun's knee in her back, lacing her into the jacket as if into an old corser.

"None of it made sense," she says, her eyes brimming. "But I never thought I was insane. I never believed I was retarded."

In the summer of 1960, a Montreal psychiatric team began a series of investigations that would prove her right. At one of the institutions, Mont Providence, an examination of about 500 boys and girls aged 4 through 12 revealed that most were of normal intelligence but being impaired by institutionalization.

"One of the conclusions of the report was that many children were perfectly intelligent but perfectly ignorant," says Dr. Jean Gaudreau, one of six doctors who evaluated the children. "In one of the tests, we showed the children objects—keys, a flag, a stove, a refrigerator. Many of the children couldn't name them, not because of a lack of intelligence but because they had never seen one." Gaudreau, now a psychology professor at the University of Montreal, recalls his shock at the pervasive stench of urine, at seeing a 5-year-old boy in a straitjacket, tied to a drainpipe, and teenagers drugged with tranquilizers. "Most of them were not retarded when they went in," he says. "Some of them were by the time they got out."

## Government Ordered Children's Release

That investigation was the beginning of the end of the program. After psychiatrist Denis Lazure headed a wider investigation in 1962, inspecting 15 of the province's hospitals, a new government declared that the children did not belong in institutions and released them that year. The younger ones went to other orphanages or foster homes. The older ones were on their own.

"Contrary to the popular belief of some, there is no exaggeration in the accounts of the sufferings of the Duplessis orphans," says Lazure, who became the Quebec health minister after the study. "If anything, they've been understated."

But though the orphans were released, their trauma was not over. For people who had lived for years within walls, with no education, whose social circle was mental patients, who didn't recognize a refrigerator, the freedom of the outside world was no freedom at all. What's more, their records still classified them as mentally deficient, which made it difficult for them to later find jobs.

"All I could do for a year after I got out was to huddle quietly and hope I wouldn't get hit," says Clarina Duguay, 63, who was interned in St.-Julien when she was 11 after her mother fell ill with tuberculosis. "It took a long time to build up the confidence to walk down the street, or to find a job." Today, Duguay is married and has six children, though she didn't tell any of them until a few years ago that she was one of the Duplessis orphans, who were beginning to get national attention.

"I always wanted to be a flight attendant," she says. "Any one of the kids there could have been anything. Today, too many of them are nothing. Their lives were stolen from them."

Bertrand, now a plumber, is frustrated by the religious orders' denials, then and now. He describes repeated sexual abuse: When the nuns went to church, a guard would come and get him, strap him in a straitjacket and sodomize him. "I told the nuns," he says, "but they didn't believe me." His hospital records from Mont Providence describe rectal damage so severe that surgery was recommended.

Even today, nuns who ran the orphanages refuse to comment on what happened in that era. Last February, Cardinal Turcotte, a senior representative of the Catholic Church in Canada, said, "I wholeheartedly defend the devoted religious women who gave 40 to 50 years of their lives working in the institutions." Turcotte called the orphans "victims of life," and declared, "They don't deserve an apology."

While some Quebeckers agree that the issue is

nearly half a century old and should be left behind, Bertrand emphasizes that the orphans' entire lives, not just their childhoods, were affected. When his children were born, he says, he re-encountered the shadows of his youth. "I was not a good father. I was too aggressive. I slapped the children because I did not know how to discipline them kindly. I thought I could leave the past behind, but I still have all that in my head."

Bruno Roy, 56, who was in Mont Providence with Bertrand, is one who has reclaimed his life. Born out of wedlock, he lived in another orphanage until he was transferred to Mont Providence at age 7. Before the institution converted to a psychiatric facility, his medical chart read: "This child demonstrates normal intelligence and is capable of being educated—he is fairly well adapted and has achieved the emotional maturity of children his age." After Mont Providence's status changed, his record declared him "severely mentally retarded."

Today, Roy has a doctorate in French literature and teaches at a Quebec college. A burly man whose black beard is stippled with gray, he has written 12 books on poetry and literature—and one about his childhood experiences that brought attention to the whole issue.

"Yes, it's true. I'm a mental defective," he says, leaning back in a chair and laughing. Roy has become an effective spokesman for the rest of the orphans, many of whom he describes matter-of-factly as "damaged goods." He was saved, he says, by one kind nun who recognized his spark and put him in a vocational training program when he was 15, just to get him outside the compound's walls. He worked in a cardboard box factory and tried to make up for lost time. He realized he had no vocabulary for the outside world.

"In the years inside Mont Providence, I saw the violence and absurdity, yet I didn't see it, because to me it was normal. I didn't have anything to compare it to," he says. At first, he says, it was easier to bury his experience. For 30 years, while he became a successful scholar, he did not talk about his past.

"Then one day, one of my [Mont Providence] classmates called and said: 'You made it, but we're still less than human. Won't you help defend us?' "I went to a meeting and saw the faces of people who were totally destroyed. These were my old playmates, who were normal when we were kids. Now they are broken. They had no voice. They had no credibility. No one would believe their horrible stories."

In 1994 he wrote a book, *My Memories From the Asylum*, to document what had happened. . . . "I became a writer because of one sentence by our national poet, Gaston Miron: 'One day I will have said yes to my birth.' " It was a turning point not only for Roy but for other Duplessis orphans. But though their case began to receive national attention, justice continued to elude them.

A class-action lawsuit was rejected by a provincial court in 1995 on the grounds that it would be too difficult to determine individual damages in the hundreds of different cases. Later that year, a police investigation of 321 complaints, including Bertrand's accusation of rape backed up by medical documents, concluded that the evidence of abuse was too old and unreliable. So in 1997, the Duplessis orphans tried a different tactic. They formed a committee to ask for a public inquiry, plus compensation and apologies from the church and government.

The government assigned an ombudsman, Daniel Jacoby, to examine the matter. In March 1997, extrapolating from settlements in similar cases in other provinces, Jacoby suggested a compensation package equal to $56 million in U.S. currency—about $700 for each patient for each year he or she spent in an institution as a result of a wrongful diagnosis, and an additional indemnity for those who were physically or sexually abused.

"It's a violation of human rights, and as a democracy we have an obligation to compensate for any harm we caused," Jacoby says. Although the government accepts about nine out of 10 of his proposals, he says, it rejected this one, and he remains puzzled by the sudden parsimony. "I won't abandon this dossier," he promised in December, "because it is a matter of fairness, a matter of humanity and a matter of moral obligation."

Last March, Premier Bouchard did apologize on behalf of the Quebec government and offered a fund equivalent to $2.1 million to provide social services for the orphans who need them—about $700 total per victim. But the offer included no direct compensation for individuals or acknowledgment of pain and suffering. The orphans committee declared it an insult.

"Although they had to endure that situation, many of them are still quite well off, so we decided to put our limited resources this way," says Dominique Olivier, a spokeswoman for the Office of Citizen Relations. "We do not plan to look into it again." Msgr. Pierre Morissette, head of the Assembly of Quebec Bishops, told a news conference in September that an apology by the church "would betray the work of those who dedicated their lives to the poorest in society."

A spokeswoman for the assembly, Rolande Parrot, said in a December interview that the church does not take any responsibility for the transfer of children to psychiatric hospitals and does not consider the religious community to have done anything wrong. She dismissed the orphans committee's protests and its vows that it will pursue the matter all the way to the Vatican. "There are no plans to reopen the case," Parrot said. "They will probably never be satisfied."

# RESPONSES TO NERVOUS BREAKDOWNS IN AMERICA OVER A 40-YEAR PERIOD: MENTAL HEALTH POLICY IMPLICATIONS

## Ralph Swindle, Jr., Kenneth Heller, Bernice Pescosolido, and Saeko Kikuzawa

*Data from large surveys conducted in 1957, 1976, and 1996 were used to capture trends in mental health problems and the steps people take to feel better. This article reviews these surveys and gives us some clues about what the landscape of mental health and illness might be like in the future. For example, the surveys showed that increasing numbers of people report some form of mental breakdown, that people are taking greater advantage of the informal support that is available to them, and that there is decreasing reliance on traditional medical care for psychological problems. As the authors are careful to acknowledge, the focus on "nervous breakdown" as the primary dependent variable in this study is somewhat crude. This focus may also lead respondents to think more about stressful life situations and disorders involving anxiety and depression, rather than severe psychopathologies such as schizophrenia and bipolar disorder. Nevertheless, the findings indicate a growing disconnection between the increasing acceptance and use of nonmedical mental health professionals, on one hand, and the rise of managed care and health maintenance organizations, which employ primary care physicians as gatekeepers, on the other hand. A second important message of this reading is that our social relationships, while serving as a common source of impending nervous breakdowns, also represent an essential source of consolation and compassion. Our mental health and illness resides within the relationships we have with other people. Maximizing the benefits of our personal relationships—as might be achieved with strategically timed preventive interventions at the time of a change in jobs, impending parenthood, or discharge from a hospital—thus emerges as a promising task for mental health professionals.*

## Suggested Readings

Christensen, A., & Jacobson, N. S. (1994). Who (or what) can do psychotherapy: The status and challenge of nonprofessional therapies. *Psychological Science, 5,* 8–14.

Kelleher, K. J., McInerny, T. K., Gardner, W. P., Childs, G. E., & Wasserman, R. C. (2000). Increasing identification of psychosocial problems: 1979–1996. *Pediatrics, 105*, 1313–1321.

Putnam, R. D. (2000). *Bowling alone: The collapse and revival of American community.* New York: Simon & Schuster.

*American Psychologist, 55*, 740–749. (2000).

*The 1957 and 1976 Americans View Their Mental Health surveys from the Institute of Social Research were partially replicated in the 1996 General Social Survey (GSS) to examine the policy implications of people's responses to feeling an impending nervous breakdown Questions about problems in modern living were added to the GSS to provide a profile of the public's view of mental health problems. Results were compared for 1957, 1976, and 1996. In 1957, 19% of respondents had experienced an impending nervous breakdown; in 1996, 26% had had this experience. Between 1957 and 1996, participants increased their use of informal social supports, decreased their use of physicians, and increased their use of nonmedical mental health professionals. These findings support policies that strengthen informal support seeking and access to effective psychosocial treatments rather than current mental health reimbursement practices, which emphasize the role of primary care physicians.*

Questions concerning the public's response to mental health problems have been informed in previous generations by the Americans View Their Mental Health (AVTMH) surveys. In both 1957 and 1976, these surveys provided directions and benchmarks for national mental health policy (Gurin, Veroff, & Feld, 1960; Kulka, Veroff, & Douvan, 1979; Veroff, 1981; Veroff, Kulka, & Douvan, 1981). The replication of some of the AVTMH questions in the General Social Survey (GSS) of 1996 provided a further opportunity to clarify and direct policy for mental health services. Specifically, it provided information on how Americans today are interpreting and responding to mental health problems and how these reactions have changed relative to the past two surveys.

## Mental Health Themes Over the Past 40 Years

Professional and self-help resources for problems of mental health were few in 1957. The ability of professionals to recognize, diagnose, and treat mental health problems was limited, and their ideas about coping and help seeking were mostly theoretical (Cowen, Gardner, & Zax, 1967). Community mental health center legislation in the 1960s represented an attempt to remedy these problems with goals of destigmatizing mental illness through educational campaigns, encouraging professional help seeking, and developing new interventions (Joint Commission on Mental Illness and Health, 1961). Professional resources became more available through a nationwide federal initiative to support community mental health centers, staffing grants, and expanded professional training opportunities (Chu & Trotter, 1974). Also, treatment advances, such as the development of effective psychotherapies and pharmacotherapies, were fueled by the expansion of basic research (Kopta, Lueger, Saunders, & Howard, 1999; Nathan & Gorman, 1998; Russell & Orlinsky, 1996; Seligman, 1994; Thase & Kupfer, 1996).

In contrast, preventing mental health problems by helping people develop more adaptive coping strategies and by using informal caregiving resources has been a developing but minor subtheme of the public mental health debate (Caplan, 1964; Felner, Jason, Moritsugu, & Farber, 1983; Price, Ketterer, Bader, & Monahan, 1980). Only in recent years has prevention research actually demonstrated that greater coping skills and the development of self-help and indigenous support for individuals are important building blocks for national mental health policy (Institute of Medicine, 1994; Muehrer, 1997; Sandler, 1997). In light of these advances, an important challenge today is bridging the conceptual gap between the emerging prevention field and the long-standing treatment field, with its emphasis on already existing mental health problems. To meet this challenge, it will be necessary to have accurate data on the public's relative preferences for professional treatment on the one hand and self-help and indigenous support on the other.

## The AVTMH Studies and the 1996 GSS

The 1957 and 1976 AVTMH studies were landmarks in defining mental health policy. The 1957 study asked hundreds of mental health and lifestyle questions. These revealed that significant numbers of Americans perceived their problems in psychological terms and that they were willing to seek help for them from both clergy and physicians. The results of the 1957 study also provided empirical underpinnings for the mental health education and training movements of the 1960s. As one report stated.

> AVTMH thus indicates the potential value of attempts to reach more people and different classes of people with mental health information. But the recognition of this fact merely begs the question of where we will get the manpower to meet increased demand for mental health services. (Joint Commission on Mental Illness and Health, 1961, p. 108)

The 1976 study revealed an acceleration in these trends, with researchers concluding, among other things, that "people who in 1976 reported having felt an impending nervous breakdown were much more likely than people who reported such feelings in 1957 to accept the possibility that they might have a problem that would require professional help" (Veroff et al., 1981, p. 85).

The 1996 survey offered a unique opportunity to assess the prevalence of these feelings for the current generation and to examine how people's responses to them have changed over the past 40 years. In turn, these results should help inform current mental health policy. This seems especially important today for two reasons. First, epidemiological evidence shows that rates of mental disorders such as depression are on the rise (Klerman & Weissman, 1989), which suggests an increased need for services. Second, recent studies have

found that only 40% of Americans with a diagnosable disorder have ever received any formal care, and that only 25% of those with a disorder received care from mental health specialists (Kessler et al., 1994). Both these findings suggest that understanding how individuals are managing their mental health problems is as important today as it was in 1957 and 1976. Specifically, how are individuals coping with the feeling of an impending nervous breakdown, and what might be the role of informal sources of help? Only longitudinal or panel data, such as those reported here, can answer these types of questions.

As such, this article examines the following public health questions: Is the current generation of Americans experiencing a greater sense of impending nervous breakdown than did the previous two generations? Have the reasons underlying the experience of impending nervous breakdown changed over the past 40 years? Are sources of mental health problems more or less conducive to formal help seeking? What differences are there, if any, in how Americans of the current generation are dealing with impending nervous breakdowns compared with the previous two generations? Specifically, is the current generation more likely to seek professional help and receive medications? What does the term *nervous breakdown* mean to the current generation when compared with more modern terms such as *mental illness*?

## Method

Questions asked in the 1956 and 1976 AVTMH national surveys, together with demographic information from the present 1996 GSS, provided the basis for this particular study. The GSS was an in-person, 1.5-hour interview conducted by the National Opinion Research Center of the University of Chicago. The GSS, funded primarily by the National Science Foundation, used a cluster sampling design to provide a nationwide, representative sample of adults living in noninstitutionalized settings. The response rate was 76.1%. The 1996 survey included a number of topical modules. The focus of the mental health module in this survey, the Problems in Modern Living module, was designed to provide a current profile of the public's view of mental health problems. This portion took about 20 minutes of the full GSS interview.

RESPONDENTS    A total of 1,444 respondents were surveyed in 1996 and asked the target question of whether they had ever thought they were having a nervous breakdown. Despite its crudeness as an indicator, the term *nervous breakdown* has a resonance with the public and, of several subjective mental health measures, bore the strongest relationship to help seeking in the 1976 study. In 1957 and 1976, the sample sizes were 2,460 and 2,264, respectively. Given the changes that have taken place in the composition of the American adult population over the past 40 years (as noted in other surveys), it is not surprising that there were statistically significant differences in the characteristics of the samples. The 1996 sample had a higher family income and was more racially diverse. Participants also tended to be non-Protestant, suburban, nonrural, better educated, less likely to be married, and less likely to profess any religious preference (all differences were significant; $p < .001$). It was therefore important to control for these changes.

DATA    . . . After a few questions about the respondent's knowledge of other people's use of mental health services or of people who were hospitalized because of a mental illness, the full sample was asked, "Have you ever felt that you were going to have a nervous breakdown?" (*yes* = 1, *no* or *don't know* = 0). This is the same question asked in the 1957 and 1976 AVTMH studies. If respondents answered "yes," they were then asked the remaining questions that formed the basis for this study: "Could you tell me about when you felt that way?" "What was it about?" From responses to this latter question, up to three external precipitating factors perceived by respondents to be related to the nervous breakdown were coded. The categories were as follows: own health problem, social network events, others' health problems, work or school problems, financial problems, and housing

problems. A respondent could report multiple precipitating factors for the nervous breakdown. Explanations that were likely to be synonymous for an impending nervous breakdown, such as stress, depression, self-doubt, and personal adjustment problems, were excluded as factors to avoid obvious confounding.

Those who responded in the affirmative to the nervous breakdown question were then asked, "What did you do about it?" (the probe "Anything else?" was repeated until the respondent said "no"), and then they were asked, "Which of these things did you do first . . . second . . . third . . . ?" Answers to the former question provided information about coping and help seeking in response to an impending nervous breakdown. As suggested by the coping theory of Moos (Moos & Schaefer, 1993), coping and help seeking responses were coded as approach coping responses (1 = *any use of logical analysis, positive reappraisal, or problem solving*; 0 = *no mention of any of the three approach coping responses*), avoidance responses (1 = *combining any use of cognitive avoidance, alternative rewards, emotional discharge, and doing nothing*; 0 = *no mention of any of the avoidant coping responses*), informal support seeking (1 = *seeking of any friends, family, or self-help groups to deal with the nervous breakdown*; 0 = *no mention of informal support seeking*), or formal support seeking (1 = *any seeking of primary care physicians, psychiatrists, counselors, mental health specialists, etc.*; 0 = *no mention of formal support seeking*).

Each respondent could have as many as three coping responses and three help sources coded. If more were provided, the interviewer chose the first three in the order in which they occurred, with the first being the most immediate response following the feeling of an impending nervous breakdown. . . . Finally, respondents who said they had never felt they were going to have a nervous breakdown or did not know were asked, "Have you ever felt you had a mental health problem?" (*yes* = 1, *no* = 0, *don't know* = 8).

Original complete respondent protocols for the 1957 and 1976 surveys were obtained from the Institute of Social Research, University of Michigan, where the original researchers provided permission to reuse the items and gave guidance on coding. All data from 1957, 1976, and 1996 were recoded into categories developed by the original AVTMH researchers. Master's-level staff at Indiana University were trained to provide consistent coding of responses. Using the categories from the earlier studies reduced the possibility that the temporal changes would be due to cultural differences in the understanding and interpretation of responses by the coders for each of the three study years. . . .

## Results

\* \* \*

IMPENDING NERVOUS BREAKDOWNS  Significantly more Americans reported feeling an impending nervous breakdown in 1996 than in 1957 or 1976. The endorsement of the nervous breakdown question increased from 18.9% in 1957, to 20.9% in 1976, to 26.4% in 1996, $\chi^2(9, N = 1,302) = 30.05$, $p$ <.0001, with the largest increase occurring in the past 20 years. To account for changes in demographic factors, adjusted prevalence rates were calculated using the result of logistic regression for each year (Long, 1997). The adjusted prevalence rates for persons with average characteristics are 17.0% in 1957, 19.6% in 1976, and 24.3% in 1996, which still represents a progressive increase over the past 40 years. Demographic factors that consistently increased the likelihood of reporting an impending nervous breakdown over the three study years were being White, being a woman, having no religion, having less family income, being younger, having children, and not being married. . . .

Recall that those who responded that they had never experienced an impending nervous breakdown were asked the follow-up question, "Have you ever had a mental health problem?" (which was not done in the AVTMH surveys). This added another 7% to the number of individuals reporting a mental health concern, such that about one third of all American adults surveyed in 1996 admitted to having felt at some point either that they were going to have a nervous breakdown or that they had had a mental health problem.

PERCEIVED PRECIPITATING FACTORS OF IMPENDING NERVOUS BREAKDOWNS  . . . Americans who felt they were going to have nervous breakdowns over the three survey years had somewhat different explanations for these feelings. . . . The most consistent trend was for the category of participants' own health problems, which were less likely to be given as an explanation in later surveys. Although events affecting loved ones (i.e., network events) did not significantly change from 1976 to 1996, they remained highly prevalent as explanations. In 1996, the most frequently cited network events related to impending nervous breakdowns were divorce, marital strains, marital separation, and troubles with members of the opposite sex. Work and educational problems as precipitating factors were also generally stable over time and most commonly represented tension in the work site and course load pressures. The unadjusted prevalence of financial precipitating factors, such as not having enough income or loss of income, increased over time but did not increase in the pooled demographic analysis when family income (as a collinear factor) was controlled. Housing precipitating factors were lowest in prevalence and were essentially stable over time; these most often reflected relocation or other difficulties related to one's residence.

RESPONSES TO IMPENDING NERVOUS BREAKDOWNS  There was only one overall change in participants' responses to impending nervous breakdowns, namely, the use of informal supports. . . . Demographic controls for changes over time made no difference in this finding. Reliance on informal supports, such as family and friends, showed a strong increase over the past 20 years. Seeking formal sources of help remained essentially unchanged in overall percentage, remaining the dominant response to an impending nervous breakdown. There was no evidence of changes in reported use of approach or avoidant coping responses.

Within the category of formal support advisors

. . . there have been some major changes. The role of physicians in helping with an impending nervous breakdown declined dramatically, from 44% in 1957 to 18% in 1996; also, between 1976 and 1996, seeing a psychiatrist declined from 8% to 3%. By contrast, there was a total increase in seeking the services of counselors, social workers, and psychologists, from 0.6% in 1957 to 18% in 1996. For those individuals who saw a physician for an impending nervous breakdown, there was a significant increase in the use of medications, from about 34.5% in the first two study years to about 57% in 1996. . . .

## Discussion

We found that more Americans had at some point felt an impending nervous breakdown in 1996 than in 1957 or 1976. This finding cannot be accounted for by demographic changes and suggests either a change in the prevalence of psychological problems or a lessening of the stigma associated with admitting that one is going to have a nervous breakdown (or both).

We also found some changes in the reasons Americans gave for feeling they were going to have a nervous breakdown. Explanations related to health declined, those related to events affecting significant others continued to be high from 1976 to 1996, and those related to external events remained common. Because health events appear to be a less common explanation for feeling an impending nervous breakdown, mental health problems today appear to be less conducive to formal medical help seeking than those of 20 and 40 years ago. That is, it makes less sense to go to a primary care physician if the problem is not seen as precipitated by a health concern.

Americans today appear to be more oriented toward dealing with their feelings of impending nervous breakdowns through informal supports from family and friends, combined with an increased use of nonmedical professionals, such as counselors, social workers, and psychologists. These findings cannot be fully attributed to demographic changes or to differences in reasons attributed for having the feelings of an impending nervous breakdown. It does appear, however, that nonmedical professionals are increasingly sought in response to network events by both younger and divorced (or separated) respondents.

Finally, with the rise of new medications and new medical care reimbursement policies, we expected more Americans to have consulted a primary care physician for medication or to have used this as an entry point to obtain reimbursable mental health specialty care. However, relative to both 1957 and 1976, there was a decline in 1996 in the percentage of Americans seeking a physician as an aid in coping with feelings of a nervous breakdown.

POLICY IMPLICATIONS   A goal of American mental health educational policy over the past 40 years has been to normalize mental disorders so that the public would seek treatment for psychological distress as easily as they do for physical illnesses (Joint Commission on Mental Illness and Health, 1961). A second goal has been to increase the supply of mental health specialists who could meet the anticipated increased demand for mental health services (Joint Commission on Mental Illness and Health, 1961). The results of this study suggest some progress has been made toward these goals, at least for less severe mental health problems. Americans appear to be more willing to admit to having feelings of an impending nervous breakdown than they were 40 years ago, and nonmedical mental health specialists are increasingly seen as appropriate resources for these problems.

Despite the latter trend, a variety of mental health reimbursement models have emerged in recent years, many of which emphasize a role for primary care physicians as mental health providers. It is estimated that as many as 162 million Americans were covered under some form of managed care contract by the end of 1998 (Strum, 1999). For mental conditions, this often entails having a primary care physician as the initial provider of mental health care for the kinds of problems likely to be considered nervous breakdowns (Depression Guideline Panel, 1993; Katon & Gonzales, 1994). It seems somewhat ironic to us that although the public appears more accepting of mental health services from nonmedical providers, they may have to access services through physicians, who they see as less appropriate sources of help for mental health problems.

A second recent development involves research on empirically supported psychological and pharmacological treatments. Efficacious treatments are now available for many of the mood and anxiety disorders that would fit within the rubric of nervous breakdown (Barlow & Lehman, 1996; Beutler, Kim, Davison, Karno, & Fisher, 1996; Christensen & Heavey, 1999; Hollon, 1996; Mynors-Wallis, Davies, Gray, Barbour, & Gath, 1997; Nathan & Gorman, 1998; Seligman, 1994; Thase & Kupfer, 1996). Brief psychotherapies are particularly appropriate for these less severe problems (Munoz et al., 1995). Unfortunately, these promising procedures are not widely disseminated to the public at large and are still rarely used in many applied settings (Hollon, 1996; Task Force on Promotion and Dissemination of Psychological Procedures, 1995). A further problem is that physicians are not likely to be aware of these developments either. They tend to dramatically underdiagnose psychological disorders (deGruy, 1996; Goldberg, 1995; Klinkman & Okkes, 1998) and are reluctant to make referrals voluntarily for psychological treatment.

Finally, we believe that a mental health policy emphasis that is prevention centered—focused on building coping skills, fostering stress resilience, and strengthening ties with family and friends—is in keeping with the present results (Institute of Medicine, 1994; Muehrer, 1997; Sandler, 1997). Self-help and seeking indigenous support are becoming increasingly common responses to feelings of impending breakdown. The National Institute of Mental Health's emphasis on primary prevention appears timely and in step with a considerable portion of the public that turns to community-based nonprofessional help providers (Kolbe, 1997; Reiss & Price, 1996).

STUDY LIMITATIONS When considering these findings overall, it is important to stress that they speak to a concept of nervous breakdown that is considered a less serious condition than mental illness. Our findings are consistent with those of Pescosolido, Monahan, Link, Stueve, and Kikusawa (1999), who found that Americans make distinctions among disorders, with disorders such as depression and anxiety considered much less serious conditions than schizophrenia. Thus, we think these findings may be generalized only to the milder end of the spectrum of mental health problems and help-seeking preferences. Moreover, although asking about nervous breakdowns may have made sense in 1957 given the methods of the day, it is suspect in the light of 1996's structured diagnostic interviews and sophisticated symptom scales. Single-item scales are prone to a variety of interpretations, and this one question bears a huge burden in this study.

Another worrisome issue is whether the meanings of the words and responses to the questions have changed over the past 40 years. However, by having all responses recoded in 1996 by the same raters, we attempted to reduce the possibility that differences in the results could be due to differences in the coding systems for the three study years. Further, we consulted extensively about coding consistency and practices with Joseph Veroff, second author of the 1957 AVTMH study and first author of the 1976 AVTMH study. Our coding scheme was developed in conjunction with coding rules he and his colleagues had used previously. Thus, we feel confident that our approach to the data is in keeping with that of the original investigators. When new 1996 phrases and idioms were encountered, we sought to remain faithful to the original coding structures as we added them to the coding system. Thus, we hope to have minimized serious inconsistencies in interpretation of responses caused by differences between today's cultural context and the cultural context of 20 and 40 years ago.

SUMMARY Data from three public surveys over the past 40 years show changes in how the current generation is perceiving and responding to mental health problems. Still, it is unclear whether the number of nervous breakdowns has increased over the past 40 years, or whether the meaning of the term has changed so that the public's attitude toward psychological problems has become more accepting. We suspect the data in this study represent an attitude shift on the part of the public, although it is possible that the number of persons with diagnosable mental disorders also has been increasing. In either case, it is important to note the increased public acceptance of indigenous and nonmedical sources of help for these problems. Overall, the American public's preference for dealing with impending nervous breakdowns through informal supports and nonmedical mental health specialists appears to be at odds with trends in the practices of the mental health system. Physicians are now expected to play a more prominent role in mental health care, yet it seems that Americans are less likely to turn to their physicians with their mental health concerns. The American public's views and the health care industry's mental health care practices appear to be heading in opposite directions, when it should be a time for the further development and dissemination of effective psychological prevention and treatment programs.

# References

Barlow, D. H., & Lehman, C. L. (1996). Advances in the psychosocial treatment of anxiety disorders. *Archives of General Psychiatry, 53,* 727–735.

Beutler, L. E., Kim, E. J., Davison, E., Karno, M., & Fisher, D. (1996). Research contributions to improving managed health care outcomes. *Psychotherapy, 33,* 197–206.

Caplan, G. (1964). *Principles of preventive psychiatry.* New York: Basic Books.

Christensen, A., & Heavey, C. L. (1999). Interventions for couples. *Annual Review of Psychology, 50,* 165–190.

Chu, F. D., & Trotter, S. (1974). *The madness establishment.* New York: Grossman.

Cowen, E., Gardner, J., & Zax, M. (1967). *Emergent approaches to mental health.* New York: Appleton, Century, Crofts.

deGruy, F. (1996). Mental health care in the primary care setting. *Primary care: America's health in a new era.* (pp. 285–311). Washington, DC: National Academy Press.

Depression Guideline Panel. (1993). *Depression in primary care: Volume 2. Treatment of major depression* (DHHS, AHCPR Publication No. 93-0551). Rockville, MD: U.S. Government Printing Office.

Felner, R. D., Jason, L. A., Moritsugu, J. N., & Farber, S. S. (Eds.). (1983). *Preventive psychology: Theory, research and practice.* New York: Pergamon Press.

Goldberg, R. J. (1995). Psychiatry and the practice of medicine: The need to integrate psychiatry into comprehensive medical care. *Southern Medical Journal, 88,* 260–267.

Gurin, J., Veroff, J., & Feld, S. (1960). *Americans view their mental health.* New York: Basic Books.

Hollon, S. D. (1996). The efficacy and effectiveness of psychotherapy relative to medications. *American Psychologist, 51,* 1025–1030.

Institute of Medicine. (1994). *Reducing risks for mental disorders: Frontiers for preventive intervention research.* Washington, DC: National Academy Press.

Joint Commission on Mental Illness and Health. (1961). *Action for mental health.* New York: Wiley.

Katon, W., & Gonzales, J. (1994). A review of randomized trials of psychiatric consultation-liaison studies in primary care. *Psychosomatics, 35,* 268–278.

Kessler, R. C., McGonagle, K. A., Zhao, S., Nelson, C. B., Hughes, M., Eshelman, S., Wittchen, H., & Kendler, K. S. (1994). Lifetime and 12-month prevalence of *DSM-III-R* psychiatric disorders in the United States: Results from the National Comorbidity Survey. *Archives of General Psychiatry, 51,* 8–19.

Klerman, G. L., & Weissman, M. M. (1989). Increasing rates of depression. *JAMA, 261,* 2229–2235.

Klinkman, M. S., & Okkes, I. (1998). Mental health problems in primary care: A research agenda. *Journal of Family Practice, 47,* 379–384.

Kolbe, L. J. (1997). Meta-analysis of interventions to prevent mental health problems among youth: A public health commentary. *American Journal of Community Psychology, 25,* 227–232.

Kopta, S. M., Lueger, R. J., Saunders, S. M., & Howard, K. I. (1999). Individual psychotherapy outcome and process research: Challenges leading to greater turmoil or a positive transition? *Annual Review of Psychology, 50,* 441–469.

Kulka, R. A., Veroff, J., & Douvan, E. (1979). Social class and the use of professional help for personal problems: 1957 and 1976. *Journal of Health and Social Behavior, 20,* 2–17.

Long, J. S. (1997). *Regression models for categorical and limited dependent variables* (pp. 9–50). Beverly Hills, CA: Sage.

Moos, R. H., & Schaefer, J. A. (1993). Coping resources and processes: Current concepts and measures. In L. Goldberger & S. Breznitz (Eds.), *Handbook of stress: Theoretical and clinical aspects* (2nd ed., pp. 234–257). New York: Free Press.

Muehrer, P. (Ed.). (1997). Prevention research in rural settings [Special issue]. *American Journal of Community Psychology, 25*(4).

Munoz, R. F., Ying, Y., Bernal, G., Perez-Stable, E. J., Sorensen, J. L., Hargreaves, W. A., Miranda, J., & Miller, L. S. (1995). Prevention of depression with primary care patients: A randomized controlled trial. *American Journal of Community Psychology, 23,* 199–222.

Mynors-Wallis, L., Davies, I., Gray, A., Barbour, F., & Gath, D. (1997). A randomized controlled trial and cost analysis of problem-solving treatment for emotional disorders given by community nurses in primary care. *British Journal of Psychiatry, 170,* 113–119.

Nathan, P. E., & Gorman, J. M. (Eds.). (1998). *A guide to treatments that work.* New York: Oxford University Press.

Pescosolido, B. A., Monahan, J., Link, B. G., Stueve, A., & Kikusawa, S. (1999). The public's view of the competence, danger-ousness, and need for legal coercion of persons with mental health problems. *American Journal of Public Health, 89,* 1339–1345.

Price, R. H., Ketterer, R. F., Bader, B. C., & Monahan, J. (Eds.). (1980). *Prevention in mental health: Research, policy, and practice.* Beverly Hills, CA: Sage.

Reiss, D., & Price, R. H. (1996). National research agenda for prevention research: The National Institute of Mental Health report. *American Psychologist, 51,* 1109–1115.

Russell, R. L., & Orlinsky, D. E. (1996). Psychotherapy research in historical perspective: Implications for mental health care policy. *Archives of General Psychiatry, 53,* 708–715.

Sandler, I. (Ed.). (1997). Meta-analysis of primary prevention programs [Special issue]. *American Journal of Community Psychology, 25*(2).

Seligman, M. E. P. (1994). *What you can change and what you can't: The guide to successful self-improvement.* New York: Knopf.

Sturn, R. (1999). Tracking changes in behavioral health ser-vices: How have carve-outs changed care? *Journal of Behavioral Health Services and Research, 26,* 359–370.

Task Force on Promotion and Dissemination of Psychological Procedures. (1995). Training in and dissemination of empir-ically-validated psychological treatment: Report and recom-mendations. *Clinical Psychologist, 48,* 3–23.

Thase, M., & Kupfer, D. (1996). Recent developments in the pharmacotherapy of mood disorders. *Journal of Consulting and Clinical Psychology, 64,* 646–659.

Veroff, J. (1981). The dynamics of help-seeking in men and women: A national survey study. *Psychiatry, 44,* 189–200.

Veroff, J., Kulka, R. A., & Douvan, E. (1981). *Mental health in America: Patterns of help-seeking from 1957 to 1976.* New York: Basic Books.

# Politics of Biology: How the Nature vs. Nurture Debate Shapes Public Policy—and Our View of Ourselves

## Wray Herbert

*One theme that consistently runs through the field of abnormal psychology today is that biological factors, especially genes, exert a significant effect on the onset, expression, and course of various forms of psychopathology. As we have seen in other readings, the evidence for genetic contributions to mental illness is indeed compelling, albeit to varying degrees depending on the disorder in question. The role of other nongenetic biological bases for disorders is also impressive. But what does the future hold in store? Will we see increasingly refined and definitive statements that further emphasize just how potent genetics and biology are? Or will we see analyses that underscore the impact of environmental factors and the means by which environmental factors combine with biological processes to produce mental illness?*

*The next article argues that the latter view will prevail in the years ahead. This article also makes two important points: public opinion on the root causes of psychopathology is very influential for setting social policy, and the ability of the general public to understand finer arguments about the interplay between nature and nurture is probably outstripped by the sheer complexity of the phenomena at work. We are left to wonder whether the pendulum will merely swing back toward nurture, now that the heyday of nature is perhaps passing, or whether a new framework altogether—one that could afford a more sophisticated view of the dynamic interplay between nature and nurture—will emerge to take its place.*

## Suggested Readings

Collins, W. A., Maccoby, E. E., Steinberg, L., Hetherington, E. M., & Bornstein, M. H. (2000). Contemporary research on parenting: The case for nature *and* nurture. *American Psychologist, 55,* 218–232.
Kitcher, P. (1997). *The lives to come: The genetic revolution and human possibilities.* New York: Touchstone Books.

*U.S. News and World Report,* 72–79. (1997, April 21).

Laurie Flynn uses the technology of neuroscience to light up the brains of Washington lawmakers. As executive director of the National Alliance for the Mentally Ill, she marshals everything from cost analysis to moral pleading to make the case for laws banning discrimination against people with mental illness. But her most powerful advocacy tool by far is the PET scan. She takes a collection of these colorful brain images up to Capitol Hill to put on a show, giving lawmakers a window on a "broken" brain in action. "When they see that it's not some imaginary, fuzzy problem, but a real physical condition, then they get it: 'Oh, it's in the brain.' "

The view of mental illness as a brain disease has been crucial to the effort to destigmatize illnesses such as schizophrenia and depression. But it's just one example of a much broader biologizing of American culture that's been going on for more than a decade. For both political and scientific reasons—and it's often impossible to disentangle the two—everything from criminality to addictive disorders to sexual orientation is seen today less as a matter of choice than of genetic destiny. Even basic personality is looking more and more like a genetic legacy. Nearly every week there is a report of a new gene for one trait or another. Novelty seeking, religiosity, shyness, the tendency to divorce, and even happiness (or the lack of it) are among the traits that may result in part from a gene, according to new research.

This cultural shift has political and personal implications. On the personal level, a belief in the power of genes necessarily diminishes the potency of such personal qualities as will, capacity to choose, and sense of responsibility for those choices—if it's in your genes, you're not accountable. It allows the alcoholic, for example, to treat himself as a helpless victim of his biology rather than as a willful agent with control of his own behavior. Genetic determinism can free victims and their families of guilt—or lock them in their suffering.

On the political level, biological determinism now colors all sorts of public-policy debates on issues such as gay rights, health care, juvenile justice, and welfare reform. The effort to dismantle social programs is fueled by the belief that government interventions (the nurturing side in the nature-nurture debate) don't work very well—and the corollary idea that society can't make up for every unfortunate citizen's bad luck. It's probably no coincidence that the biologizing of culture has accompanied the country's shift to the political right, since conservatives traditionally are more dubious about human perfectability than are liberals. As Northeastern University psychologist Leon Kamin notes, the simplest way to discover someone's political leanings is to ask his or her view on genetics.

Even so, genetic determinism can have paradoxical consequences at times, leading to disdain rather than sympathy for the disadvantaged, and marginalization rather than inclusion. Cultural critics are beginning to sort out the unpredictable politics of biology, focusing on four traits: violence, mental illness, alcoholism, and sexual orientation.

## The Nature of Violence

To get a sense of just how thorough—and how politicized—the biologizing of culture has been, just look at the issue of urban gang violence as it is framed today. A few years ago, Frederick Goodwin, then director of the government's top mental health agency, was orchestrating the so-called Federal Violence Initiative to identify inner-city kids at biological risk for criminal violence, with the goal of intervening with drug treatments for what are presumed to be nervous-system aberrations. Goodwin got himself fired for comparing aggressive young males with primates in the jungle, and the violence initiative died in the resulting furor. But even to be proposing such a biomedical approach to criminal justice shows how far the intellectual pendulum has swung toward biology. . . .

As with many psychopathologies, criminal aggression is difficult to define precisely for research. Indeed, crime and alcohol abuse are so entangled that it's often difficult to know whether genetic markers are associated with drinking, criminality—or something else entirely, like a personality trait. A 1993 National Research Council study, for example, reported strong evidence of genetic influence on antisocial personality disorder, but it also noted that many genes are probably involved. Getting from those unknown genes to an actual act of vandalism or assault—or a life of barbaric violence—requires at this point a monstrous leap of faith.

Yet it's a leap that many are willing to make. When geneticist Xandra Breakefield reported a possible genetic link to violent crime a few years ago, she immediately started receiving phone inquiries from attorneys representing clients in prison; they were hoping that such genetic findings might absolve their clients of culpability for their acts.

## Mutations and Emotions

Just two decades ago, the National Institute of Mental Health was funding studies of economic recession, unemployment, and urban ills as possible contributors to serious emotional disturbance. A whole branch of psychiatry known as "social psychiatry" was dedicated to helping the mentally ill by rooting out such pathogens as poverty and racism. There is no longer much evidence of these sensibilities at work today. NIMH now focuses its studies almost exclusively on brain research and on the genetic underpinnings of emotional illnesses.

The decision to reorder the federal research portfolio was both scientific and political. Major advances in neuroscience methods opened up research that wasn't possible a generation ago, and that research has paid off in drugs that very effectively treat some disorders. But there was also a concerted political campaign to reinterpret mental illness. A generation ago, the leading theory about schizophrenia was that this devastating emotional and mental disorder was caused by cold and distant mothering, itself the result of the mother's unconscious wish that her child had never been born. A nationwide lobbying effort was launched to combat such unfounded mother blaming, and 20 years later that artifact of the Freudian era is entirely discredited. It's widely accepted today that

psychotic disorders are brain disorders, probably with genetic roots.

But this neurogenetic victory may be double edged. For example, family and consumer groups have argued convincingly that schizophrenia is a brain disease like epilepsy, one piece of evidence being that it is treatable with powerful antipsychotic drugs. Managed-care companies, however, have seized upon the disease model, and now will rarely authorize anything but drug treatment: it's efficient and justified by the arguments of biological psychiatry. The American Psychiatric Association just this month issued elaborate guidelines for treating schizophrenia, including not only drugs but an array of psychosocial services—services the insurance industry is highly unlikely to pay for.

The search for genes for severe mental disorders has been inconclusive. Years of studies of families, adoptees, and twins separated at birth suggest that both schizophrenia and manic-depressive illness run in families. But if that family pattern is the result of genes, it's clearly very complicated, because most of the siblings of schizophrenics (including half of identical twins, who have the same genes) don't develop the disorder. Behavioral geneticists suspect that several genes may underlie the illness, and that some environmental stress—perhaps a virus or birth complications—also might be required to trigger the disorder.

On several occasions in the past, researchers have reported "linkages" between serious mental illness and a particular stretch of DNA. A well-known study of the Amish, for example, claimed a link between manic-depression and an aberration on chromosome 11. But none of these findings has held up when other researchers attempted to replicate them.

Even if one accepts that there are genetic roots for serious delusional illnesses, critics are concerned about the biologizing of the rest of psychiatric illness. Therapists report that patients come in asking for drugs, claiming to be victims of unfortunate biology. In one case, a patient claimed he could "feel his neurons misfiring"; it's an impossibility, but the anecdote speaks to the thorough saturation of the culture with biology.

Some psychiatrists are pulling back from the strict biological model of mental illness. Psychiatrist Keith Russell Ablow has reintroduced the idea of "character" into his practice, telling depressed patients that they have the responsibility and capacity to pull themselves out of their illness. Weakness of character, as Ablow sees it, allows mental illness to grow. Such sentiment is highly controversial within psychiatry, where to suggest that patients might be responsible for some of their own suffering is taboo.

## Besotted Genes

The best that can be said about research on the genetics of alcoholism is that it's inconclusive, but that hasn't stopped people from using genetic arguments for political purposes. The disease model for alcoholism is practically a secular religion in this country, embraced by psychiatry, most treatment clinics, and (perhaps most important) by Alcoholics Anonymous. What this means is that those seeking help for excessive drinking are told they have a disease (though the exact nature of the disease is unknown), that it's probably a genetic condition, and that the only treatment is abstinence.

But the evidence is not strong enough to support these claims. There are several theories of how genes might lead to excessive drinking. A genetic insensitivity to alcohol, for example, might cause certain people to drink more; or alcoholics might metabolize alcohol differently; or they may have inherited a certain personality type that's prone to risk-taking or stimulus-seeking. While studies of family pedigrees and adoptees have on occasion indicated a familial pattern for a particular form of alcoholism (early-onset disorder in men, for example), just as often they reveal no pattern. This shouldn't be all that surprising, given the difficulty of defining alcoholism. Some researchers identify alcoholics by their drunk-driving record, while others focus on withdrawal symptoms or daily consumption. This is what geneticists call a "dirty phenotype"; people drink too much in so many different ways that the trait itself is hard to define,

so family patterns are all over the place, and often contradictory.

Given these methodological problems, researchers have been trying to locate an actual gene (or genes) that might be involved in alcoholism. A 1990 study reported that a severe form of the disorder (most of the subjects in the study had cirrhosis of the liver) was linked to a gene that codes for a chemical receptor for the neurotransmitter dopamine. The researchers even developed and patented a test for the genetic mutation, but subsequent attempts to confirm the dopamine connection have failed.

The issues of choice and responsibility come up again and again in discussions of alcoholism and other addictive disorders. Even if scientists were to identify a gene (or genes) that create a susceptibility to alcoholism, it's hard to know what this genetic "loading" would mean. It certainly wouldn't lead to alcoholism in a culture that didn't condone drinking—among the Amish, for example—so it's not deterministic in a strict sense. Even in a culture where drinking is common, there are clearly a lot of complicated choices involved in living an alcoholic life; it's difficult to make the leap from DNA to those choices. While few would want to return to the time when heavy drinking was condemned as strictly a moral failing or character flaw, many are concerned that the widely accepted disease model of alcoholism actually provides people with an excuse for their destructive behavior. As psychologist Stanton Peele argues: "Indoctrinating young people with the view that they are likely to become alcoholics may take them there more quickly than any inherited reaction to alcohol would have."

## Synapses of Desire

It would be a mistake to focus only on biological explanations of psychopathology; the cultural shift is much broader than that. A generation ago, the gay community was at war with organized psychiatry, arguing (successfully) that sexual orientation was a lifestyle choice and ought to be deleted from the manual of disorders. Recently the same community was celebrating new evidence that homosexuality is a biological (and perhaps genetic) trait, not a choice at all.

Three lines of evidence support the idea of a genetic basis for homosexuality, none of them conclusive. A study of twins and adopted siblings found that about half of identical twins of homosexual men were themselves gay, compared with 22 percent of fraternal twins and 11 percent of adoptees; a similar pattern was found among women. While such a pattern is consistent with some kind of genetic loading for sexual orientation, critics contend it also could be explained by the very similar experiences many twins share. And, of course, half the identical twins did not become gay—which by definition means something other than genes must be involved.

A well-publicized 1991 study reported a distinctive anatomical feature in gay men. Simon LeVay autopsied the brains of homosexual men and heterosexual men and women and found that a certain nucleus in the hypothalamus was more than twice as large in heterosexual men as in gay men or heterosexual women. Although LeVay couldn't explain how this neurological difference might translate into homosexuality, he speculates that the nucleus is somehow related to sexual orientation. The hypothalamus is known to be involved in sexual response.

The only study so far to report an actual genetic connection to homosexuality is a 1993 study by Dean Hamer, a National Institutes of Health biologist who identified a genetic marker on the X chromosome in 75 percent of gay brothers. The functional significance of this piece of DNA is unknown, and subsequent research has not succeeded in duplicating Hamer's results.

Homosexuality represents a bit of a paradox when it comes to the intertwined issues of choice and determinism. When Hamer reported his genetic findings, many in the gay community celebrated, believing that society would be more tolerant of behavior rooted in biology and DNA rather than choice. LeVay, himself openly gay, says he undertook his research with the explicit agenda of furthering the gay cause. And Hamer testified as an expert witness in an important gay-rights case in Colorado where, in a strange twist, liberals found themselves arguing the deterministic position, while conservatives insisted that homosexuality is a choice. The argument of gay-rights advocates was that biological status conveyed legal status—and protection under the law.

## History's Warning

But history suggests otherwise, according to biologist and historian Garland Allen. During the eugenics movement of the 1920s and 1930s, both in the United States and Europe, society became less, not more, tolerant of human variation and misfortune. Based on racial theories that held Eastern Europeans to be genetically inferior to Anglo-Saxon stock, Congress passed (and Calvin Coolidge signed) a 1924 law to restrict immigration, and by 1940 more than 30 states had laws permitting forced sterilization of people suffering from such conditions as "feeblemindedness," pauperism, and mental illness. The ultimate outcome of the eugenics craze in Europe is well known; homosexuals were not given extra sympathy or protection in the Third Reich's passion to purify genetic stock.

Allen is concerned about the possibility of a "new eugenics" movement, though he notes that it wouldn't be called that or take the same form. It would more likely take the form of rationing health care for the unfortunate. The economic and social conditions today resemble conditions that provided fertile ground for eugenics between the wars, he argues; moreover, in Allen's view, California's Proposition 187 recalls the keen competition for limited resources (and the resulting animosity toward immigrants) of the '20s. Further, Allen is quick to remind us that eugenics was not a marginal, bigoted movement in either Europe or the United States; it was a Progressive program, designed to harness science in the service of reducing suffering and misfortune and to help make society more efficient.

These concerns are probably justified, but there are also some signs that we may be on the crest of another important cultural shift. More and more experts, including dedicated biologists, sense that the power of genetics has been oversold and that a correction is needed. What's more, there's a glimmer of evidence that the typical American may not be buying it entirely. According to a recent *U.S. News*/Bozell poll, less than 1 American in 5 believes that genes play a major role in controlling behavior; three quarters cite environment and society as the more powerful shapers of our lives. Whether the behavior under question is a disorder like addiction, mental illness, or violence, or a trait like homosexuality, most believe that heredity plays some role, but not a primary one. Indeed, 40 percent think genes play no role whatsoever in homosexuality, and a similar percentage think heredity is irrelevant to drug addiction and criminality. Across the board, most believe that people's lives are shaped by the choices they make.

These numbers can be interpreted in different ways. It may be that neurogenetic determinism has become the "religion of the intellectual class," as one critic argues, but that it never really caught the imagination of the typical American. Or we may be witnessing a kind of cultural self-correction, in which after a period of infatuation with neuroscience and genetics the public is becoming disenchanted, or perhaps even anxious about the kinds of social control that critics describe.

Whatever's going on, it's clear that this new mistrust of genetic power is consonant with what science is now beginning to show. Indeed, the very expression "gene for" is misleading, according to philosopher Philip Kitcher, author of *The Lives to Come*. Kitcher critiques what he calls "gene talk," a simplistic shorthand for talking about genetic advances that has led to the widespread misunderstanding of DNA's real powers. He suggests that public discourse may need to include more scientific jargon—not a lot, but some—so as not to oversimplify the complexity of the gene-environment interaction. For example, when geneticists say they've found a gene for a particular trait, what they mean is that people carrying a certain "allele"—a variation in a stretch of DNA that normally codes for a certain protein—will develop the given trait in a standard environment. The last

few words—"in a standard environment"—are very important, because what scientists are *not saying* is that a given allele will necessarily lead to that trait in every environment. Indeed, there is mounting evidence that a particular allele will not produce the same result if the environment changes significantly; that is to say, the environment has a strong influence on whether and how a gene gets "expressed."

It's hard to emphasize too much what a radical rethinking of the nature-nurture debate this represents. When most people think about heredity, they still think in terms of classical Mendelian genetics: one gene, one trait. But for most complex human behaviors, this is far from the reality that recent research is revealing. A more accurate view very likely involves many different genes, some of which control other genes, and many of which are controlled by signals from the environment. To complicate matters further, the environment is very complicated in itself, ranging from the things we typically lump under nurture (parenting, family dynamics, schooling, safe housing) to biological encounters like viruses and birth complications, even biochemical events within cells.

The relative contributions of genes and the environment are not additive, as in such-and-such a percentage of nature, such-and-such a percentage of experience; that's the old view, no longer credited. Nor is it true that full genetic expression happens once, around birth, after which we take our genetic legacy into the world to see how far it gets us. Genes produce proteins throughout the lifespan, in many different environments, or they don't produce those proteins, depending on how rich or harsh or impoverished those environments are. The interaction is so thoroughly dynamic and enduring that, as psychologist William Greenough says, "To ask what's more important, nature or nurture, is like asking what's more important to a rectangle, its length or its width."

The emerging view of nature-nurture is that many complicated behaviors probably have some measure of genetic loading that gives some people a susceptibility—for schizophrenia, for instance, or for aggression. But the development of the behavior or pathology requires more what National Institute of Mental Health Director Stephen Hyman calls an environmental "second hit." This second hit operates, counterintuitively, through the genes themselves to "sculpt" the brain. So with depression, for example, it appears as though a bad experience in the world—for example, a devastating loss—can actually create chemical changes in the body that affect certain genes, which in turn affect certain brain proteins that make a person more susceptible to depression in the future. Nature or nurture? Similarly, Hyman's own work has shown that exposure to addictive substances can lead to biochemical changes at the genetic and molecular levels that commandeer brain circuits involving volition— and thus undermine the very motivation needed to take charge of one's destructive behavior. So the choice to experiment with drugs or alcohol may, in certain people, create the biological substrate of the addictive disorder. The distinction between biology and experience begins to lose its edge.

## Nurturing Potentials

Just as bad experiences can turn on certain vulnerability genes, rich and challenging experiences have the power to enhance life, again acting through the genes. Greenough has shown in rat studies that by providing cages full of toys and complex structures that are continually rearranged—"the animal equivalent of Head Start"—he can increase the number of synapses in the rats' brains by 25 percent and blood flow by 85 percent. Talent and intelligence appear extraordinarily malleable.

Child-development experts refer to the life circumstances that enhance (or undermine) gene expression as "proximal processes," a term coined by psychologist Urie Bronfenbrenner. Everything from lively conversation to games to the reading of stories can potentially get a gene to turn on and create a protein that may become a neuronal receptor or messenger chemical involved in thinking or mood. "No genetic potential can become reality," says Bronfenbrenner, "unless the relationship between the organism and its environment is such that it is *permitted* to be expressed." Unfortunately, as he details in his new book, *The State of Americans*, the circumstances in which many American children are living are becoming more impoverished year by year.

If there's a refrain among geneticists working today, it's this: The harder we work to demonstrate the power of heredity, the harder it is to escape the potency of experience. It's a bit paradoxical, because in a sense we end up once again with the old pre-1950s paradigm, but arrived at with infinitely more sophisticated tools: Yes, the way to intervene in human lives and improve them, to ameliorate mental illness, addictions, and criminal behavior, is to enrich impoverished environments, to improve conditions in the family and society. What's changed is that the argument is coming not from left-leaning sociologists, but from those most intimate with the workings of the human genome. The goal of psychosocial interventions is optimal gene expression.

So assume for a minute that there is a cluster of genes somehow associated with youthful violence. The kid who carries those genes might inhabit a world of loving parents, regular nutritious meals, lots of books, safe schools. Or his world might be a world of peeling paint and gunshots around the corner. In which environment would those genes be likely to manufacture the biochemical underpinnings of criminality? Or for that matter, the proteins and synapses of happiness?

# SCIENCE AND THE FUTURE OF PSYCHIATRY

## Huda Akil, Ph.D., and Stanley J. Watson, M.D., Ph.D.

*With the start of a new millennium, many scholars in the mental health professions took the opportunity to evaluate progress in the field and identify new challenges. Their articles often make for stimulating reading, as the authors articulate broad themes and trends that they believe will shape the field in the future. Drs. Huda Akil and Stanley Watson observe that those of us interested in psychopathology confront unique obstacles to understanding the workings of the human brain, which, by its very nature, grows and changes with experience. They argue that an important task for the future is to clarify the details of how and why brains differ and how it is that these differences—which they refer to as a neuronal phenotype—mediate between our genetic endowment and pathological behavior. They also criticize the "unrelenting reductionism" of recent years and make the important point that genetic identification of individuals at risk for specific forms of psychopathology may cause more harm than good if effective interventions are not also provided.*

## Suggested Readings

Drabick, D. A. G., & Goldfried, M. R. (2000). Training the scientist-practitioner for the 21st century: Putting the bloom back on the rose. *Journal of Clinical Psychology, 56*, 327–340.

Frank, E., & Kupfer, D. J. (2000). Peeking through the door to the 21st century. *Archives of General Psychiatry, 57*, 83–85.

Garfinkel, P. E., & Dorian, B. J. (2000). Psychiatry in the new millenium. *Canadian Journal of Psychiatry, 45*, 40–47.

---

*Archives of General Psychiatry, 57*, 86–87. (2000).

If humanity is lucky, the evolution of our knowledge of the living world will result in the elaboration of more perfect scientific eyes to probe the nature of the human brain and to understand the complexities of the human mind. This seems to be the best path to truly helping individuals who are battling psychiatric illnesses and to actually preventing many brain-related disorders. For such accomplishments to take place, the trajectory of our science has to change, to move from its unrelenting reductionism to a serious attempt at integrating knowledge that spans from the structure of the gene to the expression of complex cognition. The tension between the biomedical and the psychotherapeutic approaches in psychiatry needs to be eliminated and transformed into a fully integrated approach that is mindful of the biological, emotional, cognitive, and social complexity of each individual.

There is little doubt that the explosion of knowledge in the life sciences at the end of the millennium will yield heretofore unimagined tools for the increased understanding we need. The challenge will no longer reside in the availability of fundamental information, but in its thoughtful integration. The avalanche of data on the sequence and variation of the human genome may be staggering, but understanding how such variation might relate to behavior, personality traits, or psychiatric illness will truly challenge our scientific skills. It will require all our intelligence in framing questions, recognizing profiles and patterns, and establishing criteria for determining cause and effect relationships.

While our colleagues in other fields of biomedical research will also have to address the issues related to complex genetics and gene-environment interactions, we in brain research will face this problem most acutely. This is because we deal with a complex organ whose very function is to learn and change through experience. All along, we will need to be mindful of the impressive plasticity of the brain not only during development but throughout life. The genes, while they set the parameters of the program, do not by any means fully determine the outcome. At the same time, it is critical to understand the parameters that lead to the dysregulation of brain function, as diseases of this organ alter our very identity and our place in the world.

It will likely be necessary to elaborate an intermediate level of knowledge that can serve as a stepping-stone between specific genetic information about an individual and the behavior of that person. We term this a *neuronal phenotype*, which consists of understanding patterns of gene expression and function within the brain, presumably as the critical mediators between the original genetic endowment and the expression of behavioral patterns. These neuronal phenotypes represent unique patterns of gene expression, in the context of known brain circuits, that are the end result of interactions between the genetic endowment of the individual and the impact of various developmental and experiential events on the brain. Thus, identical twins with identical genetic endowments may have differing neuronal phenotypes owing to their unique experiences, leading to the differential likelihood of suffering from a psychiatric disorder. It is only by having a much fuller understanding of the neuronal phenotypes that we will be able to perceive the critical differences that lead to the expression of an illness or its avoidance.

But the concept of neuronal phenotype can be broadened to be more dynamic and *inclusive*. Thus, while these phenotypes can be described in terms of patterns and magnitude of gene expression in a particular circuit at rest (e.g., how much corticotropin-releasing hormone is expressed in the amygdala and glucocorticoid receptors in the hippocampus), they can also be described in terms of neuronal activity in response to a challenge (e.g., how much dopamine is released in the prefrontal cortex vs the nucleus accumbens during a particular task), as well as the impact of an event on subsequent neuronal events (e.g., how much induction of immediate early genes or of other signaling events takes place in a circuit because of exposure to a stimulus and for how long). Optimally, we would become much more sophisticated at obtaining whole profiles of activity in the context of these neuronal phenotypes, coordinating information about starting levels of activity and reactions to input over neuronal space and time.

Thus, our more perfect scientific eyes would be able to fully probe the human brain in action, at various phases of life and under different conditions, and to understand the functional dynamics of this organ. This understanding would go far beyond the knowledge we now obtain from neuroimaging tools to simultaneously relate the global regional activities that we currently measure to the activities of the specific genes, proteins, and circuits being brought into play at any given instant. In this idealized world, we would literally be able to follow a perception, a thought, or a learning process through its key molecular and anatomical stages and see its repercussions at subsequent time points.

It is likely that such tools will simultaneously lead us to revisit some fundamental assumptions and reveal misconceptions about the nature of psychiatric disorders. For example, they may lead us to the notion that many mood disorders have a stronger cognitive component than previously anticipated. They may allow us to detect preverbal or nonverbal variables that nevertheless play a key role in social and emotional responsiveness. Even more likely, they will lead us to reorganize our most fundamental views of brain function, moving us away from the old Cartesian categories to entirely new functional neuronal entities.

Why would such a level of understanding at the molecular and neurobiological level be useful in helping people? At the broadest level, it would begin to translate the real implications of the fact that psychiatric illnesses are the result of complex genetics. In the last few years, we have come to realize that most psychiatric disorders are not due to a single gene but result from gene-gene interactions, involve gene-environment interactions, and exhibit a great deal of heterogeneity, such that the same disorder can be the result of different combinations of genetic predispositions. While this makes our work in understanding the genetics of psychiatric illnesses much more arduous, it also gives our field and our patients much hope. It says that biology is not destiny, and vulnerabilities if identified and understood need not turn into psychiatric disorders.

But to truly understand how complex genetics come into play in leading to psychiatric disorders, we need to watch various genetic programs in action during development, maturation, and aging, following various stressors with or without the illness before and after treatment with either pharmacological agents or psychotherapy. We need to grasp how certain events at critical times alter the course of development. We need to comprehend how experience in the adult brain, including social interactions, modify particular circuits in reversible and irreversible ways. We need to measure the impact of the illness itself on the expressions of specific genes in the specific individual in the context of the unique vulnerabilities of that brain. Only then would we have sufficient and systematic information to attempt to stem or reverse the critical neurobiological events that may spell the difference between normal emotionality and full-blown depression or between interesting thoughts and florid psychosis.

The day may come, sooner than we might like, when a newborn would receive full information about his or her genetic structure, including various polymorphisms that may make him or her more vulnerable to depression, autism, or Alzheimer disease. This would be a huge burden on the individual unless we could couple this information with knowledge of what one can do to help prevent the expression of these disorders. In the case of severe disorders, such as autism, what may be needed is early and fairly aggressive intervention using a range of tools from particular drugs to gene therapy. But in the case of numerous brain disorders, including many of the mood disorders and even possibly some of the age-related disorders, much could be accomplished by understanding the role of environmental modulation on these processes. In some cases, the changes may be nutritional; in others, they may well be behavioral. Social interactions, and therefore talking therapies, can change brain structure and function just as drugs can. A thoughtful combination of approaches would need to be elaborated and would require our combined efforts at the scientific and ethical levels. Huge efforts in education would be necessary to help people implement these strategies for themselves, their children, or their students. Careful public policy decisions would need to be made to ensure that this knowledge remains private and is not abused. But the greatest gain that psychiatry could offer, through a more enlightened scientific basis and a greater wisdom in its application, is something that humanity has been seeking throughout the ages—self-knowledge coupled with greater acceptance of ourselves and of others, and a way of dealing with this great gift of self-consciousness that can carry with it the burden of the deepest human suffering.

# CREDITS

## Articles

**p. 12:** From "The Challenge to Psychiatry As Society's Agent for Mental Illness Treatment and Research," *American Journal of Psychiatry, 156,* 1307–1310, 1999. Copyright © 1999, the American Psychiatric Association. Reprinted by permission.

**p. 16:** From "Comparative Efficiency of Informal (Subjective, Impressionistic) and Formal (Mechanical, Algorithmic) Prediction Procedures: The Clinical Statistical Controversy," by W. M. Grove and P . E. Meehl. In *Psychology, Public Policy, and Law, 2,* pp. 293–323. Copyright © 1996 by the American Psychological Association.

**p. 25:** From "How Psychiatry Lost Its Way," by Paul R. McHugh. Reprinted from *Commentary,* December 1999, by permission, all rights reserved.

**p. 35:** From "Dream Warriors," by Lisa Birk, originally published in *The Boston Phoenix.* © Lisa Birk.

**p. 42:** Reprinted with permission. From N. C. Andreasen, "Linking Mind and Brain in the Study of Mental Illness." Copyright © 1997 American Association for the Advancement of Science.

**p. 49:** From "Psychiatry's Global Challenge," by Arthur Kleinman and Alex Cohen, March 1997. Reprinted with permission. Copyright © 1997 by Scientific American, Inc. All rights reserved.

**p. 55:** Used by permission of the *Skeptical Inquirer.*

**p. 63:** From "Nightmare of the Mind," by Julie Cart. In the *Los Angeles Times* 1/20/93.

**p. 68:** From "The Biology of Obsessions and Compulsions" by Judith L. Rapoport, March 1989. Reprinted with permission. Copyright © 1989 by Scientific American, Inc. All rights reserved.

**p. 76:** From "Panic Disorder—It's Real and It's Treatable," *Journal of the American Medical Association, 283,* 2573–2574. Copyright © 2000 by the American Medical Association. Used by permission.

**p. 80:** From "High Anxiety," in *Consumer Reports,* January 1993, pp. 19–24. Copyright © 1993, Consumers Union of U.S., Inc.

**p. 189:** From "Birth Complications Combined with Early Maternal Rejection at Age 1 Year Predispose to Violent Crime at Age 18 Years," *Archives of General Psychiatry, 51*, 984–988. Copyright © 1994 by the American Medical Association. Used by permission.

**p. 196:** From B. Knutson et al. "Selective Alteration of Personality and Social Behavior by Serotonergic Intevention," in *American Journal of Psychiatry, 155*, 373–379. Copyright © 1998, the American Psychiatric Association. Reprinted by permission.

**p. 207:** From J. Powell, "First Person Account: Paranoid Schizophrenia—a Daughter's Story." In *Schizophrenia Bulletin*, 24, 175–176. Copyright © 1998 Jackie Powell.

**p. 218:** From C. M. Harding and J. H. Zahniser, "Empirical Correction of Seven Myths about Schizophrenia with Implications for Treatment." In *Acta Psychiatrica Scandinavica, 90* (Suppl. 384), 140–146. Copyright © 1994 by Munksgaard.

**p. 227:** From "On the nature and mechanisms of obstetric influences in schizophrenia: a review and synthesis of epidemiologic studies," by T. D. Cannon, 1997, *9*, 387–397. In *International Review of Psychiatry*, Taylor & Francis Ltd, http://www tandf.co.uk /journals.

**p. 235:** From *Hard to Forget: An Alzheimer's Story*, by Charles P. Pierce, copyright © 2000 by Charles P. Pierce. Used by permission of Random House, Inc.

**p. 242:** From "Focus on Senior Health: The Burdens of Love," by Jane Allen. In the *Los Angeles Times* 1/30/93.

**p. 246:** From "Piecing Together Alzheimer's," by Peter H. St. George-Hyslop, December 2000. Reprinted with permission. Copyright © 2000 by Scientific American, Inc. All rights reserved.

**p. 253:** From "Alzheimer's Treatments that Work," by M. Barinaga. In *Science, 282*, 1030–1032. Copyright © 1998 by the American Association for the Advancement of Science.

**p. 259:** Reprinted with permission, from the *Annual Review of Medicine*, Volume 51, © 2000, by Annual Reviews, www.AnnualReviews.org.

**p. 266:** From "Out of Control," by K. Hubbard et al., in *People Weekly*, 4/12/99, pp. 52–72. Copyright © 1999 by *People Weekly*.

**p. 270:** Reprinted courtesy of *Sports Illustrated*: "Dying to Win" by Merrell Noden, *Sports Illustrated*, August 8, 1994, copyright © 1994, Time Inc. All rights reserved.

**p. 277:** From "Watching Volunteers Eat, Psychiatrists Seek Clues to Obesity," by E. Goode. Copyright © 2000 by the New York Times Co. Reprinted by permission.

**p. 285:** From "Unusual Case Report: Nonpharmacologic Effects of Sildenafil," by D. Mintz. In *Psychiatric Services, 51*, 674–675. Copyright © 2000, the American Psychiatric Association.

**p. 288:** From "Through the Gender Labrynth," by Michael Hiltzik. In the *Los Angeles Times* 11/19/00.

## Figures